AN INTRODUCTION
TO JAPANESE
CIVILIZATION

*Prepared
as one of the
Companions to
Asian Studies*

WM. THEODORE DE BARY

EDITOR

Edited by Arthur E. Tiedemann
Columbia University Press · New York and London
1974

An
Introduction
to
Japanese
Civilization

Clothbound edition published by Columbia University Press.
Paperbound edition published by D. C. Heath and Company.

Portions of this work were prepared under a contract with the U.S. Office of
Education for the production of texts to be used in undergraduate education.
The texts so produced have been used in the Columbia College Oriental
Studies program and have subsequently been revised and expanded for
publication in the present form. Copyright is claimed only in those portions of
the work not submitted in fulfillment of the contract with the U.S. Office of
Education. The U.S. Office of Education is not the author, owner, publisher, or
proprietor of this publication, and is not to be understood as approving by
virtue of its support any of the statements made or views expressed therein.

Paperbound edition published simultaneously in Canada.
Printed in the United States of America.

Paperbound International Standard Book Number: 0-669-52878-1
Clothbound International Standard Book Number: 0-231-03651-5
Library of Congress Catalog Card Number: 74-2782

*The calligraphy for the title was prepared by Professor Fujieda Akira, Jimbun
Kagaku Kenkyūsho, Kyoto University.*

Contributors

JAMES L. ANDERSON
Stein Roe & Farnham, Chicago

KOYA AZUMI
Department of Sociology, Rutgers, The State University of
New Jersey

ARDATH BURKS
Department of Political Science, Rutgers, The State University of
New Jersey

E. S. CRAWCOUR
Faculty of Asian Studies, The School of General Studies, The
Australian National University

WM. THEODORE DE BARY
Department of East Asian Languages and Cultures, Columbia
University

NORTON GINSBURG
Department of Geography, University of Chicago

ROGER F. HACKETT
Department of History, University of Michigan

DAN F. HENDERSON
School of Law, University of Washington

DONALD KEENE
Department of East Asian Languages and Cultures, Columbia
University

MARLENE J. MAYO
Department of History, College of Liberal Arts and Sciences,
University of Maryland

HUGO MUNSTERBERG
Department of Art, State University of New York College at New
Paltz

LAWRENCE OLSON
Department of History, Wesleyan University

RICHARD STORRY
Far East Centre, St. Anthony's College, Oxford University

ARTHUR E. TIEDEMANN
Department of History, The City College, The City University of New York

CONRAD TOTMAN
Department of History, College of Arts and Science, Northwestern University

H. PAUL VARLEY
Department of East Asian Languages and Cultures, Columbia University

Preface

The present volume consists of nine essays comprising a brief history of Japan and nine topical essays on selected aspects of Japanese civilization. Of course, it was not possible to devote a separate essay to every major area of Japanese culture and undoubtedly there can be differences of opinion as to which are the best areas to include in a book like this and which can be omitted. Still, the reader will find that most of the more important aspects, if not given a full chapter in themselves, are touched upon in one place or another. However, Japanese thought was deliberately not accorded a coverage proportionate to its importance, for it was anticipated that the present volume could be supplemented in this respect by Ryusaku Tsunoda, Wm. Theodore de Bary, and Donald Keene, compilers, *Sources of the Japanese Tradition,* Columbia University Press, New York, 1958.

This book is meant to be an introduction to Japanese civilization for lower division college students. Portions of the work were prepared under a contract with the United States Office of Education for the production of texts to be used in undergraduate education. Each contributor was asked to present the facts and concepts indispensable to a beginner's informed understanding of the assigned topic. With that as a guide, each was given complete freedom to develop his presentation as he saw fit. Inevitably this has led to some structural differences among chapters, but it has also assured the reader a variety of viewpoints and approaches.

Special thanks are due Hugo Munsterberg for selecting and securing the art illustrations.

A. E. T.

NOTE ON PRONUNCIATION

Japanese words and names have been transcribed in this book according to the Hepburn system of Romanization. Japanese names are given in the Japanese order, with the family name first and the personal name second.

Vowels in Japanese can be pronounced approximately as follows:

a	as in	arm
i	as the first e in	eve
u	as in	rude
e	as the a in	chaotic
o	as in	old

Consonants can be pronounced roughly as in English (g is always hard) with the exception of r, which is rendered like the unrolled r of Spanish. A Japanese syllable usually consists of either a consonant + vowel or a simple vowel. Long marks or macrons over u and o (ū, ō) require that the sound be held for twice its normal duration. (In this book macrons have been omitted from geographic names and from Japanese words, like shogun, which have been acclimatized in English.) Since there are no true diphthongs in Japanese, two vowels occurring together should be pronounced as separate syllables. For example, the word *kai* is pronounced in two syllables ka-i. When two consonants appear together, always remembering that ts, ch, and sh are symbols for single consonants, the first consonant is sustained as a full syllable. The same holds true for an n serving in any capacity other than the initial consonant of a consonant-vowel syllable. In ambiguous cases an apostrophe is frequently placed after the n to show that it is to be disjoined from the following vowel. Thus *hokku* would be ho-k-ku, *nembutsu* would be ne-m-bu-tsu, Kan'ami would be Ka-n-a-mi. An exception to this, however, is y. When y appears between a consonant and a vowel, it is not given full value but blends lightly with the preceding consonant and the succeeding vowel so that all three form one syllable. For instance, the Kyu of Kyushu is pronounced like the English word cue.

Based on H. Paul Varley, *A Syllabus of Japanese Civilization,* 2d edition (New York, 1972), p. 91.

Contents

AN INTRODUCTION
TO JAPANESE
CIVILIZATION

PART ONE

The History

of Japan

I

Early Japan

BY

H. PAUL VARLEY

Prehistory: The Jōmon and Yayoi Cultures

Japan's position just off Asia has often been compared to that of England near the northwestern coast of Europe. Both countries have enjoyed a protective insularity in relation to their respective continents. For both, invasion has been infrequent in historic times. In Japan's case, the only large-scale armed intrusions before World War II were the unsuccessful invasions by the Mongols in the thirteenth century.

Yet in at least two important respects the English and Japanese situations have differed. First, England is far closer to the coast of France (about 20 miles) than Japan is to Korea (about 115 miles); and the English have from earliest times played an active role in continental affairs. Isolation, in short, has been a much more significant fact of life for the Japanese. Second, whereas England's Europe evolved into a continent of diverse peoples and states, East Asia has traditionally been dominated by the pervasive culture of China. The Japanese of premodern times were largely restricted to the Chinese sphere in their foreign relations and in their opportunities for cultural borrowing. Until recent centuries, contacts with the outside world were made almost exclusively through China or through Korea, the latter a country far more fully within China's cultural orbit than Japan.

Geographic isolation has undoubtedly been one of the most important determinants in the shaping of Japanese history. Remote in their island kingdom, the Japanese have ever been acutely conscious of the differences between themselves and outsiders. Their aggressive phase of foreign expansion in the recent past should not be allowed to obscure the fact that noninvolvement in overseas activities has been a far more frequent policy guide for Japanese governments through the ages. Moreover, the relative absence of outside military threat has tended to make evolution a more characteristic process in Japan's historical development than either social or political revolution. The Japanese have been cultural borrowers, from China in premodern times and from the West during the past century. They have taken eagerly from others those things they have found appealing or useful. Yet Japan's cultural borrowing, apparently indiscriminate at times, has usually proven in the long run to be highly selective, and the resultant advances in its civilization have usually been more the product of synthesis than outright imitation.

In some remote geological age the Japanese islands were connected by land to the Asian mainland. Proof of this has been provided by discovery of the fossilized bones of elephants and other continental mammals no longer indigenous to Japan. These animals apparently wandered or migrated to Japan during a time when the climate of Asia was far different from what it is today. In a later epoch the coastal land area that was to become Japan sank below the ocean and still later, after several violent shifts of the earth's surface, it reemerged as an archipelago in roughly the geographic configuration that we know it today.

Until very recently archaeologists believed that the origins of human habitation in Japan postdated substantially the formation of the country into an island chain. Man seemed, in fact, to have been quite a latecomer, not appearing on Japanese soil until perhaps 4000–3000 B.C. The best hypothesis was that this "first arriver" came from northeast Asia, perhaps through the Korean Peninsula. His culture was already advanced, since he was the possessor of polished stone tools and the maker of a sophisticated and highly artistic style of clay pottery.

Then late in the 1940s dramatic finds were made at Iwajuku north of Tokyo. From a stratum of the earth considerably below that which contained the earliest previous human remains were extracted the rough, chipped-stone tools of an obviously much older culture. Within a decade or so several hundred paleolithic, or old stone age, sites had been uncovered from Hokkaido in the north to Kyushu in the southwest and the archaeological frontiers of Japanese history were pushed back to a vastly more ancient time. So far, only the stone tools and implements of paleolithic man have been found: there are no known skeletal remains (apart from a few bone chips) or other signs of his physical or cultural presence. Nevertheless the evidence on hand is sufficient to suggest that man may have inhabited Japan as long ago as many tens and perhaps even hundreds of thousands of years. It is possible that he, like the prehistoric animals, came first by foot to Japan when it was still attached to the Asian mainland. If so, he may have been directly related to the earliest humans of the north China plain, one of the cradles of mankind and of civilization in East Asia.

Greater knowledge of paleolithic man must await future research and, let us hope, discovery. The remains of Japan's first neolithic culture, on the other hand, have been steadily unearthed, studied, and classified for nearly a century. This earliest neolithic culture is known as the Jōmon or "rope-pattern" culture from the rope-like designs which its people either incised or impressed into their clay pottery. Modern scientific techniques of measuring the age of archaeological materials have helped to revise the date of the beginning of Jōmon culture in Japan from the 4000–3000 B.C. figure mentioned above, which was generally accepted before the Pacific War, to around 8000 B.C.

Jōmon culture lasted in Japan from approximately 8000 until 300 B.C. and during this long age evolved through a number of stages. Its pottery, which was made by hand without a potter's wheel, is extraordinarily varied, with types and surface designs differing according to both time and place of construction. Typical pieces of early Jōmon pottery have bottoms like bullet or projectile heads and were apparently pushed into the earth or sand to make them stand upright; later types, on the other hand, tend to be much more elaborate and even bizarre, often having widely flared and ornately formed sides and rims.

The Jōmon people, whose sites have been found principally in the northern and eastern regions of the country, hunted animals and gathered roots, nuts, and berries. They also had canoes and were rather skillful coastal and even deep-sea fishermen. They lived at first in caves and later in shallow pit dwellings, each of a size (about two feet deep and about fifteen feet in diameter) sufficient to accommodate a family of four or five. Among the most prominent features of their settlements, which they usually occupied only briefly, were huge refuse piles or "kitchen mounds" composed mainly of the remains of shellfish, a food they apparently consumed with voracious appetite.

We have no way of knowing at this time the relationship, if any, between Jōmon man and his paleolithic predecessor. The Jōmon people may have immigrated as newcomers to Japan, but no one has been able to say with any certainty when and from just where. Perhaps they came in waves from different directions: from the north, via the islands of Sakhalin and Hokkaido; from Korea to Kyushu; or from Southeast Asia or the South Seas by a process of "island-hopping." The last suggestion is particularly intriguing. In historical times the route from Korea to northwestern Kyushu has been the most important means of entry into Japan. Yet there is a quite distinct "southern element" in Japanese culture that is not likely to have come from that direction. Certain Shintō myths, for example, are remarkably similar to those of Indonesia, New Zealand, and other island countries of the South Pacific, while early marriage customs and architectural styles are like the customs and styles of Polynesia.

Sometime around 300 B.C. Jōmon culture began to be displaced by a new culture, called Yayoi from the site in present-day Tokyo where its remains were first found. The Yayoi people used polished stone tools, wove cloth, and produced, with the aid of a potter's wheel and with a better firing technique, a technologically more advanced, although perhaps artistically less satisfying, type of pottery than that fashioned by the Jōmon people. In addition, the Yayoi people practiced agriculture and knew the use of metals.

There are, however, nearly as many unanswered questions about the transition from Jōmon to Yayoi as about the shift from paleolithic to Jōmon cultures. The tendency among Japanese scholars today is to stress the similarities between late Jōmon and early Yayoi and to hypothesize that in the former age the way had already been partially prepared for the introduction of the culture of the latter. Some scholars point out, for example, that late Jōmon man seems already to have had knowledge of a primitive kind of agriculture. Even if this were so, its importance in terms of socio-economic change should not be overestimated. The extensive adoption of agriculture and the establishment of farming villages would lead us to expect the emergence of new property-holding and social class distinctions. In fact, larger and more permanent settlements did appear in late Jōmon times; but the continuing general uniformity in the size of Jōmon pit dwellings and burial chambers indicates that, if property-holding and class distinctions arose, they were slight indeed.

Perhaps more fundamental in considering the transition from Jōmon to Yayoi is the question of how Yayoi culture originally came to Japan. It was once widely believed that the Yayoi people, whose sites are principally in the west and east, came to Kyushu from the continent (via Korea) and moved gradually into Honshu. One theory linked their arrival in Japan with the unification of China under the Ch'in and Han dynasties during the third century B.C. The theory was that the completion of the great wall of China caused migratory tribes in north Asia to move east and south through Manchuria and Korea and eventually to Japan. In the process of migration these people supposedly acquired some of the culture and technology, especially agriculture, of the Chinese.

Although there are ample grounds for dissent, the inclination among scholars at present is to reject the idea that there was any substantial "invasion" or migration such as this and to view Yayoi as essentially an important new set of cultural and technological advances on the continent which the Jōmon people adopted for themselves. This view is especially plausible in light of the later historical distinction which the Japanese earned for their capacity to adopt, voluntarily and in wholesale fashion, the superior cultures of others.

The development of agriculture during the Yayoi period (*ca.* 300 B.C.–A.D. 300) had profound and lasting effects on the course of Japanese civilization. Permanent farming villages were founded and grew in size. It became possible and desirable to accumulate wealth in the form of land and stored grain. The need for cooperative effort in tending fields and sharing available facilities gave rise to new kinds of organization. The family in particular became a more tightly knit economic as well as social unit; and above the family level increasingly larger communities made their appearance. Whereas a typical Jōmon settlement may have consisted of a relatively few households, some Yayoi communities contained a hundred or more.

The agriculture adopted by the Japanese in the early Yayoi period was the wet-rice culture of central and south China. This kind of agriculture requires a heavy input of human labor and has, until recent times, made of the mass of the Japanese people a highly sedentary farming society. Such a society tends to inculcate a strong sense of hierarchy with its stress on obedience: of children to parents, of younger to older brothers, of followers to superiors. And indeed the history of the Japanese until the modern era has to a great extent been governed by an acute consciousness of the gradations of status ascribed by birth.

Yet in at least one important way Japan has developed agriculturally quite differently from China. In China the need to undertake massive public works to control the distribution of water on a large scale for agricultural purposes has been a crucial factor in the tendency toward highly centralized "despotic" government. A similar need for truly massive public works has never existed in Japan. Water is, for the most part, abundant and evenly distributed by short, fast rivers and streams. There are no great water systems such as that of the Yellow River, which dominates the north China plain. Political and social control has been far more important on the local or regional, rather than the national, level. Hence, strong central government (to say nothing of despotism) has not been a conspicuous feature of Japanese society until modern times.

In addition to advances in agriculture, the use of metals also stimulated the rapid development of Japanese civilization during the Yayoi period. Since bronze and iron were both introduced virtually simultaneously from the continent, Japan did not have a true bronze age. Iron became the material for everyday use, while bronze was employed largely in the making of ceremonial and ornamental objects. By the mid-Yayoi age the Japanese had abandoned stone and were making their agricultural tools exclusively of wood and iron. They were, moreover, experimenting with new types of grain and moving outward from low-lying wetlands to other farming areas where they were obliged to evolve more complex methods of irrigation. Late Yayoi sites show the remains of highly developed systems of irrigated paddy fields as well as extensive storage facilities which attest that material accumulation, at least on the village level, was considerably advanced by the second and third centuries A.D.

There were three principal cultural areas in Japan during mid- and late Yayoi times: an area in northern Kyushu distinguished by the variety of bronze objects found in its burial sites, including coins and ornamental mirrors of Chinese Han dynasty origin and Korean-made spears, swords, and halberds; another area in the central provinces of Honshu in which innumerable bronze bells have been discovered scattered about; and, finally, a more remote area in the Kanto where no significant bronze findings have been made. The bronze bells of the central provinces are a great curiosity and, indeed, a mystery. Ranging in height from about five inches to four feet, these elongated objects are usually heavily ornamented both with abstract designs and with crudely sketched pictures of animals, houses, boats, people performing farming chores, men hunting with bow and arrow, and so on. Nobody has been able to explain their use (they are not functional as bells) or why they were apparently so indiscriminately discarded or left lying about by their owners. Perhaps they were used in certain religious rituals of which we no longer have knowledge or possibly they served as symbols of tribal headship. In any case production of them ceased abruptly in the early fourth century when the cultures of northern Kyushu and the central provinces began to merge.

Chinese Accounts of Early Japan

Our knowledge of Japan in the latter half of the Yayoi period—
that is, during the first three centuries A.D.—is not restricted to the
archaeological record. Valuable information is contained also in the
contemporary dynastic histories of China. The entries in these histories concerning Japan, which the Chinese chroniclers made in the
sections devoted to barbarian affairs, give us clues to aspects of early
Japanese society about which we would otherwise be quite ignorant.

The Chinese called Japan the land of Wa (a name which they
wrote with the character for "stunted" or "dwarfed") and recorded
that about the beginning of the first century A.D. Wa was divided into
a hundred "countries." Although we may hypothesize that these countries were in fact only tribal groupings, we have no way of knowing
whether they numbered precisely one hundred or whether the character "hundred" was intended to mean "a myriad." Moreover, it is
impossible to determine their distribution. Were they all concentrated in northern Kyushu around Hakata, the nearest stopping point
from the continent, or were they spread over other parts of the country, perhaps as distant as the Kansai?

In the year A.D. 57 an official group representing the countries of
Wa journeyed to China and was received in audience by Emperor
Kuang-wu, the founder of the Later Han dynasty (A.D. 25–220),
who presented it with a golden seal. More than seventeen hundred
years later, in 1784, a seal matching the description of the one presented by Kuang-wu was found by a farmer in a field near Hakata.
Not all scholars accept its authenticity, but for some this seal has
been an important factor in confirming the general reliability of the
accounts of Japan in the Chinese dynastic histories.

During the second century A.D. there appears to have been widespread disorder in Wa. Perhaps this disorder was part of a process
of political consolidation made possible by rapid technological advances in agriculture and metallurgy. Whatever the case, we are
told in the Chinese histories that by the following century the number of countries of Wa had been reduced to thirty and had come
under the general hegemony of a queen named Pimiko (or Himiko).
An especially detailed description of the land of Wa and its queen
during the early third century is contained in the *History of the Kingdom of Wei* which was compiled sometime around 297. From the
observations of the Wei history we learn, among other things, that

the people of Wa ate raw vegetables and went around barefooted; they covered their graves with earthen mounds and practiced scapulimancy as a means of divination; they clapped their hands in worship; and they conveyed messages either squatting or kneeling with both hands on the ground. Even these few entries illustrate the value of the Wei history in casting light on the origins and antiquity of certain later Japanese customs and practices. Clapping hands in worship, for example, is still common at Shintō shrines; and the covering of graves with earthen mounds presumably led to the construction of gigantic earthen tumuli in the Tomb period (discussed below). In matters of etiquette, kneeling on the ground bent almost double remains today the most deferential posture that a Japanese can assume.

Pimiko, who lived in the Wa country of Yamatai, seems to have been more of a religious than a political leader. Although advanced in years, she was unmarried and remained in guarded seclusion, where she engaged in magic and sorcery, and "bewitched" the people while her younger brother handled actual matters of administration. The temptation is strong to connect Pimiko's role as a kind of shaman or high priestess, who communicated with the gods on behalf of her people, with the origins of the most sacred ritual function of the Japanese sovereign in later historic times. Yet apparently Pimiko's personal charisma was also an important factor in maintaining Yamatai's control over Wa about the mid-third century, for after her death there was at least a temporary return to disorder.

The location of Yamatai is one of the most vexing problems in Japanese historiography. The Wei history contains explicit instructions on how to travel from Korea to Yamatai. But, although they direct us smoothly enough across the Korean Straits to Kyushu, these instructions then call for a sharp turn southward that leads ultimately through Kyushu and into the Pacific Ocean. Reluctant to dismiss the Wei instructions as utterly worthless, Japanese scholars have argued that either the distances which the Wei chroniclers give or the general line of direction they propose after reaching Kyushu must be wrong. If, for example, the instructions had said to turn *east* instead of *south* in Kyushu, then Yamatai must have been somewhere in the central provinces of the Kansai. If, on the other hand, the distances listed from one place to another in Japan were substantially less, Yamatai was most likely in Kyushu itself.

The important point is this: if Yamatai was located in the Kansai about the mid-third century it would mean that the land of Wa, from Kyushu to at least the Kansai, was even at that time loosely unified or centralized under a single "country," whose ruler (Pimiko) maintained official contact as Wa's representative with the Wei kingdom of China. But if, as seems more plausible despite what the Wei history says, Yamatai was simply the leader of "thirty countries" of Kyushu, then the merger or unification of the Kyushu and Kansai cultural zones had yet to take place.

In fact, this merger—and with it the founding of the historic Japanese state with its seat in the Kansai—seems to have occurred sometime between 250 and 400. Regrettably, the fall of the Wei kingdom in 265 brought to an end references to Japan in the Chinese histories until the fifth century, and we have no other written records for this time span of a century and a half. Rulers of the "countries" of Wa had from at least the first century A.D. repeatedly sought official recognition and backing from the Han and Wei regimes of China; but with the fall of the Wei and the beginning of disunion in north China, the Wa people apparently abandoned their efforts to maintain formal ties with the continent.

The Tomb Period

From about the year 300 Japan entered a new age of material development, most distinctive in the construction of earthen and stone tombs. Thousands of these tombs still lie widely scattered throughout Japan. Some appear to be little more than small knolls of land; but others are of truly stupendous proportions, in particular the one near present-day Osaka that is alleged to be the burial place of a semi-legendary emperor of the early fourth century named Nintoku. Although these tumuli have various shapes, some patterned on similar tombs found on the continent, Nintoku's is in the form of a giant keyhole, a shape that is unique to Japan. Surrounded by three moats, it occupies a land area of some eighty acres and is exceeded in sheer geographic size only by the tomb of the third century B.C. founder of China's Ch'in dynasty.

The appearance of these tombs from the fourth century testifies that Japanese society had reached a stage of differentiation in which an aristocratic class was able to mobilize the manpower and material resources necessary to build such gigantic monuments for its leaders. The largest and most imposing of the tombs are, like Nintoku's, in and around the Kansai and it was plainly here that the new rulers of Japan centered their efforts to unify the country under their rule.

Within the burial chambers of the tombs have been found a great variety of objects, including bronze and iron weapons, tools, and body ornaments. Of these funerary pieces, three—the long-sword, the Han-style mirror, and a type of curved "jewel" known as *magatama* —later became the sacred regalia, or symbols of emperorship, of the Japanese Imperial House.

Scholars have long puzzled over the origins of Japan's new rulers of the early tomb period. Some have even speculated that a group of horseriding warriors from northeast Asia invaded Kyushu shortly before the fourth century and militarily subjugated the country from at least Kyushu to the Kansai. One thing is clear: the rapid centralization of power in the Kansai during the fourth century was made possible only by important new advances in military technology and methods of fighting, whether or not these were directly received from northeast Asia or elsewhere. The Wei chroniclers, commenting on conditions in the early third century, had noted that the people of Wa either did not have or did not make use of horses. Yet the Japanese rulers of the fourth and fifth centuries were not only horseriders, but highly professional warriors on horseback. Despite an absence of written records, we have concrete proof of this in the collection of marvelously artistic and historically invaluable clay figurines known as *haniwa* that date from this age.

The *haniwa,* which show no readily identifiable foreign influences, constitute probably the most thoroughly "native" art form that the Japanese have produced. Usually a few feet in height, they have been found pressed into the earth around and on the tombs. The earliest *haniwa* are cylindrical in shape and may have been employed either to reduce erosion or to mark off certain areas on the tombs for symbolic or ceremonial purposes. Later, *haniwa* were molded into a whole variety of depictive forms, including houses, people, boats, animals, fish, and birds. The best assumption is that these depictive *haniwa* were intended to provide for the deceased representations of the things, both animate and inanimate, with which he was most closely associated during his lifetime. The traditional theory that the *haniwa* were first used as substitutes for people in order to end the gruesome practice of burying men alive with their dead masters is obviously erroneous, since the cylinder and house *haniwa,* to name just two, were made long before the human ones.

Warriors and horses are quite prevalent among the *haniwa* and it is these that most vividly attest to the strongly military orientation of the ruling aristocracy of the fourth and fifth centuries. The warrior figurines are elaborately clad in body armor and helmets and possess a variety of weapons, including swords, spears, daggers, and bows and arrows. Their horses are outfitted with ornamented saddles and harnesses and occasionally with metal face protectors. The impression presented by both man and beast is one of formidable preparedness for military combat. And indeed the newly organized fighting power of Japan's leaders is reflected not only in their internal centralization of rule around this time but also in the expansionist policy which they pursued in Korea from about the mid-fourth century.

Relations between Japan and southern Korea had been close for at least several centuries. Quite likely there was at first no clear political distinction between the two places, as immigrants to Kyushu maintained ties with relatives who had remained in southern Korea. With time, of course, "nationalistic" distinctions naturally arose. By the fourth century, three kingdoms were vying for supremacy in Korea: Koguryŏ in the north, Paekche in the west, and Silla in the east. Increasingly the Japanese became involved in the endless struggles among these Korean kingdoms, more often than not siding with Paekche against the others.

Around 369 the Japanese secured a territorial foothold in Korea at Mimana on the southern tip of the peninsula. Japanese sources tend perhaps to exaggerate the size and importance of Mimana. It may have been anything from a lonely outpost or military garrison to a kind of colony. But there can be little doubt that Japanese armies were deeply committed in Korea. In the history of the Liu Sung dynasty (420–479) of southern China it is recorded that on five separate occasions between 413 and 478 rulers of Japan petitioned the Liu Sung court for confirmation of various titles related to Japan and the countries comprising Korea, including those of "King of Wa" and "Generalissimo Who Maintains Peace in the East Commanding with Battle-Ax All Military Affairs." The first of these Japanese rulers has been identified by some scholars as the Emperor Nintoku for whom, as we have seen, the most gigantic of the earthen mausoleums was constructed in the Kansai. It is not known precisely which titles Nintoku wanted to have confirmed, but at least two of his successors were recognized by the Chinese in their claims to be military hegemons of Korea.

The Mythological Tradition

Before turning to the sixth century, when Japanese history becomes sharply clearer, let us examine briefly the mythological tradition of primitive Japan. The mythology of a people, quite apart from any literary pleasure it may provide, is of potential value to the historian for at least two reasons: because of the light it may shed on early customs, styles, habits, and the like; and because it may contain tales that are either literally or allegorically true. Japan's mythology is exceptionally rich and varied. Yet any meaningful analysis of it must be premised on an awareness of the time when and the conditions under which it was first put into writing. Scholars generally agree that the mythology as it first appears in the oldest extant written records of the Japanese—the *Kojiki* and *Nihon Shoki* of the early eighth century—is based chiefly on two works, an imperial genealogy and a book of "ancient words," that were written sometime in the sixth century. Japan by the sixth century, if not sooner, was indisputably ruled by a single dynastic line of emperors and almost certainly the traditional myths were arranged, and perhaps new ones were added, to cast special luster on the founding deity (*kami*) and lineage of the Imperial House. Moreover, the period from the sixth through the early eighth century, when its mythology was being put into writing, was also an epoch when Japan was profoundly under the sway of Chinese civilization and was almost completely reliant on the Chinese language for permanent, written expression. Inevitably, the compilers of Japan's mythology were influenced by Chinese philosophy and literary style and even by specific Chinese legends.

Only a brief sketch of the principal stories of Japanese mythology can be given here. In the beginning heaven and earth were separated. After six generations, the brother and sister *kami,* Izanagi and Izanami, appeared on the "plain of high heaven" and were commissioned to produce a "drifting land." Izanagi thrust a spear into the ocean below and as he withdrew it brine dripped from the tip and the small island of Onokoro was formed. Izanagi and Izanami went down to Onokoro by means of a bridge from heaven and, after giving birth to the remainder of the Japanese islands, produced a vast pantheon of *kami,* including *kami* of the sea, rivers, wind, woods, and mountains. In the process of giving birth to the *kami* of fire, however, Izanami was badly burned and went down to the "world of darkness." Izanagi, in an Orpheus and Eurydice type of sequence, went in search of his sister-wife. He was asked not to look upon her, but did and saw her in a horrible state of putrefaction.

Fleeing from the outraged Izanami, Izanagi returned to the upper world and went directly to a river to cleanse and purify himself. Among the *kami* he produced while disrobing and washing were the sun goddess, Amaterasu, and the storm god, Susanoo. Izanagi directed Amaterasu to ascend to heaven to be supreme ruler of the universe and Susanoo to assume dominion over the sea. Before taking up his duties, however, the unruly Susanoo went to heaven to say farewell to his sister and, while there, broke down the dividers of her rice fields, filled in her irrigation ditches, defecated in her palace, and committed other outrages. Shocked and dismayed, Amaterasu withdrew into a cave—plunging the world into darkness—and had to be lured out by the other *kami* of heaven.

Amaterasu eventually ordered her grandson, Ninigi, to descend and establish rule over the land of "luxuriant rice fields," bestowing upon him as symbols of his mandate the regalia of mirror, sword, and jewel. Ninigi arrived in southeastern Kyushu. Some time later his great-grandson, Jimmu, undertook a punitive campaign against aboriginal tribes to the east. Jimmu's expedition carried him through the region of the Inland Sea to what was to become the province of Yamato in the Kansai, where he conducted ceremonies to his ancestress, Amaterasu, and proclaimed himself the first emperor of Japan. The date of these ceremonies and of Jimmu's enthronement is regarded as the Foundation Day of the Japanese Empire and was calculated by historians of the seventh century A.D. to be equivalent to February 11, 660 B.C.

The myths contained in the *Kojiki* and *Nihon Shoki* collectively constitute the "scriptures" of Shintō or the "way of the *kami,*" Japan's native faith. Many bear a strikingly close resemblance to tales from widely dispersed regions of Asia, the Pacific, and even the West. The story of Izanagi's production of the island of Onokoro by dipping his spear into the ocean, for example, has a strong Polynesian flavoring: in various parts of Melanesia, Micronesia, and elsewhere, islands are mythically supposed to have been brought into being by primordial deities who "fished" them out of the ocean.

Unlike the Greeks and many other ancient peoples, the early Japanese gave little thought to the underworld or to man's state after death. Hence, in the episode in which Izanagi went in search of Izanami, the "world of darkness" is very indistinctly depicted. Shintō places great stress on cleansing or lustration, and death was regarded as simply one of a number of forms of pollution that demanded purification. Izanagi's visit to the river after returning to the upper world was thus in the best Shintō tradition. His thoughts were not at all with Izanami's sad state nor with what might become of her spirit, but rather with how to terminate the whole messy business as quickly as possible by performing lustration.

Amaterasu, the sun goddess, is the supreme *kami* in the Shintō pantheon. In the view of many scholars she was probably elevated to this position at a fairly late date—possibly as late as the sixth century—in order to give her, as the tutelary deity of the Imperial House (which we may henceforth for the sake of convenience call the Yamato family), primacy over the deities from which the other aristocratic families claimed descent. This implies that the Yamato family, after securing military and political hegemony, sought also to enhance its sacerdotal position by having the mythology rearranged to show that the sun line of Amaterasu had been ordained by heaven to found the Japanese state and to rule over it eternally. Although it is intriguing to speculate that the third-century Queen Pimiko of Wa was incorporated into the native mythology as Amaterasu, it is very unlikely that Pimiko was historically the founder of the Yamato line. There is, in fact, good reason to believe that several families held the emperorship successively during the fourth and fifth centuries. Many specialists contend that the present Yamato line was not founded until the early sixth century when, after a period of some twenty years of disorder, a provincial chieftain from the Hokuriku region ascended the throne as Emperor Keitai.

Susanoo, the storm god, has been thought by a number of scholars to represent the enemy or enemies whom the Yamato family had to overcome in order to consolidate its rulership. The outrages that he committed—destruction of field-dividers, filling in of ditches, defecating in the palace—were regarded as "heavenly" transgressions, in contrast to others, such as bestiality and the casting of spells, which were labeled "earthly" transgressions. Of the two types, the heavenly transgressions were by far the more serious, since they were held to threaten the welfare of the community as a whole.

The story of Ninigi's descent from heaven parallels similar myths from northeast Asia and has been cited as "proof" that Japan was indeed invaded during some age by people from this region of the continent who, under an "Emperor Jimmu," militarily asserted their mastery over Japan. Yet the myth of Jimmu's campaign from Kyushu to the Kansai contains many elements that suggest that it, like the Amaterasu myth, was not constructed until the sixth century and was thus also aimed at strengthening the claims to divine rulership of the reigning Yamato family.

There are, in various episodes of the mythology, references to re-calcitrant tribes or nations of people who opposed the Yamato court. We know that historically the court was obliged to deal with certain "barbarians" as it sought to expand its rule ever farther outward from the Kansai. The chief among these were the Kumaso of southern Kyushu and the Emishi of eastern and northern Honshu. The Emishi in particular have long puzzled historians, who have advanced many theories about their origins and identity. It was once widely believed that the Emishi of the early myths and records of Japan were none other than the Jōmon people, who were gradually pushed eastward and forcibly dispossessed of their land by the bearers of Yayoi culture (assumed to be the historical Japanese). Yet we have already noted the strong probability that the transition from Jōmon to Yayoi sometime about 300 B.C. did not involve a large-scale displacement of one people by another but rather the adoption of a more advanced culture from abroad by the existing inhabitants of Jōmon Japan.

The Emishi tribesmen have also frequently been identified with the Ainu, a caucasoid people who now live in Hokkaido. Recent studies of the mummified bodies of individuals known to be at least partly of Emishi extraction, however, show these individuals to have none of the physical characteristics of the Ainu. Other historical researches, moreover, point to the strong likelihood that the Ainu never settled south of Hokkaido. Far from being the Emishi, the Ainu were probably the natural enemies of the Emishi and may periodically have conducted sea raids southward against them in Honshu.

Theories such as these about the Emishi and the Ainu are ad-mittedly still highly conjectural. Nevertheless, it appears that the Emishi, against whom campaigns of subjugation were conducted in the eastern and northern provinces until the early ninth century, were in fact people of the same general ethnic stock as the followers of the Yamato court but were culturally so backward that they came to be regarded as barbarians and veritable aliens.

The Yamato Period

It was during the sixth century that Japan entered, if not fully, at least substantially into the light of written history. It is possible now to discuss with much more assurance than heretofore the evolution of Japanese culture and socio-political institutions.

The Imperial Court of the sixth century, located in or near the province of Yamato in the Kansai, exercised a kind of hegemony over a number of territorially based extended families, or *uji,* ranging from Kyushu in the west to the border of Emishi-land in the eastern provinces of the Kanto. Each *uji,* which was composed of blood relatives as well as people incorporated as fictive kin, was headed by a patriarch or chieftain (*uji no kami*) whose role, like that of the emperor at the head of the Imperial House, was both political and sacerdotal. As part of his rulership, the chieftain was called upon to perform certain sacred rites to the tutelary deity (*ujigami*) of the *uji* that were considered essential to its social cohesion and generational continuity.

Of the *uji* that constituted Japan's ruling aristocracy at this time possibly a quarter or more were of foreign—that is, Chinese or Korean—origin. For a century or more these foreign families had emigrated steadily to Japan where, with their special skills and knowledge of continental civilization, they easily acquired high social status and position. Without these foreign families, the sweeping reforms of the seventh century that transformed Japan from a backward country on the edge of Asia to a remarkably flourishing China in miniature would have been impossible.

We do not have sufficient records to determine precisely the degree of hegemony or authority that the Yamato court was able to exercise over the *uji.* Undoubtedly it varied from region to region and from one period to another. The court appears from perhaps the fourth century to have bestowed certain titles on the *uji* chieftains, such as *kuni-no-miyatsuko* (provincial commander), in an attempt to draw them more fully under central jurisdiction. In the course of putting down rebellions and otherwise expanding its activities into the provinces during the fifth and sixth centuries, moreover, the court was able to acquire certain agricultural lands, known as *miyake,* within the territorial domains of the *uji*. Although we do not know how extensive the *miyake* holdings were, it appears that they came to constitute a substantial public domain on which the court was able to base a far more radical policy of land nationalization in the mid-seventh century.

In addition to the above provincial titles, some of the more prominent *uji* chieftains received hereditary rankings, or *kabane,* that signified their right to participate in central affairs as ministers at court. The origins of the *kabane* are obscure. They may at first have been simply terms of respect used by *uji* members toward their chieftains, and only later adopted by the court as its principal ministerial designations. By mid-sixth century in any event, certain *kabane,* especially those of *omi* and *muraji,* were held by chieftains whose power at court rivaled that of the Imperial House.

Below the aristocratic or *uji* level, the great mass of Japanese society was formed into occupational groups or *be.* By far the largest of these groups were farmers, but others were comprised of fishermen, weavers, potters, and the like. Each *uji* controlled the *be* within its territorial domain and the Imperial House, in addition to the usual *be,* had special occupational groups (e.g., the Mononobe or "armorers," the Nakatomi or "attendants," the Imbe or "ritualists") that were in themselves great *uji* whose chieftains held *kabane* rankings at court.

The late sixth and seventh centuries, to which we turn our attention now, were a time of great vitality in East Asia. China's unification under the Sui (589–618) and T'ang (618–907) dynasties provided the impetus and the model for similar efforts toward unification and centralization in both Korea and Japan. After more than four centuries of disunion, China had emerged, restructured and reinvigorated, as the great "Middle Kingdom" of East Asia. One of the most important forces in China during the period of disunion and subsequent unification was Buddhism, which had been introduced to China from India sometime about the first century A.D. It is entirely appropriate to label the years from approximately the third until the eighth century as the great Buddhist age in East Asia. Buddhism at that time and at that place undoubtedly seemed as vital an ingredient of civilization and progress as, say, the Christian value system did to the Western peoples of the nineteenth century. The introduction of Buddhism to Japan, therefore, implied far more than simply the introduction of a new and purportedly efficacious body of religious doctrine. It meant the exposure of a geographically remote and still culturally backward people to all the glories and achievements of Chinese civilization.

The date traditionally given for the introduction of Buddhism to Japan is 552, when the Korean king of Paekche is supposed to have sent some scriptures and Buddhist statuary to the Japanese court in the hope of securing Japanese aid in his efforts to check the expansion of the state of Silla. Certainly the Japanese knew of Buddhism long before 552. Nevertheless, it is convenient to use this date as the point from which to study the ensuing process of 150 years of reform that brought the establishment of an impressively centralized state in Japan by the early eighth century. The reform process took place in two stages: a preparatory stage from about 552 until 645, and a stage of actual reform from the great Taika land reform of 645 until the founding of the first fixed capital at the city of Nara in 710.

During the period of reform in the sixth and seventh centuries Buddhism functioned as the principal carrier of Chinese culture and institutions to Japan. The issue that arose at the Yamato court about mid-sixth century over whether to "accept" or "reject" Buddhism was in reality a debate over the desirability of undertaking central reform on Chinese lines. Those who came most vigorously to oppose Buddhism were the families that had the largest vested interest in the *status quo,* particularly the *muraji* family of Nakatomi and the Great *Muraji* family of Mononobe. The Nakatomi claimed descent from a *kami* who, according to the mythology, had "attended" Ninigi on his descent from heaven to establish rule on earth. Along with the Imbe, they were responsible for the performance of sacred Shintō rituals at court. The Mononobe, on the other hand, were concerned chiefly with military matters and persisted in advocating a warlike, rashly imperialistic policy in Korea even though, since Japan had steadily lost ground there throughout the sixth century, such a policy was no longer tenable.

The most progressive family, and the one that most forcefully urged espousal of Buddhism, was the Great *Omi* family of Soga, which came to power with the accession of Emperor Kimmei in 531. The Soga, who were especially interested in matters of taxation and finance, appear to have established the first national treasury (*ōkura-shō*) in Japan and to have introduced various rudimentary practices of fiscal responsibility at court. They seem, moreover, to have regarded Korea far less as an arena for territorial expansion than as a bridge to China and a potential source of foreign trade.

The struggle between the pro-Buddhist and anti-Buddhist factions at court is told in fanciful and picturesque terms in the *Nihon Shoki*. When the court granted the Soga permission to build a private chapel to house and worship a Buddhist image, a pestilence swept over the land and was interpreted as a sign of disfavor on the part of the native *kami*. The Nakatomi and Mononobe thereupon destroyed the Soga chapel and threw the Buddhist image into a canal. Some two decades later, in 585, the Soga resumed their devotional practices. Once again there was a pestilence and once again the anti-Buddhists destroyed the Soga chapel and image. But this time the pestilence did not cease and the Soga were allowed to continue their worship. They now clearly held the upper hand at court. In 587 they attacked their chief rivals, the Mononobe, defeated them decisively, and inaugurated a period of ascendancy that was to last until the mid-seventh century.

What was the extent of the ascendancy or supremacy achieved by the Soga? Unlike the *muraji* families of Nakatomi and Mononobe, who had long functioned at court as service *uji* for the imperial family, the *omi* family of Soga was a great provincial or "outside" *uji* which had only relatively recently become active in central affairs. In the competition for power at court the Soga had a great advantage in that the Imperial House usually married with women from the *omi* families, which were apparently regarded as more on a level of social equality with it, and only rarely with women of the *muraji* or service *uji*. By the time of the Soga victory in 587, Soga blood flowed freely in the veins of many of the most prominent members of the Imperial House.

To consolidate the Soga's newly won position, the family chieftain Soga Umako first installed his nephew as Emperor Sushun and, when the latter proved insufficiently amenable to Soga control, had him murdered and replaced in 592 with a niece, Suiko (r. 592–628). Suiko, the first historical empress of Japan, was clearly intended to be a figurehead for Umako; yet her appointment to the throne does not mean that the Soga were able completely to dominate the Imperial House at this time. There were still a number of imperial princes who were very active politically. Chief among these and one of the towering figures of Japanese history was Prince Shōtoku, who came to hold the dual positions of crown prince and regent for his aunt, Empress Suiko.

Later generations, in celebrating Shōtoku as the great intellectual of his age and the principal precursor of central reform in Japan, have badly distorted his figure historically, so that we cannot be sure precisely which of his "achievements" are real and which are later attributions. There seems little doubt, however, that he was a man of considerable learning and erudition for his time and probably had a voice, along with Soga Umako, in most of the major decisions and policies of the final years of the sixth century and the first two decades of the seventh. Shōtoku is credited, among other things, with having written an exegetical text on Buddhism and the first national history of Japan, neither of which survives today. He is also supposed to have been chiefly responsible for the building of the Hōryūji, a temple on the outskirts of present-day Nara which remains one of the country's greatest architectural masterpieces.

Among the administrative measures traditionally attributed to Shōtoku is the institution in 603 of the Twelve-Cap Ranking System, whereby ministers at court were to be distinguished by differently colored headpieces. This system has long been interpreted as an attempt by the prince to challenge the monopoly of ministerial positions held by the Soga and other leading families through the granting of cap ranks to individual officials more on the basis of merit than of birth. Yet modern scholars tend to doubt this interpretation, which derives from the view that the previously "progressive" Soga, once in power, were content to perpetuate unchanged a loose system of central government that allowed ministerial participation only to the holders of the particularistic *omi* and *muraji* ratings. It appears, in fact, that there may have been a substantial broadening of ministerial recruitment and even bureaucratization—i.e., the regularization, rationalization, and differentiation of governing functions—at court under the Soga in the late sixth century. Soga Umako, moreover, may have been as much responsible as Prince Shōtoku for the introduction of the Cap Ranking System (which was apparently modeled on similar systems in the Korean kingdoms of Koguryŏ and Paekche) in order to give hierarchical designations to the many new middle and lower grade officials who had come in recent years to serve at court.

In 604, the year following inauguration of the Cap Ranking System, Shōtoku is purported to have issued his famous Seventeen Article Constitution. The word Constitution is misleading, since this document as it is reproduced in the *Nihon Shoki* does not contain what we would consider fixed laws or administrative provisions. One article calls upon the people to pay reverence to the Three Treasures of Buddhism (the Buddha, the Law, and the Religious Community); but essentially the Seventeen Article Constitution is a collection of maxims based on Han Confucianism that outline the qualities necessary for a virtuous officialdom. Although the admonitions that ministers must be frugal, industrious, prompt, impartial, obedient, and the like may seem to us simplistic and of only elementary value in dealing with practical matters of state, they are epochal in that they constitute the first statement in Japanese history of the need for government by ethical men.

A number of scholars strongly question whether Prince Shōtoku actually wrote or could have written the Seventeen Article Constitution. They base their doubts essentially on the number of seeming anachronisms that the document contains in references to conditions and institutions of the late rather than the early seventh century. Article XII, for example, calls upon the *kokushi* and *kuni-no-miyatsuko* to refrain from levying exactions on the people without specific authorization from the court. We have noted that the title of *kuni-no-miyatsuko* or "provincial commander" was of ancient origin; but *kokushi,* which later became the standard designation for provincial governor, does not appear to have been used in Japan before the Taika Reform. Phrases such as "the lord is heaven and the minister is earth" (Article III) and "there are not two lords in heaven just as there are not two masters on earth" (Article XII) are also viewed with suspicion because they suggest a degree of centralized authority under the throne that simply did not exist in Japan before the Taika Reform period. In short, if Prince Shōtoku was the original author of the Seventeen Article Constitution, his manuscript was without doubt considerably amended and revised by others prior to its inclusion in the *Nihon Shoki.*

One extremely important area of court activity in which Prince Shōtoku seems to have played a key role was the dispatch of official missions and students to China. The court sent a total of four missions to Sui China: in 600, 607, 608, and 614. Ono no Imoko, traditionally regarded as Japan's first overseas student, led the 607 and 608 missions. Among the fellow students and priests who traveled with him, several remained abroad for two or more decades and a few returned to play prominent roles in the Taika Reform. The journey to the continent was a dangerous one in this age. Boats were frequently sunk or blown far off course. Yet the rewards of a firsthand

Chinese education were great, as attested by the number of people during the next two centuries who gained fame and fortune after studying on the continent.

On the mission of 607 Ono no Imoko carried a message, generally attributed to Prince Shōtoku, to the Sui emperor that began: "From the Son of Heaven of the Land of the Rising Sun to the Son of Heaven of the Land of the Setting Sun." This terminology, needless to say, was not appreciated by the Sui emperor, who without doubt regarded the Japanese as little more than impertinent barbarians in the eastern sea. And indeed, so far as we know, the Japanese from the time of the first references to the land of Wa in the Later Han and Wei histories had freely and even eagerly accepted an inferior, tributary relationship vis-à-vis China. Shōtoku, if he was in fact the author of the 607 message, appears thus to have been the first Japanese leader to assert that Japan's national status was on a level with that of China. Prewar Japanese scholars chauvinistically overstressed the importance of this. Yet the fact remains that the Japanese, alone among the peoples of East Asia, were, with one exception, never again to accept subordinate treatment in their official dealings with China.

After the fall of the Sui Dynasty in 618 Japan allowed another dozen years to elapse before it sought to renew ties with China. The first mission to T'ang China departed in 630. During the next two centuries or so the Japanese sent a total of twelve such missions to China, usually consisting of from two to four boats and from 100 to perhaps as many as 600 people. The varied adventures of the government officials, students, priests, and others who participated in the missions make fascinating footnotes to this age in East Asian history. To the Japanese these missions, even though sporadically dispatched, were absolutely essential to the continuance and completion of their tutelage in the ways of Chinese civilization.

In 600, the very same year that Shōtoku sent the first mission to Sui China, the Japanese had also dispatched an army of some 10,000 troops to Korea in an attempt to recover their position in Mimana, which they had lost to the incursions of Paekche and Silla in 562. Although the Japanese expeditionary force soundly defeated Silla in 600 and exacted from her a pledge to pay the tribute which Mimana had formerly rendered to the Yamato court, Silla never honored the pledge and in 602–3 the Japanese gathered a much larger contingent of approximately 25,000 men to send over. It never left Kyushu, however, owing to the sudden death of its first commander (Shōtoku's brother) and subsequent misfortunes.

Prince Shōtoku died in 622 and Soga Umako in 626. These two men had provided superior leadership for Japan during the early stages of governmental and cultural reform in the late sixth and early seventh centuries. In a still primitive and underdeveloped society a few men of their calibre can, by virtually their efforts alone, implement changes and reforms whose importance the vast majority of their countrymen can only dimly, if at all, perceive. Japan during this age had, of course, the special advantage of numerous skilled personnel among its large immigrant population. Nevertheless, the roles of Shōtoku and Umako in providing direction for the great process of reform on Chinese lines launched at this time seem to have been crucial and their deaths unquestionably slowed its momentum.

The Taika Reform

Umako's successors as Great *Omi* were his son Emishi and his grandson Iruka, to whom Emishi relinquished the title in 643 for reasons of health. We are greatly hampered in our attempts to evaluate the period from 626 until 645, when Emishi and Iruka managed the affairs of the land, because the authors of our only source, the *Nihon Shoki,* have depicted these men in such highly stereotyped terms as Chinese-style bad last rulers. It appears, in any case, that Emishi and Iruka devoted little if any of their time to innovation. Rather, they concentrated on keeping the throne supplied with nonentities and in crushing the political ambitions of promising imperial aspirants, such as Shōtoku's son, Prince Yamashiro no Ōe, whom Iruka attacked and forced to commit suicide in 643.

The most heinous offense of Emishi and Iruka, in the eyes of the *Nihon Shoki*'s authors, was to covet the throne for themselves. In quest of it they purportedly built huge personal mausoleums that rivaled those of the Imperial House, constructed grand homes which they referred to as "palaces," and spoke of the children of their households as "princes." Whatever the truth of these allegations by the authors of the *Nihon Shoki,* it is quite possible that Emishi and Iruka did conceive of usurping the throne for their own family. The later deliberate efforts, as we shall see, of emperors after the Taika Reform to reaffirm and to heighten the sacred character of the imperial position may initially have been motivated by fears that the

Yamato family had indeed, on the eve of the Taika Reform, been perilously close to supplantation by the Soga as Japan's ruling dynasty.

By the late 630s and early 640s Emishi and Iruka had become, if not potential usurpers, certainly the principal obstacles to further reform. A clandestine group became convinced that only their forcible removal from power could make possible a further reduction in the autonomy of the provincial *uji,* including the Soga, and true centralization of rule under the throne. The leaders of this group were Nakatomi Kamatari, a member of one of the families that had most strenuously opposed the Soga a century before on the issue of Buddhism, and Prince Naka, son of the reigning empress. They were eventually joined by men from nearly all the factions at court, including a ranking Soga minister, indicating that the widespread antipathy toward Emishi and Iruka may have been as much personal as ideological.

The reform group of Kamatari and Prince Naka had as its theoreticians men who had traveled to China and had studied intensively the institutions and thought of the newly founded T'ang dynasty. Among them were Takamuko Kuromaro, Minabuchi Shōan, and the priest Min, all of whom had journeyed to the continent in the mission of 608. They had been in China during the momentous period of transition from the Sui to the T'ang dynasty, and were not only profoundly impressed by the vigor and brilliance of the new T'ang government but also alarmed by the possibility of future T'ang military expansion in the direction of Japan. Although the T'ang rulers had continued the Sui policy of aggression against northern Korea, the likelihood that they would attempt to invade Japan must have been slim indeed, if not entirely nonexistent, at this time. Nevertheless, Japan's leaders throughout the seventh century seem to have felt an acute sense of foreign crisis and potential outside threat. The group led by Kamatari and Prince Naka saw the specter of T'ang military might as one of the more compelling reasons to overthrow the Soga and to get on with centralization of the Japanese state.

Accordingly, on the occasion of a high state function in the sixth month of 645, Prince Naka and his cohorts undertook a coup by slaughtering Soga Iruka at the imperial palace in full view of the empress and her attendants. The following day Emishi set fire to his mansion and perished in the flames. With remarkable swiftness, some six decades of Soga ascendancy came abruptly to an end. The vic-

torious conspirators immediately declared the commencement of a
new epoch, which they called Taika (Great Change) in imitation of
the Chinese practice of designating calendrical eras. And on New
Year's Day of the following year, 646, they issued an edict which
set forth the general intent of the Taika Reform.

As in the case of Prince Shōtoku's Seventeen Article Constitution
and other statements and manifestoes of the seventh century, we have
the text of the Taika Reform Edict only as it appears in the *Nihon
Shoki,* most likely considerably revised and edited. It is nonetheless
clear that the Reform in its earliest stages was intended to be primarily
a land reform. The reformists wished first of all to destroy the existing systems of landholding and social organization by means of which
the great *uji* had exercised virtually autonomous control over their
territorial domains and over the people of the various occupational
groups, or *be,* that lived on them. These "private lands and private
people" were now declared to be "public lands and public people."
In this way the reformists sought to assert the right of public domain
over land everywhere and to affirm the status of all people as direct
subjects of the throne.

The new land and tax systems inaugurated at this time were modeled closely on the "equal field" and "triple tax" systems which had
been perfected by the T'ang dynasty in China. Henceforth farming
lands were to be allotted equitably on the basis of one plot per adult
male and specified lesser plots for others. Individuals were to occupy
and work these lands during their lifetimes (after which they were to
revert to the government for reallotment) and were to be responsible
for three kinds of taxes: a harvest tax, a "special products" tax (e.g.,
silk, cotton cloth, thread), and a corvée labor tax, including military
conscription.

It is not at all clear how widely this new land system was enforced.
Quite likely the degree of enforcement varied according to region. We
do know that from the outset a number of concessions in the form of
special allotments were made to members of the former ruling *uji,*
which gave them vastly larger holdings than the average peasant, and
also that the periodic inspections tended to become less and less frequent. The whole idea of an "equal field" system was excessively
idealistic for Japan of the seventh century. That it worked for as
long as it did is perhaps remarkable and is attributable in part to the
fact that even before the Taika Reform the court had begun, as we
have noted, to extend its right of public domain over an increasingly

larger portion of the country through the acquisition of special *miyake* holdings. Nevertheless, the Taika land system did contain inherent flaws and it began to break down during the eighth century.

The leaders at court during the early years of the Taika Reform period did not devote a great deal of attention to enlargement and reorganization of the central bureaucracy, but preferred to leave these matters until a time when they should feel more secure in their power. The old *kabane* titles (including those of Great *Omi* and Great *Muraji*) were, however, immediately abolished and three ministers— a minister of the left, a minister of the right, and a minister of the center—were appointed to be the chief assistants to the throne in government. Prince Naka also granted the minister of the center, Nakatomi Kamatari, the new surname of Fujiwara in recognition of his extraordinary services to the Imperial House. As Fujiwara Kamatari, this distinguished statesman became the first of a family line that was subsequently to rise to the highest circles of prominence in the court aristocracy of ancient Japan.

In 645, at the same time that the new calendrical era of Taika was proclaimed, the court for the first time used the national designation of "Nihon." This designation, which has entered English as "Japan" from its Chinese pronunciation of "Jih-pen," literally means "source of the sun" and was most likely derived from the phrase "Land of the Rising Sun" which Prince Shōtoku used in his communication to the Sui court in 607.

According to the Taika Reform Edict, Japan or "Nihon" was to be divided into the new geopolitical units of province (*kuni*), district (*gun*), and township (*ri,* consisting of about fifty households). Each province was to be headed by a provincial governor (*kokushi*) and each district by a district governor (*gunji*). Whereas the provincial governors, who were given four-year terms of office, were usually men sent out from the court, the district governors were selected from among local magnates and appear from the first to have occupied their positions on a more or less permanent, hereditary basis. Those who became the new district governors were, by and large, members of the class of lesser *uji* chieftains who had formerly held the *kuni-no-miyatsuko* (provincial commander) rankings. The awarding of district governorships to them was simply one means by which the court sought to ensure their support for the over-all policies of reform. But such a major concession to outside interests clearly indicates at the same time that the court reformists, despite their success in overthrowing the Soga, were not in a position to press for too drastic changes in regional administration.

Society during the Taika Reform period came to be divided into two general categories, the so-called good people and mean people. The "good" people included: 1) the vast majority of peasant workers, craftsmen, and artisans who had formerly constituted the occupational groups, or *be;* and 2) the ruling families of the aristocracy, whose positions were distinguished by their right to hold court ranks. The "mean" people, who comprised about ten percent of the population, were chiefly slave-like personal servants. Marxian historians, in particular, are interested in the "mean" people and the question of slavery in this early period of Japanese history. In seeking to demonstrate that seventh-century Japan had a strong slave coloration they point to the fact that, of the three taxes levied on the peasantry at this time, by far the most onerous was the corvée or labor tax. They further note that, with the shift to a feudal society several centuries later, the ruling class minimized its direct, chattel-like exploitation of human labor and concentrated instead on extracting heavy harvest rents from the peasants, who were by then locked in serfdom.

The single most powerful individual at court during the early decades of the Taika Reform period was without question Prince Naka. Curiously, however, he did not actually ascend the throne until 668. Rather, he allowed his uncle and mother (for the second time) to reign while he occupied the position of crown prince. Naka, in his apparent reluctance to accept the final exalted rank to which he was so eminently entitled, even permitted the throne to remain vacant for some seven years after his mother's death in 661.

None of the theses that have been advanced to explain Naka's attitude toward the throne is entirely convincing. It has been suggested, for instance, that he wished to follow the example of the former crown prince and regent, Prince Shōtoku, who he believed had deliberately kept the Empress Suiko removed and aloof—like a later-day Pimiko—from the practical matters of state. Yet if Naka liked the idea of a nonacting sovereign whose principal role was passively to sanctify the acts of others, he certainly reversed his thinking when he finally took the throne and became a forceful emperor in his own right. Perhaps more plausible is the view that Naka sincerely felt he could better maintain a consensus among his followers during the delicate early phases of the Taika Reform if he did not immediately become sovereign and expose himself to the charge that he sought only personal power and glory.

Whatever Prince Naka's private feelings about it, the Japanese imperial institution during the late sixth and seventh centuries was in an important stage of development owing to the influence of Chinese theories of kingship on existing native practices. Around mid-sixth century the Yamato ruler had been known principally as *ō-kimi* (Great *Kimi*), a title that appears to have been very similar to the *kabane* designations of *ō-omi* (Great *Omi*) and *ō-muraji* (Great *Muraji*). Moreover, just as there were lesser *uji* chieftains ranked as *omi* and *muraji,* there were still others who had the title of *kimi.* Perhaps, then, *ō-kimi* was simply the highest of the *kimi* just as the *ō-omi* and *ō-muraji* were respectively the most important of the *omi* and *muraji.* If so, the paramountcy of the Yamato ruler or *ō-kimi* in the sociopolitical hierarchy of mid-sixth century Japan was obviously nowhere near that of, let us say, the awesome Chinese emperor who, according to Confucian theory, enjoyed a "Mandate of Heaven."

Sometime in the early seventh century the Japanese, probably at Prince Shōtoku's instigation, replaced the title *ō-kimi* with the Chinese-style one of *tennō,* or "heavenly sovereign," in an obvious attempt to upgrade imperial prestige. Moreover, when Prince Naka finally ascended the throne as the Emperor Tenji in 668 he did so amid proclamations of portents and omens that indicated that he had received heaven's mandate. As adumbrated earlier, he most likely did this to elevate the imperial rank to an even higher realm of sanctity beyond the reach of any ministerial family that in the future might harbor the kind of aspirations once held by the Soga.

Several years prior to his accession Prince Naka had suffered the most severe setback of his political career. At the urgent pleading of Paekche, which was nearing national extinction under the relentless aggression of Silla, the prince had dispatched to Korea an expeditionary army that was decisively defeated by the combined forces of Silla and T'ang China in 663. As a result, Paekche perished, Korea was unified under Silla, and the Japanese were finally obliged to abandon their dreams of power in the peninsula. Apart from certain pirates during the medieval age, no Japanese were to fight overseas again for more than 900 years until the Korean invasions of Toyotomi Hideyoshi in the 1590s.

When Emperor Tenji (formerly Prince Naka) died in 671, a succession quarrel erupted between his son and his brother. In the violent fighting that ensued, the forces who supported the brother prevailed and the latter became the Emperor Temmu in 672. Temmu, who was probably the most powerful sovereign in Japanese history, made special use of Buddhist concepts of heavenly protection in seeking to propagandize the majesty of his rulership.

Scholars of a few generations ago were inclined to look upon Temmu's reign (672–86) as a period of conservative reaction to the more radical aspects of the Taika Reform. But more recently the tendency has been to credit Temmu with having consolidated the Reform in terms of its most fundamental goal, which was to centralize state power as fully as possible at court. Temmu's support in the succession struggle had come largely from the former *kuni-no-miyatsuko* class of lesser *uji* chieftains, who collectively were able to inflict severe defeat on several of the greater *uji* supporting the son's cause, including remnants of the once great Soga clan. Thus the Imperial House under Temmu found itself more secure than ever before from challenge by the other leading families that had formerly been joined loosely in the Yamato hegemony.

Both Tenji and Temmu are credited with having compiled important legal codes, although neither has been preserved until today. Nevertheless, it appears certain that the legal work undertaken during their two reigns and the reign of Temmu's wife and successor, Empress Jitō (r. 686–97), made possible the issuance of the great Taihō Code of 701, which became the fundamental law of the court for the next eleven and a half centuries. In addition, the period of Temmu and Jitō also witnessed a considerable acceleration in the regularization and bureaucratization of central government. By the turn of the century the stage was clearly set for the culminating accomplishments of early Japan's half-century of epochal reform: the compilation of the Taihō Code and the founding of a new imperial capital at Nara.

II

The Age

of the Court

Nobles

BY
H. PAUL VARLEY

The Structure of Nara Japan

The compilation in 701 of the Taihō Code, named after the calendrical era of Taihō or "Great Treasure," and the founding of a new capital at Nara in 710 ushered in the age of the court nobles, a period which lasted until the late twelfth century. Although no copy of the Taihō Code remains today, later commentaries and supplements enable us to reconstruct most of its contents and thus to see the basic legal structure of Japan during this period.

The provisions of the code were divided into two major categories: *ritsu* (penal provisions) and *ryō* (administrative provisions). The former, closely patterned on T'ang law, prescribed generally light punishments in accord with the Confucian ideal of seeking good government through the inculcation of virtue rather than the imposition of harsh penalties. The administrative provisions, on the other hand, reflected a fairly conscious attempt on the part of the Japanese to adapt Chinese administrative practices to indigenous sentiment and conditions. This can perhaps best be seen in the establishment of a Department of Rites (*Jingikan*) directly below the throne on the same level as a Chinese-style Department of State (*Dajōkan*). Devoted exclusively to native Shintō and the court ritual associated with it, the Department of Rites constituted an important concession to purely Japanese attitudes toward rule. While it enjoyed little real power, this department served to bolster the traditional sanctity of the throne and to enhance the emperor's role as national mediator to the gods.

The Department of State, which was the chief administrative body under the Taihō Code, was divided into eight ministries: Central Administration, Ceremonial, Civil Affairs, People's Affairs, Military Affairs, Justice, the Treasury, and the Imperial Household. Among its leading officials were a chancellor (*dajō daijin*), a minister of the left, and a minister of the right. Since the chancellor's office was usually left vacant during the eighth century, the business of the Department of State was generally supervised by either the minister of the left or the minister of the right.

The Taihō Code said nothing about the emperorship or rules for selecting a sovereign. During the eighth century, as during the seventh, several empresses occupied the throne; but after the death of the Empress Shōtoku in 770, the succession (for reasons we shall see) was restricted to males. Even then, no strict procedure was adopted for choosing successors from among the various qualified princes of the Imperial House. Although there was a general tendency from about the mid-ninth century to have the line of succession pass from father to son, a number of brothers, uncles, and other male relatives also ascended the throne.

Following several changes in the arrangement of ministerial rankings from the time of the institution of Prince Shōtoku's Twelve-Cap System in 603, the Taihō Code set forth a scheme of eight major ranks, with various subgradings, that was to remain virtually unchanged for courtier society during the remainder of the premodern period. Of the eight ranks, the first, second, and third were reserved for the very highest ministers at court and for members of the Imperial House; most officials could not aspire to rise above the fourth or fifth ranks during their careers; and members of the provincial officialdom (apart from provincial governors) were usually restricted to the seventh and eighth. Ranks held at court, moreover, were designated as "inner," whereas those possessed by functionaries in the provinces were labeled "outer." This discrimination between inner and outer officeholders and the overwhelming preference in rank given to the former contributed importantly to the steady decline in provincial administration during the age of the court nobles.

One of the most characteristic institutions of Chinese life from the period of the great Han dynasty (206 B.C.–A.D. 220) had been the system of civil service examinations. These examinations, based on knowledge of the Confucian Classics (themselves the repository of traditional Chinese morality and ethics), constituted the most important channel for entry into China's ministerial class. Japanese reformers from the time of Prince Shōtoku were well aware of this system; indeed the authors of the Taihō Code sought to inculcate the ideal of bureaucratic preferment through Confucian scholarship by providing for the construction of a central college and various branch colleges in the provinces.

Yet strong native sentiment militated against acceptance of this method of ministerial recruitment. Although special circumstances during the eighth century enabled a number of men from relatively modest social backgrounds to attain prominence either through the Buddhist priesthood or through Chinese studies, birth continued to be the overriding qualification for membership in Japan's aristocracy. The new system of court ranks set forth in the Taihō Code soon became tightly hedged by considerations of birth and family connections. So rigidly controlled had both court rank and government office become by the Heian period (894–1185) that members of all but the smallest group of aristocratic families were completely denied access to them.

Shortly after issuance of the Taihō Code, the court decided to build a new capital at Nara in the northern part of the Yamato Plain. Until this time the seat of imperial authority had frequently been moved, usually in and around the central provinces. One reason for this (at least before the Taika Reform) was the Shintō belief that the death of a sovereign caused the pollution of a site; but decisions to move had also often been based on political and strategical considerations. In any case, the frequency and apparent facility with which its location was changed suggests that there was still a very limited administrative establishment. With the rapid bureaucratization of government during the Taika-Taihō period, however, the need for a more permanent ruling center became increasingly obvious.

The site of Nara was selected for various reasons. It was in a spacious location and it met the requirements of geomancy (in Chinese, *feng-shui*): that is, its mountains, rivers, and such were situated in the correct relationship to each other. Moreover, it was near certain important Buddhist temples, among them the Hōryūji, closely associated with the name of the venerated Prince Shōtoku.

Construction was begun in 708 and the court was moved to Nara in 710. Fashioned as a miniature of the Chinese capital of Ch'ang-an (present-day Sian), it captured perfectly the spirit of an age in East Asian history dominated by the pervasive influence of the great empire of the T'ang dynasty. As at Ch'ang-an, the focal point of Nara was the palace compound in its northernmost precincts where the emperor, in the traditional Chinese manner, could "look southward" toward his subjects. A grand thoroughfare extending south from the palace divided the city into eastern and western halves, each laid out symmetrically in a grid-like pattern of intersecting north-south and east-west avenues.

Little remains today of the original Nara (the present city of that name has grown up almost entirely in its northeastern suburbs). Yet Nara in its age of glory was an imposing metropolis and was, as far as we know, the first truly urban center in Japanese history. About one quarter the size in land area of Ch'ang-an, it rose to a population of some 200,000, about 10,000 being employed directly in government service. Japan's total population at this time is estimated to have been between five and six million people.

The founding of Nara was accompanied by a great burst of economic and administrative activity. Transportation and supply facilities were set up to link the provinces with the capital; post roads and service stations were constructed in each of the great circuits or ways (*dō*) into which the country was divided; [1] new officials were appointed to oversee the collection of taxes; and the government even minted coins (known as Wadō coins from the calendrical era 708–14) to facilitate the inflow of revenue to the treasury.

Although they helped to provide for the needs of the new leisure class of the capital, these measures of the early eighth century did not stimulate any substantial commercial development in the country as a whole. The government had great difficulty, for example, in getting people to exchange the Wadō coins for goods rather than simply holding onto them as curios or hoarding them. Outside the central provinces the coins were scarcely used at all, and the practice of barter remained almost universal. The minting of coins was continued sporadically in Japan until the ninth century, when it was discontinued, not to be resumed until the latter part of the sixteenth century. A fundamental reason for the failure of commerce to develop significantly beyond the capital region during the age of the court nobles was, as we shall see, the decay of the equal-field system of land tenure and the rise from about the mid-eighth century of private estates, which promoted localism and strengthened the principle of economic self-sufficiency throughout the provinces.

Several groups, apart from the sovereigns, contended for power at court during the Nara period (710–84). These included other members of the Imperial House, ministers of the leading courtier families (such as the Fujiwara, the Tachibana, and the Ōtomo), and Buddhist priests. The constant factional clashes, intrigues, and plottings that occurred suggest a fundamental instability in ruling institutions; yet the participation of people from varying backgrounds at least gave a diversity to political affairs in Nara times. A century or so later power came to be monopolized by one family, the Fujiwara, which dominated the throne and presided over a kind of government quite different from that set forth in the Taihō Code.

1. Of the seven circuits of early Japan the best known was the Tōkaidō (Eastern Water Way) that extended from the central to the eastern provinces. The Saikaidō (Western Water Way), which comprised the island of Kyushu, had a separate administrative center known as Dazaifu. Hokkaidō (Northern Water Way), the northernmost of the main islands of Japan today, was not one of the original *dō* but was given this designation in 1869.

The rise of the Fujiwara was not sudden or accidental. Kamatari, the first holder of the name, had been one of the chief architects of the Taika Reform and his son, Fubito, played a leading role in the drafting of the Taihō Code. A daughter of Fubito was made the ranking consort of the Emperor Shōmu (r. 724–49), the first person outside the Imperial House to achieve this status, and his four sons reached ministerial rank. The death of all four sons from plague in 739 was a severe setback to the Fujiwara, but before long the family was once again providing leaders at court and by the end of the century it was clearly ahead of its rivals in the competition for power.

Buddhism in Nara Japan

The Emperor Shōmu and his Fujiwara consort were fervent Buddhists and greatly encouraged the propagation of the foreign faith. Indeed, Shōmu and his chief advisers, some of whom were Buddhist priests, even aimed to use Buddhism as the "guardian of the state" to strengthen Japan institutionally. Such an aim may seem completely antithetical to the original spirit of Buddhism, which held this world to be a place of misery and suffering and was little concerned with sociopolitical institutions. But Buddhism in China during the Sui and early T'ang dynasties had great wealth and power and its adherents were the chief transmitters of Chinese culture to other lands. To Japanese of the Nara period the idea of having Buddhism serve as the "guardian of the state" must have seemed eminently fitting.

In 737 Shōmu, following the precedents of both the Sui and T'ang dynasties, ordered the construction of a temple and nunnery in each of the provinces of Japan; and to serve as the center for this network of officially sponsored provincial religious bodies, he had the Tōdaiji (Great East Temple) built in Nara. Housed within the central building of the Tōdaiji was a huge bronze statue, some fifty-three feet in height, of the Buddha Vairochana. The casting of this Daibutsu (Great Buddha) was an impressive technological feat for eighth-century Japan. It was begun in 747 under the direction of craftsmen of Korean descent and, after seven unsuccessful attempts, was completed in 749. In that year the court received news from the northern province of Mutsu that gold had been discovered in Japan for the first time and that several hundred pounds of it were to be donated as gilding for the Daibutsu.

It appears likely that the official who made this report actually brought the gold over from Korea and offered it to the court in order to gain special favor. Shōmu, however, was overwhelmed with the auspiciousness of the "discovery." To celebrate it he went to the Daibutsu and performed a remarkable act.

Assuming a seat facing northward toward the statue, as a subject would face a sovereign, Shōmu declared himself to be a "Servant of the Three Treasures of Buddhism." In so doing he brought the throne to a crossroads in its history. Kingship in Japan was based on the emperor's claim of direct blood descent from the Sun Goddess; yet sovereigns from the time of Tenji and Temmu had also sought to use both Confucian and Buddhist tenets to strengthen their hold on the throne. It is possible that Shōmu considered making Buddhism the state religion of Japan. But he stopped short of taking the step that might have led to the establishment of a Buddhist church superior to the throne. And never again was a Japanese sovereign to humble himself in the manner of Shōmu to any outside authority or creed.

At the "eye-opening" ceremony for the Daibutsu in 752, during which the statue was symbolically given life by having the pupils of its eyes painted in, all the great dignitaries of the Nara court were in attendance. In addition there were visitors from China, India, and other distant lands and some 10,000 Buddhist priests. It was without doubt one of the grandest occasions in all of early Japanese history.

Near the Tōdaiji, and originally part of it, is an extraordinary building called the Shōsōin. Constructed like an elongated log cabin with its floor elevated high above the ground by large wooden posts, the Shōsōin is a repository of things from the eighth century and earlier. It contains thousands of objects, including paintings, lacquer, glassware, weapons, musical instruments, decorative screens, costumes, masks used in ritual dances, mundane household articles, and a variety of written documents. Many of these things belonged personally to Emperor Shōmu, while others were used in the dedicatory ceremony for the Daibutsu. Among the objects of art, a number are either imports from China or works produced in Japan in imitation of T'ang models; still others show influences from regions as distant as Persia and Greece.

In 749 Shōmu abdicated in favor of his daughter, Kōken, who in turn relinquished her position to a nephew in 757. While in retirement Kōken came under the influence of a faith-healing Buddhist priest named Dōkyō. The relationship that developed between the former empress and Dōkyō led to one of the most bizarre incidents in Japanese history. In 764 Kōken deposed the emperor, reascended the throne as Empress Shōtoku, and elevated Dōkyō to several high Buddhist and secular positions, including that of chancellor.

So infatuated did she become with Dōkyō that Shōtoku appears even to have considered placing him on the throne. Only the empress's death in 770 brought an end to Dōkyō's overweening ambitions. His downfall was total and pointed up an important fact of political life in Japan during the age of the court nobles: without strong family ties, such as those enjoyed by the Fujiwara, one could not hope to establish a lasting position of power at court. Dōkyō, who had risen from relatively modest provincial origins, was simply no match for the hereditary aristocrats at court who opposed him after the death of his patron.

The Shōtoku-Dōkyō affair came as a severe shock to Nara society. It seems to have been tacitly agreed that women should henceforth be excluded from succession to the throne. (After Shōtoku there were only two female sovereigns, one in the seventeenth and one in the eighteenth century.) At the same time a number of Buddhist priests were removed from positions of political authority and, within a decade or so, the decision was reached to abandon the capital city itself.

It is unlikely that this decision was based solely on the desire to escape what was considered the baneful influence of the Nara priesthood. In any case, the capital was relocated at Heian or Kyoto some twenty-eight miles north of Nara in 794. The move was costly and temporarily disruptive of the functioning of central government; but Heian did possess several advantages over Nara, among them better facilities for river transport to the sea and more direct access to the eastern and northern provinces, where Japanese armies were engaged in a struggle to dispossess the Emishi.

Buddhism during the Nara period is usually discussed in terms of "six sects": Sanron, Kusha, Jōjitsu, Kegon, Ritsu, and Hossō. None of these sects, however, was to find a broad following among the Japanese people. The cosmologically oriented Kegon (Flower Wreath) sect inspired Shōmu and his advisers to undertake construction of the Tōdaiji with its great statue of the Buddha Vairochana and its provincial branch temples, each symbolically represented by a petal of the lotus blossom upon which the massive Buddha sat. Yet by and large the abstruse doctrines of Indian and Chinese metaphysics advanced by the six Nara sects did not appeal to the Japanese people.

The Buddhist sects that were to become most firmly rooted in the soil of Japan were all introduced or propagated in later centuries.

If the Japanese of the Nara epoch were not generally attracted to specific sects, they were increasingly influenced (as revealed in their literature) by the basic tenets of Buddhism: e.g., that this is a world of suffering; that all things are impermanent; and that, in accord with the law of karma, one's present life and fortune are determined by behavior in previous existences. Moreover, they responded directly and wholeheartedly to the great world of continental art which Buddhism brought to their shores. The construction of wooden temples, begun in the seventh century, was continued and accelerated. The Tōdaiji was simply one of a multitude of monastic structures erected in Nara, many of which contain today, like the Shōsōin, priceless sculpture, paintings, and other treasures of the eighth century.

Although many prominent Buddhist priests of the Nara period appear to have been more concerned with political than religious matters, others sought to apply themselves sincerely and unselfishly to their holy calling. The best known was Gyōki, a popular priest who traveled about the countryside seeking converts and helping with public works, such as the construction of roads and bridges. Gyōki was also one of the early proponents of the merger of Shintō and Buddhism through the identification of Shintō deities with Buddhas and Bodhisattvas. The Sun Goddess was, for example, equated by Gyōki with the cosmic Buddha Vairochana, whose name in Japanese (Dainichi) means, appropriately enough, "great sun."

One reason for the relative meagerness of scholarly and literary output during the Nara period was the continuing problem of how to adapt the Chinese written script to the Japanese language. The court had launched a historiographic project in the late seventh century and, after numerous delays, produced the *Kojiki* in 712 and the *Nihon Shoki* in 720. The former recounts the age of the gods and traces the "history" of Japan from Jimmu to the reign of Empress Suiko, whereas the latter, after covering the same ground, continues the record until nearly the end of the seventh century. (Both works are discussed in the chapter on literature along with the great poetic anthology of the Nara era, the *Manyōshū*.) Of the two chronicles, only the portions of the *Nihon Shoki* that deal with the late sixth and seventh centuries can be considered reasonably reliable history.

The *Nihon Shoki* became the first of six "national histories" of Japan, compiled between the eighth and early tenth centuries. Discontinuance of these officially sponsored histories constituted, as we shall see, part of a much broader shift away from continental modes of government, social organization, and culture that occurred in mid-Heian times.

Decline of the Equal Field System

Any discussion of provincial affairs in the Nara period must inevitably center on the decline of the equal field system of landholding. A paucity of sources makes it unlikely that we will ever be able to reconstruct fully the extent to which this system was implemented. We do know that the Taika reformists had never intended to apply the principle of equal field allotments to all people, but only to the great mass of peasant producers. The court nobles were granted a variety of special allotments (rank lands, office lands, merit lands), some of which were tax-free. Moreover, very substantial parcels of land were bestowed on religious institutions, either by the government or by pious individual donors.

The equal field system, then, had an inherent flaw: it was in no sense equal. It appears that the vast inequities in economic wealth that existed between ruler and ruled in pre-Taika Japan were largely perpetuated during the course of reform. A minister at court during the Nara period, for example, might hold several thousand times as much land as the average peasant.

Another difficulty with the equal field system was that it required periodic inspections to maintain the desired balance in basic allotments. Since land was not heritable, it was necessary to repossess the holdings of deceased persons and to make provision for youths as they came of age. The Taika Reform Edict called for inspections every six years, but from the first these proved difficult for the government to carry out. During the eighth century inspections became less and less frequent and by the ninth they were discontinued altogether.

For the peasantry, the most onerous feature of the new land system was the corvée or labor tax, which included recruitment for military service as well as for construction and other work projects. The enlistment of a family head for frontier duty, for example, could result in the financial ruin of the family. Not only was the enlistee required to outfit and supply himself for duty; his dependents were obliged to continue payment of all other taxes in his absence. As a result, peasants from an early date sought to avoid the tax registers and many, in desperation, even abandoned their fields. By the eighth century we find references to the growing problem of *rōnin* (literally, "wave people")—that is, people who had left their allotted stations in life and who were officially unaccounted for.

One of the means by which the Nara court tried to aid the hard-pressed peasants was to have the provincial governors grant them loans, generally in the form of rice from the provincial granaries, during the periods of shortage between spring planting and fall harvesting. These loans, however, were advanced at exorbitant rates of interest (usually between 30 and 50 percent, but sometimes much higher) and in many cases were even made compulsory by avaricious provincial officials. They became, in practice, simply another form of tax and had the reverse effect of inducing an even greater number of peasants to join the ranks of the *rōnin*.

The tendency was for larger landholders, such as court nobles and religious institutions, to grant private employment to these *rōnin* and, in so doing, to violate the Taika principle of "public people." One of the tasks to which *rōnin* were put was the opening of new fields. The government itself was at first most vigorous in its encouragement of such land reclamation, since it hoped thereby to increase tax revenue. But it soon found that it was able neither to control the manner in which reclamation was pursued nor to assert effectively its claim to dominion over the newly productive lands. Since few peasants had the means to undertake the opening of fields, this profitable task fell largely to others. Among the most active were the emperor's own ministers, who were able to exert strong pressure for permanent title to their new lands and for varying degrees of tax exemption.

The abandonment of fields, most of which were probably absorbed covertly by larger holders, and the increase in *rōnin* among the peasantry caused a steady decline in governmental revenue during the eighth century. At the same time the large-scale acquisition of reclaimed, tax-free lands by court nobles and religious institutions further reduced the national percentage of land fully classifiable as public. By the end of the Nara period the reversion to "private lands and private people" was a marked trend everywhere.

Shortly before the move from Nara, the government had sought to lessen its financial burdens by dismissing a number of nonessential officials. It also responded to voices of discontent in the provinces by reducing corvée labor demands. Finally, in 792, the emperor took the momentous step of abolishing universal conscription and of directing district governors to provide for local policing needs through systems of private militia. It was noted in the first chapter that district governors were usually selected from among the leaders of families long resident in the provinces. The relinquishment of military initiative to these officials even before the establishment of the new capital at Heian had much to do with the later decentralization of rule and the rise of a provincial warrior class.

Heian Japan: Fujiwara Dominance

Heian or Kyoto, the newly constructed city to which the government moved in 794, remained the capital of Japan for more than a millennium (until the Meiji Restoration of 1868). But the Heian epoch of Japanese history is usually taken to mean the period of four centuries from 794 to the year 1185, when a new military government was established at Kamakura in the eastern provinces by the warrior family of Minamoto. The achievement of national power by the Minamoto toward the close of the twelfth century brought to an end the age of the court nobles and ushered in nearly seven centuries of dominance by warrior houses.

Heian was built on much the same pattern as Nara, although the plans called for it to be substantially larger. The western half of Heian, however, was never fully developed, and the modern metropolis of Kyoto consists of the eastern portion of the ancient capital plus that part of its suburbs, mainly in the northeast, to which the city has expanded.

Despite signs of decay in the Taika-Taihō system of administration and land tenure, the government continued to demonstrate considerable vigor in the early years of the Heian period. The emperor responsible for the move to the new capital was Kammu, one of the most forceful sovereigns in Japanese history. As has already been noted, a likely reason for moving the seat of government from Nara was to obtain more direct access to the eastern and northern provinces. Paradoxically, although it was he who had abandoned the system of universal conscription in 792, Kammu now took the initiative in stepping up the military offensive against the Emishi in the north.

During the Nara period the government had tried various methods of dealing with the Emishi, including attempts to force them onto enclosed reservations. Yet toward the end of the eighth century the Emishi rose in revolt and obliged the government to take more stringent measures. Kammu sent expeditionary forces northward in 789 and 794, but the first was badly defeated in battle and the second scored only temporary gains. In 797 the emperor selected as his commander the redoubtable Sakanoue no Tamuramaro and bestowed upon him the commission of *seii taishōgun* (generalissimo for subjugation of the eastern barbarians). Four years later, in 801, Tamuramaro achieved such a resounding victory over the Emishi that they were never again to pose a serious problem to the Japanese nation.

For slightly more than a hundred years, until the death of Kammu in 806, the system of central government set forth in the Taihō Code had functioned more or less as envisioned by its founders. During the ninth century, however, Japanese leaders began to make significant modifications in this system. One reason was their desire to streamline the elaborate and cumbrous Chinese-style structure over which Kammu and his predecessors had presided. Quarrels among Kammu's sons, three of whom followed him on the throne, set the stage for the creation about 810 of two new offices: the Emperor's Private Office (*Kurōdo-dokoro*) to enable the sovereign to issue administrative edicts more directly and with greater security than before; and the Metropolitan Police Board (*Kebiishi-chō*) to assume the function of maintaining order in the capital in the place of the imperial guard units, which had become largely ornamental.

Although these new offices may temporarily have strengthened the position of the emperor, the tendency from this time to bypass or alter the institutions of the Taika-Taihō system had the ultimate effect of diverting real power away from the throne. Significantly, it was a Fujiwara who was first appointed head of the Emperor's Private Office. Throughout the ninth century this family sought to consolidate its position at court, both through the acquisition of formal authority and through marriage ties with the Imperial House. In 858 Fujiwara Yoshifusa had himself appointed regent (*sesshō*) to the child emperor Seiwa (r. 858–76), who was Yoshifusa's own grandson. Heretofore the office of regent had been occupied only by members of the Imperial House. From the time of Yoshifusa and his son Mototsune, who became senior regent (*kampaku*) to an adult emperor, the Fujiwara fashioned the status of *sesshō-kampaku* into a new center of state power.

Several emperors toward the end of the ninth century attempted to check the rise of the Fujiwara by turning for support to ministers from lesser families. The most illustrious of the latter to receive imperial patronage about this time was Sugawara no Michizane, a former provincial governor who became minister of the right in 899. Later to be revered as one of the great "scholar-officials" of early Japan, Michizane was among the last to rise in official circles more on the basis of personal merit than through family connections. Yet even he was unable to compete for long with the Fujiwara. Accused of participating in a subversive plot in 901, Michizane was exiled to Kyushu and died there two years later.

The long reign of the Emperor Daigo (r. 897–930), whom Michizane served, has been regarded as a golden age in Japanese history. Culturally, Daigo's period was distinguished by compilation of *Kokinshū* (Collection of ancient and modern poetry), the first great officially sponsored poetic anthology, and *Sandai Jitsuroku* (True records of three reigns), the last of the six national histories. Politically, Daigo ruled without a regent, a fact that led later generations to believe that he, in contrast to his Fujiwara-dominated predecessors, exercised power firmly and directly. Yet the Fujiwara were in no sense humbled by Daigo. If anything their position was strengthened by the continuing decline of public administration in the provinces and by their own acquisition of ever larger private estate holdings during the early tenth century.

The first phase in the formation of estates (*shōen*) during the Nara period had been characterized chiefly by the opening of great new tracts of productive land by court nobles and religious institutions. The aim of the latter was to secure full autonomy for their holdings, which they could do through the procurement of documents from the court granting proprietorship in perpetuity, waiver of taxes, and immunity from intrusion by government officials. As the great estates began to take clear, and indeed legal, form by this means in the early Heian period, smaller holders everywhere saw the advantage of joining their lands with those of their powerful neighbors. The practice of commendation, which became so widespread during this second phase in estate formation, was a way both to avoid government taxation and to ensure local protection, which the court's provincial apparatus had shown itself increasingly unable to provide. Commendation required the smaller holder simply to transfer his title in land to an estate. He continued to work his fields as before and, in return for estate protection, rendered a portion of his harvest income—a portion which usually constituted much less of a drain on his resources than the government's triple tax—to his new estate overlord. The average small holder had between five and seven acres of land which he cultivated with the aid of both his family and various types of farm laborers subordinate to his control. Small holder families that entered estates became members of self-sustaining economic units. They also placed themselves in theory, and largely in fact, entirely beyond the jurisdiction of the central government.

The steady rise of the Fujiwara and the growth of the estate system of landholding brought by the mid-tenth century the evolution of a new state structure that was in many respects similar to the type of loosely federated society which had existed before the Taika-Taihō Reform. Much of the public domain was converted into private estate proprietorships and the flow of tax revenue dwindled to the point where it was insufficient to finance even the minimum needs of government. Meanwhile, the great courtier families—especially the Fujiwara—became enormously wealthy through income from their private holdings in land.

Within several decades of the death of Daigo in 930 the Fujiwara secured absolute control of the court. At the peak of their power and glory under Michinaga, about the year 1000, the members of this family dominated virtually every aspect of aristocratic society in Kyoto. They elevated sovereigns to the throne and deposed them at will. Emperors chosen during the century of Fujiwara supremacy, from 967 until 1068, were almost always children and were invariably the offspring of Fujiwara mothers. In this way the Fujiwara rendered the throne impotent. They also left little authority in the hands of the traditional officialdom of the Department of State. Public affairs in the Heian capital were handled by the regents through private administrative organs of the Fujiwara family. The striking similarity between Soga rule before the Taika-Taihō Reform and Fujiwara political practice in the late tenth and early eleventh centuries suggests the extent to which the Japanese in the intervening succeeding centuries had reversed the T'ang-inspired governmental reforms of the eighth century.

Heian Religion and Culture

The entire Taika-Taihō Reform phase had been infused with the spirit of Buddhism. Yet this great carrier of continental culture to Japan, which the leaders of the Nara period had even envisioned as the new "protector of the state," soon became in China a victim of the very process of state centralization under the Sui and T'ang that Japan's leaders had so much admired. The revival of empire after centuries of disunity had gradually turned the attention of the Chinese back to Confucian questions of social order and ethical rule and away from Buddhism. The widespread Buddhist persecutions of the mid-ninth century were in part a reaction against a foreign system that Chinese society on the whole no longer needed and in part a deliberate policy to deprive Buddhist temples of the wealth they had accumulated in preceding centuries.

Although Buddhism was thus largely rejected by the Chinese state at this time, it did not suffer a similar fate in Japan, despite general displeasure with the political meddling and unbecoming this-worldliness of the Nara sects. Interference by the latter in court politics was successfully eliminated by the move to Heian; yet no concurrent attempt was made to reduce the sizable holdings in land which they had already acquired. Indeed the Nara temples and later the temples of other sects continued to be among the most prominent and wealthy organizations in the country for another seven centuries or more.

Fundamental to the continued prosperity of Buddhism in Japan was the fact that it had become, by the end of the Nara period, both the principal intellectual system and one of the most important institutional systems in Japanese life. By contrast, Confucianism had not yet established an independent existence in Japan, while Shintō was in the process of being at least partly assimilated by Buddhism, not only through the identification of Shintō deities with Buddhas and Bodhisattvas but also through the practice of merging Shintō shrines with Buddhist temples.

Emperor Kammu had seen the advantage of encouraging the development of a new type of Buddhism at Heian that would be free of the influence of the Nara sects. The man he patronized for this purpose was Saichō (posthumously known as Dengyō Daishi or Great Teacher Dengyō), a priest who had already broken with the older sects and had established his own Buddhist center on Mt. Hiei, a few miles northeast of the new capital. Saichō journeyed to China in 804 and a year later returned to found Tendai, one of the two major sects of Heian Buddhism. He preached the importance of discipline to those who joined his order and inaugurated on Mt. Hiei a rigorous program of training. With court backing, he was soon able to elevate Tendai to a position of first importance in Heian life.

The principal text of Tendai Buddhism was the Lotus Sutra, purportedly the final discourse of the historical Buddha before his death and entry into Nirvana. In this discourse the Buddha informed his disciples that his teaching had until then been concerned solely with individual salvation (the teaching of Hīnayāna or the "Lesser Vehicle"). They were now prepared to know the ultimate truth that all beings had the potentiality to achieve buddhahood or enlightenment (the teaching of Mahāyāna or the "Greater Vehicle"). Saichō labeled the doctrines of the Nara sects inferior—Hīnayāna or, at best, quasi-Mahāyāna—and asserted that only through Tendai could the true universality of Buddhism be known.

Saichō's contemporary, Kūkai (Kōbō Daishi or Great Teacher Kōbō), revered as one of the great culture heroes of Japanese history for his brilliant scholarship and wide-ranging interests, was more indulgent toward the Nara sects and stressed the importance of acknowledging their "partial truths." A member of the same mission to China that Saichō had accompanied in 804, Kūkai returned to Japan to found the Shingon (True Words) sect of Tantric Buddhism at a monastery on remote Mt. Kōya south of the old capital of Nara. Shingon based its claim to Mahayanist universality on the all-embracing nature of its central divinity, the cosmic Buddha Vairochana (the same deity revered in Kegon Buddhism), of whom the historical Buddha was only an earthly manifestation. As a type of Esoteric Buddhism, it placed a premium on the intimate relationship between master and pupil and on the transmission of secret formulae concerning the mysteries of "mind, body, and speech," for proper performance of ritual. Iconography also formed an important part of Shingon practice and it was perhaps this aspect of the new sect that made it most appealing to the aesthetically inclined court nobles.

Kūkai became even more popular at court than Saichō. So eagerly did the nobles embrace his Shingon teachings that the rival Tendai sect soon developed an esoteric branch of its own. In the middle and late Heian periods, however, esotericism began to degenerate. Increasingly men sought to use it simply as a magical means to prolong life and to acquire immediate riches. Moreover, despite the emphasis of both Saichō and Kūkai on monasticism and the need for discipline, the Tendai and Shingon temples (along with those of the Nara sects) began to accumulate large numbers of monks who, although little interested in religious matters, were happy to serve as members of rather undisciplined and motley private armies. Through much of the Heian period these temple armies not only fought among themselves but, on numerous occasions, marched into the capital to force the government to grant their demands for special ecclesiastic appointments or for choice pieces of land to add to their holdings.

The last official mission to T'ang China was dispatched in 838. Undoubtedly one reason why the government declined to send others after this date was its dismay at reports of growing disorder in China. The Tendai priest Ennin, who accompanied the 838 mission, has left a detailed account in his diary of conditions during the decline of the T'ang dynasty, including a graphic description of the great Buddhist persecutions of 841–45. Yet probably a more fundamental reason for the cessation of missions at this time was that most prominent Japanese no longer felt a particular need or desire to go to China.

The long period of cultural borrowing from the continent, begun several centuries earlier, had at length come to an end. China's impact during these centuries had been great; yet Japan had clearly withstood cultural inundation of a sort that might have obscured its national identity. In certain areas, such as political organization and landholding, the Japanese had already begun, as we have seen, to shift to institutions and practices more in keeping with their indigenous traditions. In other areas, such as literature and the writing of history, they were evolving new styles quite distinct from the Chinese models to which they had long been exposed.

An important development of the early Heian period was the invention of *kana,* a phonetic script consisting of some forty-seven syllabic signs derived from Chinese characters. Until this time the Japanese had been obliged either to write in pure (or their idea of pure) Chinese or to attempt, as had the authors of the *Kojiki* and the *Manyōshū,* to reproduce the sounds of spoken Japanese with a variety of phonetic elements from Chinese. *Kana* (in effect, a reduced and standardized list of such phonetic elements) provided a new and essential freedom of expression for the Japanese; and indeed some of the finest works of Heian literature were to be written within the next century or so almost entirely in this script.

This does not mean that the Japanese abandoned completely their use of the Chinese writing system. Most scholars and officials continued to prefer it to what they considered a rather vulgar device for transcribing the native vernacular. Others sought to use a mixture of Chinese characters (to represent most nouns, verbs, and adjectives) and *kana* (for other words and for the grammatical inflections of Japanese). In fact, it has been this mixed style that has evolved over the centuries into the complex written language of Japan today.

The high point of cultural flowering during the Heian period coincided with the time of greatest Fujiwara prominence under Michinaga around the year 1000. Michinaga, as the emperor's first minister, presided over a small (less than one percent of the national population) and highly inbred group of families at court that constituted an aristocracy extraordinary for its exclusiveness and degree of withdrawal from the outside world. Official contact with the continent had been allowed to lapse more than a century and a half earlier. By 1000 the court had even reduced to a minimum its relations with provincial society in Japan. We know from records of the period, for example, the dread with which the Heian noble faced appointment to a provincial post and his extreme hesitancy to journey even the slightest distance from the capital.

The court noble of Michinaga's time lived in a world enormously remote from us today, not only in time but also in attitudes and behavior; and indeed, when one thinks of the historic Japanese, it is not the court noble who is likely to come first to mind, but the intrepid samurai of later ages. Such qualities as military aggressiveness, austerity of habit, and an exaggerated concern for personal honor, which have characterized the Japanese in their turbulent modern era, were utterly alien to the court nobles of the tenth and eleventh centuries. The latter lived in a world governed by standards of form and beauty. They were passionately concerned with rank and status, which were assigned almost exclusively according to birth and family standing; and they admired nothing so much as the ability to compose a graceful poem, to contrive an elegant costume, or to write in an artistic hand.

It may be charged that these nobles, who troubled themselves scarcely at all with matters of pure intellect or social morality, had a value system that was superficial and false. Yet they have left us a wonderful cultural legacy, especially in the field of literature; and we may well conclude that, in their case, beauty indeed needed no other excuse than itself for being.

Much of the best literature of the Heian period was produced by women, who had little if any training in Chinese and were content to write in the vernacular. A number kept personal diaries; others jotted down miscellaneous anecdotes and impressions. Sei Shōnagon, a lady in waiting, has left a miscellany called *The Pillow Book,* which gives in intimate detail the style of life at court around 1000. But the finest achievement of Heian literature, and in fact the greatest single work in all Japanese literature, was *The Tale of Genji,* a lengthy novel by another lady in waiting, Sei Shōnagon's contemporary Lady Murasaki.

Murasaki's book deals with the life and amorous adventures of Prince Genji, the son of an emperor by a low-ranking court lady and a model of all the qualities of taste and refinement most admired by the Heian aristocracy. Genji and his friends, who were burdened with few administrative responsibilities, spent their days largely in the search for pleasure and novel experience. They attended countless ceremonial functions, recited poetry endlessly, and moved facilely from one romantic affair to another.

The prevailing mood in Genji's circle of friends was one of subdued melancholy and nostalgia for the passing of lovely things. In later chapters of the book which depict the generation after Genji's, however, we find a growing sense of pessimism, as though the author and through her the principal characters had become acutely aware that their entire world of aesthetic perfection was itself a fleeting phenomenon that could vanish in a moment.

Court Power Struggles and the Rise of the Military

The first serious threat to Fujiwara political hegemony came not from the outside but from within court society itself. For several centuries the Fujiwara had successfully put down every attempt by other families to share in the practical affairs of government. One remarkable thing was their capacity to produce a seemingly endless succession of really first-rate statesmen and of nubile young girls to marry into the Imperial House.

The importance to the Fujiwara of their marital ties to the Imperial House was clearly revealed in 1068 when, for the first time since the ninth century, an emperor ascended the throne who did not have a Fujiwara mother. At the time of his coronation, the Emperor Gosanjō was thirty-five and had been crown prince for some twenty-five years. During this period he had been poorly treated by the Fujiwara and he now determined to check, if possible, their long-standing monopoly of power at court. Shortly after becoming emperor, Gosanjō opened a Records Office (*Kirokujo*) for the purpose of compiling estate documents and establishing criteria to judge their validity. Gosanjō's aim was to assert some kind of general administrative control over the estate system. At the same time he saw the opportunity to place pressure on the Fujiwara, who had many estates that were known to lack such documents.

In 1072 Gosanjō abdicated, possibly to rid himself of the ceremonial burdens of being emperor or possibly because of poor health. In any event he had little opportunity to demonstrate what he might have done as retired emperor, for within a year he died. Gosanjō's son and successor, Shirakawa, also abdicated at an early date, took Buddhist vows (as did many retired emperors), and soon became active in court politics through his Office of the Cloistered Emperor (*Inchō*).

It has traditionally been thought that Gosanjō and Shirakawa deliberately maneuvered to create a "system of cloistered emperors." But in line with a general reversion to the patrimonialist sentiment of a former age, senior retired emperors, rather than reigning sovereigns, had come to be regarded as the true heads of the Imperial House from the early years of the Heian period. They were publically venerated by the throne, and they utilized the equivalent of what later became known as the Office of the Cloistered Emperor for the handling of their personal affairs. Thus no radically new administrative structure was contrived in the late eleventh century to challenge the Fujiwara-dominated court. Rather, the senior retired or cloistered emperors from Shirakawa on assumed political powers in large part as a result of the need to fill a governing vacuum created by the decline of the Fujiwara, who were openly quarreling among themselves and unable to assert the type of firm leadership they had in the past.

The age of supremacy of the cloistered emperors lasted from 1086 until 1156. In one sense the rise of the cloistered emperors meant the re-entry of the Imperial House into competition for political power. But more significantly it brought a broadening of opportunity for new families, especially provincial families, to participate in the business of the court. Among the staunchest supporters of the cloistered emperors were lower provincial officials who had acquired considerable wealth, prestige, and influence in their home regions but who, until now, had had no way to make their voices heard in Kyoto.

Provincial officialdom of the late Heian period included various elements. At the district level most officials continued to be the heads of families that had been in local residence for generations. The existence of such locally based and hereditary officeholders had always been fundamentally antithetical to centralized rule. Moreover the court, by abolishing its military conscription system in 792 and ordering the district governors to organize militia locally, had given further impetus to the decentralization of national power. Although we know little about the organization of provincial society until the tenth century, it seems very likely that from the beginning of the Heian period, if not before, the district governors and their kind had begun to assume leadership of the warrior bands (*bushidan*) that were to become the fundamental units of the military class of Japan in later centuries.

Appointment to posts on the top provincial level, on the other hand, usually went either to Fujiwara ministers, who were likely to designate deputies to represent them, or to men from lesser Fujiwara branches or from other noble families that simply had no chance to advance administratively in the capital. Some men who went down to the provinces did so with serious intent, performed their duties faithfully and, in a number of cases, remained as local or regional magnates even after their terms of office had expired. Other appointees did not behave so admirably. The dispatch of deputies to the provinces was often simply for the purpose of collecting taxes for personal gain. Appointments were commonly sold and various illegal means were employed to falsify tax records, extend terms in office, and so forth. The high calibre of provincial administration set in the early Nara period had sadly deteriorated by middle and late Heian times.

One important group that went into the provinces as officials during the Heian period was comprised of distant members of the Imperial House. To prevent their numbers from becoming too large and therefore too much of an economic liability to the central government, it became the practice periodically to reduce princes who had no real hope of succeeding to the throne to nonroyal status. Those so reduced were given surnames (the Imperial House itself had none), the most prominent of which were Taira and Minamoto. A number of Minamoto, in particular, remained in the capital; but from at least the early tenth century we also hear of Taira and Minamoto acquiring influence and assuming leadership roles in the provinces. The progenitor of the provincial Taira was Prince Takamochi, who received his surname in 890 and went to the east as the vice-governor of Kazusa Province. In 939 (less than a decade after the Emperor Daigo's supposedly golden age) Taira Masakado, Takamochi's grandson, rose in armed revolt in the eastern provinces and even proclaimed himself the "new emperor." Although Masakado was killed the following year and a nearly simultaneous uprising in the Inland Sea area led by an outlaw of Fujiwara stock was also put down, the government was rudely shaken by these signs of unrest and challenge to authority beyond the confines of its insular world of the capital. To us, in retrospect, such incidents are early indicators of the formation of new power groups in the country, based on *bushidan,* that were eventually to bring to an end the supremacy of the Heian court and to usher in a largely decentralist age of dominance by provincial warrior houses.

The *bushidan* that emerged in the provinces during the Heian period may be defined as hierarchical military organizations based on extended family units. In Taira Masakado's day such warrior bands were still in an early stage of development. Masakado and his contemporaries, for example, relied mainly on their kinsmen for fighting support; moreover, their armies were loosely formed and tended to dissolve quickly after battles and at such times as the gathering of the harvest. By the eleventh century, however, *bushidan* had become much more complex and tightly organized. They included not only members of the chieftain's main family and its branches, but also men who were not related by blood (although the latter were commonly given fictive kinship designations such as *kenin* or "housemen" and *ie no ko* or "children of the house").

Whether blood relatives or not, the members of warrior bands came to be bound by feudal lord-vassal (*shujū*) ties. These ties were not based simply on the blind loyalty of vassals toward their lords, but were distinctly bilateral: vassals fought for rewards (usually in the form of land won in battle) and for protection. Even when they forfeited their lives in combat, they did so in the expectation of posthumous reward through compensation paid to their families.

It was especially in the agriculturally rich Kanto, which had been frontier-land in the early years of the imperial state, that the warrior class rose to prominence during the middle and late Heian period. The chieftains of some warrior bands in the east gradually formed territorial hegemonies by bringing other *bushidan* under their sway; and by the twelfth century several of these hegemonies had come to embrace whole provinces. Although the Taira entered first and became the more numerous, it was the Minamoto who ultimately developed the most powerful base in the Kanto. In a series of military campaigns carried out in the northern provinces during the late eleventh century, the Minamoto established a great fighting reputation and attracted as their followers scores of Kanto warriors, including many of the Taira clan. These vassalage-type commitments were to prove, two or three generations later, invaluable to the Minamoto when they finally sought to impose a hegemony over the entire Kanto.

The fighting of the late eleventh century was initiated by Minamoto Yoriyoshi who, operating from his Kanto base, conducted a campaign from 1051 to 1062 against the Abe family in the north. More than twenty years later Yoriyoshi's son, Yoshiie, undertook another series of battles in the same region, against the Kiyowara family that had arisen after defeat of the Abe. The reasons behind these wars are not fully clear. It has been said that the Abe, who had intermarried with the Emishi, were deliberately disrupting provincial administration. Other records suggest that the Abe did everything they could to cooperate with the Minamoto and that the latter provoked them to battle simply to destroy their influence in the north. A similar motive may have been behind Yoshiie's action against the Kiyowara. In any event, this fighting during the latter half of the eleventh century manifestly established the dominance of the Minamoto in the east and north.

The Kyoto government became increasingly apprehensive about the expansion of Minamoto power in these distant regions. Although it gave supplies and backing to Yoriyoshi in his struggle with the Abe, it did not grant similar aid to Yoshiie in his wars. Yoshiie financed the fighting himself and rewarded his warriors from his own resources. So great did his fame become that leaders of smaller families in the east began to commend their lands directly to Yoshiie, known also as Hachiman Tarō or "first born son of the war god Hachiman," and to enter into fictive kinship relations with him by adopting the Minamoto surname. In 1091 Kyoto forbade the commendation of holdings to Yoshiie; and shortly thereafter the Cloistered Emperor Shirakawa sought further to counter the influence of the Minamoto by engaging several prominent Taira as his personal aides.

A century earlier Michinaga had called the Minamoto the "claws and teeth" of the Fujiwara. From this remark and from other evidence we know that leading court nobles had for some time relied on chieftains of the new warrior houses to settle their disputes. During the eleventh century, moreover, it became common practice to appoint warriors to act as constabulary officers in the event of disorder or rebellion in the provinces. Thus the military families, although still quite subordinate to the Fujiwara and socially disdained by the latter, came to play an increasingly important role in public affairs. When Shirakawa opened his Office of the Cloistered Emperor in 1086, members of the Minamoto clan were among his earliest supporters. The later decision by Shirakawa to replace the Minamoto with members of a branch family of the Taira from Ise Province, which lay between the capital region and the Kanto, was a significant turning point for both these clans. Under Shirakawa and his successor, Toba (cloistered emperor 1129–56), it was the Ise Taira who gained most and who rose highest in court circles.

Thus even while the Minamoto were gradually consolidating their control over the Kanto, the Taira, under successive heads of the Ise branch, acquired large estate holdings in the central and western provinces, especially in the area of the Inland Sea. In developing such a "westward" orientation, the Ise Taira never exerted great influence among their distant kinsmen in the east, many of whom, as we have just seen, formed feudal bonds of loyalty to the Minamoto. Nevertheless by the time of Kiyomori, who became family head about mid-twelfth century, the Ise Taira were clearly in a stronger position, at least in the world of Kyoto politics, than their principal warrior rivals for power.

Conditions in the capital had become dangerously unstable by the 1150s. The Cloistered Emperor Toba was an important controlling influence; but serious rifts were growing among members of the Fujiwara family as well as between Toba's own sons, the ex-Emperor Sutoku (r. 1123–41) and the reigning Emperor Goshira-kawa (r. 1155–58). When Toba died in 1156 there was a sudden and violent outburst between two armed camps that formed around Sutoku and Goshirakawa. The brief conflict that ensued, known as the Hōgen incident, ostensibly brought victory to the forces of Go-shirakawa. But the main issues of the day were by no means settled. The principal result of the Hōgen incident was the transfer of initiative in central affairs from court nobles to the military. No longer could the court nobles use warrior chieftains as their armed lackeys. Taira and Minamoto had been engaged on both sides in the recent fighting and it was the leaders of these two clans who, as supporters of Goshirakawa, now dictated the terms of peace. One of the most dramatic signs of the change in times was the execution of ring-leaders among the vanquished, a kind of bloodletting that had rarely been seen in the Heian capital since its founding. Yoshitomo, a leader of the Minamoto, killed his own father, and Taira Kiyomori put his uncle to the sword.

In the aftermath of the Hōgen incident Kiyomori became one of the most powerful figures at court. The favor that he received, combined with a corresponding lack of favor for Minamoto Yoshitomo, set the stage for another ferocious encounter in 1159 (the Heiji incident). This time the lines were more clearly drawn: it was a struggle of Taira against Minamoto. Not only were the Taira victorious, they almost completely destroyed the leadership of the Minamoto in several days of hard fighting. Kiyomori became the new master of Kyoto and inaugurated a period of Taira supremacy that was to last for more than twenty years.

To all subsequent generations the rise and fall of the Taira has been the classic story of tragedy in Japanese history. The fatal flaws of the Taira were their pride and arrogance. Kiyomori and his clansmen lived in opulence and splendor at their Rokuhara headquarters in eastern Kyoto. They took for themselves many of the highest offices at court—indeed Kiyomori even became chancellor—and dealt in highhanded fashion with the Fujiwara as well as the Imperial House, and in 1180 Kiyomori's infant grandson ascended the throne as the Emperor Antoku. The Taira, who had risen through the patronage of cloistered emperors, now found themselves aligned with the throne in opposition to Goshirakawa, who had become cloistered emperor in 1158 and who, after two decades, was their foremost opponent at court.

Seen more dispassionately and in broader perspective, the principal mistakes of the Taira were their overinvolvement in court politics and their failure to attempt to deal with the problems of military leadership in the provinces. The Taira were themselves provincial warriors, yet once in power they were content to take up residence in the capital and to imitate the governing practices of the court nobility. Kiyomori was progressive in his efforts to develop trade with Sung China, mainly through the seaport of Fukuhara (present-day Kobe). By and large, however, he seems to have ignored the pressing need for a new type of national administration in an age when central control had become minimal.

The most serious threat to the Taira was the reemergence of Minamoto power in the eastern provinces. In the late 1170s several plots, involving anti-Taira ministers at court and leading religious institutions of the home provinces, were put down. But in 1180 a full-scale revolt erupted in the eastern provinces. The leaders were Minamoto chieftains, the most prominent of whom was Yoritomo, who had been spared at the time of the Heiji incident, when his father Yoshitomo and others had perished, and had been sent into exile. Yoritomo centered his operations in the seaside town of Kamakura (south of modern Tokyo), where the Minamoto had long maintained residence. He gave first priority to the assertion of control over the warrior families of the east and, in fact, remained in that region throughout the years of warfare against the Taira. The historical importance of this decision by Yoritomo to devote himself chiefly to the establishment of a lasting hegemony over the Kanto can hardly be overstated. The Kanto, where the Minamoto had their traditional base of power, was some ten times wealthier in agricultural lands than any other region of Japan and was the true birthplace of the samurai. Under the leadership of Yoritomo, the numerous and fierce fighting men of the Kanto became an irresistible force against the Ise Taira and their supporters in the west. Other Minamoto captains, most of whom eventually acknowledged the overlordship of Yoritomo, carried the fighting to the Taira. In 1183 the latter were driven from the capital. Kiyomori had died two years earlier and the Taira were without forceful leadership. They had backers in the west, but were unable to marshal sufficient support to counter the armies of the Minamoto.

The great field commander of the Minamoto was Yoritomo's half brother, Yoshitsune. A resourceful and daring fighter, Yoshitsune defeated the Taira in one key battle after another. The end came in the third month of 1185 when Yoshitsune led a naval force against the Taira at Dannoura in the Straits of Shimonoseki. The child Emperor Antoku, whom the Taira had taken with them when they fled westward, was among those who perished in this final encounter that brought the downfall of the proud but seemingly ill-fated Ise branch of the Taira. Yoshitsune's splendid victory, on the other hand, ushered in a new and dynamic era for the Minamoto and for Japan.

III

The Age

of the Military

Houses

BY
H. PAUL VARLEY

The Kamakura Shogunate

The year 1185 marks the transition from ancient to medieval Japan. The medieval epoch (until 1568) was distinguished by such fundamental developments as: the dispersal of political power to regions outside the Kyoto area, especially to the eastern provinces; the spread of culture and learning to the provinces, which came to participate in the creation of new modes of artistic and intellectual expression strongly influenced by the growing warrior ethos of society; the founding of simpler and more universally appealing sects of Buddhism; the decline and disappearance of the estate system of landholding, paralleled by formation of the fief and more direct relations between warrior proprietors and peasant producers; and the evolution of a largely self-governing peasant village, which provided the foundation for extraordinarily stable rural conditions by the Tokugawa period (1600–1867).

Minamoto Yoritomo called his new government in Kamakura the *bakufu,* a term usually rendered in English as shogunate. The founding of this military government, while epoch-making, had much about it that was fully within the scope of traditional political practice. Like leaders of prominent families in the past, Yoritomo sought to justify his assumption of power as a delegation from the throne, ultimately (in 1192) securing for himself the title of *seii taishōgun* (usually abbreviated, for convenience, to "shogun"). This title had first been held by the great Tamuramaro in the late eighth and early ninth centuries.

In imitation of the house governments of the Fujiwara and other court families, Yoritomo adopted typically family-type offices for his shogunate: an Administrative Board (*Mandokoro*), a Board of Retainers (*Samuraidokoro*), and a Board of Inquiry (*Monchūjo*). Victory over the Taira in 1185 enabled him to expand his economic base through the confiscation of Taira estates in the central and western provinces. By forcing the court to agree to the appointment of his followers as stewards (*jitō*) to other estates and as constables or protectors (*shugo*) to the various provinces, Yoritomo was able to extend his network of authority even farther afield from the eastern provinces, his original base. He himself was made steward-general and constable-general.

We must not assume, however, that the Kamakura shogunate became at this time a fully national regime. Yoritomo and his followers constituted an eastern military clique that was able to seize certain lands directly and to appoint representatives to the holdings (estates) of others in the west. Since there was from the outset strong resistance to the stewards—especially in the region of Kyoto—a number of these appointments had to be withdrawn. In 1189 Yoritomo conducted a successful campaign in the northern provinces to destroy a branch family of the Fujiwara which had held dominant authority in that region for several generations. Even so, throughout the Kamakura period (1185–1333), military control over both north and west remained incomplete. The old regime, including both court nobles and religious institutions, continued to share land and jurisdictional rights with the newly organized military families centered at Kamakura.

One of the most important sources of the shogunate's strength lay in its network of lord-vassal relations, which formed the matrix of eastern military society. Moreover, Yoritomo's own background of descent from the Imperial House gave him a superior claim to leadership. By exploiting this personal qualification as well as the intimate relations of military society, he was able to assemble an elitist following of retainers, or shogunal housemen (*gokenin*), willing to accept his command absolutely. This gave him tight organizational control over the eastern provinces and facilitated the assignment of stewards and constables to other regions. The eastern provinces had long been developed to the point where they had the potential, socially as well as economically, to challenge the centrality of the Kyoto region. Yoritomo's special role, as we have seen, was to assume leadership there and to bring unity where for years petty chieftains had struggled and feuded, unable to achieve any over-all political settlement.

Yoritomo proved an exceptionally able ruler of men, but in the end he failed to consolidate the leadership of his family on a lasting basis. By the twelfth century the Minamoto, like the Taira, had become a widely dispersed and multi-branched family. In the early years of struggle against the Taira, Yoritomo had been only one of several Minamoto chieftains who sought to assert their claims to headship of the family. Even after his appointment as shogun, Yoritomo remained wary of relatives and inordinately suspicious that they might attempt to challenge his own leading position at Kamakura. Under one pretext or another, he liquidated several of his most illustrious kinsmen, including his half-brother Yoshitsune, the brilliant field commander of the final stages of war in the west.

When Yoritomo died suddenly in 1199 the succession of his young son Yoriie as shogun had not been smoothly prepared. Yoriie became the nominal head of a Minamoto family whose leadership was weakened and divided. In the absence of strong shogunal direction, leaders of other warrior families in the east began to contend openly for power. Final victory in this power struggle went to the Hōjō, whose principal advantage lay in their marriage relationship to the Minamoto. Yoritomo had married Masako, a daughter of Hōjō Tokimasa, one of his guardians and supporters from the early years of exile in the east. Even after her husband's death the widow Masako remained, along with her father and her brother Yoshitoki, a prominent figure in shogunate circles. Within a decade or so the Hōjō, with Yoshitoki at their head, assumed control of the shogunate. In 1219 when Yoritomo's second son, the shogun Sanetomo, was assassinated, possibly at the instigation of Yoshitoki, the last barrier to Hōjō command of the shogunate was removed.

The Hōjō were one of several provincial branches of the Taira who had decided to support Yoritomo in 1180. Perhaps because of their relatively obscure family status, even within the Taira clan, the Hōjō were reluctant to accept high office and title. They remained content to exercise their authority as shogunal regents (*shikken*), while securing first members of the Fujiwara family and later imperial princes to act as figurehead shoguns.

During the period of struggle for power at Kamakura, which lasted nearly two decades, relations between the shogunate and the Kyoto court became increasingly strained. After Yoritomo's death there was little real contact between the two centers of government. A distinctly anti-shogunate clique, headed by the Cloistered Emperor Gotoba, came to feel that the opportunity was at hand to strike down the warrior usurpers of the east and to restore the court to preeminence in fact as well as in theory. Gotoba gathered a select group of court favorites and of warriors from the central provinces who were discontented with Hōjō rule. In 1221 he declared the regent Yoshitoki a rebel and called upon all subjects of the land to rise against him. After a brief period of indecision, Yoshitoki dispatched a huge army from Kamakura, which easily broke through Gotoba's inadequate defenses and occupied Kyoto.

This brief struggle, known after the calendrical era as the Jōkyū (or Shōkyū) incident, tells us much about the realities of power and personal loyalty during the early Kamakura period. Yoshitoki had openly flouted a cloistered emperor, yet still received wide support from the shogunal housemen. Gotoba, on the other hand, found himself with little real backing. Many criticized him for selfishly and arbitrarily jeopardizing the peace of the realm. Few protested when the shogunate exiled Gotoba and his two sons (both former emperors) and inflicted punishment on their leading confederates.

Success in the Jōkyū incident enabled the Hōjō to impose military rule over the land on a much broader basis than before, both politically and economically. Minamoto Yoritomo, while exercising personal influence at Kyoto, had not attempted to bring the court under direct shogunal administration. Accordingly, the court had retained considerable administrative authority, not only over local matters in Kyoto, but also in the provinces through its provincial governors, who continued to function alongside the new military constables. Gradually the constables absorbed the powers of their civil counterparts; but in the early years of the Kamakura period they were restricted largely to activities of a purely military or police nature. As part of the Jōkyū settlement Yoshitoki appointed two deputies (*tandai*) as permanent shogunal administrators in Kyoto. These deputies were always high-ranking Hōjō, who came to exercise their authority over all of the central and western regions of Honshu. Along with a similar deputy appointed later in Kyushu (Kyushu *tandai*), they became the ranking officials of the shogunate outside the eastern provinces.

Henceforth virtually all acts of the court needed approval of the shogunate. The Hōjō dictated the line of succession and chose those candidates least likely to assert themselves politically against Kamakura. Significantly, Yoshitoki allowed members of the Imperial House to retain extensive estate holdings. Although reduced to political impotence, the court was not yet deprived of its economic base.

When Hōjō Yoshitoki died in 1224 he was succeeded as regent by his son Yasutoki, who had been cocommander of the shogunal army during the Jōkyū struggle and had remained in the capital as one of the newly appointed Kyoto deputies. Yasutoki was an outstanding leader, even among the Hōjō regents, a group who on the whole provided the most stable period of administration during the medieval age.

Yasutoki's regency, from 1224 to 1242, was especially noteworthy for two events: the founding of a Council of State (*Hyōjōshū*) in 1225; and promulgation of the first military code of law, the Jōei

Code of 1232. Minamoto Yoritomo's rule as shogun had been distinctly autocratic. The boards that he established were strictly advisory bodies: final decision in all matters remained with him. The Hōjō under Yasutoki, on the other hand, sought to broaden the base of participation in shogunal affairs by inviting other eastern chieftains to sit on the Council of State, which now became the highest source of judicial and legislative authority at Kamakura. Yasutoki also inaugurated the office of cosigner (*rensho*) to assist the regent in presiding over the council and to issue edicts jointly with him. As with the Kyoto deputies, the cosigner was always a high-ranking Hōjō.

The Jōei Code was a remarkable document for its time, reflecting in its provisions the profound changes that were taking place in the transition from a court-centered to a predominantly military society in Japan. Legal practice of the Kyoto court was still based on the Confucian principles of ethical government found in the codes adopted from T'ang China, which, even though supplemented in later centuries, were scarcely sufficient. Little attempt had been made in later centuries to supplement or to amend these T'ang-style codes to meet the expanding needs of society, especially the needs of the new military class forming in the provinces. The Jōei Code, by contrast, was designed specifically for the warrior. It was a highly legalistic document, stressing such things as the duties of stewards and constables, the means for settling the all-important disputes over land, and the rules governing inheritance. In nearly every instance provision was made for the punishment—including confiscation of property and execution—of those who failed to obey. In contrast to the elaborate prose of the T'ang-style codes, the Jōei Code was written in direct and more easily understood language. From the standpoint of legal development, there could scarcely have been a more dramatic change than that inaugurated by Yasutoki and his advisers. Yet in fact these men simply codified practices that were already well developed among the provincial military. The measure of their success as compilers is attested by the influence of the Jōei Code on military law for the next six centuries.

Kamakura Religion and Culture

The Kamakura period was the great age of popularization for the Buddhist religion in Japan. The complex sects of Nara Buddhism had held little appeal for any but a small group of intellectuals. Heian esotericism, with its stress on assiduous practice and intimate personal instruction, was perhaps ideally suited to the leisured aristocracy of the Heian capital, but could scarcely provide a base sufficient for the religious conversion of provincial society. Apart from the activities of certain government officials and regional military families, we know in fact very little about the provinces and their needs before the Kamakura period. We do know that the twelfth century was a time of widespread pessimism. Warfare was becoming endemic and even in the capital itself administration had declined to the point where Fujiwara ministers, cloistered emperors, and temple rowdies were constantly quarreling among themselves. Both man-made and natural disasters were accentuated and intensified by the increasing inability of the court to cope with them. These mounting ills seemed to accord with predictions that the country had entered a period of the "end of the Buddhist law" (*mappō*). The fact that it was a group of eastern warriors that finally restored order only lent further credence to the belief that times of extremity demanded extreme measures.

The esoteric sects of Buddhism had emphasized the importance of individual effort in the search for enlightenment. During the struggle and turmoil of the final years of the Heian period, such striving on the part of the individual seemed futile. As men began to question the methods of the Heian sects, they came also to criticize the warlike and this-worldly behavior of their priesthoods. Clearly Heian Buddhism was in need of institutional as well as doctrinal renovation.

It was under these conditions that the idea of mass salvation became widely popular in Japan. During a period which society considered degenerate, faith in individual effort gave way to the conviction that salvation could be achieved only by throwing oneself on the saving grace of another. The Japanese did not have far to look for an articulation of this way to salvation. The *nembutsu* (invocation of the name of Amida Buddha) had been introduced from China as early as the ninth century, and about the year 1000 Genshin had expounded the merits of Amidism in his *Essentials of Salvation*. In the later books of *The Tale of Genji* we find ample evidence that this style of Buddhism enjoyed more than just a passing vogue among the members of court society. But it was not until the late twelfth century that Amidism, through the efforts of the priest Hōnen, was firmly established as the Pure Land sect and began to spread rapidly through the country.

According to scripture, Amida had vowed to save all who would call upon him through the prayer *namu Amida butsu* (hail Amida Buddha). His grace was to be granted universally and unconditionally, and salvation was to be realized immediately upon death through admission to the western paradise of the Pure Land. It can be seen that Amidism had the simplicity and directness of the type of religious creed most likely to hold mass appeal during an age of social stress and political disorder. The promise of salvation at the end of this life was certainly far removed from the original Buddhist prediction of a cycle of deaths and rebirths before the achievement of Nirvana. Moreover, the view of Amida as the great savior came close to a theistic position, which was also atypical of original Buddhism.

Hōnen's great disciple was Shinran, who in the thirteenth century founded a new branch of Pure Land Buddhism known as the True Pure Land sect. It was under Shinran that the universal implications of Amidism were most fully developed. Whereas Hōnen had allowed that good acts, meditation, and repetition of the *nembutsu* might be of some merit, Shinran rejected utterly all forms of self-effort. He asserted that salvation could be insured without even verbalizing the *nembutsu* but by simply making a silent commitment to Amida.

Shinran did much to help spread afield the new Buddhism of salvation by concentrating his proselytizing efforts on the poorer classes of the eastern provinces. Rejecting the need for priestly celibacy as simply another manifestation of self-concentration or egoism, Shinran himself married and bequeathed the headship of the True Pure Land sect of his descendants. In the fifteenth century the sect became one of the most powerful organizations in the land, even mustering sufficient military strength to seize control of a province—Kaga—which the sect administered for nearly a century.

During the thirteenth century popular Buddhism found another champion—but of a considerably different stamp from the self-effacing Shinran—in the remarkable person of Nichiren. The son of an eastern fisherman, Nichiren became the great prophet of doom during the Kamakura age. Strongly influenced by the doctrine of the "end of the Buddhist law," he predicted violent destruction of the country, a prediction that seemed to be near fulfillment during the Mongol threat of the 1270s and 1280s. Nichiren blamed Japan's fallen state on the decline of the universal Tendai church and the propagation of doctrines distortedly drawn from the Tendai synthesis by the new Buddhist sects. Salvation, he insisted, could only be realized through complete rejection of all these demonic groups and exclusive acceptance of the fundamental teachings of the Lotus Sutra, the principal repository of Mahayanist universalism. Nichiren, in exaltation of this ultimate scriptural source, formulated the prayer *namu myōhō renge kyō* (hail the marvelous law of the Lotus Sutra).

Nichiren was one of the most remarkable men in Japanese history. His religious intolerance was certainly unusual within the context of receptivity and nonexclusiveness so characteristic of philosophical and religious attitudes in East Asia. Perhaps more than anyone else in premodern Japan, Nichiren came closest to being the true social rebel. On countless occasions he demonstrated a resolute willingness to defend principles—alone if necessary—in the face of severe pressure from the military authorities. Moreover, despite his predictions of doom, Nichiren was ardently concerned with preserving nationhood. His concept of nationhood (not generally shared by others in this feudal age of localism and particularism) was based on the premise that Japan could be saved only by acceding to his demands for religious renovation.

Unlike the popular Buddhist sects of the Kamakura period, the Zen or "Meditation" sect emphasized individual practice and discipline. Zen had been introduced to China from India about the sixth century A.D. and now, more than 600 years later, was officially brought to Japan. Practitioners of Zen sought to develop personal powers of meditation and intuitive response in the quest for enlightenment. The stress they placed on self-control made Zen especially attractive to the medieval warrior, and indeed shogunate leaders during both the Kamakura and subsequent Muromachi (1336–1573) periods enthusiastically supported Zen temples and institutional activities. The impact of Zen on Japanese culture was also profound, although discussion of this is more appropriately left for the Muromachi period.

There were two main streams of literary production during the Kamakura period: continuation of the ultra-refined Heian style, as epitomized by the *Shin Kokinshū* (New collection of ancient and modern poems; 1205) and the development of a new and more vigorous genre of war tales based on the ethos and values of military society.

The *Shin Kokinshū,* long admired for its craftsmanship and polish, is in the great tradition of official court anthologies dating back to the *Kokinshū* of the early tenth century. Perhaps the most striking thing about the *Shin Kokinshū* is the contrast it reveals between the gentle world of courtly elegance, with which its antiquarian-minded authors were solely concerned, and the realities of Kamakura militarism.

A work more in keeping with the times is the *Hōjōki* (An account of my hut; 1212), the miscellany of Kamo no Chōmei, a recluse who had once been a member of court society. In both content and style the *Hōjōki* marks a literary transition from one age to another. Although its author does not directly recount the fighting between Taira and Minamoto, he speaks vividly of the turmoil and disorder of his times. Buddhist pessimism is a central theme of the *Hōjōki* and the description of fires, famines, and other natural disasters seem quite appropriate to the "end of the Buddhist law." Stylistically the *Hōjōki* is characterized by a heavier preponderance of abstract Chinese vocabulary, deemed necessary to express effectively the more philosophical themes that had come to concern men.

One of the best known and most popular works of the Kamakura period is the *Heike Monogatari* (The tale of the Heike), a lengthy narrative centered on the rise and fall of the Taira (Heike) family. Eposodic in nature, the *Heike Monogatari* is a later compilation based on a long oral tradition. Along with the other war tales produced in the centuries to follow, it describes in detail the lives and deeds of the medieval samurai. Although their value as history is sometimes questioned, these war tales constitute one of the great repositories of Japan's military heritage.

The Mongol Invasions and the Fall of the Kamakura Shogunate

The dispatch of official missions to China had been terminated in the mid-ninth century, owing in part to the deterioration of political conditions in China and in part to the growing introversion of Heian society. Thereafter Japanese leaders, with the notable exception of Taira Kiyomori, were not inclined to renew official continental ties. Certain families and local officials of Kyushu continued to deal privately with the foreigners; but, apart from Kiyomori's attempts to channel trade with Sung China through port facilities in the Inland Sea, Kyoto remained officially aloof. The shift in military hegemony to the eastern provinces in 1185 brought to an end even Kiyomori's semiofficial intercourse with Sung China.

The Kamakura shogunate in its early years showed little concern for and acquired little knowledge of overseas affairs. It was during this time that most of Asia, including north China, was brought under the domination of the Mongols, led first by Genghis Khan and later by Khubilai Khan. The rapid expansion of Mongol power on the continent had no immediate effect on Japan. In 1227 there arrived in Kyushu a note from the kingdom of Koryŏ concerning a dispute involving some Japanese in Korea. The note, duly forwarded to Kamakura, marked the first known instance of communication between the shogunate and a foreign country. Thereafter the shogunal officials in Kyushu continued to handle in desultory fashion whatever foreign exchanges there were until 1268, when another Koryŏ messenger brought word from the new Mongol regime at Peking demanding that Japan enter into tributary relations. It was clear that failure to do so would bring punitive action.

The Kyoto court was thrown into a state of panic, but Kamakura stood firm. The regent Tokimune, to the undying gratitude of later Japanese nationalists, summarily rejected the Mongol demands. Even among those who have since reviled the Hōjō for their shabby treatment of the Imperial House during the Jōkyū incident, Tokimune has remained an object of praise for his fortitude in the face of an awesome threat from the world-conquering Mongols.

The Mongols attempted twice to invade Japan, once in 1274 and again in 1281. On the first occasion a combined force of Mongols and Koreans overran the islands of Tsushima and Iki and tried to land near Hakata on the north coast of Kyushu. After a day of sanguinary fighting in which the warriors of Kyushu barely managed to check the foreign invaders, a storm arose that decimated the Mongol fleet and forced abandonment of invasion plans. During the next few years the shogunate continued to resist Mongol overtures and on two occasions even beheaded the Mongol envoys. Infuriated, Khubilai dispatched a much larger force in his second attempt to bring the Japanese to heel. Again the point of battle was Hakata, but this time the Mongols were far more determined and better prepared. The second campaign lasted nearly two months and sorely tried the Japanese defensive capacity. Once again, however, the native forces were saved by a storm that arose fortuitously to drive the Mongols out to sea.

The invasion attempts were a unique experience for the Japanese of the medieval age. Insularity had always been a dominant fact of life in the island country and nothing in its past provided a precedent to which such experience could be related. Coincidentally it was at this time that, after centuries of neglect, intellectuals had begun to turn once again to the study of Shintō and to examination of texts such as the *Nihon Shoki,* which recounted the sacred origins of Japan. When the heavens responded during both Mongol attacks with "divine winds" of destruction (*kamikaze*) against the enemy, it seemed indeed that Japan was the recipient of special protection by the gods. Later generations of Japanese were profoundly influenced by these concepts of kamikaze and divine protection, made so meaningful by the experience of the Mongol invasions.

Yet it is difficult to assess the immediate effects of the Mongol invasions on Japan of the Kamakura period. Since the Kamakura shogunate continued in existence for another half century, the invasions can scarcely be regarded as a proximate cause for its final collapse. Nevertheless, among historians analyzing the decline of the shogunate, it has been traditional to place great stress on the cost of prolonged foreign defense (which was maintained until nearly the end of the century) and on widespread dissatisfaction over claims for reward which the shogunate could not adequately meet. In fact the burden of defense was carried almost entirely by a group of warriors in Kyushu, so that dissatisfaction on the part of the military was probably limited mainly to those of the westernmost island. Certain temples and shrines also complained that their ministrations for heavenly intercession had not been duly compensated. Apparently the phenomenon of the kamikaze convinced many that prayers had been more efficacious than arms against the Mongols.

But the true impact of the Mongol invasions can only be understood within the context of certain larger social and economic processes that were at work in late Kamakura Japan and that would ultimately have brought the shogunate's downfall without the intrusive factor of foreign attack. Examination of these processes reveals, among other things, that: 1) agrarian-based military regimes are ill-equipped to handle the problems of commercial progress that are invariably created by the establishment of order and tranquil conditions; 2) the Kamakura shogunate itself was overextended and could not indefinitely maintain national control without expanding its base of warrior support beyond the existing shogunal housemen, a group which was primarily eastern in its composition.

These shogunal housemen had fixed incomes based on annual harvest levies. As the cost of living mounted during the thirteenth century they found it increasingly difficult to maintain their obligations and their positions. Many were forced to turn to the moneylender, often pledging their lands and incomes as security for usurious loans. Shogunal authorities inveighed against the pledging (and in many cases the alienation) of land by their elitist followers, but only with partial success. The condition of many housemen was further exacerbated by the custom of divided inheritance, which caused the parceling out of family property among all children, female as well as male. Toward the end of the century the shogunate even tried to aid the housemen through outright debt cancellation decrees, known euphemistically as "virtuous administration" (*tokusei*). Although some housemen may have benefited temporarily from these decrees, the *tokusei* could not provide a permanent solution to their growing financial problems.

The need for defense against the Mongols in the west, where the shogunate had its smallest following, also placed considerable strain on the houseman system. Estate holders in the central and western provinces were finding it increasingly difficult to maintain control of their landed interests in the face of incursions by local warriors, who were both housemen functioning as stewards and non-housemen holding other estate posts. In many cases the non-housemen combined into "rowdy bands" (*akutō*) and became a distinct threat not only to the estate holders but to local order in general. The shogunate tried to distract these restless warriors by recruiting them for the defense of Kyushu. Certainly the idea of bringing more men under allegiance to Kamakura was a good one, but the rather casual manner in which shogunal officials allowed non-housemen to perform duties that had heretofore been reserved exclusively for housemen caused strong resentment among the latter. The Hōjō reacted to this and other problems by attempting to draw shogunal power more fully into their own hands. Yasutoki's ideal of assembly government was destroyed when the later Hōjō regents gradually transferred the shogunal decision-making process from the Council of State to their private family meetings.

A further complicating factor in politics of the late thirteenth century was the emergence of a dispute over succession to the throne. When the Cloistered Emperor Gosaga died in 1272 without making clear the order of succession, two of his sons—the ex-Emperor Gofukakusa and the reigning sovereign Kameyama—claimed that the throne should go to their respective descendants. There were many personal and legal points of argument on both sides. It appears, however, that Gosaga's intent had simply been to allow the shogunate to decide on succession as it had since the Jōkyū incident of 1221. Undoubtedly a strong stand by the shogunate in the beginning would have settled the matter in favor of either Gofukakusa's or Kameyama's line. But shogunal leaders were deeply absorbed with the Mongol invasions and other problems and quite possibly felt that the encouragement of division within the Imperial House might be a good means for reducing any latent threat that Kyoto still held for the Kamakura regime. In any case they soon sanctioned a compromise agreement whereby the junior line (Kameyama's) and senior line (Gofukakusa's) were to succeed alternately to the throne. Within time nearly all of court society came to be divided into hostile camps behind the two lines.

In 1318 a member of the junior line ascended the throne as the Emperor Godaigo. Three years later his father abolished the Office of Cloistered Emperor and allowed authority to be concentrated exclusively in Godaigo's hands. Godaigo was at the time a mature and vigorous man in his thirties. He deeply resented the subordinate role of the court in national affairs and, like the Cloistered Emperor Gotoba a century earlier, began to scheme to overthrow the military regime in Kamakura. In 1324 and again in 1331 he encouraged plots against the shogunate, but on both occasions they were unsuccessful. After the second plot shogunal authorities, also recalling the case of Gotoba, exiled Godaigo to the Oki Islands in the Japan Sea. But the matter was not so easily settled, for by this time anti-Hōjō sentiment was mounting in the central and western provinces. Shogunal troops were unable to deal effectively with the guerrilla bands that constantly harassed them in the hills around the capital. Prominent among the guerrilla leaders was a warrior named Kusunoki Masashige, whose valor and unswerving devotion to the cause of Godaigo have made him one of the paragons of loyalty to the throne in Japanese history.

In 1333 loyalist supporters engineered the escape of Godaigo from the Oki Islands. Simultaneously the shogunate dispatched a great army westward under a leading eastern chieftain, Ashikaga Takauji. Marching into the central provinces, Takauji suddenly changed sides, announcing his allegiance to Godaigo and attacking the shogunate's deputy offices in Kyoto. As he did so, another eastern chieftain, Nitta Yoshisada, rose to destroy the Hōjō administration at Kamakura. With surprising suddenness the military system founded by Minamoto Yoritomo a century and a half before was reduced to ruins. The Emperor Godaigo returned in triumph to Kyoto to inaugurate what he hoped would be a new era of imperial rule.

There has been a strong tendency during times of instability for the Japanese to think in terms of "restoration" and, like their Confucian counterparts in China, to seek ideals for rule in the past. In its simplest terms restoration in Japan has always meant a return to the emperor of powers and privileges that were his by birthright and that he had formerly enjoyed. Implicit has been the charge that others have usurped or somehow perverted the exercise of these powers and privileges. Godaigo, by selecting his own posthumous name of the "Later Daigo," indicated his desire to restore the practices of the early tenth century—before the consolidation of power by Fujiwara regents and before the rise of cloistered emperors, shoguns, and shogunal regents—when the Emperor Daigo had supposedly exercised direct imperial rule.

The Ashikaga Shogunate

Godaigo interpreted victory over the Hōjō as a personal mandate to reinstitute direct and personal imperial rule. During a two-year period beginning in 1333 he undertook a restoration of imperial rule (known as the Kemmu Restoration) based on a series of policies, some of them pathetically naïve, to strengthen his own position and to reassert the primacy of the court nobles over the warriors. In reality Godaigo's position was tenuous from the start, for he relied on a highly unstable coalition, including many warriors who had joined his cause simply to oppose the Hōjō. When it became obvious that the Kyoto court could not effectively handle their claims for reward and other crucial matters, these warriors became disenchanted and began to look elsewhere for leadership

The two most prominent warriors under Godaigo were Ashikaga Takauji and Nitta Yoshisada. Both were heads of Minamoto branch families and were natural rivals for military leadership after the defeat of the Hōjō. Yoshisada, who was in a weaker strategical position, intrigued against his rival at court and finally forced Takauji into revolt. To secure a measure of legitimacy for himself, Takauji announced support of a member of the senior line of the Imperial House. In 1336 he drove Godaigo and his followers to the hills of Yoshino south of the capital and thus set the stage for the protracted period of dynastic schism known as the war between the courts. Although the southern (junior line) court managed to sustain itself in the region of Yoshino until 1392, after the first decade or so it held little hope of being ultimately victorious. Its greatest leader was the courtier-general Kitabatake Chikafusa, author of the *Jinnō Shōtōki* (Record of the direct descent of the divine sovereigns), a work important both for its views on medieval Shintō and as a polemical tract in support of the legitimacy of the southern court.

The northern (senior line) court meanwhile became simply a façade for the Ashikaga shogunate, whose headquarters Takauji established in Kyoto.

Regionalism became an increasingly important factor during the opening years of the Ashikaga shogunate. In contrast to the earlier Minamoto and Hōjō, the Ashikaga were able to achieve a hegemony little better than that of *primus inter pares*. The need to bring at least partial order when warfare between the courts seemed unending forced them constantly to make concessions in the form of rewards in land and greater administrative authority to newly appointed constables and allied commanders who were themselves striving to establish control in the provinces. It was not until the period of the third Ashikaga shogun, Yoshimitsu, whose rule commenced in 1368, that some semblance of a cohesive system of central and regional military government reemerged.

Constable authority during the Kamakura period had been limited to certain police powers and to responsibilities related to the mustering of shogunal housemen for guard duty. During the early Muromachi period (so named because from Yoshimitsu's time the shogunate's offices were located in the Muromachi section of northeast Kyoto) the constables, or constable-daimyō [1] as they are designated by modern scholars, became virtually autonomous rulers of one or more provinces. The Yamana family at one point held as many as eleven. To maintain command of their regional domains, however,

1. The term *daimyō* means, literally, "great name." From about this time on it increasingly came to be used to signify regional magnates.

the constable-daimyō were obliged to rely to some extent upon the support of the shogunate and upon cooperation with each other. Under Yoshimitsu a balance of power between shogunate and constable-daimyō was evolved which proved workable for nearly a century. The key to this balance was the participation on an alternating basis of leaders of the three most prominent constable-daimyō families—the Hosokawa, the Hatakeyama, and the Shiba—as shogunal deputies (*kanrei*) at Kyoto.

Yoshimitsu's administration from 1368 until 1408 was the high point of shogunal rule in the Muromachi period. Yoshimitsu was a shrewd and forceful leader who not only helped develop and maintain the balance of power with the constable-daimyō, but also succeeded in 1392 in bringing about a reunion of the courts. Actually, support for the Yoshino court had by then nearly vanished. Yoshimitsu promised a return to the old order of alternate succession, but never honored it, and from that time all emperors have been from the senior (northern) line.

The Ashikaga shogunate, because of its insufficient holdings in land, was constantly plagued by financial problems. To increase government revenue Yoshimitsu and his advisers sought, with only partial success, to impose a variety of levies on acreage, households, and commercial lending concerns. Toward the end of the century they found still another source of income in trade with Ming China. The Ming dynasty had first made contact with Japan to gain support in the suppression of Japanese-led pirates (*wakō*) who were ravaging the coastal waters and mainland of China.

In the absence of normal maritime relations among China and her neighbors, piracy was a recurrent problem in East Asia throughout the premodern period. From the end of the thirteenth century *wakō* became increasingly active, first toward Korea and then toward China. The *wakō* of this period ranged from groups of petty seamarauders to supporters of the southern court, who held out in Kyushu until the 1390s and made frequent raids on the continent to commandeer men and supplies for their continuing struggle against the Ashikaga shogunate. Yoshimitsu's willingness to cooperate in action against the *wakō* arose from the twofold desire to establish friendly relations with the Ming rulers for the purpose of trade and to eliminate one of the last outposts of the southern court.

To the great chagrin of later Japanese historians, Yoshimitsu appears to have accepted precisely the type of tributary relationship with

China that the Hōjō had so resolutely refused a century earlier. In correspondence with the Middle Kingdom he accepted the use both of Chinese calendrical designations and of the personal title of *kokuō* (king of the country), which the Chinese traditionally bestowed on the heads of tributary states. In designating Yoshimitsu as *kokuō,* the Ming were either unaware of or chose to ignore the fact that the Ashikaga shogun, whatever his power, was still theoretically subordinate to the emperor in Japan's ruling hierarchy.

The trade with China (called the "tally" trade from the use of tallies or markers to identify official ships) which Yoshimitsu promoted lasted for nearly a century and a half, from 1401 to 1549. To the Chinese it was not trade at all, but the rendering of tribute by Japan in return for gifts from the Chinese emperor; as such it was to be kept within strict limits (e.g., one tribute mission every ten years). The Japanese, on the other hand, sought profit, and hence frequently violated the Chinese-imposed limits. Among the principal Japanese exports in the tally trade were sapan wood, sulphur, copper ore, swords, and folding fans; imports included silk, porcelains, books, and Chinese copper coins, which the Japanese used widely as a medium of exchange in the medieval period.

With his power and prestige secure by the early years of the fifteenth century, Yoshimitsu dominated both court ministers and warrior chieftains in Kyoto. He encouraged the constable-daimyō to take up permanent residence in the capital under his surveillance and seized every opportunity to enhance his personal stature. In 1394 he had turned the office of shogun over to his oldest son, only to assume for himself the exalted court title of chancellor, which Taira Kiyomori alone among the military had previously held. After his death in 1408 he was given, for a brief period, the honorary posthumous designation of "retired emperor"; and indeed from certain acts shortly before his death Yoshimitsu gave indication that he might be scheming to place another of his sons on the throne and to assume for himself a role similar to that of a cloistered emperor. Perhaps he sensed that the inherent weakness of the Ashikaga shogunate demanded extraordinary measures to guarantee its continuance as a legitimate and effective governing center.

The balance of power between the Ashikaga shogunate and the constable-daimyō, so carefully constructed during the final decades of the fourteenth century, began to deteriorate after Yoshimitsu's death in 1408. In their efforts to govern large regional bases the constable-daimyō had been obliged to seek the support of local warriors in their provinces and to appoint the more important of these as deputies or other domain officials. As the constable-daimyō, at Yoshimitsu's urging, spent more and more time in the capital, they delegated greater shares of provincial administration to these prominent local warriors. Before long a number of the latter exercised authority sufficient to endanger or even to upset the political hegemonies of their absentee lords. This danger became reality in the series of succession disputes that erupted among the constable families in the years leading to the Ōnin War of 1467–77. Indeed, it was the phenomenon of the succession dispute that became symptomatic of the impending collapse of the entire shogunate-constable structure from about the mid-fifteenth century.

Under Yoshimitsu's firm hand succession disputes within the constable-daimyō families had been largely avoided by prompt shogunal confirmation of new family heads (although in one or two cases Yoshimitsu had encouraged disputes in order to weaken and reduce the strength of families that had become a threat to the Ashikaga themselves). During the fifteenth century, however, and especially from the time of the shogun Yoshimasa, who assumed office in 1443 at the age of eight, the shogunate lost much of its power to control or to direct the constable-daimyō. Yoshimasa's interests lay in the arts and in courtly pleasures and not at all in military matters. During his tenure of office the shogunate became little more than an observer of the struggles among the regional magnates. Under such conditions shogunal confirmation could no longer serve as an effective check to internal quarrels upon the deaths of these magnates.

Failure to provide effectively for transference of the headship of a constable family often presented the family's vassals with the opportunity to back opposing candidates and to set in motion a protracted contest over succession in which the candidates themselves were apt ultimately to become mere pawns. Among the families victimized by disputes about this time were the Hatakeyama and the Shiba, two of the three shogunal deputy houses. In the case of the Hatakeyama, the dispute began in the 1450s, continued through the Ōnin War, and lasted until the deaths of both candidates for family headship in the 1490s. By that time the regional power of the Hatakeyama had vanished.

The immediate cause of the Ōnin War in 1467 was a dispute over succession to the office of shogun itself. The constable-daimyō, led by the Hosokawa and the Yamana, massed their armies into two rival camps in Kyoto in support of the candidacies of Yoshimasa's brother and son. In fact, the question of who would succeed Yoshimasa at the head of an already impotent shogunate was scarcely more than an excuse for these chieftains to contend openly among themselves. The war, which lasted for a decade, brought fearful destruction to Kyoto; it also caused the decline, if not the collapse, of most of the constable-daimyō houses. Certain of these houses, already riven by internal disputes (such as the Shiba and Hatakeyama), participated on both sides in the fighting. Others lost part or all of their provincial bases to vassal deputies who had remained at home. By the time the war in the capital ended in 1477, the whole structure of central and regional control over which the Ashikaga and their constables had presided was irreparably damaged.

Even at their height the Ashikaga had not exercised firm jurisdiction over areas distant from the home provinces. The failure of their governing system during the Ōnin War inaugurated a century of virtual anarchy through much of the country. Yet this was also a time of important social change and institutional development from the local level up that was to make possible a new national unification at the end of the sixteenth century.

Muromachi Culture

Although the Muromachi period was an age of political instability and nearly constant warfare, it was also a time of considerable cultural brilliance. One characteristic of Muromachi culture was its diversity, both in content and in the social range of those who participated in it. The Kamakura period witnessed the expansion of culture outward from the world of the Heian aristocrat to the society of the provincial military. During Muromachi times a truly national culture first began to take shape as this expansion came to include the rural peasantry as well as the rising merchant class of the larger urban centers.

A second characteristic of Muromachi culture was the key role played in its formation by Zen Buddhism and Zen priests. With the renewal of contact with China and the Asian mainland from late Heian times on, Japanese adherents to Zen became actively engaged in the importation of new ideas and styles from abroad. And after the founding of the Ashikaga shogunate the more prominent Zen Temples of Kyoto (known as the *Gozan* or "Five Temples") assumed a leading role, under the patronage of the Ashikaga, of what was at first a quasi-official and then an official trade with China. Among the intellectual and artistic pursuits first introduced to Japan about this time by Zen priests who journeyed to China were Sung Neo-Confucianism and monochrome ink painting.

Zen canons of simplicity and restraint and the Zen stress on intuitive response proved eminently congenial to the Japanese of the Muromachi period. It is incorrect to suppose that the culture of Muromachi Japan became exclusively a "Zen culture," for the aesthetics of this age also owed much to tastes cultivated by the Japanese long before their formal exposure to Zen. Nevertheless, so much of Muromachi culture did become intimately associated, if not imbued, with the Zen spirit that it is impossible fully to appreciate its development apart from the historical course of Zen in Japan during the Muromachi period. From a purely religious standpoint, on the other hand, it is doubtful that Zen Buddhism ever secured a very large following of exclusive practitioners, for even among those of the court and military aristocracies most devoted to Zen methods and ways there seems to have been a generally felt need to turn to the faith sects (especially Amidism) for ultimate spiritual comfort.

The location of both court and shogunate in Kyoto made this ancient city once again preeminently the cultural as well as the political heart of the land, at least until the Ōnin War. Under the earlier Kamakura shogunate, military leaders had attempted to minimize the contacts between warrior and court. Housemen were forbidden, for example, to accept court titles without the express approval of the shogunate. During the Muromachi period, on the other hand, there was much intermingling of warrior leaders and courtiers, stemming partly from the proximity of their offices in Kyoto and partly from the conscious policy of merger pursued by Yoshimitsu. As a consequence, military rulers like Yoshimitsu and Yoshimasa felt completely at ease among a wide range of acquaintances and confidants, including daimyō, Zen prelates and prominent clergy of other sects, court nobles, and even members of the Imperial House. They "held court" for the leading political, intellectual, and artistic figures of the day and became themselves the highest arbiters of taste during the two most brilliant cultural phases of the Muromachi period.

Even before the full flowering of Muromachi culture in the late fourteenth and fifteenth centuries, a literary work of high distinction, the *Tsurezuregusa* (*Essays in Idleness*), was produced by Yoshida Kenkō in the 1330s. Kenkō, a court noble skilled in letters and verse, wrote this book in middle age after taking Buddhist vows and withdrawing from the responsibilities of everyday life. A collection of anecdotes, critical comments, and sundry notations, the *Tsurezuregusa* is in the best tradition of the Japanese miscellany. It is unrealistic, perhaps, in that it contains not a word about the political and military disorder of the times. Kenkō preferred, rather, to discuss such matters as ancient ceremonial and the elegant amenities of court society. Yet, unlike the author of the *Hōjōki* a century or more earlier who spoke with anguish of the disasters that beset late Heian Japan, Kenkō appears to accept with greater resignation and philosophical equanimity the uncertainties and upheavals of his own age.

Yoshimitsu's phase of cultural flowering at the end of the fourteenth century is known as the Kitayama, or "Northern Hills," period from the location of his monastic retreat (the Kinkakuji, or Golden Pavilion) in the Kitayama section of northern Kyoto. A number of factors—including stabilization of the constable-daimyō domains, unification of the courts, the opening of trade with Ming China, and Yoshimitsu's own proclivities—contributed to the stable and cosmopolitan conditions that proved so favorable to the renewal of intellectual and artistic pursuits at this time. Nearly all the scholarly, and much of the literary, output of the period flowed from the small group of *Gozan* Zen temples, whose prelates, as part of their multifarious activities, wrote Buddhist texts, composed Chinese-style poetry, and undertook the compilation of dictionaries.

The finest cultural achievement of the Kitayama period was the development and perfection of the Nō (literally, "talent" or "ability") drama. The origins of Nō are obscure, but they appear to be deeply rooted in folkways. Entertainments of a secular and earthy nature, consisting of composite forms of song, dance, and mimicry, are known to have been held at harvest and other festival times from at least the mid-Heian era. In the later stages of their evolution these entertainments were called "field music" and "monkey music" and were frequently performed at shrines and other popular meeting places. For half a millennium or more artistic modes and styles had emerged almost exclusively from the aristocratic sectors of Japanese society. In field music and monkey music as forerunners of Nō we see the first important stages in the broadening of cultural horizons to include the creative impulses and tastes of virtually all classes of the Japanese people. Nō was brought to its highest level of perfection by the playwrights Kan'ami and his son Zeami, who enjoyed the generous patronage of Yoshimitsu. In their hands Nō became a highly stylized and refined form of art.

The custom arose of having programs of several Nō plays offered at a sitting and, to lighten what would otherwise have been a somber succession of narratives, interspersing the plays with brief offerings known as *kyōgen* (mad words). The *kyōgen* are comic sketches in which servants and other humble people frequently spoof and outwit their superiors. Unlike the Nō plays, which were elevated at this time to the tastes of the highborn, the *kyōgen* retained their essentially popular flavor in both subject matter and style of presentation. Some Japanese historians have attempted to find in *kyōgen* signs of conscious resistance or challenge to the upper classes by the lower. The records do indeed show occasional annoyance on the part of the authorities at the irreverent character of certain *kyōgen*. But apparently these authorities were never aroused to the point of imposing general restrictions on their composition and performance.

Japanese culture during the Muromachi period was, to a greater extent than ever before, a culture of participation. Theatrical presentations brought people together as performers; other pursuits, such as poetry-writing, united them as composers. From the fourteenth century on, the composition of linked verse (*renga*), which had formerly been little more than a source of amusement to court poets, became enormously popular. At social gatherings versification, in which two or more persons took turns composing brief units of poetry that could be joined in nearly endless fashion, was apt to be the center of attraction.

Tea drinking also gained wide vogue in the socializing process of this age. Commoners may have been the first to organize tea parties; yet, in the same fashion that popular theater was elevated by aristocrats to the level of Nō, so the preparation and consumption of tea came to be formalized into the classical tea ceremony. To the connoisseurs of Yoshimasa's time participation in this ceremony was perhaps the most satisfying of all aesthetic experiences. Gathered in tranquil and severely simple surroundings to observe the careful movements of the ceremony and to comment on the utensils in use and on artistic matters in general, they were apparently able to achieve a remarkable sense of withdrawal from the cares of a troubled age.

Before the Ōnin War the shogun Yoshimasa had been little more than a flamboyant pleasure-seeker, who delighted in elaborate flower-viewing processions, lengthy Nō programs, and sumptuous feasts. After the war his tastes, if not his spending habits, seem to have been greatly tempered or purified, owing no doubt in part to his growing sense of futility in the realm of politics. The Higashiyama period (so named from the location of his retreat, the Ginkakuji or Silver Pavilion, in the "Eastern Hills" section of Kyoto) refers specifically to the postwar era when Yoshimasa and his coterie provided in Kyoto an atmosphere conducive to a variety of cultural and artistic pursuits, which were much influenced by Zen and which included, in addition to the tea ceremony, landscape gardening, monochrome painting, and flower arranging.

The postwar period also witnessed a wave of nostalgia for the past, reflected in various reanalyses and exegetical studies of Heian masterpieces such as *The Tale of Genji* and the *Kokinshū* and in the appearance of new cultural centers in the provinces. Court nobles in Kyoto had by this time been almost completely dispossessed of their sources of income from landed estates. Many were forced to seek a livelihood by giving instruction in the arts. Disturbed conditions in the capital, moreover, prompted a number to accept the invitations of warrior chieftains to visit them at their provincial seats. In this way some of the most prominent intellectuals and artists of the day, including the incomparable painter Sesshū, traveled far afield and gave further impetus to the growth of national culture, which was so characteristic of the Muromachi period.

A Century of Provincial Wars

Japanese scholars sub-label the last century of the Muromachi period, from the end of the Ōnin War in 1477 until approximately 1568, the *Sengoku jidai,* or "period of warring states," in imitation of the age of disunity (403–221 B.C.) so designated in Chinese history. In Japan's case, it might be more appropriate to render *Sengoku jidai* as the "period of war in the provinces," inasmuch as there were few clearly defined states or provincial domains until well into the sixteenth century. In outlying regions, such as northern Honshu and southern Kyushu, certain daimyō did manage to hold their positions throughout the turbulence of these years. But in the great majority of instances the pre-Ōnin domains were obliterated or fragmented and a general struggle for land and power ensued among lesser warrior chieftains that was not fully resolved until the emergence of a new pattern of daimyō holdings in the provinces about the mid-sixteenth century.

A term frequently used to describe the process of rapid social and political change during this late Muromachi or provincial wars period is *gekokujō* (those below overthrow those above). With varying degrees of aptness, *gekokujō* is applied to the complex of revolt and upheaval at all levels of society—from peasants rising against oppressive landlords to vassal warriors dispossessing their lords— that typified the age. Central control became virtually nonexistent. The Imperial House was reduced to a state of near poverty, in which on one occasion insufficient funds forced postponement of an emperor's coronation for twenty years—and on another, it is said, an emperor sold his signature for cash. Ashikaga shoguns fared little better. By the turn of the century they had become mere puppets in the hands of contending chieftains in Kyoto.

Institutional developments in the provincial wars period took place chiefly on two levels: the regional level, where provincial domains, usually smaller but more tightly controlled than those of the constable-daimyō, were forged by a new class of daimyō; and the local level, where a long-evolving process of separation of warriors from their countryside was accelerated and where self-governing peasant villages, which became characteristic of the Tokugawa period, took final form.

Many of the daimyō of the provincial wars period were deputies of constable-daimyō, who, by the process of *gekokujō,* had overthrown their former lords and had asserted their own claims to independent territorial rule. In the anarchy of the times the new daimyō sought first to fortify and defend their domains against attack by others. Their aim was to "enrich their states and strengthen their arms" (*fukoku kyōhei*); accordingly, they constructed powerful castle towns and gathered their warrior followers into permanent military units in them. Aware that only prosperous states could support such full-time fighting establishments, they adopted positive economic policies to encourage commercial as well as agricultural developments—e.g., they granted incentives for the opening of new lands, undertook cadastral surveys, improved methods of internal transporta-

tion and communication, and sought to exploit available mining resources.

The degree to which the daimyō could impose despotic controls
over their domains depended on the intensity of resistance likely to
be aroused by such controls. In general, the daimyō of the provincial
wars period showed themselves to be extraordinarily forceful and
aggressive. Since they lived in a violent and predatory age, without
such qualities they could not have survived for long. They were also
progressive men for their time. We can see in the "house laws" (i.e.,
domain codes) which they compiled a surprisingly practical approach
to administration. These laws contain a minimum of Confucian
rhetoric and pontification on the need for moral and harmonious
government. Instead, they tend to deal with precise duties and rules
of behavior and to threaten severe punishment in cases of violation
or nonperformance. Virtually all of the house laws, moreover, call
for the employment of "men of talent," to be selected less on the
basis of their birth and familiarity with the Confucian Classics than
on their capacity to perform specific and differentiated functions,
from fighting in the field to managing fiscal affairs at the domain
capital.

The daimyō were as alert to the problem of maintaining internal
order as they were to defending themselves against and challenging
the leaders of other domains. They sought, for example, to prevent
the formation of unauthorized leagues among their vassals by setting
forth strict rules about marriage and other contractual arrangements.
At the same time they took elaborate steps to protect their borders
and to guard against "foreign" attack or infiltration. In their relations with neighboring states, the daimyō were guided by considerations of power and advantage; and, as the records clearly show, they
were capable of deceit, cruelty, and deception in the highest degree
when in pursuit of victory over an enemy.

It was during the provincial wars period that conditions most
closely resembling the feudalism of Western Europe prevailed in
Japan. Aristocratic society was by the late fifteenth and early sixteenth centuries overwhelmingly a military society, in which men
were joined hierarchically by ties of vassalage and in which social
status and political power were fused and made dependent solely on
one's position in the military hierarchy. The last vestiges of the complex and outmoded estate system of land tenure were at length swept
away; court nobles and other absentee holders were everywhere dis-

possessed by warriors who established more direct, fieflike proprietorships over land. Although warriors held superior proprietorial rights, it was the peasantry, of course, who actually worked the soil. The tendency was for one peasant and his family to assume responsibility for the farming and management of one plot of land. The peasant's status became that of a serf inasmuch as he was permanently attached to the land he worked and was obliged to render a portion of his harvest as rent to his warrior overlord. The latter, on his part, protected the peasant from outside intrusion, but otherwise interfered as little as possible in the personal labors and affairs of peasant society. By the late sixteenth century peasants throughout the country had formed themselves into virtually autonomous villages where they lived, worked together, and provided for their own needs.

Little has been said thus far about commercial developments during the medieval age. In view of the great burst of activity in domestic commerce and overseas trade that accompanied political unification in the second half of the sixteenth century, however, it is appropriate here to comment briefly on progress in the nonagricultural sector of the Japanese economy.

From the beginning of the Kamakura period there had been a marked growth in the number and size of handicraft trades and in market and transportation facilities. The gradual obliteration of estate boundaries, which had prevented the expansion of commerce earlier, was one factor in this growth. The spread of a money economy was another. Although government leaders of medieval Japan refrained from issuing their own currencies, imported coins from China were widely circulated as media of exchange from at least the twelfth century.

The concept of an expanding economy in an age of mounting struggle and political anarchy, such as the Muromachi period, may seem paradoxical. While no simple explanation can be given, several reasons may be suggested. Many of the armed conflicts from the fourteenth century on were not especially destructive in an economic sense. Armies tended to engage in brief battles and to move on without remaining long enough to become a burden to local communities. On the contrary, the frequent movement of fighting men from one region to another undoubtedly served to stimulate growth in both transportation and communication.

Rulers and others in positions of authority during the medieval age often sought additional revenue by levying passage fees at barriers that they erected on main transportation routes. Needless to say, this practice had an inhibiting effect on commerce, as did the border controls imposed by daimyō of the provincial wars period. Yet the unusual concentration of commerce in the central provinces and in certain port cities on the Inland Sea made such barriers and controls less inhibitive in these key areas than they might otherwise have been. No daimyō, for example, was able to impose his hegemony over the central region around Kyoto from the end of the Ōnin War until the rise of Oda Nobunaga in the 1560s and 1570s. Powerful commercial interests in the home provinces were able collectively to resist the more onerous checks to their activities and to account for a large portion of the nonagricultural growth of the national economy. At the same time many of the daimyō, while of necessity restricting traffic over the borders of their domains, showed themselves to be decidedly "unfeudal" in their attitudes toward commerce by encouraging the development of markets and handicraft trades. A few favorably situated daimyō, such as the Hosokawa on the Inland Sea and the Ōuchi at the Straits of Shimonoseki, even took an active part in the overseas trade with China and Korea after the Ōnin War.

Some daimyō appear to have been commercially more progressive than the medieval merchants and artisans themselves. The basic unit of organization among the latter was the guild, or *za,* formed by members of a particular craft or trade for mutual protection, market advantages, and such. These guilds, which typically acquired the patronage of court nobles in Kyoto or of religious institutions, were inclined after reaching a certain size to become highly restrictive— that is, they concerned themselves primarily with the protection of their existing privileges and with the prevention of interference from the outside. Oda Nobunaga, for one, sought to dissolve these older guilds and to encourage the formation of new groups, known as "free guilds" (*rakuza*), which would be more liberal in their attitudes, their activities, and their membership policies.

Unification: Nobunaga, Hideyoshi, Ieyasu

Political unification, or reunification, in the latter part of the sixteenth century was the final stage in a long and dynamic process, which we have observed, of institutional growth at the regional (daimyō domain) and local (peasant village) levels in Japan. By the 1550s daimyō throughout the land had brought to their domains a high degree of order and were on the verge of contending with one another for supremacy. The necessary building blocks were, so to speak, at hand and were ready to be combined into a new system of national hegemony.

It was precisely at this time, when unification appeared imminent, that European traders and Catholic missionaries first arrived in Japan. There is little doubt that unification would have taken place with or without the novel factor of Western intrusion. Nevertheless, the particular challenges presented by the foreigners and the responses of the Japanese to these challenges had a profound effect on the final form that unification took.

The Portuguese, who led the way in European exploration around the coast of Africa to Asian waters, had reached India in 1498 and had continued on to establish bases both in Southeast Asia and in China. In 1543, when a Portuguese ship ran aground on the small island of Tanegashima off the southern coast of Kyushu, its occupants became the first non-Asians, so far as we know, to set foot on Japanese soil. Within a few years Portuguese trading ships were making regular calls at ports in Kyushu and had helped launch Japan on the most flourishing phase of foreign intercourse in its premodern history. The Portuguese, governed by European mercantilist thinking, were especially anxious to acquire Japanese bullion. Since the Japanese on their part desired silk, the newcomers inaugurated a system of triangular trade whereby they brought Chinese silk to Japan in exchange for silver.

With the Portuguese traders came Portuguese missionaries. In their dealings with the Japanese, the Portuguese (and later the Spanish) never wavered in their insistence that trade and missionary work go hand in hand. Herein lay the fundamental difficulty in relations. Japanese leaders came increasingly to regard Christianity as inimical to their interests and indeed harmful to Japanese society as a whole. They were constantly obliged to balance their distaste for Christianity against their mounting desire for foreign trade.

The great Jesuit Francis Xavier arrived in Japan in 1549 and remained until 1551. During his stay, Xavier was most impressed with the Japanese people and, upon departure, rated missionary prospects in Japan as excellent. But he was frustrated in his attempts to make contact with the Japanese "ruling elite" and to obtain permission to proselytize on a national scale. A trip to Kyoto revealed to him the disappointing fact that no central ruling group existed that could effectively grant such permission. Returning to Kyushu, Xavier spent the remainder of his time in Japan seeking converts among the various classes in that westernmost part of the country.

Later missionaries were to have greater success than Xavier in the capital region. In their diaries and papers these men have provided us with vivid and intimate accounts of Church activities in and around Kyoto and of their personal contacts with the great figures of the age of unification. Kyushu, however, remained the most fertile ground for propagation of the Christian faith in Japan. The missionaries were most effective in appealing to members of the poorer peasantry of Kyushu, although they also included several daimyō among their converts. The daimyō may have embraced Christianity more from a desire for commercial profit in their trade with the foreigners than from any compelling religious urge. It was, nevertheless, estimated in 1582 that the number of native Christians had reached approximately 150,000 and that there were some 200 churches in Japan. If these and other figures compiled during the next few decades are at all accurate, they imply that Christianity enjoyed greater favor among the Japanese of the late sixteenth and early seventeenth centuries than it does among their descendants today.

In addition to Christianity, the Portuguese introduced firearms, tobacco, and a variety of other exotic things to Japan. Firearms did not immediately revolutionize warfare, although they did give a distinct advantage to those diamyō who were able to acquire them in sufficient numbers for key battles. By the time they could be widely produced, about 1600, unification was completed and fighting had ceased.

One of the most interesting products of foreign influence at this time was the style of painting known as Namban (southern barbarian) because the Europeans approached Japan by sea from the south. Namban artists, who painted mostly on folding screens, were fascinated by the strange looking foreigners and depicted them with extremely elongated bodies, tiny heads, and outlandishly baggy clothes.

While the Japanese were undergoing this unique premodern experience of exposure to things and people non-Asian, political unification was proceeding apace. Unification from the 1560s on was to a large extent the work of three great men, the first of whom was Oda Nobunaga, a daimyō from the province of Owari, located midway between the Kyoto region and the eastern provinces at the site of modern Nagoya. The Oda family had provided deputy constables to the Shiba at the time of the Ōnin War and their rise to prominence during the provincial wars period was a classic example of *gekokujō*. Nobunaga, after consolidating the headship of his own family about the mid-sixteenth century, began to expand outward from his Owari base by destroying certain opponents and by bringing others into alliance with him. One key to his success was the pact he formed in 1560 with Tokugawa Ieyasu, a young chieftain from adjacent Mikawa Province, who provided Nobunaga with an indispensable shield of protection in the rear as he moved westward toward the capital.

When Nobunaga entered Kyoto in 1568, he did so with the blessing of the emperor and in the company of a fugitive member of the Ashikaga family, whom he installed as the fifteenth and last Muromachi shogun. But Nobunaga had little real need for the legitimizing seals of either imperial or shogunal approval, since his position was based on the reality and not the theory of power. When in 1573 he decided that the shogun had become excessively bothersome, Nobunaga simply dismissed him and thus extinguished the line of Ashikaga rule founded nearly two and a half centuries earlier by Takauji.

Nobunaga did not seek special titles or offices for himself and, indeed, dealt with administrative matters in the generally *ad hoc* fashion of a military commander still absorbed mainly with combat in the field. By occupying Kyoto he took the first step toward unification, but the country was still far from his. Among the more prominent of his adversaries were several of the great temples of the home provinces. In 1571 he surrounded and destroyed the complex of some 3,000 buildings that comprised the Enryakuji on Mt. Hiei, in the process slaughtering most if not all of the many inhabitants of that ancient Buddhist center. Nine years later, in 1580, he achieved perhaps his greatest military victory when, after long siege, he successfully reduced the mighty True Sect fortress at Ishiyama in Osaka.

In his efforts to unify the country Nobunaga demonstrated the type of progressive attitude toward commerce and trade characteristic of the more prominent sixteenth-century daimyō. We can see in his policy toward the city of Sakai, for example, Nobunaga's determination to secure and maintain the economic as well as human resources necessary to wield power in an age of mobile armies, mass battles, and national military strategy. Sakai, located at the eastern end of the Inland Sea, was at the time the principal entrepôt port in the overseas trade with Ming China. During most of the sixteenth century it had been managed by a well-organized group of merchants who had repeatedly thwarted the efforts of petty daimyō in the central provinces to assert their mastery over the city. The status of Sakai was very much like that of a European "free city." Only in the face of Nobunaga's overwhelming might did it finally submit to military overlordship. Yet Nobunaga was careful not to upset the commercial functioning of Sakai. His aim was to keep the city flourishing as before and to use it as a major source of arms and supplies in future campaigns.

Nobunaga constructed his principal fortress at Azuchi on Lake Biwa east of Kyoto. To encourage its growth as a castle town, he directed a number of his warrior followers to move to Azuchi and issued orders guaranteeing a high degree of commercial freedom and opportunity in the town's newly established markets.

Nobunaga did much to bring a kind of rough order to central Japan, but before he could complete the task of national unification he was struck down by an assassin in 1582 at the age of forty-eight. His death at the hands of one of his leading generals, Akechi Mitsuhide, was promptly avenged by another general, Toyotomi Hideyoshi.

Hideyoshi, who pursued and destroyed Mitsuhide, was one of the true military geniuses of Japanese history. The offspring of a fairly well-to-do peasant family of Owari, Hideyoshi had risen in the ranks of Nobunaga's army from sandal bearer to a position of prominence sufficient to enable him to seize power after his lord's death. Within a decade he completed the job of unification in a series of campaigns ranging from Kyushu in the west to the northern provinces of Honshu. By 1590 daimyō throughout the country, including the reluctant Tokugawa Ieyasu, had acknowledged his suzerainty and Hideyoshi was the undisputed master of Japan.

Hideyoshi built several castles, including an especially mighty one at Osaka and another at Momoyama to the south of the capital. Linked with Azuchi, Momoyama has given its name to the art period coterminous with the ages of Nobunaga and Hideyoshi. The Azuchi-Momoyama period is noted not only for its impressive castles, but also for its heroic and rather ostentatious art style, a style in keeping with the spirit of an epoch of great military and political exploits.

Like Nobunaga, Hideyoshi made no attempt to assume the title of shogun. He was always sensitive to his humble origins and sought in at least two ways to improve his social standing: by adopting the aristocratic-sounding name of Toyotomi (his original family name was Kinoshita); and by taking a series of high court titles, including those of chancellor and regent, the latter of which had until then been the exclusive property of the Fujiwara.

Hideyoshi never secured a truly dominant base in agricultural holdings in the central provinces. His income from rice-producing lands has been estimated at less than a third of that later enjoyed by the Tokugawa in the east. This relative poverty in land caused Hideyoshi, like the Ashikaga and to a lesser extent Nobunaga, to turn his attention to overseas trade. Following Nobunaga's practice of commissioning official ships, he launched Japan on an expanded phase of competitive maritime commerce that carried Japanese ships as far afield as the Philippines, Malaya, and Siam, and that provided a welcome new source of governmental revenue. In 1584 the Spanish, sailing out of Manila, appeared in Japanese waters, and soon became active participants in the bustling Kyushu trade of the early years of Hideyoshi's rule. It was also during this time that the port of Nagasaki, founded as recently as 1570, became one of the chief contact points between Japan and the outside world.

Although he remained to the end an enthusiastic advocate of foreign trade, Hideyoshi became progressively disenchanted with Christianity. Nobunaga had been favorably inclined toward the Christians, owing chiefly to his desire to check militant Buddhism in the central and northwestern provinces. Hideyoshi, on the other hand, apparently came to suspect that Christianity was potentially subversive to the system of loyalties that held the Japanese, especially members of the ruling military class, together. Undoubtedly he found distasteful the prospect of his own followers diverting their allegiance to Rome. He may also have become apprehensive that Catholic Christendom harbored territorial designs on Japan. On several occasions Hideyoshi threatened to expel the missionaries, and he even went so far as to crucify some of them; but he could never bring himself to take the final step of proscribing the foreign religion and thus jeopardizing trade relations with the European countries.

Hideyoshi's own rise from peasant to military hegemon had been a spectacular instance of upward social mobility during the provincial wars period—the ultimate, one might say, in *gekokujō*. Yet his case must be considered an exception to the general trend toward separation of peasant and warrior which developed from at least the mid-sixteenth century. Ironically it was Hideyoshi himself who took the final steps to institutionalize this separation in his famous "sword hunt" of the late 1580s aimed at the confiscation of all weapons from peasants and other nonwarriors and in several nearly concurrent decrees dividing the warriors from the other classes of Japanese society.

Hideyoshi also undertook the first public minting of coins since the mid-Heian period. But perhaps his most ambitious project was the series of land surveys he implemented during the period between 1582 and approximately 1594. The information gathered in these surveys, which were carried out on a national scale, provided the statistical basis for the later calculation of domain holdings during the Tokugawa period.

In the last years of his life Hideyoshi was absorbed to a large extent with two grandiose and ill-fated attempts to invade the mainland of Asia through Korea. It is doubtful whether we can ever determine his precise motives for the two Korean campaigns of 1592 and 1597. Perhaps he sought new worlds to conquer; or perhaps his desire for trade drove him to seek by force new markets outside Japan. In any event the first campaign was terminated when the Japanese drive up the peninsula of Korea was stalled by the intervention of Chinese troops and the second ended in withdrawal upon Hideyoshi's death in 1598.

Hideyoshi had the chance to devote much more attention than Nobunaga to central administration, yet he too was unable to establish a government sufficiently stable to withstand the shock of his own passing. Chief among his administrators were the so-called Five Commissioners (go-bugyō), lesser daimyō who had risen in Hideyoshi's service and who owed direct and absolute allegiance to the Toyotomi family. Since these men alone could not be expected to hold things together, Hideyoshi in the last year of his life appointed the greatest of the other daimyō (who were closer to being his allies than his vassals) as a council of Five Elders (go-tairō) to maintain a regency for his son and heir, the five-year-old Hideyori. A similar council had been arranged upon Nobunaga's assassination, but Hideyoshi had at that time himself quickly assumed all its powers. Now, on his deathbed, Hideyoshi sought desperately to commit a new group of elders—consisting of the daimyō of the houses of Tokugawa,

Maeda, Mōri, Uesugi, and Ukita—to the future loyal service of his infant successor.

Yet rivalries among the leading daimyō emerged into the open as soon as Hideyoshi died. By far the most powerful single chieftain was Tokugawa Ieyasu, whose domain in the eastern provinces was already larger than that of the Toyotomi. Before long Ieyasu took control of the council of Five Elders and began making moves clearly aimed at extending his own territorial and political influence. Foremost among Ieyasu's opponents was Ishida Mitsunari, one of the Five Commissioners. After some two years of maneuvering, the Tokugawa and anti-Tokugawa forces, the latter led by Mitsunari, met in 1600 in a great showdown battle at Sekigahara in Mino Province. Aided by defections in the enemy's ranks, the Tokugawa and their allies were triumphant at Sekigahara and as a result of their victory were able to inaugurate a period of more than two and a half centuries of peaceful hegemony over Japan.

IV

Tokugawa Japan

BY
CONRAD TOTMAN

The society of Tokugawa Japan was officially conceptualized in Confucian terms as a four-class society consisting of warriors, peasants, artisans, and merchants, in order of descending status. In essence, however, Tokugawa society consisted of two classes: the warriors (samurai), who ruled, and the common masses, who were ruled. The rulers maintained a political system that gave Japan peace for more than two centuries, and the commoners worked with enough diligence and ingenuity to make Japan one of the most populous and prosperous societies of its day.

The Tokugawa Political System

Most of the families that ruled Tokugawa Japan had risen from obscurity during the sixteenth century. They had achieved power initially on the basis of military skill, but they did not retain it on that simple and hard basis. Rather, they remained in power from 1600 to 1868 by transforming their military organizations into elaborate civil administrative structures and justifying these structures on the basis of an ethical system rationalized in terms of Confucian philosophy.

The basic political unit in the warrior class was the house (ie). A house normally consisted of three groups: the members of the main family, who were descended patrilineally from the founder of the house; closely related branch families; and an organized group of usually nonconsanguineous subordinate or vassal families, whose positions were hereditary. The head of the main family was the head of the house. All members of the house consciously regarded it as the political entity to which they belonged and on whose behalf they served. The house had a headquarters and as its economic base a territory governed by the house head and his vassals. A system of offices, house regulations, and administrative practices gave order and effectiveness to the house as a governing body.

Tokugawa Japan was governed by a number of such houses organized pyramidically on the basis of practices developed during the half century before Ieyasu's great victory at Sekigahara in 1600. At the apex of the pyramid was the government of the Tokugawa house, called the bakufu after 1603 when Ieyasu received from the emperor the traditional hegemon's title of shogun. In return the bakufu or shogunate guaranteed the dignity and welfare of the powerless but symbolically important Kyoto court. From the great castle at Edo the shogunate governed directly, or indirectly through trusted vassals of modest rank, about a fourth of Japan. In addition, it maintained a suzerain role over the major warrior houses that governed the other three fourths of Japan. There were about 250 of these houses, each of whose lord or daimyō administered a domain (*han*) that presumably sustained anywhere from perhaps 10,000 to as many as 1,000,000 people.[1] The greatest of these domains were held by families that had created them during the decades before 1600, whereas the smaller ones were mostly granted to lesser men by the shogun or daimyō during the century after Sekigahara.

The daimyō were initially categorized according to their relationship to Ieyasu, and their relationship to the shogunate was thereafter predicated on this basis. Throughout the Tokugawa period daimyō houses with only limited private power but strong traditions of loyal service to Ieyasu enjoyed much influence at Edo whereas houses with much private power and weak traditions of service to him had minimal influence on the shogunate. More specifically, those 150 or so daimyō whose ancestors had been vassals of Ieyasu before Sekigahara were known as *fudai* or vassal daimyō. Most of them held relatively modest domains, but these fiefs were generally located close to the vast directly governed lands of the Tokugawa in central Japan, and these daimyō staffed all major shogunal offices. Those twenty odd daimyō descended from cadet offspring of Ieyasu or his successors were known as *shimpan* or related daimyō. They held domains, including a few large ones, on the periphery of the Tokugawa lands and served as military buffers, but they had only advisory, not administrative, positions in the shogunate. The remaining 100 or so daimyō, whose ancestors had sworn fealty to Ieyasu only after the Tokugawa triumph of 1600, were known as *tozama* or outside daimyō. This title indicates that they were not considered members of the great Tokugawa house. They held most of the large domains, but these were situated far from Edo. And these daimyō were excluded from a political role in the shogunate because they were never regarded as truly reliable vassals. Among the outside daimyō, those whose ancestors had fought Ieyasu at Sekigahara, such as the Shimazu

1. Technically a lord possessing a domain that produced 10,000 or more *koku* (1 *koku* = 5.11 American bushels) of rice or other produce of equal putative value was a daimyō. The 22,000 or so Tokugawa "trusted vassals of modest rank," that is, direct retainers, were known as *hatamoto* and *gokenin*, but only about 2,500 of their greatest members had fiefs, the rest receiving stipend rice from shogunal warehouses.

of Satsuma or the Mōri of Chōshū, seem especially to have preserved a residual discontent with Tokugawa hegemony.

The Control System

Besides maintaining these elemental categories of vassal, related, and outside daimyō, the shogunate developed a complex control system that preserved Tokugawa hegemony and the Tokugawa peace for well over two centuries.

During the century before 1600, great daimyō had associated with each other on the basis of temporary political alignments of a very tenuous nature. The Tokugawa peace was essentially a product of Tokugawa success in replacing these frail political ties with a very complex and persuasive set of strategic, institutional, and ideological connections that bound shogunate and domains together in a very stable and mutually reinforcing relationship.

Perhaps one of the most crucial aspects of the total control system was the establishment and maintenance of a policy of isolation. Whereas Hideyoshi in the 1590s had undertaken a program of overseas expansion that sent much of the samurai manpower out of Japan, the shogunate's leaders chose instead to keep the warriors at home, controlling them by sturdy institutional arrangements and directing their energies into unwarlike enterprises. This policy of isolation had the corollary effect of shutting Japan away from the tides of change that swept Europe between 1600 and 1850. By successfully forbidding all but token European contacts after about 1640, the shogunate discouraged the introduction into Japan of disruptive ideas, military technology, or trading patterns. In addition, the early Tokugawa insistence on national isolation set important precedents. Although the scope of shogunal authority in foreign affairs was not completely defined, the shogunate did establish the principle that there could be only one policy for all Japan. And more specifically it established that as long as the shogunate insisted on a policy of isolation the daimyō must abide by it. On the other hand, no strong precedent instructed the daimyō on how to behave should the shogunate reverse its traditional policy, and in the 1850s this reversal undercut the principles of two centuries.

Besides defining the outer boundaries of Japanese politics, the shogunate established the general lines of internal political relationships. After the smashing victories of 1600, of course, Tokugawa military power was enough to intimidate stubborn men, and the advantage was immediately strengthened by shifting daimyō about in such a manner as to juxtapose enemies, so that anti-shogunate coalitions could not easily form. To reinforce this adjustment, Ieyasu and his immediate successors then created large domains for their cadet offspring on the periphery of the shogunate's territory in central Japan. These domains lay athwart the major approaches to Edo and were designed to impede an attack upon the main center of Tokugawa power. By edict, moreover, the shogunate also required the outside daimyō to spend great sums of money on behalf of the Tokugawa, in this way reducing the ability of potential enemies to acquire armaments.

On a more permanent basis, the shogunate issued extensive regulations restricting castle construction and limiting the size and armament of domain military forces. Formal inspectorates and a periodic inquest system were also established. But fully as important as these formal methods of surveillance were the informal lines of communication along which news of domain affairs was passed by domain vassals to Tokugawa vassals and eventually to shogunal officials.

This informal communications network was one important by-product of that most important control mechanism, the *sankin kōtai,* or alternate attendance system. This system required that the daimyō himself spend every other year in Edo, making therefore a very expensive annual progress between his own castle town, wherever in Japan it might be, and the shogunate's headquarters. The system had several advantages for the Tokugawa. It imposed expenditures that kept domain governments from growing too wealthy and induced daimyō to spend their wealth at Edo, where it was subject to shogunal exploitation. It kept daimyō families, key domain vassals, and half the daimyō in *de facto* captivity at all times. It created a duality in domain government—one headquarters at Edo and another at the domain castle—that enabled shogunate leaders to manipulate domain officials more easily. Finally, it kept a vast number of domain warriors in Edo where inevitably they talked of domain affairs and so helped keep shogunate and domain more closely informed of each other's affairs and policies. More than any other mechanism the *sankin kōtai* system turned shogunate and domain into a single interacting political system.

The *sankin kōtai* system also created a nationwide communication network that permitted the rapid development of an ethical consensus and agreement on political legitimacy. The Tokugawa argued and the warriors in general agreed, first from necessity and later from conviction, that the Tokugawa shogun had the right to stand above the daimyō and regard them as subordinates because Ieyasu had pacified Japan, and so had earned imperial appointment to the traditional role of protector of the emperor and executor of his wishes.

The isolation of Japan, the territorial adjustments, the imposition of levies, the issuance of regulations, the ranking and rewarding, punishing and pressuring, and manipulating through *sankin kōtai* all served to stabilize and balance the political forces in Japan. It was the combination of these institutional devices and the general acquiescence in the Tokugawa claim to authority that enabled the "great peace" to endure for so long.

Tokugawa leaders had stabilized the political order midway between the poles of anarchical localism and complete centralization. The Tokugawa house had appeared on the historical stage during the tumultuous Sengoku or Warring States period (*ca.* 1477–1568), when daimyō, in expanding their domains, had permitted vassals to control lands and warriors personally, thus creating dangerous centers of partial autonomy within their own domains. During the half century before Sekigahara, however, leaders such as Nobunaga, Hideyoshi, and Ieyasu had increasingly deprived their great vassals of private military forces, and after 1600 this practice was further developed. But though there was during the seventeenth century a distinct tendency to reduce the amount of land and manpower controlled by vassals, this tendency was never pushed to a conclusion. The shogun allowed the great daimyō to retain their mighty castles, thousands of vassals, and extensive self-sufficient territories, subject to modest regulations. And many of these daimyō in turn allowed their chief vassals to keep men and land of their own, subject also to some limitations. Shogun and daimyō were evidently confident that their own directly administered lands and warrior forces were sufficiently massive to prevent rebellion. As a consequence, despite the power and influence of the shogunate, its position never became comparable to that of those contemporary European monarchies that had gradually displaced the private power of medieval feudal lords with centralized political systems.

The Bureaucratic Character of Government

In terms of centralization, then, the Tokugawa system differed less from prior governments of Japan than did contemporary European monarchies from their predecessors. But in another sense the Tokugawa system represented a more radical change. Government in Tokugawa Japan was highly bureaucratized and in many ways resembled the government of present-day Japan more than it did the governments that had preceded it. In the Kamakura period a small number of warriors at Kamakura had settled disputes involving Minamoto vassals, while other warriors serving as stewards and constables had kept the peace throughout Japan. In the Muromachi period a shogun with often only nominal power watched nervously while a number of great regional magnates jousted and quarreled among themselves. But in the Tokugawa period elaborate bureaucracies of stipendiary officials administered clearly delineated territories. The shogunate, for example, ruled its domains through a force of over 17,000 officials and guards, and the daimyō had comparable battalions of officials administering their lands and peoples.

These bureaucracies were staffed by a closed, stratified, hereditary warrior elite. At all but the lowest levels they were closed to non-warriors, and within the warrior class as a whole men of high hereditary family rank had exclusive access to the highest, most responsible offices, while medium and low-ranking warriors had access respectively to medium and low-level posts.

This characteristic is clearly evident in the shogunate. Only vassal daimyō could hold the eight or so major supervisory offices, such as senior councilor (*rōjū*), Kyoto deputy (*shoshidai*), or keeper of Osaka castle (*jōdai*). At an intermediate level were some 5,000 vassals (known as *hatamoto* or bannermen) who had substantial incomes and retainers of their own but who were not of daimyō rank. They held crucial administrative positions such as commissioners of finance (*kanjō bugyō*), inspector or inspector general (*metsuke* or *ōmetsuke*), or commissioners (*bugyō*) for the several cities under Tokugawa control. They also monopolized many elite shogunal military positions. At the lowest level were an estimated 18,000 minor vassals (*gokenin* or housemen) with modest stipends, few or no retainers, and access only to the large number of insignificant clerical, guard, and menial attendant positions in the shogunate.

Governmental practices in the domains closely paralleled those in the shogunate, many office titles and procedures being essentially the same. One important consequence of this was that, although decentralized in terms of authority, the political system of Tokugawa Japan was homogeneous in terms of practice, giving Japan a high level of operational uniformity that no doubt helped considerably in the political consolidation of the 1870s.

To some extent the governmental offices of the shogunate and the domains had proliferated in the seventeenth century as a means of employing warriors who no longer had wars to fight. It was one of the prices of peace. One result of the warrior's quest for satisfactory jobs seems to have been a great and general concern to preserve one's position and pass it on to one's heir, creating the close rank-office nexus discussed above. This interest in job security reduced concern with operational efficiency and occupational competence, so that some routine administrative processes lost flexibility and became politically obsolete. At the highest levels shogun and daimyō found themselves occupied more and more with ritual duties, and at lower levels men formally responsible for many administrative functions found their hands tied by practices sanctified by time and tradition.

Offsetting this debilitating trend, however, was a development that helped house governments bypass both restrictive hereditary office privileges and inflexible administrative practices. This was the emergence within the shogunate and domains of bureaucratic factions, alliances of officials and would-be officials who jockeyed for power, whether in hopes of changing policy or of simply enjoying the fruits of office. This factional rivalry prevented hereditary privilege from becoming fully established in some crucial administrative posts such as those of senior councillor and commissioner of finances. It also led to the development of numerous informal governing techniques such as the creation of *ad hoc* committees or special posts whose incumbents could carry out important policies quite independently of the regular bureaucracy. In short, those trends that reduced governmental efficiency were sufficiently offset by other developments that increased efficiency so that the shogunate and domains retained the capacity to cope with day-to-day problems reasonably successfully.

The Fiscal System

One crucial aspect of Tokugawa government was the fiscal system. In accordance with the predominant form of Confucian political theory, which will be discussed below, shogunate and domain leaders believed that ideally only agricultural production should be taxed. They felt that taxes levied on commerce would only serve to push up consumer prices, evidence of poor government in principle and self-defeating in practice, since the governments would then have to spend their tax income on goods selling at inflated prices. Accordingly, shogunate and domains alike made extensive land surveys to determine the total agricultural productivity (*kokudaka*) of their domains, and then levied taxes on the basis of this measure, thereby taking from the peasants anywhere from 25 to 60 percent of their production, usually about 40 percent.

After 1700 or so land surveys became more infrequent and uncovered little new taxable production, and the more or less fixed income of the shogunate and the domains was thereafter usually insufficient to meet their expenses. Frequently governments could not, for example, afford even to make needed castle repairs. More painful than such physical maintenance problems were the personal problems generated by the gap between warrior income and expenses. Much of the land tax income was used for sustaining shogunal and domain warrior forces, and the hereditary stipends and office salaries that came from this source could not be increased enough to meet the family wants of these warriors. Indeed, from time to time stipends were reduced by one means or another as governments tried to keep their expenses under control. This forced the samurai to curtail domestic expenses wherever possible and accept a lower standard of living or go into debt, often both.

This fiscal dilemma compelled governments to look elsewhere for income, and as the Tokugawa period progressed, shogunate and domain leaders slowly developed a variety of devices that in fact channeled money from commercial activities into government coffers. Some governments, for example, set up monopoly control over certain enterprises, funneling their profits directly into the treasury. Others issued monopoly licenses for fees, and still others obtained loans and outright gifts from merchants. Many of these practices, however, tended to generate political criticism because they ran counter to orthodoxy, and in consequence fiscal policy became one of the basic issues of dispute between rival bureaucratic factions. And in any case, as fast as new sources of income were found, the warrior ruling class spent the monies, and the basic problem remained unsolved. To meet immediate needs warriors privately and their governments institutionally turned to moneylenders, with the result that a vast and permanent warrior indebtedness developed, creating an enormous bond of mutual dependence between the warrior class and the commercial houses that furnished the funds. The implications of this intimate warrior-creditor relationship are suggested a bit later.

Warrior Class Orthodox Values

Tokugawa Japan throbbed with intellectual vigor. In all segments of society one could find men discussing the meaning of experience as well as the nature and the content of propriety and wisdom. This intellectual activity continued and even diversified throughout the period despite the fact that only one school of thought enjoyed the shogunate's approval as orthodox learning while all other interpretations were labeled heterodox and were tolerated by the shogunate and domains with fluctuating liberality.

The officially accepted doctrine was that articulated by Chu Hsi and other Confucian scholars who flourished in the Sung dynasty of eleventh- and twelfth-century China. These scholars wove basic Confucian ideas into a complex metaphysical construct, thereby giving potent support to the social ethics that they advocated. These ethics by and large served to justify and reinforce the *status quo* as it existed in seventeenth-century Japan, and this made the doctrine particularly attractive to leaders of both the shogunate and the domains.

The teaching of Chu Hsi was basically rationalistic in the sense that it encouraged the "investigation of things," the study of human affairs and political problems. This study, however, was not to be pursued independently of ethical considerations, but was to be conducted with a constant concern for human values because, it was argued, only such compassionate study could ultimately lead to true understanding of the cosmological principles underlying the "myriad things" of the material world. And only through such complete understanding could man perfect his fundamental goodness and so be at one with "the Way," the ultimate and ideal Confucian reality. There was thus a close bond between knowledge and morality, and the human values that constituted this morality were those of the classical Confucian gentleman: the five Confucian virtues (inner integrity, righteousness, loyalty, altruism, and love); adherence to the "mean," or avoidance of extremes; understanding of the proper forms of social order and discourse; and good manners.

One of the fundamental characteristics of the social order was the inequality of men, an inequality which characterized life's most basic human associations, notably those of ruler and subject, of father and son. In all such associations, the superior was to practice benevolence and the inferior respect. When all people behaved in this fashion, society would become harmonious, which was characteristic of the Way. To achieve this harmony it was first necessary for the ruler to practice the Confucian virtues, because if he did this, his inferiors would be inspired to do likewise and gradually virtue would percolate downward until all men were in proper harmony, that is, knew and practiced the Way. A ruler could not hope to know how to behave, however, unless he too had a model to emulate, and accordingly he was to study the Chinese Classics, in which he could learn about the virtuous governance of certain ancient Chinese rulers who lived in the golden age of antiquity, when the Way was fully established in this world. In this glorious age when rulers were benevolent and subjects respectful, the people tilled the soil and lived in modest, stable security. One of the unfortunate developments of later decadent ages was the proliferation of merchants who produced nothing, created social disorder, and fostered greed and selfishness. The virtuous ruler, therefore, among other things, endeavored to prevent the growth of a merchant class, and instead tried to keep his subjects fruitfully employed on the land.

In a number of ways this set of ideas was attractive to the leaders of seventeenth-century Japan. The doctrine of Chu Hsi gave rational justification to the existing hierarchical social structure and permitted the shogun to insist that his example should be emulated by the daimyō and lesser Tokugawa vassals, and theirs by their vassals, and so on down to the lowliest warrior. The adoption of the Confucian four-class theory of society then made this idea of rule-by-example applicable to commoners as well and enabled the warriors to equate themselves with the Confucian literati as a social elite having a philosophically justified right to rule. The stress on the inferior's obligation to serve loyally helped strengthen the hierarchy after the bonds of the battlefield had disappeared. Chu Hsi's emphasis on the need to respect the outward forms of social procedure and structure reinforced the privileges and practices of the rulers. The interest in learning induced the now inactive warriors to turn their energies to scholarship, and the idea that learning must be judged on the basis of its relevance to Confucian ethics also placed a strong limitation on the scope of study and the attitudes one brought to it. The belief that the ideal society lay in the past served to discourage conscious political innovation and encouraged men to turn to history for guidance. Thus throughout the Tokugawa period shogunate and domain leaders repeatedly spoke of reestablishing the splendid conditions of Ieyasu's day, and when they did innovate, it was in the belief that this would help to restore a better prior condition, or it was justified as the reinvigoration of an older practice that had been abandoned. The Confucian anticommercial bias in particular became deeply involved in operational politics. The chronic fiscal problems of the shogunate and the domains generated intense concern and endless discussion of means to resolve the problems, and these debates were as a matter of course couched in terms of Confucian attitudes toward commerce.

Heterodoxy

The teachings of Chu Hsi were preferred by the shogunate and enjoyed the position of orthodox learning. But the quest for understanding that had led Japanese to the doctrines of Chu Hsi also led them to other teachings. Collectively these other teachings constituted the heterodox thought of the Tokugawa period, and though they appeared as soon as did the study of Chu Hsi and steadily diversified thereafter, they did so despite an attitude of official disapproval that from time to time resulted in spasms of persecution and suppression of scholarly activities.

In twelfth-century China the growth of the Chu Hsi school was paralleled by the growth of another school of philosophy which, like that of Chu Hsi, derived from classical Confucian teachings. This philosophy is known by the name of one of its later proponents, Wang Yang-ming (or Ōyōmei in the Japanese pronunciation). Whereas Chu Hsi had insisted that one could know the Way only through study of the external world, Wang argued that one could know the Way only by intuitive perception. Moreover, he contended, one must act directly upon the basis of his perception of right and wrong, not on the basis of his understanding of the temporal order as manifested in its evidential form. This basic orientation predisposed adherents of the Wang Yang-ming school to autonomous action and could serve to rationalize defiance of the Tokugawa regime. But at the same time the philosophy offered no substantive operational guidance and consequently in itself could not sustain programmatic social action.

Of more ultimate consequence in Tokugawa Japan was a return to the study of the most ancient texts of the Confucian Classics themselves. Scholars of these texts concluded that Chu Hsi's teachings were a serious distortion of true Confucian thought. This, of course, put them in the position of defying shogunal leadership in things philosophical, but more importantly, it stimulated the broader study of history, Japanese as well as Chinese, by implying that through careful scholarship one could come ever closer to a true understanding of the proper order of society.

In fact, Tokugawa period scholars had from the very outset been confronted by the knowledge that they were Japanese, that they had inherited an extensive literature on Shintō and Buddhism, and that somehow this had to be either harmonized with Confucian thought or shown to be inconsequential. Some scholars were able to accept the second choice, but most were unprepared to acknowledge that the heritage of their own society was of no consequence and could properly be ignored. Instead they tried to work out a philosophical synthesis, in order to show that the classic virtues of Japan and China were identical and hence that the Way was indeed universal. The result, however, was never entirely satisfactory, though the efforts of these scholars served to introduce variety into Tokugawa thought.

Much of this scholarly inquiry, following the Chu Hsi ideal of "investigating things," consisted of highly rational analyses of nature and society. The study of nature eventually led to an interest in Western medicine, astronomy, and other physical sciences. Since the only source of information was the restricted Dutch trading post at Nagasaki in southwest Japan, Western studies came to be called "Dutch studies" (Rangaku). However, continuing government suspicion of these studies discouraged their widespread development.

More important was the study of Japanese history and society. This gradually created a group of scholars and a body of literature dealing both with Japan's origins, as recorded in such ancient records as the *Kojiki,* and with the country's history, especially the history of the Imperial House. This study came to be known as the School of National Learning (Kokugaku), and as it developed in the eighteenth century, it abandoned the rationalism of Chu Hsi and acquired a highly irrational ethnocentric character.

This growing irrationalism was particularly manifest in the revitalized study of Shintō mythology, which resulted in an extensive literature extolling the special virtue of Japan. The key to this special virtue lay in the "fact" of Japan's eternal Imperial House, which was unique in the world. Belief in this uniqueness led some scholars to denounce foreign studies, and Confucianism in particular, as degenerate and unworthy of pursuit. Moreover, by focusing attention on the Imperial House, these scholars brought to the center of the stage the question of the proper relationship between emperor and shogun. Here, as in the question of the proper relationship of Japanese and Chinese tradition, a number of answers were given, and for most of the Tokugawa period these answers were more or less satisfactory. At least the question remained an academic one until the nineteenth century. But again, just as some forms of heterodoxy laid an intellectual foundation from which one could criticize orthodoxy, so this study created a basis on which one could criticize the Tokugawa hegemony in Japan, if for any reason one felt such criticism warranted.

In its totality, thought in Tokugawa Japan was remarkable for both its extent and its diversity. And yet, despite the variety of views that were held, Tokugawa Japan was an exceptionally stable society. This intellectual vigor did not prove disruptive of society for a number of reasons. One obvious reason was the durability of the institutions of control. By and large these served to discourage any who might wish to put radical ideas into practice, not so much by harsh punishments as by making it very difficult for like-minded men to coordinate and sustain their efforts long enough to effect lasting changes.

But perhaps this institutional aspect was less important than the core values which were integral to the thought of almost all these thinkers. There was general agreement that the warrior class should retain its special prerogatives, that within this class it was right to have stratification and a general correlation between status and office-holding. It was agreed that the Tokugawa should, on one ground or another, keep the peace and that this peace should safe-guard the well-being of daimyō, warriors in general, and commoners in the mass. No one doubted that the Imperial House deserved respect and protection. There was also agreement that frugality, restraint, self-discipline, loyalty, diligence, and responsibility were virtues that everyone, at least everyone else, should cultivate. And there was agreement that the object of policy was the maintenance of a virtuous, vigorous, prosperous, peaceful society.

About what then did people disagree? Essentially they disagreed on whether these goals were being attained and, if not, on how to achieve them, and in part this disagreement stemmed from the differing philosophies discussed here. But since people generally seemed to agree on the objectives of their efforts, disagreements were deprived of much heat and usually operated at a level of tolerable intensity. For a long time few among the warriors of Tokugawa Japan found the evils of their day so great as to make reform worth serious personal risk.

Commoners' Values

The warriors who ruled Japan were numerically a small minority of the population. The vast majority, over 90 percent of the populace, were commoners. Officially they were divided into farmers, artisans, and merchants, but for purposes of study a more fruitful division is between the villagers, most of whom tilled the soil, and the urban residents of the towns and cities. Slightly less than a tenth of the commoners lived in cities and towns; the rest lived in the villages and countryside. Just as the small warrior elite set the tone and pattern of political life and ideals, so this small minority of urban dwellers set the tone of cultural life. And in one way or another the political patterns, the ethics, and the cultural tastes of these two urban minorities gradually penetrated the vast population of the villages (from which, in primitive form, these patterns, ethics, and tastes had largely arisen). In the process Japan was given a level of social homogeneity that seems surprising in view of the fixed social and geopolitical boundaries of the Tokugawa system.

The value system of Tokugawa commoner society was essentially that of the warrior class. As among warriors, so among commoners basic concern was given to one's obligations, not to one's rights. Superiors were expected to show benevolence, and in return inferiors were expected to fulfill their obligations to be loyal, to accept their positions in life, and to eschew the thought of advancing socially at the expense of others. Most of the important relationships in Tokugawa society were familial, whether the kinship was real or fictive. Farming units, business enterprises, handicrafts, or artistic activities were generally family operations, and the highest commoner ideal of day-to-day consequence was the ideal of sustaining the prosperity of these operations. To achieve this end, great emphasis was laid on personal frugality and on the performance of duties to the very best of one's ability.

It was a stern ethic and derived strength among commoners, as among warriors, from its integration with religious sanctions of one sort or another. During the Tokugawa period, the Jōdo Shin or True Pure Land sect of Buddhism, for example, denounced excesses—of consumption, profit making, or ambition—as detrimental to the understanding of Buddha's teachings and hence to personal salvation. The popular Shingaku doctrine of the eighteenth century based itself on more characteristically Confucian premises, arguing that loyalty, diligence, and frugality all helped to eliminate selfishness and reveal to oneself one's true nature, and "knowing one's nature one knows heaven." In the nineteenth-century peasant doctrine of Hōtoku, diligence and thrift were encouraged as the necessary means of repaying a burden of universal obligation inherent in one's very creation and upbringing.

The significant consideration here is that all these doctrines served to reinforce social stability rather than encourage social adventurism. They led a commoner to regard his ascribed social function, be it clerking, farming, fishing, carpentering, selling, or whatever, as a respectable and socially indispensable undertaking. The doctrines all strengthened social efficiency by discouraging disputatious or irresponsible conduct and by encouraging a persistent but unspeculative economic productivity. Their political upshot was to leave political authority and initiative to the warriors while directing the commoners' energies into other channels.

Urban Society

By standards of the day Tokugawa Japan, with some 15 percent of its populace living in cities, was an unusually urbanized society, more urbanized, for example, than most of western Europe. Half of these city folk were the ruling warriors; the other half were the urban commoners, the social pacesetters of the day. Their zestful new taste was founded on the radically new character of Tokugawa cities.

The older towns of Japan—the temple towns, the small trading centers, and even the few large port towns and the old political centers of Nara, Kyoto, and Kamakura—nearly all declined or were eclipsed before or early in the Tokugawa period. Only Kyoto retained a preeminent role. The large towns of the period were mostly castle towns consisting of a daimyō's splendid castle, the homes of his warriors, and the homes and businesses of the common people who flocked around to serve these warriors-in-residence. These towns were basically politico-military units, and though commercial activities later became very important, the towns generally retained about as many warriors as commoners, which gave them a highly consumer-oriented character.

Despite this general homogeneity, however, it is possible to speak of "regional" and "national" towns or cities. The castle towns of daimyō tended to keep a strong local or regional flavor, serving as centers of their own domains and having limited outside contact except for the goings and comings associated with *sankin kōtai* and commerce. But the three great cities of Kyoto, Osaka, and Edo were truly national centers, although the first two were not characteristic castle towns. They were all directly controlled by the shogunate, drew residents from throughout Japan, and had political and economic ties to people throughout the country. Kyoto revived as a cultural center, Osaka mushroomed as an entrepôt, and Edo became the hub of Tokugawa political life. The three also differed from regional towns in size, the first two having about 500,000 people apiece and Edo well over 1,000,000, while the regional cities were smaller, few if any exceeding 100,000 in population.

The national cities were not only much larger; they were also more cosmopolitan, serving as centers of the gay new life, as models to be emulated by the regional cities. It is worth noting again that in the world of art and literature, if not in that of scholarship, this meant emulating the commoners in these great cities, rather than the political elite. By contrast, in earlier Japanese cities those who ruled also had been the arbiters of taste and the consumers of the artist's production. The more fortunate commoners of Tokugawa cities had a sufficiently high level of literacy as well as enough wealth and leisure to enjoy amenities that had previously been restricted to the aristocratic few.

Even among the national cities, however, there were subtle differences richly appreciated by the Tokugawa connoisseur. Kyoto, teeming with artisans and proud of its past glories, was known for its urbane polish and decorum, for the quality and restraint of its culture. The resident of Osaka, home of flourishing commercial enterprises, boasted of his townsmens' stability, sharp financial acumen, aesthetic vigor, and cultural respectability. The Edo dweller, or Edokko, was more rowdy, boisterous, and unrestrained. Viewed as a boor by the Kyotoite, and as a spendthrift by the Osakaite, he returned these slurs by dismissing the former as passé and the latter as a pinchpenny.

Urban Culture

The merchant culture of the Edo period first flowered during the late seventeenth century, the Genroku period. In both its social origins and its substance it was very unlike the culture of the preceding Muromachi period, especially the fifteenth century. The Momoyama warriors of the late sixteenth century had swept away the subtlety and delicacy of Ashikaga Yoshimasa's day, replacing it with the bold splendor of Hideyoshi's castles and tea parties. The merchants inherited this *joie de vivre* but combined it with the severe canons of the day to evolve a more complex, more enduring taste in which pride, pathos, irony, delicacy, refinement, and masterful vulgarity all were to be found. Buddhist sensibility, so basic to earlier taste, survived primarily in the form of a stereotyped secular didacticism.

Genroku taste found expression in drama, art, and literature, all of which tended to overlap and draw inspiration from the "gay quarters," those sections of town, such as the Yoshiwara in Edo, in which entertainment was permitted to flourish. In these quarters the secularized Buddhist world of evanescence, the *ukiyo* or "floating world" was a reality. Here money bought its greatest—and briefest—delights; here beauty and grace won wide—and fleeting—fame; upon entry here, responsibility abruptly vanished—only to descend again heavier than ever when the gallant left the quarter and returned to his daily world of obligations and duty.

The popular Kabuki theatre attracted large audiences. In contrast to the stately Nō of the Muromachi period, Kabuki was bright, boisterous, and noisy.

To a very great degree the most popular art and prose of the Edo period were two facets of one activity, the publishing of popular books portraying the exciting if meretricious life of the gay quarters. Pictures and text were incised on wood blocks and printed on sheets that were then bound into volumes for sale. Or the prints might be distributed singly as art or advertisement. In books the ukiyo-e prints reinforced the narrative of the *ukiyo-zōshi,* the "tales of the floating world." Like Kabuki, the *ukiyo-zōshi* flowered during the Genroku period, the works of Ihara Saikaku typifying the genre. His stories focused on the tension between the obligations of life and the temptations of love·and pleasure, the floating world. It was the adventures of love and pleasure that gave his works such popularity, but it was the care he took to treat such adventures as examples of improper behavior and to bring the errant to their consequent and deserved suffering that carried his works past the official censors.

Tokugawa poetry also sometimes took the urban commoners' life as subject, yet the greatest poet of the Genroku period, Matsuo Bashō, is best known for his crisp evocation in haiku of his own travel experiences. The haiku, with its cryptic style, was popular throughout Tokugawa society and may be regarded as an art form that combined the ascetic Muromachi taste and the acutely perceptive Edo taste.

The extent to which literature and art focused on the gay quarters is a proper measure of the importance of these quarters in the total life of urban dwellers. Their lives were humdrum, uneventful, and tightly hedged about by obligations involving practically everyone they knew. Whether warriors serving in the government, retinue, or guard service of their daimyō, or townsmen working as clerks, laborers, or any of a hundred minor professionals, the course of life was charted, the alternatives known, and apart from natural disasters, little was left to chance or imagination. Just as dramatic productions and novels permitted wives, daughters, and the poor to escape for vicarious joy into the risqué or dangerous escapades of heroes and heroines, so the gay quarters provided more fortunate husbands and fathers with an area in which they could escape momentarily the net of daily obligations and enjoy with nominal real risk the adventures of a world in which they were not eternally accountable.

Commerce

Humdrum daily life in its totality added up to a booming commercial society, and it was the urban wealth generated by this vigorous population that financed much of the floating world, whether directly through the expenditures of townsmen or indirectly through the liberality of warriors who had borrowed their funds from the townsmen. In both scope and complexity this commercial activity was sharply different from earlier commerce in Japan. Previously the only nationwide trade had been in luxuries while the bulk of trade had been local in nature, but during the great peace intensive trade in daily necessities reached a national scope. Coastal shipping channels ringed Japan, and ports of call existed all along the coast, especially on the long convoluted coastline between Edo and Kyushu. On land, too, there was ceaseless travel along the main highways, and the combined traffic of *sankin kōtai* retinues and commerce was sufficient to sustain chains of post towns along all the main thoroughfares. This network was tied together by an officially sponsored post horse system that carried news between the major cities and towns.

Along these lines of communication flowed the goods, people, negotiables, and information of Tokugawa commerce. The awkwardness of transporting barter goods early encouraged the use of money, and the shortage of specie fostered the use of convertible notes. Businesses opened branches, formed combinations, licensed subordinate firms, and gradually created a highly complex commercial structure that bound the major cities and production areas together in one extensive web of transactions.

Tokugawa commercial enterprises were highly specialized and elaborately structured. Entrepreneurs might deal only in a particular type of product, such as lumber, oils, or fish, or limit themselves to a particular location or locations, or to a particular phase of activity such as wholesale purchase, shipping, storage, or finance. These various enterprises might be coordinated in great or minor degree, and they tended to form monopoly operations, such as the giant shipping monopoly on the Osaka-Edo sea route. These monopolies limited competition, fixed prices, distributed business or the profits of business, regulated the quality and quantity of production, protected the credit of members, prevented abuses by members—in short, served to stabilize and regulate activity in their jurisdiction. At first they had appeared despite governmental opposition, but by the mid-Tokugawa period they generally had official backing and in return paid regular license fees to the shogunate and the domains in order to keep this backing.

Skillful merchants in advantageous positions accumulated huge fortunes through the operation of these commercial organizations, and the shogunate and the domains relied heavily on them for governmental loans. Government indebtedness grew to massive proportions and proved a chronic problem for the administrators. A potentially more explosive issue, as suggested earlier, was the personal indebtedness of the warriors. Their indebtedness was frequently to small-scale moneylenders, not to the great monopoly merchants, and if anything these small operators were more usurious and unrelenting than the great merchants because they ran a greater personal risk of bankruptcy if warriors defaulted or if warrior debts were modified by government edict, as happened occasionally.

This pattern of merchant wealth and warrior indebtedness had a number of consequences. In the first place it bound merchant and warrior together; neither could function in the accustomed manner without continued cooperation from the other. But at the same time, as lender the merchant had at least a psychological advantage that tended to conflict with the theoretical relationship of superior and inferior, and this, together with the merchant's frequently more comfortable standard of living, created a certain warrior resentment that could be repaid with merchant disdain. And at another level the merchant wealth struck the rulers as evidence that society was out of order. The merchant condition was not in accord with his low social place and, particularly in hard times when food was scarce or fire had laid waste the city, popular suffering stood out sharply against merchant affluence. This in turn led to occasional popular assaults on the homes of moneylenders and merchants, and such violence troubled the rulers because while they tended to sympathize with the populace, they needed the merchants and in any case could not condone violence. In short, the flowering of the Tokugawa economy led to social strains as well as to a generally more prosperous and glittering society.

Rural Society

The warriors gave order to society and the urban commoners gave it flavor, but it was the vast body of rural people, fully 85 percent of the total population, who gave it life. These rural folk lived in villages, most of which had existed for centuries, surviving the chaos, the famines, and the plundering soldiers who came and went. They managed their own affairs as much as possible, and yielded to outsiders as little as possible, whether of authority, manpower, or produce. The villagers traditionally had organized themselves, settled their own disputes, looked after their own needy, and maintained their own temples, shrines, paths, and paddies.

During the Tokugawa period, too, this pattern of village self-government was largely preserved, since both warriors and villagers wished it that way; the latter because they had long ago learned that outside control meant outside exploitation, the former merely because they wished the village to serve at minimal cost as a peaceful, reliable source of foodstuffs, goods, and obedient manpower. Because of this convergence of interests the governments of Tokugawa Japan simply imposed a formal administrative structure above the villages and allowed the villagers to go on managing affairs much as before, subject, of course, to specific regulations, such as those levying taxes, proscribing weapons, or requiring registration at the local temple. Despite or perhaps in part due to this policy of qualified laissez-faire, village life in the Tokugawa period actually experienced fundamental changes in terms of both village social structure and the village economy.

In earlier centuries the basic unit in the villages had been the house (*ie*). It was, indeed, this house pattern that the Tokugawa expanded into a system of government. The village house was ideally a patrilineage, a group of families claiming real or fictive descent from a single ancestor and organized among themselves hierarchically, the main family having the most land, the most wealth, and the greatest say in house discussions. Other descendants were ranked in terms of kinship, their land and influence generally varying in accordance with their affinity to the main family, the most distant kin and any attached hereditary households in effect being tenants or permanent hired helpers. The members of such a house cooperated on its behalf, exchanging labor and assistance in proportions and ways determined by their standing in the house. And in village affairs they tended to act as a bloc, interacting with the several other houses in the village, the head of each main family being spokesman for his house's interests, the group of spokesmen serving as village leaders.

During the Edo period, however, this village structure seems slowly to have changed, initially in central Japan and later in the outer areas of the northeast and southwest. In this process of change the several families in a house gradually cooperated less and less and began to function as more fully autonomous production units. They ceased habitually to help one another on the assumption that such aid was a house obligation; instead they sought assistance, whether in manpower, land, or equipment, from whoever would provide it most cheaply or conveniently. And in village affairs, families also began to give support to one another across house lines, thus upsetting the old equilibrium and undermining the position of old village leaders.

An important factor in this trend was the increasing importance of money in intravillage transactions and in transactions between the village and the outside world. Money was first used in the villages of central Japan, where trade had early put it into circulation, but its use gradually spread until most of Japan was involved. The growth of cities and of the nationwide trading network created a market that encouraged villagers to diversify their output and sell such products as cotton, silk cocoons, or handicrafts for cash, and the villagers accepted money because they had learned that it could be used advantageously.

For one thing, paying taxes in money might be cheaper than paying in kind, depending on the harvest. For another thing, it might be more satisfactory to hire labor, or rent equipment or land for cash, than to arrange it through the house, especially if one's standing in the house were quite low. On the other hand, if one's house status were high, one could simplify a host of chronic responsibilities for poor relatives by satisfying one's own labor or other requirements through direct cash payments. In short, money provided an alternative medium of exchange which for many transactions was felt to be preferable to payment in goods or services, and hence it came to be used for much, although never for all, or even most, village exchange.

This process of socio-economic change had complex consequences for villagers. It destroyed the old structure of monolithic personal ties, introducing flexibility, room for greater initiative and choice. But this coin has two sides, and the other face showed village tensions, conflict, and insecurity. In material terms, the poorer villagers, who had previously been granted a bit of land or assured work by their house betters, found themselves with no protectors, and in hard times many had to sell or mortgage their small plots in order to survive. The long-term result was on one hand an increase in tenantry and the creation of a more mobile supply of landless, hired laborers accustomed to working for wages. On the other hand there appeared a wealthy peasantry with large landholdings, only a portion of which they worked themselves, men who used their modest reserves of capital to develop small village industries in order further to strengthen their situation. Here were two basic elements favorable to the later development of an urban industrial society: a manipulable labor force and a source of available capital.

At the same time, the new village wealthy were not necessarily the old main families, and this created friction between these old families jealous of traditional privileges and newly prospering families eager to reap the social fruit of their material success. The concern of these disputants had a hard economic dimension, too, because village leaders settled most local disputes and determined how the village tax burden was to be divided among families. Understandably, in such decisions the unrepresented could expect to fare worse than did the represented. These rivals would then jockey for the support of the other villagers, who had lost much of their sense of house loyalty, and so village politics became a more competitive, less smoothly structured, and less manageable affair than hitherto.

Out of these conditions grew a rather widespread and chronic tension in rural Japan, and these intravillage difficulties were often complicated by a number of external factors. The transportation system, although splendid in contrast to former ages, did not connect villages, districts, or provinces together so completely as to make bulk goods shipments everywhere possible. This limitation was reinforced by the government's proscription of vehicular traffic and by the political boundaries maintained by the shogunate and the domains. Where trade was physically possible it was sometimes restricted by domain leaders too concerned with their own domains to respond to distress in neighboring regions. A third external factor was taxation. Some domains seemed to follow the old adage that the peasants should be so taxed that they could neither live nor die. These practices left villages in some areas with a very thin margin for survival from harvest to harvest. When extreme weather conditions ruined the harvest locally, villagers, especially the poorer or politically unrepresented villagers, might face famine, and because of political boundaries and poor transport they could not obtain relief from other areas. This combination of factors frequently led to outbreaks of local violence as villagers fought among themselves or struck out in protest at local representatives of higher powers, whether merchant or governmental.

Looking then at Tokugawa commoners as a whole, one can see that their values reinforced stability, making the ethical consensus of the warrior class a nationwide consensus. This gave great cohesiveness to Tokugawa society and contributed to the remarkable duration of the great peace. But at the same time the processes of commercial growth in the towns and socio-economic change in the villages introduced a series of disruptive factors that begged for solution but found none. They were kept under control by the institutional system and the ethical consensus that reinforced it, but they generated a moderate level of ongoing turmoil that was, according to the ethics of the regime itself, an indication of its failure to meet the obligations inherent in the right to rule. For the warrior elite it was an embarrassing situation, one potentially disruptive to the great peace.

A Century of Change

Clearly Tokugawa society was not static. In many ways it underwent major changes, growing more populous and complex as time passed. Focusing more directly on the process of change itself, one may speak of two main phases: a century of rapid growth and settling down after the brutal Warring States period, and another century and a half of persistent flux within an over-all social equilibrium. It took the better part of a century, or roughly the passing of three generations, before Tokugawa politics was thoroughly routinized, but the basic political relationships of the Tokugawa system were defined during Ieyasu's lifetime.

An undertaking of great initial importance was disarming the peasants and binding them to the soil because it permitted leaders to regulate the size of armies and turn most manpower to productive activities. This process was actually carried out in much of Japan before 1600, as Hideyoshi, Ieyasu, and many other regional leaders imposed law and order on their domains by making land surveys and population censuses, by collecting weapons of war from the peasants, by regulating peasant movement and activity, and by placing trusted men in charge of agricultural districts. After Sekigahara thorough inspections and censuses completed the job. This policy deprived commoners of the tools of rebellion and made it difficult for them to move about at will. It secured the human base of the Tokugawa regime.

On a higher level, the leaders of Ieyasu's day devised ways to control the armies already in existence. These ways were mostly developed before 1600; indeed their development was a necessary prerequisite to unification. One essential innovation was the organization of fighting forces in such a manner that lower-level subordinates of a regional magnate could not use their immediate followings as an independent base of power. For example, from the 1570s until his death Ieyasu created more and more military units whose leaders were appointed officers with limited tenure, rather than personal lords of the fighting men in the units, and these units became the most trusted forces in the Tokugawa army.

At the highest level, during Ieyasu's day the relationship of daimyō and shogunate was determined by territorial adjustments, most of which were made after Ieyasu's victory at Sekigahara in 1600 and his destruction of Hideyoshi's son, Hideyori, at Osaka in 1615. These relationships were consolidated by the growth after 1603 of the practice of daimyō attendance on the shogun at Edo, and they were formalized in 1615 in a set of regulations for the daimyō.

Basic domestic political relationships were thus generally established by 1616, but the process of isolating Japan from European influence was not completed for another three decades. Before his death in 1598 Hideyoshi had become distrustful of the Christian missionaries, particularly the Portuguese, and Ieyasu too seems finally to have concluded that loyalty to Edo, as he thought of it, was incompatible with loyalty to Rome, as he understood that. Accordingly, in 1614, after three years of increasing restrictions, he ordered the expulsion of all Christian missionaries, but the order was not completely enforced. Under the two succeeding shoguns, Hidetada and Iemitsu (ruled 1616–32, 1632–50), however, the shogunate intensified its effort, expelling most missionaries and executing a few. Concurrently the government undertook to suppress domestic Christianity, using decidedly harsher measures such as threats, torture, execution, and population movement.

Fear of the foreign religion as harbinger of foreign conquest or promoter of domestic rebellion gradually led to opposition to foreign trade and foreign contact in general. Hidetada first restricted trade with the Portuguese and Spanish in his efforts to stamp out Christianity, and in the 1630s Iemitsu extended the policy to the Dutch (the English having departed from Japan in 1623). This development reached a climax in 1639 after the suppression of a massive rebellion on the Shimabara peninsula in Kyushu, an area in which Christianity had taken strong hold. This outbreak seems to have been provoked mainly by local economic suffering and political abuse, but the rebels soon adopted Christian slogans to rally themselves, and they were regarded by Edo as Christian rebels. They were ruthlessly suppressed, and shortly afterwards nearly all remaining European contacts were severed. Only the Dutch were permitted to keep a small trading post at Deshima, a water-girt depot in Nagasaki, and their trade volume was sharply restricted.

Accompanying this gradual suppression of European contact with Japan was a complementary effort to stop Japanese from going overseas. A brisk Japanese trade with East and Southeast Asia had flourished for decades, but by 1640 it, too, was ended and Japanese shipbuilders were forbidden to construct vessels large enough to make long ocean voyages. Chinese traders were restricted to Nagasaki and Okinawa; and Korean traders, to Tsushima, an island midway between Korea and western Japan. Thus by the 1640s the shogunate had succeeded in nearly stamping out Christianity, in limiting trade and discouraging its use as an avenue of foreign influence, and in preventing Japanese from going abroad. As a result Japan was untouched by the political turmoil that disrupted much of the world between 1600 and 1850. And the rapid changes in thought and technology that remolded Europe operated independently of the changes that remolded Tokugawa Japan.

In the realm of foreign affairs, then, the policies of Hidetada and Iemitsu resulted in major changes. Domestically, during these years the problem of warriors without lords (*rōnin*) was solved. The establishment of peace and the frequent shifting about and punishing of daimyō had created large numbers of lordless warriors who by the 1630s constituted a major disruptive element in society. By the 1640s both the shogunate and the domains were taking steps to absorb them, simplifying requirements for service, creating positions and stipends for them, and encouraging them to take up scholarship and other fruitful pursuits. By the time of Iemitsu's death much had been done, and an abortive rebellion of lordless warriors in 1651 finally prodded the authorities to find places for those who were still without lords or occupations.

The solution of this problem was only one part of the larger process by which warriors in general were domesticated by being used in a host of nonmilitary duties. By the time two or three generations of them had lived without war, most had lost both the will and the skill to fight effectively. In essence, by 1700 they had surreptitiously been turned into civil bureaucrats whose real nature was hidden beneath swords, pikes, military titles, and a host of routine guard duties.

The process of controlling warrior forces thus blended imperceptibly into the broader process of routinizing the general patterns and relationships of political life. At first the shogunate and the great rival outside domains had regarded one another with well-justified distrust, but as the decades passed, they more and more took one another and the content of their relationship for granted. In the

1630s the *sankin kōtai* system was standardized, and the annual journeys, life at Edo, and ritual visits to the shogun became a routine part of warrior existence. The heavy burdens of construction and the ready punishments that the early shoguns had heaped upon the outside domains had nearly ceased by 1650 and thereafter shrank to almost a token ïevel.

Within the shogunate and the domains, too, the procedures of government became regularized and offices and personnel policies standardized. At the highest level, for example, it was generally agreed by 1700 that shoguns were succeeded by their eldest sons and that when no sons were alive, the successor was to be someone from a small number of Tokugawa related houses. Similarly the shogunate recognized the succession practices of the domains and as long as these were of a stable nature usually accepted domain decisions. And at all lower office levels there were reasonably stable means of maintaining continuity in office: through factional interaction in important offices, through hereditary preference in offices of no political import.

During this century the shogunate and the domains also worked out reasonably effective means of assessing the land and collecting and disbursing revenues. The shogunate, for example, made land surveys during Ieyasu's day, expanded its financial machinery during Iemitsu's day, surveyed the land again and overhauled its machinery during the 1680s, and discarded one assessment system for another during the 1720s. During the same century the need for income had also prodded the governments to set up monopoly enterprises, sell licenses, and borrow funds, in the process creating new fiscal organs to handle the transactions.

This growth of political institutions was paralleled by the growth of political ideology. A Zen monk introduced Chu Hsi's teachings to Ieyasu, and later Hayashi Razan taught his doctrines to Ieyasu, Hidetada, Iemitsu, and even the fourth shogun, Ietsuna (1651–80). By mid-century the Hayashi school enjoyed an unrivaled position at Edo, and students of Razan were spreading across Japan, teaching these doctrines to whatever daimyō and domain vassals would listen. During the 1650s the vigorous daimyō of Mito, Tokugawa Mitsukuni, started a major historical project inspired by Confucian scholarly ideals, and the final product of the Mito effort was the monumental *Dai Nihon shi* (History of Great Japan).

Accompanying this process of institutional and ideological development was a broadly ranging social growth that continued on into the eighteenth century. During the first thirty years of Tokugawa rule the daimyō gradually built their elegant mansions at Edo and worked out the procedures of their *sankin kōtai* progresses. As this system developed, it stimulated the growth of post towns, portage crews, shipping services, and in Osaka and Edo extensive service facilities such as those of rice traders, dry good merchants, and a host of entertainment establishments.

This trend, of course, involved major changes in the population. In gross terms, the over-all population of Japan grew from perhaps eighteen or twenty millions in about 1600 to some thirty millions in 1720 or so. But more importantly, this population acquired a distinct urban element, as Osaka and Edo in particular grew from towns with a few tens of thousands in the early seventeenth century to metropolises of half a million souls in the Genroku period. By 1700 the population of Japan had far more diversity, far more skills, and far more sophistication than its ancestors of 1600.

Change within a Stable Framework

The rapid pace of development which marked the seventeenth century was not maintained during the latter part of the eighteenth and first half of the nineteenth century. Rapid and dramatic change gave way to more subtle forms of development.

Philosophical speculation in particular branched out into a number of vigorous and more clearly delineated schools. During the seventeenth century philosophy had been relatively undifferentiated. Men had accepted Confucianism as the finest philosophy, placing emphasis where they chose and trying moderately to reconcile Chinese ideals and Japanese history in whatever ways seemed personally satisfactory. But during the eighteenth and nineteenth centuries differentiation occurred, with apologists for the native tradition becoming clearly distinguished from the increasingly segmented Confucianists, while a few scholars took an ardent interest in Dutch studies, in the process falling out with both Sinophiles and Japanophiles.

During the eighteenth century several scholars brought a more rational or critically analytical attitude to their studies. Some raised searching questions about ancient Japanese myths and their relationship to the religions of other societies; others argued on behalf of a more scholarly study of nature; and still others dealt with political problems, suggesting changes, for example, in the policy of exclusion or the attitude toward merchants. During the rule of the eighth shogun, Yoshimune (1716–45) and the era when the shogunal favorite Tanuma Okitsugu led the shogunate (1767–87) these new views spread. However during the conservative administration of the senior councilor Matsudaira Sadanobu (1787–93) the growth of heterodox thought was slowed by the Kansei edict of 1790, a shogunal decree designed to restore the preeminence of Chu Hsi thought and stop the spread of unauthorized opinion.

Following Matsudaira's dismissal and during the remainder of the shogun Ienari's long reign (1787–1835) heterodox thought gradually revived. Dutch studies acquired more adherents, and economic revisionism developed further. But most striking was the advance of Shintō studies and of the School of National Learning. During Ienari's reign, Hirata Atsutane carried Shintō thought to an irrational extreme, arguing vigorously, for example, that Japan was not only superior to China but unique in the world, superior to all other lands, and literally the land in which the gods had been born. Hence, he argued, Japan correctly was known as the Land of the Gods.

Besides diversifying in content and forming distinct and irreconcilable schools, later Tokugawa philosophy also spread out socially to be embraced and taught by commoners as well as warriors, as was noted in the discussion of Shinshū, Shingaku, and Hōtoku.

On a political level, a gradual change in the nature of shogunal leadership took place. Until 1650 shoguns had clearly led the shogunate by consulting with and giving orders directly to key advisers. But the growth of bureaucratic complexity and customary shogunal duties gradually reduced the shogun's capacity directly to manage affairs. Then in 1684 a senior councilor was murdered in Edo castle, and to prevent any assassin from reaching the shogun his office was physically separated from the offices of major shogunal officials. For most of the next century shoguns depended on personal favorites of modest origins who were able to oversee the administrative structure more directly than they. After the fall of Tanuma and rise of Matsudaira in 1787, however, the favorites were discredited and displaced by leaders who were vassal daimyō and regular high-ranking officials in the shogunal bureaucracy. This long-term trend favored the shogunate insofar as it kept political leadership and administrative leadership united and functioning smoothly despite the shogun's isolation and loss of direct administrative control. It weakened the shogunate, however, in that a vassal daimyō was much less secure in office than a shogun and so less able to innovate boldly lest in making political enemies he risk his own and his followers' positions at Edo. In short, this long-term trend improved the shogunate's capacity to administer ongoing affairs efficiently, but it reduced the government's capacity for rapid adaptation to new needs.

At an administrative and fiscal level, changes continued to be made, but they had little of the sweep or clarity of direction evident in seventeenth-century developments. Leaders like Yoshimune and Tanuma constantly tinkered with their administrative machines, especially with the fiscal mechanisms, trying one thing and then another in their ceaseless quest for funds. During Yoshimune's administration the older shogunal opposition to monopolies gave way to approval and exploitation. Thereafter the old aversion to commercial taxes yielded to a readiness to levy these taxes through diverse subterfuges such as calling the funds gifts, loans, or fees. The fiscal result was to make governments ever more dependent on income from commercial sources, money rather than produce income. And while this did help the governments finance their operations, a price was paid in ideological obfuscation, greater fiscal complexity, and further dependence on merchant cooperation, strengthening the symbiotic relationship of warrior and merchant.

This gradual drift from a rural to an urban fiscal base was not, however, a steady trend. On the contrary, it would proceed for a time, in the process generating an ever higher level of indignation among the virtuous political outsiders. Then, under a reformist regime, efforts would be made to revive the virtues of frugality and Spartan discipline, to reduce government expenses, warrior debt, the role of money in government finances, and the social influence of the urban merchants. The greatest of these periodic reforms was led by the shogun Yoshimune during the 1720s and 1730s. The next reform was led by Matsudaira Sadanobu in the 1790s. His effort was briefer, less pervasive, and less successful, but nevertheless more shrill in tone and more frenetic in pace. The third major shogunal reform was led by the senior councilor Mizuno Tadakuni in 1841–43, and this was the most frantic, the briefest, and the least effective of the three. Between these efforts shogunate leaders like Tanuma pursued less dramatic policies of partial adaptation to the flourishing commercial economy and partial adherence to the Confucian norms of the day.

One interesting aspect of this cyclical pattern of vigorous reaction and limited adjustment was that it was not merely a phenomenon limited to the shogunate. Rather, the waves of reformism and adjustment in Edo tended to accompany similar waves in the domains. One should also note that at first the initiative came from Edo, but later it came from the domains. Thus many domains diligently and consciously modified their government structures to make them more like Ieyasu's in the early 1600s, and a century later Yoshimune's effort set off a chain reaction throughout Japan. But Matsudaira took office partly as a result of agitation by men outside the shogunate in defiance of its leaders; and in the nineteenth century a decade of reform among the domains occurred before Mizuno undertook his ill-fated effort at Edo. This strongly suggests the extent to which political initiative had slowly shifted from the cumbrous government at Edo to the smaller administrations in the castle towns throughout Japan.

Another area of persistent change was rural Japan where, as was suggested earlier, the social and economic restructuring of the villages continued to advance. Whereas urban merchants had pretty well stabilized their techniques and fields of activity by the mid-eighteenth century, rural entrepreneurs continued to develop new enterprises as the ongoing village change increased their opportunities and cast up new and more ambitious landowners. One consequence of this seems to have been that by the late Tokugawa period economic initiative had shifted from the cities to the villages much as political initiative had shifted from Edo to the domains. Both trends were species of decentralization; both meant that innovations could not be converted easily into nationwide policies, but both also meant that a host of different and even mutually incompatible experiments could proceed concurrently. It was a situation ill-suited to perpetuate a uniform *status quo* but well designed to permit local adjustments to new conditions.

If these developments laid the groundwork for adaptation, others just as surely revealed the gradual accumulation of problems for which the Tokugawa system had no satisfactory answers.

As suggested earlier, the School of National Learning touched upon the question of how the shogun could rightly rule if the emperor were the legitimate ruler. During most of the seventeenth and eighteenth centuries it was usually argued that the shogun was appointed by the emperor to rule on his behalf because experience had shown that the Imperial House itself was unable properly to do so, whereas military rule had brought peace and tranquillity to the emperor's people and land. But what if someone became convinced that Tokugawa rule did not really secure Japan's peace and tranquillity? In the late eighteenth and early nineteenth centuries the question operated largely in the realm of academic speculation, upsetting only a few court nobles and some domain scholars. During Matsudaira's administration, for example, a few scholars at Mito were able to inject the question of respect for the emperor into the political contest at Edo and their criticism helped to drive Matsudaira from office. Yet even this flurry of activity failed to raise the underlying question of shogunal authority. Should a situation arise, however, that challenged Tokugawa ability to maintain peace and tranquillity, then the matter of legitimacy could become a real issue.

At a lower social level a material problem was slowly undercutting the status structure of the Tokugawa system. During the seventeenth century, as low-ranking warriors had gone into debt governments had devised ways to assist them, but by the mid-eighteenth century this practice had ceased, and the indigent warriors had to find relief elsewhere. One method was to borrow from moneylenders; another was to marry into wealthy commoner families. Affluent merchants and farmers had become numerous, and some of them welcomed ties to families of warrior status. Warriors began to adopt sons or marry daughters of wealthy commoners in return for financial aid. This practice confused status lines, but it did not in fact allow merchants to rise to positions of political influence. On the contrary, it probably released some pressure by helping impoverished and potentially disruptive warriors and by appeasing ambitious commoners even while it enmeshed them in the existing warrior social structure. But for all this, like borrowing, it continued to be regarded as an immoral practice and may well have generated feelings of frustration and resentment among both those who crossed status barriers and those who merely watched in disapproval.

A related problem was the intensifying rural and urban violence of the later eighteenth and nineteenth centuries. This violence sprang from a complex set of economic and social dislocations and was frequently aggravated by the values and institutions of the regime. Even when they involved thousands of dissidents and major conflicts with government forces, these violent outbursts were local and temporary in nature, never threatening to topple the regime. But, like marriage across class lines, the outbursts violated the premises of the regime;

after all, the shogun as executor of the emperor's will and as Confucian ruler was expected to keep the peace and maintain the welfare of the people. Should he obviously fail to do so, one could question his right to rule. But here again, in practice the incidents were of local scope, and the very fact that Japan was broken into some 250 major political units made it difficult for these matters to appear issues of nationwide consequence; instead they discredited lesser men: daimyō, domain administrators, or simply town and village leaders.

It was, rather, the recurrence of a problem that by its very nature was inescapably nationwide in import that finally subjected Tokugawa legitimacy to serious question. This was the reappearance of foreigners exploring, drifting ashore, seeking provisions, and finally demanding trade and diplomatic intercourse. When foreigners demanded the repudiation of the established Tokugawa policy of isolation, they struck at the very roots of the great peace, and when foreign contacts were established, the other problems—of imperial prerogatives, warrior distress, merchant excesses, and popular unrest—were aggravated and transformed into issues involving Tokugawa legitimacy. Suddenly the shogunate found itself denied its consensual basis, damned by the very success that for two and a half centuries had kept Japan's problems boxed up in tight little particularistic categories. By the 1860s they were all intertwined, all blamed on the shogunate, all demanding solution.

V

Late Tokugawa

and Early Meiji

Japan

BY

MARLENE J. MAYO

The Strength of Tradition

More than a century ago, well before the West's reappearance, Japan's potential as a modern society was already high, although this is more obvious to us now than it was to the Japanese who lived in the tottering world of the Tokugawa shogunate or to the many foreign admirals and diplomats who badgered Japan into accepting first diplomatic and then commercial relations with their countries. All of East and South Asia experienced the Western advance, but only Japan, for better or for worse, began to transform itself in the latter half of the nineteenth century. By 1900 Japan was vastly different from the country of 1800, and its emergence as a modern power amazed foreigners as much as its traditional arts and customs intrigued them.

Puzzling questions persist as to the basic nature of the changes, their significance, and why and how they took place. We have a fascinating set of conflicting characterizations of early-nineteenth-century Japan: a regimented police state, an obscure agricultural kingdom, a decaying feudal organism, or a highly developed traditional society on the verge of modernization—if indeed not already modern. All of these views contain some measure of truth. Even more to the point, they reflect either hindsight or the changing concerns and methods of successive generations of Japanese and Western scholars who have seen Japan in many guises and tended to either emphasize its failures as an industrial democracy or laud its over-all success. They have asked if modernization primarily was self-generated, originating with the reform programs of the domain governments and the shogunate in the 1830s and 1840s. Or did it really begin with Commodore Perry and his black ships, whose visits to Edo Bay in 1853 and 1854 served both as a symbol and concrete evidence of an intruding, menacing, but also alluring West? Or still later with the political coup of 1868, known as the Meiji Restoration, which opened the way for new leadership and radical policies? Whether we emphasize change or continuity, internal or external forces, it is clear that Japan's modernization, although accomplished in a short span of time, was made possible, as in the West, by the accretion of centuries. The problem here is to recognize the contributions of Tokugawa tradition (and even earlier times) without detracting from the subsequent Meiji achievements, belittling the impact of the West, or ignoring the even greater changes of the twentieth century.

As a beginning, advances in Tokugawa education offer an excellent illustration of the strengths and weaknesses of late traditional Japan. Today, the Japanese are among the world's most literate people. By 1800, however, Japan's literacy rate was already high, whether measured by standards elsewhere in Asia or even in Western Europe. The estimate of functional literacy is startling: 30 percent or higher for adult males. Japan's warrior elite, from shogun and daimyō to the lowest foot soldier, was well schooled in the Neo-Confucian classics of statecraft and ethics. On the whole, this was a rather dull education, but if it did not stir profound intellectual curiosity it at least had the virtue of instilling a strong sense of political responsibility in the samurai. The military arts were still practiced but mainly as sports or highly stylized aesthetic exercises. Merchants and clerks in the shogunal cities and domain castle towns—and village headmen as well—had also acquired the rudiments of a classical education along with the practical learning required to do their jobs. Late Tokugawa Japan was a place of publishing houses, best sellers, lending libraries, circulating manuscripts (including technical treatises), and above all of schools, ranging from the orthodox Confucian academy of higher learning in Edo to hundreds of official domain schools, thousands of private institutions, and more than ten thousand primary schools in the countryside, usually quartered in Buddhist temples. Here peasant children, too, learned to read simple characters and the syllabary, to count on the abacus, and to memorize Confucian maxims.

Although the Confucian Classics and the traditional military arts dominated Tokugawa curriculums, many of the domain schools and especially the private academies (often comprised of just one man and his devoted disciples) offered a wide range of specialization, either in heterodox Confucianism, Japanese literature and history, or Dutch studies. There was an increase in general knowledge and in the number of people acquiring that knowledge. Serious doubts exist as to the relevance of this primarily Confucian education to the needs of Japan's modernization; and Tokugawa rationalism and empiricism were not the counterpart of the Newtonian or scientific world view. Nevertheless, the Japanese had accepted formal education as vital to the proper performance of their duties and as a key to professional and occupational advancement. They were accustomed to the routine of systematic training outside of the home, at regular intervals, and through several levels of proficiency. And they had sophisticated concepts with which to analyze the world of nature and of man.

There had also been an intensification of national consciousness among the samurai aristocracy and a considerable blurring of class lines. Although Tokugawa laws prohibited changes of occupation or residence and closely regulated travel between the domains or from castle towns to shogunal cities, there was a steady flow of people, goods, gossip, and information. Transportation and communications improved remarkably, contributing to an expanding vision of life outside of the village, the domain, even Japan—through books, woodblock prints, tales of itinerant peddlers, religious pilgrimages, sightseeing trips, and news from those who had left their native places to seek adventure or try their fortunes elsewhere. For the daimyō and those of their samurai retinue who regularly made the trip to Edo, there was a common upper class urban culture and in time a common apprehension of decay within and danger without. Awareness of other countries and cultures, however, was more than matched by a deep love, almost mystical in quality, for Japan as unique in spirit and values.

Harder to analyze and much more controversial is the extent of economic development and changes in village society by the mid-nineteenth century. The essence of the modern transformation is the creation of an industrial society, and theorists of all schools, ranging from orthodox Marxist to laissez-faire capitalist, have made widely varying assessments of late Tokugawa agriculture, commerce, and manufacturing. One line of argument is primarily concerned with the point Japan had reached by the 1850s in the assumed universal transition from feudalism to capitalism. Was it commercial capitalism or incipient industrialism? Some detect a union of interests between rural manufacturers and lower-status warriors, a combination which by its very nature would inevitably produce a repressive social and political system in Meiji Japan. Another line of argument centers on stages or preconditions of economic growth: whether Japan was ready for "economic takeoff" or the transition to modern economic growth; whether Japan was comparable to, say, Elizabethan England although lacking its extensive international trade, or to the even more advanced England of the 1750s. A better analogy might be Germany, where national unification and industrial growth came at approximately the same time as Japan's, after a long period of preparation.

All parties to the dispute can at least agree on the vigor and complexity of Tokugawa Japan's economic life. By 1850 the Japanese had apparently expanded and diversified their economy about as much as was possible without foreign trade, science and technical progress, and more sophisticated notions of economic development. However, if the late Tokugawa economy was not precisely a capitalist market system, neither did most Japanese live at the subsistence level of semiserfs. There was instead an unequal distribution of increased rural and urban income among a people who were coming to expect and demand much more in their material lives. Also, there were values and habits which, as it turned out, were basic to sustained economic growth: discipline, hard work, high savings, the ability to cooperate and organize, and relatively honest civil administration.

In the art of government, too, the Japanese were highly advanced. The shogunate operated through an intricate bureaucracy in Edo, and there were lesser ones modeled on it in the castle towns. The shogun, like the emperor, was busy with ceremonial routine and isolated from practical politics. In a sense this was fortunate, for the shoguns who reigned from 1837 to 1867 suffered from severe physical or mental afflictions. The Senior Council of vassal daimyō made the decisions but occasionally solicited advice from other influential daimyō on an informal basis. The shogun's power as the legitimate deputy of the emperor was absolute in theory, but in practice both the man and his administration were prevented by custom and precedent from a totally dictatorial exercise of authority. Neo-Confucianism stressed government by ethical men and good example as superior to laws and coercion, but in Tokugawa Japan there was considerable appreciation and use of law. Furthermore, the autonomy of most domains was very real, and the village leaders enjoyed a modest degree of discretionary power under samurai supervision. Within the elite there was a growing tendency to reward talent, but there were more samurai than posts to fill and there was an almost total exclusion of merchants from political power. Duplication, delays, and cumbersome checks and balances hampered administration, but practical-minded officials managed to circumvent some of this by resort to informal committees and petitions. Experience with specialized duties and standardized office routine would assist in the transition to the functional ministries of a modern bureaucracy. In politics, then, as in economics and scholarship, the Japanese displayed a rational spirit: an appreciation of order, coherence, and efficiency which served them well in absorbing the shocks of social change and in creating an industrial society.

By 1850, although only a portion of the population was under direct Tokugawa control, Japan was in many ways—culture, language, expanding markets, and political practice—a unified nation. It would be historical license to go further and call this system in its latter-day form a centralized state in all but name or to ignore the intensity of regional and local attachments. Credit for devising Japan's modern nation state must be given to the early Meiji leaders, but many of their skills, procedures, and attitudes were valuable legacies of the Tokugawa age. Nor was late Tokugawa Japan necessarily evolving into a modern society. It is stimulating, but in the end not totally satisfactory, to explain Japan's rapid modernization by pointing to a feudal history which made it more like Western Europe than China. This can easily deteriorate into the assertion that Japan became what it was by 1900 because it was already headed that way. Unless one accepts historical determinism or sees a single pattern in world history, there is little reason to believe that Japan would have inevitably of its own momentum generated industrial growth, instituted parliamentary constitutionalism, or engaged in empire building if it had not been for the confrontation with the nineteenth-century West and the policies of the men who took power in 1868. However much we may appreciate the strength of tradition in assisting modernization, it is still quite possible that much was done in Japan's case in spite of and not because of the past. What happened was a still imperfectly understood process of interaction between Japan and the West and between the old order and new requirements, with the Japanese displaying remarkable resolution and a capacity for change and adaptation which went far beyond mere imitation of the current models offered by the West.

Although historians have done much to restore Tokugawa Japan's reputation, the subsequent Meiji political and intellectual leadership, out of conviction as well as for political reasons, would speak of their predecessors with disgust, even hatred. Later generations would learn to despise Tokugawa Japan as a closed society and a feudal system bedeviled by internal contradictions. Conceivably, however, with some restructure the Tokugawa shogunate could have provided effective national leadership. This is an "if" question, but nevertheless important in assessing the Meiji program as a new view of society or merely an elaboration on a national scale of shogunal reforms. The Tokugawa regime was in terrible trouble by mid-century, but the shogunate did not collapse of its own weight or corruption. Its demise was engineered by a political conspiracy within the privileged class, specifically by samurai from strong outside domains in southern Japan in league with court nobles and a few daimyō related to the Tokugawa family. With some justice they attributed a long list of ills to Tokugawa misrule and ineptitude: inflation, samurai impoverishment, exorbitant taxes, limited opportunities for men of talent, social disorder, foreign insults. There was no widespread mass movement, but adding to the unease was popular agitation. Since the 1790s peasants, out of frustration and misery, had exploded in riots of increasing frequency and size against their exploiters, sometimes the officials but more often the local moneylenders and landlords. By the 1830s and 1840s, a time of natural disasters and crop failures, a new source of violence was unrest in the cities, where mounting food prices provoked uprisings. Osaka was a city of starving people in 1837, and the streets of Edo were clogged with corpses. New popular religious cults emerged, whose founders, often peasant women, spoke in oracles, went into trances, or claimed revelations. Some converts sought solace in worship and prayers; others in faith healing and charms. A few took to direct action like the peasants near Nagoya in 1867 who broke into wealthy homes or storehouses and demanded food while chanting religious slogans and dancing themselves into a frenzy. The despair was real and evident, but most critics saw the solution in a change of men or policies rather than the system of rule. Until the 1860s Tokugawa Japan tolerated a high degree of financial insolvency, social upheaval, and political uncertainty.

Reforms and Reformers

Officials, however, were neither blind nor indifferent to the suffering and rallied to the cause of reform. In the 1830s and 1840s, first several of the domains and then the shogunate as well worked out a series of measures named for the Tempō era (1830–43), though not confined precisely to those years. In tackling fiscal and administrative problems, the Tempō reformers, like their predecessors in the eighteenth century, were motivated primarily by Confucian values and sentiments—concern for the general welfare, for morality in statecraft, and for preservation of the natural order. Although many of them displayed considerable imagination, their intention was to arrest moral decay and not to revamp institutions. They sponsored reform to save the system, not alter it. Samurai, peasants, artisans, and merchants, it was argued, could find relief for their distress if only they would stay in or get back to their proper places and perform their proper duties. The Tempō reformers could not afford to be complacent for another reason, foreign pressures. Since the late eighteenth century when reports, not always accurate, of Russian activities in the north had filtered down to Edo and the early nineteenth century when British ships in search of Dutch prizes of war or food and water had appeared off the southern coast, officials grew increasingly wary of foreign designs in East Asia. Even before the shocking news came in 1842 of China's defeat in the Opium War, coastal defense had become a major concern of the reformers despite disagreement on whether the external menace or domestic ills should be given priority.

In their attempts to improve finances for administrative and defense needs, domain and shogunal officials explored all sorts of devices. Expenditures were trimmed, stipends were cut, debts to merchants were totally or partially canceled, interest rates were reduced, coins were debased, luxurious display was prohibited, taxes were increased or their collection made more efficient, peasants were ordered back to their villages, monopoly guilds were more closely regulated or dissolved, and the simple frugal life was extolled. Some of the domains in their relentless search for new sources of revenue used their authority to promote production and control the economy. The results, in most cases, were land reclamation projects or domain monopolies in cash crops and famous local products. To meet the external threat, there were experiments in the manufacture of improved guns and cannon and in Dutch-style military drills and exercises. In Mito, for example, temple bells were melted to provide metal for guns. In Hizen, one of the two domains alternately responsible for the defense of Nagasaki, technicians built a reverberatory furnace (1848) to cast iron for cannon, and Satsuma constructed a blast furnace (1854) to improve the quality of pig iron. The daimyō of Mito and Satsuma, and some shogunal retainers, urged the removal of the ban against building large ships and supported the training of a navy and merchant marine. A few voices promoted international trade or overseas expansion, the latter to relieve population pressures and to check the foreign advance. There was broad recognition of the need to improve education and acquire more technical information from Dutch books.

The reforms were not restricted to economic and military measures. Some involved adjustments in the social and political system. There were suggestions that men of talent and ability (mainly from the samurai ranks) be better employed and that the shogunate allow a wider group of daimyō and retainers to participate in the making of policy on a regular basis. The rationale was that all were servants of the emperor's country and had a moral duty to defend it. The Toku-gawa should not think selfishly only of their own position, and the daimyō must work to save Japan and not merely their own domains. Implicit—but very weak at this point—was an attack on samurai privilege and military despotism.

The Tempō reforms and those which followed in their wake after 1850, when knowledge of Western technology and methods increased, represented a vigorous if largely unsuccessful effort to meet Japan's needs. Several of the domains, however, showed themselves to be either more creative and daring or simply better organized, and came out stronger than the shogunate, whose measures failed and cost it confidence and support. Its problems and responsibilities were greater and its freedom to maneuver perhaps less than in the domains, or so it may have seemed to timid bureaucrats. Commercialization of the economy, for example, was more advanced in the Tokugawa territories than almost anywhere else in Japan. Poverty, indebtedness, and rural tenancy were also extensive. Some of the areas least touched by social and economic change, such as the large outside domains of Satsuma and Chōshū, were the most successful in restoring fiscal solvency and utilizing talented middle and lower samurai. This was to have profound repercussions in the future, for in the 1860s Satsuma and Chōshū would be powerful enough to challenge and end Tokugawa rule.

Chōshū, which overlooked the Straits of Shimonoseki in southern Honshu, was very large, very rich (perhaps fourth or fifth in actual production of rice though officially ranked ninth), and a little above average in its proportion of samurai population. Chōshū, an enemy of the Tokugawa at the battle of Sekigahara in 1600, had never forgiven the shogunate for subsequent reductions in its holdings. During the Tempō era, it had published a domain budget, abolished commercial monopolies (in salt, sake, and cotton, for example) in favor of chartering local merchants for a fee, and fallen back upon an institutional innovation of an earlier era, a savings and investment bureau set up to accumulate emergency reserves. The financial reforms did help the samurai and raise their morale. In the 1860s, Chōshū would have the funds to equip its newly reorganized militia units with foreign guns.

Satsuma, located at the southern end of Kyushu, was also very large and even more remote. It was officially second in rice income and had subfiefs and even its own dependency, the Ryukyu Islands, a source of rice, sugar, and Chinese goods. The Ryukyuans had been conquered by Satsuma early in the seventeenth century but continued to pay regular tribute to China as well. The Shimazu family had been rulers in Kyushu since the twelfth century and like the Mōri family in Chōshū resented their loss in lands after 1600. One of the unusual characteristics of the domain was the high ratio of samurai to the general population, almost 25 percent compared to five or seven percent elsewhere. Many lived in the country and were available for all kinds of police and administrative work. The domain obviously could field a large army. In the Tempō years, Satsuma built up reserves by monopolizing the profits from cash crops in cotton, wax, and especially sugar from the Ryukyus, where harsh measures were employed to force an increase in production. The Shimazu family produced several competent rulers, and Shimazu Nariakira, daimyō from 1851 to 1858, was almost as prominent in the inner circles of national politics as Tokugawa Nariaki of Mito, though both were excluded from the Senior Council. Nariakira, like his father and grandfather, sponsored Dutch studies to strengthen his domain, ignoring charges that he was an eccentric or Dutch-crazed daimyō. Under him, there were experiments in electricity and gas lighting, the construction of a model steam engine and a steam locomotive, and the introduction of water-powered weaving machinery.

The Tempō reforms reflected only a portion of the broadened learning and intellectual pursuits of late Tokugawa Japan. Intellectuals, most of whom were samurai, were in a troubled, questioning mood, and many reform proposals were in circulation. The dominant strain was orthodox Confucianism, but the School of National Learning, the Mito school of history, and scholars of Dutch studies contributed new ideas and emphases. Much of what they said was at first not very startling or subversive, but in time their anxieties were to produce more profound answers to Japan's problems and a deeper commitment to radical reform and change, by force if necessary.

Confucian economic thought, in particular, was not very distinguished, certainly not as inventive as economic practice. Most scholars and reformers (as in the case of the Tempō reforms) equated welfare and virtue with a natural or agrarian economy and were content to ask the merchants to charge less interest or lower prices, the peasants to work harder and be frugal, and the samurai to set a better example in simple, disciplined living. Very few preached respect for merchants and profit-making. Even those who called for an increase in production were not theorists of economic growth but advocates of sound fiscal practice to fund military expenditures. Their slogan, *fukoku kyōhei,* enriching the country and strengthening its arms (or wealth and power), came from the Chinese classics of the Legalist school and meant little more than improving coastal defenses through new sources of income. The belief was deeply engrained that contact with the barbarian, Christian West was bad; for in the West inferiors and superiors did not know their proper places, merchants acted like officials, men and women reversed their natural roles, and profit was valued over duty. Confucians of a more heterodox persuasion, however, emphasized practical or real learning (Jitsugaku). Contemporary problems, they taught, required realistic, workable, practical solutions. Knowledge without action was meaningless, moral platitudes must not be substituted for actual improvements in the people's welfare, and the world of nature was worthy of study.

Jitsugaku also reinforced Dutch studies, which had made great advances by the 1850s. As a serious scholarly pursuit, such learning had become respectable in the late eighteenth century when Dutch anatomy texts and works on natural sciences were deemed superior to Chinese sources. By the Tempō era, Japan's economic and defense needs had also turned the attention of Dutch scholars to military technology. Some of these men, like Sakuma Shōzan, who called upon Confucian men of talent to master Western military science and strategy in defense of the country, were remarkably bold and courageous, but most were content simply to study and conduct small experiments, without worrying too much about the political implications. Few were interested in Western culture itself. Besides, the shogunate met open political criticism with censorship, imprisonment, and even execution.

Dutch learning was not considered to be particularly dangerous since much of it was technical and conducted under domain and shogunal sponsorship. Whatever their other failings, the officials were not total obscurantists and made some use of the new knowledge while keeping it under supervision. The shogunate had set up a bureau to translate barbarian books in 1811 and would expand its operations after 1850. Several of the domains had academies of Dutch studies; others sometimes had at least a library of Dutch books and translations. In the official academies the Dutch curriculum was narrow and only a few applications for study were accepted. But it bears repeating that the scholars, both private and official, were often as limited in their curiosity as the government was restrictive in the conditions it imposed on their work. Instead of becoming heretics or advocating change, they remained convinced of the essential superiority of the Neo-Confucian world view and Eastern wisdom. They had persuaded themselves that the Confucian investigation of things (moral essences, ethical principles) could include the study of the laws of nature (the measurable, quantifiable principles of physics and chemistry). In the end, Tokugawa empiricism and rationalism, whether nurtured by Jitsugaku or Dutch studies, were not fully cognizant of science as systematic theory and method or of the premises upon which Western technology rested but did prepare many Japanese to appreciate the bases of modern science when contacts with the West expanded. The scope of Dutch learning continued to widen and became Yōgaku or "Western learning" as scholars turned in the 1850s to English and other languages and began to pursue a broader search for knowledge and to speculate about the relationship between values or institutions and advances in technology. Because of their interest in foreign learning, Dutch scholars tended to be critical of strict seclusion but, like their colleagues, wanted any relations with the West to be favorable to Japan.

By mid-century, therefore, knowledge of the West, while not extensive, did exist, based mainly on Dutch books and reports from the Dutch at Deshima and supplemented by the tales of Japanese castaways, interrogations of shipwrecked Westerners, and items in Chinese gazetteers. Scholars and shogunal officials, accordingly, had a general idea of world geography, of variations in national customs, and of Western military power, and their perceptions and insights would continue to deepen.

One important thing to be noted about the Confucian and Dutch scholars is their intense love of country. Since the mid-eighteenth century, scholars of the School of National Learning had contributed enormously to a revival of interest in Shintō and ancient Japanese literature and history. They stressed the unique characteristics of the Japanese spirit, culture, people, and above all of the Imperial House. They had an inordinate, almost irrational pride in a single, unbroken line of emperors stretching back into antiquity and reaching ultimately to the Sun Goddess. They spoke of Japan as *shinshū,* the divine land, or as *kōkoku,* the emperor's country, and insisted along with Confucian reformers that moral purification was more pertinent to the country's salvation than all the chatter about technology, military drills, or reverberatory furnaces. Quite naturally, they feared contamination of the Japanese spirit and subversion of the natural order by foreign trade, Christianity, or Western mores. To spread the emperor's glory (not necessarily by force) would, they sincerely believed, benefit the whole world. However, even the most extreme of these scholars, who reviled both China and the West as inferior to Japan and claimed to find in Shintō a complete culture and theology, had some interest in Western technology, if only to fend off the West. The School of National Learning thus helped intensify the strong sense of nation with which the samurai faced the West. Perhaps because of their emotional identification with the divine land, along with better information about the West, Japan's leaders feared the loss of political independence more deeply than the Chinese, who bore the main brunt of the Western advance. Consequently, they acted more rapidly to adopt counter measures. The Japanese had a tradition of borrowing from other peoples but no experience of alien rule and never developed the Chinese conviction that alien conquerors would ultimately be absorbed and the native culture continue unchanged.

Among the slogans, ideas, and reforms of the period, those generated by the Mito school of history were extremely influential. To be precise, it was the Mito synthesis, for it embraced Neo-Confucianism and Shintō though tending to spurn Buddhism as alien. Mito was a Tokugawa-related domain located on the coast about seventy-five miles northeast of Edo. Its Tempō reforms, though unsuccessful, were the inspiration for attempts elsewhere; its daimyō from 1821 to 1844, Tokugawa Nariaki, was one of the most striking political personalities of the period and the hero of dissidents; and its school of history was a major source of mid-century loyalist, antiforeign, and restorationist thought. The Mito scholars had revived work in the 1790s on a project dating back to the seventeenth century, the *Dai Nihon shi* (History of Great Japan), a chronicle of Japan from its legendary origins to the fourteenth century, centering on the emperor in the fashion of Chinese historiography. In their widely read essays and commentaries, the Mito historians also worked out a rather primitive theory of state. In developing the theme of *sonnō*, reverence for the emperor, they argued that the right emperor, that is the legitimate sovereign by blood descent from the Sun Goddess and by possession of the Three Imperial Regalia, must be on the throne, for only then was good government possible. This was originally not meant as an attack on the position of the shogun (to whom the Mito daimyō was related) but was rather a reminder that the emperor symbolized rule by universal principles of law and morality, the orderly continuation of government, and the unity of the Japanese people. Direct rule by the emperor was not necessary. Loyal ministers at the actual level of power would put into practice the precepts which the emperor as the ultimate sovereign upheld. As in orthodox Confucian thought, the shogun was therefore viewed as a loyal and virtuous minister, the lawful delegate of the emperor with full authority to rule so long as he kept the peace and protected the country. Loyalty to the emperor transcended all other loyalties but did not conflict with respect for the shogun or duty to the daimyō.

Mito theorists, like the Shintō scholars, were convinced of the unique qualities of their country. One of them proudly asserted that "there had never been a land like Japan" in its purity and beauty. Japan was even closer than China to the ideal Confucian state because it had been spared both alien conquest and internal rebellion against the dynasty of the sun line. As troubles mounted after 1830, Mito scholars called upon all virtuous men, including the shogun, to put aside private interests and work selflessly for the good of the entire country, for the realm of Japan was His Majesty's realm. They next drew the conclusion that the emperor himself should take a personal interest in the problems and welfare of his people. In projecting back to a time of enlightened rule in antiquity, they spoke in praise of the Nara court, a time when several emperors did rule in their own right but ironically also a time when Japan was not in seclusion but busily assimilating the foreign culture of T'ang China. This early form of "restoration" thought was vague but would evolve into the notion first that on all important matters the emperor should be consulted by the shogun, next that he should participate in decisions, and finally in the 1860s that there should be a restoration of direct rule. In fact, the restoration in 1868 was merely nominal. Historically, the emperor had rarely been identified directly with state power, either in theory or in practice. He had been above politics and enveloped in ceremony. In addition, the Mito school adapted other Confucian teachings to Tokugawa Japan, such as respect for classical learning, the necessity of behavior appropriate to one's lot in life, and the interdependence of force and moral suasion in effective government.

Mito scholars also developed in their writings the theme of jōi (expel the barbarians), originally meaning to repel the foreign ships. There had been much excitement in Mito in 1824 when some British sailors had landed and asked for food and water. As more and more ships were sighted or shipwrecks occurred, the theme of jōi was further expanded into a rejection of foreign customs and contacts. This was the logical corollary of reverence for the divine land. There must be no insults, no pollution of Japan. A rigid policy of seclusion must be maintained. Such ideas were eloquently expressed in a famous political tract of Aizawa Seishisai, *Shinron* (New proposals), written in 1825. It circulated throughout Japan in manuscript and when printed at mid-century became one of the most widely read works in domain academies. Arguing from the premise that Japan was superior by virtue of the "Heavenly Sun Succession" and the descent of all Japanese from the gods, Aizawa challenged the shogun to arrest moral decay, to improve defenses, to unite the country in the face of external danger and so discharge one of his basic duties as the deputy of the emperor by driving away the barbarians. Thus Japan's unique political order would be preserved. His word for the state was *kokutai,* or national essence, a term destined to receive great attention from Meiji ideologues and twentieth-century militarists. Aizawa was in complete agreement with the 1825 shogunal edict ordering that foreign ships be driven off "without second thoughts."

Less scholarly but more popular were the essays of Aizawa's younger Mito colleague, Fujita Tōko, who joined *sonnō* to *jōi* in the most potent political slogan of the mid-century. *Sonnō-jōi,* he wrote in the 1840s, was the ultimate duty of men of determination and high purpose. For true patriots, reverence for the emperor automatically entailed rejection of the barbarians. In their support of *jōi,* Mito scholars did not totally reject Dutch learning. They would take the guns and the ships; it was the barbarian's religion and culture that they could not abide. But many of the samurai loyalists who read the Mito essays interpreted *jōi* to mean that anything or anyone Western was evil. Kyoto and subsequently Edo, just after the beginning of treaty relations, were crowded with young men who were eager to prove their love for Japan and reverence for the emperor by cutting down Westerners, assassinating unpopular officials, and setting fire to foreign compounds. They were extremists only in the sense of wishing to overthrow the shogunate but were not social revolutionaries. A few, however, who managed to survive the terror and violence of those years revised their earlier positions and turned to Western learning as a better way of defending Japan.

But what of the emperor himself and his court, the object of such adulation? In the Tokugawa period, the shoguns had kept the emperors and court nobles in virtual isolation in Kyoto, confined to the environs of the palace or their mansions, but had substantially improved their material lot. Rituals were again conducted with the ancient splendor and magnificence. Court nobles lived comfortably if not as luxuriously as the wealthier daimyō. In the 1840s, as the education of the nobility began to improve, many of the courtiers too would read or hear of the recent Mito and Shintō works and grow politically ambitious. Further information on the domestic and world scene was supplied by sympathetic daimyō who were well connected at court through marriage alliances.

The Emperor Kōmei, who ascended the throne in 1846, turned out to be strong of will and interested in politics. When it occurred to the critics of shogunal policies to act according to the emperor's opinion rather than simply use his name, political intrigues became infinitely more complicated. In 1846, for the first time in two centuries, an emperor spoke out on a matter of national policy. He, or more likely his advisers (Kōmei was about fifteen at the time), was reacting to the foreign menace. It was only a few years after China's defeat, and there had recently been several incidents involving foreign whalers and merchant ships. Now, in a letter to the shogun, Kōmei berated him for inadequate coastal defense and exhorted him to protect the "land of the gods," thereby diminishing His Imperial Majesty's anxiety.

The Foreign Crisis

The shogunate at mid-century was trying to deal responsibly with domestic and foreign crises, even after the failure of the Tempō reforms. National officials, no less than local ones, were worried and searched for workable solutions and men of talent. The new leader of the Senior Council after 1845, Abe Masahiro, often solicited the opinions of outside and related daimyō. More and more, the Senior Council had to contend with a restless court, resentful daimyō, disaffected samurai, and an increasingly insistent West. Their policies, however, seemed to have little effect in alleviating internal distress, and military defense remained inadequate. Tokugawa officials had been afraid to let the domains become too powerful but had not done enough in their own territories. The foreign problem would now become uppermost and thoroughly perplex them.

In diplomacy, the shogunate was quite realistic, if not resolute. It, not the domains, had the problem of dealing with the Western requests, which by the 1850s were thinly disguised demands, and it had to take the blame or credit for the aftermath. For a century, as the Russians and British had expanded their interests in East Asia, the shogunate had vacillated as to the wisdom and practicality of strict seclusion. In the 1780s some advisers were sympathetic to legalization of trade with Russia in Hokkaido and further north. In 1804–5 Edo turned down the requests of a Russian envoy at Naga-saki, but had misgivings. In 1825 the policy had hardened again to the "no second thoughts" edict but was relaxed in 1842, following the Opium War, to permit cautious assistance to ships in distress—but nothing else. In the late 1840s, when French activities were reported in the Ryukyu Islands, Abe decided to let Satsuma supervise trade relations between the islands and France if the French attempted to force the issue. The most dramatic and ultimately successful Western attempts to break Japan's seclusion were made by two Americans, Commodore Matthew C. Perry, in 1853–54, and Townsend Harris, in 1856–58. After decades of Western probes and academic debates, Japan was at last confronted with a clear-cut choice of opening the country or "repelling the barbarians." And it was obvious this time that the foreigners would not take "no" to their requests for regular and formal contacts.

The relatively well-informed shogunate ignored boasts about the superiority of Eastern spirit over Western matter and yielded as gracefully as it could. But the senior councilors were trapped in an impossible situation. In their judgment, Japan could not and should not risk a clash with the foreigners, but at the same time the Toku-gawa could not afford to appear submissive to the foreigners and thereby disgrace the nation and throne. The shogunate tried to avoid direct and immediate answers (interpreted as oriental duplicity by ill-informed or unsympathetic Westerners); it sought to seem to give while not giving, and to play for time in order to build Japan's defenses. When pressed by Perry, alternately magnanimous and militant, and just as determined as the Japanese to brook no insults, Abe and the other senior councilors gave in and reluctantly granted the 1854 Kanagawa Treaty of Navigation and Friendship. It opened two ports (Shimoda and Hakodate) as provision stations, promised humane treatment of shipwrecked Americans, permitted an American consular official to take up residence in Shimoda after a lapse of eighteen months (not so clearly stated in the Japanese as in the English text), and pledged most-favored-nation treatment. As noted, Abe had previously gone out of his way to consult the opinion of lead-ing daimyō who were not formally entitled to sit in the Senior

Council. Now, after Perry's first visit in 1853, he requested advice from all of the daimyō, the shogun's direct retainers, and the leading scholars, an act which has invariably been interpreted as an admission of the government's weakness. The move was unprecedented, but so was the combination of Perry's request and the display of power. Abe's tactics should also be viewed as a response to a decade-old demand to base important decisions on open discussion and recruit men of ability into the administration. Great numbers of those consulted would advise polite rejection or limited compliance, for few wanted to risk a war. But Tokugawa Nariaki, who thought war might serve to invigorate and purify the declining samurai spirit, publicly called for expulsion to encourage resistance and spur military reforms. A subtle politician, he later accepted the inevitable. He saw much worth in Western technology but was never reconciled to extensive trade or friendly relations.

Perry had not held out for a full-fledged commercial treaty, but Townsend Harris, who arrived in 1856 as the American consul-general, persisted against great odds and finally won such a treaty in 1858, the model for others with Britain, France, Holland and Russia. It provided for consular jurisdiction, a minister-resident in Edo, fixed and limited shipping and tariff charges, and religious freedom for Americans living in Japan. There was again wide solicitation of opinion, and as before most did not want to fight but fretted at the concessions. In 1858 the issue was more dangerous politically, for the fortunes of the Kyoto court had risen and the emperor refused to give prior confirmation. Beyond that, the actual presence in Japan of foreign envoys, sailors, merchants, and missionaries, although few in number and very restricted in movement, increased the potential for conflict and focused even more attention on the emperor as a unifying force in the face of Western pressures. Reverence for the emperor at this point had come to signify much more than gratitude for the unique Imperial House and pride in being Japanese. Somehow, he should participate in the political process. All factions, of course, believed themselves loyal to the emperor. The question was whether loyalty was best expressed by supporting seclusion or the opening of the country. Extreme *jōi* now meant rescind the treaties and expel the foreigners. The moderate *jōi* camp simply wished to hold the line against new concessions. Among advocates of opening the country (*kaikoku*), the extreme wing had expanded its ideas to include foreign trade as beneficial and increased foreign contact as useful and stimulating, mirroring Sakuma Shōzan's famous aphorism,

"Eastern morality and Western techniques." The moderate wing, however wanted Japan not to remake itself in the Western image but only to accept the treaties as a lesser evil than war and certain defeat with the likelihood of even more humiliating treaties. Limited contact would give Japan the financial and technological resources it needed to decide later how little or how much it wished to welcome the outside world. On both sides, then, the moderates were really not very far apart.

Fifteen years after Perry's intrusion, the shogun's rule ended. Even with the perspective of more than a century, politics during those years seem a bewildering maze in which internal and foreign issues are completely entangled and intrigues at Kyoto and in domain castle towns become as crucial as those in Edo. Undoubtedly, dealing with the West hastened the demise of the shogunate and undermined its legitimacy in the eyes of imperial loyalists. The shogunate, however, far from losing its nerve or playing the role of a discredited regime, came under the control of men who either attempted to reassert Tokugawa authority or seriously considered how to share power with the court and all of the daimyō. And politics would be played against a backdrop of continuing economic and social change. Throughout this period technology advanced, education expanded, and defenses improved. The shogunate's projects in manufacturing and shipbuilding were as elaborate as those in any of the domains. Foreign teachers and technicians were hired, perhaps as many as 200 in all. A few students went abroad, either secretly and in defiance of the ban on foreign travel (ended in 1866) or with the official blessing of their daimyō or the shogun. The shogunate enlarged its bureau for barbarian books into an institute (1857) offering instruction in foreign languages and techniques of diplomacy. Its doors were at first open only to Tokugawa retainers, but soon samurai from all over Japan were admitted. It was renamed the Institute for Enlightenment in 1863, a small but significant sign of changing attitudes toward barbarian learning. By then, the curriculum included physics, chemistry, mathematics, and even oil painting. The shogunate's Western scholars had begun the struggle to understand the history and social systems of the West and to master its science and technology. By 1866 some of the brightest of the Tokugawa overseas students, those who had studied law and politics in Holland, had returned to Japan and been put to work. They were respected, however, more for their language and technical skills than for their political opinions and were not necessarily employed to the best advantage. Later on, it would come as a most pleasant surprise to many of them that the early Meiji government valued their training and desired their services and thus was more enlightened than they had anticipated.

In spite of all of this, the shogunate did not lead Japan into a new era. To ambitious men in the outside domains and at the Kyoto court, its politics and institutions were bankrupt and losing authority. It was too much identified with the shame of yielding to the foreigners, even by those who welcomed the ideas and goods of the West. More to the point, by 1868, the shogunate had still not made much headway in solving purely domestic problems.

Its troubles had really begun in 1858 when the Senior Council had decided that the determined Townsend Harris must be given his treaty of commerce. The American's arguments were cogent: the British and French, then engaged in another war with China, might not be as generous as the United States if they made the first commercial treaties, and furthermore Japan might actually profit from international trade. Complicating the settlement with Harris was a domestic issue, which to many was even more important, the dispute over the shogunal succession. The shogun, who was without an heir, lay ill and dying. There were two candidates for his office, Hitotsubashi Keiki, a son of the daimyō of Mito and the choice of those who wanted an able man capable of providing intelligent leadership, and Tokugawa Iemochi, the boy daimyō of Wakayama, whose claim by heredity was slightly better but whose chief assets were youth and malleability. Among the leading daimyō, there was more agreement on Keiki than on the treaty. Tokugawa Nariaki naturally supported his son and denounced concessions to Harris as a further humiliation; but Ii Naosuke, the wealthy and powerful vassal daimyō of Hikone, who had never liked Nariaki for personal and political reasons, backed both Iemochi and the treaty. Ii was mildly in favor of the further opening of Japan but passionately dedicated to keeping the shogunate under the control of the vassal daimyō. Keiki, in spite of his ability, was therefore unacceptable to him.

As tension mounted, the chief senior councilor, now a vassal daimyō named Hotta Masayoshi (1810–64), undertook a mission to Kyoto to win approval of the Harris treaty. He soon found himself embroiled in more of a conflict than he had expected. The court indicated a preference for Keiki and little enthusiasm for the treaty. Hotta wavered, for he was closely associated with Ii. Finally, hoping to win approval for his foreign policy, he yielded on the succession

dispute. In the uproar which followed, Ii took over the shogunal administration as *tairō* (great councilor or regent), a title reserved for
emergencies. He then decided the shogunal succession in favor of
Iemochi and forced through acceptance of the treaty without waiting
for Kyoto's approval. He also inaugurated a purge which reached
into Edo, Kyoto, and several domains and resulted in arrests, confine-
ments, and executions.

Ii's autocratic and brutal actions turned many critics of the
shogunate into active enemies. Up to that time they had confined their
objections to the shogunate's personnel or certain policies but had
managed to remain loyal to existing institutions. But when the
shogunate disobeyed Kyoto and accepted the treaty, patriots in
disgust, shock, and hatred concluded that it was not worthy to lead
Japan in reform—and that it had compromised Japan's security. They
did not consider that Ii too honored the emperor or what might have
happened to Japan if he had not gone ahead with the treaty. For
these men, *sonnō* had reached its logical conclusion, overthrow of the
shogunate and rule by the emperor. They were not yet part of an
organized movement or widespread conspiracy; few of them had any
positive ideas about reforms, but they did resort to isolated acts of
violence. One young Chōshū samurai whose loyalty had held firm up
to this point, though severely tested, was Yoshida Shōin. No narrative
of these years is complete without reference to him, for he was a
student of Shōzan and teacher of many of the first generation of Meiji
statesmen. More important, he became a folk hero whose words,
deeds, and sincerity were said to embody a pure Japanese spirit. His
execution in 1859, when he was only twenty-nine, made him a martyr
to the loyalist cause. In one of those strange twists of history, his
name and example were subsequently used less by his students as they
matured and acquired power than by conservative opponents of the
Meiji government.

Shōin's views reflected, in large part, the advanced Mito teachings.
He was antiforeign but sufficiently aware of the value of Western
studies to try, without success, to board one of Perry's ships and
slip abroad. His love for Japan as the emperor's realm and desire
to learn more about the people and conditions of his country had
earlier prompted him to leave Chōshū (1851–52) without permission. He had little faith in the existing leadership and thought the
lower ranks would produce heroes, like himself, who would save
Japan by reforming the shogunate. He did not apparently envision

a radically new society, but he did suggest in his voluminous writings that Japan should and must change. He also argued that it was Japan's destiny—as well as a good defense measure—to expand onto the continent and create an East Asian empire. When he heard about Ii's acceptance of the Harris treaty, Shōin plotted to assassinate a shogunal emissary to Kyoto but the plan was discovered and he was sentenced to death. Many acts of violence followed, including the assassination of Ii Naosuke himself in 1860 by a band of samurai and commoners. In the meantime, Ii had won imperial approval of the Harris treaty and commissioned envoys to travel to Washington for ratification ceremonies.

The thought of Yokoi Shōnan was even more significant in the 1850s and 1860s than Shōin's, especially when expulsion proved impossible, and provides evidence that Japan's brand of Confucianism was not so great a barrier to innovation and modernization as was China's. Shōnan's reputation as a great teacher and scholar in the outside domain of Kumamoto spread all over Japan and his readers included wealthy farmers and merchants as well as samurai. From 1858 to 1863 he was a political adviser to the Tokugawa-related daimyō of Echizen, Matsudaira Shungaku, who was promoting reforms in the domain's education system and becoming an important figure in Edo politics. Samurai who were active in the restoration movement and even some of the shogunal officials were very much influenced by Shōnan's ideas on the promotion of wealth and power. He should perhaps be classified as a Jitsugaku scholar, which in his case meant a search for the truth of things or the reality behind things and stress on the practical implications of Confucian ideas. Shōnan stretched and strained the meaning of righteous government in Confucian theory to incorporate Western learning, to proceed from dependence upon scriptures and introspection to observation of actual conditions, and to find solutions to contemporary political and social problems. Shōnan went back to the legendary sage kings of China to find models for political leadership. They, he said, had studied nature, that is, the real world, and used their knowledge to improve the people's welfare. Furthermore, wisdom and ability, not birth, were what counted.

In the 1850s, Shōnan supported the shogunate's policy of opening Japan, for this he said was in accordance with universal principles. To enrich and strengthen Japan, it was necessary to give up antiquated ideas and learn from other nations. Shōnan did not ever fully comprehend or appreciate science, technology, and the Western industrial order, but he advocated as practical solutions the expansion of agricultural production and international trade, encouragement of domain industries, creation of a navy, and open discussion of reform proposals. In 1867 he also proposed the establishment of a national deliberative assembly of daimyō and samurai. One of his suggestions, to the daimyō of Echizen, subsequently acted upon in Edo, was that the shogunate end the system of alternate attendance to ease the financial strain on the daimyō and promote national unity.

The Failure of Reconciliation Attempts

Shōnan's ideas mirrored the moderate reform efforts made by shogunal officials, influential daimyō, and court nobles to patch up the differences between Kyoto and Edo after Ii's assassination. *Kōbu gattai,* or the union of civil and military officials (sometimes rendered as the union of court and camp), as this movement was called, like all the other catch-phrases and slogans of the period meant different things to its many advocates. The general intention was to promote harmony between Kyoto and the shogunate—and equally important between the vassal daimyō in control at Edo and the great outside and related daimyō—in order to deal with the West and domestic disorder.

The origins of the movement can be traced back to at least 1858 when a high-ranking court noble suggested to a shogunal representative that Edo and Kyoto symbolize their desire for reconciliation by a marriage between the shogun and the emperor's young half-sister, Kazunomiya. The emperor agreed to the marriage but made his consent conditional on a promise from the shogunate to stop hedging on the foreigners and get rid of them and their treaties. Only then would there be real unity in Japan. The new leaders of the shogunate, feeling more vulnerable after Ii's death, agreed to the conditions but made their promise as vague as possible. Expulsion would be carried out, perhaps in seven, eight, or ten years, but first Japan's military defenses must be improved. How could there be ejection of the foreigners before there was unity in Japan? Kazunomiya married the shogun in 1862 and the shogunate was forced to set a specific time for action against the foreigners: July, 1863. Few leaders, of whatever faction, however, expected a literal implementation of this promise. The domains supporting *kōbu gattai* were more interested in who would control the shogunate. Satsuma, for example, hoped that the outside daimyō would gain a permanent voice in the highest shogunal councils. Its aim was not to destroy the shogunate's power but to reallocate it so that the vassal daimyō should not have the exclusive right to determine national policy. More extreme than this were the reformers who enthusiastically promoted government by assembly, inspired by half-digested information about Western parliamentary practices and older Confucian notions of rule by discussion and ability. It seemed to them that participation by able daimyō—and able samurai—should be institutionalized to allow meetings at regular intervals of a national council in which the shogun would be first among peers, or perhaps even reduced in rank to daimyō.

Another practical question for the *kōbu gattai* party was the degree of deference the shogun should show toward the emperor as a sign of his loyalty. Twice (in 1863 and 1864) the shogun made trips to Kyoto, breaking a precedent of two centuries and risking some loss in prestige. Kyoto sent two missions to Edo (in 1862 and 1863), which resulted in several new appointments. Keiki became guardian of the shogun, and Matsudaira Shungaku of Echizen became in effect the shogunate's senior minister. Several outside and related daimyō were made advisers to the court and waited, but in vain, for inclusion in the Senior Council. The duty of alternate attendance was relaxed to one hundred days every three years.

It was at this point that the union of court and shogunate was severely tested by the foreign issue. As mentioned, the court under the influence of extreme antiforeign elements from Chōshū had maneuvered the shogunate into ordering the expulsion of foreigners in the summer of 1863. To Kyoto this meant using force if necessary. To Edo this meant holding the line against further intrusion and reliance upon negotiations with Western governments to postpone for several years the opening of additional ports and cities to foreign trade and residence, as promised in the treaties. Special shogunal missions to Europe were dealt with rather sympathetically and won postponements, though only to January 1, 1868, for the last of the sites, Hyogo (present-day Kobe) and Osaka. Otherwise the foreigners, instead of allowing themselves to be expelled, became more deeply entrenched. The foreign diplomats insisted on strict observance of the treaties and demanded stiff indemnities whenever legation property was destroyed or one of the foreign community was killed or injured. In the fall of 1863 a British squadron destroyed the shore batteries of Kagoshima, following an incident the previous year when enraged Satsuma retainers had cut down an Englishman for refusing to dismount from his horse and stand politely at the roadside as the procession of Shimazu Hisamitsu, father of the daimyō and a leader in the *kōbu gattai* movement, passed by. The British took action on their own when the shogunate seemed unable to force the domain to make a proper settlement—punishment of the murderers and payment of an indemnity to the victim's family.

In the meantime Chōshū had taken literally the expulsion order and fired on American and French ships passing through the Straits of Shimonoseki in July, 1863. Chōshū then proceeded to close the passageway. Within a year an allied expedition of British, French, Dutch, and American ships had also seen to Chōshū's punishment, though the Western ships took a good pounding in the process. The Western envoys in Japan, more and more aware of the reviving influence of the court, insisted on and got in 1865 the emperor's sanction for the treaties. This came after they had gone to Hyogo with a fleet of five ships. In 1866 the shogunate agreed to a general tariff convention, which fixed import and export duties at a very low rate of approximately five percent of the product's value. In particular, the British and French ministers to Japan, respectively Sir Harry Parkes and Léon Roches, closely guarded their country's treaty rights. Both tried to divine the future direction of Japanese politics, with Roches leaning to the side of the shogunate, and Parkes, who was kept well informed by a brilliant legation staff, placing more and more faith in Kyoto, Satsuma, and Chōshū. These two outside domains had abandoned the explusion policy as naïve after the Western displays of military power at Kagoshima and Shimonoseki. Furthermore, they now seemed more progressive and better able to advance the cause of British trade.

In the early 1860s Satsuma and Chōshū had been jealous and suspicious of each other and vied for the favor of Kyoto. The political position of each shifted frequently according to which faction currently was in power within the domain. In general, Satsuma, under Shimazu Hisamitsu, was more successful in politics at Kyoto and Edo. Its line was softer and more in tune with that of moderates from other domains. Chōshū had an able bureaucracy but did not have an outstanding daimyō to help its cause. Its *sonnō* behavior in 1862–63 was so excessive that even the emperor grew alarmed and named the domain an enemy. At his bidding, Chōshū troops were driven out of Kyoto in 1863 by a combined force from Satsuma and the Tokugawa-related domain of Aizu, then repulsed again a year later when they attempted a counterattack. To Chōshū extremists this was total humiliation for a domain which had produced Yoshida Shōin and regarded itself as motivated by the purest loyalty to the emperor. A group of tough, realistic bureaucrats, deeply concerned by the setbacks in Kyoto and the Shimonoseki bombardment, began plotting to gain control of domain policy. Many of them were young progressives from the lower and middle samurai ranks.

The shogunate now made things worse for Chōshū by sending a punitive expedition in late 1864—in the emperor's name, of course. Chōshū managed, after a little fighting, to secure a truce on moderate terms, but there were serious aftereffects. Civil war broke out in the domain in 1865, and the progressives, many of whom had been employed in defense projects, had the edge. They purchased Western rifles; moreover, they ignored both old methods of warfare and class divisions in organizing several auxiliary militia units of mixed samurai and peasant soldiers. The peasant volunteers may have been more interested in the status they acquired as soldiers than in the politics of their commanders, but they were trained in drill formation and the use of modern weapons, and fought well. A new faction came into power in Chōshū, including many who would soon be involved in the Meiji Restoration. They continued publicly to mouth the old slogans of "revere the emperor" and "expel the barbarian" in order to undermine the shogunate, but in fact had made up their minds to pursue policies of wealth and power based upon improved knowledge of the outside world.

By this time Tokugawa officials had come to realize that the shogunate's structure must be reorganized if their rule was to continue. Some advocated that the emperor be designated as head of state and the Senior Council be replaced by a representative assembly of daimyō directly under the shogun. One or two of this group even suggested that the shogun resign his office for an important but lesser role in a new national administration. A second group wished to create a unified state by destroying the domains. The latter faction won out and the shogunate undertook several measures to reassert its authority, including an attempt to reestablish a strict *sankin kōtai* system. It also decided in early 1865 to launch a second expedition against Chōshū, not only to unseat the domain's leaders but also as a means of centralizing the shogunate's power.

However, there was no military action till August, 1866, since the related and vassal daimyō were slow in supplying their quotas of troops. During this time Satsuma and many other domains had become as concerned as Chōshū about the shogunate's ultimate intentions. Danger to one was an obvious threat to them all. For years intermediaries from Tosa and elsewhere had been trying to reconcile Satsuma and Chōshū so that the two could more effectively concentrate their wealth and energies on national questions. This time the Tosa men were successful. By the time the fighting began, the two domains had concluded a secret alliance through meetings of their representatives in Kyoto. Kido Kōin for Chōshū and Saigō Takamori and Ōkubo Toshimichi for Satsuma agreed in March, 1866, that Satsuma would mediate with the emperor for Chōshū's reinstatement and under extreme conditions give military aid. They pledged to work together in the future for the restoration of the emperor but did not specify whether this meant the military overthrow and destruction of the shogunate.

The second expedition against Chōshū went badly for the shogunate. Although it had imported Western guns and ships and solicited foreign military advice, its troops were outfought by the Chōshū militia units. When Iemochi unexpectedly died in August at Osaka, Keiki at last became shogun in his own right (in January, 1867 with the reign name Yoshinobu) and called off the expedition on the pretext of mourning for his predecessor. With a great deal of advice from the French minister, the new shogun outlined a program to promote trade and tap commercial wealth through regular taxes on merchants, negotiate foreign loans, set up specialized departments in the national government, recruit men of ability, adopt new codes and regulations, and receive foreign envoys with Western-style etiquette. Construction was continued on an elaborate arsenal and dockyard at Yokosuka. French and British military advisers were hired. Keiki also sent one of his younger brothers to Paris in 1867 to attend the international exposition and remain for study and travel.

Keiki apparently had in mind political and economic reforms of a fairly comprehensive nature. There had been riots in Edo in 1866, a sad reminder of the high prices of food and commodities, and the treaty powers were pressing hard for the opening of Hyogo and Osaka on schedule. But many of the daimyō and upper samurai were beginning to lose interest in reform of the shogunate, even with Keiki at the helm. His views seemed to have hardened over the years as guardian of Iemochi, and there was little role for the outside domains in his proposals. And very little too for the Kyoto court, where there was now a new emperor. Kōmei's sudden and mysterious death early in 1867, while recovering from smallpox, removed a major source of antiforeignism and was followed by the naming of a fifteen-year-old youth as his successor. This was Mutsuhito, the future Emperor Meiji. Keiki's reforms were scarcely under way when Satsuma and Chōshū, with allies among the court nobles, began to plot his overthrow.

The Meiji Restoration

By the summer of 1867 the loyalist reformers in Satsuma and Chōshū were quite certain that whatever program the shogunate adopted would not go fast or far enough to meet Japan's needs or their own ambitions. A change of government was imperative, and they were ready to resort to military force to achieve it. By November their plans were well advanced. Through connections in Kyoto the conspirators obtained decrees exonerating Chōshū and authorizing loyal daimyō to launch a punitive expedition against the shogun. It is quite possible that the documents were taken secretly from the court without ever having been submitted to the young emperor. They were in large part the handiwork of the court noble Iwakura Tomomi, a consummate politician who had shifted to an extreme *sonnō* position while under house arrest for political errors in 1863–67. During that time he had been secretly in touch with friends at the court and many of the samurai reformers, particularly Ōkubo Toshimichi. He had come under the influence of scholars in Confucian studies and National Learning who directed his attention to the Nara period and still further back in history to the lore surrounding the founding of the empire in 660 B.C. They urged a restoration in reality, not in name, and intimated that the new leaders should think of themselves as creators on the same order as those who originally established the Japanese state.

Keiki learned of the plot, and in November voluntarily offered to resign first his duties and then his title. The surprised Kyoto court was not prepared to assume direct rule and asked him to remain in power until a council of daimyō could be assembled. Keiki's decision, the final motives for which are still unclear, was probably made with the expectation that he would stay on at a high level in whatever new political settlement was adopted. Satsuma, Chōshū, and their allies were thrown off balance temporarily by Keiki's petition but then decided to go ahead with their own plans. On January 3, 1868, in the early morning hours the transfer was easily and swiftly made when troops from the four related and outside domains of Satsuma, Aki, Owari, and Echizen, under the command of Saigō, replaced the Tokugawa guards at the gates of the imperial palace. Chōshū troops were just outside Kyoto but could not yet approach the palace. Tosa did not at first participate. The outside daimyō of Hizen was another who hesitated, much to the disgust of domain loyalists. That same day, the emperor announced his acceptance of the shogun's resignation and decreed the restoration of imperial rule. Other crucial decisions were to deprive the shogun of his title, drastically reduce his lands, abolish court offices by which high Kyoto nobles had controlled the emperor after the Nara period, and designate new national political posts. Promises were made to consult the opinions of men of talent, without regard to rank or origin, and to end the distress of the people as they underwent "renewal in all things." In effect, the restoration of virtuous government of the distant past was linked to the rejection of evil customs of the recent past. The events of the day amounted to the abolition of the shogunate and the establishment of a new government with the emperor as the source of authority and ultimate power but not the actual ruler.

Keiki, startled at the severity of the measures, was persuaded by loyal retainers and vassal daimyō to put up a fight. The civil war which resulted dragged on for over a year, until the last of the Tokugawa holdouts surrendered in the northern island of Hokkaido. The outcome, however, had been fairly clear ever since February, 1868, when 120,000 men had clashed in battle not far from Kyoto and the new government had won. This was soon followed by the peaceful surrender of Edo Castle and Keiki's decision to refrain from encouraging further resistance. In some parts of Japan, there were large-scale troop movements and considerable loss of life. The Japanese did pay a price in blood for the Meiji Restoration, although in extremes of violence and terror it was not the counterpart of the French, Russian, or Chinese revolutions or the American Civil War.

Just how much of a turning point was the seizure of political power by new leaders in January, 1868? Was it the necessary prelude to Japan's modern transformation, however limited the original motives may have been? It has become conventional to distinguish between the Restoration coup (ōsei fukko) and the subsequent Renovation (Meiji ishin) and further to point out that those who cooperated to destroy the shogunate did not necessarily envision a totally new government and society. Most of the samurai and daimyō who fought in the Restoration battles anticipated little more than a transfer of authority to the Kyoto court. They were confident that loyalists like Saigō would set things right and did not expect to lose their status or domains. Yet within three or four years, the new government had embarked upon a program of such basic change that Japan would become by the turn of the century a full-fledged nation state in the initial throes of an industrial revolution. The reforms came faster and were far more thorough than anything previously attempted by the shogunal or domain governments. The Meiji restorationists were not social theorists and did not have a master plan, but they did have a general idea of what they wanted: political unity, national wealth, secure defenses, and equality with the Western world. They were heir to a set of specific proposals dating back to the debates of the 1850s and 1860s on the abolition of the domains, military training for commoners, open discussion, government by council, improved education, international trade, and machine technology. They accepted change as essential, in some cases even as a positive good rather than a necessary evil. There was, of course, much confusion and hesitation at first, but while struggling to hold power and organize a new government with wide support, the Meiji leaders also tried to identify Japan's needs, determine priorities, and work out an integrated program of reform. They had the will and ability to refine abstract notions into concrete measures. They were essentially realistic, pragmatic men who were willing to make quick decisions, and who were often quite ruthless despite all the Confucian rhetoric about harmony. A constant spur to their actions was fear of a predatory West, but much of what they did went beyond the requirements of self-defense. There is some evidence (more obvious by the early 1870s) that they wished to fit their measures into a new world view and give transcendent meaning to what they were doing, to combine power with enlightenment. The Western historical experience was a rich source of new ideas, and the Meiji assessment of progress was at first based on recent American and European accomplishments. In that sense, Westernization as both a profound and a superficial process had begun but was transmuted along the way into modernization as Japan created out of tradition and change its own version of an industrial society with a new assortment of satisfactions, tensions, and dilemmas.

As a group, the Meiji leaders did not represent the rise of a new class to power. Instead, it was secondary elements within the old ruling elite which took over, a disaffected, alienated wing—in short, the least representative of the old class. They were not landed gentry but products of castle towns and in a few cases of Kyoto mansions. Most of them came from the middle and lower ranks of the samurai in the outside domains of southwestern Japan, specifically Satsuma, Chōshū, Tosa, and Hizen during the first six years and later mainly Satsuma and Chōshū. They had been men of privilege and learning if not of comfortable incomes. With few exceptions, they had made their way up in domain or court politics by utilizing every opportunity to master administrative skills or acquire Western learning, whether from books, foreign teachers, or study and travel abroad. They made allies whenever they could of sympathetic members of the upper samurai ranks and the commoner elites—wealthy farmers, rural merchants, village leaders, or urban financial houses—but for political and not ideological ends. Some of the original leaders of the Restoration remained firmly in power until their deaths, providing continuity in leadership while undergoing changes in outlook; some grew uneasy about tactics and timing but approved of the basic aims of the reforms; and some were horrified, for liberal and conservative reasons, at the course Japan was taking and either dropped out or were forced out.

The Meiji Restoration has an existence in the popular and intellectual mind, quite apart from the actual events, motives, and results. Such an image is as important in a people's history as a meticulously detailed narrative of events which purports to reconstruct the past as it really was or an analysis of underlying forces. Present views of the Restoration have been colored by Japan's mixed record of great power status, war, defeat, and humiliation—but also by magnificent recovery. Scholarly interpretations are as varied as those made of revolutions and major upheavals in other parts of the world: a revolution from above, a movement from below, an abortive bourgeois-democratic revolution, a revolutionary restoration, and a limited conservative revolution. The Meiji leaders have been called everything from modernizing bureaucrats to despotic oligarchs. There has been sharp controversy over the degree of continuity and discontinuity with the past.

To some, continuity means lingering feudal remnants; the Meiji leaders were militarist, reactionary, and absolutist. Their program of artificially accelerated change encountered weak democratic forces and distorted the "normal process" of liberal modernization, thus inevitably producing a fascist rather than a free society. It was they who initiated, whether consciously or not, the politics of suppression at home and aggression abroad. Skeptics reply that such judgments stem from formulas based entirely upon European history and not fully applicable to Japan in spite of its feudal inheritance. Furthermore, liberal modern societies have also engaged in imperialist expansion. Continuity signifies that the Meiji leadership began with a set of positive preconditions for modern economic growth and nation-building. They had Western experience to draw from but no set formula or precise model of change. They began to build their state and refashion society with immense skill and imagination, breaking with the past more often than they utilized it. What they did was an extraordinary achievement. Finally, by continuity and evolution, some mean Japan's rational, orderly response to the West and internal problems. The new leaders did not kill the shogun. There were no complete disinheritance of the old elite, no mass jailings, few executions of political and class enemies, little violent upheaval. To others, this is the heart of Japan's subsequent tragedy. Gradualism was a mistaken policy. The leaders did not go far enough (and could not because of their class origins) in destroying the old (reactionary) conditions of peasant life and did not therefore undertake a true revolution or work for social justice. The union of reactionary landlords and industrialists under an authoritarian bureaucracy would prevent the emergence of an industrial democracy. To use the language of our own time, there was neither a total destruction of the system nor a widespread belief that there should be.

Much of the criticism is not unlike talk about the unfinished business of the American Revolution or the contribution of the Civil War and Reconstruction to the dilemmas of modern America. The Japanese public mood was ambivalent during the centennial year of the Meiji Restoration, 1967–68. There was an uncertain mixture of pride and regret. Many of the events of the Restoration years were forgotten, and many of the statesmen only dimly or inaccurately remembered. Scholars held seminars and conferences on the problems of modernization. Radical historians accused the government of faking history with its plans for an official celebration and of glorifying absolutism and imperialist expansion. However, exhibitions of memorabilia and documents drew large crowds. Popular television dramas and documentaries recreated the exploits and great moments of the Restoration years. A new statue of the Emperor Meiji was unveiled. The grandsons of the Meiji leaders gathered to reminisce about their illustrious forebears. A school for flower arrangement announced that it had kept pace with the changes symbolized by the Restoration. But somehow all of this did not express the same depths of emotion as parades in Red Square on the fiftieth anniversary of the Russian Revolution, or the celebrations of Bastille Day, July the Fourth, and the Chinese Double Tenth.

However, dictionary and partisan definitions aside as to the nature of modernization and true revolution, Japan did begin to undergo a profound transformation. There was considerable disruption and disorientation. The populace had to be taught that the emperor was a symbol of continuity and tradition. There was innovation from above, as the leaders pushed and prodded Japan in the direction of radical change, but the nation was not unwilling or unable to follow or, sometimes, to go its own way. The people often were better prepared to take the initiative than the leadership was willing to concede. Although agrarian riots continued, soon to be joined by samurai protest, many others in the cities, towns, and countryside were enthusiastic about the reforms in the belief that better times were coming and great things would be accomplished. Some of the change was shattering; some of it was taken in stride; and some was welcomed. To those who lived through the 1870s, it was a dizzying, exhilarating, disturbing time.

The Early Meiji Changes

Let us turn now from ideas about the Restoration and its significance to the events themselves. One of the first acts of the new Meiji government was to inform the foreign powers that it would honor the shogunate's treaty obligations. An announcement appeared on public notice boards that henceforth Japan would be a member of the world community and act in accordance with the principles of international law. Men who had come to power by manipulating the slogan of *sonnō-jōi* now linked the emperor's rule to an open country. Later that year, the era name was officially changed to Meiji (enlightened government), and plans were made to transfer the emperor's permanent residence from Kyoto to Edo, now renamed Tokyo. For economic and strategic reasons, Tokyo was considered superior to Kyoto. Moreover, a change in the site of the capital would dramatize the change in government. In the meantime, the leaders had stated their aims in a very general way through the emperor's Five Article Oath of April 6, 1868—better known as the Charter Oath. It would before long take on the character of a sacred document and be as important for what was read into it—parliamentary government, a modern economy and education, social leveling—as for its immediate purpose, which was to win broad support for the government and encourage financial contributions. The oath was made to the emperor's ancestors and read to an assembly of court nobles, daimyō, and samurai officials, who then pledged in writing to support it. It included promises to convoke an assembly and decide all matters by open discussion, strengthen finances, improve the general welfare, end the antiquated laws and evil customs of the past, and search for knowledge all over the world. Its language echoed the sentiments of many late Tokugawa debates and memorials. Implicit in it was criticism of the arbitrariness and narrow political base of the shogunate. But the promise to consult public opinion meant little more than listening to the views of well-informed samurai and leading commoners.

The new leaders had many things to do all at once but tended to concentrate on consolidation of their political power and national unification. Here perhaps Tokugawa experience and samurai political consciousness made the task both obvious and somewhat easier than social and economic change. Moreover, most of the leaders agreed that little else could be done until a unified nation had been forged. Political centralization entailed the creation of a national bureaucracy centering on the emperor, the extension of direct rule into the former Tokugawa territories and the domains of the daimyō, and the transfer of loyalty from village and domain to the national government.

The Meiji leaders operated through a Council of State (*Dajōkan*), which they reorganized several times in the first few years while groping for the most effective ways to channel power. They were very much interested in the question of an ideal and permanent structure but for the moment had to experiment. By 1871 the Council of State had been divided into a central board, a prestigious and powerful body of imperial advisers who made national policy; an administrative section composed of heads of the various executive departments or ministries; and a deliberative assembly which discussed but did not make laws. This was a reflection of interest in the theory of checks and balances and separation of powers. The ministries of the early Meiji bureaucracy were functional, organized to handle specialized tasks, such as finance, foreign relations, military affairs, or education, and subdivided into numerous boards and bureaus. The junior men, most of whom were recruited from favored key domains or carried over from shogunal employment, could be called professionals. They had administrative skills and Western learning, and they followed routine office procedures. Frequently, they had more radical ideas than their seniors and wielded much influence. The "legislative" division, one of a series of early experiments in deliberative assemblies, was little more than an advisory body of government appointees, but it did just barely keep the promise of the Five Article Oath. It was indirectly representative of domain opinion in that the members tended to be local leaders. During the first four years there was considerable reshuffling of jobs and a turnover in personnel as samurai replaced the daimyō and court nobles in the highest and most important posts. Commoners also became eligible to serve in government. Instead of a political system dominated by one man or a few, there was group leadership, an emphasis on consensus, and much informal maneuvering. It was not, however, a faceless bureaucracy. The political partnership, for example, of Iwakura, Ōkubo, and Kido and their respective factions was crucial.

Within four years these men had brought most of Japan directly under the control of the central bureaucracy in Tokyo. In 1868–69, as troops from loyalist domains pushed back the shogunal forces, former Tokugawa lands were divided into prefectures and officials were appointed to supervise them. In March, 1869, the daimyō of Satsuma, Chōshū, Tosa, and Hizen, under the influence of former samurai retainers who were now with the central government, agreed to the voluntary return of their land and census registers to the emperor. By this gesture, they made the point that all of the land and the people in Japan fell under the emperor's jurisdiction. Their cooperation was secured when they were confirmed in their hereditary positions in the domains but with the new title of governor. Also they were to receive a handsome salary while the central government assumed the burden of administrative expenses and annual samurai stipends. A few months later, all daimyō who had not followed suit were ordered to surrender their registers. Then in August, 1871, after taking care to sound out opinion in key domains and organize a ten-thousand-man imperial guard with contingents from Satsuma,

Chōshū, and Tosa, the emperor announced the abolition of the domains and the establishment of prefectures. In 1868 the shogunate had been destroyed; now, the domains. It was feared there would be bloodshed, but the samurai did not yet mount a serious protest. Barriers between the domains were to be taken down; daimyō were to move to Tokyo; and prefectural governors were to be appointed by the central government without regard to their region of birth or rank. Several years were necessary to standardize perfectural administration and organize the local police, but the imperial government had begun, in fact as well as name, to rule the whole of Japan.

At the same time there were major economic and social reforms. Political unification was hardly possible without dismantling the Tokugawa class system; economic growth, in turn, required a new social and political framework. Ultimately, all of these measures depended upon a climate of opinion conducive to fundamental change. Quite apart from the question of economic growth, the new government was desperate for revenues to pay off the Tokugawa and domain debts and finance the numerous projects of its steadily expanding bureaucracy: harbor improvements and the erection of lighthouses (undertaken at the insistence of the foreigners), imports of machinery, construction of schools, studies of overseas students, salaries of foreign teachers and advisers, diplomatic and consular establishments, a modern army and navy, a railroad, and a telegraph network. The chief sources of income were irregular. Other than taxes on the confiscated Tokugawa lands, there were contributions and loans from wealthy peasants and a handful of rich urban merchants, customs duties (limited, however, by treaty regulations), and two foreign loans. The latter were reluctantly negotiated and quickly repaid, for the Meiji leaders were apparently fearful of political interference if they relied too heavily upon foreign capital.

For proper budgeting and financing, the government needed a dependable annual tax revenue. After several years of discussion and studies of foreign practice, a series of land and tax laws was enacted, 1871–73. These laws confirmed existing trends and legalized private ownership in order to facilitate taxation. Title deeds were issued to those who could prove ownership, and values of rice land were computed at what was considered to be a fair market price. The yearly tax was set at three percent of the land value (reduced to two and a half percent in 1877) and was to be paid in cash, in contrast to the Tokugawa practice of taking a fixed proportion in kind of the assessed output of the land. Agricultural production in Japan was already very high, and landowners, as a class, probably paid no more than before 1868. The estimate is that from 60 to 80 percent of the Meiji government's revenues in the first two decades came from this land tax. The reforms assisted the transfer of capital and savings from the former Tokugawa aristocracy, which had tended to spend mainly on goods and services, to a government which channeled the wealth into investment and production and encouraged private capital to do the same. But there was no land reform. The new laws did nothing to relieve the problem of tenancy, or the difficulties of small farmers. In fact, they probably worsened conditions by making it easier for landowners to threaten foreclosure. There were more agrarian riots after the Restoration than before. Some could be attributed to the same old reasons: high rents, taxes, and interest rates, but others grew out of new grievances: the payment of taxes in money, military conscription, tuition charges for compulsory education, or the adoption of the solar calendar. In the abstract, agriculture and the wealthy farmers could afford to pay for the government's initiation of industrialization and still have surplus left for private investments, but vast numbers of peasants remained in poverty.

Closely related to these land and tax reforms was a series of measures adopted from 1869 to 1873 with the intention of freeing the Japanese for more productive pursuits and correcting the social abuses of the past. All persons were to have the right to choose their occupations and places of residence. They were entitled to surnames. Farmers could decide which crops they wished to plant. The Tokugawa class divisions of warrior, farmer, artisan, and merchant were abolished (1869–71), and the Eta and *hinin* (untouchables and outcastes) were elevated in status. Technically, all Japanese were equal before an impersonal, impartial law, but of course old prejudices and sensitivities to status continued. The government perpetuated this by creating the three new divisions of *kazoku* (peers or nobility: former daimyō and former court nobles); *shizoku* (gentry: most of the former samurai families); and *heimin* (commoners: everybody else from foot soldiers to untouchables). These designations were mainly nominal, however, and carried few privileges. And soon the samurai would lose their hereditary incomes and exclusive claim to the military function, just as they had already lost their monopoly on government posts.

In continuation of its attack on social privilege, but with an even deeper interest in reducing unproductive financial obligations, the government worked out a voluntary commutation scheme in 1873 by which former samurai and daimyō could commute their pensions and allowances into lump settlements and interest-bearing bonds. This was made compulsory in August, 1876. There were very few officials at this point who defended the right of the old samurai class to permanent support, but many did think the settlement was unduly harsh, bordering even on confiscation of private property. On the whole the daimyō managed very well with their capital sums and bonds. But for the lower ranks it was a case of finding new kinds of work or of starvation. To them, the government was ruthless and a cruel disappointment. Further proof, if needed, of the government's lack of sympathy was the ban in 1876 on the wearing of the two swords in public. This was a tremendous affront to the samurai sense of honor and self-importance.

In fact, there were many new opportunities for former samurai as bureaucrats, teachers, army officers, police officials, journalists, scholars, or colonists in Hokkaido, occupations closely related to their education and previous status, and further opportunities, if they could stomach the thought or had the talent, as bankers and businessmen. This absorbed a certain amount of the discontent. A few managed to acquire greater fortunes and personal power than would have been possible under the Tokugawa, but many more floundered around unable even to profit from the government's rehabilitation schemes. Such men were obviously a prime source of discontent, and by the mid-1870s either they were involved in assassination plots and uprisings or they joined political associations.

The internal dissent very much disturbed the Meiji leaders, but they went ahead as rapidly as they dared and used a substantial portion of their revenues for public works projects and industrial ventures. Major accomplishments of the early 1870s were cable connections with East Asia; telegraph lines linking Tokyo, Yokohama, Osaka, and Nagasaki; and rail transportation between Tokyo and Yokohama. By 1880 there were still only 150 miles of railways, but their construction furthered the initial modest spurts of economic growth by stimulating large capital outlays, iron manufactures, and improved technical education, especially in engineering. The government also sponsored other projects which required more skill and capital than private investors could then marshal, for example, shipyards, munitions, mining, and textiles. It set up a few model factories and agricultural experiment stations, not so much to make great profits as to show the way, for it was also anxious to encourage private individuals to assume these burdens and initiate new enterprises as quickly as possible. It also contributed as much, if not more, to economic growth by establishing a rational political order and praising investment in modern enterprise as honorable and patriotic.

Security and national independence were a constant concern of the early Meiji leaders but not an obsession. For men who had come to power by playing upon fears and dislike of the Western barbarian, they showed remarkable restraint in planning Japan's modern military establishment. The foreign threat was very real to them, but not sufficient cause to build a military state. Their initial discussions on security revealed a wide range of opinion about the size, training, and recruitment of a national army. Although peasants in Chōshū had proven their fighting mettle in the 1860s, there was still a strong conviction that only samurai should be soldiers. Some argued for an officer corps of samurai and an enlisted force of commoners, while others insisted on recruitment and promotion regardless of class. In 1870–71 studies were made of the relative merits of the Prussian and French military systems and conscription laws, and in 1872 a French military mission arrived to help train the army. The final decision, as announced in the Conscription Act of January, 1873, was to create a relatively small standing army with large reserves by recruiting able-bodied males from the age of twenty for three years of active duty and four years in the first and second reserves. Exemptions were provided for students, government officials, heirs and heads of households, those who wished to and could pay a substitute fee in money. Criminals were not eligible. All men between the ages of seventeen and forty were to be organized into militia units.

This law was largely the work of Yamagata Aritomo of Chōshū and his staff in the Army Ministry, and their prime considerations had been the defense of Japan against external aggression (Russia at that time being the chief worry), preparation against future emergencies, and the maintenance of internal order. For financial reasons, they applied the law at first only to a limited area and set as their goal a modest-sized peacetime standing army of approximately 32,000 men. Conscripts were given training in modern weapons and drill formation. A military academy modeled upon St. Cyr was opened for the training of junior officers, and a select few were sent abroad to study in European military schools. Army duty was not at first welcomed with great joy or patriotic fervor by the commoners, but in the long run conscription would assist enormously in social leveling, the education of the peasants, and the spread of emperor-centered nationalism. Much attention was also given to the building of a modern navy. British advisers were hired, cadets were sent to the British and American naval academies, and ships of the most advanced military design were purchased abroad; but the navy would remain subordinate to the army in over-all military planning until the 1890s.

Although the main motive in organizing the early Meiji army was the defense of Japan, rather than imperialist expansion in East Asia, the Council of State was very sensitive to boundary questions. A combination of force, Western-style diplomacy, and colonization was used to secure control over territory considered to be historically and legitimately Japanese. Government officials were alert to the usefulness and hypocrisies of Western international law, and very early the Foreign Ministry made a point of mastering the new diplomatic etiquette and sending ministers and consuls to the major treaty countries. In 1870–71 an extensive ten-year program was adopted for the colonization of Hokkaido, with the dual purpose of checking Russia and developing natural resources. In 1872 the Ryukyu Islands were taken over from Satsuma and incorporated into Japan. The Manchu court, accustomed to receiving tribute from the islands, objected, as did many of the islanders, but in a series of complicated negotiations stretching over ten years and a resort to force in 1874 the Japanese vindicated their claim. In the meantime they were in actual possession of the Ryukyus, which they reorganized into a prefecture. With little protest from the Western powers, Japan annexed the Bonin Islands in 1875, placing them under the government of the district of Tokyo. That same year, in a treaty with Russia, it gave up its claims to southern Sakhalin in return for control of all of the Kurile Islands. If the government harbored imperialist ambitions, they were modest by comparison with Western practices in East Asia and the claims of the vast though crumbling Manchu Empire. In these first years of the Meiji state, security was defined as the defense of the frontiers and not as international power politics or expansion abroad. Dissent was loud but would not seriously influence foreign policy until the 1890s.

Education and the Search for Enlightenment

Mass education was another priority of the Meiji leaders, who saw it as vital to the transformation of Japan. A trained and well-informed citizenry would make Japan secure and wealthy, certainly as much as, if not more than, political solidarity and a modern army. The Education Act of 1872 outlined an ambitious scheme of education from the elementary through intermediate and higher levels. "Learning is the key to success in life," read the very liberal preamble to the law. "There shall, in the future, be no village with an illiterate family, and no family with an illiterate person." All Japanese children, male and female, commoners and former samurai, were to receive a minimum of four years of compulsory elementary education. This was to be financed through tuition and local funds, a provision which considerably dampened enthusiasm for the law. Some very poor communities could manage only with subsidies. Although there were many practical problems to solve, including teacher training, the compilation of textbooks, and the acquisition of buildings and classroom equipment, the Japanese made good progress toward their goal within the next decade. World history and geography, sciences, and foreign languages were introduced into the curriculum. Numerous elementary schools, although only half of the number promised, were constructed. Higher technical schools were founded, and in 1877 Tokyo Imperial University opened its doors. To skeptical conservatives it seemed as though Japanese history and traditional ethics were being neglected, and further reforms in curriculum, financing, and administration would follow after 1879, culminating by the end of the Meiji period in six years of compulsory, tax-supported education.

Adoption of the mass literacy program provoked much discussion, both in and out of the government, about the ultimate meaning of the new education for the individual and the state. The preamble to the 1872 law said that education was to build character, develop the mind, and cultivate talents. Among the numerous private essays on the subject were the writings of Fukuzawa Yukichi, founder of Keiō Academy (the future Keiō University), confidant of many government officials, and subsequently a prominent journalist. His basic premise, which reflected his reading in the primers of British and French liberalism and also observations made during trips to the United States and Europe in the 1860s, was that politics and government were only a small part of human affairs. The driving force of the new Japan must be independent, self-reliant individuals who regarded themselves as citizens rather than subjects and whose learning embraced science, logic, and mathematics. Thinking for oneself and acting on ones own initiative were a measure of patriotism. But this was the younger Fukuzawa speaking. Later on he would place more emphasis on state power and the requirements of national defense than on individual liberty and popular rights.

Early Meiji Japan's modern education also included studies abroad. A few students went to the United States or Europe on their own, but many more were sponsored by the government. After some bad experiences, official regulations were revised in 1872–73 to ensure that mature students, those who could presumably profit both themselves and Japan, would be selected. The minimum age was set at eighteen, there was to be no change in the subject of specialization without the consent of the Education Ministry, and all scholarship recipients were to conduct themselves as loyal Japanese while abroad. These young men returned to responsible positions, good incomes, and high status. By the end of the century the need to send students to foreign preparatory schools or universities had considerably diminished, for Japan had made such remarkable strides that it could educate the bulk of its scientists, engineers, technicians, and professional men at home.

During these years the central and local governments employed thousands of foreign advisers, teachers, and workers. Some of the foreign helpers were given positions of considerable importance, and as a group they did much to build the railroads, hospitals, schools, industry, and modern administration of Meiji Japan. They assisted in the colonization of Hokkaido, the compilation of law codes, and the writing of the Meiji Constitution. They contributed to Japan's advances in agriculture, medicine, and science. They even encouraged the Japanese to reverence and preserve their traditional arts and crafts. Their function, however, was limited to offering expert advice; the Japanese retained at all times full control of final decisions and policy. The government was willing to divert substantial funds from its tax revenues into high salaries for these advisers but simultaneously arranged for young Japanese to acquire the education necessary to assume such roles so that these foreigners could be dispensed with.

The Japanese spoke proudly and sometimes humorously of the

1870s as a time of *bummei kaika* (civilization and enlightenment). The slogan was used by the government, intellectuals, and the populace as a whole. Amidst the turmoil and dislocation there were great hopes for a better life. The Japanese saw themselves as throwing out all the evil things of the past along with the Tokugawa system of rule. They were joining the mainstream of world history and building a new nation which would take its place on a level of equality with the most advanced nations. Young intellectuals read Montesquieu, Rousseau, Spencer, J. S. Mill, Bentham, Guizot, and Buckle in translation or in English and French. They were interested in Western social theory, economic thought, natural sciences, literature and art, and in the laws of history, and did not always ask whether the new ideas were already outmoded in their original setting let alone applicable to Japan. Most intoxicating of all was the idea of progress, the notion that all mankind was developing through several stages of culture and history from primitive beginnings to a complex and fully enlightened utopia. Pragmatists were inclined to break the old molds anyway, but the doctrine of progress greatly eased the psychological tensions of departing from hallowed tradition.

Some intellectuals joined societies of like-minded men to educate each other and reach the literate public. By far the most famous of these groups was the Meirokusha (Meiji Six Society), founded in 1873, the sixth year of the Meiji era. It lasted about a year and a half, from 1873 to 1875, held an average of two meetings a month, sponsored a few lectures, and published a journal of limited circulation in which such issues as the function of scholars, reform of the Japanese language, representative assemblies, and freedom of conscience were debated. Like the government, the Meirokusha hoped to spread cultural enlightenment and destroy ignorance so that Japan could become truly progressive. Most of the members were bureaucrats, but they tried to walk the delicate line between enthusiastic support of official policies and detached criticism of errors. When censorship laws were passed in 1875, the society voted to disband rather than compromise its position.

All manner of practical pursuits and ludicrous fads were followed in the name of *bummei kaika*. "New," "enlightened," "civilized," "fashionable," and "Western" merged in an indiscriminate whirl. It was "enlightened" to promote industry and commerce, to agitate for popular rights, to study science and mathematics, to publish newspapers, to aim for success in life, to change to the solar calendar, to sprinkle one's conversation with foreign words, to sit in chairs, to eat meat, to use the *kana* syllabary instead of characters in writing, to wear leather shoes and cut one's topknot if a man, or to cease blackening one's teeth if a married woman. In 1873 the Meiji government had also concluded that it was enlightened to end the persecution of Japanese Christians and harassment of Buddhists. While still giving preferential treatment to Shintō to bolster the emperor's prestige, it ordered the removal of public notices banning the worship of Jesus. It denounced violent attacks on Buddhist temples and art works, such as had followed in the wake of the forcible separation of Shintoism and Buddhism.

There was much that was light and frivolous in *bummei kaika,* but the Japanese were the first to joke about it and to caricature themselves. Superficial equation in Japan of enlightenment with a Western diet or clothing was matched by superficial equation in the West of the Japanese spirit with cherry blossoms or the tea ceremony. And despite talk of the old as wicked or outmoded, new Confucian study groups were founded at the end of the decade. While the *avant garde* experimented with new techniques, traditional craftsmen and artists continued to make their wares, write their poems and stories, and paint their pictures with great pride. Kabuki and Nō theater acquired new patrons. All of the talk about elevating the position of women, however, did little to alter marriage customs or the family system.

Perhaps the most remarkable venture in Western learning and the expression of *bummei kaika* was the Iwakura embassy to the United States and Europe, 1871–73. It included some of the most powerful men in the Meiji government and was to play an important part in the process of modernization. At the head were Iwakura Tomomi, as chief ambassador, and his long-time colleagues Ōkubo and Kido as vice-ambassadors. Another vice-ambassador was Itō Hirobumi, a young official who was destined to become one of the most famous of the Meiji statesmen. There were special commissioners from each of the ministries and numerous secretaries and interpreters, in all about fifty men. The mission's aims were threefold: to pay the respects of the Emperor Meiji to the heads of state of the treaty powers, to engage in preliminary discussions on the vexing question of treaty revision, and to see what the West was really like and what it might have to teach Japan. Although the Japanese often spoke resentfully of consular jurisdiction and the loss of tariff autonomy as infringements upon Japan's national sovereignty, the government had decided that it would be best to postpone the revision conferences scheduled for 1872 until a time when Japan should have undergone further reform and would be in a stronger position to bargain for equal treaties. In the meantime the embassy was to find out exactly what the treaty powers thought and what the prospects for a favorable revision were. Beyond this, the government wanted to undertake a more systematic program of reform than in the past, and the embassy hoped to gain knowledge and perspective which would be of assistance in establishing priorities and in working out long-range solutions. A pledge was signed by the ambassadors and those remaining behind to keep each other well informed and to refrain as much as possible from major reforms and new appointments until the embassy returned with its reports and a grand policy debate could be held. This stricture did not apply to those reforms necessary to carry out the abolition of the domains and the establishment of the prefectures. The embassy and the caretakers did keep in very close touch, and most of the important laws adopted in the ambassadors' absence had their approval.

Although they knew in general what needed to be done even before they left Japan, the journey was nevertheless an eye-opener and gave them a deepened understanding of the world outside Japan and of the immensity of the task they had undertaken. It was an advanced course in Western studies for Iwakura, Kido, and Ōkubo, and made them a little less dependent on the young men who were specialists in Dutch or Western learning. The commissioners completed elaborate studies on Western laws, schools, industry, commerce, agriculture, and military power. As a group, the embassy did not view the West as a monolith but instead learned to appreciate the many national differences. The United States, England, and France seemed to be the most enlightened and advanced countries, while Germany rose in their esteem and Russia fell. They returned home less frightened of Russia's capacity for immediate and sustained expansion in East Asia though still wary of its ultimate intentions. They remained convinced of the need to preserve Japan's security through a strong military establishment but sensed they had time to build up a conscript army. They saw even more clearly the importance of mass education and of general economic development. They shed any lingering Confucian biases against the profit motive and government by laws. They supported the eventual adoption of a constitution, which, however, they saw as the best means to rationalize the political order and restrain arbitrary actions rather than as a way to share legislative power with a representative assembly. They concluded that Western enlightenment was the result of respect for history and tradition and of centuries of gradual growth as well as of the drastic technological changes since 1800. The key to Western wealth and power was not so much individualism or initiative as mastery of science, long-range planning, and a highly developed talent for organization in economics and politics. It seemed obvious that the wisest course was a policy of gradualism, which to them meant a middle path of steady progress and fundamental change between the extremes of moribund conservatism and reckless radicalism.

The Crisis of 1873 and Its Aftermath

In the autumn of 1873, when the last of the embassy had returned, instead of an over-all policy debate there was a furious controversy over whether or not Japan should send a punitive expedition to Korea. For the past five years the Korean court had refused to receive Japanese envoys or to recognize the Meiji government. This was taken as a grave insult by many former samurai, who were ready to settle the question by warfare and very much wanted a militant foreign policy—for reasons of national glory, as well as for their own security and employment. In the absence of the embassy, Saigō Takamori, with support from Itagaki Taisuke, a member of the Council of State from Tosa, and Foreign Minister Soejima Taneomi, a former Hizen samurai, won the backing of the Council of State for still another diplomatic mission, with himself at its head. Should Saigō, the personal emissary of the emperor, be killed, Japan would have an excellent justification for invasion. Many motives have been attributed to Saigō: a desire to brake the reforms if not stop them, and perhaps open the way for military men to take over; compassion for the former samurai, who should have a last moment of glory before absorption into the general populace; the wish to atone for his support of the Restoration; the hope of purifying the Japanese spirit, which had been polluted by excessive *bummei kaika*. Saigō's role in this will probably continue to invite speculation, for he was and continues to be a folk hero almost without peer. Those who joined with him were, if not similarly motivated on the Korean issue, at least hopeful of using the crisis to gain more influence. During the same time Charles LeGendre, former American consul at

Amoy and now an adviser to the Japanese Foreign Ministry, had been urging the government to undertake an expedition to aboriginal Taiwan and avenge the recent murders of shipwrecked Ryukyuan fishermen—Japanese subjects—while giving assurances that this was in complete accord with international law and not a violation of Chinese jurisdiction. He warned the Japanese to stake out a claim to Taiwan and Korea as well before the major Western powers could move in. Some Japanese officials, including the commissioner of colonization in Hokkaido, were more concerned about troubles to the north in Sakhalin where there had been serious incidents involving Japanese and Russian settlers.

Iwakura, Kido, and Ōkubo were appalled at the prospect of war and furious to learn of internal disorders and agrarian protests which had occurred during their absence. Much of this they blamed on mismanagement by the caretakers and hasty, incessant legislation. In the angry quarrels of October, all three were eloquent spokesmen against the proposed expedition, Kido from his sick bed, Ōkubo at meetings of the Council of State, and Iwakura in a decisive audience with the young emperor. Korea was an important issue in itself, but the debate turned into a power struggle and a showdown on basic national policy in both foreign and domestic affairs. Japan, the ambassadors and their supporters argued, needed to concentrate its resources and energies on internal reconstruction and could not afford to squander its wealth on questionable military ventures or provoke the antagonism and possible intervention of the major powers. To support a war for the sake of the former samurai was to place an unfair burden upon the rest of the population. The actions of the Koreans were insulting, but must be interpreted as the deed of ignorant, foolish people who did not know any better. War should be undertaken only when there was just cause and when a country was well equipped militarily. When the chief minister of state collapsed under the strain, Iwakura moved into his place and went directly to the Emperor Meiji with a lecture on the importance of real accomplishments and actual power in contrast to expensive and empty heroics. Saigō's plan was defeated, and he and his allies (Itagaki, Soejima, Gotō Shōjirō, and Etō Shimpei) resigned.

The outcome of the crisis of 1873 was of fundamental importance. The government was controlled by a smaller group, and one in greater agreement as to what should be done. Japan was to concentrate its resources and energies on internal reform for the next twenty years. Policies on compulsory education, taxation, military conscription, legal and judicial reform, and the promotion of industry were to be refined, qualified, and carried out by a government comprised mainly of Satsuma and Chōshū men with some Tosa and Hizen representation. Also, Japan's foreign policy for the next twenty years was, on the whole, cautious and restrained. The difficulties with Korea and Russia were settled by diplomacy. The major exception was an expedition to aboriginal Taiwan in 1874, but it was a small-scale operation motivated less by designs for a colony than by worry over samurai discontent. It served primarily as an outlet for samurai frustrations and came after an attempt on Iwakura's life, a rebellion in Hizen led by Etō Shimpei, and a flood of critical memorials.

Since the victors in the 1873 debate have been labeled latent imperialists who disagreed with their adversaries only on timing and tactics and simply postponed aggression to a later date, it must be stressed that Iwakura remained to his death in 1883 an advocate of cooperation with China and Korea. The imperialist impulse was never very strong in Ōkubo and weakened in Kido after his trip abroad. Their argument was not for the reconstruction of Japan so that it might later engage in expansion but for the conversion of Japan into a powerful, wealthy, and enlightened country which could then take whatever action it deemed necessary to ensure security and equality. The emergence of Japanese imperialism cannot be attributed to inherent militarism or ancient dreams of empire. Western imperialism was a fact of life in East Asia, and the behavior of the European powers, the United States, and the China under the Ch'ing, as well as that of Japan, must be examined with greater care. In 1874 China's objections to the Taiwan expedition led to some tense moments, but war was in the end averted by skillful negotiations. Although Japan won an indemnity and strengthened its claim to the Ryukyu Islands, the expedition had almost ended in disaster and was deemed a dangerous mistake. Thereafter, Japanese diplomacy, as noted, was extremely cautious—much to the disgust of militant dissidents.

In the meantime Ōkubo had taken over the new Home Ministry, and his performance in that office, 1873–78, far more than the Taiwan fiasco, was the test of his sincerity in arguing for domestic reconstruction. Ōkubo is remembered today as a harsh, calculating, and ruthless oligarch, but perhaps more than any other member of the Iwakura embassy he had profited from his journey and was changed by it. His ministry was at the center of efforts to consolidate Japan's political unity and encourage economic growth. With his staff, he standardized prefectural administration, established the metropolitan police, reorganized the postal services and census records, ordered topographical surveys, improved public sanitation, and promoted light industry, model factories, agricultural experiment stations, and the export of Japanese handicrafts. Ōkubo recruited talent from all over Japan and promoted his men on the basis of merit. Along with Iwakura and Kido, he supported the gradual adoption of a constitutional system.

There was uneasiness among conservatives and radicals about the direction in which Japan was heading. Such policies and equally the authoritarian manner in which they were carried out aroused organized political opposition in the form of a "people's rights" movement, and provoked several uprisings culminating in a large-scale samurai rebellion in 1877. The Satsuma Rebellion was the most serious challenge to authority faced by the Meiji government. Agrarian disturbances and the earlier samurai revolts had been put down with relative ease. Stern press and public association laws had kept independent-minded journalists and agitators under a fair degree of control. But Kyushu, in particular Satsuma with its large population of former samurai, seethed with discontent under the new regime just as it had under shogunal domination. Local leaders charged that the government was un-Japanese, extravagant, and arbitrary. Saigō had returned to Satsuma after his resignation in 1873 and had become involved with private schools specializing in military education and token instruction in the Confucian Classics. Apparently only with reluctance did he accept leadership of the unhappy samurai in his home province, and then only after the mandatory commutation of pensions and Tokyo's attempt to remove guns from its Kagoshima arsenal to a safer place. The Satsuma Rebellion was put down, but just barely and at an enormous cost. The army, reserves, military cadets, police, and volunteers had to be called out. The Satsuma troops, even with inferior equipment and communications, fought well but in the end lost out to a mixed peasant-samurai army with modern weapons. Nevertheless, when it was over, the Meiji generals sat down to a serious review of their command and supply systems and of military training. Saigō, trapped with 500 of his followers and wounded by a bullet, committed suicide. Even as the leader of the opposition, he enjoyed great adulation and was never branded a traitor. In time he would become the special hero of ultranationalists. Ōkubo's fate was assassination in 1878 and diminished fame.

The government which survived the Satsuma Rebellion was now in firm and unquestioned control of the whole country. Doubts over who was to lead Japan or in what direction it would go were ended by the victory, although the grumbling and criticism continued. There were now important new questions to solve, particularly those of treaty revision, finance and a permanent political structure. Already there were signs of much greater selectivity in drawing from the Western experience and of a renewed interest in Japanese history and culture. In retrospect, the Meiji government in its first ten years had been remarkably venturesome and open to new ideas. It had faced up to crucial decisions and built much of the foundation for a modern state and society and the transition to modern economic growth. This had been done with a mixture of persuasion and coercion but without systematic resort to brutality or terror. There was considerable suffering and some bloodshed but little sense of cataclysmic upheaval. A century later the argument would still rage as to whether the Meiji leaders had gone too far or not far enough in reshaping Japan.

VI

The Era of

Fulfillment:

1877–1911

BY
ROGER F. HACKETT

The thirty-five years from the suppression of the Satsuma Rebellion to the death of Emperor Meiji in 1912 forms a period of stunning progress in the modern history of Japan. When the government forces succeeded in quashing the rebellion the last serious domestic challenge to national unity had been met and a new era was inaugurated. The new era was characterized by the fulfillment of the original goals of the Meiji leaders—the gaining of national security and international equality. The nation continued to modernize its institutions and took giant strides to build up its economic and military power. The unmistakable evidence that Japan had succeeded in meeting the Meiji goals by developing a "rich country and strong military" is found in the revision of the unequal treaties, the far-reaching military victories, and an alliance on equal terms with a major power of the West. Domestic progress and international success had enabled Japan to achieve security and equality and to emerge as a world power. From a nation beset with fears of being colonized by the dominant Western nations Japan at the end of the first decade of the twentieth century stood self-assured as the dominant state of East Asia, confident enough to join the Western powers in the scramble for empire.

A survey of the history of Japan between 1877 and 1911 brings landmark events in this era of fulfillment readily to mind: the enactment in 1889 of a constitution that created a new framework for politics; the rapid economic development that narrowed the technological gap between Japan and the West and provided the sinews of military power; the victory over China in 1894 that launched a new chapter in foreign relations; the ending by 1899 of the unequal treaties that crowned a generation of effort to free the nation from humiliating inequality; the equal alliance with Great Britain in 1902, the military triumph over Russia in 1905, and the annexation of Korea in 1910 that together raised Japan to first rank as an imperialist power. These events proved that Japan had in thirty-five years achieved the goals of the Meiji Restoration.

The Development of a Constitutional System

A conspicuous feature of the development of Japan following the Satsuma Rebellion was the evolution of a constitutional political system. This was in part a result of the pressure exerted by those outside the government who were opposed to the authoritarian nature of the regime, but more significantly it came about because the governing group was persuaded that representative institutions would strengthen the nation just as they seemed to contribute to the dominance of the advanced countries of the Occident. In any case, a major feature of the political history of the second decade of the Meiji period was the creation of a new political structure capped by the enactment of a constitution in 1889 and the meeting of the first Diet in the following year. The new political system evolved slowly and deliberately, and its final form was shaped primarly by those in power, although the tempo and scope of political reforms were influenced by the opinions of leading public figures outside the government.

As we have noted, the failure of the Satsuma Rebellion ended the overt threat to the stability of the Meiji government. But Itagaki Taisuke, a Tosa samurai prominent in the Restoration, and other important leaders resigned from the government over the issue of a war with Korea in 1874 and waged a political offensive against the monopoly of power held by the Satsuma and Chōshū leaders. The general line of attack was stated in 1874 when Itagaki and his followers presented a memorial that criticized the unbridled power of officials and called for the immediate creation of a popularly elected national assembly so that the government would share power with the people. What began as a protest movement among disgruntled samurai excluded from the center of power gained momentum through the organization of political societies advocating democratic rights, local self-government, and a national assembly. With the spread of this "movement for freedom and people's rights" (*jiyū minken undō*), as it came to be known, from Tosa to other parts of the country, anti-government political associations mushroomed. Counterparts to the Tosa political society, which was known as the Risshisha and had been founded in 1874 as a "self-help" club for former samurai, cropped up rapidly. By early 1875 they had been amalgamated into a nationwide Society of Patriots (Aikokusha) to support the political program of the 1874 Tosa memorial.

The response of the government leaders to these political demands was conditioned by three factors. The first was their preoccupation with the violent threats to stability which had followed the serious split in the leadership over the Korean War issue. Memorials could be received and set aside, but revolts had to be put down. In large part because of the menace of violent opposition, the government had agreed to an armed expedition against Formosa in 1874 as a way of diverting the militancy of former samurai. But even this decision had caused dissension within the government and the resignation of Kido Kōin, who firmly adhered to the position that domestic reforms must precede any foreign ventures. Dissent within the Council of State and revolts by disaffected samurai were far more serious matters to the government than demands for "people's rights."

A second factor influencing reaction to the parliamentary movement was the general acceptance among the government leaders of the idea that constitutional government should eventually be adopted. Before the demands for popularly elected assemblies were presented by the opposition in 1874, Kido had argued in favor of a constitutional form of government, and several proposals had been drafted within the government envisioning a political system based on a constitution with some guarantees for popular rights. So it is apparent that the first proposals for a reorganization of the political system along constitutional lines did not arise as a result of demands by the political "outs."

A third and related factor affecting the government's response to the popular movement was the determination to maintain firm control, to keep the movement in check by stern measures if necessary. Constitutional niceties were, in the minds of the leaders, secondary to the needs of stability through strong central authority and the building of national strength to carry out the long-range goals of the Restoration. Pressures for democratic rights forced them to consider the issue of a national assembly more seriously, but the determination to impose a stable, unified order led them to give even more attention to devising means of controlling the popular movement.

Under these circumstances, the Meiji leaders compromised. They took modest steps toward constitutional government while they passed legislation to contain the disruptive influence of radical demands for immediate political changes. As an example of the former, a conference was held in Osaka in 1875 to reestablish unity between government leaders and Kido and Itagaki. As a result of this meeting, the government was reorganized to provide for an independent judiciary in the form of a Supreme Court (*Daishinin*). In addition, an appointive Chamber of Elders (*Genrōin*) was established to review the legislative proposals of the government. It was also agreed that to avoid excessive concentration of power there would within the Council of State (*Dajōkan*) be a strict separation between members responsible for policy formulation and those responsible for the executive administration of the various ministries. This reorganization was accompanied by an imperial rescript which declared that "constitutional government shall be established in gradual stages" and instructed the Chamber of Elders to draft a constitution. From the Osaka agreement came the first tentative steps in the direction of representative government since it provided for the summoning of a conference of prefectural governors. Out of the second conference of these local officials in 1878 came the decision to establish elected prefectural assemblies. Prefectural assemblies were elected in 1879 by adult males paying at least five yen in land taxes. These bodies were limited to discussing local budgets, while the governors retained all rights to initiate legislation, dissolve the assembly, and veto its decisions. Nevertheless, their establishment represented a move in the direction of representative government, and by 1880 assemblies had been formed in the towns and villages as well.

The Osaka Conference of 1875 had produced only modest results, but nevertheless Itagaki agreed to rejoin the government and disband the Society of Patriots. However, when many of the measures agreed on were not carried out, Itagaki again left his government post, disturbed by the continuing domination of the Satsuma-Chōshū clique and annoyed at the authoritarian means adopted to control the growing "people's rights" movement.

An illustration of the government's techniques of controlling the movement while granting small concessions is to be found in the 1875 laws forbidding newspapers and journals to criticize the government or even to discuss national laws. Despite these control measures the "people's rights" movement gained momentum after the Satsuma Rebellion and in 1880 delegates representing over 87,000 members of political associations in twenty-two prefectures met in a national convention to create the League for the Establishment of a National Assembly. The movement gained headway for several reasons: the growing participation of prosperous landlords and rural merchants who resented their heavy tax burden, the ability of the leaders to organize and coordinate political activity, and the popularization of constitutional government in the newspapers and journals of the day. Many prominent intellectuals, most of whom were inspired by the liberal ideas of French and British political philosophers, spread knowledge of democratic institutions and won support for antigovernment pressures. To counter the clamor for a national assembly and the agitation of antigovernment political groups, the authorities passed a Public Assembly Law in 1880. This law severely limited public gatherings by requiring police permission for all meetings and approval of the subjects to be discussed; it forbade public servants— soldiers, policemen, teachers—to attend such gatherings and granted local authorities the power to suppress political agitation.

The small concessions which had been made to public pressure generated further demands: local assemblies were used as forums for radical speeches, and repressive measures against political agitation often bred further demonstrations. The leaders of the government, as we have seen, were not opposed to moving in the direction of parliamentary government, but they did not agree on what kind of constitutional system should be created. They were against radical proposals for immediate action and resented the pressure brought against them by the opposition. Despite this bitter attitude toward the clamoring radicals, the government itself was giving increasing attention to the drafting of a constitution. The promise of an eventual constitution made at the Osaka Conference of 1875 was followed by the drafting of a constitution by the Chamber of Elders. This draft followed the general pattern of European constitutional monarchies: some limitations were placed upon the power of the central government and the monarch, some powers were conceded to a legislature, and recognition was given to the rights of individuals. Iwakura Tomomi, the leading member of the Council of State, was dissatisfied with this proposed constitution. As an archconservative he was alarmed at the liberal tone of the document and requested the other councilors to express their views on the issue of a constitution.

Between December, 1879, and the spring of 1881 seven councilors, including Yamagata Aritomo, Inoue Kaoru, Ōkuma Shigenobu, and Itō Hirobumi—those who really controlled the government under the general supervision of Iwakura—submitted their opinions on the advisability of a constitution and a national parliament. Most of the responses of the councilors were conservative and cautious. They agreed, in general, that a constitutional system should be worked out that would safeguard the sovereign power of the emperor and preserve the authority of the administration, but allow the gradual establishment of a popular national assembly with limited powers. This apparent consensus on a gradual approach to a constitutional system was shattered, however, by the last opinion to be submitted, that of Ōkuma.

Ōkuma Shigenobu, councilor, minister of finance, and distinguished

Meiji leader from Hizen, adopted the radical approach of the "people's rights" movement. Influenced by advisors who were enthusiastic students of English-style constitutional government, he advocated government by political parties, that is, cabinets organized by the majority party and responsible to a national assembly. Although, like his colleagues, he felt that a constitution should be granted by the emperor, he insisted that elections for a national assembly should be held in 1882 and the body convened the following year. The extremism of Ōkuma's proposals precipitated a political crisis which was compounded by his opposition to and public disclosure of the decision to sell, at a fraction of their value, the assets of government enterprises in Hokkaido to a private company owned in part by a fellow councilor who had headed the Hokkaido Colonization Bureau.

As a result of this "crisis of 1881" the Hokkaido sale was canceled, an imperial rescript was issued announcing a national assembly in 1890, and Ōkuma was dismissed from office. In the history of the development of the Meiji political system this crisis was a turning point. For one thing, a definite date had been set for establishing a national assembly, although the delay of nine years was more consistent with the gradual approach of the government leaders than with the demands of the opposition for quicker action. For another, the ousting of Ōkuma further restricted the top leadership of government to a tight Satsuma-Chōshū oligarchy.

Although Ōkuma was to add weight to the liberal currents in Meiji society, his removal left the conservative element at the center of power. The result is well illustrated by a document Iwakura submitted to his colleagues in which he outlined the fundamental principles to be included in the constitution. He was determined to rebut those features of the British constitutional system reflected in Ōkuma's startling proposal. With the aid of a second-level bureaucrat, Inoue Kowashi, who was influenced by German constitutional philosophers, Iwakura drew up a plan of government which borrowed heavily from the Prussian system and laid down what proved to be the essential features of the Meiji constitution of 1889. Among them were the basic points that the constitution would be granted by the emperor, that the legislature would be bicameral with a lower house popularly elected by a limited franchise, that the cabinet would be responsible only to the emperor and wholly independent of the legislature, and that the previous year's budget would remain in effect if a new one was not approved by the legislature.

Although the final constitution was prefigured by Iwakura's general principles, until its enactment in 1889 there were eight years during which both the government and the outside forces prepared for a new political system. As a result of the pledge of a constitution the "people's rights' movement was transformed by the birth of national political parties. In the fall of 1881 Itagaki reorganized the League for the Establishment of a National Assembly into the Jiyūtō (Liberal Party). The party adopted a platform favoring popular sovereignty and responsible parliamentary government. As successor to the Society of Patriots of 1875 it continued to reflect the influence of French doctrines on its Tosa leaders by stressing individual rights and civil liberties. The party drew its major support from landowners and businessmen in the villages and small towns. In March, 1882, Ōkuma and his followers formed the Rikken Kaishintō (Constitutional Progressive Party), advocating more moderate positions than the Jiyūtō and oriented to the concepts of British parliamentary liberalism. It drew its support from urban intellectuals and students, particularly those associated with the ideas of Fukuzawa Yukichi of Keiō University, and businessmen, including the head of the large Mitsubishi Company. A pro-government party, the Rikken Teiseitō (Constitutional Imperial Party), was founded in 1882 by bureaucrats, local government officials, and conservative journalists in sympathy with a Prussian-style constitutional monarchy.

Through political meetings, party declarations, and the drafting of private constitutions widely publicized in the expanding antigovernment press, both the Jiyūtō and Kaishintō engaged in a running struggle to influence the government toward a more liberal regime. At times, radical thinkers in the parties led violent demonstrations against the heavy hand of the authorities. As party agitation grew and violence erupted, the government issued more ordinances to restrict political activities. Under these ordinances police permission was required to hold a political meeting. Moreover, political associations had to disclose the names of their members and refrain from disturbing the public peace. New press laws placed harsh controls on the opposition newspapers. In 1887 a Peace Preservation Law was adopted that led to the expulsion of hundreds of party members from the Tokyo area because they were declared to be "a threat to public tranquillity."

Under these circumstances it is not surprising that the party movement was soon crippled. But there were internal reasons which are as important if not more important in explaining the collapse of the parties. Both the Jiyūtō and the Kaishintō were torn by factionalism, financially weakened by the depression of the 1880s, and divided between radical and moderate wings. Moreover, rather than forming a common front against the government, they attacked each other with accusations of corruption that further weakened the parliamentary movement and discredited it in the eyes of the public. By 1884 the Jiyūtō had dissolved itself and Ōkuma had resigned as head of the Kaishintō.

As the parties waned, the government proceeded to reorganize the administrative structure and prepare the constitution. Itō was charged with responsibility for developing a constitutional system along the lines outlined by Iwakura in 1881. As a first step, he led a mission to study the operation of constitutions in Europe. The mission spent the major part of its time overseas studying with leading German scholars of constitutional law. These jurists recommended a Prussian-style constitution and an authoritarian system of government stressing the supreme power of the emperor. They urged representative institutions but argued against party cabinets, which they considered divisive. Most of what Itō heard was consistent with the basic principles outlined by Iwakura and provided European precedents for the development of a conservative political order acceptable to the Meiji leaders.

The final drafting of the constitution was preceded by several important structural changes in the political system that prepared the way for a constitutional regime. First, in 1884 a peerage of over 500 persons in five ranks was created from among the old court nobility and former daimyō. Former samurai who had rendered valuable service to the state, including the oligarchs themselves, were also ennobled. The purpose of establishing a peerage was to provide a basis for selecting the members of the proposed upper house of the legislature. It was also a way of building the support of many conservatives as a check against the lower house. Second, in 1885 the Council of State was replaced by a modern cabinet under a prime minister. The prime minister was made responsible to the emperor for all state affairs while the other cabinet ministers were accountable to the prime minister for the work of their ministries. This reform removed the three court nobles who advised the emperor as chief ministers (chancellor and ministers of the left and right) under the Council of State and who exercised ill-defined control over the departments supervised by the councilors. It also had the effect of strengthening the oligarchs' base of power before the convening of a national assembly. Itō became the first prime minister, and seven of the remaining nine ministers were from Satsuma and Chōshū. At the time the cabinet system was introduced, all bureaucrats except the top two levels were placed under a merit system based on a civil service examination. Third, several posts were created outside of the cabinet ·—the lord keeper of the privy seal and the Privy Council—as personal spokesman and advisory body, respectively, for the emperor.

In the military as well as in the political sphere changes were introduced to strengthen the authority of the state. In the face of political unrest and liberal doctrines Yamagata Aritomo, the major figure in the development of the army, wished to strengthen the discipline, the organization, and the autonomy of the military services. Morale and discipline were developed by proclamations stressing the traditional virtues of loyalty and obedience to the emperor. The "Rescript to Soldiers and Sailors" issued by the emperor in 1882 emphasized the duties and the guiding ideals of the military. Military organization was strengthened by adopting the German general staff system with the chief of staff independent of the army minister and civil officials in matters of command. The autonomy of the military was established when the chief of staff was allowed direct access to the emperor, who alone was given supreme command over the army and navy. Yamagata also served as home minister for five years and built up the power of the central government by developing a national police force under the control of the ministry. The same goal of strengthening central power was served by his reorganization of local government in 1888 and 1890.

All these institutional innovations added strength to the power of the central government and presaged the conservative character of the constitution. The Meiji Constitution was written by a small group of able men under Itō's supervision and with the consultation of a German jurist, Hermann Roesler. Great secrecy surrounded the work of the committee in order to avoid the criticism or interference of political opponents and the distraction of publicity. The draft was completed in 1888, ratified by the Privy Council under Itō's presidency early the next year, and promulgated by the emperor on February 11, 1889.

The Meiji Constitution, composed of seven chapters and seventy-six articles, and the subsidiary administrative laws issued at the same time, became the fundamental law of the nation for the next fifty-eight years. The distinguishing feature of the new political system was its authoritarian character. Sovereignty rested with the emperor by right of his mythical divine descent. He was invested with supreme political power, held all executive authority through a cabinet and other organs responsible solely to him, and exercised legislative power with the consent of the parliament. He was designated the commander of the army with the power to declare war, make peace, and conclude treaties. He could veto laws passed by the Diet, dissolve the House of Representatives, and issue ordinances, when the Diet was not in session, that had the effect of law.

But these starkly conservative features of the constitution were combined with more liberal elements. The promise of a national assembly was met by the establishment of a bicameral parliament, or Diet, with a House of Peers made up of members of the nobility and imperial appointees, as well as a House of Representatives chosen by a limited electorate of adult males paying at least fifteen yen in national taxes. Legislation required the consent of the Diet, which also had the authority to initiate laws, make representations to the government, and submit petitions to the emperor. The constitution required that the annual budget be approved by the Diet, although it was stipulated that failure to vote a budget would continue in effect the budget of the previous year. A bill of rights was included which guaranteed such things as freedom of religion, press, and association. However, here again, these rights were qualified by such phrases as "within the limits of law" or when "not prejudicial to law and order."

In sum, the constitution combined conservative and liberal principles, but it was weighted heavily on the side of an authoritarian system that reserved to the government overwhelming power and preserved the principle of the political sovereignty of the emperor. At the same time, minimal concessions were made to popular rights and parliamentary government; the participation of parties in the political process was recognized. The end product was not too far from the political system envisioned by most of the Meiji leaders a decade earlier. It represented a blending of authoritarianism and constitutionalism in which the demands of the opposition forces were partially met while the ruling group retained the upper hand. It is noteworthy, however, that in the conflict of ideas regarding the new political order both camps accepted the traditional theory supporting the unique position of the emperor and the principle of imperial sovereignty. Yet both sides were deeply influenced by the Western example of constitutional government. By mixing these elements Japan in 1890 reached a new stage in its political development. The constitution was written, in part, as a result of the "people's rights" movement, but it is more accurately seen as the capstone of a long process of political evolution, the result of the interaction between the ruling elite's vision of a modern constitutional state and the political ideals of the impatient opposition.

Politics under the Constitution

The next twenty years of Japan's history revealed the strengths and weaknesses of the Meiji Constitution. From 1890 to 1910 dominant power remained in the hands of a small ruling group but as the parties in the Diet grew steadily stronger compromises had to be worked out. Although the constitution placed supreme political authority in the person of the emperor he did not take part in the administration; actual executive power was controlled by the Satsuma-Chōshū elite and exercised through their positions in the cabinet and in the armed forces. Of the seven prime ministers between 1885 and the end of the Meiji period all except two were from Satsuma or Chōshū. This same Satsuma-Chōshū group became institutionalized as an informal, extraconstitutional body known as the genrō (elder statesmen). The genrō, in practice, became the source of ultimate executive power. They collectively made the decisions reserved for the emperor and replaced the emperor in his role as coordinator of political power.

This new stage of constitutional government was symbolized by the first national election in Japan. In the summer of 1890 almost all of the 460,000 eligible voters (slightly over 1 percent of the population) went to the polls to elect 300 members to the House of Representatives. The Jiyūtō and Kaishintō had been revived in anticipation of the election and they won well over half the seats in the house, with the rest representing small parties and independents. The House of Representatives now became the arena for the renewal of sharp opposition between the government and the parties.

Contention centered on matters of principle, and the "budget issue" became the focus of the struggle. The constitution was ambiguous on the degree of control the Diet could exercise over the administration. The popular parties adhered to the principle that the cabinet should be responsible to the elected legislature which, they felt, had every right to interpret the "will of the emperor." The ruling oligarchs, on the other hand, subscribed to the principle that the cabinet and administration should "transcend" the conflicting political forces, be unaffected by the position of the Diet parties and accountable only to the emperor whose executive power they claimed to exercise.

These clashing views on how the new political system should operate concentrated on the problem of the annual budget. The constitution required Diet approval of the budget. This power had been qualified by the stipulation that certain fixed administrative costs could not be cut and by the provision that in the event that the annual budget was not passed the previous year's budget would operate. Even this qualified power over the budget gave the parties an effective weapon in their opposition to the government, because national expenditures were rising rapidly and any excess over the preceding budget, as well as the taxes needed to raise funds for the increase, had to have the approval of the Diet.

This power was quickly wielded. In the first Diet the parties made a substantial cut in the budget proposed by Prime Minister Yamagata Aritomo. Subsequently each prime minister was faced with similar slashes in the budget. In confronting the antagonism of the opposition parties, the cabinets used a variety of measures: suspending or dissolving the Diet, splitting the opposition by bribing party men for their votes, attempting to influence elections, invoking the emperor's instructions. While all these measures and others were employed with varying success by the rulers, the conspicuous feature in the running struggle was the solution by compromise. In this development it was clear that the political parties, even with their internal divisions, susceptibility to bribes and force, and their disadvantages under a constitution that granted overwhelming authority to the administration, gradually increased their power to extract concessions from the government and won a steadily larger role for their participation in the political process.

The twenty-year history of relations between the cabinet and the Diet from 1890 to 1910 is divided into three periods; in each the oligarchy retained ultimate control only by yielding a steadily greater role to political parties. The first, from 1890 to 1894, was marked by bitter hostility between the executive leaders and the opposition parties. The second, from 1895 to 1900, following a period of wartime unity and unusual cooperation, was distinguished by a series of coalitions in which a cabinet led by one of the oligarchs included a few members from one or the other of the two major opposition parties. The third, from 1900 to the end of the Meiji era, was a period when the original Meiji oligarchs or their protégés maintained political power through more direct cooperation with or actual leadership of political parties. Throughout the twenty years the parties were repeatedly reorganized, often fought each other, and at one point merged. Likewise, the oligarchy did not remain united in its attitude toward parties, as seen by Itō's decision to form a party government in 1900.

From 1890 to 1894 three successive oligarch prime ministers capitalized on the advantages of their entrenched power and legal position to safeguard the administration from parliamentary encroachment. In the first Diet, for example, when the finance committee of the house cut the proposed budget by over 10 percent and attacked the government for its arrogance, Yamagata prorogued the lower house, intimidated Diet members, and bribed his party antagonists to split the opposition. Moved by his desire to demonstrate to Westerners that constitutional government could succeed in Japan, Yamagata did not carry out his threat to dissolve the House of Representatives. Instead, he lured enough votes from the Jiyūtō to pass a budget, but only after agreeing to accept more than half the cuts the Diet had made. The austere, inflexible Yamagata found this experience with democratic institutions painful, and when Itō criticized his tactics he resigned. But the first Diet had set a pattern for relations between the government leaders and the legislature: the high-handed and repressive tactics used by the executive to force their views; the verbal violence of the parties and their use of their limited power to strike at the government's budget; and in the end some compromise between the two sides to prevent the collapse of the constitutional system.

Matsukata Masayoshi, the Satsuma genrō who had for many years served ably as finance minister, succeeded Yamagata as prime minister. When in 1891 the second Diet slashed his budget, he dissolved the lower house and supported measures to weaken the opposition during the ensuing election. Repressive police and local government powers were used to terrorize candidates and to intimidate the electorate. Election violence resulted in at least twenty-five deaths, but the brutal government campaign failed completely. Matsukata faced a new house in which the opposition parties held an absolute majority, and the battle was renewed. The parties not only cut the budget again but passed resolutions condemning the election interference. When a split developed within the cabinet Matsukata resigned and Itō took his turn as prime minister, leading a cabinet that included most of the other genrō.

Itō espoused a flexible approach to the Diet and by temperament was more inclined to work out compromises. He had even given thought to abandoning the principle of "transcendent" cabinets in favor of organizing a government party to control the house, but his fellow genrō had sternly rejected such an approach. Despite his political skill, Itō was unable to deal with the assaults of the parties. His budget was severely clipped and after fruitless negotiations he prorouged the Diet. Next, he was confronted with a memorial to the throne impeaching the cabinet. To this he responded with an unprecedented measure: he had the emperor issue a rescript supporting the cabinet. The emperor deflated the parties' opposition to the budget by promising to reduce his own income and by ordering civil and military officials to sacrifice one tenth of their salaries. This dramatic introduction of the emperor into the dispute stilled the opposition. But the parties, forced to compromise on the budget issue, shifted their attack to other issues such as the government's failure to get the unequal treaties revised. In January, 1894, and again in June, Itō dissolved the Diet. It was just at this point of deadlock between the cabinet and the parties that war broke out between Japan and China. Without doubt the constitutional crisis was a factor in Japan's decision to go to war. Moreover, those who welcomed a foreign war to unite the nation seemed justified, for the Diets that met during the war passed without dissent a vastly expanded war budget.

War had produced unusual calm and cooperation and when, after its victorious conclusion, the struggle between the oligarchs and the parties was renewed, the political climate had changed. From 1895 to the end of the century each prime minister concluded some type of agreement with one of the parties, an entente which included concessions to the party in return for votes to approve government policy. These shaky alliances represented a step away from the concept of "transcendent" cabinets and a realization that party support was the most sensible way of passing national programs. Itō formed an alliance with the Jiyūtō and rewarded their support by giving Itagaki the post of home minister. The Kaishintō, after March, 1896, called the Shimpōtō, countered by joining other groups in the lower house to oppose the alliance and by developing relations with other members of the oligarchy, in this case allying themselves with the Satsuma genrō, Matsukata. When Itō resigned after four years as prime minister,

Matsukata organized the next cabinet with the acknowledged support of the Shimpōtō and with their president, Ōkuma, as his foreign minister.

But these alliances failed to produce political stability. The oligarchs had achieved greater success in passing their budgets and other programs, but they were still subject to vigorous attacks on both their domestic and their foreign policies and were quick to take stern steps to quell opposition—as four dissolutions of the Diet between 1895 and 1900 attest. The parties slightly increased their participation in the administration but did not gain much in their unrelenting effort to make cabinets responsible to the Diet. Party members were disillusioned by the low returns for their cooperation and were convinced that the genrō attached no real importance to the parties. Out of this frustration and disillusionment grew the belief that the parties must be united to check the power of the genrō. When the Matsukata-Ōkuma coalition fell apart, the two leading parties finally submerged their differences in the spring of 1898 and joined together in the Kenseitō (Constitutional Party) to advance the principle of cabinet responsibility and other party policies.

This shift in the opposition precipitated a split within the oligarchy. Faced with this overwhelming strength in the hostile house, Itō, who had replaced Matsukata as prime minister, proposed to his fellow genrō either that he be permitted to organize a party to support government policies, if necessary by giving up his position, or that they turn the reins of government over to Ōkuma and Itagaki, the joint leaders of the new Kenseitō (Constitutional Party). Yamagata was incensed at the proposal and refused to accept either alternative; the other genrō were almost as unhappy with the choices, and when no decision could be reached Itō resigned. In the absence of a willing successor among the genrō, the Kenseitō leaders were invited to form a cabinet.

In the history of Meiji politics the formation of the Ōkuma-Itagaki cabinet was a landmark in the struggle between the oligarchy and the parties. Yet its significance was quickly dissipated by the utter failure of the new cabinet. The service ministers, who continued from the previous cabinet, refused to cooperate, and the civil bureaucrats, the majority of whom were loyal to the concept that the administration should be free of party control, obstructed the work of the party cabinet. A more serious drawback was that the Kenseitō cabinet had promised an expansion in the military establishment but was unable to agree on the necessary tax program to support it. Most deleterious, however, were the battles over the spoils of office waged by factions within the party. Four months after it was formed, the cabinet, forced to recognize its incapacity to bear the burdens of executive responsibility, resigned, and the party split, with one group under Itagaki retaining the name Kenseitō and the other, led by Ōkuma, assuming the name Kenseihontō (Real Constitutional Party).

Yamagata now once again became prime minister and attempted to reassert the control of the oligarchy. As a military man and an uncompromising advocate of executive power free of parliamentary influence, he conducted a counteroffensive to repair the damage done to his concept of a limited constitutional government. He held a wide base of power in the military establishment and the bureaucracy from which to assert his point of view. Yet above all else Yamagata was a realist. His own previous experience as prime minister as well as the experience of subsequent cabinets convinced him of the need to win support in the Diet for his policies. In the pattern of the other genrō prime ministers since the Sino-Japanese War, he formed an alliance with Itagaki's Kenseitō and worked out a legislative program that included a reform in the election law which more than doubled the electorate by reducing the tax qualification, expanded the size of the house to 369 members, and provided for a secret ballot. In return, his budgets and bills for increased taxes were passed.

It was through imperial ordinances issued when the Diet was not in session that he reinforced the power of the central government. His objective was to curb party infiltration into the bureaucracy through appointments to office and to strengthen the independent position of the military. The former was achieved by new civil service regulations which brought all but the top posts under an examination system. The latter was assured by an order stipulating that the army and navy ministers must be active officers of the top two ranks of their respective services. The Meiji Constitution had granted the military autonomy and the chiefs of each service's general staff had direct access to the emperor. The new measure reasserted the principle that civil authority should not interfere with the command decisions by guaranteeing the military's control over two important cabinet posts, thereby providing a check on any cabinet which did not accept the military's wishes.

Yamagata's counteroffensive had been remarkably successful but his stubborn resistance to the demands of the Kenseitō that it be given cabinet representation and further concessions for continued co-operation destroyed the alliance. When members of the party sought an alliance with Itō instead, a third phase of politics under the Meiji Constitution was inaugurated.

The pattern of constitutional politics that developed during this third phase departed from the overbearing dominance of "transcendent" cabinets in the first period and the uneasy ententes of the second. This period was characterized by the development of parties which became, in effect, administration parties supporting the policies of the ruling elite. These parties were led either by Itō and his protégé, Saionji Kimmochi, or by Katsura Tarō, a Chōshū general supported by Yamagata. Itō evolved this pattern of politics after he extracted the approval of his reluctant fellow genrō for his old notion of organizing a government party. He had responded favorably to the overtures for cooperation made by members of the Kenseitō who were disenchanted with their alliance with Yamagata. In September, 1900, he agreed to form a party, known as the Rikken Seiyūkai (Association of Friends of Constitutional Government), and persuaded many of his followers in the bureaucracy to join. The exhilaration felt by the old party men over the promising road ahead was tempered by their acceptance of his condition that the party must include representatives of all groups in the nation and that it must obey his orders. This meant that the party had accepted a powerful oligarch as its leader with the prospect of gaining access to administrative authority. By yielding the leadership of the party to an oligarch they made it possible for Itō to insert his own interpretation of constitutional government into the center of the party movement. On the other hand, as time would tell, the involvement of many able former bureaucrats in a party was to have a profound effect on politics. In any case, the other major party, the Kenseihontō, bitterly criticized what its members claimed was abject submission to the oligarchy, and vowed to obstruct any Seiyūkai government. Added to this was the opposition of Yamagata's military faction and the hostility of the conservative bureaucracy to Itō's activities.

When Itō formed his Seiyūkai cabinet in October, 1900, all except the foreign minister and the two service ministers were members of the party, although the majority of them were former bureaucrats recently turned party men. Predictably, with a Seiyūkai majority in the lower house the cabinet encountered few problems there, but the forces of conservatism in the House of Peers, who were heavily influenced by Yamagata, blocked a large tax bill. When his genrō colleagues refused to use their influence to help him, Itō resorted to an imperial message instructing the Peers to pass the bill. In this way the immediate legislative problem was overcome, but the conflicts between internal factions evaded his harmonizing talents. When Itō, wearied by discord, resigned in mid-1901, it seemed only natural to assume that Yamagata would resume control of the government.

By 1900 Itō and Yamagata were clearly the two leading political figures, and their rivalry was a conspicuous feature of the political scene. They clashed over differing interpretations of how the constitution should operate and their personalities and political styles were miles apart. Each had a large following and the contest between their two factions was central to the politics of the following decade. But it is well to note that their differences were never as strong as their common interest in fulfilling the Meiji dream of building a strong nation, independent, secure, and respected. Both manipulated and strove to have their own views prevail, but they tried to compose their disagreements so as to avoid a fatal conflict that would destroy the hopes they shared. Yamagata went along with many of Itō's policies regarding constitutional politics and Itō accepted Yamagata's belief in the independence of the armed services and supported the expansion of the military. When Yamagata was unwilling to bear the burdens of leading the government after the Seiyūkai cabinet resigned in 1901, Itō approved, along with other remaining genrō, the appointment of Yamagata's protégé, Katsura. Thus, for the first time in Meiji history the prime minister was not one of the original participants in the Restoration.

Katsura formed a cabinet of bureaucrats but Itō persuaded the Seiyūkai to give him the vital support he needed in the Diet. When Katsura encountered Seiyūkai opposition to his scheme for financing military expansion, Itō was able to bring about a compromise settlement. When the Kenseihontō called for a vote of nonconfidence against Katsura the Seiyūkai majority defeated the motion. Although Katsura had difficulties with the Diet and aroused bitter antagonism by his tendency to be arrogant and high handed in the manner of Yamagata, the success of his cabinet, which remained in office for an unprecedented four and a half years, was in part because of the Seiyūkai support he received. It was also attributed in part to Katsura's success in reducing Itō's political power, which was based on the latter's acknowledged executive authority and his presidency of the majority party. This dual role, which enabled Itō to have a strong voice in decisions, irked Katsura and Yamagata because they felt that his role as a genrō, impartially advising the emperor, was incompatible with his party presidency. In late 1903, by a piece of neat maneuvering, Yamagata and Katsura were able to get the emperor to instruct Itō to give up his party affiliation and resume his old position as president of the Privy Council.

Itō resigned from the Seiyūkai, turning over the reins of the party not to the old-line politicians but to his protégé, Saionji, scion of a court family, with experience as a cabinet minister and privy councilor. A close friend of Itō, he had been a prime mover in the organization of the Seiyūkai and as Itō's successor he continued the trend of prominent bureaucrats emerging as party leaders. Saionji's chief lieutenant in party affairs was the gifted political manager Hara Kei, another former bureaucrat.

The last decade of the Meiji period is sometimes referred to as the Katsura-Saionji era because the two took turns as prime minister. This seesaw arrangement produced a degree of political stability, as both relied on Seiyūkai support to advance policies that were not strikingly different. Unity on the home front characterized the years of the Russo-Japanese war, but public attacks on the Katsura government for its failure to get an indemnity in the Treaty of Portsmouth forced the cabinet's resignation. Saionji then took office as leader of the majority party, but his moderate approach received the cooperation of the military faction, appreciative of the earlier support Saionji and the Seiyūkai had given Katsura. The political calm was interrupted in 1908 when cooperation broke down over financial policies—Saionji favored retrenchment in the face of the large budget deficit; the military favored tax increases to pay for expansion—and Katsura again became prime minister. After three years in office Katsura encountered growing difficulty in gaining party support in the lower house and once more surrendered the prime ministership to Saionji.

The ease with which Katsura and Saionji passed office back and forth reflected their ability to cooperate. Both were reasonably flexible: Saionji was by nature cautious and moved very slowly toward achieving party control of the cabinet while Katsura became estranged from Yamagata's more uncompromising stance and acknowledged the need for party participation in the political process to the point where, in 1913, he was to form his own political party. Stability was also enhanced by the increasing number of former bureaucrats who found party politics an attractive route for their ambitions.

This surface stability did not mean that the fundamental division between the oligarchy and the parties regarding constitutional government had been solved. Indeed, many disillusioned veteran party politicians left the Seiyūkai because of the slow pace toward genuine responsible government and the opportunistic compromises with the entrenched bureaucracy which they felt did nothing to dislodge but in fact strengthened the power of the oligarchy. On the other hand, the incessant demands of the military for ever larger budgets to meet Japan's new status as a world power, and the impatience of conservative forces with party opposition and discord, reinforced the desire of the military-bureaucratic establishment for stronger executive power and autonomous authority to fashion if not dominate national policies. The inner conflict of principle was resolved with some success because of the talent for compromise, the over-all unity of national purpose which exceeded the divisions within society, and the stable collective leadership provided by the Meiji statesmen at the summit of the power structure. The next decades, however, witnessed an open clash between the conflicting forces within the political system as time and changing circumstances eroded the old unity of purpose and the coordinating leadership at the top that had distinguished the Meiji period. Nevertheless, by 1910 the political system embodied many of the features of constitutional representative government envisioned by the Meiji leaders and clamored for by the "people's rights" movement. Although the governing characteristic of Meiji constitutional politics was the primacy of the ruling elite, power was retained in the last analysis only through compromises with the opposition. The political parties, on the other hand, with all their internal weaknesses, had become a permanent part of the political scene and had evolved from confrontation through alliances and ententes with oligarchs to bureaucrat-led parties responsible for national policies.

Foreign Affairs

It is the history of Japan's foreign relations between 1877 and 1910 that most convincingly records an era of fulfillment. While the building of a strong, modern nation through political and economic reforms was the means, the end was the attainment of national security and international equality. All efforts were bent to gain national independence and to rid the nation of the unequal treaty system imposed by Western power. Equality was to be won by unremitting diplomatic efforts; national security was gained through military triumphs and reinforced by an alliance with Great Britain.

The major problem that demanded the attention of every foreign minister in the nineteenth century was the revision of the treaties made in the 1850s and 1860s. Under these agreements foreign nations had secured extraterritorial rights and special trading privileges which compromised Japan's independence. In the 1870s Japan took her first diplomatic steps to get rid of the unequal aspects of the treaties and thereby regain economic autonomy and the lost sense of political self-confidence. But these efforts were unsuccessful and the Japanese were reminded that revision would be acceptable only when their legal codes reached Western standards. This led the government to compile new codes and to stimulate the adoption of Western customs and practices in order to win acceptance as an advanced nation. When Foreign Minister Inoue Kaoru renewed the quest for equal treaties in 1886, Japan had advanced far in the development of a modern legal system and the adoption of Western ways. Cabinet members even resorted to such exaggerated demonstrations of the "progress" of the nation as attendance at masquerade balls in a specially constructed social hall. In return for treaty equality, Inoue proposed a temporary arrangement of mixed courts of foreign and Japanese judges and offered to grant unrestricted residence to foreigners. These provisions aroused antigovernment nationalist sentiment on the part of both the "people's rights" movement, which used it as an additional political weapon to attack the administration, and conservative Japanese piqued by the indiscriminate mimicking of Western customs. Ironically, Inoue was forced to terminate negotiations because of this simultaneous nationalist attack from the political left which clamored for Western constitutionalism and the extreme right which decried the headlong rush to follow Western political and social patterns. The same combination of liberal and reactionary forces also caused the defeat of Foreign Minister Ōkuma's treaty revision negotiations in 1888, and an ultranationalist fanatic attempted to assassinate Ōkuma.

Nevertheless, the government doggedly persevered in its diplomatic efforts to revise the treaties. Finally, in 1894, after Japan had completed her new legal system and persuaded the world of her progress, Great Britain, which had been particularly stubborn in refusing to yield treaty rights, signed a treaty ending extraterritoriality as of 1899. The other major powers signed similar treaties. These treaties also recognized Japan's tariff autonomy and provided for complete independence in this area by 1911.

While the successful revision of the unequal treaties satisfied the nation's aspiration for acknowledged independence and equal treatment in the international order, it was to a large measure the by-product of the general success of modernization. The desire for national security was more dramatically and more definitely met by military victories, foreign alliances, and territorial expansion.

In the course of the nineteenth and early twentieth centuries, while much of Asia fell under the domination of Western imperialism, Japan acquired great power status and an empire of her own. In striking contrast to the frequent conflicts in domestic politics, the government and people were almost completely united in external affairs. Diplomatic efforts and military clashes with foreign powers were unanimously supported as steps to full autonomy and national security. Paradoxically, politicians who were radical liberals on the home front were frequently flaming nationalists on foreign issues, while arch-conservative leaders of the government often proved to be more realistically, but nonetheless firmly, committed to expanding Japan's influence in East Asia and the world.

The world in which Meiji Japan grew up was dominated by the expansion of the Western powers. It was an age of vigorous empire-building, and large areas of Asia became colonial, or semicolonial territories of the imperial powers. A second factor confronting the Meiji statesmen was the decline of the Manchu empire. As Chinese power waned, areas such as Korea, which had lived within the orbit of the Chinese tribute system, became the victims of great power pressures. Finally, the reemergence of Russian power in the Far East became a factor of prime importance as Japan attempted to secure her place in East Asia. East Asia had become a major area for an intensified imperialist rivalry that led to the division of China into spheres of influence. In large measure, Japan defined her foreign policy in terms of the relationship between her security needs and the strategy of the imperial powers in East Asia.

In 1876 a treaty with Korea opened three Korean ports to trade and provided for diplomatic relations with an "independent" Korea. The opening of her door to Japan, and then to the Western powers, caused serious internal repercussions in Korea. The desire for independence and modernization was ill served by conflicting foreign influences and endemic factionalism at the Korean court. Meanwhile, China strove to retain her traditional role as Confucian protector and asserted her ascendancy at Seoul by self-serving intervention in palace disputes. Japan also became more deeply involved in Korean politics by siding with a reform-minded faction in the government which favored sweeping changes on the Meiji model. Factionalism and foreign pressures, palace plots and assassinations, attacks on legations, and a popular antiforeign movement to restore "Eastern Learning" combined to produce in Korea bewildering and volatile conditions.

Inevitably, Japanese activity conflicted with China's determination to strengthen her position in Korea. A series of incidents, including a clash between Japanese and Chinese troops in Seoul, and a mob attack on the Japanese legation after the fall of a pro-Japanese faction at court, were followed by a temporary diplomatic solution. By the Tientsin Convention, signed by Itō and Li Hung-chang in 1885, both nations agreed to withdraw their forces from Korea and not to send troops without notifying each other. But the nub of the Korean problem remained unchanged: the Manchu government's claim that the historical "tributary status" of Korea accorded China special rights versus the Japanese assertion that her relations were with an independent Korea with whom she could pursue policies calculated to advance her own interests. Each rightly accused the other of interfering in Korea's internal affairs.

In the years following this agreement, Japanese economic activities in Korea grew steadily, but China succeeded in strengthening her political controls in Seoul and thereby the claim of Korea's dependent status. At this point new factors emerged to complicate further a difficult situation. First, Russia's aspiration to build an empire in the Far East led her to seek economic advantages and an ice-free port in Korea. This imperial ambition in the east was symbolized by the 1891 decision to complete the construction of the Trans-Siberian Railway by 1903. Second, to counter Russian actions, Japan devised a strategy which called for the military defense of what Yamagata called the "line of advantage." For Japan's security, he argued, defense of the territorial homeland, the "line of sovereignty," was not enough; the control of Korea, where the "line of advantage" ran, must also be denied to any unfriendly power. Japan's own ambitions were furthered by the mischievous activities of Japanese expansionists in Korea and the growing belief of military bureaucrats that a foreign war would most effectively quiet the obstreperous antigovernment actions of the political parties in the Diet thereby producing unity on the home front. Thus the conflicting interests and rival ambitions of three nations, as well as the hopeless weakness of the Korean government, provided the background for a major collision.

The outbreak of a Korean domestic rebellion in 1894 became the occasion of the intervention of Chinese and Japanese troops that led to the Sino-Japanese War. The Korean king was unable to quash the rebellion and turned to China for help. In accord with the Tientsin Convention, China informed Japan that a small force was being sent to protect her "tributary state," whereupon Japan countered by dispatching forces to Korea, which, she reminded China, was not a Chinese protectorate. The Koreans were finally to quell the insurrection but now hostile foreign troops faced each other in Seoul. To put an end to incessant troubles, Japan demanded that Korea accept a broad program of reform under Sino-Japanese auspices, but China would have no part of it. By late June, 1894, the Japanese government had decided to take independent action and, if necessary, to resort to war against China. Hostilities finally broke out after the Japanese had seized the Korean government and forced it to order the expulsion of the Chinese officials and troops. War was declared on August 1, 1894.

The war was short and Japan won a spectacular victory. Land forces captured Pyongyang, crossed the Yalu River into Manchuria, and took the naval base of Port Arthur on the Liaotung Peninsula. Sea forces shattered the Chinese navy and secured control over North China waters. Upsetting the predictions of the Western powers, a small but efficient Japanese army had in three months crushed the large but scandalously incompetent Chinese forces. The extent of Japan's triumph was revealed in the terms of the Treaty of Shimonoseki that formally ended the war in April, 1895. China was forced to recognize Korea's independence; to cede Formosa, the Pescadores, and the Liaotung Peninsula in South Manchuria; to negotiate a commercial treaty granting Japan all the privileges Western powers had gained in China plus a few more; and to pay an indemnity of 200,000,000 taels (about 360,000,000 yen).

Military victory had produced impressive territorial and diplomatic gains, but less tangible consequences were fully as important. The dash and competence of the military was a gratifying measure of Japan's success in building the sinews of modern power; the Meiji reforms had proved their effectiveness. Furthermore, the war bred national purpose and patriotic pride in the military forces; the triumph produced an exhilarating feeling of confidence and self-esteem which went far to remove the national fears and anxieties of the mid-nineteenth century. Internal political divisions, as we have seen, were healed as huge war budgets were passed without a dissenting voice.

Japan's startling victory also upset the balance of power in East Asia and involved her in the complex rivalry of the great powers. The defeat of the Middle Kingdom precipitated a new phase in the age of imperialism as the Western powers advanced their own ambitions by demanding new concessions from China to build up their spheres of influence. But because of this intensification of great power rivalry Japan was to suffer a humiliating setback just as she had emerged to take her place alongside the leading powers in Asia. Russia, in particular, became alarmed at the possibility that her ambitions in Korea and Manchuria could be obstructed by Japan. As a consequence, Russia won the aid of France and Germany in forcing Japan, through diplomatic pressure, to relinquish the rights to the Liaotung Peninsula she had gained in the Treaty of Shimonoseki. Japan, in no position to resist this Triple Intervention, returned the area to China. The bitter resentment she felt at this turn of events was deepened a few years later when China ceded railway rights in Manchuria to Russia and granted her a twenty-five-year lease on the very area that Japan had been forced to give up. Great Britain, for her own reasons and in contrast to the other powers, had not been a party to the Triple Intervention. Instead she chose to cultivate a policy of friendship with Japan. This shift in British policy, the legacy of national humiliation for Japan in 1895, and the aggressive Russian policy in northeast Asia therefore were to set the scene for the next major steps in Japan's foreign relations.

At the turn of the century Japan walked in stride with the Western powers. With colonies of her own, a commanding position in Korea, and broad interests in North China, her security and national interest were vitally affected by the complex rivalry between the powers in East Asia. She had joined the other powers in agreeing to the American doctrine of the Open Door to protect their equal commercial opportunity and to preserve China's integrity as a nation. At the same time, she felt that Russian activities in Manchuria and Korea were the major menace to her establishing her security and supporting her national interests. This belief was strengthened during and after the

Boxer Rebellion in North China when Russian armies occupied a large part of Manchuria, an area already penetrated by Russia through economic activities and the building of the Chinese Eastern Railway. Great Britain also became apprehensive over the Russian encroachment in Manchuria and north Korea and turned to Japan to gain support for their common interests.

In Tokyo the government was divided between those who, like Itō and Inoue, believed that Japan's paramount power in Korea could best be gained by an agreement with Russia, and the opposing view, urged by Yamagata and Katsura, that Russia must be blocked by the force of an expanded army and navy. While the first group formulated plans for a treaty with Russia, recognizing each other's special interests, the second pressed for the expansion of the military forces and an alliance with Great Britain that would isolate Russia in the event of a conflict. At this juncture, Russian pressure on China for further concessions in Manchuria played into the hands of the military faction and the decision was taken to sign an agreement with Great Britain.

The Anglo-Japanese Alliance of 1902 readjusted the balance of imperial power in East Asia. Aside from the ritual pledge not to disturb either the *status quo* in East Asia or the independence of China and Korea, the important part of the treaty was the promise to come to each other's aid if either was attacked by more than one power, and the acknowledgment of Japan's special interests in Korea and each other's special interests in China. In effect, Great Britain had gained Japanese recognition of her dominant position in China and prevented a Russo-Japanese agreement that would menace her East Asian interest. Japan, on the other hand, had gained acknowledgment of her special position in Korea and the assurance that should a war break out with Russia, Great Britain would come to her support if France or Germany sided with Russia. The alliance meant that Great Britain recognized Japan as an equal partner in the age of imperialism and confirmed Japan's position as a world power. Under these changed circumstances, Russia declared that her military forces would be withdrawn from Manchuria in three stages over eighteen months. But declarations were not deeds.

Even though the Anglo-Japanese Alliance did not preclude a Japanese agreement with Russia, as subsequent attempts at negotiations testify, both Russia and Japan seemed to be caught in a chain of developments that must lead in the course of time to a military showdown. Russian expansion into East Asia had involved railway building (the Trans-Siberian was completed in 1903), economic penetration, commercial installations, the settlement of nationals to exploit these new opportunities, and the need to protect both the people and the capital invested. The economic rewards, however, had not been commensurate with the enormous drain on the nation's treasury; even the 6,000 mile haul across the Trans-Siberian took longer and was more costly than sea transportation from Europe to the port of Dairen on the Liaotung Peninsula. Nevertheless, the expansionist spirit in the age of empire-building was difficult to check, and Russia seemed prepared, if necessary, to protect her investments and support her ambitions with force.

Japan, on the other hand, appeared equally trapped. The early concern for security had emerged into a desire for an empire to equal the presumed economic and political advantages of the empires of the Western powers. Expansionist societies, emboldened by Japan's victory over China and the alliance with Great Britain, agitated for an extension of Japan's sphere of influence as far north as the Amur River. Some espoused an ideology that advocated an imperial mission to save China from predatory Western nations. Others supported the notion that Japan should carry modern civilization to fellow Asians. Japan's strategic thinking had pushed the "line of advantage," within which potential enemies must be excluded, well into Manchuria so that her dominant interests in Korea would be protected. Aided by the large indemnity of 1895, her economy and trade had grown rapidly, and military expenditures had increased commensurately.

Given these pressures and ambitions on both sides, it is not strange that all attempts to compose Russian-Japanese conflicts in Korea and Manchuria were of no avail. Japan's demands for a recognition of her upper hand in Korea were linked with an offer to recognize Russian rights along the railways in Manchuria provided the administration of the area was restored to China. Russia found this effort to confine her interests unacceptable, and Japan could not agree to the Russian counterproposals. In due course, mutual distrust and suspicious maneuvering on both sides undermined all diplomatic efforts to forestall hostilities.

Japanese forces attacked the Russian fleet at Port Arthur on February 4, 1904, and a declaration of war followed. The world was taken by surprise at this action and was even more surprised at the decisive victory that ensued. Japanese armies landed in Korea, crossed the

Yalu River into Manchuria, and won a series of engagements; other forces landed on the Liaotung Peninsula and captured Port Arthur after a long and costly siege. As the main Russian forces withdrew to the north they were relentlessly pursued. In March, 1905, a critical battle was fought at Mukden, where again the Russians were defeated and forced to withdraw. Meanwhile, Russian reverses on land were duplicated by naval disasters. In desperation the Russians sent their Baltic fleet of over thirty vessels around Africa to East Asia waters for a showdown on the high seas. But in May, 1905, Admiral Tōgō's fleet caught the Russian fleet as it tried to run through the Tsushima Straits, which separate Korea from Japan, and destroyed all but a few of the enemy's vessels. By the time of Admiral Tōgō's spectacular victory, both Japan and Russia were exhausted. Casualties had been heavy on both sides, the financial drain had been enormous, and Russia was confronted by revolutionary disorders at home. Both nations were eager to respond to President Theodore Roosevelt's initiative in arranging a peace conference.

The Treaty of Portsmouth, signed in August, 1905, was a major landmark in East Asian history. By it Japan acquired southern Sakhalin, the Liaotung leasehold, and Russian railway and economic rights in South Manchuria; in addition, China's sovereignty was restored in Manchuria. Russia also acknowledged Japan's supremacy in Korea but refused to pay an indemnity. The failure to gain any monetary payment had, as we have seen, serious political repercussions in Japan. Despite this, the victory of Japan over Russia represented a major step in Japan's rise as a world power. Now a full-fledged imperial power with acknowledged supremacy over Korea and vastly expanded holdings on the Asian continent, Japan found her nationalism greatly intensified by her victory, a victory which also was to stimulate the rise of nationalism throughout Asia.

In the aftermath of the victory over Russia, Japan began a new phase in her imperial expansion on the continent. Korea was converted from a nation dominated, with international approval, by Japanese political and economic power to a protectorate under which the last vestige of nationhood were destroyed. As a final step, Japan absorbed the peninsula by annexation in 1910, organized the area as an integral part of her empire and pursued policies geared to Japan's national interests, paying no regard to the aspirations of the Korean people for independence. In Manchuria, Japanese economic penetration, based on newly acquired rights and territory, was vigorously pushed through the exploitation of the South Manchurian Railway Company. Ironically, from the Treaty of Portsmouth flowed Russian-Japanese collaboration in Manchuria; the relations of the two countries were stabilized in a treaty signed in 1907 that made a north-south division of the region into mutually recognized spheres of influence and control.

The Meiji era had seen an unparalleled transformation in Japan's international position. She had risen from a frightened island-nation threatened by the Western powers to the level of a proud, extensive empire allied to the leading power of the West. As a result of her rise, the structure of great power relations in East Asia was dramatically altered. The high point of Western imperialism had passed, for from this point on Western domination over East Asia receded and the Western nations turned their attention more to their relations within Europe. For a generation the actions of the imperial powers of the West had been the main determinant in the course of events in the international relations of East Asia, but during the fifteen years following the Sino-Japanese War an important initiative and the determining influence in the affairs of East Asia was gained by Japan. The aim of the Meiji leaders of building a strong, secure nation equal to the Western powers had been fulfilled beyond their dreams.

The Transformation of Meiji Japan

Thus far the narrative of political events from 1877 to 1910, showing the evolution of the Meiji political system, has been presented, and over the same period the attainment of national goals through the achievement of great power status has been traced. These internal political events and external relations cannot be understood, however, unless they are viewed against the background of an over-all process of modernization that transformed every aspect of Japanese civilization in the Meiji era—the economic structure, the social patterns, the educational system, the thought, literature, and fine arts. Every aspect of Japanese life, from clothes and habits of speech to social customs and philosophical concepts, was profoundly influenced by the tidal wave of Westernization that engulfed Japan. This does not mean that traditional ways were completely cast aside. But few corners of Meiji Japan went untouched or unchanged. There was a fundamental uniformity in the myriad changes: the effort to learn the techniques, institutions, and ideas of the West and to adjust them to fit local conditions.

Fundamental to the development of Meiji Japan was the introduction of Western technology and the growth of industrialization. Rapid progress had already been made along these lines by the late 1870s. Government initiative and funds had constructed arsenals, shipyards, and communications systems which were strategically important for the building of military power. They had also built factories for the manufacture of such things as bricks, glass, and cement. While the use of public funds and government supervision is characteristic of early economic growth, there was considerable scope for private capital and initiative. In the fields of mining, textiles manufacturing, especially in silk production, and in the many enterprises requiring limited capital, private investment played the major role. By the 1880s cotton spinning, which became Meiji Japan's largest industry, was almost entirely privately controlled. Government sponsorship combined with private enterprise to stimulate rapid economic growth. An additional factor which boosted industrialization was the employment of hundreds of foreign experts to teach, advise, and train a generation of Japanese on how to build and run modern industries.

The steady, if slow, increase in factories and industrial production in early Meiji was accompanied by the growth of other sectors of the economy. Most conspicuous was the rise in agricultural output. Acreage expanded and with the development of new techniques, often stimulated by government argicultural extension services, agricultural yield doubled between the 1880s and 1910. This meant a higher rate of increase than the expansion of the population, which moved from slightly less than thirty-seven million in 1880 to about fifty million in 1910. Trade also grew apace, with silk and cotton textiles as the major exports, and a favorable balance was recorded in the mideighties. So although the government fostered the development of strategic industries and built model factories and public services, the rest of the economy grew under private entrepreneurship. Moreover, growth in the traditional enterprises accompanied the development in the modern sector to provide a balanced foundation for the more rapid growth of the later decades.

By 1880 the government's ambitious economic plans were in difficulties. Many of the government enterprises were unprofitable, the effort to develop Hokkaido had been costly, the price of paying off the samurai was high, and the financial burden of the Satsuma Rebellion had drained the treasury. The consequence of this state of affairs was a serious inflation that drove prices up and the value of the land tax, the government's main source of income, down. One solution suggested was to seek a large foreign loan, but the Meiji leaders steered clear of all but a few minor loans to support their economic program in order to avoid the possibility of foreign control. Instead, Matsukata, the finance minister, decided in 1881 to cut back the government's economic involvement in industry and adopt a policy of deflation.

Economic retrenchment through the sale of government industries coincided with a major political crisis; this gave rise to accusations that the policy was politically motivated to favor wealthy industrialists so as to gain support for the government. Although many of those who bought the plants and mines at bargain rates were closely connected with government leaders, the decision was undoubtedly made for sound fiscal reasons. In any case two results ensued: first, the purchases placed large sectors of the economy in private hands and laid the foundations for the emergence of such zaibatsu combines as Mitsui and Mitsubishi; and second, the policy succeeded in restoring the financial health of the government, a stable monetary system was created, and the way was paved for impressive economic growth.

The late 1880s were boom years; all the economic indicators rose. The number of plants doubled by 1890, production expanded, trade increased, and there was a rush of entrepreneurs into new industries. The war against China stimulated another surge. The demand for goods grew and production spurted while the war was paid for by the Chinese indemnity. By the turn of the century Japan's economy had grown, with occasional pauses, to an impressive point in its technological development. Modern industries had burgeoned but at the same time agriculture and small enterprises responding to the demands of traditional tastes had also expanded.

The third and much more impressive economic boom came after the Russo-Japanese War. Electrical industries grew, the government-founded Yawata Steel Works diminished the need for heavy iron and steel imports, shipbuilding expanded—in short, heavy industries became a major component of the economy. The capital invested in industries of all description multiplied by leaps and bounds.

The rate at which Japan adopted Western technology and industrial institutions in the Meiji period was matched by the speed at which new knowledge and skills were acquired and a modern educational system developed. The search for appropriate Western models and the yearning to understand the Occident had produced many books and translations which acquainted the people with the ideas as well as the exotic customs of the West. The adoption of foreign ways was a product of mixed motives: realization that social and intellectual changes were a necessary part of modern innovation and the conviction that conformity to Western practices was one way of avoiding the shame of backwardness. Therefore, along with the more significant institutional and organizational shifts, Meiji society went wild in experimenting with and adopting the more superficial signs of Westernization. Brushing teeth with powders, shaking hands instead of bowing, dressing in Western clothes and wearing Western-style haircuts all became fashionable marks of the proper modern citizen. One prominent intellectual was met by raised eyebrows when he asserted his egalitarian ideals by marrying in a ceremony where he and his wife exchanged rings and concluded a formal understanding that pledged them to an equal relationship. Along with trolleys, trains, and the telegraph came a fad for Western art, architecture, and attire. And all these changes, both the serious and the whimsical, were pursued in a quest for progress, advancement, and self-improvement that characterized the temper of early Meiji.

As in other aspects of Meiji society, government leaders often led the way in borrowing from abroad. Almost all of the ruling circle traveled to Europe and America to study the secrets of Western success, and many on their return built at least partially Western-style houses for themselves. For the political elite, Westernization was seen also as a way of hastening the end of the unequal treaties. This was the prime reason for building in 1883 the Rokumeikan, a Western-style public hall where international balls and other social events attended by government dignitaries and the diplomatic corps were held.

By the late 1880s, however, the craze for things Western had generated conservative countercurrents. Attacks were made against the indiscriminate emulation of foreign ideas and the submerging of traditional tastes by the flood of crass imitation. The swing away from exaggerated Westernization was encouraged by those who argued that the weakening of traditional culture and values was a disservice to the goals of national unity and strength. Furthermore, they asserted, the West was not a single cultural unit, and only through a critical selection of those elements that would blend with tradition could the state find secure independence. The renewed interest in the past coincided with the debates on what form the constitutional system should take. It was pointed out by conservative thinkers that there were as many ideas in Western thought that could be adopted in support of an authoritarian imperial system as there were theories to justify a liberal parliamentary policy. As we have seen, by the late 1880s the Meiji leaders, with confidence stemming from the success of their institutional changes, were justifying their political stand by the concepts of conservative Prussia. The promulgation of a constitution centered on the traditional imperial system, the formulation of a Confucian-oriented ethical standard in the Rescript on Education of 1890, and the upsurge of patriotic pride during the war against China were major landmarks in the recrudescence of traditional values at the heart of nationalist sentiment. Relative political stability, victorious wars, and industrial progress undergirded the vigorous nationalism that aided in the fulfillment of the goals of the state.

The rapid acquisition of new knowledge and modern skills as well as the inculcation of traditional values in support of national goals is most vividly seen in the educational system that evolved in Meiji Japan. In the early stages, emphasis was placed on building an educational system that would educate all the people and spread Western knowledge to all levels of society. French and American models influenced the early Meiji school system, with the centralized structure of the former combined with the ideal of independent self-development of the latter. By 1880 the sixteen months of schooling made compulsory for all children in 1872 was extended to three years and later to six years. At the time the requirement was raised to three years, only about 50 percent of the male and less than 20 percent of the female children were in school. By 1900 these percentages had risen, respectively, to 90 and 70, and by 1910 the figure had risen to over 95 percent for both sexes.

By the turn of the century the government educational structure reached its mature form. Above the compulsory six-year elementary schools were the five-year middle schools along with girls' high schools and various technical schools. These levels produced a literate population and provided limited technical skills for boys, and all the education it was felt that girls needed. At the next level were higher technical schools and the three-year higher schools which led to the three-year government universities. Thus, by the end of the Meiji era, the Japanese literacy rate was one of the highest in the world, and the people were well educated to meet the requirements of modern society. This was a dramatic illustration of the fulfillment of a national policy. The parallel development of a system of private schools and universities, including many founded by Christian missionaries, added diversity to an impressive educational structure.

At the same time that the quantity of education increased, the orientation of the content of the system was altered. Most conspicuous was the swing away from the goal of self-improvement and self-advancement to the aim of fitting education to meet the needs of the state. During the 1880s, when skepticism and opposition rose against the excessive orientation to the West, a shift in policy was made as a step in consolidating support for the goals of the nation. Based upon the Confucian concepts of the close link between morality, education, and government, greater emphasis was placed on ethics courses and the principle of loyalty to the state. The new policy received emphatic definition in the Rescript on Education issued by the emperor in 1890. The ideals of social harmony, respect for law and order, and service to the nation in order to "guard and maintain the prosperity of Our Imperial Throne coeval with heaven and earth" were set forth as the aims of education. Thus we see that in the reorientation of the educational system, no less than in the changing intellectual climate of the 1880s and after, Western influences were tempered and modified by a reinvigoration of traditional values.

VII

Taishō

and Early Shōwa

Japan

BY

ARTHUR E. TIEDEMANN

On the night of July 29, 1912, the broad plaza in front of the Tokyo imperial palace was filled with thousands of people, most of them prostrated upon the ground in prayer. Within the palace the sixty-year-old Emperor Meiji lay dying of uremia. A few hours after midnight the gathered multitude learned the emperor had died and from them as if from a single throat, there rose a great wail of lamentation. To the Japanese it seemed as if not simply a reign but rather an era had ended.

The death of the Emperor Meiji was the point at which people looked around and for the first time became fully aware of the tremendous changes which had overtaken Japanese society in the preceding two decades. Japan had ceased to be simply a rural, agricultural country whose foreign trade was directed to supplying raw materials to the West. Increasingly it was becoming a manufacturing nation whose interest focused on purveying Western style light industrial products to the markets of Asia, especially China. The first long steps toward industrialization and urbanization had been taken, and all the economic, social, and political forces and problems attendant on such a change had been called into being. Some Japanese eagerly welcomed the passing of the old Japan and confidently looked forward to reshaping Japanese life in accordance with the most advanced and progressive thought currents in the West. Many others regarded with horror the heterodox ideas, the extravagant ambitions, the vulgar indulgence, and the brassy self-centered opportunism which seemed the inevitable concomittant of the new era. In their eyes the abandonment of the traditional virtues was rotting away the very fabric of Japanese society and could bring nothing but disaster. It was as a warning against this that, as the Emperor Meiji's funeral cortege left the palace, General Nogi, the Russo-Japanese War hero, ceremoniously committed hara-kiri.

The Taishō Political Crisis

The sense that the ascension of the new Emperor Taishō (Great Righteousness) represented a moment of profound change was heightened by a great political crisis which developed shortly after the Emperor Meiji's death. In 1912 the prime minister was Saionji Kimmochi, the court noble who had become president of the Seiyūkai party, but the real power in the cabinet and the party was the home minister, Hara Kei. By a judicious exploitation of the pork barrel Hara had developed the Seiyūkai into a disciplined party firmly rooted among the locally powerful interests in every part of Japan. He had also used his first term as home minister (1906–8) to create a loyal following among the bureaucrats. In the election of May, 1912, promises of funds for local development and the application of pressure by prefectural governors enabled the Seiyūkai to obtain a substantial majority in the House of Representatives. Hara hoped to use government funds to expand his party's influence even further. However, in the fall of 1912 it became clear that the nation had been brought to the brink of financial disaster through the huge budgets produced by the Hara system, by arms expansion, by domestic capital investment, and by the development of Japan's newly acquired overseas possessions. These expenditures had been financed largely through constant resort to foreign and domestic borrowing, but by 1912 the nation's credit was nearly exhausted. The problem was that while much of the spending was economically sound it had been for projects which did not yield immediate returns. Moreover, there had been an overly optimistic development of productive capacity beyond the needs of the available markets. Foreign trade in particular did not expand at the anticipated rate, so that Japan was experiencing great difficulty in meeting its foreign payments.

Faced with these difficulties the Saionji cabinet decided that the only way to restore confidence in the nation's finances was to hold down expenditures in the budget for 1913. Determining the precise areas in which expansion plans would be cut back immediately became a political problem. Hara, fearful that any reduction in economic development funds would adversely affect the fortunes of the Seiyūkai, managed to confine most of the cuts to the administrative and military portions of the budget. The chief sufferer was the army, which was once again asked to postpone the creation of two new divisions long promised it by the government. For Yamagata and the other army leaders this was a difficult decision to accept since they were convinced that the situation unfolding in China as a consequence of the October, 1911, revolution made two additional divisions absolutely necessary. They argued that China was disintegrating and Japan must be able to intervene militarily to protect its interests in Manchuria and Inner Mongolia. The Saionji cabinet felt that the gains of such a military intervention would be more than offset by the hostility it would arouse among the powers and by the probable exclusion of Japan from the markets of China proper. The cabinet could not, therefore, concede the immediate necessity for the two divisions and adamantly refused the army's request. In a last desperate attempt to get their way the army leaders had the army minister resign and then refused to supply another candidate until their demands were satisfied. Unable to function without an army minister and unwilling to accept the army's terms, the Saionji cabinet resigned on December 5, 1912.

Saionji's unexpected choice caught Yamagata unprepared with an alternative candidate for the prime ministership. At first he tried, unsuccessfully, to persuade Saionji to resume the post. As consultations among the flustered genrō dragged on inconclusively day after day, the outraged public was given an opportunity to crystallize its opposition to the military's highhanded treatment of a cabinet which just a few months before had won an overwhelming election victory. The Kōjunsha, a social club of politicians, journalists, and businessmen (mostly Keiō University graduates) took the lead in launching a movement to "protect constitutional government." The fury of the public rose to even greater heights when with Saionji's concurrence the genrō finally in desperation decided to call upon Katsura Tarō to leave his nonpolitical palace post as lord keeper of the privy seal and organize his third cabinet. The anger was further exacerbated when Katsura secured an imperial order directing the reluctant navy to supply him with a minister. To the public the action appeared to be the most blatant reassertion of the Chōshū clique's hegemony and a flagrant abuse of the emperor's prestige. At mass rallies addressed by the veteran parliamentarians Ozaki Yukio and Inukai Ki it was demanded that Chōshū-dominated genrō politics be replaced by party cabinets.

Though individual Seiyūkai members joined the swelling anti-Katsura tide, Hara Kei held off committing the party itself until he could discover whether Katsura was willing to resume the old working arrangement with the Seiyūkai that had characterized his first two cabinets. If the Seiyūkai's access to power and government funds could be preserved, Hara was quite willing to overlook the constitutional issue. Katsura, however, had long since decided that the Seiyūkai's cooperation came at too high a cost. When he had last left the prime ministership in August, 1911, he was resolved to found a political party and end his dependence on the Seiyūkai. He had been thwarted in this design by the disapproving Yamagata, who took advantage of the Emperor Meiji's death to remove Katsura, a one-time protégé, from active political life by securing his appointment as lord keeper of the privy seal and grand chamberlain to the Emperor Taishō. Once summoned back to the political scene, Katsura, defying both Hara and Yamagata, began to implement his long delayed plans. His invitation to join his party met with an eager response from many members of the smaller Diet parties. These men felt they were doomed to futility and extinction if they could not settle their minor differences and organize a united opposition to the Seiyūkai. Katsura's bid seemed a golden opportunity to obtain the money and the bureaucratic patronage necessary to build a strong party capable of rivaling the Seiyūkai and destroying its dominance. To these Diet recruits Katsura was able to add his many followers among the bureaucrats, for example, Gotō Shimpei, Katō Kōmei, Wakatsuki Reijirō, Hamaguchi Osachi. He was convinced that by the time the Diet reconvened on February 5, 1913, enough Seiyūkai members would have deserted their party to give him a majority.

In this he was mistaken, for when the Diet reassembled his opposition still controlled a majority and Ozaki Yukio loosed a famous tirade in which he accused Katsura of hiding behind the throne and ambushing his foes with imperial rescripts. Faced with the certainty of a no-confidence vote, Katsura quickly prorogued the Diet and began maneuvering to neutralize the Seiyūkai opposition. With what he thought to be Saionji's agreement, Katsura obtained from the emperor an order directing Saionji to bring the Seiyūkai into line. On February 10, just a few hours before the Diet was to reopen, Saionji presented the message to the Seiyūkai caucus. By an overwhelming voice vote the imperial command was rejected. The decision stunned Katsura, who had gone to the Diet building brimming over with confidence in his victory. Reluctant to face the turmoil of a general election, he immediately decided to resign, and postponed the Diet meeting. The crowds surging around the Diet building, knowing merely that the Diet had been suspended, were transformed into a mob which rampaged through central Tokyo and was suppressed only by the use of cavalry and thousands of policemen. The Tokyo riots spread to the other main urban centers but soon petered out, since the anti-Katsura parties, having obtained their objective, provided no leadership or organization.

The Seiyūkai's resolve to resist Katsura had been stiffened at the last moment by the news that Yamamoto Gombei, the Satsuma admiral, was willing to accept the prime ministership. The Satsuma group, which had not supplied a prime minister since 1897, sought by this means to restore its flagging influence. The genrō finally, with some reluctance, did turn to Yamamoto, and upon entering office he established a working agreement with Hara much along the lines of the one Hara used to have with Katsura. Hara also exacted two administrative reforms from Yamamoto: 1) a very small number of top bureaucrat positions were removed from the civil service list and thus made available for patronage; 2) eligibility to serve as army or navy minister, which had been restricted to generals, lieutenant-generals, admirals, and vice-admirals on active duty, was now extended to retired officers of the same rank. No prime minister ever made use of this second provision, so it must be admitted that the sound and fury of the movement "to protect constitutional government" effected very little change in the structure of the Japanese government. However, after this date it was impossible to settle a political matter by invoking a personal imperial decision. Moreover, despite Katsura's fall from power and sudden death shortly thereafter, the politicians and bureaucrats he had gathered under his banner stuck together and formed the nucleus of a second party. They organized the Dōshikai (Association of Like-minded Persons) and accepted as its president Katō Kōmei, a former bureaucrat who not only had several times been foreign minister and thus was prime ministerial timber but who had also married into the Iwasaki (Mitsubishi) family and therefore had access to money. With this there emerged a party whose members possessed the administrative talent, the political influence, and the financial support necessary to effectively challenge the Seiyūkai's monopoly and thus create a real two-party system.

The Yamamoto cabinet had fairly smooth sailing until suddenly in January, 1914, the Japanese press printed a Reuter's dispatch reporting that Berlin court proceedings had revealed evidence of Japanese naval officers accepting bribes to facilitate contract negotiations between the navy and Siemens, Schuckert Company. The report immediately brought to the fore the smoldering resentment against the large budgetary sums with which the navy had been favored in recent years and against the continuous high taxes these grants had necessitated. In the lower house of the Diet the Dōshikai and the other opposition parties on February 10 presented a no-confidence motion, which the Seiyūkai majority easily voted down. On the same day there were several violent clashes between the crowds and the police but Hara, as home minister, quickly restored order. Nevertheless, the

Yamamoto cabinet had to resign in March, 1914, when the House of Peers expressed its distaste for Yamamoto and the Seiyūkai by obstinately refusing to pass the budget. A hostile House of Peers backed by general public hostility was too much for the cabinet to face even though it had a lower house majority.

After over three weeks of inconclusive discussions the genrō, among whom by this time Saionji was numbered, finally settled on the old warhorse Ōkuma Shigenobu, who had several years before retired from active political life. Katō Kōmei was brought in as foreign minister, assuring the new cabinet of the Dōshikai's support. Ōkuma's appointment was hailed by the public as a step toward liberal government. The reactions might have been more reserved if the public had known that Yamagata and other genrō had accepted Ōkuma on the understanding that he would give the army its two divisions and destroy the Seiyūkai party. When the Seiyūkai secured the Diet's rejection of the two new divisions in December, 1914, Ōkuma dissolved the lower house. In the subsequent election, Ōura Kanetake, a former police official whom Ōkuma had made home minister, used bribery and every kind of government intimidation to break the Seiyūkai. The Seiyūkai was able to return only 104 members and the Dōshikai with 150 members became the largest party. Ōura was impeached at the first session of the new Diet, but this came to nothing, since Ōkuma's adherents had a majority and rallied to the support of the man who had secured their election. Nevertheless, in July, 1915, Ōura had to resign when overwhelming evidence of his bribing Diet members was presented in the Tokyo District Court. At this time Katō Kōmei and some other ministers expressed their disapproval of Ōura by resigning. However, the Dōshikai's public image had already been tarnished by its vote against Ōura's impeachment in the face of his flagrant election interference and on the matter of moral principle the public saw little to choose between the Dōshikai and the Seiyūkai. The new Diet, of course, gave the army its two divisions.

Foreign Relations During World War I

In the field of foreign affairs, within a few months of taking office, the Ōkuma cabinet was confronted with the outbreak of the European war. Anxious to avoid the spread of hostilities to China, England asked that Japan restrict her assistance under the Anglo-Japanese Alliance to preventing German raiders from operating in the China

Sea and undertake further military action only if English bases in China were attacked. Foreign Minister Katō insisted that Japan must seize this opportunity to drive the Germans from East Asia. The English, fearful of the American and Australian reaction if Japan should step into Germany's place in China and the Pacific, withdrew their request for aid. Even some highly placed Japanese were reluctant to enter the war too quickly: to them the outcome was not at all clear and they feared Japan might be betting on the wrong side. Katō would not yield and on August 23, 1914, Japan declared war, using in her ultimatum the very phrases the Germans had employed toward Japan in the 1895 intervention. By November the German base in Shantung and the German Pacific islands were in Japanese hands. Thereafter, except for some token convoy duty in the Mediterranean, Japanese participation in World War I ended.

The Chinese government tried to limit Japanese activity in Shantung to the Kiaochow naval base and its environs, but the Japanese army pushed ahead to seize the German-built Shantung Railroad and in effect occupied the whole province. Japan was determined that all the German rights in Shantung were to be transferred to herself. The foreign minister, Katō Kōmei, had also decided that now was the time to settle all outstanding issues with China. For some time the Japanese had been concerned by the fact that their position in Manchuria depended upon rights which had in 1898 been granted the Russians for twenty-five years. This meant that by 1923 there would be no legal basis for the huge interests which Japan was building up in Manchuria. Now, while the Western powers were distracted by the European war and Japanese forces were on Chinese soil, there seemed to be an excellent opportunity to press the Chinese not only to transfer the German rights to Japan but also to expand Japanese rights in Manchuria and Inner Mongolia and to extend the time limit on those rights to ninety-nine years. These points constituted Group One and Group Two of the famous Twenty-one Demands secretly presented to President Yuan Shih-k'ai on January 18, 1915. Perhaps to test just how much could be squeezed out of the rickety Chinese government, Katō Kōmei also included three other groups of demands which, if granted, would have made China a virtual Japanese protectorate: Group Three in essence turned over the Han-Yeh-P'ing Company's steel and iron production to Japan; Group Four prohibited the ceding or leasing of any part of the Chinese seacoast to a third power; Group Five provided that the Chinese were to employ Japanese political, financial, and military advisers, that Japan would aid in policing certain Chinese cities, and that the mine, harbor, and railroad development in Fukien be turned over to Japan.

Though the Japanese had enjoined strict secrecy upon the Chinese government, Yuan Shih-k'ai arranged for the demands to be leaked in the hope that public opinion would be aroused. In this he was not mistaken for both in China and among the Western nations the Japanese action called forth universal condemnation. Even in Japan itself some of the genrō and other political leaders felt that Katō Kōmei had gone too far and risked permanently alienating the Chinese. They argued that a softer policy would do more to improve Japan's position in China than the present bullying. In the face of this opposition Katō Kōmei gradually modified Japan's demands, withdrawing in particular Group Five. Finally, on May 25, 1915, the Chinese government, having been faced with a forty-eight hour ultimatum, signed a series of treaties embodying most of the demands of the first four groups. Japan had assured her legal position in Shantung, Manchuria, and Mongolia, but she had inflicted an injury on Chinese pride which would not be forgotten and which would contribute significantly to giving an anti-Japanese twist to the newly rising tide of Chinese nationalism.

At this time, however, the attitude of the Western powers was of more concern to Japanese diplomacy than the reaction of a weak and disorganized China. Some day the war would end and the powers would resume their game in East Asia; Japan wished to make certain that when that day came the gains she had made in the 1915 treaties would not be snatched from her. Since it was not clear in 1915 who would emerge victorious from the war, Japan did not reject out of hand a German approach which offered to accept Japan's possession of Shantung and the Pacific Islands, to give Japan a free hand in China, and to grant the Japanese extensive loans. In return the Germans asked that Japan cease forwarding military supplies to Russia. Exploratory conversations were actually held in Stockholm during the early months of 1915 and 1916. On both occasions the Japanese informed the various Allied Powers and the danger of a Japanese-German agreement undoubtedly helped Japan secure from England, France, and Russia recognition of Japan's new rights under the 1915 Sino-Japanese treaties. In July, 1916, Russia signed a defensive alliance with Japan directed at any third power which should threaten either country's interests in China, especially in Manchuria and Inner Mongolia. This treaty was regarded by the Japanese as the bulwark of their position in China. Later, in early 1917, Japan made agreements with England and France which sanctioned her gains in China and the Pacific. Even the United States appeared to accept the inevitable when Secretary of State Lansing in November, 1917, signed with Ambassador Ishii a statement which recognized "that territorial propinquity creates special relations between countries, and consequently . . . Japan has special interests in China, particularly in the part to which her possessions are contiguous."

The tightrope Japan was walking in her foreign policy had caused a number of Japanese leaders to conclude that a high degree of domestic political unity would be necessary if the country was to get safely and profitably through the dangers of the war and the postwar period. They were reluctant to entrust this delicate task to the Ōkuma cabinet, which had already demonstrated such ineptitude in its bungled handling of the 1915 negotiations. Consequently, in the fall of 1915 talk arose of establishing a national union cabinet. In the spring of 1916 the leaders of the three largest political parties—Katō Kōmei, Hara Kei, and Inukai Ki—consulted together and issued a statement pledging to place foreign policy and national defense beyond political discussions. The genrō Yamagata, who was convinced the country needed a government around which all Japanese could rally and therefore one above all parties, did not favor any of these party leaders for prime minister. His choice fell upon General Terauchi Masatake, who had since 1910 been governor-general of Korea. Yamagata regarded him as a strong, forceful man who would bring to the prime ministership not only military and administrative experience but also considerable knowledge of how to deal with the Chinese. Turning aside Ōkuma's attempt to have Katō Kōmei named as prime minister, Yamagata in October, 1916, ushered the supraparty Terauchi cabinet into office. Almost immediately thereafter the Dōshikai joined with the various groups which had supported Ōkuma to organize, under Katō Kōmei's presidency, the Kenseikai (Constitutional Government Association). The new party controlled a majority in the House of Representatives and Katō Kōmei plainly indicated he did not intend to withhold his criticism of the new cabinet. When the Diet met in January, 1917, Terauchi dissolved it. In the ensuing April elections the "unnatural majority" of the Kenseikai was destroyed and the Seiyūkai reemerged as the largest party in the house. No party, however, had a majority, although with the tacit support of the

Seiyūkai and its other supporters the Terauchi cabinet was able to obtain what it wanted from the Diet.

In its new approach to China the Terauchi cabinet decided it would stop relying upon Western style imperialist agreements and turn instead to an arrangement based on traditional Confucian ideals laced with an appeal to the solidarity of the "yellow race" against the "white race." Terauchi believed that Japan could deal with the new military men who had gained control of Peking after Yuan Shih-k'ai's death in June, 1916. His advisers felt that if China were handled sympathetically by Japan she would be a natural ally in the coming global struggle between the races. In his dealings with the Peking leaders Terauchi bypassed the normal foreign ministry machinery and operated instead through his personal aide Nishihara Kamezō. It was Nishihara's plan to develop economic cooperation between China and Japan and eventually create an autarkic economic sphere. To further this end he negotiated with Peking in 1917 and 1918 something like 145,000,000 yen of what were called economic development loans. The granting of such huge loans by a nation which in 1914 was itself heavily in debt was made possible, of course, by the huge profits the war boom had brought Japan. In actual fact very little if anything of these unsecured loans was used for economic purposes. They were diverted rather to building up the military and political power of the Tuan Ch'i-jui government. It was the hope of the Terauchi cabinet to strengthen Tuan to the point where he could unify China politically and then to develop a military, political, and economic coalition with him which would give Japan an "elder brother's" predominance in China.

Hardly had the Terauchi cabinet begun to implement its China plans when the fall of the tsar's government confronted it with a radically altered situation. The Japanese army regarded the disorder in Russia as a golden chance to move into Siberia. It had soon drawn up a plan calling for seven divisions to occupy Siberia up to Lake Baikal. The marvelous opportunity to seize Siberia's riches relegated China to a position important primarily as a staging area for the control of Siberia. Japanese efforts in Peking were now directed toward obtaining an agreement from the Peking government for Sino-Japanese military cooperation ostensibly aimed at preventing the Germans and Austrians from taking advantage of Russia's trouble to disturb the peace of East Asia. By May, 1918, an agreement was signed giving Japan the right to move troops freely about on Chinese soil. Although it was fully prepared to act, the Japanese army had great difficulty persuading the Terauchi cabinet to take the plunge and invade Siberia. England and France, wishing to maintain an Eastern front in Russia, and seeking to prevent the tons of supplies in Siberia from falling into German hands, had for some time been urging Japan to act. However, the Wilson administration was very reluctant to see Japan turned loose in Siberia and had persistently vetoed the move. Some members of the Japanese government, feeling that Japan was still not strong enough to risk antagonizing the United States, refused to go along with the decision to invade unless American consent was secured. A head-on collision was shaping up within the Japanese government when suddenly the crisis was ended in July, 1918, by an invitation from President Wilson to participate in a joint allied expeditionary force to Siberia. In Wilson's mind the need to rescue the stranded Czech troops in Siberia had come to outweigh the dangers of Japanese troops entering the region. Wilson's invitation was accepted and the Japanese army, disregarding suggested limits on contingent size, threw 75,000 troops into Siberia, three times the number sent by their allies. Thus began an expensive four-year-long attempt upon the part of Japan to gain control of eastern Siberia or at least to detach it from Russia and establish there a cooperative buffer state.

The Hara Cabinet: Domestic Affairs

As has been indicated, Japan was able to undertake her costly foreign adventures only because of the tremendous change wrought in her economy by World War I. The war rescued her stagnating industry and allowed her to put to work her overbuilt production capacity. The Allies, especially Russia, were begging for war materials, and price was no object. In many instances, the Allies themselves supplied the Japanese with raw materials and asked merely that they be processed. As European suppliers of civilian goods dropped out of neutral markets, the Japanese filled the gap, particularly in Asia. The physical volume of exports increased 40 percent; the money value 300 percent. Japan entered new lines of production and greatly diversified as well as expanded her industry. Factory workers increased by over 70 percent and urban centers swelled. Japanese maritime tonnage doubled and income from shipping increased tenfold. By the end of the war

Japan had switched from a debtor nation to a country whose international account showed a net credit of more than a billion yen.

The heavy demand for labor entailed by the rapid wartime expansion of industry led, of course, to rising wages for the factory worker and miner. But inflationary pressures drove prices up even more rapidly and in the end the real wage actually declined. Some of the traditional sectors of the economy, fishing for instance, did not fully participate in the general prosperity. These groups were gripped by something akin to desperation as during the course of 1918 the ever-soaring price of rice began to place the cost of their staple food beyond their reach. Finally, on August 6, 1918, the fishermen's wives of a small village in a fairly remote part of Japan (Toyama) rioted in protest against the rising rice price. Within a matter of days, in an almost spontaneous manner and with absolutely no incitement by radical agitators, rioting spread to over 300 cities, towns, and villages. Rice dealers and the wealthy were attacked and their warehouses sacked. In many localities troops were required to suppress the violence. The Terauchi cabinet, the whole Japanese establishment was shocked to its core. Never before had there been anything quite like this widespread outburst of elemental rage against grievances with which the government had proven incapable of dealing effectively. In September the humiliated Terauchi cabinet resigned.

When the surviving genrō—Yamagata, Matsukata, Saionji—met to pick the next prime minister, their choice fell upon Hara Kei, the Seiyūkai president. Yamagata would have preferred a nonparty man but once Saionji refused the position he could see few alternatives to Hara. Besides, Hara had managed over the last few years to convince Yamagata that their ideas were pretty much in tune, a point which Hara's loyal support of the Terauchi cabinet seemed to bear out. In addition, there was the lurking fear that if Hara were now refused his chance and passed over in favor of some bureaucratic protégé he might very well combine with the Kenseikai to bring the new cabinet down. Thus Japan for the first time received a prime minister who was, by deliberate choice, without a title of nobility and who had a seat in the lower house of the Diet. As prime minister Hara proved very adept at gaining the support of the various segments of the Japanese power structure. In Tanaka Giichi he found an army minister who appreciated that times had changed and the army must draw closer to the general public if it was to maintain its power. By a judicious sprinkling of cabinet and para-cabinet jobs among the members of the House of Peers he succeeded in maintaining an amicable working relationship with that body. His long-standing connection with the bureaucracy assured him full cooperation in that quarter.

Unfortunately, however, Hara's great political skills were not addressed to solving the numerous domestic, social, and economic problems which confronted Japan during his term of office: the inflation; the readjustment of the Japanese economy to the realities of the postwar world; the influx of ideas from abroad generated by the wartime propaganda of the Allies and the Russian Revolution; the growing demands of the rapidly expanding labor movement. Although many greeted Hara as the herald of a new era, his gaze was really directed backward toward the political problems of the prewar period and his main interest was in furthering the old policies he had found so successful in building power for himself and the Seiyūkai. Only slight changes were made in the governmental structure to which Hara had so skillfully adapted himself. The colonial governorship, hitherto reserved for military men, were opened to civilians, but in Korea no effort was made to implement this new policy. A few positions were taken off the civil service list, but these were mostly technical jobs and could not be used to expand party control in the bureaucracy. Far more important to Hara than structural changes was his deeply felt need to secure a crushing Seiyūkai majority in the Diet. To this end he obtained in 1919 the passage of a new election law which maintained a tax qualification for voters and which brazenly rearranged election districts so as to give every possible advantage to the Seiyūkai. To prepare the ground for the next election Hara provided lavish government funds for railroad building, new schools, and local economic development. By 1920 government expenditures were double those of 1917 and there had been a tremendous expansion in the national debt.

This obvious manipulation of governmental policy in the selfish electoral interest of a narrow political group was very disillusioning to the public. Moreover, the continuation of a tax qualification for voting ran counter to the growing demand for the adoption of universal manhood suffrage, a cause behind which many of the newer forces emerging on the Japanese scene had placed themselves. The liberal intellectuals among the university professors and the journalists saw in universal suffrage a device which would destroy the old network of interests in the election districts, thereby purifying the political parties and making them representative of the whole population rather than merely the propertied classes. These intellectuals also felt that universal suffrage would channel popular discontent into constructive paths and avoid a repetition of the senseless destruction of the rice riots. The labor unions, now numbering over 200, fastened on universal suffrage as a means of obtaining the legal right to organize, the repeal of oppressive police regulations, the eight-hour day, and the improvement of working conditions. The farmers' unions, organized in increasing numbers among the landless tenants after World War I, likewise regarded expanded voting rights as an important step toward solving their economic dilemma. Also vitally concerned with universal suffrage were the university students. In 1919 students at Tokyo University founded the "New Man Society" (Shinjinkai), an organization devoted to the study of social thought and social problems which soon became a model for similar student groups at other universities. Under the influence of their voracious and often ill-digested consumption of democratic, socialistic, communistic, anarchistic, and every other conceivable type of Western thought, these upper- and middle-class students developed a humanitarian concern for the welfare of the broad mass of Japanese and set about actively to improve conditions of life in Japan. To them universal suffrage seemed an appropriate place to begin.

On February 11, 1919, and on the same day in 1920 huge but orderly public demonstrations demanding universal manhood suffrage were held in Tokyo. Impressed by the support the measure drew, the Kenseikai and other opposition parties introduced manhood suffrage bills in the Diet meeting held during the winter of 1919–20. The Kenseikai had even begun to move toward preparing legislation to deal with some of the social and economic problems the Seiyukai had ignored. Hara's response was to dissolve the Diet on February 26, 1920, in order that an election might be held under his own carefully drawn election law before the opposition parties could swing public opinion behind themselves. In the election Hara's painstaking arrangements paid off handsomely. Despite the fact that the country was in the midst of an economic recession, that the Siberian affair was going badly, that members of the cabinet had been engaged in flagrantly corrupt acts, that public opinion was hostile, Hara's intricately woven alliances among local interests held firm and the Seiyūkai won 281 of the Diet's 464 seats.

The defeat of universal suffrage and the election of 1920 represented for many Japanese the final disenchantment with the traditional political parties; for some, with the parliamentary process itself. Henceforth no one could take seriously the idea of the parties being the champion of the people; they were seen to be just one set of interest groups among many others. Many liberal intellectuals adopted critical positions of almost cynical detachment. Disillusioned students drifted more in the direction of Marxism and devoted themselves to organizing labor and farmers' unions. Unions either retreated entirely from political activity and confined themselves to specific economic goals or tried to set up new "proletariat" parties. In 1920 the Japan Socialist Union came into being, only to be quickly suppressed by the police; on July 5, 1922, the Japan Communist Party was founded and was also fairly quickly put out of business.[1] Some dissidents adopted a policy of "direct action" and advocated assassinating the representatives of what they considered an outrageous system, an example of the actual implementation of this being the murder in 1921 of the head of the Yasuda zaibatsu. By their failure to develop a positive relationship with the new groups that began to emerge and organize in the postwar period, the Japanese political parties missed a golden opportunity to develop popular support for themselves and to provide a constructive leadership for the satisfaction of popular discontents. The field was left free for more radical leadership and the political parties remained like a tree without roots, ready to fall before an adverse wind.

The Hara Cabinet: Foreign Affairs

The Hara cabinet was also a period of important change in the field of foreign affairs. The cabinet was barely settled in office when the war ended and Japan was summoned to take her place among the "big five" at the peace conference. This consummation of Japan's long-hoped-for admission into the magic circle of the world powers was confirmed by the grant of a permanent seat on the council of the League of Nations. Japan felt, however, that this new prestige was somewhat tarnished by her inability to secure a declaration of racial equality in the Covenant of the League. Still, her failure in this matter undoubtedly facilitated the acceptance in the peace treaty of

1. There was a very small socialist movement in the first decade of the twentieth century, but it became quiescent after the execution in 1911 of Kōtoku Shūsui and others for allegedly plotting to assassinate the Emperor Meiji.

the transfer to Japan of all Germany's rights in Shantung, an act which further embittered the Chinese and led to anti-Japanese riots and boycotts. At Versailles Japan also received as a mandate the German Pacific islands north of the equator, under the usual pledge, of course, not to fortify them. As a result of her extremely limited participation in World War I, Japan had considerably enhanced her international prestige and had substantially advanced her position in East Asia and the Pacific.

Yet the new position which Japan had achieved fell far below the ambitions entertained during the war by many of her leaders. The expected predominance in Chinese affairs had run afoul of the emerging Chinese nationalism; the dream of controlling eastern Siberia was vanishing before the hard reality of Bolshevik reassertion of Russian power and unity. The Japanese anticipated that soon the United States would reenter the East Asian scene with the full force of the military and economic power it had developed during the war. "American expansion in China," said an Army General Staff report, "is the inevitable trend of events and given our present power it is very difficult for us to stop her." Stopping America would, in the first instance, have meant building a naval strength capable of keeping the American navy out of East Asian waters. But any naval race with the United States was virtually impossible for Japan, given the economic plight the country found itself in during the postwar period. The war prosperity was gone and by 1919 imports were exceeding exports. Within three years of the war's end 60 percent of Japan's huge foreign earnings had vanished, largely wasted in her Chinese and Siberian adventures or used to finance a splurge of spending on consumption goods by the Japanese public. By 1920 Takahashi Korekiyo, Hara's finance minister, was asking the nation to curtail consumption and to expand production directed at export markets. It was obvious to Japanese economic leaders that successful competition would require a further development and modernization of Japan's industrial facilities and that in the absence of an extensive Japanese machine tool industry this would in turn necessitate the import of a great deal of foreign capital goods. Given Japan's shrinking foreign balance, these imports would have to be paid for with foreign loans, and the chief capital market had become the United States.

Convinced on one hand that Japan could not effectively exclude America from Chinese affairs and on the other hand that Japan would have to turn to America for development capital, opinion amongst

Japanese leaders began to swing toward the idea of a *rapprochement* with the United States. Prime Minister Hara, who had for several years past expressed the view that Japan could accomplish little in China without an accommodation with the United States, moved vigorously to implement the new policy. As his ambassador to Washington Hara appointed Shidehara Kijurō, a career diplomat prominent among the many Foreign Ministry officials opposed to Japan's recent highhanded, go-it-alone policy. Understanding that closer relations with the United States were impossible until China policy was changed, Hara suspended political loans and arms shipments to the Peking faction and adopted a neutral attitude in China's civil wars. The new approach was to avoid any opposition to Chinese nationalism and to encourage the unification of the country under one government. It was hoped that then Japan would be able to develop friendly relations with whatever group emerged as the new rulers and thus secure a favorable climate for Japanese economic penetration.

Hara's chance to demonstrate Japan's changed attitude came during the negotiations for the new China loan consortium proposed by the United States in July, 1918. Under the American proposal all economic and political loans to China would be made by a joint banking group representing America, England, France, and Japan; all existing rights to make loans to China, including those for railway construction, would be surrendered to China or the consortium; there would no further political intervention in China; and the open door policy would be maintained. After extended negotiations the Hara cabinet accepted all these conditions, asking only that the South Manchurian Railway and seven other lines in Manchuria and Mongolia be excluded from the scope of the agreement, a request to which the other governments acceded. Thus, when Japan entered the consortium in 1920, the basic decision had been taken to cooperate with the Western powers in China proper, to forgo any attempt to secure special privileges there, and simply to compete in economic terms under the open door policy. Only in Manchuria and Inner Mongolia was a special position to be maintained. This basic shift in policy was accepted by even the military leadership. The army minister, Tanaka Giichi, speaking to a meeting of reservists, said, "Present world trends do not permit the old style of imperialist expansion, things like seizing new territories as we have done in the past or enlarging spheres of influence. Therefore we must endeavor to attain our same ends by peaceful means, by purely economic expansion." From this new orientation followed naturally the concessions which Japan was willing to make at the Washington Conference.

The Washington Conference, held in the winter of 1921–22, produced a series of agreements embodying the new order which was shaping up in the Pacific. Much to the relief of the British dominions, the Anglo-Japanese Alliance was replaced by a Four Power Pact (France, Great Britain, Japan, the United States) in which the signatories agreed to respect each others' rights in the Pacific. In addition, there was a naval agreement which set a 5:5:3 capital ship ratio for the United States, Great Britain, and Japan, limited the size and armament of battleships and aircraft carriers, halted plans for naval expansion, and actually secured a reduction in tonnage. To this was added an agreement that the United States and Great Britain would not build any new fortifications between Singapore and Hawaii. These two accords, plus the fact that Japan eventually took greater advantage of her building privileges than the United States did, in effect gave the Japanese navy supremacy in East Asian waters. Thus Japan was able to obtain naval security at a cost within her means.

The most probable cause of war in the Pacific, the China problem, was dealt with in the Nine Power Pact. The signatories promised to respect China's independence and integrity, to avoid interfering with the Chinese people's attempts to create a stable government, to refrain from seeking special rights in China or doing anything which threatened the security of other nations, and to support a policy of equal opportunity for the commerce and industry of all nations throughout the territory of China. Provision was also made for the reexamination of the problems of extraterritoriality and tariff autonomy. To show her good earnest in this matter Japan consented to open to the consortium the previously excluded Manchurian railroad lines. In addition, she promised not to appoint Japanese advisers to the local Manchurian government though there was, of course, full understanding that she was not surrendering her special privileges in Manchuria. Japan also signed a bilateral accord with China, agreeing to withdraw her troops from Shantung and to give up all but purely economic rights there. To cap the Washington settlement Japan privately conveyed her intention to evacuate Siberia, a promise which she fulfilled, except for northern Sakhalin, in October, 1922.

Party Government under Katō Kōmei
and Tanaka Giichi

On the eve of the Washington Conference Prime Minister Hara was cut down by the knife of a deranged railway worker. To avoid jeopardizing the conference Takahashi, the finance minister, was quickly made president of the Seiyūkai and installed as prime minister. Takahashi, who was a banker and had no real roots in the Seiyūkai organization, found it very difficult to manage the factional disputes within the party. As soon as the conference had been safely concluded, he left office. For the next prime minister the genrō wanted a strong leader who could enforce the changes in the military sphere necessary to implement the Washington treaties and who could also push through the retrenchment program deemed necessary to slim down Japan's overexpanded economy for competitive world marketing. They choose Admiral Katō Tomosaburō, Hara's navy minister and the chief naval delegate to the Washington Conference. Admiral Katō at first wished to establish a national union cabinet with the participation of the political parties, but Katō Kōmei and Takahashi Korekiyo refused his offer and he therefore had to organize a purely bureaucratic cabinet. He did receive, however, the tacit support of the Seiyūkai majority in the Diet. Though the admiral was very effective in facilitating Japan's adjustment to the limits set at the Washington Conference, little success attended him in the economic field, where he was reluctant fully to apply his restrictive measures lest the whole edifice collapse. When he suddenly died in August, 1923, the Japanese economy had still not made the necessary adjustments to the postwar world. In choosing Admiral Katō's successor the genrō, now really only Saionji, again ignored the parties. This time Saionji picked Admiral Yamamoto Gombei, believing that it was necessary to have a supraparty cabinet in office if economic adjustment were to be achieved and the regular Diet elections that would be held in May, 1924, conducted fairly. Again the original aim had been a national union cabinet, but again Katō and Takahashi had declined to serve.

Just as the Yamamoto cabinet was being organized, the Great Earthquake of September 1923 struck the Tokyo-Yokohama region, causing widespread physical devastation and killing about 150,000 persons. In the confusion following the disaster attacks were made upon Koreans and a number of Japanese radicals were murdered by the police. It may have been resentment of this which a few months later led Namba Daisuke to attempt the assassination of Crown Prince Hirohito, then acting as regent for his father, who died a few years later in 1926. In any event Admiral Yamamoto took upon himself the responsibility for the failure to properly protect the prince and resigned. As Yamamoto's successor, Saionji recommended Kiyoura Keigo, a former bureaucrat who organized his cabinet from among his fellow bureaucrats in the House of Peers. Furious at being passed over in favor of a comparative nonentity, Katō Kōmei (Kenseikai), Takahashi Korekiyo (Seiyūkai), and Inukai Ki (Kakushin Club) proclaimed their united opposition to the new cabinet and organized a three-party league for the protection of constitutional government, that is, for the recognition of the principle of party cabinets. At this point the anti-Takahashi forces within the Seiyūkai, somewhat more than half the Seiyūkai Diet representation, bolted the party and, calling themselves the Seiyū Hontō (True Seiyūkai) offered their support to Kiyoura. All during the spring the three-party league fiercely denounced the Kiyoura cabinet as a violation of proper constitutional politics. However, they aroused little enthusiasm in the public, which regarded with a cynical eye the parties' claim to be fighting on behalf of the people. Nevertheless, a well-planned electoral cooperation allowed the allied parties to decisively defeat the Seiyū Hontō. In the May election the Kenseikai emerged as the largest party, winning 155 seats. This, added to the Seiyūkai's 101 and the Kakushin Club's 29, gave the three-party league a clear majority in the new Diet. In June the Kiyoura cabinet, which Saionji had probably intended to be only a caretaker government anyway, resigned and at long last Katō Kōmei was summoned to organize a coalition party cabinet.

The members of the Katō coalition cabinet assumed office filled with plans for action on a wide range of matters. They wished, for instance, to alter substantially the structure of the House of Peers and make that branch of the legislature more amenable to party influence. Since the consent of both the House of Peers and the Privy Council was necessary for this and since the public was not interested enough to bring irresistible pressure to bear on these bodies, the changes turned out to be modest: a slight reduction in the number of nobles; an increase in the wealthy taxpayers eligible to elect representatives to the upper house; and the token addition of four members selected by the Imperial Academy. The coalition was more successful in putting through a universal manhood suffrage bill which set the voting age at 25, a quadrupling of the electorate. This was neatly balanced by a new Peace Preservation Law which made it a crime punishable with ten years' imprisonment to advocate either a change in Japan's political structure or the abolition of private property. Most of the party politicians, the bureaucracy, and the business community were fearful that the new voting qualifications would widen the opportunity for radical left-wing political activity, particularly since Japan's resumption of relations with the USSR might facilitate the entry of communist propaganda. These fears were undoubtedly heightened by the older generation's bewilderment at the rapid cultural change that was occurring in Taishō Japan. In the 1920s the popular mass culture of the West began to spread widely among urban Japanese, particularly upper- and middle-class youth. Radio, the motion picture, the phonograph, new advertising techniques and picture journalism disseminated all the latest fads and crazes with an unprecedented speed and immediacy. The style of the Western flapper was reduplicated by the Japanese *moga* (modern girl) with her bobbed hair and daringly high hemline. The *mobo* (modern boy), when he was not at the baseball field, sought his amusements in the beer halls or in the dance halls where he could hear the newest jazz or practice his Charleston with a taxi dancer. In that era of *ero-guro-nansensu* (eroticism-grotesquerie-nonsense) the young and even the not so young seemed capable of any selfish frivolity or extravagance. Behind the *mobo* might lurk the "Marx boy."

The Katō cabinet also turned its hand to the as yet unresolved problem of Japan's postwar economic readjustment. Japanese prices were still at a level much higher than those in the other major trading nations. This situation encouraged an excess of imports over exports and was rapidly depleting Japan's foreign exchange balances. Every move on the government's part to lower prices had brought a rash of business failures and thus threatened the solvency of the Japanese banking system, which had too much of its assets out on loan to Japanese companies. The Great Earthquake of 1923 had further exacerbated the situation by forcing the government to authorize large extensions of credit with a consequent further rise in prices. The only thing that averted an economic disaster was a series of large foreign loans which the Japanese began contracting from March, 1923, on.

The Katō cabinet was determined to bring down prices, expand exports, reduce imports, and create a favorable balance of trade. To this end it campaigned for reduced consumption at home and raised import duties on consumer goods. It also made substantial cuts in the budget, primarily in administrative and military costs. Twenty thousand employees were pared from the government payroll, four divisions were cut from the army, and two thousand military officers were retired. Not all of the military savings were realized, however; the army minister, Ugaki Kazushige, in return for his cooperation in reducing the military forces managed to get some of the money used to modernize the army's equipment and to introduce military training into the universities and secondary schools. Certain of the fiscal measures advocated by the Kenseikai members of the cabinet led to a growing estrangement from the Seiyūkai. General Tanaka Giichi succeeded Takahashi as Seiyūkai president in April, 1925, an event significant in itself as showing where even for a military man the path to power lay in the 1920s. Since Tanaka was ambitious for the prime ministership, he declined to serve in the cabinet, and the two wings of the coalition (the Kakushin Club had merged with the Seiyūkai) moved toward a break. Finally, in August, 1925, Katō reorganized his cabinet as a purely Kenseikai affair and the Seiyūkai entered into opposition. The Kenseikai cabinet secured a majority in the Diet by obtaining the cooperation of its old opponent, the Seiyū Hontō. When Katō died in January, 1926, power passed smoothly to his home minister, Wakatsuki Reijirō, a former finance ministry official.

The foreign policy of the Katō-Wakatsuki cabinets was in the hands of Shidehara Kijurō. In general, Shidehara pursued a policy of cooperation with the Western powers and of conciliation in China. Eschewing force and seeking always to settle incidents through diplomatic channels, Shidehara aimed at creating a friendly atmosphere which could facilitate the expansion in China of Japanese economic interests. He was willing, he asserted, to accept the reasonable demands of Chinese nationalism, but he defined "reasonable" as the acceptance by the Chinese of a relationship of "coexistence and co-prosperity" with Japan. His intransigent refusal to give up what he considered to be an absolutely vital special position for Japan in China is quite evident in his policy toward the Chinese demand for tariff autonomy. As the price of tariff autonomy he consistently pressed for a preferential tariff rate agreement which would give Japan a competitive position equal to that of the Chinese producer and superior to that of the other foreign nations. He also tried to tie in tariff reform with a repayment of the loans Japan had made China during World War I (Nishihara Loans). He never for one instant, of course, considered surrendering any of the special privileges Japan had in Manchuria.

Criticism of the conciliatory aspects of Shidehara's policy grew in Japan as it became evident that the large increase in exports to China which had been anticipated had not materialized. With the movement of the Kuomintang armies into central China the fear grew that Japan's substantial economic stake in Shantung and in Manchuria was threatened and must be protected by strong actions. The Sei-yūkai was in the fore in criticizing the government's "weak" policy and offered their own president, General Tanaka, as a man who would know how to take the strong measures necessary to deal with Chinese recalcitrance. However, the Wakatsuki cabinet was brought down not directly by the China issue but by a financial crisis which developed in the spring of 1927. The crisis resulted from an inadvertent remark by Wakatsuki's finance minister that set off a series of runs on the shaky Japanese banking system and threatened to smash it. The Privy Council refused Wakatsuki permission to issue an emergency decree authorizing the Bank of Japan to extend large credits to the banks in difficulty. The cabinet resigned and on Saionji's recommendation General Tanaka succeeded as prime minister. By that time the crisis was so serious that the Privy Council was willing to allow Tanaka over three times as much money as Wakatsuki had requested. The affair ultimately strengthened the economy by eliminating many marginal companies, but the large credits pumped into the system further delayed the long-sought-for price readjustment. The major zaibatsu, who had been relatively unaffected, also took quick advantage of the opportunity to consolidate their position by acquiring numerous valuable properties fairly cheaply.

Soon after taking office the Tanaka cabinet sent troops to Shantung on the plea that Japanese lives and property had to be protected against the disorders attendant on the northward advance of the Kuomintang armies. The troops were withdrawn in a few months but returned in the spring of 1928, at which time there was a full-scale military clash with the Chinese troops. Tanaka's main concern was to prevent the civil war and Kuomintang authority from extending to Manchuria and Inner Mongolia. For this reason he forced the warlord of Manchuria, Chang Tso-lin, to withdraw from the civil war in north China and return to Manchuria. On the way Chang was killed by a group of Japanese officers who hoped to use the incident as a cover for the seizure of Manchuria by Japan's Kwantung Army.[2] This move was, however, quickly suppressed by Tanaka. On the whole the Tanaka cabinet's "strong" policy accomplished little beyond rousing the Chinese to anti-Japanese boycotts which further depressed Japanese business.

At home Tanaka continued the vigorous policy of repression begun against the left wing, particularly the Communists, by the preceding party cabinets. In March, 1928, and again in April, 1929, a nation-wide police dragnet rounded up thousands of suspected Communists and other Marxists. Many of those arrested disappeared for years into jail to reemerge only after a long period of indoctrination or, in some instances, not until 1945. The suppressive measures begun by Tanaka were continued with increasing severity by later cabinets and effectively eliminated the Left as a viable alternative in prewar Japanese politics. Tanaka, however, did allow left-wing candidates to run in the first universal manhood suffrage election, which was held in February, 1928. In that election, marked with numerous irregularities, the Seiyūkai and the Minseitō (the Kenseikai merged with the Seiyū Hontō) won just about the same number of representatives, thus making Tanaka's position in the Diet very shaky.

To manage the Diet Tanaka had to engage in highly questionable practices which brought both him and party politics into bad repute with the public. Discontent with his "positive" economic program also developed. His huge budgets kept prices up but did nothing to relieve the economic distress of the countryside or the unemployment of the cities. Imports continued to exceed exports, and by early 1929 Japan's foreign balances had just about vanished. In addition, it became obvious that the stream of foreign loans, which had been bridging the payments gap, was drying up. The situation could be saved only if Japan put her finances in order and returned to the gold standard, which she had left in 1917. This question was particularly important since Japan was soon to be confronted with the problem of refunding some of the huge loans she had secured during the Russo-Japanese War. In the spring of 1929 Tanaka was moving toward a reversal of his major policies, but before very much could be done he was forced to resign by the displeasure of the emperor and court officials over his failure to secure from the army adequate punishment for the murderers of Chang Tso-lin.

2. The Kwantung Army was Japan's garrison in the Kwantung Leased Territory, a small peninsula at the end of the larger Liaotung Peninsula which in its turn juts out from south Manchuria.

The Hamaguchi Cabinet: A Last Chance for Party Government

As Tanaka's replacement Saionji selected the Minseitō president, Hamaguchi Osachi, a former finance ministry official with a reputation for fiscal orthodoxy who seemed eminently qualified to lead the nation out of its economic difficulties. The Hamaguchi cabinet's solution to the economic crisis was a classical retrenchment program and a return to the gold standard. Immediately on assuming office in July, 1929, the cabinet set about reducing government spending and curtailing deficit financing, measures intended to cut public and private demand for goods and thus induce both a lowering of the price level and a reduction in imports. Reduced prices would, it was assumed, lead to an expansion of exports and an improvement in the balance of payments. In addition, the government launched a large-scale rationalization program designed to effect a more permanent reduction in production costs and insure that Japanese prices should be competitive with those of the other industrial nations. The return to the gold standard would reestablish the mechanism for keeping those prices in line with world prices. It was also the indispensable condition if Japan was to obtain from the London and New York money markets the loans the government felt necessary to tide the nation over the present crisis.

The Hamaguchi cabinet warned the Japanese people that they would have to endure a period of belt-tightening and hardship but promised that soon afterward prosperous times would come without fail. Concerned that the prospect of future economic gains might not provide strong enough motivation for the sacrifices being asked of the public, the government conducted a propaganda campaign to arouse nationalist sentiment in support of its economic policies. The campaign elaborated upon the peculiar virtues of the "national polity" and pointed up the obligation of all to make sacrifices for the state and the emperor. In a sense it would not be an exaggeration to say that the Hamaguchi cabinet's effort to enlist nationalistic shibboleths in aid of its economic program prepared the ground for the ultranationalist and expansionist propaganda of the 1930s.

Nothing, of course, could have been further from the intentions of the Hamaguchi cabinet, whose own foreign policy was pacific and based on the principle of cooperation with the Western powers. Convinced that Japan's economic future depended on maintaining harmonious relations with Great Britain and the United States, the cabinet assiduously sought to avoid any serious difference of opinion with these powers. In China Shidehara Kijurō, once again in office as foreign minister, reinstituted his policy of refraining from military intervention and searched anew through diplomatic negotiations for a modus vivendi with the Kuomintang government which would assure Japan's economic interests and treaty rights. Perhaps the most symbolic instance of the Hamaguchi cabinet's accommodating spirit was the London Naval Conference of 1930. The success of this conference was very important to the cabinet, since a reduction in naval armament would provide substantial budgetary savings for the retrenchment program and in any case Japan's economic plight precluded her engaging in an all-out naval race. Moreover, it was feared that a failure of the conference would endanger Japanese bond issues soon to be floated in London and New York. Therefore, even when it became clear that a treaty could be obtained only by yielding on the principle of Japanese naval hegemony in the western Pacific, Hamaguchi and Shidehara were ready to make the sacrifice.

Hamaguchi was able to convince the leading officers of the Navy Ministry that the diplomatic and economic situation absolutely required Japan to sign the treaty, that the navy would have to be patient until the 1935 naval conference, by which time the nation would probably have recovered its economic strength and would be in a position to make stronger demands. With the aid of Navy Ministry officers and certain other senior naval officers, Hamaguchi managed to bypass the fierce opposition of the Navy General Staff and secure the signing and ratification of the treaty. But the very victory destroyed any possibility of its repetition in the future. The officers who had cooperated with Hamaguchi were driven from positions of influence in the navy. It was explicitly ruled that the official navy estimate of strength requirements must be approved by the chief of the Navy General Staff. In addition, the army began to prepare its defenses against a similar cut in its own budget. And finally, the extremists were given an issue around which to rally ultranationalist sentiment.

To the charge of "surrender" at London was soon joined the cry of failure in China. Shidehara had been able to make little headway against the intransigent nationalism of the Kuomintang government. The Chinese would not make the slightest concession to him and were adamantly pressing for the end of extraterritoriality, for the restoration of their control over coastal and inland waterways navigation, for the recovery of railway rights, and even for the return of the South Manchurian Railway Zone and the Kwantung leasehold. Both Sei-yūkai and Minseitō policies appeared incapable of securing that special position in China which almost all Japanese had come to believe was absolutely essential to the future of Japan. Indeed, the party politicians seemed on the verge of losing for the nation every gain which had been made since 1895.

To the seething discontent with foreign policy was added the social tensions generated by the spread to Japan of the effects of the great world depression. Japan could not have escaped this, of course, but the institution of deflationary measures at almost the very moment the depression broke undoubtedly made the impact upon Japan much worse than it might have been. Unfortunately, the Hamaguchi cabinet stubbornly persisted in its deflationary policy long after the magnitude of the economic disaster had become evident. Worst of all, the cabinet obstinately refused to take any adequate measures to relieve the victims of the depression. The ordinary Japanese, especially the farmer, suffered terrible hardships, and political discontent flared violently, in the end costing Hamaguchi his life.

The impact of the 1930–31 was much the worse for many Japanese because it came as the culmination of a decade of depressed economic conditions. In the 1920s a slow rate of economic expansion plus technological improvements increasing output per worker meant that the number of jobs available failed to keep pace with the growth of population. Not only did many urban workers have difficulty securing work but the surplus labor of the agricultural regions could no longer find an adequate outlet in the factories. This made the condition of the small farmer and tenant farmer quite desperate, for the 1920s was also a period when the price of rice was being held down as the result of an increasing flood of rice from Taiwan and Korea, a flood created by a governmental cheap food policy designed to keep down the labor costs of industry. In the face of low prices the Japanese farmer tried to maintain his income by increasing his yield through the use of artificial fertilizer (zaibatsu manufactured), but this only increased his costs and by enlarging the rice supply further depressed prices. The farmer was not alone in his suffering. The small industrial producer, too, was finding it hard going in the 1920s since he could compete less and less effectively with the technologically modern and increasingly large-scale operations of the zaibatsu. He could survive, when he did, only by reducing the return to himself and his workers to the vanishing point. Zaibatsu marketing operations, particularly the new department stores, also cut heavily into the livelihood of the many small neighborhood retailers. Even among the educated elite the 1920s saw a growing unemployment problem and there were suggestions to reduce the numbers of those attending universities and higher technical schools. In short, when the world depression struck, many segments of the Japanese population had little material or psychological reserves left with which to meet the blow.

The economic debacle of 1930–31 was a major factor in undermining the Japanese people's confidence in the ability of party politicians and party government to solve the nation's problems. In a country where democratic traditions had deeper roots party government might have survived these failures in domestic and foreign policy, but in Japan the cultural and institutional environment gave no moral sanction to party cabinets. Nor, in the eyes of the Japanese people, had the conduct of party politicians earned them any moral claim to power. The numerous political scandals which had filled the press over the years had fostered a public image of the typical party politician as corrupt, unprincipled, and devoted solely to the interest of himself and his zaibatsu allies. When the political parties failed to meet the test of practical success, they forfeited any claim they might have had to political leadership, and the Japanese people did not hesitate to turn elsewhere for guidance. The stage was cleared for the advocates of a more aggressive foreign policy and a more tightly organized domestic structure. Still, despite its failures in its own time, the prewar party movement did provide a heritage of habits, skills, and ideas which contributed significantly to the development of parliamentary government in postwar Japan.

VIII

The Road to

War: 1931–1945

BY

RICHARD STORRY

Prelude in South Manchuria

In a famous injunction to his fighting men, the Rescript to Soldiers and Sailors of 1882, the Emperor Meiji had warned them "not to meddle with politics." This august command was broadly obeyed by all but a few officers until the beginning of the 1930s, so far as Japanese domestic politics were concerned. Beyond the borders of the homeland, on the continent of Asia, it was a different story. For example, the Siberian Expedition (1918–22) had provided opportunities for political intrigue; and South Manchuria was an area in which the Japanese Kwantung Army played a decidedly political role. And South Manchuria in 1928 was the scene of an ominous event, creating a sensation at the time, although the details of the affair were not made public until after World War II. During the early morning of June 4, 1928, the Chinese warlord of Manchuria, Marshal Chang Tso-lin, was killed when an explosion wrecked his train as it steamed under a bridge in the suburbs of Mukden.

Since the railroad was guarded by Japanese troops there was, to say the least, a suspicion that the Japanese must have engineered Chang's death. In fact, the assassination was the work of a small band of military men headed by a senior staff officer of the Kwantung Army named Colonel Kōmoto Daisaku. The assassination was the first move in a plot to secure the seizure of part if not all of Manchuria beyond the South Manchurian Railway Zone. The plan was that, after the wrecking of Chang Tso-lin's train, troops of the Kwantung Army in Mukden should be mobilized and should then open fire on Chang's bodyguard, thus provoking hostilities with the Chinese. This would give the Japanese a pretext for advancing beyond the Railway Zone. But Kōmoto's superiors, who had been kept in the dark about the affair, refused to countenance the mobilization, and put a stop to any further action against the Chinese.

This particular episode is interesting for several reasons. In the first place, it foreshadowed what would happen in that same city of Mukden a little more than three years later, on September 18, 1931, when officers of the Kwantung Army, again following a railroad explosion, would launch an attack on the Chinese, thereby sparking off the famous Manchurian Incident. Second, although the assassination of Chang Tso-lin was carried out by a mere handful of officers and men, without the foreknowledge of senior commanders, little retribution was visited upon those responsible for the crime. This Manchurian plot of 1928, the first striking example of terrorist activity by the younger officers of the modern Japanese army, was hushed up and therefore implicitly condoned by the General Staff, despite the efforts of Prime Minister Tanaka to obtain some assurance that Colonel Kōmoto and his confederates would be punished. So an evil precedent was set. It seemed that officers who "meddled with politics," even to the point of terrorist violence, would not necessarily have to face anything much worse than a severe reprimand.

Third, the entire affair was wrapped in a cloak of secrecy. The Japanese press was forbidden by the police, acting on orders from the Home Ministry, to print news concerning the incident "which might be detrimental to the state and which might embarrass the international standing of Japan abroad." This kind of censorship, ocurring in the comparatively liberal 1920s, was to be highly characteristic of the next decade, when ultranationalism hit its stride and terrorist plots became endemic. Thus rumor and gossip took the place of hard news; and the development of an informed and responsible public opinion was gravely frustrated.

Ultranationalism in the 1920s

Yet in 1928 Japanese ultranationalism was very much a minority movement, this being still the age of Diet politics and party governments. At least in the big cities and towns right-wing extremism was out of fashion. The cliques and coteries of fanatical nationalists seemed unrepresentative of anybody but themselves. They lacked both power and prestige. They frequently broke up due to internal jealousies, only to emerge again under another name. Their members were a diverse collection of fierce reactionaries, old and young radicals disenchanted with Marxism, former anarchists, unprincipled adventurers, opportunists, idealists, and plain gangsters.

There was also, as early as 1927, at least one secret, conspiratorial group of junior army officers. This was the Kinkikai, or "Society of the Imperial Flag," which aimed at the establishment of a military dictatorship through revolutionary violence. Its very existence was of course a flagrant breach of the Emperor Meiji's rescript. The leading figure in this clandestine act of defiance was Major Hashimoto Kingorō. Possibly because his political activities had become known, he was sent to Turkey as military attaché. But he was to turn up again in Japan before long, proving to be a constant troublemaker.

For a feature of Japanese ultranationalism is the way in which the same persons reappear on the scene as the years go by. One or two even straddle the prewar and postwar periods—for example, Akao Bin, who was involved in a bomb attack on the Soviet Embassy in Tokyo in 1928 and who was still an energetic and well publicized nationalist agitator nearly forty years later. A noted survivor from the Meiji period, already venerable in the 1920s, was Tōyama Mitsuru. With a history of intrigue and terrorism going back for years, he was the doyen of ultranationalists. But it could be argued that this old rogue, with his white beard and portentous air, was a shade old-fashioned. More in tune with the twentieth century, perhaps, were men such as Kita Ikki and Ōkawa Shūmei, who can be described as fascists of a type peculiar to Japan.

Kita Ikki is important in the modern development of Japanese ultranationalism, because in so far as this decidedly irrational and destructive movement had any intellectual substance it was thanks to Kita and his ideas. This is why Kita Ikki has been called "the ideological father of Japanese fascism." Kita, who was born in 1884, was influenced by Marxist socialism in his youth. He went to China and was caught up in the revolutionary movement in that country. For a time at any rate he seemed to have worked in China on behalf of Japanese military intelligence. His first major piece of writing, published in 1906, was an attempt to harmonize in one synthesis, which he called "pure socialism," the concepts of nationalism, liberalism, and individualism. Later he wrote a history of the Chinese Revolution of 1911. Then, in 1919, he published his most famous work, *A General Outline for the Reconstruction of Japan,* which, it has been said, "brought socialism and Japanese imperialism under one umbrella." The book was strongly anticapitalist, advocating the nationalization of all wealth above a certain fairly limited amount. At the same time it preached the doctrine of armed expansion overseas, notably into Siberia and the southern Pacific. For Kita claimed that with her scattered fringe of islands Japan was "a proletariat among the nations." She had the right, therefore, to rearm with vigor and to make war for what he called "the rectification of unjust international frontiers." In his "reconstructed" Japan the emperor would be the cornerstone of the nation, the supreme representative of the people. But those who would carry out the task of reconstruction would be a military junta. The armed forces, in other words, were to take over the running of the state.

Kita Ikki, when young, had been impressed not only by Marxism but also by the Meiji Restoration, which he interpreted as the successful effort by an inspired group of men to change the course of Japanese history. One of their achievements had been to persuade the daimyō class to "restore" to the emperor his administrative powers over all the provinces of the land. Similarly Kita's proposals for drastic nationalization were interpreted to suggest a second restoration—a Shōwa Restoration. For rich men and institutions would be compelled to "restore" their wealth to the emperor. The same applied to the Diet, which under Kita's proposals would be dissolved while the work of reconstruction was being carried out. The surrender of power by party politicians would be an act of "restoration" to the emperor. So Kita's program came to be known as "the Shōwa Restoration." It represented a new force in the nationalist movement, and one that can be regarded, in the Japanese context, as recognizably fascist.

Ōkawa Shūmei was one of Kita's disciples, whose main employment was with the South Manchurian Railway Company. He worked both in Tokyo and in Manchuria for their East Asia Research Institute. A man of a great many contacts, particularly among army officers, he was an indefatigable promoter of patriotic societies. Although he quarreled with Kita in the 1920s, Ōkawa was certainly influenced very deeply by Kita's ideas. Yet he was less anticapitalist than Kita, much more pragmatic. Ōkawa was a vocal chauvinist, interested above all in the expansion of Japanese national power; and it may be noted that he was on close terms with Colonel Kōmoto, the assassin of Chang Tso-lin.

Another significant figure, in terms of the influence he exerted on ultranationalist ideology, was Gondō Seikyō. This influence came from his ideas rather than his actions; for he was a thinker, not a man of practical affairs. His fame rested on his championship of village life. Gondō's ideal was a Japan based not on centralized power and urban industrialism but on a confederation of autonomous village communities. He was the author of several works in praise of agrarianism and was profoundly critical of the existing bureaucratic structure of the state, centered in the huge and (in Gondō's view) parasitic metropolis.

It may seem bizarre that patriots obsessed by dreams of national glory should have paid much attention to Gondō's ideas, so redolent of Ruskin, Tolstoy, and the anarchist Kropotkin. But, as a Japanese scholar has explained, in the ultranationalist movement there were "those who advocated an intensive development of industry and who wished to increase State control for this end, and those who flatly rejected the idea and thought in terms of agrarianism centered on the villages. Many members of the right wing held both these views." Japan's "superpatriots," indeed, were often astonishingly naïve, following the promptings of the heart rather than the head. Young officers, more than most people, tended to be moved by simple emotions; and since a great many of them came from country districts they found Gondō's attacks on the evils of city life very much to their taste.

In the manifestations of extreme nationalism, as we shall see, there was usually a strain of savage destructiveness. Terrorists could always identify with eloquence the institutions which they wanted to destroy. They were far less articulate as a rule when it came to an explanation of what they hoped to see established once the work of destruction was done. Here they resembled those European anarchists who were driven much more by the passion to break with an oppressive past than by any serious reflection on what they wanted to build up in its place. A faithful reflection of this attitude is the admission made in his postwar autobiography by Kodama Yoshio, a terrorist of the 1930s: "We did not possess nor did we attempt to form any concrete plan as to how the nation was to be developed. . . . We did not realize then the stupidity of preparing for destruction without any preparation for the work of construction to follow." [1]

When, on November 14, 1930, Prime Minister Hamaguchi received the wounds from which he was never to recover, the shots that rang through Tokyo Station symbolized the beginning of a new and terrible era for Japan. The prolonged controversy over the London Naval Treaty had stirred up misgivings and fears all over the country, providing a considerable stimulus to nationalist feeling. More momentous was the impact of the world depression. This struck Japan in 1930, a year in which quotations for rice and silk fell catastrophically, to levels unknown since the nineteenth century. Desperate times seemed to call for desperate remedies. Extreme nationalism of the radical kind began to attract many more adherents.

It was in this climate of growing economic distress and general public anxiety that at the end of September, 1930, there was formed in Tokyo a secret association of army officers known as the Sakurakai, or "Cherry Society," taking its title from Japan's most celebrated

1. Yoshio Kodama, *I Was Defeated* (Tokyo, 1951), p. 4.

blossom. But the overtones here were far from flowery. The readiness of the cherry blossom to fall to the ground after a few brief days of glory had a powerful symbolic significance for Japan's warriors. The beauty of the blossom was invested with a peculiar pathos, suggestive of courageous self-sacrifice.

Certain officers from the General Staff and the Army Ministry were the founding members of this society. Prominent among them was Hashimoto Kingorō, back from Ankara and now a lieutenant colonel. Since the aim of the society was to discuss ways and means of reforming Japan, it is not surprising that the Shōwa Restoration should have been a central theme of their deliberations. There were just over a hundred members. It would be unfair to suggest that all of them were active conspirators planning a *coup d'état* that would rid their country of the evils they deplored. But a militant party in the Sakurakai, led by Hashimoto, did make detailed preparations to this end; and this reached an advanced stage in the early spring of 1931, after Ōkawa Shūmei and other civilian firebrands were brought into the plot. Certain senior officers, also, had been approached. One or two of them were quite sympathetic; and it seems that Major General Tatekawa, of General Staff Intelligence, was fairly deeply involved in the whole operation.

What was planned was a *coup d'état,* to take place on March 20, 1931. Thus the affair is always known as the March incident. The coup was to be carried out in the following way. A mob, organized by Ōkawa and comprising hired vagrants together with a large muster of right-wing stalwarts, would march on the Diet. At the same time "death-defying bands" of fanatics would hurl bombs at the prime minister's house and the offices of the Minseitō and Seiyūkai. The next move would be the mobilization of the Tokyo garrison, followed by the proclamation of martial law, the establishment of a military government, and the dissolution of the Diet.

However, less than a fortnight before this drama was to have been staged, the operation was called off. General Ugaki, the army minister who had been designated by the plotters to head the "Restoration" government, insisted that all plans be canceled. Ugaki's exact involvement in these plans remains a matter of conjecture to this day; but presumably there was at one stage a reasonable expectation by Hashimoto and the others that the general would favor their scheme. It seems true that not only Ugaki but also certain other generals had early information of the plot; and the conspirators felt that they had at least the tacit backing of some senior officers. Accordingly there was a sense of shock and disillusionment when these generals appeared to change their mind as soon as the moment for action arrived.

Although it never erupted to disturb the peace and was kept secret at the time, the March incident had important consequences. Some historians have argued persuasively that the abortive March conspiracy led to a determination to press ahead with plans for a coup outside Japan, in Manchuria, and that therefore a direct link exists between the conspiracy and the Manchurian Incident six months later. Others have denied this. What is beyond dispute is the connection between the March incident and the growth of military indiscipline, in other words the further involvement of army officers in political intrigue, propaganda, and the plotting of violence. For, since at least some officers in high positions were implicated, if only passively, in the March plot, it would have been embarrassing for the military authorities to take disciplinary measures against Hashimoto and his "Cherry Society" colleagues. So once again, as after the assassination of Chang Tso-lin, terrorism was tacitly condoned by the very persons whose duty it was to preserve discipline in the emperor's office corps.

The Manchurian Incident

The next conspiracy involving army officers was by no means abortive. This was the coup at Mukden on September 18, 1931, when the Kwantung Army attacked the local Chinese garrison, thus setting in train a series of military and political events that culminated in the establishment of Manchukuo, a state in name but wholly subservient to Japanese interests and effectively administered at all but the lowest level by Japanese personnel.

In what is known to history as the Manchurian Incident the initiative lay, from start to finish, with a group of colonels, majors, and captains of the Kwantung Army. It was these officers who fabricated the excuse for military action against the Chinese—namely an alleged Chinese attempt to sabotage the South Manchurian Railway at Mukden. It was these officers who stiffened the resolve of their commander in chief, Lieutenant General Honjō, when he appeared to waver in his determination to take strong measures. Again, it was these officers who organized a "spontaneous" movement by the inhabitants of Manchurian towns in favor of self-determination and a break away from the Nanking government. It was the same group which by coercion and bribery induced various prominent Chinese residents to become Japanese puppets.

Not only the Wakatsuki cabinet but also the Army Ministry and General Staff in Tokyo were perplexed to know how to restrain the Kwantung Army. After the first military action in Mukden, followed by a further advance, Tokyo was able to halt operations for a few weeks. But in fact the Japanese army's behavior in Manchuria won growing popular support, especially when it became clear that the League of Nations was unlikely to accept Japan's official assurances that the Manchurian action had been taken for reasons of self-defense. It was not so much any question of principle, such as the issue of military discipline, that worried the army authorities in Tokyo, as the reaction of the Soviet Union. They were afraid that any advance into northern Manchuria might provoke Soviet intervention. However, the Soviet Union adopted a very cautious policy, and it became evident that the Japanese could push toward the north without serious risk of conflict with the Russians.

Just a month after the Mukden coup there occurred the so-called October incident in Tokyo. This was a conspiracy in which Hashimoto Kingorō played the dominant role. The plot envisaged the assassination of Prime Minister Wakatsuki and his colleagues, and the establishment of a dictatorial government to be headed by Lieutenant General Araki, with Hashimoto as home minister and Ōkawa Shūmei as finance minister. When the police forestalled this coup, only a few days before it was due to take place, they discovered that more than a hundred army officers, together with a few naval officers, were involved.

This was a very serious affair, of which the public had little inkling at the time, because news of it was heavily censored. The ringleaders were treated with great leniency. The severest punishment was awarded to Hashimoto, who was given twenty days' confinement. Later he and other officers were transferred to posts outside Tokyo. There was no question of depriving them of their commissions. This October incident was undoubtedly the product of some collusion between officers in Japan and others in the Kwantung Army. For the latter wanted to make Manchuria a kind of national socialist "paradise" and hoped to see a similar state of affairs established in the homeland.

General Araki, it seems, did not approve of this plot that would have placed him in a position of supreme power. But like several other generals he had much sympathy with the radical ideas of the politically minded younger officers. When the Wakatsuki Minseitō cabinet resigned in December and was followed by a Seiyūkai cabinet headed by Inukai, Araki became army minister. This was one of many signs that the days of temperate Shidehara diplomacy were now over, and that henceforth the army would play a greater part in shaping Japan's destinies.

Indeed, by the end of that year, 1931, a new and heady atmosphere of patriotic fervor pervaded the land. Most people had now come to feel that the Kwantung Army had acted with a bold incisiveness that the emperor's advisers and Diet politicians had always lacked. The Manchurian adventure, in other words, was generally popular. Even many of Japan's socialists now gave the army their enthusiastic backing.

The new prime minister, Inukai Ki, had many good contacts with China, for in earlier days he had been closely associated with Sun Yat-sen's movement for national regeneration. Soon after taking office he began secret talks with the Chinese government through a trusted intermediary. Inukai certainly had no intention of yielding an inch of newly occupied territory in South Manchuria, but he doubted the wisdom of further armed action at that juncture, and he was eager to reach an understanding with the Chinese. Furthermore, on his appointment as prime minister he had been told by the emperor that the army's interference in domestic and foreign policies was causing anxiety; and it is known that Inukai was worried about the way in which junior officers of the Kwantung Army had taken the law into their own hands. Apparently he contemplated asking the emperor to dismiss certain troublemakers from the army, and it seems that he had at least a vague plan to prepare with his cabinet an imperial rescript ordering the Kwantung Army to cease operations in Manchuria.

Such schemes were not hidden from Inukai's chief cabinet secretary, who was on close terms with extreme nationalists in the army and outside. It is probable that it was through him that terrorist fanatics learned that the prime minister might try to call a halt to Japan's bid to control the whole of Manchuria.

Nationalist feelings were greatly stirred by the fighting that broke out in Shanghai at the end of January, 1932. The Shanghai hostilities lasted for no more than some six weeks, but they were ferocious while they endured. In those days humanity was not yet accustomed to the concept of the air bombardment of civilians. The spectacle of Japanese air attacks was very shocking, for these took place in full view of the large foreign population living in Shanghai's International Settlement and French Concession. The Chinese troops, who had no air power to back them up, resisted with tenacity, and it was only by bringing in much superior forces that the Japanese compelled their opponents to give way. A truce was then arranged by neutral representatives on the spot. The Shanghai battle, in which the Chinese seemed to play the role of heroes and the Japanese that of brutal invaders, made much more impact on world opinion than the erratic fighting in more remote areas of Manchuria. American opinion in particular hardened against what was seen as Japanese aggression; and in this period the attitude of Stimson, Hoover's secretary of state, became decidedly hostile to Japan.

At home in Japan two politically motivated murders shook society. In February the former finance minister, Inoue Junnosuke, was assassinated. The following month the same fate befell Baron Dan, the managing director of the Mitsui interests. Both were victims of young men who belonged to an ultranationalist group called "The League of Blood" (Ketsumeidan). It became known that more than a dozen other persons, prominent in business or politics, had been marked down for assassination. Among them was Prime Minister Inukai.

The End of Party Government

On May 15, 1932, in broad daylight a group of young naval officers and army cadets burst into the prime minister's official residence and shot Inukai dead in his own reception room. Behind this act of terrorism there appears to have been no constructive aim whatever. The participants in the May Fifteenth incident did not have any concrete ideas about the type of government to be set up after Inukai's death. They were interested only in his destruction.

The prevailing attitude of the military authorities was one of sympathy with the assassins. General Araki, for example, declared just after Inukai's murder that, although the crime must be punished, the young officers concerned had acted from patriotic and unselfish motives. This kind of reaction found plenty of echoes among the public at large; and when the murderers were brought to trial they were widely regarded as heroes and potential martyrs. Not immune, perhaps, to the dominant atmosphere of patriotic excitement, the judges handed down sentences of imprisonment, of which the longest was fifteen years. In fact none of those convicted remained in custody for even ten years.

An important consequence of the May Fifteenth incident was the demise of party government in Japan. Had Prince Saionji, the surviving genrō, attempted to recommend a Seiyūkai leader as Inukai's successor the army could have prevented any serving general from joining the new cabinet as army minister. Not until after World War II would there be another cabinet headed by a Diet politician. Inukai's successor, in fact, was a retired admiral, Saitō Makoto, a man of rather enlightened and moderate views who yet felt obliged to bow to the army's demands. Accordingly his government, later in that summer of 1932, formally recognized the new state of Manchukuo. Thus the seal of approval was given to the work of the Kwantung Army, which by this time controlled all Manchuria.

Manchukuo, apart from its economic value to Japan and its supposed utility as a promising haven for Japanese immigrants, was cherished by the army as an essential springboard for operations against Siberia. War with Russia was thought to be inevitable. In 1932 the school of thought represented by Araki was in the ascendancy. Araki, an ebullient publicist, was always preaching the ineffable virtues of "the Imperial Way" (Kōdō), which exalted the confused, mystical ideal of "direct rule by the emperor." The concept owed something to Kita Ikki's writings; and the advocates of the Imperial Way were often radical reformers of a national socialist kind; but at the same time they were passionately anticommunist, with a particularly strong detestation of the Soviet Union. Thus the Imperial Way faction (Kōdōha) believed that a struggle with the Russians could not be avoided and was likely to occur in the mid-thirties.

For the moment, however, it was the League of Nations that posed the most serious foreign policy problem for the Japanese. The League's Commission of Inquiry into the Sino-Japanese dispute, under the chairmanship of Lord Lytton, completed its investigations during the first half of 1932 and published its report at the beginning of October. The verdict, although phrased with tact and moderation, was a condemnation of Japan's actions in Manchuria. Early in 1933 the League of Nations formally endorsed the Lytton Report, whereupon Japan withdrew from that body. The country was now isolated diplomatically in a way unknown since the time of the Triple Intervention in 1895. The more thoughtful were seriously worried by this turn of events. The withdrawal from Geneva, it is said, caused the emperor many sleepless nights. Symbolic of his anxiety, and of his impotent idealism, was the emperor's request that an expression of a desire for world peace should be included in his edict announcing Japan's withdrawal from the League.

In 1933 there was a temporary settlement with China. Japanese troops by now faced the Great Wall along a great part of its length, and had penetrated deeply into Inner Mongolia. A locally negotiated truce brought an uneasy peace. Chiang Kai-shek was more concerned to suppress his Communist opponents than to continue the struggle against the Japanese. In a famous aphorism he was to declare: "The Japanese are a disease of the skin. The Communists are a disease of the heart." But the truce did not mean the end of Sino-Japanese friction; and North China was the object of unremitting Japanese interference and pressure for the next four years, until the outbreak of full-scale fighting in the late summer of 1937.

The four years from 1933 to 1937 had witnessed a complicated, confidential but not always well-concealed struggle for power within the Japanese army. Araki's group, the Imperial Way faction, began to lose ground after Araki himself resigned as army minister, due to ill health, in January, 1934. Those competing to replace the dominant Imperial Way faction were many. The army in fact was as riddled with jealousies as a girls' boarding school. Cliques grew up on the basis of friendships formed in the Military Academy, or on that of a shared regional background. Certain factions were knit together, like "the Cherry Society," by a common enthusiasm for political and economic reform. While some groupings were mutually hostile, others shared the same basic aims and were linked in some form of alliance. The Imperial Way faction, for example, was usually associated with the young officers pledged to achieve the Shōwa Restoration. The most influential group opposed to the Imperial Way faction was commonly known as the "Control faction" (*Tōseiha*); and it was this group or clique which eventually prevailed. But to see internal army rivalries solely in terms of a struggle between the Imperial Way faction and the Control faction would be, no doubt, an oversimplification of a highly complex issue. Nevertheless, many historians, including Japanese historians, have interpreted the story broadly in such terms.

The Suppression of Dissent

On certain questions all military factions were in full agreement. Apart from their keen dislike of Marxism in all its forms, they had a profound distrust of other ideas considered to be alien to "Japanism" —such as liberalism, academic freedom, individualism, and indeed Christianity. Thanks to what had happened in Manchuria the soldier was restored to his old position at the apex of society, at least in the esteem of the masses of the people. Accordingly, it is not surprising that there should have developed an atmosphere of patriotic conformism, which bore down hard on independent minds, an atmosphere of which the so-called McCarthy era in the United States, twenty years later, was a very pale echo.

Consider the case of Dr. Minobe Tatsukichi, professor emeritus of Tokyo Imperial University and a member, by imperial appointment, of the House of Peers. Minobe for years had been the leading expert on Japanese constitutional law. A whole generation of administrators, diplomats, scholars, and business tycoons had sat at his feet in their student days. He had offered an authoritarian but rational interpretation of the Meiji Constitution. His general outlook could be described as that of an enlightened conservative. Nobody appeared to be less subversive. But he had always discussed the constitutional position of the Japanese monarchy in terms of political science rather than in those of mysticism or theology. On such grounds he had been criticized in the past by a lunatic fringe of ultranationalist academics; but in general his views had long been accepted, at least among thinkers outside the armed services. It might be added that the emperor himself thought highly of Minobe.

This respected old gentleman, however, came under new and sharp attack in 1935, first of all in the House of Peers, where a fellow member launched a diatribe against him. This attack, and those that followed, tended to concentrate on a phrase first used earlier in one of Minobe's books. In this work Minobe had stated that the emperor was "the highest organ of the State." Minobe's critics believed or pretended to believe that this comment was little short of blasphemy. No cool legal definition, in the ultranationalist view, was appropriate to describe the emperor's status, since this rested on the inherited divinity of the monarch and was associated with a throne the prosperity of which was (to use the words of the Rescript on Education) "coeval with heaven and earth."

Minobe's "organ theory" (*kikan setsu*) became in 1935 a widely known and much reviled phrase. No patriotic gathering, no reunion of army veterans, seemed properly conducted without some speech execrating the "organ theory" and calling for "the clarification of the national polity." Minobe himself at first put up a vigorous and courageous defense. But he was forced to resign from the Diet, and he was driven into complete seclusion—with police protection supplied—in spite of the sympathy felt for him by the emperor and his advisers as well as at least some members of the government and higher bureaucracy—none of whom, however, felt ready to come out publicly in his defense. He escaped assassination by mere chance; for he was wounded, in what was intended to be a lethal assault, by an ultranationalist fanatic.

The Minobe case, let it be remembered, was only the most famous of many instances of victimization. Other scholars all over the country suffered in various ways during the 1930s for what they had said or written.

It was in the midst of the national hysteria over the "organ theory" that the Imperial Way faction in the army incurred a setback, with the forced resignation of one of its leaders, General Mazaki, from the important post of inspector general of military education. Mazaki was on close terms with Araki. Like Araki he was greatly admired, even idolized, by many restless young officers, disciples of Kita and his ideas. Such was the indignation created by Mazaki's removal that one field-grade officer, Lieutenant Colonel Aizawa Saburō, traveled up from the provinces to Tokyo, strode into the Army Ministry, and hacked to death Major General Nagata, who was held to have been active in intrigues against Mazaki. This sensational event was followed in due course by the scarcely less sensational trial of the assassin. As in the case of those who killed Inukai, the positions of prosecutor and accused seemed curiously reversed. It was Aizawa, not the judge or prosecutor, who dominated the courtroom, which was treated to lectures from him on the current evils of the day, notably the prevalence, especially in high quarters, of the pernicious "organ theory."

Incident of February 26, 1936

This trial had not ended when there occurred the most serious of all Japan's domestic "incidents" of this century. Early on the morning of February 26, 1936, amidst a severe snowstorm, a group of captains and lieutenants led the troops immediately under their command, about 1,500 in all, out of their barracks into the deserted streets of the city. Some detachments occupied buildings in the government quarter, adjoining the palace grounds; others set out on missions of murder, to the prime minister's official residence and to the homes of other prominent men. Those killed included the emperor's day-to-day political adviser and former prime minister, the venerable Admiral Saitō; another former prime minister, currently finance minister, the aged Takahashi Korekiyo; and Mazaki's successor as inspector general of military education, General Watanabe. The prime minister of the day—Admiral Okada, who had succeeded Saitō in July, 1934—had a remarkable escape. When the assault on his residence came, he sought refuge in a cupboard. The mutineers shot dead Okada's brother-in-law whom they mistook for Okada, since the two men happened to resemble each other very closely. Admiral Suzuki Kantarō, the emperor's grand chamberlain, was left for dead but in fact recovered from the many bullet wounds he received. He was to become Japan's last wartime prime minister. Both the genrō, Prince Saionji, and Count Makino, another important adviser of the emperor, had lucky escapes from assassination.

These acts of revolutionary frenzy were intended to usher in the Shōwa Restoration. The young officers believed that the uprising would soon be legitimized when sympathetic seniors, such as Mazaki, established a new regime, to be followed by the needed reform of the state structure. In this respect, as in many others, they revealed a characteristic naïveté. For if certain generals appeared to encourage the young officers before the coup, these same generals sat on the fence once the explosion had occurred. Yet there was evidently a period of great uncertainty for very many hours after the outbreak of the mutiny. The first press announcement, for example, did not condemn the mutineers but spoke of them in quite neutral terms. Had the insurgents thrown a cordon round the imperial palace, and had risings in sympathy taken place in other parts of Japan, things might well have turned out differently.

But from the first the emperor reacted to the crisis in a forthright manner. So did the navy. The emperor made it clear that he looked upon the insurgents as rebels. He declared that they must be suppressed without delay. The navy, for its part, adopted an extremely firm stand. Warships steamed into the port of Tokyo, landing parties of armed bluejackets who were soon in position facing the rebels. The guns of the First Fleet were ready to fire on the buildings in rebel hands. The army authorities adopted the double course of parleying with mutineers and concentrating reliable troops against them.

Martial law was proclaimed. But Tokyo was spared the shock of civil war. On the fourth day of the mutiny an appeal to surrender proved effective. One rebel officer shot himself. The others gave themselves up, expecting perhaps that their eventual court-martial would be given the publicity accorded that of Aizawa. However, the trials of the mutinous officers and of civilians linked with them, such as Kita Ikki, were secret. Seventeen of the accused, including Kita, were condemned to death and executed by firing squad, as was Aizawa.

In the first weeks following the mutiny a popular revulsion against the army, for ever having allowed such an insurrection to occur, seemed to foreshadow some reduction in the political influence of Japan's military. The Imperial Way faction, at any rate, was discredited. Its chief figures were soon deprived of their posts. But the generals who carried out this purge were not ready to ease the army's pressure on government policy. On the contrary they increased it very sharply. They could now exert a form of blackmail, warning both the emperor's entourage and the cabinet that if attention was not paid to the army's wishes a second and more serious mutiny could very well take place. So the army had much say in the composition of the cabinet formed by the new prime minister, Hirota Kōki, on March 9, 1936, to succeed the Okada administration. General Terauchi Hisaichi, Hirota's army minister, made it plain that the army would not cooperate with the prime minister if he invited persons with liberal leanings to join the cabinet. And by the late summer of 1936 the basic policies of the government, in education and finance as well as national defense and diplomacy, were being dictated by the army minister, acting as mouthpiece for his military colleagues and principal aides.

The consequences of this state of affairs were to be momentous. In illustration of the point we may turn to the confession of the celebrated secret agent, Richard Sorge. In 1936 Sorge had been a German press correspondent in Tokyo for some years, while simultaneously head of a clandestine Red Army spy ring. (He was arrested in 1941 and eventually executed in 1944.) Sorge is discussing the detailed report on the February Mutiny which he sent by courier to Moscow. The essence of this report is summed up by Sorge in these words:

There were two ways in which the Japanese Government could handle the aftermath of the February 26 Affair. They could either introduce social reforms, at the same time imposing strict discipline on the army, or they could adopt the policy of permanent expansion.

This phrase, *permanent expansion,* is my own invention. It came to me from Trotsky's phrase, "permanent revolution."

Japan adopted the second course. Whether the direction of this permanent expansion was to be China or Russia was a question of the greatest importance to the Soviet Union.

I remember that I reported to Moscow that the direction would be China. For I had in mind a tradition of Japanese expansion that went back to the days of the Empress Jingu.[2]

Indeed, all the indications in 1936 in Japan pointed in one direction, namely armed expansion. The size of the defense budget, the plans for new naval construction, the government's economic program, the measures to enhance patriotic indoctrination in schools throughout the country, the new national slogan of "the time of war preparation" (*junsenji*), and finally the Anti-Comintern Pact—all carried the same message for those who dared to look ahead: sooner rather than later Japan would be at war.

The eclipse of the Imperial Way faction seemed to decrease the likelihood that this war would be with Russia although that country remained in the army's view a potential enemy. The growing involvement in North China, however, was very ominous. Sorge's prediction might have been no more than intelligent guesswork. Yet it was clear that if one accepted the hypothesis of "permanent expansion" China rather than the Soviet Far East was the more vulnerable target.

The Eruption of the China Hostilities, 1937

Unlike the Manchurian Incident, the hostilities that broke out in 1937 were probably not the result of a conspiracy on the part of Japanese officers in the field. The first clash, between the Chinese and the Japanese North China garrison (long stationed in the Peking-Tientsin area under the terms of the Boxer Protocol), took place at the Marco Polo Bridge outside Peking on July 7, 1937. Its origins remain obscure. In any case the first spate of fighting was followed by a cease-fire; and it looked as though a local dispute would be patched

2. F. W. Deakin and G. R. Storry, *The Case of Richard Sorge* (New York, 1966), pp. 175–76.

up locally, as others had been, on terms favorable to the Japanese. In Tokyo the chief of the general staff advised the cabinet that "inasmuch as the government's policy of localizing the incident is thoroughly understood by the field commander, all necessary measures in connection with this matter will be left to the discretion of the commander stationed in China."

But the situation in China had changed. Chiang Kai-shek and the Kuomintang were no longer at odds with the Communists. That rather mysterious affair, Chiang's incarceration at Sian by Chang Hsueh-liang in December, 1936, had as its aftermath the formation of an anti-Japanese united front by the Kuomintang and the Communists. The latter, so far as we know, secured Chiang Kai-shek's release on the understanding that Chiang abandon his campaign against them, joining with them to resist the Japanese. Certainly Mao Tse-tung, about a year later, was to refer to the Sian Incident as an epic event in Chinese history since it led to the establishment of the united front.

So in the summer of 1937 there was a new temper in Nanking, and Chiang Kai-shek was not prepared to acquiesce in a local settlement of the North China hostilities. This was a matter that must be negotiated at government level, between Nanking and Tokyo. Meanwhile he began sending troops in considerable numbers to North China.

The Japanese government at this time was headed by Prince Konoe, the most popular prime minister the country had known for many years. This comparatively young and handsome member of the age-old court nobility was believed to be a truly disinterested statesman, immune to the temptations of the ordinary politician and free from the mental rigidity so often associated with bureaucrats and officers. His intellectual abilities were highly esteemed. He enjoyed the reputation of being at the same time a nationalist and a man with a realistic understanding of the contemporary world. Here was someone, it was widely agreed, who had both a taste for tradition and a real sympathy with all who favored change by legal and constitutional means. The emperor's advisers hoped and believed he would be able to restrain the army. The army's view, needless to say, was just the reverse. They saw in Konoe an ideal figurehead behind which military intervention in political and economic affairs might continue unchecked.

In his handling of the crisis of July, 1937, and indeed in his handling of relations with China during the next sixteen months,

Konoe appeared always to take, in public, a position of considerable intransigence, although in private he would bemoan the unreasonable stand adopted by the army minister and other army leaders. His initial public attitude toward China was decidedly uncompromising. So there was popular support for the muster of reinforcements called for by the army in response to China's movement of troops to the north. After the fighting deteriorated into full-scale warfare both in the north and in Shanghai, followed by a Japanese advance up the Yangtze and the storming of Nanking, Konoe helped to kill the hopes of successful German mediation in the conflict. Indeed, he went further than the General Staff in the severity of the demands made on the Chinese. Then, in January, 1938, he committed himself to a public condemnation of Chiang as a leader with whom the Japanese government would have no further dealings. It is a measure of Konoe's self-awareness that later he felt some burden of responsibility for the tragic "China Incident"; and perhaps this was one reason why he took his own life in December, 1945.

The Japanese never clarified, even to their own satisfaction, their precise war aims in China. What began as a skirmish developed into a series of military campaigns, affecting more and more of the vast Chinese terrain. Within two years of the clash at the Marco Polo Bridge Japanese troops were in occupation of nearly all the important cities of China from Peking to Canton. Among the professed purposes of the Japanese army were the chastisement of Chiang Kai-shek and the delivery of China from the menace of Communism. But Chiang Kai-shek stubbornly refused to submit; and the horror and social chaos that accompanied Japanese military invasion greatly promoted the Communist cause. As much as any other factor, Japanese aggression helped to bring about the success of the Chinese Communist Revolution.

Hopes of a quick termination of the war after the fall of Nanking at the end of 1937 and after the fall of the Wuhan cities in October, 1938, gave way to the realization that the struggle might drag on for years. Meanwhile relations with the United States, Great Britain, France, and the Soviet Union grew steadily worse. Considerations of both humanity and self-interest led Washington and London to condemn the repeated bombing of cities such as Chungking, Chiang's capital after the loss of Wuhan, and the often brutal treatment of Chinese civilians by Japanese troops. British and other foreign business activities up and down the China coast suffered loss, damage, and interference. The Japanese army in the field, on the other hand, became increasingly anti-Western, since they blamed the West, especially Great Britain with her extensive interests all over China, for Chiang Kai-shek's continued resistance.

Prince Konoe, who had been reluctant to take the prime ministership in the first place, resigned at the beginning of 1939, being succeeded by the convinced but cautious nationalist, Baron Hiranuma. But before leaving office Konoe added a phrase to the political vocabulary of the Orient. Early in November, 1938, he had made what was intended to be a serious peace offer to China. But its terms were harsh; and the only thing to be said in their favor is that they did not include the demand for an indemnity. It was at this point that Konoe declared Japan's "immutable policy" to be the establishment of "a New Order in East Asia." This meant the creation of an anti-Communist bloc composed of Japan, Manchukuo, and China, the three countries to be linked in close political, economic, and cultural union.

In Chungking Chiang Kai-shek publicly rejected the offer and announced that he would carry on the fight. However, one of his most celebrated colleagues, Wang Ching-wei, had become pessimistic about China's prospects and believed the war could be ended without too much loss of face. Since this was not a proposition that he could persuade Chiang to accept, Wang contrived to slip out of China secretly to Hanoi. With Japanese help, he traveled to Shanghai and and began long negotiations with a variety of Japanese "China experts," both military and civilian, first in Shanghai and then in Tokyo. Wang Ching-wei cannot be accused of conscious treachery, although it is fair to call him a defeatist. There is no doubt that he regarded his dialogue with the Japanese as being in the best interests of his countrymen. He was, after all, a powerful figure with a long record of responsible leadership in the Chinese Nationalist movement. He had no intention of becoming a Japanese puppet, like Pu Yi, the last Ch'ing emperor of China, who had been placed on the synthetic throne of Manchukuo by the Kwantung Army. Yet in the end Wang Ching-wei, too, was to be no more than a Japanese satellite. In due course he was assisted in the formation of a government in Nanking, and in 1940 Japan recognized this regime as the legitimate government of the Chinese Republic, considering this an important step on the road to the creation of the New Order.

Relations with the USSR and Germany

While war burned its way across China, Japanese-Soviet relations remained as tense as ever, and there were continual minor clashes at many points on the Manchukuo-Siberian border. In the summer of 1938, and again a year later, these erupted into major battles. The first, at Changkufeng, close to Korea, was short but severe. Neither Tokyo nor Moscow wanted war; and a settlement was fairly quickly arranged. The second battle was much more prolonged and serious, lasting on and off for five months, from May to September of 1939. It took place in the Nomonhan area, in a region of steppe where Manchukuo bordered on Outer Mongolia. Here the Russians won a clear victory. A Japanese infantry division was cut to pieces. The strength and firepower of Soviet armor surprised and impressed the Japanese army. Eventually, since the two sides were not prepared to engage in outright war, a truce put an end to the fighting.

The efficiency of Zhukhov's tanks at Nomonhan was not the only unpleasant surprise in store for Tokyo that summer. The government was astonished to learn that Hitler's foreign minister, Ribbentrop, had flown to Moscow to sign a pact with the Russians. This action was indeed regarded as a slap in the face by Japan, for Japanese-German relations were those of particular friendship, thanks to the Anti-Comintern Pact. This bound the two countries in an ideological bond against a common foe—nominally the Comintern, in reality the Soviet Union. So cordial were German-Japanese relations that there had been long, although ultimately unsuccessful, confidential talks between the two powers about ways and means of transforming the Anti-Comintern Pact into a military alliance. Therefore, the sudden announcement of a Nazi-Soviet *rapprochement,* of which Tokyo had been given no warning, made Japanese diplomacy look very foolish. The loss of face was hard to endure; and the Hiranuma cabinet resigned within a week of Ribbentrop's visit to the Kremlin. Pro-German officers in the Japanese army—that is to say, the majority—knew they had been caught off balance, and at a moment when their forces were not doing very well in combat against the Russians at Nomonhan.

Thus when World War II broke out in Europe a few days later, Japan's attitude was one of genuine neutrality. Germany for once was out of favor.

The situation changed, inevitably, in the following summer. Nazi triumphs in Scandinavia, the Low Countries, and France gave keen encouragement to those in Japan who had been so downcast in the previous August. It seemed the path of wisdom to seek closer association with the all-conquering victors of Europe. And in September, 1940, Japan signed a treaty of alliance with Germany and Italy.

The Tripartite Pact was welcomed not only as a warranty of future cooperation with the now seemingly invincible power of Nazi Germany, but also because it appeared to place an effective check on strong action by the United States, which showed signs of practical sympathy with Great Britain and the exiled governments of Poland, Norway, and the Netherlands. Prince Konoe was back in office as prime minister when the pact was signed. Indeed, his return had been engineered by the army precisely because they wanted him to be the man to sign the new treaty. The previous government, under the temperate Admiral Yonai, had been considered pro-British. It was characteristic of Konoe, however, that he should have regarded the Tripartite Pact with mixed feelings.

These were not shared by his foreign minister, Matsuoka Yōsuke, a voluble pro-German nationalist, who proceeded to purge the foreign service of those whom he suspected of not sharing his enthusiasm for the fascist powers. Such persons were finding the pervading atmosphere increasingly uncongenial. For although Japan was not a fascist state the general climate was becoming markedly totalitarian. Konoe had agreed to organize a mass national party "to assist Imperial Rule"; and the Diet political parties then went into voluntary self-liquidation. In November, 1940, a further stimulus was given to both ethnocentric and totalitarian trends by the national celebrations commemorating the putative 2,600th anniversary of the empire's foundation.

In the early spring of 1941 Matsuoka undertook a much publicized trip to Europe, traveling there and back by rail across Russia. While in Berlin he found Hitler and Ribbentrop eager to extract from him a promise, which he could not give, of a Japanese attack on Singapore. But Matsuoka does not seem to have caught any whisper of Operation Barbarossa, the projected German assault on the Soviet Union. On his way back through Moscow Matsuoka found Stalin very ready to be friendly to Japan; and a Neutrality Pact was signed in the Kremlin with little, if any, preliminary bargaining.

The new relationship with Russia was well received in most circles in Japan, for it was believed that ever since the Polish campaign

German-Soviet cooperation had continued without much friction. Furthermore, it was thought that the Germans themselves were looking forward to the day when the Tripartite Pact could be enlarged, by the adherence of Russia, into a four-power alliance. Finally, Japanese eyes were now gazing with great interest on what was loosely called "the southern zone"—namely, the area, stretching from Hanoi to New Guinea, occupied by French, British, and Dutch colonial possessions. Japanese expansion into that area would be made a more attractive and feasible proposition if Tokyo could feel that relations with the Soviet Union were stabilized.

Japan Moves South

When the German onslaught on the Soviet Union occurred in June, 1941, the Japanese—like the Russians themselves—were taken by surprise. But Matsuoka refused to be abashed by this latest example of Nazi dynamism. On the contrary, as though he had always foreseen what was going to happen, he immediately pressed for active Japanese participation in Hitler's new war.

This was too much for Konoe, whose main concern at the time was to improve Japan's relations with the United States. Common sense, too, carried the day even in the Japanese army. For although some officers may have accepted the view, sedulously put about by the German Embassy, that this was the ideal moment for Japan to settle old scores with the Soviet Union, the prevailing opinion was that it would be best to wait and see what happened in the Nazi-Soviet conflict. The army, therefore, did not insist that Matsuoka be retained at the Foreign Ministry. In order to be rid of Matsuoka, Konoe resigned together with his cabinet. Being reappointed prime minister he formed a fresh cabinet without inviting Matsuoka to join it, the new foreign minister being a retired naval officer, Admiral Toyoda Teijirō.

But if action against Russia were to be deferred, action elsewhere seemed desirable. And an area ripe for penetration was French Indochina, where the Japanese army already had a foothold. For after the fall of France in 1940 Japan had secured a number of bases in the north of Indochina, on the pretext of ensuring that supplies did not reach Chiang Kai-shek through Haiphong. But the southern part of French Indochina was not affected by these arrangements. In July, 1941, however, Japan delivered an ultimatum to Vichy France, demanding the right to move air, sea, and land forces to the region of Saigon and the Mekong delta.

Seen from Washington and London, this new advance appeared to suggest only one thing—a clear intention to threaten Malaya and the Dutch East Indies, not to mention Thailand. The governments of the United States, the British Commonwealth, and the Netherlands imposed what amounted to an economic embargo on Japan. This meant that Japanese imports of raw materials from a large segment of the globe would come to a standstill. It meant, above all, that Japan would find it impossible to replenish her stocks of oil. These stocks, carefully built up over the years, were thought sufficient to meet normal requirements for at most two years, and this estimate was regarded as optimistic.

Economic sanctions, which the United States and the League powers hardly considered seriously at the time of the Manchurian crisis, were now enforced against a Japan much stronger and more determined than she had been nine or ten years earlier. It was considered that Japan would probably bend before this pressure. There was a general impression abroad, in America and the countries of the British Commonwealth, that Japan was (to use the phrase current at the time) "bogged down in China" and would be unlikely, when it came to the point, to go to war with both the United States and Great Britain.

The Crisis Between Japan and the United States

Certainly the government in Tokyo faced a grave impasse. There were, it seemed, but two choices open. The economic embargo would be lifted, of course, if the Japanese called a halt to their policy of expansion. In practice this would involve at least a measure of withdrawal, of retreat, from both China and the Indochina peninsula. This would be a diplomatic setback and one which nationalists would see as a great humiliation, reminiscent of what happened at the time of the Triple Intervention in 1895. The other alternative was to break the embargo by force, the Japanese seizing for themselves the rubber and tin of Malaya and the oil of the Dutch East Indies.

This was the course of action chosen by the general staffs of the army and navy, and accepted by the cabinet. But all agreed that every effort should be made to reach some reasonable settlement with "the encircling powers." In practice, from the Japanese point of view, the issue of peace and war rested on the series of talks which the Japanese ambassador, Admiral Nomura, was having with Secretary of State Cordell Hull in Washington, D.C. On the question of raising or maintaining the trade embargo, the governments of the British Commonwealth and the Netherlands were ready to delegate to the United States the main responsibility of negotiating with Japan.

There can be no doubt that the Japanese leadership—including, of course, the most powerful sector of that leadership, the army—genuinely hoped that a peaceful solution of the crisis would emerge from the Washington talks. As for Konoe, he wanted to avoid war with America at almost any cost; and for this reason he proposed that he and President Roosevelt should meet, in either Hawaii or Alaska. The suggestion was at first welcomed by the president, but on taking further advice he decided that a "summit" of this kind would be undesirable unless the two countries first reached some kind of agreement on fundamental issues, with the Japanese showing evidence of a real change of heart. The American leadership, we must remember, was hagridden by recollections of Chamberlain at Munich. What guarantee was there that Japan, which had broken many promises, would abide by commitments made at a meeting between the prince and the president?

Konoe himself was convinced that any freely negotiated Japanese-American agreement, reached at such a meeting, could be enforced on the refractory armies in the field. He would take with him to a meeting with the president generals and admirals of sufficient authority and determination to ensure that any orders—to withdraw from French Indochina, for example—were strictly obeyed.

Yet one may doubt whether a Konoe-Roosevelt conference would have been successful. The disparity of aims and opinion on the two sides was, after all, immense. Still, it seems tragic that the frail possibilities of reaching an understanding at such a meeting were never put to the test.

At bottom what separated Tokyo from Washington was the question of China. As part of a bargain the Japanese army would have been prepared, admittedly with great reluctance, to evacuate the southern part of French Indochina or even perhaps the whole of that country. But any retreat, save of a very nominal kind, from China was absolutely unacceptable to the army. On this point military opinion was unanimous. The question of moving troops out of China might be discussed once Chiang Kai-shek was induced to make peace on Japan's terms. If Washington wanted to see a Japanese withdrawal from China, then American influence must be used on the side of Japan and the Wang Ching-wei government to persuade Chiang to make peace. Such was the reasoning of the Japanese army. Pending this kind of end to the China war there could be no evacuation of the occupied areas of that country. On this the soldiers were adamant, none more so that Lieutenant General Tōjō Hideki, the army minister.

Between July and September, 1941, a formidable mobilization of men and resources took place in Japan. Some of the mobilized formations were equipped, it seemed, for cold weather conditions. It was not difficult to guess that their destination was Manchukuo. (The Germans were still advancing. Who could be sure that the Soviet Union might not collapse?) But other regiments and divisions embarked for the south. Their tropical gear suggested at least some reinforcement of the garrisons in Formosa, South China, and French Indochina.

Some months earlier, as we now know, the navy had begun planning the surprise attack (a Japanese specialty) that they felt would be required if there was to be war with the United States. On Japan's prospects in such a war the navy was more realistic than the army. It is significant that, while the admirals felt they could deal crippling blows in the first round, they were exceedingly doubtful whether Japan could prevail in a long war. The army, on the other hand, grossly underestimated the vital importance of America's huge industrial power and totally misjudged the temper of the American people, believing that they would not stomach a prolonged struggle; and a prolonged war could be expected, if the Americans, having lost the first battles, seriously intended to expel the Japanese from the territories they had seized.

It was at the beginning of September, 1941, that the Konoe cabinet and the chiefs of staff, meeting in the emperor's presence, formally decided to go to war if no agreement with the United States could be reached through diplomatic talks. The operative passage in this top secret decision reads: "In the event that there is no prospect of our demands being met by the first ten days of October through diplomatic negotiations, we will immediately decide to commence hostilities against the United States, Britain, and the Netherlands." [3]

But when October arrived, with still no prospect of success in the Washington talks, Konoe was not willing to authorize the next step,

3. Nobutake Ike, ed., *Japan's Decision for War* (Stanford, 1967), p. 135.

namely, the decision to go to war. This caused a bitter crisis in his relations with Tōjō, the army minister, and led to Konoe's resignation and Tōjō's appointment as prime minister, but on the understanding that the October deadline should be canceled. A new time limit was set—the end of November. Meanwhile a final effort was made to break the deadlock in Washington. A special envoy in the person of Kurusu Saburō, a former ambassador to Germany, was sent to join Admiral Nomura in the United States. After the attack on Pearl Harbor it was believed in America that Kurusu's mission was an example of diabolical Japanese cunning, a deceitful maneuver to lull Washington into a false sense of security. This interpretation, while understandable in the circumstances, was incorrect. Nomura, a man of great goodwill in his attitude to the United States, was a sailor, not a diplomat. It was at Nomura's pressing request that Tokyo sent a senior diplomat to help him in the last critical weeks. It should be noted that, although all concerned appreciated the imminent danger of war, nobody outside a small group of navy officers—not even Tōjō himself—had prior information of the plan to attack Pearl Harbor. (Tōjō and the army were informed, certainly, that the navy had an effective plan of action in the event of war. But this was all they knew, and—in the navy's opinion—all they needed to know.)

Kurusu brought with him proposals for a compromise, if only a temporary one. Counterproposals came from the State Department. Neither side, however, would make the minimum concession deemed essential by the other.

The American stand was basically one in defense of a free China. If Washington had been prepared to "sell China down the river," to make a deal with Japan at Chiang's expense, the Pearl Harbor holocaust would never have occurred. In a real sense the United States became involved in World War II because of China.

Japan, on the other hand, was the victim of her unbalanced constitutional and administrative structure, which gave very great influence to the armed services; an influence which, as we have seen, the army enlarged enormously during the 1931–41 period. A national structure of this type called for a strong coordinating power at the top, one that would make the final decisions and see that these were carried out. This ultimate authority was lacking. For on one hand the last genrō (Saionji), who died in late 1940 at the age of ninety-one, was too old to fill the role; and on the other the emperor was not equipped to take the lead, for he had been taught by all his mentors never to act except on the advice of the appropriate civilian and military officials.

The nation, therefore, lurched forward from one venture to the next, until in 1941 it was landed in a situation where it had no choice but to retreat or fight. The choice was revealed in the early hours of December 8, 1941 (Tokyo time) when the Japanese struck simultaneously at Pearl Harbor, Hong Kong, and Malaya.

War and Surrender

The course of the bitter struggle that ensued, raging from the Aleutians to the doors of Australia, need not be recounted here. The story has been told and analyzed many times. It is certain that history can show few comparable examples of such rapid and overwhelming victories, such vast initial gains, followed by a total reversal of the fortunes of war, and terminated by a dramatically swift and cataclysmic defeat.

The mood of the Japanese people swung from tremendous elation at the beginning to intense gloom at the end. By August, 1945, it looked as though the Japanese at home, armed with little more than courage and bamboo spears, faced inevitable extinction. One can only speculate about what would have happened if the surrender had not occurred in mid-August, 1945. Would the Russians have overrun Hokkaido? Would other cities have suffered the fate of Hiroshima and Nagasaki? Would an Allied landing in Kyushu have faced the kind of desperate, costly resistance that was encountered at Saipan, Iwo Jima, and Okinawa? Would revolution and anarchy have destroyed forever the monarchy and all traditional institutions and beliefs? Would civilians have committed mass suicide, as happened at Saipan and Okinawa? The answer, surely, is that all these things might well have occurred. So, in conclusion, a word perhaps should be said about the circumstances of the surrender that saved Japan from such ultimate horrors.

It had become clear by the spring of 1945, even to the army authorities, that fanatical courage, of the kind displayed by the suicide pilots of the kamikaze squadrons, could not make up for the losses, especially in shipping, already incurred. Thus attempts were made to seek some kind of armistice, short of surrender, through the mediation of Moscow. Stalin, however, procrastinated in his dealings with the Japanese. His representatives listened to what the Japanese had to say but would commit themselves to no positive action. Meanwhile, as spring gave way to summer, the pounding of Japan by enemy planes and ships was slowly bringing the economic life of the country to a standstill. Malnutrition, too, was beginning to take its toll.

Yet, even after the dropping of two atomic bombs, and a Soviet declaration of war and the invasion of both Manchukuo and Korea, the nation's military and civilian leaders remained divided on the question of whether or not to accept the terms of the Potsdam Proclamation, the stern ultimatum that had been issued on July 26, 1945, by the American president and the British prime minister. There was a deadlock between those ready to bow to the ultimatum, provided only that the monarchy remained, and those who could not tolerate the prospect of "the unconditional surrender of all Japanese armed forces." The issue was settled by the emperor, who was invited to give what was in effect a casting vote. He declared that the ultimatum should be accepted; and he adhered to this decision after an Allied reply seemed to leave uncertain the question of the monarchy's survival. So it was that an unprecedented imperial broadcast was heard over radios throughout Japan on the morning of August 15, 1945. The rather high-pitched, unfamiliar voice of the emperor told the people that he was ready to bear "what was unbearable." In other words, the war was over. Japan had surrendered.

Members of the emperor's family were sent to the various force headquarters overseas, sometimes to areas where large bodies of men had seen no fighting for years and felt themselves fresh and undefeated. These imperial messengers were dispatched to make sure that the army obeyed the decision to surrender. It is a striking fact that, with the exception of a tiny handful of men in and near Tokyo, nobody tried to defy the emperor's command. Far too late in the day the voice of reason was allowed to prevail. This must provoke the sobering reflection that if Saionji and Wakatsuki could have arranged for a similar imperial command to have been issued, in September or October, 1931, it might possibly have been generally obeyed. If this had happened, the whole course of events would have been different —with results beneficial to Europe as well as the Orient. For the League of Nations would have felt an access of renewed confidence and strength, and the foreign ministries of the powers would have placed greater trust in that organization and in the principle of collective security. Japanese ultranationalism in that event need not have become a monster, devouring half Asia and almost destroying, in the end, the Japanese themselves.

IX

Japan

Since 1945

BY
LAWRENCE OLSON

Some Statistical Measures

In the quarter-century since World War II Japan has moved with stunning speed from near-collapse, through an undreamed-of regeneration of its economy, to face by the 1970s Japanese versions of environmental pollution, urban sprawl and social pathology characteristic of high industrial development elsewhere. At the same time, the Japanese people, wishing mainly to be left alone to enjoy the fruits of their new-found prosperity, are already once more being pressed by their complex perceptions of their own national identity as well as by the expectations of others to play a more visible political role in the world. For more than a century the Japanese have been trying constantly to catch up with the latest that has been achieved in the technological realm by the nations of the modern West. Today those goals have been largely achieved, while the attitudes underlying them, though still dominant for a majority of leaders and people, are increasingly being brought into question.

By the end of the 1960s Japan's gross national product was the third largest in the world, between 1965 and 1970 growing at a rate of over 12 percent. The population today is the world's sixth largest and has passed 103 million. Less than a fifth of the labor force is in agriculture, which accounts for less than 10 percent of the national income. Textiles, which twenty years ago were nearly half of all Japanese exports by value, now are less than a fifth. Annual steel output has reached about 80 percent of American production, and Japanese steel-making capacity is not being fully used. Metals and machinery are more than half of total exports. The Japanese lead the world in shipbuilding, and their electronics and optical industries are universally famous for quality and efficiency. Already by the early 1960s expenditure on research and development in private industry equaled in percentage of national product the amount being spent by France, and exceeded that of West Germany. But while other nations allocate up to three fourths of their research funds to military and space uses, Japan at present spends only some 5 percent for these purposes. For the last decade the defense budget has not exceeded 2 percent of national income or 15 percent of the annual budget.

Other indices of Japan's current stage of development may be found in demographic statistics. The birth rate, which in the late 1940s was 34 per thousand per annum, currently is 19, and the population grows at a mere one percent annually. It used to be said in Tokyo that the only thing that would bring down the birth rate was night baseball, but it is obvious that the Japanese long ago resorted to other and more effective expedients. Life expectancies also are "Western": about 68 for men, 73 for women. And when people die, they die of much the same things that Westerners do: the three main causes of death are heart disease, cancer, and automobile accidents; rather than tuberculosis, yaws, beri-beri and other diseases more commonly associated with the agrarian parts of the Asian world.

Another measure of Japanese development is in education. The habit of going to school is far more than a century old. The literacy rate for males a century ago has been estimated authoritatively at about 45 percent, a higher rate than one finds in many "underdeveloped" countries today. For generations virtually all Japanese have been able to read and write. Universal compulsory education through the ninth grade is well enforced. Seventy-five percent of those Japanese who graduate from junior high school enter high school, and more than 25 percent of male high school graduates enter a university of some sort. Japan has long been a meritocracy heavily stressing education: and a university education is today considered essential for entry into most of the elite positions in the society. Moreover, political leaders do not have to contend with the education of immense and diverse minority ethnic groups; except for some 600,000 Koreans and much smaller numbers of Chinese, Americans and Europeans, there are few foreigners in the country, and none of the small minorities that do exist has any particular political significance.

In many other ways Japan is strictly comparable to Europe or America rather than to Asia. The savings rate, for instance, is remarkably high. Urban wage earners regularly put aside from 10 to 15 percent of their disposable income. In the sphere of consumption, standards of living and purchasing power approach or exceed European levels: per capita income in 1973 exceeds that of Great Britain and is approaching one half of that of the United States. Tastes in food have long been changing, especially in the cities, where more meat and milk and other dairy products are widely consumed. The family car is a reality for increasing numbers of people, to the point where a "no car" movement has begun in Tokyo. Japanese automobile production is now about 60 percent that of the U.S. The communications network, the transport grid, the shipping fleet, the newspapers and other mass media are all the most sophisticated outside the Western world and in many ways surpass in modernity anything in the West. More books and more movies are produced than anywhere else on earth. And another sign of Japan's progress is that all these statistics are Japanese: Japan is one of the few places outside the West where reliable statistics can be obtained.

Consider the Japanese accomplishment, then. Twenty-eight years ago the country was in ruins, psychologically demoralized, the economy almost totally stalled, nationalism fragmented and atomized, with intellectuals groping for existential solutions like everybody else. People in the towns were grubbing in the ruins for surviving possessions to exchange for food in the countryside. In this bleak era the people were sustained by their habits of cohesiveness, endurance, and small expectations. With the mythology of their uniqueness at a sudden end, and the meaning of Japaneseness more than ever dispersed into the general modern uncertainty, it might be supposed that they would have gone to pieces entirely. Another people with different politics or a different temperament might have chosen revolution. However, for the most part the Japanese survived to blame the war on their military leaders; they learned quickly how to make the most of a benevolent American Occupation to get themselves on their feet again economically and politically. It took them longer to get their spiritual and psychological bearings, perhaps. But today there are clear signs of a new assurance in those spheres as well as in more measurable ones. Japan has rebuilt itself despite a very narrow resource base, through the vigor and dynamism of its ordinary people. It is the people who have been and are Japan's greatest and most abundant resource. They have endured, they have worked and built on the strengths of their traditional qualities, in spite of their shortcomings and inadequacies and their peculiar liabilities as citizens of the world. However, other peoples work hard too; and without leaders to rally such qualities Japan's comeback would hardly have been possible.

Conservative Continuity and Dominance

Japan is a highly organized society with skilled leaders, the best of them immensely talented economic managers. What they lack in charisma is more than made up by drive and world-famous commitment to group and national goals. Since the end of World War II conservatives of one party label or another have dominated Japanese political life. Their programs and policies have set the country's course at home and abroad. It has rarely occurred to these conservative leaders that what they wanted and stood for might not be best for their country as a whole. While they may eventually be proven wrong in this, with one unimportant exception conservative parties have never been unseated at the polls since 1946. The most interesting political questions today are still those that probe conservative intentions in the domestic or foreign sphere, and ask whether and how and when they can meet the needs of their swiftly diversifying and complicating society, change with it, and direct its change, modernizing their politics along with the more tangible machineries of production.

Three intertwined elements comprise the conservative elite. The first is the civilian bureaucracy, which survived the war essentially intact. Though methods of personnel selection were somewhat liberalized after the war, educational channels into the appointive services remained narrow. A few universities, with Tokyo University preeminent among them, still furnish the majority of such recruits.

At the head of the bureaucracy stands the prime minister, who, in a system of responsible government such as Japan has had since 1945, also heads the government party, today called the Liberal-Democrats. Around the prime minister are ranked his cabinet. Since according to the 1947 Constitution at least two thirds of all cabinet officers must be members of the Diet, and since in practice all are so selected, ambitious and able bureaucrats must retire from appointive office to stand for election if they wish to reach the top. This has contributed to the "bureaucratization" of politics, which had begun before the war. One might prefer the parties to produce more politicians of stature, and the Japanese have themselves been aware of this problem. The fact remains that the senior Japanese bureaucrat is typically an educated and incorruptible man, whose talents have been well exploited in the service of Japan's secular goals. He is a tried and tested administrator with skills which, until very recently at least, have been appropriate to the technological future.

The second element in the elite is the managerial class in large business firms. Japan is a capitalist society, and commerce and industry lie at its heart. Agriculture has always been regarded as vital to national success but, as Sir George Sansom long ago remarked, agriculturists were somewhat less important to the leaders than agriculture. Farms provided food, factory labor and taxes for early modern progress in the cities. Today's elite reflects the long priority placed on commerce and industry as well as the postwar land reform. Japan has no class of landed gentlemen, and although some business leaders may have been born in the countryside, they left home early to be educated in the cities and are for the most part preoccupied with urban industrial concerns. The success of their enterprises has of course extended the market in the rural sector and raised rural standards of living to "non-Asian" levels. It has also drawn workers in floods from country to city, reducing rural populations in many prefectures. Unlike the bureaucrats, businessmen less often go openly into politics, but prefer to exercise influence behind the scenes. Election expenses for conservative politicians are largely provided by business firms or individual businessmen, and irregularities connected with such contributions are one of the characteristic forms of "corruption" in Japan.

The third element in the elite consists of elected politicians of conservative parties in the national Diet, prefectural governors and influential members of prefectural assemblies. "Pure" politicians who came up through local party offices have not been on the increase in recent years, but they represent a long tradition and have often contended with ex-bureaucrats for power in party factions and councils.

Probably the most significant thing that can be said about the conservative leadership is that its temper is pragmatic, and that it is more given to action than to speculation. These qualities obviously relate to the Japanese people as a whole. As a newspaper poll in Tokyo revealed, what the people admire most of all in politicians is the capacity to act, if possible for the greater benefit of Japan and all its citizens. What is perhaps least esteemed is theory that leads to no action. In view of the tradition of violence in politics that has unfortunately survived the war, this predilection for acts above thoughts may be disquieting, but it is characteristic, and it goes along with other such typical traits as emotionalism and a compulsion to hide individual responsibility in the group. At any event, since 1945 the conservatives have shown a talent for *ad hoc* programs and policies that have anticipated and undercut those of the opposition sufficiently to keep the latter from power.

There has been, then, some continuity of political structures and indeed of political individuals from prewar times. For this, Allied (meaning principally American) Occupation policy was responsible.

The Occupation in its early years set out to remake Japan in a "democratic" image. It reformed the system of landholding to drastically reduce farm tenancy. It gave women the vote along with the legal right to hold property and to divorce their husbands. It abolished the legal basis of the old family system, opened the jails and freed political prisoners, encouraged labor unions to organize and achieve legitimacy, allowed opposition parties to thrive (including the Communist in the first postwar years), and reformed the content and methods of primary and secondary education. It sponsored and provided the draft of a new constitution, which became law in 1947, establishing popular sovereignty, abolishing war as an instrument of national policy (Article 9), and granting a wider range of personal freedoms than Japanese had ever possessed before. Rights of free speech, press, and religion were guaranteed. A new system of courts was set up, a new civil code written. The old military establishment was abolished, and until the early 1950s even the police were decentralized and put under the jurisdiction of local entities. The emperor was retained as the symbol of the state, but the cult of state Shintō was wiped out, and Shintō as a religion was deprived of state subsidies. The zaibatsu were broken up and their assets scattered. Purges of Japanese associated with the era of militarism reached deep into the society in the Occupation's early years.

This dramatic era of reform was characterized by a very real and sometimes excessive, though short-lived zeal. But the Occupation was not prepared to govern Japan directly; it chose to rule through the "indigenous" machinery it found intact. Thus the civilian bureaucracy of government remained, though perforce infused with a new spirit of reform under pressure from the Occupation. Political parties that had written themselves out of existence in 1940 were rapidly rebuilt after 1945. Some new faces appeared in the top posts after prewar politicians fell in the purge. Thus Yoshida Shigeru, a former diplomat, emerged in 1946, and gathered round him a coterie of ex-officials from the Foreign Ministry and other agencies of the government. But Yoshida, for all his ability, was not in any real sense a "new man," the product of a social upheaval. Likewise his protégés, Ikeda Hayato and Satō Eisaku, both later to become prime minister, were veterans of the appointive bureaucracy with little or no party experience before 1945. Five times prime minister between 1946 and 1954, Yoshida was destined to become the strong man of postwar Japanese politics. He did much to bring his country out of ruin, but from first to last he showed a regal impatience toward his opponents, and his arrogance toward the electorate was sometimes ill concealed. He skillfully played upon the contradictions of the Occupation to maintain Japan's security from internal and external enemies and insure a conservative continuity in postwar Japanese governments.

Yoshida, the Occupation, and the Socialists: 1946–1952

The Occupation period was filled with ironies and incongruities. Most obvious of these was the spectacle of an alien military command enforcing sweeping social and political reforms on a people with radically different traditions from their conquerors. This was not lost on thoughtful Japanese, many of whom deplored the inappropriateness of some of the reforms even when they were sympathetic with Occupation goals in general. Yet the Occupation was destined to leave indelible marks. Though many of its innovations were later to be adulterated in letter or spirit, those for which some pressure already existed within Japanese society—and they included many of the most important ones—were taken up by Japanese with a stake in their success. There is little reason to believe that the dramatic land tenure reform, the new constitution, and much other legislation would have been introduced on Japanese government initiative alone. Today these and other measures have taken root and had pervasive effect. The longer the new constitution and other measures remain on the books, the less likely they are to be removed on grounds that they are alien. Japan may not yet be a really liberal society, but it is more nearly so because of Occupation influence.

However, the reform era was extremely brief, and during its early years Japanese political power returned to conservative hands. The first election with universal suffrage was held in April, 1946, and shortly thereafter Yoshida Shigeru became prime minister. He and his colleagues were hardly social reformers, but they had a realistic view of their people's capacity to endure defeat and rise to a position of renewed dignity and stature in the world. The goal of the conservatives from the early postwar years was to hold the country together, to rely upon traditional qualities of good sense, sobriety, humor, and hard work, and to look toward a better place in the world for Japan. As much as their grandfathers, they wanted wealth and power for

Japan and themselves. But military adventures had wrecked the country. In 1945 production stood at about 10 percent of 1934–36, and early Occupation plans called for sending what industrial plants remained to Southeast Asia as war reparations. (A few shipments were actually made before this policy was reversed.) In the burned-out cities the new public mood was viscerally opposed to war; all the built-up hatred of the people was turned upon the discredited Japanese military; and peace, as one Japanese put it, became the "mainstream of the national soul." Novels of wartime horrors sold heavily, along with escapist literature of the erotic and the grotesque. In such an *après-guerre* atmosphere (or *apure,* as the Japanese called those times), Yoshida and his colleagues had the insight to see that Japan had no choice but to cooperate with the Occupation and to align Japan with America's interest in Asia if the nation were to survive without social revolution and the elite who remained were to be given the chance to build a sound, conservative, and capitalistic future.

However, in spite of shiploads of American flour and other basic commodities, the Liberal Party, which Yoshida headed, was unable to cope with inflation, food shortages, and economic paralysis during this period. The new labor movement, encouraged by Americans to organize in the first place, was quickly penetrated by leftists now freed from jail. By the end of 1946 widespread work stoppages increased the economic confusion, and unions of government workers called for a general strike to begin on February 1, 1947. This date marks perhaps the first clear shift in American policy away from reform. Fearful of chaos, the Supreme Commander for the Allied Powers, General MacArthur, whose word was the real law of the land, issued an order barring the strike and calling for a new general election. In the May, 1947, election the Socialist Party won a third of the total vote. For the next eighteen months Japan was governed by a shifting coalition of Socialists and anti-Yoshida conservatives. From May, 1947, until February, 1948, Katayama Tetsu served as prime minister, the only Socialist to do so in Japanese history to date. Then from February, 1948, until his resignation that October, the cabinet was led by a conservative ex-diplomat, Ashida Hitoshi, who formed a coalition with the Socialists.

The word "socialism" covers a wide set of meanings in Japan. For some it has long meant little more than a moderate parliamentary reformism and the extension of welfare measures to cover more and more people. This version of socialism had its origins in humanitarian concern for the poor in the slums of Kobe and other industrial cities of the early twentieth century. Other Socialist leaders got their start after World War I as organizers of farmers' unions. In those days about half of all farmers were landless tenants; but the American-sponsored land reforms of the 1940s reduced that figure to about 5 percent and eliminated most of the basis for peasant unrest.

Still other Socialists came to prominence in the labor union movement. Unions have been organized in industry for more than fifty years, but only since 1945 have they been legal. Local unions have provided an important channel of upward mobility for some able men, who today have become the bureaucrats of the labor movement. Some are postwar types with university education, products of the current technological age. Others are more rough-hewn prototypes of the "labor-hero." Such men have run for office as Socialist Party members, while their intellectual colleagues for the most part have remained in their universities and magazine offices. Some Socialists come from very humble backgrounds; Sasaki Kōzō, the party chairman in 1967, was the son of a charcoal burner in the backward northern provinces.

The real arena for Japanese Socialist activity has been the cities, especially since World War II, when more and more people concentrated there. Perhaps 80 percent of the labor force works in city occupations today. Here socialist theory had old champions among intellectuals, most of them of bourgeois origins and conservative personal values and habits. A tradition of Marxist protest among university professors goes back to the Russo-Japanese war; but intellectual Marxism really took root after 1917, when intellectuals trained in Europe or in German-style Japanese universities read Marx, Lenin, and other European writers and translated them into Japanese. Feeding upon imported theories, such men embraced class struggle and anti-imperialism and called for worker participation in production decisions. Some had visions of a united front of peasants and workers that would take over the state and produce a classless Elysium. Yet it was usually a Japanese Elysium; few were able to transcend their stubborn nationalist attitudes. Threatened before the war with repeated arrest, imprisonment, torture, or even execution, some became Communists, some recanted, others died in prison, or remained silent, or collaborated openly with the military, or equivocated endlessly over the problem of how to fit proletarian revolution to the Japanese social and historical case. The Japanese intellectual has had an agonizing time being honest with himself and with others; often he has failed, and often he has worn his agony on his sleeve and postured self-pityingly. But dissent by a vocal minority of intellectuals from the rule of the conservative elite is a main fact of Japanese political life and has an important bearing on postwar Japanese history.

The Socialists could hardly have come to power at a worse time than 1947. Economic conditions continued to deteriorate, and the Occupation began to insist upon stringent measures to cope with inflation. The Socialists were required to stop inflation and get production going at the same time. Occupation policies took a generally more conservative turn as the cold war grew in intensity. Communist victories in China and the confrontation of America and Russia in Europe helped to change the official U.S. view of Japan from a laboratory of democracy to an industrial base to be rebuilt and denied to the Communist bloc. Perhaps worst of all from a Socialist standpoint, their leaders proved inadequate to the task of governing. Forced into a coalition with conservatives, right-wing Socialists took most of the cabinet posts, while their left-wing rivals won many key party and Diet positions. Without real experience in administering the country before the war, the party allowed old factional and ideological disputes to undermine its chances. Socialist legislation, such as nationalization of the coal mines, was watered down or passed in meaningless form. Left-wing unions in government and heavy industry, many of them infiltrated by Communist agitators, led strikes and demonstrations, undercutting the moderate Socialist leadership. In the midst of its troubles, the coalition government of Ashida was brought down by an unsavory political scandal involving the deputy prime minister.

Socialist failure in the 1950s had a disastrous effect on the party's later chances for power, led to deep controversy over the "class versus mass" nature of Japanese socialism, and contributed to a formal schism of the party in 1951. The most immediate result of the Socialist debacle, however, was the return of Yoshida to power. In the general election of January, 1949, Socialist seats declined from 143 to 48. Profiting from Socialist losses the Communist Party won 35 seats. But the conservative Democratic-Liberal coalition party under Yoshida came in with 264 of the 467 lower house seats, and 44 percent of the total vote.

For the next three years Yoshida was at the height of his power. With the outbreak of the Korean War in June, 1950, economic conditions rapidly improved. Standards of living and foreign trade still were not up to the levels of 1934–36, but the country was clearly getting back on its feet and moving forward. Instead of shipping

Japanese industrial plants overseas as reparations, America now poured technical assistance, industrial raw materials, and machinery into the country, helped to retool key industries, such as oil refining and steel, granted loans and industrial credits to private industry, and otherwise supported the balance of payments by trade and by offshore purchases of goods for military use in Korea and for civilian aid in other countries as well.

At the same time, America sought to bring its Occupation to an end. By 1950 or 1951 its personnel had quite lost the high quality of its first representatives and, as one American writer has put it, had taken on more the manner of carpetbaggers than reformers. Negotiations were begun in this period leading to the San Francisco Peace Conference in the fall of 1951, where a peace treaty was signed between Japan and the Western Allies. In April, 1952, the treaty came into effect with the United States, and the Occupation formally ended. As the price of the peace treaty Japan signed a security treaty with the United States and an agreement governing the maintenance of American military bases on Japanese soil, and thus was brought formally under the military protection of the United States.

The peace treaty with its explicit alignment with the West stirred controversy in Japan and was the proximate cause of the Socialist split into two parties. Right-wing Socialists voted to accept the peace treaty but not the security agreement. Their left-wing colleagues rejected both and demanded that Japan sign a peace treaty that included the Communist powers. On this disagreement the party foundered. But Yoshida based his acceptance of the treaty and the bases on the judgment that most Japanese were more eager for the restoration of independence than for anything else; that they would perforce go along with a postponement of settlement with the Communist powers and would accept, however reluctantly, the political fact of alignment with the West and protection by American military power during a time of Japanese military weakness, when the outcome for Japan of the revolution on the continent of Asia was by no means certain.

The "Reverse Course" and the Rise of "Confrontation Politics": 1952–1960

With independence, the themes characteristic of Japanese national life ever since 1952 began to emerge. Though their strength gradually grew as the decade of the 1960s passed, the Socialists did not again reach power, even in a coalition. The conservatives, for their part, set about consolidating themselves in power, building up the nation's economic strength at home and its prestige abroad.

In the mid-1950s strong sentiment developed for revision of many of the reforms of the Occupation era. About some of these measures there was relatively little dispute; for example, local elective school boards, an innovation which had gained little understanding, were abolished without serious protest. The trend toward reconcentration of economic power was obvious, though there were more large firms competing for the market, and their credit arrangements differed from those of prewar times. Other revisionist steps were less popular. However, Yoshida succeeded in recentralizing the police authority. His administration also altered labor laws to deny government workers the right to strike. In 1950 he established the National Police Reserve, which in 1952 became the Security Forces and later the Self-Defense Forces. Although the Constitution quite plainly forbade it, the conservatives claimed the right to rearmament for purposes of self-defense. American officials encouraged steps toward rearmament and spoke of the American-sponsored Article 9 of the Constitution as a bad idea that should be amended. Such statements inflamed many Japanese intellectuals, who felt betrayed by changes in American policy; they also gave comfort to Socialists, who won many votes among the nervous population by advocating disarmed neutrality and nonaggression pacts of the Locarno variety. Constitutional revision became a major domestic issue. Until now the Socialists and their allies had controlled enough Diet seats to block revision; however, some conservative leaders always had been in favor of doing away with Article 9 and changing the Constitution in other ways. A deputy prime minister in the 1950s declared that if he could have his way the vote would be taken away from women, and many aspects of the prewar family system legally restored. Such reactionary changes were not likely to occur; but against this sort of thing the Socialists cried out in defense of the Constitution, which was their charter of legal existence, written, ironically, by the "imperialistic" Americans. They fought the reconcentration of power in conservative hands, in 1955 reuniting in one Socialist Party to improve their chances. But this merely provoked the conservatives into reuniting their own divided forces a month later into the Liberal-Democratic Party, and the polarization of political forces continued without pause. Left confronted right in an often sterile and frustrated posture of opposition.

Socialist appeals had most effect where foreign policies were concerned; but domestic issues also were fought bitterly and did not always result in a conservative victory. Thus in 1958 Prime Minister Kishi Nobusuke abruptly proposed legislation widening the powers of the police to search and arrest individuals and enter private premises. Kishi's police bill revealed a greater concern for public peace and order than for the individual's right to protection from abuse of police power. Even though there was certainly room for improvement in Occupation-sponsored police legislation, and many Japanese were alarmed by the spread of crime and by police inability to cope with it successfully, Kishi misjudged the temper of the postwar public. He had been a cabinet minister in the government of General Tōjō during the war; he was associated with Japanese colonial exploitation in Manchuria and after the defeat had spent two years in Sugamo prison as a "war criminal." His policies were feared by many people who had no special fondness for socialism but who valued their new-found freedom from the hated police methods of the past. Kishi had a kind of talent for stirring memories of that past; in the police bill dispute the Socialists got hold of an issue that inflamed the public, and by not overplaying it they forced the conservatives to back down and withdraw the legislation. It has not been reintroduced.

The police bill controversy revealed that while more Japanese vote conservative than Socialist, they do not necessarily approve of everything their leaders do after being elected. The temper of the people is conservative, but it is not reactionary; city dwellers especially are sensitive to any threat to freedom from the kind of harassments to which they were formerly exposed.

Along with a massive increase in the mobility of people from country to city after the Korean War, there had grown up in the cities a kind of hedonistic mood based not so much on a Western sense of individual worth as on the right of the individual to be left alone at a distance from authority. Respect for the obligations that accompany rights in a truly liberal society was often lacking. But the self-centered pursuit of one's own designs came to characterize much of urban Japanese society. Many observers commented on this hedonism, especially of the younger generation; at the same time many were struck by the lack of personal autonomy, the almost instinctive reliance on primary groups and acceptance of hierarchical relationships modeled on the family in most of the contexts of daily life.

The search for peace in a different sense continued to be a principal motif of this period. Pacifism for some people meant a principled rejection of war and violence, emphasized by the miseries of Japan's modern experience. For many others pacifism was a mode of escape from a world they fancied they never made, a desire for noninvolvement in the crude power struggles of the cold war. Even as the economy recovered and the population began to feel less self-pitying about economic conditions, sporadic violence continued to characterize political life; assassins, often described after the fact as deranged, stabbed Socialist Secretary General Asanuma Inejirō to death and attacked Prime Minister Kishi and other public figures. Student fanatics like the killer of Asanuma were just as ready to take the law into their own hands as the young officers of the Japanese army had been in the 1930s, though students in today's Japan are fortunately less able to convince others of the rightness of their cause.

Socialists and their allied "ban the bomb" organizations fastened on the peace theme. American bases in Japan could, of course, be counted upon to provide incidents to inflame xenophobia, and conservatives had no monopoly on nationalist feeling. In the 1950s the "peace nationalism" of the Socialists was more appealing to many than the still somewhat disreputable conventional imagery of conservative nationalist goals; national interest was seen by many to be best served by the permanent neutrality of Japan and withdrawal from its American ties. But although this issue was to come to a head in 1960, and cause a conservative government to fall, Prime Minister Yoshida's reading of public sentiment regarding the American relationship was proved justified throughout the period. The Socialists could agitate and obstruct, students could snake-dance in the streets, and this would get headlines, especially in the United States; but the Socialists could not come to power on appeals for peace or conservative mistakes alone. They needed more positive domestic policies and better leaders, and organization to reach more people, and they had none of these during this decade.

In the 1950s the economy rose to prewar levels and surpassed them in many respects. As production and gross national product leaped forward, conservative governments turned to restoring Japan to a position of influence in international politics. During the regime of Prime Minister Hatoyama Ichirō Japan took the initiative to reach agreement with the Soviet Union ending the state of hostilities between them. This was, indeed, the principal accomplishment of the otherwise undistinguished Hatoyama government. In this period negotiations were also concluded with four countries in Southeast Asia—Burma, South Vietnam, Indonesia, and the Philippines—for reparations agreements to settle war damage claims. Soon goods and services began moving southward as reparations. to help in the rebuilding of those economies and also to reestablish Japanese commercial ties. The Japanese would have to work long and hard to regain the trust of the people of that area, but a beginning was made in the mid-1950s. Under U.S. sponsorship, too, Japan was readmitted to various international organizations, and was voted full membership in the United Nations and its associated agencies. The process of recovering respectability was well advanced by the close of the decade.

Meanwhile, conservative leaders concerned with foreign policy formulation were content to watch international developments and to wait, maintaining ties with the United States and trading with as wide a world market as possible; Japan prospered while allowing the United States to foot the bill for its defense. With less than two percent of the national income spent for their own military uses this was an understandable policy. At the same time political discourse toward the end of the 1950s was steadily exacerbated by the continued presence of American bases in Japan and Okinawa and by growing differences on China policy between conservatives and Socialists and even within the conservative party itself. Most Japanese did not really want to become involved actively in American wars in Asia. Most were still suffering in some sense from the shock of defeat, still wishing passionately to pursue their own economic concerns in peace, still feeling their impotence to do anything to change their dependence on America and play a more active role in the world. The discrepancy between economic prosperity at home and Japan's insignificance as a world power rankled in many minds. The late 1950s was the era of the great "Jimmu boom," the highest level of prosperity since the founding of the nation, when all the gadgets and amusements and symbols of the new "mass society" seemed to come onto the market at once. One fad replaced another; the "Jimmu boom" gave way to the "leisure boom"; people in large numbers began skiing and taking to water sports; wages went up and clothing styles improved; boys and girls grew taller than their fathers and mothers; and the less tangible gaps between the generations grew steadily wider year by year. Conservative politicians deplored the lack of "moral education" for youth.

But the old men in control of the mechanism of politics seemed to be falling behind the moods and trends of their own society. This applied to Socialists as well as conservatives. Television, radio, and newspapers all proclaimed an era of affluence for the "new middle class" of white-collar workers and their families, but the bureaucrats grumbled about lack of "morality" and took what appeared to be an increasingly passive stance in foreign policy.

Out of such complex anxieties, feelings of frustrated nationalism, and pride in postwar accomplishments came the Tokyo riots of May and June, 1960, when to many Japanese and foreign observers the collapse of parliamentary government in Japan seemed possible. These fears now seem overdrawn. Kishi, a prime minister of proven un-popularity, groping in his own clumsy way to come up with something that would satisfy the needs of the new national self-awareness, attempted to negotiate a more favorable security treaty with the United States than the treaty that had been signed in 1952. Kishi sought to limit the rights of Americans to move whatever men and material they wished into and out of Japan without prior Japanese knowledge or consent; he sought for some kind of time limit on the new treaty, for a more explicit American commitment to come to Japan's aid if attacked, and other concessions that might put his gov-ernment in a better light with the public. His aims were unexception-able; they might even be said to have been patriotic; but in the process of working out the treaty details with the United States enough time elapsed for the opposition to get hold of the treaty issue and turn it into an occasion for protest. The Socialists and Communists, with their supporters among the students, labor unionists, and intellectuals, formed a common front against any new treaty. Forcing the treaty through the Diet in the middle of the night by dubious parliamentary tactics, Kishi again misjudged the public mood and further confirmed the suspicions of many city people that he wanted to bring back the whole nightmarish paraphernalia of the police state. However unlikely this might appear in present-day Japan and however obvious the leftist exploitation of the treaty issue, the fact remained that many people could be easily persuaded to oppose the prime minister, who personified all the reactionary "reverse course" tendencies of a decade of uninterrupted conservative rule. All the "progressive elements" thus were momentarily enabled to rise up against the government in Tokyo. The riots which resulted were an outburst of emotional pro-test against the frustrations of Japanese existence in a world over which Japan seemed to have less control than it had ever had in modern times. But while the rioters were able to let off a lot of steam, they were not able to change the outcome; the new treaty was passed and ratified; American bases remained on Japanese soil, though with a few new restrictions; and the ultimate question of Japan's independence, which as much as anything lay buried beneath the shouts and the rioting, was left for the future to decide. Kishi himself was forced to resign after President Eisenhower's visit to Japan had to be canceled at the height of the uproar, but Japanese voters returned another conservative, Ikeda Hayato, to power in the general elections that followed. The political temper of the public once again was shown to be conservative but not reactionary.

The 1960s

By the early 1960s conservative welfare programs, though inadequate in amount and coverage of the population, were beginning to rob socialist promises of much of their appeal. Gross national product was increasing at more than 10 percent annually, and rising purchasing power was beginning to turn Japan into a consumer-centered society. Modern advertising techniques imported from the West helped to create new tastes and demands; most people expected to own electric washing machines and television sets as a matter of course, and many had their minds set on other treasures: air conditioners, hi-fi sets, and even family cars figured largely in many dreams. As financial restrictions were relaxed, more Japanese tourists traveled abroad. The steady shift of industrial priorities toward more sophisticated products and processes made for shortages of skilled labor in some fields, while many less efficient smaller industries were forced to raise wages to keep their workers. In the universities complaints were heard about the lack of appropriations for scientific research. Japan had rebuilt its industries largely on imported know-how after the war, but many persons now lamented the derivative nature of Japanese technology and called for more basic research and development at home. Funds for such research increased rapidly as the decade passed, although coordination of research among universities, private industry, and government agencies was poor.

Prime Minister Ikeda, in power from 1960 to 1964, through a combination of political luck and skill was able to turn the people's minds from political confrontations and struggles toward more tranquilizing economic matters. He adopted what was called a "low posture" toward the Socialists and refrained from introducing Diet measures or using tactics that would inflame the opposition any more than was unavoidable. For their part, the Socialists had taken a severe setback in the security treaty affair as well as in the great coal mine strike in Kyushu in 1959–60. They were preoccupied with post-mortems and self-criticism; some intellectuals admitted publicly that Marxism as a methodology was dead and should be discarded by the Japanese left. Within the Socialist Party new proposals were advanced for "structural reform," meaning more realistic tactics that might have a chance of bringing the party to power. However, such "revisionism" was still sternly opposed by the orthodox Marxists, who remained in control of the party apparatus. The vocabulary of socialist action programs showed little change.

Ikeda's years were a period of relative political quiet. This is not to say that they were without interest. Just before Ikeda took office, the Democratic Socialists, a right socialist group, had split from the parent party. It continued as a small but significant force and showed signs of gaining strength toward the middle of the decade. Perhaps more interesting was the rise of Sōka Gakkai, the lay arm of a Japanese Buddhist sect (Nichiren), which in the 1950s, on a program of faith-healing and easy happiness, won millions of adherents among the less privileged citizens of Japan's great cities. Significant enough as a social force, Sōka Gakkai also organized its own party, the Kōmeitō, and entered politics. With its religious faith in a Japanese savior and its proselytizing zeal, Sōka Gakkai had a messianic cast about it that appeared sinister to some observers, who saw in it neo-fascist tendencies. Its platform in politics was what it thought the voters wanted: peace, lower taxes, clean government, and the like. With 25 seats in the lower house and 20 in the upper house by 1967, it was potentially a significant force in politics. But, whatever its ultimate meaning, Sōka Gakkai was able in the years after the security treaty riots to take advantage of public disenchantment with the established parties; and it especially presented a challenge to the conservatives to modernize their politics and rid themselves of factionalism and corruption.

However, the best word to describe the 1960s in Japan was economism. Ikeda focused national attention on the government's "double the income" plan. As the symbol of the Kishi years had been street riots, the symbol of Ikeda's administration was the Olympics of 1964, which brilliantly signified Japan's phoenixlike rebirth and marked the real end of the postwar period. Economic confidence had clearly returned: Japan was a member of the prestigious OECD (Organization for Economic Cooperation and Development), belonged to the consortium to aid India, took the lead in setting up the Asian Development Bank, and in other ways acted as one of the "have" nations of the world.

As the 1960s slipped by, new nationalistic opinions appeared in public and private discussions, new versions of history were debated in books and magazines. It was plain that the Japanese wished to have a position of prominence in the world to match the nation's economic power. At the same time Japanese society was growing steadily more pluralistic. What was really striking was the diversity of points of view and their expression. Except for a small right-wing fringe, few wished to be identified with any ultranationalistic mystique in the prewar sense. Most conservative leaders still saw their own and their nation's interest best served by cleaving to the United States while trading with whomever they could. With Asia still in revolutionary tumult, with Japanese public opinion skittish toward rearmament, and with the nation dependent upon America for its defense, there was perhaps little for the leaders to do but wait and pursue "economic diplomacy." Yet by the middle of the 1960s differences of opinion about Japan's role in the world had appeared, not only between Socialists and conservatives but among conservatives, between groups of politicians and groups of businessmen, and between age groups within each segment of the elite. Such pluralism made it difficult to detect trends in the midst of all the noise, but some clues could be found in specific issues.

Japanese magazines and newspapers were full of articles on national defense and national purpose. A whole new breed of "defense intellectual" emerged in the 1960s, many of them professors in universities, top-ranking journalists, or lecturers in the Defense Academy in Tokyo. This debate was stimulated by the Chinese nuclear explosions in 1964, the 1965 Communist take-over attempt in Indonesia, and the war in Vietnam, all of which disturbed many people, confirming their desire for noninvolvement but at the same time helping to widen the sanction for rearmament. But the defense debate was related more profoundly to the thaw in the cold war that led to what one Japanese writer called the Cold Alliance between Russia and America. It was a product of the Sino-Soviet split, the emergence of De Gaulle, and other centrifugal movements in world politics. New possibilities for Japan were now talked about and written about. The participants in this discussion were not merely leftists: some were right-wing revisionists; others were simply moderate nationalists who did not necessarily question the soundness of Japan's continued association with America, at least for the time being. But many people began to wonder aloud about Japan's relations with China and the Soviet Union, and about what degree of rearmament might be necessary for Japan and when.

The rearmament question was, of course, closely linked with domestic politics. Within the Liberal-Democratic Party one group, which might be called the "hawks," openly favored revision of Article 9 of the Constitution to permit conventional rearmament for offensive as well as defensive purposes. The main body of the party was reluctant to come out for rearmament before the voters. Popular sentiment still favored peace and noninvolvement, and the Self-Defense Forces were not esteemed as a career, especially during a period of prosperity. Conscription still was a political impossibility. Thus, in spite of the wider discussion of rearmament, there was not much evidence of any widespread will to take action to defend the country against outside dangers. The mission of the Self-Defense Forces was merely to provide for brief deterrence against conventional attack. The principal reason for this was not any peculiar pacifism in the Japanese spirit but rather the fact that most people simply did not believe, or did not want to believe, in the existence of an outside danger. This was true even after the Chinese nuclear tests. In fact, most Japanese felt that the danger of America's involving them in a war against Asians was much greater than any threat to their national safety from China. They did not want to be pushed to take a stand openly on one side or the other in ideological conflicts.

It was reasonable to assume that, given an increase of national self-awareness, Japanese opposition to rearmament would slowly disappear. Statements by government officials to the effect that nuclear weapons might some day be designed for defensive purposes and that, if they were, Japan might have some of them, were not met by any particular cries of anguish, even among the Socialists. Socialist leaders privately admitted that Japan must have some kind of armed forces, if only for defensive purposes. Nationalism had never been a monopoly of the conservatives.

Prime Minister Satō Eisaku, who came to power at the end of 1964, was extremely sensitive to the defense issue, and especially to atomic weapons. He and his government continued to rely on the American nuclear umbrella and probably would want to do this and to spend less than 15 percent of the annual budget on defense for as long as was politically feasible. It made sense to suppose that the time would eventually come when Japanese armed forces would be willing and able to take over American bases. In the meantime, it seemed likely that the Japanese government would want to let the Security Treaty run beyond 1970.

Few Japanese advocated a nuclear weapons program, though there was strong sentiment for placing restrictions on the programs of the nuclear "have" nations as the price of signing the proposed international nuclear nonproliferation treaty since that treaty would bar Japan from such weapons indefinitely. A few commentators, politicians, and businessmen argued that proliferation was inevitable, and that it must include the Japanese. Some said Japan must somehow prepare for the day when Chinese missiles could reach the continental United States, and they thought that day not far off. Others suggested an eventual joint nuclear program with the United States or some kind of multilateral nuclear force. Others thought an independent Japanese program was the only safe policy and the only way to obtain the scientific and technical knowledge necessary for big-power status. Still others argued the total vulnerability of Japan to nuclear attack and urged confidence in the U.S.

Once again the variety of points of view has to be stressed. There was already a substantial nuclear research program for peaceful purposes. There was also a rocket program and a project to launch an unmanned satellite, both sources of obvious pride to the Japanese people. Japanese writers constantly repeated that their country could produce nuclear weapons if it so wished; it had the technology but refrained on policy grounds. In the press there was a good deal of groping for some means of turning abhorrence of war into a concrete foreign policy. Practically speaking, Japan had signed binding agreements with the United States for the disposal of nuclear by-products; these would have to be rewritten, or ignored, if production of such weapons were undertaken. In view of American opposition to nuclear proliferation, this would mean a radical change in Japanese policy.

With rearmament and defense was closely linked another nationalist issue: Okinawa. As the 1960s drew to a close the issue of Okinawan reversion to Japan and Japanese irredentism toward Okinawa became an increasing source of trouble for Japanese-American relations. The Satō government accepted the American bases in Okinawa, since these afforded protection against nuclear attack at minimum cost to the Japanese. However, it was confronted with the political problem created by the strong movement among the Okinawans for a return to Japanese rule. The Okinawan people spoke Japanese, they *felt* Japanese, and they appeared to prefer self-government under Japanese jurisdiction to any kind of government, even the "best," under Americans. The Okinawan desire for reversion drew widening support from the Japanese public, a support further deepened by the question of nuclear and chemical armaments on the islands. As 1970 approached, there were signs that America would have to make up its mind to return Okinawa to Japan even if this meant the establishment of restrictions upon the use of Okinawan bases similar to those imposed on bases in Japan proper. Otherwise America would run the risk of provoking a reaction that might do serious harm to the alliance with Japan. In the fall of 1970 an agreement was finally reached returning sovereignty over Okinawa to the Japanese government. Actual reversion came on May 15, 1972, with the U.S. retaining its major bases on the islands.

Both rearmament and Okinawa were closely related to the problem of Japan's long-term relations with the Communist regime in Peking. Japanese attitudes toward Communist China were very complex. Large numbers of Japanese were still alive who had lived in Manchuria or other parts of the mainland for varying periods in the past. Some of these people had rather romantic feelings about China. They felt a kind of affinity for the Chinese that they felt toward no other people, based on cultural similarities and long historical contact. At the same time they were often deeply condescending toward the Chinese.

Much more significant than any feelings of cultural affinity was the appeal of the Chinese revolution to many Japanese intellectuals, who were intrigued with the problems of Chinese modernization, with the application of modern factory industry and the division of labor to the still premodern Chinese scene, with the Chinese variant of late twentieth-century society and how the Japanese nation was to relate to it in the future. Such questions absorbed substantial numbers of younger Japanese thinkers and commentators. In 1966–67 they were shocked by purges of Chinese intellectuals and by Chinese intransigence toward the world in general during the great Cultural Revolution. But Tokyo intellectuals still felt the powerful appeal of the

Chinese revolution, a great cataclysm that was taking place nearby, and that they could have little or nothing to do with or control. While almost no Chinese visited Japan, several thousand Japanese traveled to China each year. Some were sympathetic with the Chinese on racial grounds; they saw them as Asians throwing off Western control. Pan-Asianism was still a living idea in Japan; it was implied in paternalistic attitudes toward the rest of Asia and the condescension toward China that often went along with admiration. Part of the fascination of China lay in the Chinese rejection of the Western world. Part lay in the hope of commercial profits. Some Japanese, of course, supported Chinese communism for ideological reasons, but China appealed to the unsatisfied idealism of many Japanese who were struck by the apparent contrast between the revolutionary fervor and sense of purpose there and their own rather humdrum, stodgy politicians with their imagery of economic diplomacy and conservative nationalism.

As far as the Japanese government was concerned, its official position in the 1960s was still to follow the lead of the United States and not to recognize Communist China or vote for its admission to the United Nations. On the contrary, in its 1952 peace treaty with the Chiang Kai-shek regime Japan recognized Taiwan as the legal government of China. Moreover, a brisk trade with the island had developed. Nevertheless, at the same time "unofficial" contacts grew between Japan and Peking. Japanese newspapermen were stationed there, trade fairs were held by each country in the other, and many missions of businessmen and even conservative politicians went to China. The government insisted that trade and politics could be kept separate, and it showed no signs of drawing nearer to China politically. By 1966 trade between the two countries totaled some 600 million dollars both ways. This was still less than 5 percent of Japan's total trade, and only something over 10 percent of Japanese-American trade.

Within the Liberal-Democratic Party there were some differences over China policy. A minority of perhaps eighty politicians formed the Society for the Study of Afro-Asian Problems, which favored China's admission to the UN and called for immediate peace talks with the Viet Cong. This group included some people who were often described as the "left wing" of the conservative party, but its most striking characteristic was the relative youth of its members, who represented the newer generation of political leadership that was coming up. Most of these men were not ideologically leftist but merely ambitious; they were looking for an issue that would distinguish them from their elders. A politician like Nakasone Yasuhiro, for example, for years has called for more independence from the United States and some new leverage in Japan's foreign policies. Men of this type talked a great deal but were without any clearly defined alternatives to the Satō policy of alliance with America that they could agree upon as feasible for Japan. There were rumors that this group might wish to break away from the Liberal Democrats, make common cause with the Democratic Socialist Party, and perhaps found a new coalition party of the center. Such possibilities had been raised before but had never materialized.

The majority of the conservative Japanese leadership remained with the United States on China. They saw Japan competing with China for the economic and political leadership of Asia in the next generation. As one leader put it: "in the next fifty years Japan and China will fight it out for the economic leadership of Asia. India will be a poor third. The Indians haven't got what it takes to catch up with us." Such men regarded Japan as far ahead of China economically, and aside from some anxiety over Chinese nuclear explosions, they did not fear China in any basic sense. They talked of the possibility of eventually serving as some kind of mediating force—a bridge, as they liked to call it—between China and the Western world.

Conclusion: The Early 1970s

In the summer of 1972, using the reversion of Okinawa as the occasion, Prime Minister Satō left office and was succeeded by Tanaka Kakuei, a long-time conservative politician and former party official of the Liberal-Democrats. In the later years of Satō's ascendancy his government became relatively immobilized in the face of a whole battery of problems. Pressures grew within the party as well as outside it for rapprochement with Peking, but Satō refused to risk breaking ties with Taiwan, where by the late 1960s the Japanese commercial presence was pervasive and growing rapidly. Relations with the Republic of Korea had been formally established and there was evidence of greater Japanese investment and economic activity in South Korea, even as the Japanese left wing urged renewal of ties with the North. Some conservative interests favored formation of a Pacific community of noncommunist nations. Others probed toward the north, searching for ways of doing more business with the Soviet Union: some Japanese oil refiners were tempted by Russian offers of cheap crude oil in return for Japanese pipeline and other goods. From time to time Russian trade officials held out glowing prospects of Japanese sales of plant and equipment for the development of eastern Siberia, and some timber agreements were signed, but promise was not yet matched by performance in that area.

On another front, the Japanese were expanding their economic assistance to South and Southeast Asia and had pledged to bring their aid contributions up to one percent of national income. The Japanese government was making policy probes in various directions pointing to some more independent role in Asia in a context of the global relaxation of cold war tensions and the multi-polarization of power centers that had begun in the 1960s. Yet Japan's foreign policies were still characterized by their "low posture," and the government was careful not to upset its basic alignment with the United States. Whatever moves might be made in other directions, no basic shift of policy was visible as long as Satō remained in office, in spite of much rhetoric. Moreover, despite an expansion of aid programs, to most other Asians the Japanese appeared to be more interested in the exploitation of raw materials and quick commercial profits than in genuine development assistance; while to a growing number of Americans Japan was believed to be enjoying a "free ride" at their expense, sitting under the umbrella of American military protection while refusing to open Japan's doors to unrestricted imports of goods and capital.

Thus by the early 1970s the Japanese were beginning to experience serious problems with their image in the world. Such problems had been sporadically experienced before in the postwar period, e.g., in textile disputes with the U.S. in the 1950s; but up until the late 1960s and early 1970s they could be countered by Japanese concessions and positive evidence of Japan's expanding concern for the welfare of other Asians, as well as a slowly growing willingness to undertake a larger share of Japan's own defense. By the end of the Satō era, however, the situation had been greatly exacerbated by both domestic and foreign developments.

Basic to the problem was the decline in the value of the American dollar and the consequent breakdown of the postwar international monetary system; inflation in the United States, in part attributable to the Vietnam war; and a very rapid expansion of the volume of Japanese exports to the United States. By 1968 the U.S. balance of trade with Japan, consistently favorable since the early 1950s, had turned unfavorable, and these deficits grew astonishingly until by Japan's fiscal 1972 they amounted to more than $4 billion and represented the most spectacular portion of the total U.S. trade deficit. At the same time, the Japanese business community, or important parts of it, were no longer as compliant as they had been in response to American demands for "liberalization." To Japanese conservative politicians, faced with the slow erosion of their ascendancy at the polls for many years, it seemed politically imperative to continue to protect agricultural and other interests from foreign competition. Government bureaucrats continued to demonstrate their historical reluctance to allow open and unrestricted foreign business operations—which many feared would mean foreign control—in the domestic economy. A new mood of intransigence was plain on both sides, and was quickly exploited by the mass media in both countries, where many of the stereotypes of past hostility were resurrected. Some Japanese manufacturers, e.g., in textiles, rejected government pressure to set voluntary quotas on their exports, blaming American trade problems on unreasonably high labor costs, inefficiency, and a decline in the desire to work hard and take pride in the results. A moralistic tone was more and more evident in their diagnoses of U.S. infirmities. On their side American trade negotiators and businessmen responded with demands—sometimes delivered in a strident and heavy-handed manner—that Japan show gratitude for American aid and protection by curbing exports to America and opening the Japanese market wider to American goods.

These strains clearly reflected Japan's new position as a major economic power in the world, just as they revealed the fundamental shift that had taken place in America's position as a world policeman and giver of foreign aid. Osaka's dazzling Expo '70 may be taken as a symbol of the return of Japanese ebullience. Another symbol of economic progress is the quite sudden awareness of the costs of that progress in Japan, the flood of recent articles about the "public damages" of pollution, smog, traffic jams, and the appearance of such terms as "net national welfare" and "social indicators" in the jargon of economists and other writers. In many ways Japan today has become the type case of high industrialism and its disastrous social and ecological effects, and students of these matters in the West have begun asking what the Japanese experience of urban and environmental problems may have to teach the older industrial societies.

In such an atmosphere of high export growth and rising temperatures among trade negotiators, President Nixon on August 15, 1971 suddenly announced a 10 percent surcharge on foreign products entering the United States. A few months later, in February 1972, the President visited Peking for a series of well-publicized meetings with Chinese leaders, a visit arranged without any serious consultations with the Japanese government. Whatever the reasons behind such procedures, the so-called "Nixon shocks" hurt Japanese feelings, weakened the position of Prime Minister Satō in his own party, and reinforced a feeling that the Nixon-Kissinger foreign policy took Japan for granted.

After taking office in July 1972 Prime Minister Tanaka moved swiftly to recognize the People's Republic of China and broke diplomatic relations—though not trade relations—with Taiwan. But otherwise, after a year in office there was little to show that the Tanaka government's foreign policies would be very different from earlier conservative positions. More money was scheduled to be spent on defense, but authoritative projections indicated that Japan intends to continue to rely on the U.S. nuclear deterrent, even though there may be some creeping erosion in its credibility, as long as the Sino-Soviet split continues and Japan feels no real or imminent threat from either Communist power. As far as conventional defense is concerned, the Japanese military capacity will for the foreseeable future remain modest and limited to Japan and its territorial waters. Tanaka came to power projecting the image of a relatively uneducated party politician who was very different from his Tokyo University-trained bureaucratic predecessors. But in fact Tanaka was schooled in the same goals and policies as they, and if he is a "new man" in any sense other than producing ringing new slogans about remaking the Japanese archipelago, this fact has not so far been made clear. In the last general elections in December 1972 conservative strength declined slightly as a percentage of the total vote, but the conservative absolute majority in the lower house was reconfirmed, in spite of some rather remarkable Communist Party gains. The conservative majority seems likely to continue so long as the economy grows and something, however slight, is done to improve the quality of life in the cities.

One who seeks to evaluate the Japanese future has before him a choice of approaches. He can take the sanguine view and argue that Japan has nearly a century of experience with parliamentary institutions; that party government is more stable today than ever before; that the political, social and economic situation is more pluralistic;

and that the secular drift is toward a more open society. He can argue that the leaders in Tokyo have a greater appreciation than before of the need to show some vision and to get beyond the level of commercial exploitation in their dealings with the countries to the south; that some, at least, of the leaders are beginning to see that the real problems of the world's future lie in the inequities between have and have-not nations, and that ideological disputes in Asia, as elsewhere, are in some sense a manifestation of this gulf. On this reading of Japanese probabilities, Japan will continue to see that its most intimate economic and political interests lie with the West, and will be able to extend assistance to less fortunate countries as a part of a multilateral effort that will maintain Japan's basic pro-Western alignment. Conversely, one can take the more melancholy position that party government is still weak, with the Socialists frozen in permanent opposition; that despite great changes in Japanese society in the direction of wider legal rights and of habits of greater mobility for many people, the drag of the past still pulls heavily against the development of a sense of individual autonomy and egalitarianism; consequently that the prospects for a liberal society in the Western sense are dim and that the Japanese continue for the most part to be condescending and manipulative in their dealings with other Asians. Which view the observer chooses will depend in some measure on his temperament and philosophical predilections. In any event, what seems clear is that the period of postwar client-patron relationship between the United States and Japan is ending, with some pain on both sides. The "Nixon shocks" alerted the Japanese to a certain lack of American solicitude for Japanese sensibilities in the new power games of the 1970s; it is hardly to be expected that the Japanese for their part will docilely accept whatever economic or other demands are made on them by table-thumping negotiators from America. Relations between the two countries will not return exactly to the pre-1971 formulation, at least in a subjective sense, nor should this be expected nor even be regarded as ideal. But the objective fact remains that America and Japan as nations still have more interests in common than not, and Japan is still America's principal ally in the Pacific area. Few Americans recognize Japan's greatness as a nation, just as few Japanese wish to play a more prominent political role in the world, not yet, at any rate. The time is clearly coming, however, when the Japanese government will lead the country in some new and more independent foreign policy initiatives of its own, with a Japanese stamp on them. This need not, and probably will not, signify a return to a militaristic foreign policy; and there is no reason why these new Japanese initiatives cannot coincide with American interest, if some care is given to the feelings as well as the interests of each side by the other. The best insurance of a constructive outcome for Japanese-American relations would be a period of peace and increasing economic cooperation among all parties in Asia.

PART TWO

Aspects

of Japanese

Civilization

X

Japanese

Religion

BY
WM. THEODORE DE BARY

Japanese religion is a mystery, an elusive combination of ever-changing elements that has somehow managed to preserve a distinct character. It is at once an expression of the Japanese openness to life and to the world, their readiness to adapt and change, and their tenacious conservatism. Its vitality is shown by the proliferation of "new religions" in the mid-twentieth century, while its continuity is demonstrated by the persistence in these new cults of traditional attitudes and practices. We may describe, then, the recurring features of Japanese religion and suggest its moving spirit, but any definition will tend to limit itself far more than Japanese religion itself has been willing to do.

Like Japanese life and culture, Japanese religion has been deeply affected by natural circumstances. The Japanese think of themselves as an "island" people. This means, among other things, that because they have been set apart from the Asian mainland they have managed to maintain a separate existence and preserve their own identity. At the same time it expresses their need to affirm and assert that identity in contradistinction to others. That is, the Japanese were conscious of their relation and their debt to other peoples and cultures, in contrast to the self-sufficient attitude of the Chinese, who thought of themselves as occupying the center of the world and were largely oblivious of others. For the Japanese to speak of their homeland as an island country actually suggests less an attitude of deep insularity or isolationism, of resistance to outside influences, than it does an awareness of their precarious existence in a much larger world.

Similarly, though some Japanese have stressed their own identity by insisting on the distinctiveness of their native religion or their national spirit, the fact is that, as far back as one can tell, both of these have been expressed in an international or intercultural context. The so-called Three Imperial Regalia, prime symbols of divine sovereignty and national tradition, are the Mirror, Sword, and Curved Jewel. Archaeology shows clearly that the Mirror and Sword are derived from the bronze and iron age culture of the mainland, while the curved jewel is common to Korea and Manchuria as well as Japan. Conversely, in the Confucian Classics of China we find clear recollections of religious practices—lustration, exorcism, shamanism—similar to those of early Shintō. In discussing "Japanese" religion, then, we must remind ourselves constantly of this fundamental ambivalence of the national and international in the Japanese tradition.

Furthermore, when Japan is spoken of as an "island country," this means a country of many islands, not just one; a unity based on diversity. This geographical pluralism is reflected throughout much of Japanese history in political and social pluralism, and the same is basically true in religion. Thus we have the three major traditions which have coexisted throughout much of Japan's history: Shintō, Buddhism, and Confucianism. The Japanese have generally accepted the differences among these three, while at the same time believing that each has developed a characteristic Japanese form.

Shintō

The earliest Japanese religion was already a hybrid in the sense that it included beliefs and practices not exclusively Japanese, but shared with the other peoples of East Asia. It became conscious of itself as Shintō, "the way of the gods (or spirits)," only in confrontation with Buddhism ("the way of the Buddha"), and Confucianism ("the way of the scholars [or sages]"). When this occurred, during a period of greatly increased contact with mainland Asia in the sixth and seventh centuries, the Japanese thought of "Shintō" as the pre-existing or traditional religion and the others as recent imports, but it is noteworthy that they did not make the distinction on national lines as between Japanese, Chinese, and Indian. The idea of Shintō as a pure, integral Japanese religion was a much later creation.

This pluralistic approach was evident even within what was called Shintō. It was a loose agglomeration of local and regional cults, with a diversity of gods and spirits. These cults included a variety of religious elements: nature worship, animism, shamanism, ancestor worship, hero-worship, fertility rites, phallicism, fortunetelling, and so on. Even within a given locality or shrine these elements underwent gradual change, as the emphasis shifted from one to another in different times. And similarly with the objects of worship. The culture hero of one age might take on the function of a fertility god in the next; the nature god (e.g., the deity of the sun-worshipers) might later be claimed as the ancestral deity of a certain clan (e.g., the Imperial House).

In all this there was an easy process of convertibility and adaptation in both gods and cults. There was, accordingly, no clear conception of divinity, no real attempt to articulate a theology on a rational basis, and no moral doctrine proceeding from well-defined philosophical or theological premises. These characteristics of Western religion are missing in Shintō because they run counter to the whole Japanese approach to religion. Definitions are static and limited, detached from life and feeling. Shintō was dynamic and open, immersed in life and incapable of viewing it from a distance. It accepted life, and did not ask many questions.

The classic explanation of the meaning of *kami* (god, spirit) comes from the eighteenth-century writer Motoori Norinaga, who in a more rationalistic age confronted the question and admitted that he could not make much logical sense of it:

I do not yet understand the meaning of the term *kami*. In general, however, is signifies the deities of heaven and earth that appear in the ancient records and also the spirits of the shrines where they are worshipped. Needless to say it includes human beings, and such objects as birds, beasts, trees, plants, seas, mountains, and so forth. In ancient usage anything which was outside the ordinary, possessed superior power or was awe-inspiring was called *kami*. . . . Evil and mysterious things, if they are extraordinary and dreadful, are also called *kami*. . . . Although they may not be accepted throughout the whole country, yet in each province, village, and family there are human beings who are *kami*, each according to his own proper position. . . .[1]

Two things stand out in this description. One is the strongly particularistic character of Shintō worship—its identification with particular places and objects. The other is that divinity as represented in the concept of *kami* implies no distinction from the human. It is in this light that one must understand the development of so-called emperor-worship, and that one must ask what meaning it could have for the emperor, during the postwar Allied Occupation, to renounce his divinity.

Among the natural elements or objects which have figured largely in Shintō worship there are five in particular: sun (or fire), water, mountains, trees, and stones. In the "land of the rising sun" and of the Sun Goddess, sun-worship and fire-ceremonies (the common word for sun and fire being the same: *hi*) have long been practiced. The closeness of the Japanese to and dependence upon the sea, rivers, lakes, and streams has given them a great love of water and a deep mystical sense of its purificatory properties. Mountains, too, are prominent features of the Japanese landscape that have been worshiped as gods or used as places of worship and religious sanctuaries.

1. Adapted from D. C. Holtom, *The National Faith of Japan* (New York, 1938), pp. 23–24.

Stones likewise have been common objects of worship, often as phallic symbols, and the Japanese fascination with their shapes and textures has been transferred to one of the most characteristic art forms, landscape gardening. Similarly in Shintō shrines trees of great size and age are often found marked for special reverence, and the Japanese feeling for natural wood grain and texture is another distinctive aspect of the art and architecture.

Shintō worship consists essentially of attendance upon the god and offerings to him, accompanied by invocations and prayers. Purificatory rites are an important preparation for such ceremonies, but they function independently also as means of dispelling evil and misfortune. Festivals represent special occasions for honoring the god and establishing what might be called good rapport with him (or her). The idea is to entertain him and make him well-disposed toward the worshipers by providing the best of hospitality—food, drink, clothing, music, dance, and innumerable other performances of an athletic or artistic nature. Solemnity alternates with lighthearted enjoyment, and from this combination of the formal and ceremonial with the playful and enjoyable have evolved many of the characteristic arts and sports of Japan.

Generally, but not necessarily, these ceremonies and festivals take place at a shrine, which is thought of as the dwelling place or abode of the god. Basically such a shrine consists of a single chamber or sanctuary in which an object manifesting the god's power—the so-called god-body—is installed. The sanctuary is almost always raised up and approached by a steep stairway—but approached only by the priest and not by ordinary worshipers. Auxiliary structures include almost invariably a torii or gateway which marks the entrance to the shrine precincts, and a covered basin or open stream at which the faithful purify themselves by washing before coming into the shrine. Often, too, there is an oratory before the shrine where most ceremonies, music, and dance are performed (if there is not a separate hall for the latter), and admission here is in principle open to all.

Along with these more or less uniform elements in shrines and religious practice, in many places there will be distinctive features in architecture or ceremonial which reflect local tradition and the particularistic feelings referred to above. Local priests and inhabitants pay special attention to these, not only as a matter of local pride but also out of the loving delight which they take in such details of life and nature.

In general Shintō rituals and festivals have celebrated the important occasions of life and of the agricultural year: births, marriages, the New Year plowing, planting, harvesting, and so on. Among religions Shintō is probably unique in its having almost nothing to do with death or the afterlife, except through its function of purification. Marriages have usually taken place at a shrine, funerals almost never.

Those who care for and preside over the shrines may accurately be referred to as priests, because of their basic sacerdotal function in the offering of sacrifice. There are, however, no Shintō monks or monasteries. Nor until recent times under Western influence has there been anything like the theological or pastoral functions of the priesthood. Ritual practice has always dominated over theological discussion, and with neither an explicit doctrine nor a specific moral code there has been little need for sermons!

Before the introduction of Chinese writing and ideas in the sixth century and after, the Japanese apparently had no means of recording their religious beliefs. There is little reason to believe that they had produced an articulate body of doctrine or a set of scriptures. The legends in the first histories, the *Kojiki* and *Nihongi,* often cited as containing the original deposit of Shintō mythology, are late compilations in which political considerations and Chinese philosophical and ethical conceptions intrude themselves everywhere. This fact was acknowledged by the great Neo-Shintō scholars of the eighteenth century who recognized Japanese poetry and even fiction as a better source of native attitudes than these official documents.

Similarly there has been almost nothing in the way of church organization or hierarchical authority in Shintō. Attempts to organize the shrines and priesthood on a nationwide basis have generally been political in character, as, for instance, the early legislation to impose a Chinese-type bureaucratic structure. This failed to take hold, except in a purely formal sense, and both shrines and priesthood lapsed back into the traditional pattern of hereditary family succession and local autonomy. The much later attempt in the same direction, accompanying the creation of a modern bureaucratic nation-state in the nineteenth century, came to an end with the separation of "church" and state during the Allied Occupation after World War II, when custody of the shrines returned to the hereditary priesthood.

In spite of Shintō's inarticulateness, however, and the lack of any unifying authority, certain pervasive attitudes toward life and the world have found implicit acceptance and unrationalized expression in Shintō worship. Among these we may list the following:

1. A reverence for life and creativity; and abhorrence of death and defilement.
2. An appreciation of the beauty and awesomeness of nature or divine creativity, as expressed especially in a feeling for what is "natural," pure, simple.
3. An essentially pluralistic and particularistic approach to life. Shintō is not polytheistic in the ordinary sense, because it has no well-defined consciousness of "God," monotheistic or polytheistic. The divine is a dynamic, living presence expressed in manifold forms, undergoing constant transformation.
4. A deep awareness of mystery-in-simplicity; a concomitant tendency to simplify and mystificate everything.
5. A deep sense of gratitude for blessings received and an acknowledgement of one's dependence on some greater, higher being.
6. A powerful sense of community based on reverence for the sources of the common life.
7. Ritual as essentially an enjoyment of the above, expression of gratitude for it, and renewal of one's sense of communion with divine life.

Most of these attitudes are not confined to Shintō but have found their way into the other religions which have become naturalized in Japan. Their persistence and enduring vitality are shown by their powerful resurgence in many of the "new religions" of modern times. Such new movements are no doubt a more genuine expression of Japanese religious feeling than were the artificial attempts to make Shintō serve as the basis for a nationalistic ideology in the late nineteenth and early twentieth centuries.

Buddhism

Buddhism came into Japan in the sixth century A.D. from Korea and China. By this time it was already almost a thousand years old, and a highly developed religion. One can well imagine how deep an impression it made on the relatively simple and unsophisticated

Japanese of that age, presenting to them not only a profound teaching from India but also the art and culture of China through which that teaching was now expressed.

The essentials of the teaching itself are succinctly stated in the Four Noble Truths:

1. The truth of suffering—that suffering is inherent in life. Buddhism is deeply conscious of the finite character of human life. Joy and sorrow, pleasure and pain, health and sickness are inextricably bound up with one another. The more we seek of one, the more exposed we are to the other. And so the trouble lies in the seeking. This leads to the second of the Noble Truths—
2. That suffering is caused by desire or selfish craving. It is the desiring of things for oneself that brings pain. Why? Because this desire is based on an illusion—that things, and we ourselves, have permanence. In fact, nothing does. They and we are all transitory, all constantly subject to change. To possess things is impossible. To be attached to them is to depend on the insubstantial. They come into existence by a concatenation of causes and conditions, which are themselves transitory. Dependence on things brings frustration and disappointment. But there is a way out, as the third Truth tells us.
3. Desire, and consequently suffering, can be eliminated.
4. The fourth Truth is the Noble Eightfold Path whereby one may be delivered from desire and suffering to attain the peace of Nirvana. This Eightfold Path is essentially an ethical and psychological discipline. By achieving greater self-control, greater detachment from things, greater selflessness, one achieves freedom from illusion. This is not just a freedom of the mind, like intellectual detachment, but an active, practical freedom over one's whole self and one's environment. It aims at concentrating the mind in meditation, at attaining an intuitive awareness of the Truth, in which the peace of Nirvana is found. Nirvana means simply the extinguishing of desire. It implies nothing about the extinction of self, except insofar as self is bound up with desire or craving.

In relation to the Japanese religious outlook, as we see it in the preexisting Shintō religion, there are two things that strike us. Shintō showed a cheerful, optimistic attitude toward the world. It expressed a simple joy in life. Pain, defilement, death it preferred not to talk about. These were taken notice of only by the taboos placed on them. From this standpoint Buddhism, in its preoccupation with suffering and death, would seem an extremely pessimistic approach to life. Yet this may well have been the reason why Buddhism touched the Japanese so deeply. It gave them a new insight into aspects of life which Shintō had not dealt with. At the same time it suggests why the Japanese, in accepting Buddhism, also modified it. They infused into it some of their own native appreciation of life and nature.

But Buddhism had its own positive side, as well. The third and fourth Truths express a remarkable confidence that suffering can be overcome. To some Nirvana may have seemed a pale and lifeless concept, a kind of spiritual no-man's-land. But by the time Buddhism reached Japan, it had developed more appealing ways of expressing itself. For instance, the prime objects of faith were known as the Three Treasures or the Three Refuges. These were:

1. The Buddha.
2. The Law or Dharma.
3. The Religious Community (Sangha).

1. The Buddha was he who had won the truth and shared it with others. As commonly represented in sculpture, sitting in meditation, he symbolizes the fundamentally meditative character of Buddhism.

2. The Dharma or Law—the truths or teachings of the Buddha which would bring release from suffering.

3. The Sangha—the body of those who had dedicated their lives to achieving and spreading this Truth. It is roughly comparable to holy orders or monastic orders in the West. The characteristic activity of the Sangha was study and meditation. To take up the religious life was understood as leaving the world, leaving one's household or family, leaving behind the personal cares and attachments of life, for a life apart from the world of men. It was a type of discipline Shintō had never demanded of the Japanese. Pre-Buddhist Japanese religion was, organizationally speaking, just another aspect of the dominant clan organization. The Buddhist monastery, by contrast, was a community dedicated to learning, to spiritual cultivation, and to religious worship.

In the Mahāyāna form of Buddhism, which was to be most influential in Japan, we may observe certain general trends of great importance:

1. First, the Buddha as an object of worship, rather than simply as a teacher, was increasingly the center of attention.

2. There was not just one Buddha so reverenced, the historical Buddha, but many of them—all embodiments of the Liberating Truth which they had achieved first through the accumulation of meritorious deeds, and finally through an experience of enlightenment.

3. The most popular objects of devotion were the Bodhisattvas, Buddhas-to-be, who had won Nirvana for themselves but elected to remain in the world to help others win it.

4. There was an increased emphasis in Buddhism on faith and on the saving grace of the Bodhisattvas as a means of achieving liberation. By the same token there was generally less emphasis, at least in the popular mind, upon the hope of achieving liberation through the pursuit of meditative disciplines.

5. Mahāyāna Buddhism asserted most emphatically that salvation was open to all, and that all other faiths, all other schools of Buddhism served only to bring men by different pathways to the one saving truth most fully expressed in the Mahāyāna.

One can imagine the effect on the early Japanese of these ideas and ideals, a sudden revelation to them of a new world of the spirit, of new human potentialities. Take, for example, the Buddha figure. First of all, it represented an ideal of human triumph over suffering, of the attainment of spiritual peace. Secondly it was expressed in human form with an artistry that is compelling. Before the advent of Buddhism Japanese religion had no such sculpture, no objects of veneration or inspiration modeled on the human form. But with their native sensitivity to beauty, they must have been deeply moved by the sublime representations of the Buddhist ideals of contemplation in the Buddha figure or of compassion in the Bodhisattva images.

The development of Buddhism in Japan reflects historical changes in the society itself. Its introduction was sponsored by the ruling clans of the sixth and seventh centuries, and religious institutions were closely identified with the extension of the power of these clans, especially that of the Imperial House. Under such rulers as Prince Shōtoku and Emperor Shōmu, Mahāyāna Buddhism constituted an important element in the ideology of the new state, which aimed at universal dominion. Such scriptures as the Lotus Sutra and Kegon Sutra offered a vision of a universal spiritual order corresponding to the new political order. Other texts promised blessings on the state and its subjects in return for its patronage of the new religion. Temples and monasteries were built for the Buddhas and guardian gods whose protection was sought for the rulers. To a considerable extent the dominant social ideal assumed a harmony of interests between the propagation of religion and the maintenance of peace in the land.

For the most part religious organization and practice reflected the aristocratic structure of the society. Egalitarian tendencies in Mahāyāna Buddhism were inhibited, while hierarchical attitudes developed strongly. The aesthetic aspect of religion predominated, not only because of the Japanese native sensitivity, but because the aristocratic society of the Nara and Heian period admired beauty and elegance above all things. Esoteric Buddhism, as taught especially by Kūkai (Kōbō Daishi), best exemplifies this trend in the Heian period (ninth to eleventh centuries). It held that truth was manifested in all things, physical as well as mental, material as well as spiritual. The potentiality for Buddhahood lay in all things, and all things could contribute to one's attainment of Buddhahood as they influenced the development of one's total self. Bodily training, psychological discipline, aesthetic cultivation—all aspects of one's personality were involved in the attainment of Buddhahood. Consequently ritual and art were as important as scripture and meditation. It was not just a matter of enlightening the mind but of affecting and transforming the whole man.

This view of the world and of man gave great impetus to Buddhist art. Esoteric Buddhism included innumerable gods and Buddhas in its pantheon. All were considered different expressions of the same essential truth. Represented pictorially in the so-called mandala, these gods and Buddhas embodied the whole universe and were arranged in different patterns and postures to illustrate different aspects of reality. A close *rapprochement* with Shintō was also made possible by the acceptance of its gods as manifestations of the cosmic reality. Such a catholic and all-embracing attitude went far toward adapting Buddhism to Japanese tastes, especially the love of nature and enjoyment of beauty.

The collapse of the Heian court and its civil administration in the eleventh century brought profound changes in Buddhism. Religious institutions bound up with the fortunes of the court nobility declined, while a highly aestheticized and sentimentalized religion, based on the refined enjoyment of beauty and the ennui it gave rise to, could not meet the challenge of the difficult times ahead. With almost constant warfare, famines, pestilences, and social disruption came a sense of impending doom. The mind of the new age was tragic and heroic, not aesthetic.

But the new religious situation was also a product of developments within Buddhism itself, especially the growing consciousness of a discrepancy between the Mahāyāna ideal of universal salvation and the fact that the attainment of Buddhahood seemed so difficult, and in practice limited to so few. The new forms of Buddhism, generated directly out of the old monastic center of Mt. Hiei, near Kyoto, attempted to bring salvation immediately within reach.

This was most marked in the doctrine of salvation by faith in the Buddha Amida. Amida, a common subject of meditation in Esoteric Buddhism, became increasingly an object of worship. Exclusive devotion to Amida was stressed as the one reliable means of salvation for sinful men in a corrupt and disordered world. It was only necessary to utter the name of Amida in sincere faith and then, whatever one's sins in this life, one would be taken at death to Amida's Pure Land, where all the obstacles, illusions, and temptations that prevented one from achieving Buddhahood in this world would be removed. This doctrine of salvation by faith brought Buddhism out of the monasteries, with their austere disciplines, into the households of peasants and townspeople. For the first time Buddhism became a religion of the masses. Accordingly, the temples of this sect were later built on a great scale, to accommodate the large number of devout worshipers who came to pay homage to Amida.

Amidism stressed the value of faith, not human action. Another important movement in medieval Buddhism combined faith and action in devotion to the teaching of the Lotus Sutra. This scripture proclaimed the salvation of all beings, but also insisted on the need for courageous action to spread the good word of the Lotus Sutra. Nichiren, the founder of this movement in the thirteenth century, believed that the Buddhism of his day was thoroughly corrupt, and that it was the mission of himself and the Japanese people to purify and revive it. He was an intransigent critic of both political and religious leaders in his day. For his outspokenness, he suffered arrest, imprisonment, and exile, setting an example as a fearless fighter and martyr for truth. His modern followers tend also to be great activists in the political and social sphere, and to be strong Japanese nationalists. They are well organized and an important factor in national elections. Thus Nichiren's Lotus sect is a rare example of a Buddhist movement with a political and social program. On the other hand it had the least influence on the Japanese arts in general.

One of the sects Nichiren most condemned was Zen Buddhism. He thought Zen essentially a selfish teaching because it centered around the enlightenment of the individual rather than the salvation of mankind or the nation, and because it stressed self-effort rather than salvation through faith. And Zen did indeed oppose the idea that Buddhahood was something to be sought outside oneself. Every man has a Buddha-nature, and to realize it, according to Zen, he need only look within. Self-understanding and self-reliance are the keynote of Zen.

The means by which this inner realization may be achieved is indicated by the term Zen, meaning "meditation" or "concentration." To speak of it as a "means," however, is appropriate only with reference to the specific procedure involved in the practice of meditation: sitting erect, cross-legged and motionless, with the mind concentrated so as to achieve, first, tranquillity, and then active insight.

Meditative practices of this sort were an essential feature of Buddhism from the earliest times and are related to the Yoga practices of ancient India. It was in China, however, that the practice of this type of meditation for the first time became the basis of a separate school of Buddhism. In protest against the prevailing scholasticism of Chinese Buddhism, with its attention to scripture and philosophical discussion, a movement developed stressing intuitive enlightenment and rejecting any dependence on scripture or doctrine. The sect was organized around individual masters who claimed an authoritative patriarchal transmission of vital truth from the first teacher, Buddha. According to tradition, this transmission was brought from India to China by Bodhi-dharma. He is a favorite subject for Zen painting, expressing qualities of rugged integrity, resolute courage, and penetrating insight. From him the transmission went on from generation to generation without verbal preaching or written scripture, but with cryptic signs or striking gestures as the only overt form of communication from one patriarch to another.

There is, however, a body of literature which has grown up around the Zen masters, consisting of anecdotes about them or about the steps by which disciples of Zen have gained the truth. These usually focus upon a baffling problem which will not yield a solution until the student abandons ordinary processes of reasoning and opens the doors of his mind to intuitive understanding.

But of all the means of conveying the insight of Zen to the uninitiated, perhaps the most effective have been the traditional arts of Japan, such as landscape painting, landscape gardening, the Nō drama, swordsmanship, and the tea ceremony. The pioneer teachers of Zen in Japan had a particularly close association with the cult of tea. The making and drinking of tea is one of the simplest of everyday activities. Zen turned it into a fine art. This is typical of the Zen approach to life—finding great beauty and significance in the commonplace. Everything about the tea cult is a combination of the utmost simplicity and the greatest refinement.

One may observe here, too, the permeating of Zen by traditional Shintō attitudes and values: simplicity, naturalness, love of beauty, and lack of interest in doctrine. Generally speaking, Zen developed a close association with the new military aristocracy, especially the Ashikaga shogunate. Devotion to Amida and the Lotus Sutra was stronger in the lower classes. These three forms of Buddhism tended to dominate the religious scene down into modern times, but with the rise of the Tokugawa shogunate at the end of the sixteenth century there was another major change which tended to limit the role of religion in Japanese life. The shogunate attempted to unify the extremely decentralized feudal system and strengthen civil administration. Though tolerating Buddhism it felt a need for a common political and social ethic, which Buddhism did not provide. The Tokugawa therefore encouraged the spread of Confucianism.

Confucianism and Neo-Confucianism

Confucianism, though a product of China, has not, historically speaking, been confined to a role as the national creed or cult of the Chinese, but has entered deeply into the lives of other East Asian peoples as well. Its transmission to these other countries is all the more remarkable, however, since Confucianism has had no missionaries of its own to win converts abroad. The scholar and the official, rather than the monk or pilgrim, is the usual symbol of Confucianism in action; its natural orbit is the family and the state, not the "uncivilized" world.

Consequently, when Confucianism was first introduced into Japan in the sixth and seventh centuries, Buddhist monks had to serve as the intermediaries, bringing Chinese culture with them as naturally as Christian missionaries of the twentieth century brought Western medicine, for example, to strange lands. Similarly, when the second great wave of Confucian influence reached Japan, Buddhist monks again served as intermediaries—this time the Zen monks who played such a prominent part in trade and intercourse with China, and who made their monasteries centers of Chinese studies in the Ashikaga period. Art history tells us how great an impression had been made on the Japanese by the artistic achievements of the Sung dynasty. Another outstanding product of Sung times was Neo-Confucian philosophy, which likewise attracted the attention of learned monks in fifteenth- and sixteenth-century Japan.

Nevertheless, it is to other factors than its reception by Zen monks that Neo-Confucianism owes the ascendancy which it achieved in the early years of the Tokugawa period. Neo-Confucian orthodoxy in Japan was a creation of both scholarship and state sponsorship. Circumstances had enhanced its importance to men confronted by precisely those problems which Confucianism took most seriously, and whose outlook and interests differed greatly from its original clerical sponsors. It was not long, therefore, before those who espoused the cause of Neo-Confucianism attempted to liberate themselves from clerical dominance and establish Neo-Confucianism not only as an independent teaching, but also as a creed and code having undisputed state sanction. The outstanding leader in this movement was Hayashi Razan, and characteristically the leadership of the orthodox Neo-Confucian school in Tokugawa Japan passed down through his family, on a hereditary basis, so that successive generations of Hayashis served as the chief educational advisers to the shogunate and the chief authorities in intellectual matters right down to the fall of the Tokugawa in 1868.

There is no time here for even a brief summary of Confucian beliefs or principles, and I shall confine myself to mentioning just three elements in Confucianism, or rather Neo-Confucianism, which I believe exerted special influence in Japan. These are its ethical humanism, its rationalism, and its historical mindedness. First, let us take up its ethical humanism.

The moral doctrines of this school focus directly upon man and his closest human relationships, not any supernatural order or divine law. These are expressed most concretely in the Five Human Relationships and their attendant obligations (between ruler and subject, father and son, husband and wife, older and younger brother, and between friends). Such an emphasis upon human loyalties and personal relationships was obviously congenial to the feudal society of Japan in this period, and provided a uniform, secular code by which the Tokugawa could maintain social order in all their domains, no matter how divided they might be by local loyalties or religious allegiances. It is a noteworthy fact that public morality until recent times drew more upon the ethical teachings and terminology of Confucianism than upon any other doctrine.

The Neo-Confucian philosophy imported to Japan under the Tokugawa was known as "the philosophy of reason (or principle)." It stressed the objective reason or principle in all things as the basis of learning and conduct. Intellectually this required exhaustive study of things and human affairs in order to determine their underlying principles, pursuing what the *Great Learning,* a favorite text of this school, called "the investigation of things." This positivistic and quasi-scientific approach was a notable characteristic of Japanese thought and scholarship in the Tokugawa period, which showed a new interest in observing the constant laws of nature and human society, as contrasted to the medieval, Buddhistic view of the world as subject only to ceaseless change, the Law of Impermanence.

A strong sense of the importance of human history has been a feature of Confucianism from earliest times, in contrast to Buddhism and Hinduism which have attached little importance to history. In Japan the writing of the first national histories in the eighth century was a direct outgrowth of Confucian influence on the Japanese court. Similarly, when Confucianism was revived and reintroduced in new forms under the Tokugawa, it gave a strong impetus to the writing of history. The founder of the official school himself undertook to write a general history of Japan, after centuries during which history was neglected under the dominance of Buddhism. But the significant thing here is that this reawakened sense of history should have contributed so much to the growing sense of Japanese nationalism. For it inevitably pointed to the importance and preservation of Japanese traditions. Thus perhaps the most influential Confucian school of historical writing was established at Mito by a branch of the Tokugawa ruling house. Following Confucian principles, it emphasized the principle of loyalty to the legitimate dynasty—that is, the Imperial

House in Kyoto, rather than the Tokugawa shogunate itself. It is not surprising that this same Mito branch of the Tokugawa house should have played a leading role in the Imperial Restoration of 1868.

The dominance of Confucian thought and culture in the Tokugawa period derived from its secular functions. Institutionally it was represented by the scholars and officials who served the shogunate or the various domains. These were members of the military aristocracy, but during the long Tokugawa peace their military functions gave way increasingly to scholarly and bureaucratic ones. There was a notable extension of education and cultural activity, some of it reaching out to include Western studies as learned from the Dutch in Nagasaki. By the nineteenth century the process of "civil"-izing the old warrior class had proceeded far enough that they and many of their Confucian values could adapt to the new situation confronting Japan, but the creation of a modern state eliminated the old institutional basis of Confucianism and a serious question arose as to how the latter could survive among the modern bureaucrats, technicians and university professors of a new age.

The Shintō Revival and Modern Nationalism

The emperor-centered nationalism of modern Japan, however, besides deriving from these tendencies in Tokugawa Confucianism, also owed much to the Shintō revival which took place in the eighteenth and early nineteenth centuries. The interest in history which was stimulated by Confucianism led the Japanese to reexamine the history of their country, and to exalt Japan over China. Following essentially this same line of thought and study other thinkers established the School of National Learning (as opposed to Chinese learning) and devoted themselves to "rediscovering" what they thought was the pure and unadulterated Japanese tradition. They were convinced that Japan had its own characteristic way of life, and a spirit all its own. But when they reexamined the records of the past they had great difficulty identifying anything in the early records not strongly influenced by Chinese thought. In the end they turned to poetry and novels like *The Tale of Genji* as expressing this characteristic spirit or attitude, which they identified particularly with the emotions, the feelings of man, rather than his rational faculties. Thus, opposed to

Confucian rationalism, which they identified with the Chinese, they upheld the emotional sensitivity and innocent spontaneity of the Japanese.

In the potent brand of nationalism which surged up in nineteenth-century Japan these two strains in Tokugawa thought, Shintō and Confucianist, were synthesized in a conception put forward by the later Mito school, the conception of Japan's peculiar "national polity" (*kokutai*). "Polity," of course, refers to the basic form of government in a society and the ends which it is thought to serve. According to the Mito theory, Japan's distinctive national polity was based on the divine ancestry of the Imperial House, the assurances of the Sun Goddess concerning its destiny to rule the world, and the peculiar virtues of the Japanese people in remaining faithful to this dynasty down through the centuries. In late nineteenth-century Japan and right up to the end of World War II this doctrine became almost universally accepted among the Japanese. It was the ultimate appeal and sanction invoked in support of virtually any political stand: Japanese reactionaries, conservatives, liberals, and even many social revolutionaries appealed to its authority. Embodying as it did virtually all of Japanese tradition, it served as a national symbol susceptible to some extent of divergent interpretations. Westernized liberals, for instance, tended to dwell on the example set by the young Emperor Meiji, who, in his famous Charter Oath, called for increased participation of the people in government. Conservatives emphasized disciplined loyalty to the throne. But Western political labels are inadequate when applied to the strange configurations of Japanese nationalistic thought. The extremes of left and right meet in the thinking of those who reject the bourgeois culture of the West and reassert traditional Japanese values.

In the fully developed nationalist doctrine which became orthodox state teaching in the late 1930s, as set forth in the *Kokutai no hongi* (Fundamentals of Japan's national polity), glorification of the Emperor and of the traditional virtues of the Japanese people is combined with a strong opposition to Western influences, and in particular to the individualism of the West, which is contrasted to the Japanese ideal of a harmonious society working together as one family. Western capitalism, individual enterprise, individual rights are seen as manifestations of bourgeois self-assertion, disregarding the good of society as a whole. Similarly, fascism was viewed simply as a form of racial self-assertion. It was believed that the contradictions of Western individualism, class warfare, and racial antagonism could only be resolved by pursuing the traditional Japanese ideal of the family-state or family society, in which everyone worked together, not necessarily as equals, for the good of the whole, and in which leadership represented only a higher form of self-sacrificing service to the nation. Japan's mission in the modern world, they thought, was to assert this ideal throughout the world and rescue the West from the dilemma of unrestrained individualism.

Japan's defeat in World War II completely shattered the belief in Japan's national destiny. Charges of Japanese oppression and atrocities in occupied territories were a shock to those who had believed idealistically in Japan's divine mission to lead the Asian peoples. Disillusionment brought a trend toward the abandonment of traditional ideas and practices in favor of whatever seemed to represent the superior civilization of the Western conquerors. The teaching of Confucian ethics disappeared almost entirely, and a wave of indiscriminate "Americanization" followed. But in response to this there also arose a strong undercurrent of reaction and resentment in the form of anti-Americanism. The least significant element in this was overtly traditionalistic or from the right. Most often, among intellectuals and the young it manifested itself in "Marxist" protests against "bourgeois capitalism" and "Western imperialism." In a period when Marxism was disintegrating as a philosophy, its authority shattered by de-Stalinization and the Moscow-Peking cleavage, and its economic dogmas undermined by practical failures and pragmatic compromises, left-wing movements and idealistic socialism continued to attract the young as essentially a form of moral protest against all forms of social evil.

Among a much larger segment of the population, however, traditional attitudes reasserted themselves in another guise: the new religions. As in the case of left-wing movements, wherein traditional values provided the moral dynamism behind ostensibly modern and revolutionary drives, the "new religions" have drawn heavily on the traditional sources of religious emotion (chant, song, and dance) and aesthetic appeal, while insisting on their "new-ness" and ultramodernity. One of their most important functions has been to provide a new sense of community in the midst of rapid processes of social change and urbanization. Strong group feeling, group therapy, and mutual help are found in those of a predominantly social character. Another common element is faith healing. The more political sects stress vaguely moralistic and rationalistic solutions for the complex problems of an advanced industrial society. Some are quite internationalistic: making claims to universality and exhibiting a kind of rotarian ecumenicism—while others are intensely nationalistic. In the latter case, however, no clear political trend is apparent. National self-interest in foreign policy is conceived in the form of neutralism and little sense of world mission or national destiny is evident.

In the meantime economic prosperity has brought a boom in domestic tourism. More people than ever visit shrines and temples on holiday and the affluence of religious centers is manifested in the repair and rebuilding of many historic shrines long neglected even in the earlier period of ultranationalism. The more serious adherents of such faiths, aware of the commercialism that has invaded religious institutions, are disturbed over its implications and are pondering deeply the true role of religion in modern life.

XI

The Art of

Japan

BY
HUGO MUNSTERBERG

The Prehistoric Period

Of all the aspects of Japanese culture, the arts are the most rewarding for the person unfamiliar with the language and history of Japan. Aside from the fact that the visual arts have an almost universal appeal, the Japanese themselves have always been an extremely artistic people. In fact, it has often been said that of all civilizations, that of Japan is the most sensitive aesthetically. Art was not restricted to a small elite or used exclusively for religious purposes, but permeated almost every aspect of life. This remarkable creation is the only form of Japanese culture which has had a significant influence on the West. Certainly eighteenth-century European porcelains such as Meissen, Chantilly, and Worcester would not have existed without the examples of Imari and Kakiemon wares; and the painters of the impressionist and postimpressionist movement were profoundly influenced by the print makers of the ukiyo-e school. Modern architects, beginning with Frank Lloyd Wright who freely expressed his indebtedness to traditional Japanese art, were greatly influenced by the domestic architecture of Japan, just as present-day American and European pottery has been influenced by traditional Japanese teaware and folk pottery which centuries ago developed a very similar sensibility.

The Japanese artistic tradition is one of the most ancient in the world, with origins which go back to the eighth millennium before Christ when the so-called Jōmon pottery culture began. This early phase, which lasted for several thousand years, up to the end of the pre-Christian era, is one of the most interesting and creative of all prehistoric cultures. The name Jōmon, meaning rope-impressed, is a term coined by modern archaeologists, and refers to the pattern often impressed on the surface of Jōmon pottery by rope, matting, or sticks. Interestingly enough, this impressed ware shows marked similarities to both European Neolithic and American Indian pottery, but it is very different from the prehistoric pottery of China, suggesting a north Asian rather than a Chinese connection for Jōmon civilization. It is not known who these people were, where they came from, when they arrived in Japan, or what their relationship was to the other peoples of Eastern Asia. It is also not quite clear how they are related to the Ainu, a Caucasoid race which still survives in small numbers on reservations in Hokkaido and adjacent territories.

Jōmon art is usually divided into various phases, most commonly

Early Jōmon, Middle Jōmon, and Late Jōmon, the most outstanding being the middle period. The ceramics of the Middle Jōmon period were often very imaginative in shape and design, at times bordering on the bizarre, so strange and fantastic that modern Japanese critics have referred to these jars and bowls as surrealist. The surface of this type of vessel is treated in a sculptural manner with peculiar protrusions and openings, and animal and human shapes emerging from the rim and the sides. Just what the meaning of these ornaments was is unfortunately not known, but it is safe to assume that they must have had some magic or sexual significance. This expressive, extremely original style is unique to Japan, and the very opposite of the simplicity and restraint which characterizes later Japanese ceramics, suggesting again that Jōmon art has little relation to the traditions which have evolved in Japan during the last two thousand years. Also very different from later work is the *dogū,* or clay idol, which appeared during the Middle Jōmon period and became particularly popular during the Late Jōmon. The *dogū* are female fertility deities, often with projecting breasts and large thighs not unlike the prehistoric female figures found all over Europe and the Near East. The finest of these images are expressive sculptures of great vitality, equal to the best of the European idols.

A very different kind of prehistoric culture, called Yayoi after the district of Tokyo in which the first archaeological remains were excavated, reached Japan during the third century before Christ. This new culture was technically superior to the Jōmon, for it used metal and was materially of far greater complexity. The pottery was made on the potter's wheel, a technical advance over the hand-built Jōmon ware; though it was less original, it showed the simplicity of form and design which is still characteristic of the best Japanese ceramics.

The most important difference between the earlier culture and that of the Yayoi period is the mastery of metal, especially bronze manufacture. Among the metal objects are remarkable bronze bells, sometimes with relief designs depicting contemporary life; weapons of all types; and bronze mirrors similar to those of Han China, with which Japan maintained a close relationship. The most important of these finds, which are often very beautiful works of art, were excavated in the tombs of rulers. These sites are particularly common in western Japan.

In the third century A.D., a protohistoric period began which is usually called the Tomb period, for the most impressive remains are

the huge burial mounds, some of which still exist. The most extensive are of vast dimensions, equal in size to the pyramids of Egypt
and the imperial tombs of China. From an artistic point of view, the
most remarkable features of these tombs are the hollow clay grave
figures, or *haniwa,* which were placed in a circle around the base and
the top of the mounds. Although decidedly primitive, they have a
great appeal to modern taste because of their naïve charm as well
as their feeling for abstract geometric form. Many types of human
figures, various animals, and even houses and boats were portrayed,
so that not only are they rewarding from an aesthetic point of view,
they are also valuable documents for the life of the Tomb period.

The artistic contribution that was to be the most lasting was the
development of the Shintō shrine which to this day serves as the
prototype for much of Japanese architecture. The feeling for simplicity of form and honest use of natural building materials, still characteristic of Japanese construction, is already apparent in these
sanctuaries. The great shrines at Ise and Izumo are not the buildings
erected during the Tomb period, for it was the custom to tear the
shrines down each generation and reconstruct them in the same style,
but they certainly reflect the kind of architecture introduced during
this period, an architecture showing a striking resemblance to the
chieftain huts of Southeast Asia and Polynesia, which are also raised
on stilts and dominated by huge thatched roofs.

The Asuka Period

The event that is usually credited with changing the entire cultural
history of Japan is the arrival in 552 of a mission from the Korean
kingdom of Paekche which brought Buddhist images and sutras. This
was probably only one of many such encounters not just with Buddhism but with the more sophisticated and highly developed culture
of the mainland which was to transform the civilization of Japan.
Buddhism and Buddhist art were introduced first from Korea and
then directly from China, and the result was that by the year 600
Japan was virtually a Buddhist country, producing works of art far
closer to those of Korea and China than to the *haniwa* of the Tomb
period culture. Not only were sacred icons imported from the
continent, but Buddhist craftsmen came to Japan in order to teach
the Japanese the proper way to make images and construct temples.

Only in the nineteenth century, with the introduction of Western culture, has Japan experienced so profound a revolution in her whole cultural outlook.

The first period of Japanese Buddhist art is called Asuka, after the district in which the Japanese capital was located at the time. The source of most of this art was Korea, and in some cases it is possible to tell whether the works were actually made in Korea or whether they are Japanese objects imitating Korean models. Workshops were no doubt established at the cloisters where Korean and Chinese immigrants taught the Japanese carvers, painters, and carpenters the secrets of their craft as well as the proper iconography to be used for the various types of Buddhist sacred figures. The Japanese craftsmen showed an amazing ability to absorb the foreign style, and within a period of some fifty years they were able to produce works which equaled the best of the Korean and Chinese originals. Certainly the change which took place was the most dramatic that Japanese art has ever experienced, for at the beginning of Asuka period the Japanese were making primitive clay grave figures and crude wall paintings, while at the end, in 645, they were creating sculptures and paintings of great sophistication and refinement.

The cultural centers of this period were the great Buddhist monasteries, just as the Christian monasteries were the centers of culture in medieval Europe. Among the most important was Hōryūji, located near Nara, which is still standing today and has preserved some of its original buildings, which are among the oldest wooden structures in the world. Unfortunately, one of the finest of these, the main hall (*kondō*), was destroyed by fire in 1949, but since it was reconstructed in its original form, it is no exaggeration to say that the temple complex at Hōryūji still looks much the way it did some twelve hundred and fifty years ago. The chief structures of such a Buddhist sanctuary —and this would be the same in Buddhist temples today—were the main gate (*chūmon*); the main or "golden" hall (*kondō*); the pagoda (*gojūnotō*); and the lecture hall (*kōdō*), the whole surrounded by a covered cloister which separates the sacred enclosure from the world. All the structures were built of wood which was painted red and had a large, overhanging roof made of gray tiles. This was in striking contrast to the Shintō shrines and the traditional Japanese peasant houses, both of which used unpainted wood and thatch roofs. But in both the native and the Chinese-inspired Buddhist style, there was the same blending of architecture with the natural setting, and the same preference for a modest scale, with buildings rarely of more than one story.

Along with the new style of architecture, the Buddhist missionaries introduced Korean and Chinese sculpture, painting, and decorative arts. Executed by pious craftsmen, many of whom were no doubt monks, this work was almost exclusively devoted to the glorification of Buddha and Buddhism. A variety of techniques was used, bronze casting, wood carving, and wall painting being the most common. Among the bronze images of the Asuka period the celebrated Shā-kyamuni trinity of 623 on the main altar of the *kondō* at Hōryūji is probably the finest. Interestingly enough, it was made by the grandson of a Chinese immigrant, indicating the close connection which existed between the foreign craftsmen who had come to Japan and their Japanese pupils and descendants. In fact, this trinity, in both its style and its iconography, is very similar to the Buddhist sculptures which were made in sixth-century Korea and China. Of the wooden images, the finest are probably the standing figure of the Kudara Kannon, the Bodhisattva of Mercy and Compassion, also at Hōryūji, and the seated Miroku, the Buddha of the Future, which is located in the neighboring Chūgūji nunnery. Indeed, in the eyes of some critics the Chūgūji Miroku, who is shown seated in divine meditation while awaiting his rebirth as a Buddha, is the most beautiful and spiritually moving of all the religious icons of Japanese art, for in this figure the inwardness and contemplation so characteristic of Buddhism is expressed in its supreme form. The Kannon image, called the Kudara Kannon after the Korean kingdom from which it was said to have been brought to Japan, is still foreign in style. The Miroku, on the other hand, although certainly based upon continental models, already shows a distinctly Japanese flavor, especially in its emphasis on abstract forms which to a certain extent recall the simple shapes of the *haniwa*.

Unfortunately, the painting of the Asuka period has all but disappeared, since it was usually executed either on the walls of the buildings or on perishable materials such as wood, paper, or silk. Happily, a series of paintings decorating a little shrine in the main hall of Hōryūji still survives, and this at least gives some idea of the kind of subject used and the style. Called the Tamamushi shrine after the beetle wings which at one point decorated its metal work, it is noted for its panel painting executed in oil pigments on wood and representing scenes from the previous incarnations of the Buddha which are known as Jātaka scenes. The style is very similar to that found in sixth-century China, with long, slender figures, and space which is very abstract and two-dimensional. There is a wonderful feeling for pattern and abstract design which makes these pictures aesthetically very appealing. Although little of the decorative art of the period has survived, remarkable progress was made in metal work, textiles, and pottery, indicating the stimulating effect of Chinese and Korean influences.

The Nara Period

The dominance of continental art was even more pronounced during the Nara period, which in art history extends from 645 to 794. Instead of being transmitted through Korea, the foreign influences now reached Japan directly from China, which, under the T'ang dynasty, was undergoing a period of great artistic florescence. Nara, the new Japanese capital, was laid out in imitation of the T'ang capital of Ch'ang-an, and Japanese monks, scholars, diplomats, and merchants traveled to the Middle Kingdom to study the culture and institutions of China. In fact, so close was the relationship between the two countries that often one cannot distinguish between the Japanese and Chinese objects which are still preserved in the Shōsōin, where they were deposited in the middle of the eighth century. The reason is that the Japanese craftsmen were so skillful in their imitations that even scholars cannot always decide which object was imported from China and which was a Japanese work made in the Chinese style.

While the art of the Asuka period was largely based on that of Korea, which in turn was derived from the Chinese art of the Six Dynasties and Sui periods, Nara period art was influenced directly by T'ang China. Instead of the slender, abstract forms characteristic of the earlier works, the sculptures and paintings of the Nara period are full-bodied and more naturalistic, reflecting the sensuous art current in seventh-century China, which had been greatly influenced by Gupta India. The iconography employed by the image makers also changed dramatically, exotic, many-armed deities being represented, and Amida, the Buddha of the Western Paradise, playing a prominent role.

Among the Buddhist temples established at this time, the most prominent was Tōdaiji, or Great East Temple, in Nara. Although much damaged in later periods and largely reconstructed in a somewhat different style, it is still very impressive. The present main hall, which is an Edo period structure erected after the original building was destroyed by fire, is still the largest Buddhist temple in Japan, and contains the Daibutsu, the biggest statue of Buddha ever made in the country. The construction of so colossal an image, over fifty-three feet in height, represented a major technical and artistic achievement. Its dedication ceremony, which was celebrated in 752, was one of the great religious events of the period, attracting thousands of Buddhist monks and worshipers not only from all over Japan but also from China, Korea, Central Asia, and India.

Of the surviving structures at Tōdaiji, the most outstanding are the graceful Hokkedō, so named because it was in this hall that the Lotus Sutra, or *Hokekyō,* was read; and the famous storehouse, the Shōsōin, built in log cabin style and serving as a repository for the many examples of the decorative arts which the widow of the Emperor Shōmu dedicated to the temple in 756. Other celebrated examples of Nara period Buddhist architecture which still survive in their original form are the pagoda at Yakushiji, the main hall and lecture hall at Tōshōdaiji, and the octagonal Yumedono at Hōryūji, all located in the vicinity of Nara. No doubt all these buildings are derived from Chinese prototypes and reflect the architectural style current in T'ang China, but since no such wooden structures have survived in China, these Japanese examples are not only priceless heirlooms but also key monuments in the study of Chinese Buddhist architecture.

The most remarkable artistic achievement of the Nara period, however, is the sculpture, which in the eyes of most critics is the finest the Japanese have ever produced. Certainly both the quality and the variety of images made during the later part of the seventh and the eighth century has rarely been matched and never surpassed in the long annals of Japanese art. While the earlier images had been largely bronze or wood, now other media, such as lacquer and clay, were also employed. By this time the Japanese craftsmen had mastered all the lessons of their Chinese teachers, and as a result they produced images which were not only spiritually moving but technically of the highest order.

It is difficult to select the most outstanding from the numerous Nara period images which have survived, but certainly the Tachibana shrine at Hōryūji, a charming little work representing the Buddha Amida seated on a lotus with the souls of the blessed in his paradise, and the large statue at Yakushiji of Yakushi, the Buddha of Medicine and Healing, flanked by the Bodhisattvas Nikkō and Gakkō, are among the finest of those executed in bronze. Of the hollow dry lacquer images, the most famous are perhaps the lovely figure of the many-armed Indian deity, Ashura, which belongs to the Kōfukuji at Nara, and the deeply moving portrait of the monk Ganjin, who had come from China as a Buddhist missionary and established Tōshōdaiji in Nara where his image is still preserved. Clay was often used to make guardian figures such as the Four Kings (Shitennō), who protect the four corners of the Buddhist altars, or the Two Kings (Niō), who are placed at the entrance of most Buddhist temples to ward off evil demons which might wish to harm the sanctuary. In contrast to the Buddhas and Bodhisattvas, who are always shown in relaxed positions with serene expressions mirroring the inner peace they have achieved, the guardian figures are represented as fierce warriors whose dramatic stance and contorted facial expression indicate the function they perform. Since they are ultimately Indian deities, they also reflect the racial type of the West as seen by the Japanese —namely, large bulging eyes, protruding noses, and hair which stands up dramatically.

Painting also flourished during the Nara period. However, very little has survived, and the single most important monument which had come down to modern times, namely, the wall paintings in the main hall of Hōryūji, were largely destroyed or badly damaged when the building was burned in 1949. Fortunately, a large number of photographs and copies had been made, and the museum at Hōryūji has some fragments of the originals as well as oddly transformed remains which look like strange X rays. The subject of the paintings was the four Buddhist Paradises corresponding to the four directions, and eight Bodhisattvas. The style in which the frescoes were painted clearly reflects that of T'ang China, which in turn is ultimately derived from Central Asian and Indian models. The forms are very full and sensuous, and the expression harmonious and spiritual in keeping with the religious ideals of the Buddhist faith. In contrast to the more plastic Indian style, these Japanese paintings depend primarily on line, with shading used sparingly to bring out the roundness of the form and the folds of drapery, and with colors which were delicate and subdued. The loss of these masterpieces of East Asian painting is particularly tragic since no equivalent of these works has survived in China.

Only a very few Nara paintings on silk or paper are still extant, but those which have survived suggest that a flourishing school of both religious and secular painting must have existed. Of the pictures executed on silk, the finest is a representation of Kichijōten, the Goddess of Beauty and Good Fortune, who is shown as a Nara court beauty dressed in the elegant garments of the period, and reflecting the moon faced and full-bodied ideal of feminine beauty popular at the Nara court. Similar depictions are found among the secular paintings at the Shōsōin, suggesting that the representation of T'ang beauties was a favorite subject of the artists of the Nara period. While these works are hanging scrolls (kakemono), hand scrolls (makimono) were also made, the finest being the *Inga-kyō* scrolls depicting the past and present incarnations of Shākyamuni Buddha. As the forerunners of the Yamato-e paintings of later times, these works are very important in the development of Japanese painting. Combining the sacred text with illustrations executed in a naïve but charming style, they are fresh in color and astonishingly well preserved for pictures dating back to the eighth century. Besides these scrolls, there are painted scenes on lacquer boxes, banners, and screens, all of which indicate that both figure and landscape painting must have flourished at this time, inspired by the Chinese painting of the T'ang period.

During the Nara period the decorative arts developed far beyond anything which had previously been known in Japan. We are fortunate in having thousands of well authenticated Nara period pieces which have been preserved for some twelve hundred years in the Shōsōin. Nowhere else in the world has such a wealth of objects in such good condition been preserved from an eighth-century civilization, and the result is that the material culture of this time can be reconstructed with great accuracy. There are gorgeous textiles, gold and silver vessels, mirrors, lacquer boxes, musical instruments, and ceramic wares, as well as screens, banners, hangings, writing instruments, books, maps, household furniture, armor, and magnificent masks. Every type of object used at the Nara court during the mid-eighth century is represented in this extraordinary collection, and every piece bears witness to the highly developed, sophisticated culture typical of the Nara period. It is impossible to single out specific works from the rich array of objects in the Shōsōin, but certainly the textiles are outstanding, with a great variety of techniques used in the weaving, dyeing, and embroidery; and the marvelous metal work of all kinds, as well as the glazed pottery vessels, shows an artistic and technical excellence rarely equaled in later times. The objects preserved in the Shōsōin are not the only examples of Nara period crafts which have come down to us, for numerous other decorative art works have survived.

The Early Heian Period

Although the Japanese capital was moved at the end of the eighth century to Heiankyo, the present-day Kyoto, the strong Chinese influence which had characterized the Nara period continued during the opening phase of this new epoch, which is called the Early Heian, or Jōgan period. Extending through the ninth century, it corresponded to the Late T'ang period whose culture it reflects. The most important change was the emergence of new esoteric Buddhist sects, called Mikkyō in Japan, of which the Shingon and Tendai sects were the most significant. Introduced by the famous Buddhist masters Saichō and Kūkai (Kōbō Daishi) in the early ninth century, they soon spread throughout Japan and had a profound influence not only upon Buddhist thought but also on its art.

Instead of the traditional representations of the great Buddhas and Bodhisattvas of orthodox Buddhism, strange and fearsome deities were portrayed, and magic diagrams known as mandalas were used to express the spiritual insights of the new doctrines. Here again, the influence of India was very striking, for although these concepts reached Japan through China, they were really Indian in their inspiration. In fact, in their iconography and symbolism they are closer to Tantric Buddhism and Hinduism than to the traditional Hīnayāna or Mahāyāna teachings. The central figure is now the great Cosmic Buddha Vairochana, called Dainichi, or the Great Illuminator, in Japan. All the other Buddhas, Bodhisattvas, and sacred beings were now considered manifestations of Vairochana.

These new religious ideas find their most profound expression in the mandalas, which embody the basic ideas of Shingon Buddhism in visual form. There are usually two such magic diagrams, one called the Diamond Mandala, which represents the world of essences, and the other, the Womb Mandala, symbolizing the phenomenal world. At the center of both is the figure of the great Cosmic Buddha Dainichi, whose very being fills the universe and who represents ultimate reality. His hands are locked in the gesture of supreme knowledge, with the right index finger clasped in the fist formed by his left hand, a gesture which symbolizes the union of the male with the female, and of the world of ultimate essences with the world of appearances. In these icons the emphasis is less on draftsmanship and beauty of form than on correct iconography, but the result is often very pleasing with abstract formal designs not unlike those used in modern nonobjective art.

The most impressive Shingon paintings are those representing the five great Wisdom Kings (Myōō), especially Fudō, who appears as a manifestation of the Buddha Vairochana himself. He is portrayed as a fierce, awe-inspiring god, surrounded by flames and holding a rope and a sword with which he fights evil passions and saves souls from purgatory. He is shown sitting or standing on a rock which symbolizes the fact that he is indestructible. Rendered in brilliant colors—red, blue, or yellow Fudō occur—these paintings are powerful and dramatic, very different in feeling from the gentle, serene images of the traditional Buddhist style.

Although painting was no doubt the dominant art form of the Early Heian period, sculpture and architecture also played an important role. The sculptural style was very close to that of ninth-century China, with full, heavy forms which are impressive in their bulk and majesty rather than outstanding in their aesthetic appeal. Among them are strange, exotic deities with multiple heads and limbs. Derived from Hindu sources, they are quite alien to native Japanese traditions. Such Hindu gods as Brahma seated on a goose and Shiva on his bull appear in sculptures as well as paintings, for they had become part of the pantheon of Esoteric Buddhism.

Of the Early Heian Buddhist temples, Kūkai's great sanctuary on Mt. Kōya was the most famous, but unfortunately none of the ninth-century buildings are left. The best preserved of Early Heian temples is the small but lovely Murōji in an isolated mountain village not far from Nara. Here the main hall and pagoda have survived in their original form, showing the traditional Buddhist features beautifully adapted to the picturesque mountain setting, and using the thatch roof of the indigenous style. Of the secular architecture almost nothing remains, but it is said that the imperial palace in Kyoto, although in its present form a work of the Edo period, goes back to ninth-century designs and reflects the palace architecture which was current in T'ang China.

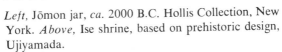

Left, Jōmon jar, *ca.* 2000 B.C. Hollis Collection, New York. *Above,* Ise shrine, based on prehistoric design, Ujiyamada.

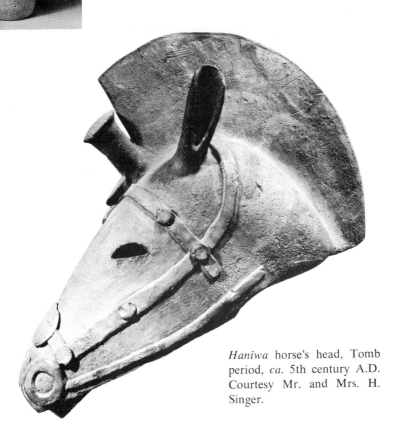

Haniwa horse's head, Tomb period, *ca.* 5th century A.D. Courtesy Mr. and Mrs. H. Singer.

PLATE 1

PLATE 2

Above, Two Bodhisattvas. From Tamamushi shrine, Asuka period, 7th century A.D. Hōryūji. Nara. *Left,* Miroku in Meditation, Asuka period, 7th century A.D. Cleveland Museum of Art, John L. Severance Fund.

Buddhist trinity, Early Nara period, 7th century
A.D., Hollis Collection, New York, photograph by
Charles Uht.

PLATE 3

PLATE 4

Above, Pagoda, Nara period, 8th century A.D. Yakushiji, Nara. *Left, Kondō* (Golden Hall), Nara period, 8th century A.D. Tōshōdaiji, Nara.

Left, Nikkō Bodhisattva, Early Heian period, 9th century A.D. Cleveland Museum of Art, John L. Severance Fund. *Right,* Standing Bodhisattva, Heian period, 10th century A.D. Wolff Collection, New York, photograph by O.E. Nelson.

PLATE 5

Paradise scene, Heian period, 12th century A.D. Cleveland Museum of Art, Worcester R. Warner Collection.

PLATE 6

PLATE 7

Above, Portrait of Priest Kakushin, Kamakura period, 13th century A.D. Cleveland Museum of Art, Purchase of Leonard C. Hanna, Jr. Bequest. *Below,* Section of a handscroll (*Yūzū Nembutsu Engi*), Kamakura period, 14th century A.D. Cleveland Museum of Art, Purchase of Mr. and Mrs. William H. Marlatt Fund, John L. Severance Fund, and Edward L. Whittemore Fund.

Golden Pavilion and garden, Mu
machi period, 14th century A
Rokuon-ji, Kyoto.

PLATE 8

PLATE 9

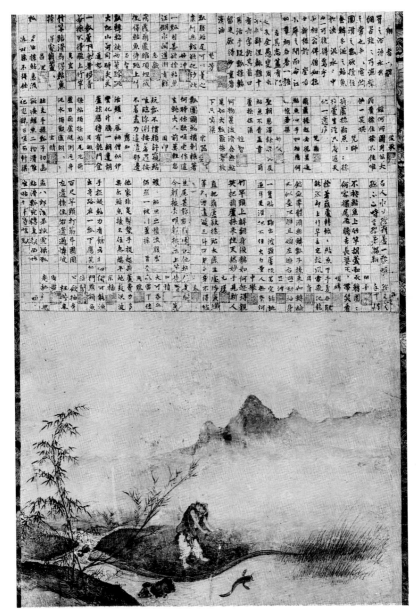

Catching a Catfish with a Gourd, by
Josetsu, Muromachi period, 15th
century A.D. Myōshinji Collection,
Kyoto.

PLATE 10

Right, Hawk screen by Kanō Eitoku, Momoyama period, 16th century A.D. Tokyo University of the Arts Collection. *Below,* Nō Mask of Beautiful Woman, Edo period, 17th century. Munsterberg Collection, New Paltz, N.Y.

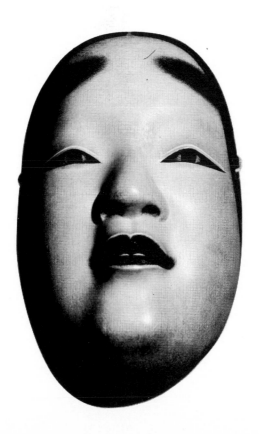

Left, Shino tea bowl, Momoyama period, 16th century A.D. Itsuō Museum, Osaka. *Right,* Karatsu tea bowl, Early Edo period, 17th century A.D. Private collection, Japan.

PLATE 11

PLATE 12

Matsue Castle, Edo period, 17th century A.D. Shimane Prefecture.

Above, Scene from the Tales of Ise, by Sōtatsu, Edo period, 17th century A.D. Bunting Collection, Shawnee Mission, Kansas, *Right,* Monkey Reaching for Reflection of Moon, by Hakuin, Edo period, 18th century A.D. Munsterberg Collection, New Paltz, N.Y., photograph by Raphael Warshaw.

Katsura Detached Palace, Edo period, 17th century A.D., Katsura, Kyoto.

PLATE 13

PLATE 14

Above, Lacquer writing box, by Kōrin, Edo period, 17th century A.D. Seattle Art Museum. *Below,* Wood-block print of Woman and Child, by Utamaro, Edo period, 18th century A.D. Morse Collection, New York.

Above, Imari ware bowl with Dutchmen, Edo period, 18th century A.D. Nakao Collection, Tokyo. *Right*, Imari ware porcelain bowl, Edo period, 18th century A.D. Private collection, Japan.

PLATE 15

PLATE 16

Ema votive horse painting, Edo period, 17th century A.D. Mr. and Mrs. James W. Alsdorf Collection, Winnetka, Ill.

The Heian Period

From the seventh to the ninth century Japanese art had been so strongly influenced by China that at times it was little more than a provincial reflection of the mainland. During the next three centuries, called the Heian or Later Heian period, a truly Japanese art was evolved. The reason for this was that T'ang China, which had been so culturally productive during the seventh and eighth centuries, had suffered a decline, and the persecutions of Buddhists and generally chaotic conditions in the late T'ang period had undermined the respect of the Japanese for Chinese civilization. By the end of the ninth century the Japanese had decided to send no more embassies to China. As a result the Japanese had to depend upon their own resources, and an art and literature evolved which were not only national in character but markedly different from that of China. Perhaps the most striking results of this change were the development of a native syllabary called *hiragana* and the emergence of an indigenous literature whose masterpiece is Lady Murasaki's *The Tale of Genji,* a novel in which the elegant court life of the Heian period is beautifully portrayed.

Painting was the dominant art form of the Heian period. A native Japanese style evolved which, fittingly enough, is called Yamato-e, or Japanese-style painting, in contrast to the Chinese style, Kara-e. Many of the characteristics which even today are considered typically Japanese are found in Yamato-e painting. The most prominent are the narrative emphasis and the decorative quality, which are also characteristic of Momoyama screen paintings and the woodblock prints of the Edo period. While the Chinese during these centuries were developing a Taoist inspired, monochrome ink painting, the Japanese were using vivid colors and producing narrative scrolls depicting Heian court life and stories about temples and shrines.

The most famous of the Yamato-e paintings is the Genji scroll, now, unfortunately, in fragments, most of which are in Tokugawa Museum in Nagoya. This scroll is one of those rare occasions where the work of a great writer is illustrated by an equally brilliant artist, and as a result the novel finds its visual equivalent in the pictures. The work is believed to be by an eleventh-century artist who was well acquainted with the life he portrays, so that he was able to give a vivid sense of that poetic beauty touched with melancholy which characterized the world of Genji and his ladies. The style is rather abstract and two-dimensional, with simple lines indicating the faces, and forms which are reduced to colorful, decorative patterns.

Another masterpiece of Heian period Yamato-e is the animal caricature scroll traditionally attributed to the Buddhist abbot Toba Sōjō. The most important parts of this scroll are in Kōzanji in Kyoto, but there are small sections in the United States. This delightful work, which pokes fun at the corruption and worldliness of the clergy, has justly been a favorite in both Japan and the West. Like Aesop, Toba Sōjō satirizes his contemporaries by presenting them in animal form, with a large frog representing the Buddha, monkeys dressed up as priests, and foxes and rabbits in the robes of pilgrims. In some scenes the animals are fighting; in others they are frolicking. In contrast to the Genji scroll, which is painted in bright colors, this work is done entirely in black and white, with vigorous and expressive brushwork. A delight in narrative is very much in evidence, and the result is a type of painting which is typically Japanese. Although these two are the most famous of the Heian narrative scrolls, several others survive either in the original or in copies, indicating that this school, which flourished in eleventh- and twelfth-century Japan, must have been rich and productive.

In Buddhist painting great changes occurred, and as a result this art was also freed from Chinese domination. Both the conventional Buddhist paintings of the Nara period and the more austere and fantastic icons of the early Heian lost their appeal, and a more sophisticated, poetic type became popular. Instead of the awe-inspiring and esoteric images of strange gods, the artists portrayed the joys of the Blessed in the realm of the Buddha Amida who welcomed the souls of the departed to his Western Paradise. Kannon, the Bodhisattva of Mercy and Compassion, and Fugen, the Bodhisattva of Wisdom and Virtue, were now depicted instead of the grotesque forms of Fudō and the other Wisdom Kings.

Perhaps the most beautiful Heian religious painting is the celebrated portrayal of the death of the Buddha Shākyamuni, in which the golden figure of the Great Teacher is shown stretched out on his death bed surrounded by his followers and sacred beings who are all lamenting his departure. In this, as in other Heian icons, delicate colors are used with the most graceful lines, resulting in a work of exquisite beauty. Although losing some of the depth of religious feeling which had marked the finest of Nara period Buddhist painting, and without the dramatic impact of the Shingon inspired Early Heian icons, the Buddhist paintings of this period are among the loveliest works of Japanese religious art, and perfectly mirror the spirit of the age.

Similar changes reflecting the different religious climate are apparent in the sculpture of the Heian period. In contrast to the bronze, lacquer, and clay images popular during Nara times, Heian period images are usually made of wood, a medium which was more suited to the softer, warmer effects which are characteristic of this sculpture. It was during this period that the technique of making carvings from several blocks of wood was first employed, a method which was to become very common during the subsequent Kamakura period. The invention of this process is usually attributed to Jōchō, who was the most celebrated sculptor of the period. His most famous work, which is generally regarded as one of the masterpieces of Japanese sculpture, is the large image of the Buddha Amida in the Phoenix Hall of the Byōdōin at Uji near Kyoto. A majestic work carved in wood and richly gilded, it is typical of the Heian period style in its elaborate detail, especially of the nimbus, and in the graceful figures of the flying angels, or apsarases, which surround the Buddha. The most characteristic sculpture of the period, however, is the carving in the Jōruri temple in Kyoto of Kichijōten, a Japanese version of the Hindu goddess Srīmaha Devi. This elaborate statue, painted in bright colors and carved with a wealth of intricate detail, shows the deity as an elegant Heian court lady, emphasizing her beauty and elegance rather than her more spiritual qualities. However, there are Heian period sculptures of Buddhas and Bodhisattvas which express a truly religious feeling, using the wood to convey spiritual rather than worldly beauty.

There can be no question that these centuries were a period of great architecture. Literary records speak of the impressive temples which were built, and of splendid palaces erected for the emperors and the nobility. Unfortunately very little of this has survived. The war between the Taira and the Minamoto destroyed many of these buildings, and others fell to fire or simple decay, since they were built almost wholly of wood. The most typical extant structure is the Hōōdō, or Phoenix Hall, in Uji, which was originally a palace of the Fujiwara family, and then a temple dedicated to Amida. Its name is derived from the fact that the ground plan resembles a phoenix with outstretched wings, and there are golden phoenixes on the roof. Although relatively small, it is outstanding for its graceful execution.

Many of these Heian buildings were richly decorated with lacquer and gold leaf, to which mother-of-pearl inlay and metal ornaments were often added, resulting in buildings of great splendor and refinement.

The architectural development which was to have the most lasting effect occurred not so much in the temple as in the house, for it was during this period that the typically Japanese dwelling evolved. In the mansions of the nobility the type of building which we think of as characteristically Japanese first appears. Known as *shoin* style architecture, these structures had raised wooden floors, removable walls, light construction, and bark roofs, features which are still found in Japanese houses today.

In the decorative arts the break with China and the prevalence of a more Japanese taste also made itself felt. Pottery, which for the most part had been dependent upon the Chinese, whose ceramics were so much more technically advanced, fell into a marked decline, but there was a flourishing of lacquer and textiles, two crafts in which the Japanese had always excelled. In fact, if there is one field of art in which even the Chinese have always been willing to acknowledge the supremacy of the Japanese, it is in the production of fine lacquers, and it was during the Heian and Momoyama periods that the finest of these were made. Heian lacquers are outstanding for both their technical excellence and their beauty of design. Gold and silver, usually applied in a fine powder, inlay of mother-of-pearl, and painted designs were all common, often used together with exquisite results. While a number of excellent lacquers survive, nothing is left of the splendid twelve-layer kimonos described so vividly in *The Tale of Genji*. The effect of these many garments, one worn over the other, each a different color and woven from the finest silk, must have been very lovely. Certainly in these fields the break with China not only helped the native industries but also resulted in works of great beauty and originality.

The Kamakura Period

In contrast to the courtly elegance of the Heian the Kamakura period, which lasted from 1185 to 1333, was a military period of great vigor. It is named after the new site of the capital, which was moved from Kyoto to the eastern seashore at Kamakura, not far from the present-day Tokyo, because, tradition says, the military rulers did not want the samurai to be corrupted by the effeminate court life of Kyoto. Reflecting this new outlook, Kamakura art was far more vigorous and realistic, with a consequent loss of some of the sophistication which had marked so much of the art of the Heian period. Both the subjects treated and the style reflect the spirit of the new age.

Among the arts sculpture was especially prominent. The Kamakura age was the last great period in the history of Japanese sculpture, for after the thirteenth century this art form suffered a decline from which it never recovered. Wood was the favorite medium of the Kamakura sculptors, who often made huge images by joining several blocks. The qualities which distinguish these statues are their expressive power and their realism, which is especially striking in the portraits. Typical of the Kamakura style are the two huge guardian figures which were made for Tōdaiji in Nara when this temple was rebuilt after having been destroyed during the civil war which ravished Japan at the end of the Heian period. These statues are the work of the two most famous sculptors of the day, Unkei and Kakei, who presided over a workshop employing a large number of carvers who often collaborated with them on their sculptures. The Tōdaiji guardian figures are very impressive, with muscular bodies, powerful limbs, and dramatic facial expressions. Even more famous is the great Buddha of Kamakura, a huge bronze image made in imitation of the Daibutsu at Tōdaiji, indicating the great influence which the sculpture of the Nara period had on that of the Kamakura. Although remarkable for its size, it is less good artistically than many of the smaller wooden sculptures which were produced during this period. Among these the most exceptional are the portraits of legendary holy men and famous contemporary abbots. In the first category are the statues of the Indian patriarchs Asanga and Vasubandhu, which are striking for both their realism and their deep spiritual feeling. In the second category, the finest is the lifelike work representing the priest Chōgen, who had been responsible for the reconstruction of Tōdaiji, and whose portrait showing him as a saintly old man with a wrinkled face is still preserved in the temple in which he was active. Here again, the marked parallels between this work and the Nara period portrait of Ganjin shows the close relationship between these two periods of Japanese art.

Among the paintings of the Kamakura period the most interesting are the Yamato-e scrolls which continue the Heian tradition but show definite changes in both the subject matter and the style. In-stead of the amorous adventures of Prince Genji, the artists portray the military exploits of great warriors, as in the well-known *Heiji Monogatari* which shows an uprising in Kyoto, or another scroll depicting the Japanese defeat of the Mongol invaders. One of the rolls of the *Heiji Monogatari* is now in the collection of the Boston Museum of Fine Arts, the only major Yamato-e scroll which has been permitted to leave Japan. It shows the characteristic style of the period, with its wealth of narrative detail and its vivid realism in the portrayal of the burning palace, the warriors on horseback, and the running figures.

Other narrative scrolls deal with the lives of famous Buddhist teachers, such as Hōnen, who is shown wandering through the coun-tryside, preaching to great multitudes who have gathered to hear him. In these pictures there is a renewed influence of Chinese paint-ing, especially in the treatment of atmosphere and space, although scenes such as the view of Fuji show that these events are taking place in Japan. The strangest of the Buddhist scrolls represent the hungry ghosts who must roam about eternally starving as a punish-ment for their wicked lives. Even more gruesome are the so-called hell-fire scrolls in which the torments of the damned are depicted in vivid and graphic detail.

Of the conventional Buddhist paintings the most interesting are the *yamagoshi raigō* scrolls in which the Buddha Amida is shown appear-ing over mountains. They usually have the golden figure of the Bud-dha flanked by two Bodhisattvas against a typically Japanese land-scape. It was said that if a dying person took hold of the silk cord hanging from the hands of Amida, he would at once enter the West-ern Paradise. Painted in bright colors with flat, decorative forms, these works are often very beautiful as art while at the same time giv-ing moving expression to the teaching of the salvation sects which flourished during the Kamakura period. Other religious pictures re-flect the Dual Shintō belief which grew up at this time and taught that the Shintō gods were really manifestations of the Buddhas.

Landscape and portrait paintings were also popular during the Kamakura period. Unfortunately, almost none of the landscapes has survived, but masterpieces like the scroll depicting the Nachi water-fall indicate that Japanese scenery was now represented in a quite realistic manner. Portraits have fared better, for numerous likenesses of both secular and religious leaders have been preserved. The most famous is the likeness of Minamoto Yoritomo, the founder of the Kamakura regime, whose portrait gives a lively sense of his appearance and personality.

Compared to the wealth of churches and castles which survived from thirteenth-century Europe, only a remnant of Kamakura period architecture has come down to us. Of all the many structures erected in Kamakura itself, among them some of the great Zen temples of Japan, the only one still standing is the relic hall (*shariden*), of Engakuji, and even this building is now roofed with thatch instead of tiles. Its style owes much to the architecture of Sung China, especially in the design of the windows and doors, an influence which reflects the renewed contact with the mainland. In fact, much of Kamakura architecture was greatly influenced by that of China, particularly in the Zen temples, for the monks were in close contact with their Chinese teachers. However, other structures were built in a more traditional style, going back to older Japanese models, such as the great Nara period temples. Among the new kinds of buildings, the most interesting is the *tahōtō,* a pagoda which is based on the traditional stupa of ancient India. It is associated with Shingon Buddhism, indicating the close relationship which existed between the esoteric sects and the homeland of Buddhism. The oldest surviving example of this type of building is the Ishiyamadera at Otsu near Lake Biwa. Generally speaking, the architecture of the Kamakura period offers a great variety of styles, some of them reflecting foreign importations and others continuing the older native traditions.

In keeping with the more practical spirit of the age, the decorative arts were less important than they had been during the Heian period. Indeed, the samurai were far more interested in fine swords and sturdy armor than in the beauty of the utensils used in the mansions and palaces. However, there was at least one medium which made great advances, and that was pottery. The reason was undoubtedly the renewed contact with China which during the Sung period had experienced its greatest age of ceramics, excelling both in porcelain and stoneware. The Japanese craftsmen, always anxious to imitate what they admired in foreign countries, at once tried to equal the Chinese wares, especially the lovely green celadons and the dark brown pottery which they called Temmoku ware. The center of this new ceramic industry was the city of Seto, which is not far from modern Nagoya and still plays an important role in the production of Japanese ceramics. According to tradition it was Katō Shirōzaemon, better known as Tōshirō, who was responsible for this development, although modern scholars tend to doubt this. Be that as it may, there is no question that the thirteenth century saw the emergence of a vigorous ceramic industry with Japanese potters producing stoneware with green, yellow, and brown glazes which were sometimes incised with delicate designs. Although these jars and bottles were still rather crude and certainly no match for the sophisticated productions of the Korean and Chinese potters, they mark the beginning of the great ceramic tradition of Japan which later was to produce such outstanding wares.

The Muromachi Period

By the end of the thirteenth century the power of the military rulers at Kamakura had begun to decline. In 1333 the capital was moved back to Kyoto, and the Ashikaga family came to power. This period, which lasted some two hundred and fifty years, is usually called the Muromachi period after the section of Kyoto in which the Ashikagas had their palace. Although a period of strife with frequent civil wars, it was also an age of cultural florescence, for the Ashikaga rulers were great patrons of the arts. Since relations with China, which had suffered during the Mongol rule, once again became very close, this was also a period when Japan was subject to strong cultural influences from the mainland. Chinese artistic ideals in general and the Buddhist sect called Ch'an in China and Zen in Japan completely transformed Japanese civilization. Many things which today are considered typically Japanese, such as ink painting, stone gardens, the tea ceremony, and flower arrangement, not to mention the cult of the subdued, are actually Chinese importations which were introduced into Japan during the Muromachi period. Most of them have ceased to be important in the country of their origin, but they continue to play a vital role in Japan, where Japanese and foreigner alike consider them part of the native artistic heritage.

The single greatest cultural influence during the Muromachi period was Zen Buddhism. The great Zen monasteries became the centers of cultural activity, and many of the greatest artists were Zen monks. They looked to China for inspiration, and several of the most famous, such as Sesshū, actually went to China to study the work of the great Sung painters and Ch'an Buddhism. Other Zen monks were sent to China by the shoguns for the express purpose of collecting and buying Chinese paintings, especially those by the Ch'an painters of the late Sung period, with the result that today this school is far better represented in Japan than in China where, under the influence of the Confucian literati, it had fallen out of favor.

So close was the relationship between Chinese and Japanese Zen-inspired ink painting that it is often almost impossible to tell if a given work is done by a Chinese painter or a Japanese working in the Chinese style. Interestingly enough, the Japanese did not copy the Ming painters of the fourteenth and fifteenth centuries, but the earlier Sung artists whose work corresponded more to their own artistic and religious ideals. To them the misty mountain landscapes of artists like Hsia Kuei and Ma Yuan, and the inspired Zen paintings of Mu Ch'i and Liang K'ai, represented the very essence of what they themselves were trying to express, and, although they never reached the level of their Chinese masters, the best of Muromachi ink painting is very outstanding.

The early Japanese ink painters imitated their Chinese models very closely, but as time went on and the artists were able to absorb the foreign influence, they evolved a style of painting which, although based on Sung work, exhibited features which were distinctly Japanese. This was particularly true of the Zen monk Sesshū, active during the second half of the fifteenth century, whom many critics consider the greatest of all Japanese painters. Although his subjects, consisting largely of landscapes and Zen scenes, are usually borrowed from Chinese sources, his emphasis on heavy black lines, his sharp contrasts between light and dark, and his flattening out of space are very different from anything in Chinese painting, while in his bird and flower screens, the decorative tendency of Japanese art is clearly evident. Here again one sees the typical tendency of the Japanese to take only what serves their purposes, and then transform it according to their own taste.

Numerous other ink painters were also active, many of them Zen monks who decorated monasteries and produced all kinds of scrolls, album leaves, and screens in the sumi-e, or ink painting. But although Sesshū had a great influence on all later Japanese painting and even had a school named after him (it is called the Unkoku after the temple in which his studio was located), the Muromachi period artists who were most influential were those of the Kanō school, which was founded by Kanō Masanobu and his son Kanō Motonobu during the later part of the Ashikaga period. Unlike Sesshū and his school, the

Kanō school painters were professional artists rather than monks. Their painting tended to be very eclectic, using a great number of styles taken from both the Chinese and the Japanese traditions. It has often been said that it was the Kanō school artists who adapted Chinese painting to Japanese ideals, and introduced more decorative and realistic tendencies into Japanese painting. This latter trend may also have been due in part to the influence of the painting of Ming China, which now became popular in Japan.

Since the prestige of Chinese painting was so great, it was only natural that Japanese style work like Yamato-e scroll painting should have declined in importance. The school which, at least to a certain extent, kept the more indigenous tendencies alive was the Tosa school, which enjoyed the patronage of the Kyoto court and continued to produce colorful narrative scrolls depicting stories about famous shrines and temples and episodes from Japanese history. Traditional Buddhist painting also declined, although Shingon mandalas, Amida *raigō* pictures, and Dual Shintō scrolls continued to be made. However, by the end of the Muromachi period all Buddhist art had declined since Buddhism itself had lost much of its appeal.

Sculpture, which had played so prominent a role during the Kamakura period, ceased to be important since Zen temples did not use religious images. The only type of Buddhist sculpture which continued to be popular was portraits of famous Zen priests, and these works were often very telling in their realism. Masks, which had been made in Nara and Heian times for the *Gagaku* and *Bugaku* dance performers, were now produced in large quantities for the Nō actors. There were many different kinds of masks, each representing a specific type, such as a beautiful woman, a priest, a mad person, a demon, or a ghost, so that the actor who put on his mask assumed the face of the role he was playing. The carving is usually of a high order, and the expressions of the masks, which change in different lights, are often very alive. Once the types were established, the various masks became part of the repertoire of Nō drama, and they are still being used in performances given today.

The Muromachi period was rich in architecture, for it was at this time that many of the great Zen temples of Kyoto, such as Daitokuji, Tōfukuji, and Nanzenji, were established. Unfortunately, very few of the original buildings have survived, since the civil strife in late Ashikaga times was very destructive. However, from the evidence of existing buildings and the views of temples in paintings, it would appear that in this area, as in so many others, the Chinese influence was very strong.

Of the buildings of this period, the most famous are the Golden Pavilion, or Kinkakuji,[1] built as a pleasure palace by the Ashikaga shogun Yoshimitsu but later turned into a Buddhist temple, and the Silver Pavilion, or Ginkakuji, built by his grandson Yoshimasa as a country villa. Both are structures of great elegance, reflecting the aestheticism of the day. It was here that the shoguns surrounded themselves with their courtiers, literary men, artists, Zen monks, and tea masters, and gave themselves over to a life of aesthetic enjoyment. These pavilions, which are light and simple in their construction, with a feeling of openness, are among the loveliest of all Japanese buildings. Beautifully adapted to their surroundings, they are set in gardens with artificial lakes, rock islands, and picturesque pines which form an integral part of the architectural design.

While the gardens of the villas were designed for the enjoyment of the aristocracy, the gardens of the Zen monasteries were religious in character. Among the most outstanding is the one at the Daisenin, part of the Daitokuji monastery, though the best known is the world-famous rock garden at Ryōanji in the northern district of Kyoto. Both are what the Japanese call dry gardens, that is, gardens constructed without the use of water, in which white sand carefully raked to simulate waves represents the sea, while the rocks stand for islands emerging out of the water. The dry gardens have none of the elements which Westerners think of as essential to a garden— no flowers, no grass, only sand, rocks, moss, and perhaps some trimmed bushes or trees. Although many of these gardens may seem quite natural, they are actually very conscious works of art in which the various elements, such as rocks or trees, are used by the garden architect to create his formal design. The authors of these gardens were often famous painters or Zen priests who saw them as works of art resembling an ink painting, with the sand being the white paper, and the rocks the black ink. What they actually represent is a miniature landscape, often a small-scale replica of a famous scene, or an imaginary landscape in which the essence of Zen Buddhism is expressed by means of a few simple forms.

Closely connected with Zen Buddhism was the tea ceremony, or chanoyu, which became popular during this period. The tea houses,

1. The original Kinkakuji was destroyed by fire several years ago, but an exact duplicate has been erected.

small buildings in which the tea ceremony was performed (an example is the Tōgudō on the grounds of the Jishōji where the Silver Pavilion is located), had a profound influence on all later architecture as well as on Japanese taste in general. The decorative arts were also very much influenced by chanoyu, for the tea masters were both patrons of art and arbiters of taste. Employing many of the best potters, bamboo workers, and iron casters, their preferences helped form the kind of aesthetic sensibility which prevailed. At first Chinese objects were much in demand, and teacups and tea caddies were imported from the mainland. Later, as the Wabi school of chanoyu became popular and a more rustic taste prevailed, Korean rice bowls of the Yi dynasty became fashionable, as well as indigenous local wares such as those from Bizen, Iga, Tamba, and Shigaraki. All of these ceramics are the very antithesis of porcelains like the celadons. They represent a folk art tradition, for they were originally made by local potters for the people of their own districts but now, discovered by the tea masters, they were used in performing the tea ceremony. Other objects which were important in chanoyu were cast-iron pots, bamboo spoons, and tea whisks; and lacquer boxes of various kinds. All this resulted in a revival of Japanese crafts which, both in the Muromachi and in later periods found their greatest patrons in the tea masters.

The Momoyama Period

The Momoyama period, named after a hill near Kyoto which was the site of Hideyoshi's great palace, was a brief but artistically very productive period. Lasting for little more than a generation, from 1573 to 1615, it had a decisive influence on many aspects of Japanese culture. It has often been said that with this period the modern age in Japan begins. In fact, the division between Momoyama and early Edo is based largely on the difference in ruling families, for, culturally speaking, the entire seventeenth century is a unified whole. Several important factors contributed to the great changes which occurred. First, after a long and bloody war, Japan was united by military dictators; second, the country was engaged in active intercourse with the outside world, especially the Portuguese and Spaniards who sent priests and merchants to Japan; and third, and perhaps most important, it was during this period that the big cities and the merchant class began to play an important role, a development which was to have far-reaching effects not only on society but also on the arts.

The Momoyama period is probably best reflected in its architecture, for the great castles and palaces which men like Hideyoshi built sum up the aspirations of the age. Palaces such as the one on Momoyama and castles like that in Osaka were structures of a size and grandeur which had never been equaled even by the great Buddhist temples of earlier times. They reflected the power and wealth of the military rulers who had united the country by subduing the local lords, and who controlled human and economic resources far in excess of those available to any previous rulers. They were able to hire vast armies of laborers (it is estimated that 30,000 workers were employed daily in the construction of Osaka castle alone) and to spend lavish sums on decoration. The most immediate purpose of such buildings was to serve as military strong points from which the positions they controlled could be defended in case of attack, but they were also symbols of power used to impress subordinates. This was no doubt particularly true of Hideyoshi, the greatest of these military men, who had risen from the humblest of origins.

Unfortunately, very little of all this grandeur is left. Osaka castle was destroyed first in 1615 when the Tokugawa forces defeated the followers of Hideyoshi's son, and again in 1868 at the time of the Meiji restoration. The great Fushimi palace on Momoyama was dismantled shortly after it was built, and parts of it are now incorporated in the Nishi Honganji in Kyoto. At least two outstanding examples of Momoyama architecture are still extant, namely, the Himeji castle in Hyogo Prefecture west of Osaka and the Nijō Palace in Kyoto. The former was built by Hideyoshi as a strong point for western Japan, and was enlarged during the seventeenth century by Ieyasu. It consists of a series of walls and moats copied from European fortifications and crowned by a huge six-story tower, or keep, which serves as the core of the castle. Although the tower itself is built largely of white plaster and wood, stone was used extensively in the walls and the foundations, and tile in multiple roofs. The result is a structure of very impressive appearance and its height, previously unequalled, completely dominates the landscape.

The Nijō palace, which is only a part of what was originally a much bigger building complex, is equally impressive, although in a somewhat different way. Built in the early years of the seventeenth century as a residence for Ieyasu during his stays in Kyoto, it was constructed on a grand scale and decorated by the finest artists of the period. Although modest when compared with the palace of Louis XIV at Versailles, which was built about the same time, it is large by Japanese standards, with splendid gates, spacious rooms, a big audience hall, and extensive gardens. Although it is built in the simple, rather severe style which is traditional for Japan, the intricately carved woodwork, the beautiful metal ornaments, and, above all, the gorgeous screen paintings give it a magnificence which expresses not only the wealth but also the excellent artistic taste of the rulers.

Celebrated painters were employed to decorate these buildings. Among the most famous was Kanō Eitoku who was responsible for decorating the great castle in Osaka as well as Nobunaga's castle at Azuchi and Hideyoshi's Jūrakudai palace. Some of the masterpieces of Japanese art are the screen paintings executed at this time. Large-scale works with bright colors and rich gold leaf applied in a flat, decorative manner, these screens were gorgeous in effect, and brightened the otherwise rather dark interiors. Although grander in scale than any previous Japanese painting, a fact which some critics have thought due to the influence of European painting, the screens are very much in keeping with Heian period Yamato-e in which there had been a similar emphasis on decorative pattern, bright colors, and gold and silver leaf.

Although bold, colorful painting was the pictorial style most characteristic of the Momoyama period, many other types were also produced. Ink painting, the dominant form of the Muromachi period, continued to be popular, although the style was somewhat different, marked by the larger scale and the broader brushwork typical of the period. The most notable artist working in this manner was Hasegawa Tōhaku, who regarded himself as a follower of Sesshū and was also very much influenced by the great thirteenth-century Chinese painter Mu Ch'i. Among his masterpieces is a pair of screens portraying pines in mist, now in the collection of the National Museum in Tokyo. This work is similar to Sung painting, especially in its feeling for ink tones and atmospheric effects, but the emphasis on the decorative and the flattening out of space show that Tōhaku was not only a man of his time but also a typically Japanese painter.

Another type of work which enjoyed considerable popularity was genre painting. Most interesting perhaps were the pictures showing the life of Europeans, a type of work known as Namban, meaning painting which portrayed the Southern Barbarians, as the Portuguese and Spaniards were called. From a Japanese point of view, these were exotic scenes showing the strange fashions and grotesque appearance of the foreigners, who are always of towering height, with very big noses. Some paintings show the foreigners arriving in their ships or worshiping in their churches; others portray scenes from Europe painted in a Western style with linear perspective and shading.

Of the decorative arts the two which best express the period are textiles and lacquers. The Japanese have always excelled in these media, even surpassing their Chinese masters in the wealth and variety of their output, and it is no exaggeration to say that the Momoyama textiles and lacquers were the finest ever made in Japan or, for that matter, any place in the world. While earlier kimonos had consisted of layers of robes, each a different color, the garments of the Momoyama period, although simple in cut, were far more elaborate in their techniques. Weaving, dyeing, and embroidery were used either singly or in combination to produce bold colorful patterns of great originality and beauty.

Among the lacquers the most magnificent are the ones sprinkled with gold powder, a technique known as *maki-e*. The finest of these lacquers are called Kōdaiji ware after the temple in Kyoto built in memory of Hideyoshi, the interior of which was gorgeously decorated with gold lacquer. Vessels and utensils of all types were made in this manner. The designs, which were usually rather simple, flowers or autumn grasses, for instance, were treated in a very abstract manner which, combined with the lavish use of gold, resulted in works that are at once opulent and refined.

Ostentatious as the Momoyama period was in some ways, in others it was the very reverse and its more restrained side found its perfect expression in the tea ceremony, or chanoyu, which played an important role in the culture of the time. Hideyoshi, who reveled in displaying his wealth and power, often in the rather obvious manner of a parvenu, not only was a great admirer of the tea master Sen no Rikyū but also practiced this art himself. The dichotomy which Ruth Benedict pointed out in *The Chrysanthemum and the Sword* is already apparent in Hideyoshi, for the bloodiest of the Japanese warlords, whose invasion of Korea is still remembered by the Koreans for its cruelty, was also a sensitive and discriminating *chajin,* or devotee of the tea ceremony. It is as if these two sides of the Japanese character must find expression simultaneously, for many a modern Japanese business tycoon, having made a fortune in the most ruthless manner, then turns around and spends his money building up a collection of beautiful works of art to which he reacts with real sensitivity. Perhaps one side compensates for the other: in any case, for the samurai involved in the ceaseless struggle of this warlike age, to leave worldly considerations behind, depositing his sword at the entrance of the tea house and humbling himself by crawling through the low opening, must have been as welcome a relief as the calm, spiritual atmosphere prevailing during chanoyu.

The artistic taste associated with the tea ceremony, often called the tea taste, can best be described by the Japanese terms *wabi* and *shibui,* meaning the cult of quietness and solitude, the plain and the rustic, the subdued and the unostentatious. The tea house itself was built in the style of a peasant hut with an interior of extreme simplicity. The only ornaments were a scroll hanging in the wall niche, or tokonoma (perhaps a Zen saying or a landscape), and a simple flower arrangement or an old bronze vessel. Otherwise the small tatami room contained nothing but the brazier to heat the water for the tea. However, the untensils for preparing the tea and the bowl from which it was drunk were of great beauty and often extremely valuable. In fact, it was during this period that the finest Japanese ceramics were made, many of them for the tea ceremony. The famous were named after the celebrated tea masters who are said to have designed them. The best known are Shino ware, which has bold designs on a thick, creamy white or gray glaze; Oribe, which uses a dark-green glaze usually covering only part of the vessel; Karatsu, made in imitation of the Korean ware of the Yi dynasty, which was outstanding for its painted designs; and, above all, Raku, a low-fired black or dark-brown ware. Perhaps most typical of all Japanese ceramics is Bizen ware which has no glaze at all, but for its beauty depends entirely upon the reddish clay and the effect of the firing. In this ware, the spirit of *wabi* finds its purest expression.

The Edo Period

The last of the great epochs in the history of traditional Japanese art was the Edo, or Tokugawa, which lasted from 1615 to 1867. It is usually referred to as the Edo period because the Tokugawa shoguns, after consolidating their power, moved the capital to Edo, the present-day Tokyo. The city, which up to this time had been a small country town with a provincial castle, now replaced Kyoto as the administrative and, to a certain extent, the cultural center of the country, and by the end of the eighteenth century it had over a million inhabitants, making it the largest city in the world. While the art of previous periods had on the whole been aristocratic in character, valued primarily by the nobility and the Buddhist clergy, now the commoners became involved, mostly the well-to-do merchants of the cities and to a lesser extent the artisans and even the peasants.

The early phase of Edo art corresponded roughly to the seventeenth century. In many ways it continued the artistic trends of the Momoyama, but while the art of this period had been bold and gorgeous, that of the Edo was more restricted and academic, reflecting the atmosphere of the Tokugawa regime which was politically repressive since the new rulers, having united the country, did not tolerate anything which might disturb their administration.

The greatest change of these years was that the broad contacts with the outside world which had proved so stimulating during the Momoyama period were now broken off, Christianity being first forbidden and then rigorously stamped out. The intercourse with foreign countries was limited to Holland and China, and even these relationships were sharply curtailed, foreigners being allowed only in the port of Nagasaki on Kyushu. However, in spite of these strict controls, European and Chinese culture became increasingly influential among Japanese intellectuals. As far as art was concerned, this isolation had the effect of turning Japan inward, and as a result, the Edo period is one of the most completely Japanese eras in the history of the country.

Although the Edo period, which lasted some two and a half centuries, was not particularly long for a period in Japanese art history, it is of major importance in the study of Japanese art, for so much material has survived that most of the Japanese art in Western museums comes from this epoch. Since the country was at peace and fairly prosperous, the actual output was no doubt larger than that of the other major periods, and because it is closer to us in time, more Edo art has come down to us than remains from all the other periods combined.

Of the great architectural monuments, the most impressive, although not necessarily the most attractive, is the mausoleum which Iemitsu built in memory of his grandfather Ieyasu, who had established the Tokugawa dynasty. Located at Nikko north of Tokyo, it was erected as a temple dedicated to the spirit of Ieyasu, who upon his death had been given the title of Tōshō Daigongen, or the Great Manifestation of the Buddha Resplendent in the Eastern Region. This complex of buildings is the most ostentatious ever built in Japan. There is a Japanese saying, "Never say *kekkō* (magnificent) until you have seen Nikko," which indicates what the Japanese think of the shrine. To modern taste, it is too gaudy and ornate, but there can be no doubt that it succeeds in what it set out to do. The Yōmeimon, or Gate of Sunlight, is regarded as one of the master-pieces of Japanese architecture. It is a twelve-columned, two-storied structure with gables at the ends and sides decorated with the most elaborate carvings. Intricate to a high degree, these ornaments repre-sent various animals, such as lions, tigers, dragons, and birds, as well as Chinese sages and children at play. The carvings are gilded or brightly colored, which increases the garish effect. Although not all the buildings at Nikko are equally elaborate, the total effect of the shrine mirrors the cult of military power and material splendor which was characteristic of the Edo period.

The other side of the national character, the cult of the simple and the subdued or, to use the Japanese term, the *shibui,* is best illustrated by the other celebrated example of mid-seventeenth-century architecture, namely, the Katsura Detached Palace located not far from Kyoto and interestingly enough built during the very same years as the shrine at Nikko. The taste which rejects the Tokugawa mausoleum as too gaudy has praised Katsura as the finest domestic building in Japan and one of the great masterpieces of world archi-tecture. Men like Frank Lloyd Wright, Le Corbusier, and Walter Gropius have made the pilgrimage to Katsura and found that it em-bodied the very principles which they themselves were striving for. Honesty, simplicity, economy, functionalism, and beauty of design and material are all combined with a sensitive feeling for the land-scape setting. Built of wood, with nothing but sliding screens, or shōji, dividing the inner space from the outer, it has the free-flowing space which modern architects have found so desirable. There is no emphasis on ornamental decoration. The forms are of the utmost simplicity, the design purely geometric, and the materials left in their natural state with the texture and color of the wood, the cypress work forming the roof, the translucent rice paper of the shōji, and the rush matting of the tatami used for their own beauty. Not only is the building itself a masterpiece, but the garden with the exquisite tea house, artificial pond, picturesque pines, old stone lanterns, and moss is an essential part of the whole.

In painting, the Edo period was one of the richest and most diversified in the history of Japanese art. Many different schools flourished simultaneously, appealing to different segments of Japanese society. Not only was the output very large, but a good part of it has survived, so that probably nine tenths of the traditional painting still extant comes from the Edo period. All types of work were produced, the most common, perhaps, the hanging scrolls, or *kakemono;* but horizontal scrolls (or *makimono*), album leaves, fan painting, and wall and screen painting all had their practitioners, with many artists working in several or sometimes all of these forms. The schools themselves were often family enterprises, like the Kanō school, which traced its origin back to Kanō Motonobu and continued down to the modern period. Others, such as the literati school of painting, called *bunjinga,* appealed to a certain class of society, or followed in the footsteps of a great master, such as Sesshū.

In the eyes of contemporary critics, the most outstanding and creative school, and certainly the one which reflects the most truly Japanese sensibility, was the Sōtatsu-Kōrin school, which was named after its two greatest practitioners, the seventeenth-century Sōtatsu and his eighteenth-century follower Kōrin. Both worked in the conventions of the Heian period Yamato-e and Momoyama screen painting, using colorful patterns and decorative forms, and depicting landscapes or themes taken from Japanese literature. In contrast to Momoyama painting, their work is usually less bold in feeling and not on so large a scale, though it is subtler and more elegant, in keeping with the changed cultural climate.

Of the traditional schools of painting, the two most important were the Kanō and Tosa schools, both of which continued to enjoy official patronage, the former working for the Tokugawa shogunate in Edo, and the latter being court painters of the emperor in Kyoto. The Kanō school was much more important, with a number of its artists, such as Kanō Tanyū and his brother Kanō Naonobu, among the great painters of the Edo period. Their style was usually rather eclectic, for they worked in a variety of manners derived from Chinese and Japanese sources, but their specialty was a somewhat modified Chinese-style ink painting ultimately derived from Sung painting but Japanized to a certain extent and also showing the influence of the realistic trend of Chinese painting characteristic of the Ming period. Other works executed by members of the Kanō school were in the more colorful, decorative style derived from Momoyama screen painting. The Tosa school suffered a great decline, and played a very minor role during most of the Edo period, since the Kyoto court had fallen on evil days and had no significant patronage to offer. In fact, the Tosa school painters even went so far as to adapt a more realistic Chinese style in order to gain more success. However, at the very end of the Edo period, when there was strong agitation for a restoration of imperial power, there was a revival of Tosa school painting based on Heian period Yamato-e, with its rich use of gold leaf, its colorful patterns, and its subjects taken from classical literature.

The school which appealed to the rich merchants of Osaka was the Ōkyō school, named after the eighteenth-century master Maruyama Ōkyō. His style combined the decorative tendencies of Japanese painting with a detailed realism derived from Chinese sources and, to a certain extent, from Dutch engravings which entered Japan through the port of Nagasaki. He specialized in elaborate decorative screens executed with a careful attention to detail. The lifelike realism for which he and his followers are noted is particularly evident in his sketchbooks with their studies from nature.

The aim of the gentlemen painters of the *bunjinga* school was quite different, for they appealed to the cultured literati, the Confucian scholar class who looked to the eccentric school of Ch'ing period China for inspiration. Using a Chinese style and Chinese literary subject matter, they portrayed not the world around them but a world of their own imagination derived from Chinese art and literature. Their style was abstract, with emphasis on line and brushwork and only sparing use of color. The best artists of this school, such as the eighteenth-century master Ike no Taiga and the early nineteenth-century painter Gyokudō, are among the most powerful and interesting painters of the period and represent the Chinese tradition in Japanese painting at its best.

Perhaps most indicative of the social changes which were occurring was the rise of a school of genre painting representing the life of the commoners and above all the Yoshiwara, the amusement district of Edo. While traditionally Japanese painting had largely been produced for the aristocracy and the temples, this type, often executed by anonymous artisans, was made for the growing urban middle class and portrayed their own life rather than scenes from Japanese history or Chinese literature. Particularly outstanding were the artists who painted the stately courtesans of the Yoshiwara district, but all aspects of contemporary life were portrayed in the rich and varied output of this school.

Finally there were the painters reflecting foreign life and foreign influences. Although contact with the outside world was practically forbidden, Europeans continued to fascinate the Japanese, and the small number of Dutch engravings and illustrated books which filtered in managed to keep the interest alive. There were painters and especially print makers who continued to produce work representing the foreigners in their native dress as they could be seen on the island of Deshima in the harbor of Nagasaki; and during the later Edo period there were artists who quite consciously imitated Western-style perspective and shading in their own work.

Although ukiyo-e originated as a type of genre painting, it is best known today as a school of wood-block printing which has enjoyed more popularity in the West than any other form of Japanese art. The Japanese themselves have always looked upon it as a rather insignificant and vulgar art, since it dealt with what is called the Floating World of Pleasure in contrast to the world of Buddhist thought or Confucian learning, but in recent years even Japanese critics have reevaluated the contributions of this school and today they admire the great masters of the color print for their very real artistic achievement.

In the West this has been true for almost a hundred years, ever since the first prints reached Europe during the middle of the nineteenth century and were hailed as outstanding works of art which were admired by artist and critic alike. Men such as Degas, Manet, Monet, and Whistler among the impressionists, and Toulouse-Lautrec, Van Gogh, and Gauguin among the postimpressionists were lovers and collectors of Japanese prints, which influenced them in their own work. The appeal which ukiyo-e had for them was two-fold. On one hand they admired the linear quality and the beautiful feeling for design; and on the other hand they found in the scenes themselves a world of esthetic delight and exotic charm which enchanted them. As a result a vogue for all things Japanese swept Europe and America, and Japanese prints were eagerly sought after, so that today the finest collections of these works are in the West.

The artist primarily responsible for turning the creative energy of the ukiyo-e school toward wood-block prints was the late seventeenth-century master Moronobu, who was the first to realize that by using the print instead of the painted scroll, the public for this kind of art could be greatly increased since the cost of the individual work would be lower. It was he who produced picture books which served as guides to Yoshiwara, showing the gay life and the beautiful women which the amusement district provided. Although Moronobu worked only in black and white, color was soon added, first by painting it in, and later by using several blocks, one for each color. The whole process of producing ukiyo-e prints was a complex one involving the collaboration of four different persons—the publisher who commissioned and financed the enterprise, the artist who designed the prints, and the engraver and the printer who were responsible for transcribing the artist's drawing into the wood-block form. Neither the printer nor the engraver were artists, but skilled artisans who were experts in their craft. The subjects were usually chosen by the publisher and consisted of themes like the beauties of the Yoshiwara district, hours in the day of the courtesans of the Green Houses, highlights of the Kabuki theater, or in later times, when landscapes became more popular, views of Edo or Mount Fuji. Since the artist had very little to do with producing the finished work, popular sets of prints could be duplicated indefinitely, and it is said that some Hiroshige prints which proved particularly successful were printed in editions of 10,000 copies.

The favorite subject of the eighteenth-century print makers was the figure, usually that of either courtesans or Kabuki actors. The early masters tended towards large compositions with a single figure, often that of a famous beauty, filling most of the space, while the later artists used more complex compositions with several figures and a greater variety of colors. Among the earlier ones, Kaigetsudo was the most outstanding, while Harunobu, who had been responsible for developing the color print, and Utamaro, who was famous for his portrayal of geisha and courtesans, were the supreme masters of the second part of the century. In their work, the elegance and beauty of the women of Edo Japan were celebrated in a manner which is as appealing today as it was in its own time.

Next to the Yoshiwara beauties, the world of Kabuki, the traditional Japanese theater, was the most popular subject for ukiyo-e prints. Entire families of wood-block artists, such as the Torii family, devoted themselves to this subject, making posters to advertise coming attractions as well as portraits of actors and sets of prints which were sold at the theater to Kabuki enthusiasts. Unlike the paintings produced by the artists of the Kanō or *bunjinga* schools, these prints were considered not works of art but cheap commercial products, printed in large numbers to be sold as souvenirs to people visiting the amusement district. Yet, in spite of their commercial origin, these prints at their best were works of art of a very high order.

By the end of the eighteenth century, the figure print had run its course. Not that artists did not continue to make all kinds of figure prints right through the nineteenth century, but the creative phase was over, and the designs became hackneyed and rather carelessly worked out. New subjects, especially Japanese landscapes and scenes from ordinary life, began to occupy the artists. Among them, the two most celebrated were Hokusai and Hiroshige, both active primarily during the first half of the nineteenth century, and the death of Hiroshige in 1858 marks the end of the great period of ukiyo-e. The output of both these artists was tremendous. It is estimated that Hokusai alone produced some 35,000 designs, and that Hiroshige made over 5,000 prints, many of which are of the first quality. These artists celebrated the beauty of the Japanese countryside as well as portraying the life of ordinary people. Of Hokusai's work, the most outstanding is probably the set of thirty-six views of Fuji, showing the sacred mountain from different places and at different times of day, while Hiroshige's best-known work represents the fifty-three stages of the Tokaido road, which linked Edo with Kyoto. While Hokusai excelled in his sense of decorative design and his vivid portrayal of people, Hiroshige was a master of mood and atmosphere and no one has ever captured as well the quality of the Japanese landscape, with its pines and mists and mountains.

Sculpture was of little importance during the Edo period. This was largely because of decline of Buddhism, which had been the chief patron of this form. The Buddhist sculpture that was produced usually continued the style and iconography evolved during previous periods, but it lacked both the spiritual fervor and the artistic quality which had marked the best of the older work. The one exception was the miniature sculpture, called netsuke, which were fastened at the waist and had tied to them small medicine containers (*inrō*). Made of ivory, bone, deer horn, or wood, the netsuke had intricate carving, often of great ingenuity. The best were made during the eighteenth and early nineteenth centuries, but others were produced even later to meet the demand of collectors. Much of the appeal of these small sculptures, which have been very popular in the West, lies in their subject matter, for they represent all sorts of scenes from Japanese life and legend.

While sculpture languished, there was an increasing demand for decorative arts. The peaceful, prosperous years of the Edo period encouraged the production of these arts, and of course far more has survived from this period than from any other. Lacquer, textiles, metal work, ceramics, and various media flourished, with both the aristocracy and the rich merchants patronizing the excellent craftsmen who were active all over Japan. Edo and Kyoto continued to be the great centers, but many local towns, such as Seto and Arita, which produced ceramics, experienced a golden age. In fact, it may well be said that in the decorative arts the genius of the age found its truest expression, for the Edo period was a time of worldly splendor and luxury rather than one of spiritual fervor or cultural refinement. The style owed much to that of the Momoyama period, especially during the early Edo, whose craft production is usually considered the finest of the period, with the late seventeenth century, the Genroku age, being the highpoint of the whole era.

The most important development in the decorative arts was the introduction of porcelain, which took place at Arita in Kyushu during the seventeenth century. Prior to this, only the Chinese and Koreans had made fine white porcelains, but now the Japanese found good supplies of the kaolin clay needed for its manufacture, and they too learned how to make this type of ware. The result was a rich and extensive production of porcelains which soon rivaled those of China and enjoyed great popularity not only in Japan but in the West as well. The enameled porcelains from Arita, called Imari ware after the place from which they were exported, were not only the first works of Japanese art to reach the European market, they were also the inspiration for the great porcelain factories of eighteenth-century Europe.

The bulk of these porcelains came either from northern Kyushu, especially the region around Arita in Saga Prefecture, or from the Kutani kilns located in the hills outside Kanazawa. Among the Arita wares, the finest were the Kakiemon made by a family of potters who excelled in producing porcelains with a very pure white body and beautiful designs painted in bright enamel colors representing birds, flowers, grasses, and other decorative motifs. The most refined and also the rarest, are the porcelains which are called Nabeshima ware because originally they were made especially for a daimyō family named Nabeshima. But the porcelains which Japanese critics have always valued most highly, and which are considered most typical of the Japanese sensibility, are the Kutani wares, especially those called Ao Kutani, which are decorated with a deep-green glaze. The colors are more subdued and the designs simpler and more abstract than those of most of the Arita wares, which were modeled on Chinese porcelains of the late Ming and early Ch'ing period.

The output of these kilns was enormous, with all kinds of bottles, jars, dishes, cups, and plates made on a mass scale. The quality and cost of the various wares differed tremendously, depending on the client for whom they were manufactured. The most refined porcelains were usually reserved for the court and the aristocracy, while the coarser wares were manufactured for the common people and for export. Many porcelains of all types were made expressly for Europe, the shapes and designs often being prescribed by the Western importers. This trade was handled almost entirely by the Dutch East India Company, which enjoyed a monopoly in this lucrative business.

The ceramic production of the Edo period was by no means restricted to porcelains; in fact, the bulk of the output continued to be pottery, stoneware as well as earthenware. The tea masters felt that the rougher, more rustic quality of pottery was better suited to the tea ceremony than any of the porcelains, and they continued to be the most important patrons of artistic ceramics. All the many kinds of tea ware which had originated during the Momoyama period, such as Oribe, Shino, Karatsu, and Raku, continued to be produced during the Edo period, but it is generally agreed that this later work never equaled the quality of the earlier tea wares. This process of gradual deterioration went on throughout the Edo period, the nineteenth-century ware being poorer in quality and weaker as art than those of the earlier centuries. The same decline took place in the traditional local kilns like Bizen, Shigaraki, Tamba, and Tokonabe, which produced more forceful and rustic work in the seventeenth century than they did in the eighteenth or nineteenth. But at all these kilns good pieces continued to be made throughout the period, and the best works are rightly placed among the masterpieces of Japanese pottery.

The single most famous Edo potter, and perhaps the most celebrated in all Japanese history, is Kenzan, the brother of Kōrin, who is also famous as a screen painter and decorative artist. Kenzan's ware is noted for its spirited designs, which consist of landscapes, trees, flowers, and grasses drawn in a spontaneous, abstract style of great beauty and expressiveness. Yet Kenzan was only one of the many fine potters who were active during this period. The best of them were much admired. They were not looked upon as mere craftsmen but as artists whose fame could rival that of a painter or a calligrapher, and who were far better known than any of the sculptors or architects.

Next to ceramics, lacquer was the most important of the decorative arts of the Edo period. Although the output was tremendous and much of it is very fine, it is generally agreed that the work of the Edo period does not quite equal that of the Momoyama, which represents the golden age of Japanese lacquer. Again, the finest pieces were made during the seventeenth century. The quality declined somewhat in the eighteenth century, and by the first half of the nineteenth century, cheap mass-produced lacquers, often with gaudy and tasteless decorations, had become quite common. Throughout the Edo period lacquer was used for many different objects, some of considerable size like palanquins, Buddhist altars, and decorations for pillars and walls. Others were small, like combs, pins, and hair ornaments, as well as all kinds of boxes, containers, and bowls. The techniques varied extensively, with gold and silver powder, inlay, and painted designs enjoying great popularity.

Among the many outstanding lacquer craftsmen, the two most celebrated were Kōetsu, the famous seventeenth-century calligrapher and swordsmith, and Kōrin, the great eighteenth-century painter who did not consider it beneath his dignity to design kimonos, decorate the dishes of his brother Kenzan, or produce writing boxes, such as the famous one with the scene of the eightfold bridge in which gold powder, lead, mother-of-pearl inlay, and silver are used to decorate the lacquer. All these works express both the material splendor of the Edo period and the decorative tradition in Japanese art.

Equally outstanding were the Edo textiles. Gorgeous kimonos of all types were made for the court, as well as robes for Nō actors and Yoshiwara courtesans. Even the well-to-do merchants vied with one another for splendid robes made from the finest materials by the best artisans available. No other civilization has ever attached so much importance to beautiful garments. The reason the Japanese valued them so highly was partly because of their traditional love for beautiful textiles, and partly because, since they did not wear jewelry, the splendor of the garments indicated the social position and wealth of the wearer. A supply of fine kimonos was an essential part of the dowry of a well-to-do bride from a good family, and kimonos were often handed down from generation to generation.

Although Western art lovers do not usually think of swords as works of art (as the Japanese do), sword accessories like the guards, or *tsuba,* and the small sharp knives known as *kosuka* have their ardent collectors even among those outside Japan. They show the skill and artistry of the Japanese metal workers at its best, for they were executed with great care and the finest of them are outstanding for the beauty of their design and workmanship. Other objects made of metal were the bronze mirrors with graceful designs in low relief on the back; the iron pots, especially those used in the tea ceremony, which had an austere and simple beauty; and the many different types of bronze vessels which were used for incense burners, flower vases, and various kinds of containers. In all these objects, the fine craftsmanship of the Edo metal workers is apparent, even if the designs, especially during the later years, were not always of the best.

The most remarkable thing about the Edo period is not so much that it produced outstanding art for the elite as that even the simple things produced for the common people were of equal artistic merit. These ordinary objects made by unknown craftsmen in provincial towns and rural areas were for years hardly considered worth saving, but today, due to efforts of the folk art movement, these folk art objects are now eagerly collected. Indeed, it is this outstanding folk art of traditional Japan which probably represents the most remarkable artistic heritage of the Japanese people. In many other Asian civilizations, such as China, India, and Persia, there are magnificent examples of fine arts made by skilled workers for the ruling classes, but in Japan alone ordinary people produced objects of the highest artistic order for their own use and pleasure.

Folk art, or *mingei,* had, of course, existed to a certain extent in earlier times, but it was not until the Edo period that the country became prosperous enough for the common people to have the leisure to produce works of real beauty. Most of them were purely utilitarian, because art for art's sake, or art as an expression of esthetic ideas, is quite alien to folk culture. Yet in the eyes of the modern *mingei* enthusiast, it is the unpretentiousness of the folk art that makes it so appealing, for among the most ordinary objects, often made by local farmers in their spare time, we find some of the masterpieces of the Edo period.

It was the potters who were the most outstanding folk artists of Edo Japan. Folk kilns sprang up all over the country, and wares of every type were made. Usually the pottery was rough stoneware with subdued glazes in brown, black, green, or white. The shapes were simple and strong, often of great beauty. Utilitarian vessels such as bottles, jars, cups, dishes, and plates were the most common. Particularly remarkable are the oil plates used to catch the dripping oil from the lamps, and the stone plates, or *ishizara,* both of which were made at the Seto kilns. Although simple, unpretentious objects made for the kitchens of peasant homes, they are extremely beautiful in their bold designs, which are painted in a spontaneous and inspired manner. None of them were considered works of art but, in spite of this, they are among the strongest and most beautiful of the Edo period ceramics.

Pottery was only a small part of the *mingei* production. Textiles, especially those made on Okinawa, were outstanding for both their colors and their design. Woven and dyed all-over patterns were preferred, and resulted in very pleasing effects. Each region tended to have a particular type of textile design, and strong and lovely kimonos, *yukata* (light summer kimono), *futon* (floor mattress) covers, hangings, and *furoshiki* (square cloth of varying size, used for covering the head or carrying things) were produced all over the Japanese islands. Hand-woven and using only natural dyes, these textiles had an individual quality which no mass-produced, machine-made cloth ever possesses.

Almost every aspect of Japanese life was in some way associated with the arts, reflecting the aesthetic sensibility which is such an integral part of Japanese civilization. The large peasant houses with their magnificent thatch roofs and beautiful woodwork, the country inns with their fine proportions and subdued elegance, and the rustic shrines all express this feeling for visual beauty which is so typical of rural Japan even in the present day. And the utensils used in the houses, whether they were of wood, bamboo, or lacquer, were made by craftsmen who took pride in their work and, without being pretentious, often produced veritable masterpieces. Today, when the market is flooded with shoddy, machine-produced goods, it is difficult to imagine the thought and care which went into the making of even the humblest utensil. But modern collectors and folk art enthusiasts, both in Japan and in America, have rediscovered these *mingei* works, finding in them an honesty of purpose and beauty of expression which have a strong appeal. The *mingei* work, when seen against the entire output of these two and a half centuries, is only one aspect of this rich and productive period, and yet it is an art which is unique to Japan. No form gives a clearer expression to the Japanese genius for making art an integral part of life, for living with it and using it, rather than setting it apart as something outside.

Modern Japanese Art

The Meiji Restoration in 1868 brought about a completely new period in Japanese art. Instead of being cut off from the outside world, artists were flooded with new impressions and experiences. A great vogue for everything Western became fashionable among the *avant-garde* of the new Japan. Not that all traditional culture disappeared overnight—on the contrary, a counterreaction began within a few years, and in more provincial places the old Japan continued undisturbed, but a new era had definitely arrived. Those who lament this change feel that the introduction of foreign ideas was a tragedy for Japanese art, since it destroyed what was genuine and indigenous and replaced it with something which was not only artificial but essentially alien. No doubt this was true to a certain extent, but it must be admitted that by this time the traditional art of Japan had become sterile and moribund, and that even for the so-called Japanese-style artists, the infusion of new life and new ideas proved beneficial. Certainly the ready acceptance of Western art and Western ideas indicated that the old ways had lost their hold on the Japanese, and that the artists themselves, especially those who were young and forward-looking, were eager for stimulation and welcomed the introduction of European culture just as their ancestors in ancient times had welcomed the new ideas from China.

So great was the craze for everything Western that traditional Japanese art was considered hopelessly out of date, and it is said that during the first burst of enthusiasm, some of the old temples were torn down and Buddhist images were actually destroyed. European artists were invited to Japan to teach the new ideas and techniques, and soon Japanese artists began to travel to Europe in order to study in the art centers of the West. The results were startling, for almost overnight the Japanese art world, which for two and a half centuries had been almost completely self-enclosed, was suddenly inundated with foreign influences. To be modern meant to be Western, to be abreast of the dramatic new developments which were taking place in all areas, for a radically different era had dawned, and the island empire, which for so long had been cut off from the outside, was now trying to catch up with the exciting new developments of the modern world. To succeed required sudden and drastic changes which could only be brought about in an authoritarian society like Japan where the hereditary ruling class with the backing of the imperial institution was able, almost overnight, to transform a backward and feudal society into a modern industrial one.

The change in the arts was also sudden and revolutionary, but it was by no means complete, for the great bulk of Japanese artists continued to work in the traditional manner. Even today, when Western-style art is more the rule than the exception, both trends are still represented in the major national exhibitions, although Japanese-style art no longer plays a leading role. At first, however, it was quite the contrary. During all of the Meiji period, which lasted from 1868 to 1912, European-inspired art continued to be the exception, although much of the so-called Japanese style work showed a certain amount of Western influence. A great deal of rivalry existed among the artists, with those advocating Western ideas regarding themselves as pioneers courageously opening a new path, while the traditional artists felt that they alone represented the true native heritage and that their opponents were selling out to the foreigners. Interestingly enough, the greatest spokesman for the cause of preserving what was indigenous was not a Japanese but an American scholar, Ernest Fenollosa, who, at a time when European ideals seemed to be overwhelming the country, advocated a return to the traditional ideals of the East. And it was Fenollosa and his disciple Okakura Kakuzō who were responsible for stemming the tide and making the Japanese aware of the greatness of their own artistic traditions. However, the dream of infusing new life into the old by combining the spiritual heritage of the East with some of the stylistic conventions of the West proved to be a stillborn rearguard action rather than the beginning of a new day.

All the different arts were affected by the changes which were occurring in Japanese life. Architects began building European-type brick structures in the revival styles current at that time in the West.

In sculpture new styles and subjects became fashionable, and artists trained in the Western manner made public statues of famous men and, what was even more startling, representations of the nude female body, a subject which had never before been treated in Japanese sculpture. But the greatest changes occurred in painting. Under the leadership of Kuroda Seiki, who had studied in Paris, Western oil painting was introduced to Japan, and the latest French art movements, such as realism and impressionism, became popular among young painters. Here again the Japanese showed their genius for absorbing outside influences, for within a generation the young artists had mastered the foreign style and were creating works in oil which compare favorably with all but the best of their European models. At the same time, others were continuing to work in the traditional manner, the most outstanding being Tomioka Tessai who favored the so-called southern or *nanga* school of ink painting. In fact, Meiji Japan was a bundle of contradictions where the old was mixed indiscriminately with the new, and people would put on kimono with Western-style leather shoes, and have no feeling of incongruity.

The areas in which the native tendencies proved strongest were domestic architecture and the decorative arts. Here the traditions were still very vital, and the foreign influences were never able to dominate them. Actually, it was during these very years that the decorative arts of Japan became very popular in Europe and America, and Japanese art was eagerly collected by Westerners. The demand for certain arts continued, for the tea masters still used traditional crafts in the tea ceremony, and people of all kinds continued to wear kimonos and use lacquer and ceramics in their daily life. In domestic architecture the European-style house never really caught on, since it was too expensive for all but the very well-to-do, and it was not really suited to Japanese life.

Unfortunately, the quality of most of this work declined, and even the best of these crafts cannot be compared to the finest work which was made during the Edo period. However, in isolated provincial places, good folk art continued to be produced throughout the Meiji period. Wood-block prints still enjoyed widespread popularity but, due to the introduction of synthetic pigments as well as the deterioration of craftsmanship, the level of the prints showed a marked decline. The most interesting are the so-called Yokohama prints which show the Westernized world of Yokohama and Tokyo, with railroad stations, customhouses, and ladies dressed in the latest European fashion.

With each generation the influence of Western ideas became increasingly dominant. Meiji men were still firmly grounded in old Japan, and the men of the Taishō era, from 1912 to 1926, stood halfway between the two cultures, but the artists of the Shōwa period were wholly modern in their outlook. Although the great art exhibitions still separated the Western and Japanese-style sections, the proportion had changed, with the Western-influenced art predominant, and even those works which were supposed to be purely Japanese reflecting the influence of European art.

While the inroads of Western civilization and Western art have been very destructive in those parts of the world where the native traditions could not compete with the more vigorous foreign influences, this has not been the case in Japan. Critics differ about the merits of modern Japanese art, but no one can deny that it has been a very vital expression of contemporary Japanese society, and that the best works produced in the twentieth century are comparable to the best of nineteenth-century Japan. This is true not only of the Western-style artists but also of those who do Japanese-style work. Painters like Umehara Ryūzaburō and Yasui Sōtarō, whose painting is derived from the postimpressionists, as well as Japanese-style artists such as Yokoyama Taikan and Maeda Seison, are today generally accepted as masters of the modern period who have a place of honor in the history of Japanese art.

The modern movement has also made an important contribution to the wood-block print. After a marked decline during the late Meiji period, the Japanese print was reborn when, under the leadership of the Japanese Woodcut Artists Association, a new and original school was developed, with artists working in a Western manner. No longer using professional wood engravers and printers as the ukiyo-e masters had done, but cutting their own blocks and making their own prints, these artists produced work which was both vigorous and interesting. Among the purely Western-style print makers, the greatest was probably Onchi Kōshirō, who was the pioneer among Japanese abstract artists and was greatly influenced by Kandinsky. Among those working in a more Japanese style, Munakata Shikō is the most forceful, producing vigorous, decorative prints which are unmistakably Japanese and yet use elements from the West.

The overriding problem for the modern Japanese artist is how to become part of the worldwide modern art movement and at the same time preserve something distinctly Japanese. Among those who have been most successful in achieving this synthesis are the great modern potters like Hamada Shōji and Kawai Kanjirō. Profoundly influenced by the traditional folk wares of the Japanese rural kilns and yet well acquainted with the modern Western tradition, these potters were able to infuse what was best in the old with the spirit of the new age.

Other artists have continued to work in a purely Japanese manner. Again, the potters are perhaps the most outstanding, with Kitaōji Rōsanjin and the Bizen potters the finest. Working largely for the tea masters, who still keep to the traditional forms of the tea ceremony, these potters make ceramics in the style of the Momoyama period and produce work of the highest quality. Another field in which traditional techniques still prevail is domestic architecture, and many modern architects continue to design private dwellings, inns, and tea houses which are completely Japanese and at the same time very successful. But even in these fields it is usually the older generation which perseveres in the time-honored way, while the younger depends more and more upon the West.

This is particularly true of the postwar generation, whose life has been deeply affected by the American Occupation with its influx of Western ideas and Western culture. In recent years, when the same art styles and fashions have sprung up almost simultaneously in Tokyo and Paris and New York, the purely native tradition has become impossible to maintain. Abstract and nonobjective art, action painting, and even pop art have their Japanese practitioners, and young artists flock to New York in ever increasing numbers to learn the latest art movements, which are quickly taken up in Japan.

It is too early to evaluate the Japanese contribution to world art, though it can certainly be said that Japan plays a far greater role in the international art movement than any other non-Western country. Although inferior to Europe and the United States in originality and power, modern Japanese art has nonetheless earned a rightful place in the international art scene. And as Japanese artists become more at home in the contemporary idiom, they will no doubt express themselves more freely and make a more vital and significant contribution. This is already the case with architects like Tange Kenzō and Maekawa Kunio, as well as abstract painters like Okada Kenzō, who are accepted not only in their native country but in Europe and America as well. And just as the ancient Japanese, having absorbed the Chinese influences, began to think of this foreign-inspired art as their own, so the Japanese of the future will no doubt feel that Western-style art is not something foreign, but a natural way to express their own artistic ideas.

Whether such a development would mean the end of all native traditions remains questionable. Certainly the overwhelming impact of Chinese art and culture did not destroy all the things that were distinctly Japanese, and today there are areas where the Japanese tradition is still vigorous, in spite of the fact that modern Japan is the most Westernized of all Asian countries. This is particularly true of the crafts, for not only do the tea masters continue to use traditional work, but in the more isolated and backward rural districts the folk arts are still alive, with anonymous craftsmen producing pots, baskets, and cloth which are distinctly Japanese. Whether this can be maintained in an increasingly urban society with an ever-growing flood of mass-produced goods is still an open question, but in light of the very traditional nature of Japan, and the pride the Japanese have always felt in their artistic heritage, it is not impossible that the native tradition will continue even after the mainstream of Japanese art has become wholly international.

XII

Literature

BY
DONALD KEENE

Characteristics of Japanese Literature

The beginnings and earliest development of Japanese literature are almost indistinguishable from the historical emergence of the Japanese people and language. The oldest book extant dates back only to A.D. 712, but it contains legends and poems which undoubtedly antedate the compilation by centuries. Our earliest information comes from the brief, cryptic notice of an unknown Chinese traveler, preserved in the *History of the Kingdom of Wei* of the late third century A.D. The Japanese communities he described cannot easily be identified in terms of modern geography, and the rulers he mentioned do not figure in any Japanese source. Yet it seems evident from the proper names and a few terms recorded in transcription that the language of the people inhabiting the islands to the east of China was Japanese; we may gather too that the religious practices observed by the traveler were accompanied by primitive songs, and that tales and legends were already in existence.

The evidence concerning the ancient Japanese language is too fragmentary to permit generalizations, but apparently it resembled later Japanese in general sentence structure and sounds. In contrast, say, to the Chinese language, Japanese was polysyllabic, an agglutinative language which built single words to sentence length. Connections with Korean and the Altaic languages have been suggested. Even a cursory examination of parallel modern Japanese and Korean texts indicates that they resemble each other in structure far more closely than either resembles Chinese, but we cannot as yet state positively that the two languages are of the same family. From the standpoint of literature, the marked dissimilarities with Chinese are more important than the resemblances to Korean. At times the native Japanese culture seemed about to be engulfed by the more advanced Chinese culture but the strikingly different nature of the Japanese language proved in the end an effective bulwark against the loss of distinctive Japanese manners of expression.

Japanese have traditionally divided words of their language into open syllables consisting of single consonants followed by simple vowels. Each syllable is given equal weight, and no stress accent marks either the individual words or whole sentences. A language with such features lacks the elements of the usual Western forms of prosody. When five open vowels are the only possible endings for words, rhyme is so easy as to be meaningless. Meter, again, is impossible in a Western sense because the language lacks a stress accent. Finally, quantity cannot serve in Japanese (as in Greek or Latin) as a distinguishing feature of poetry since the syllables are all of equal length.

Because the language failed to provide Japanese poets with easy technical devices for distinguishing poetry and prose but tended instead to blur the differences, poetic expression easily degenerated into prose unless preserved by intensely poetic language, striking syntax, or great concentration of expression—all features of Japanese poetry. A lengthy poem, identifiable throughout as poetry in a Western language if only by the prosody, presented almost insuperable difficulties in Japanese; a verse of low tension, such as those commonly encountered in Homer or Milton, would have little to distinguish it from prose. The principal Japanese prosodic device was syllabics; each syllable being considered equal in stress and length to every other syllable. The total number of syllables in a line created its shape and weight. In the most ancient surviving examples no clear preference may be detected for a particular number of syllables in a line of poetry, but even among the songs included in *Kojiki* (Record of ancient matters; 712) alternating lines of five and seven syllables become numerous as we approach historical times.

The Japanese preference for lines of five and seven syllables has been variously explained. Some scholars liken it to the Chinese use of lines of five and seven characters. However, in Chinese classical poetry each character is not only a syllable but a word; in Japanese poetry a syllable forms only part of a polysyllabic word. Moreover, Chinese poems normally consist entirely of lines of the same length, whether of five or seven characters, and do not alternate in the Japanese manner. These considerations do not rule out the possibility of Chinese influence, but the connection is by no means obvious. Other scholars have found in the alternating lines of five and seven syllables an expression of the Japanese predilection for asymmetry and irregularity; not only does each line contain an odd number of syllables, but a Japanese poem (again, unlike Chinese poems) consists of an odd number of lines. Such speculations are unlikely ever to result in positive identification of the origins of Japanese poetic forms, but we should note that alternating lines in five and seven syllables occur throughout the range of Japanese literature from the eighth century until the twentieth. Even when free verse forms were introduced from the West and longer lines became the rule, they could generally be broken down into component phrases in five or seven syllables. The classical plays—whether of the Nō, Kabuki, or puppet theater—were written largely in lines that follow this pattern, and even novels often contained extended passages, not necessarily poetic in subject, which retained a poetic form.

Japanese poetry was usually written in certain established poetic moods. If some occasion required that a poet write a verse, he adopted one of these moods, even if it was not his own, or even if (as when a Buddhist priest wrote love poetry) the mood was inappropriate. Poetry was filled with a prevailing melancholy atmosphere, at least during the seven centuries between *Kokinshū* (Collection of ancient and modern poetry, 905) and the beginnings of haiku verse. The fall of the cherry blossoms, so often described, was not merely a moment of tragic beauty but an easily employed symbol for the passage of time and the loss of the poet's good looks and happiness. The joy of seeing cherry trees in bloom was also recorded, particularly in the early anthologies, but most memorable poems were composed in a wistful, bittersweet mood. We cannot doubt that the sorrow expressed is often real, but its compass is narrow. The grief of a Chinese poet over the destruction of his city or of an earlier Japanese poet on the death of his wife was considered too direct and harsh by later poets. Moreover, the lives of the courtiers were so wanting in events of magnitude that we can easily imagine why poetry should have become less an expression of actual emotions than an affirmation of principles of poetic composition. Poetry obsessed the courtiers, and trivial "secret teachings" were guarded with a desperation suggesting matters of life and death. A staggering production of poetry flowed from the courtiers' brushes, much of it composed in conjunction with love affairs. Love is strongly emphasized in Japanese poetry, though it figures comparatively little in the works of major Chinese poets, for it served an important function in "making gentle the ties between men and women," in the phrase of the preface to *Kokinshū*. It was one theme all poets could treat, no matter how cloistered or uneventful their lives.

The Japanese language possessed a richness of shading impossible to communicate fully in translation. Particles and verb endings were manipulated to create the exact atmosphere desired by the poet. A perfectionist approach to poetry was considered desirable; rather than express new poetic conceptions, the Japanese poets preferred to express with somewhat greater skill than their predecessors thoughts already familiar to their readers, using language which was not only familiar but openly derivative. They depended on a more exact or more evocative choice of language and imagery to give freshness and value to their poetry.

Japanese poetic criticism goes back almost as far as the artistic composition of poetry. This criticism, though rarely satisfying to a person nurtured on Western poetics, is noteworthy for its insistence on purity of language and on the subtle varieties of effect obtainable by slight alterations in wording. Because the Japanese language lends itself to ambiguity of expression, a suggestive vagueness became at times an essential feature not only of poetry but of prose. The supreme masterpiece of the literature, *Genji Monogatari (The Tale of Genji; c.* 1010), is exceedingly difficult even for a Japanese scholar to decipher. The subjects of sentences often are left unstated, and sometimes, almost imperceptibly, the subject shifts from clause to clause. The only clue to the subject may be the degree of politeness of the verb, each verb possessing not only tense but a level of politeness and sometimes an indication of the sex of the speaker. A sentence such as "I urged her not to disobey his order" normally would contain no words for "I," "her," or "his," but the variety of level of politeness generally indicates who is meant. The lack of distinction between singular and plural causes other ambiguities, as in this haiku by Matsuo Bashō (1644–94):

kareeda ni	On a withered bough
karasu no tomaritari	A crow has alighted:
aki no kure	Nightfall in autumn.

But the poem *might* mean "on the withered boughs, crows have alighted"; indeed, a painting by Hanabusa Itchō (1652–1724) illustrating the poem shows eight crows perched in a tree full of withered boughs. Moreover, the words *aki no kure,* here interpreted as "twilight in autumn," could also mean "the twilight of autumn," that is, the end of autumn. Bashō probably wished both meanings to be understood. Evening is the appropriate time of day for the scene (bright sunshine would surely be incongruous), just as late autumn, when the leaves have dropped from the boughs, is better than mid-autumn, when crimson foliage would lend an unsuitable brightness to the picture.

Japanese poets and prose writers have not only accepted such ambiguity as part of the language, but have deliberately cultivated it.

Even in straightforward statement, there is a reluctance to say that a child is five years old or that a journey took eleven days; instead, the child is described as being "about five or six" and the journey as having taken "more than ten days." The lack of precision, initially occasioned by the language itself, accords with the prevailingly emotional, nonintellectual expression favored by the Japanese; evocation rather than statement was the goal of the Japanese author and constituted the distinction between artistic writing and everyday prose.

At times, of course, Japanese writers desired to achieve greater precision and intellectual conviction than ordinary Japanese syntax permits. From the eighth century onward works in both prose and poetry came to be composed in classical Chinese, sometimes in order to take advantage of the possibility of expressing abstractions or lending authority to a statement by allusion to ancient Chinese examples, sometimes merely as a proof of competence in a difficult, learned tongue. The parallel between the Japanese use of classical Chinese and the medieval European use of Latin at once comes to mind; in both cases such writings were more esteemed in their own time than they are today. Although most Japanese poetry in Chinese is hardly more than exercises in the use of recondite phrases and obscure characters, a few poets were able to profit by the opportunity of writing Chinese to describe their thoughts more precisely and powerfully than they could in Japanese.

The existence of this option undoubtedly contributed to the conservatism of Japanese poetry. A poet who felt dissatisfied with the purity of language, single-mindedness of thought, and lyricism of expression demanded by the critics could turn to Chinese rather than attempt a revolution within the domain of Japanese poetry. The introduction of new poetic forms—the *renga* (linked verse) in the fourteenth century, haiku in the sixteenth, European-influenced free verse in the nineteenth—similarly tended to preserve orthodoxy in the classic tanka by diverting to new forms poets who desired change.

The purity of Japanese writing, however, was often more apparent than real. Chinese myths and legends, suitably attired in the garb of Japanese names, passed imperceptibly into all forms of Japanese literature. Chinese literary constructions, especially parallelism of expression (in contrast to the Japanese preference for asymmetry), found their way into seemingly uncontaminated Japanese compositions. Most importantly, Chinese literary preferences were often adopted bodily by the Japanese despite differences in language and forms of expression. Japanese works of poetic criticism are burdened with lists of "maladies" to be avoided at all cost; on examination, many are seen to refer specifically to Chinese literary usage and to be virtually meaningless in Japanese. These dicta were, nevertheless, long observed with painstaking care, especially at poetry competitions where the use of a syllable at a forbidden place was sufficient grounds for disqualifying a poem. Chinese literary opinions of a more substantial nature were also adopted by the Japanese when evaluating their poets. The prefaces to *Kokinshū,* for example, praise or condemn poets in Chinese terms, finding one man "full of passion but lacking in expression" or another "beautiful in expression but lacking in sincerity." Poetry itself, the preface writers declared (following the preface to the Chinese anthology *Shih ching*), "moves heaven and earth and stirs the gods and demons." Unlike the European, who usually assumed that the gods "possess" the poet and make him their mouthpiece, the Japanese accepted poetry as a wholly mortal accomplishment.

Movements in Chinese literature often had repercussions in Japan, even within the conservative tanka. The imagery chosen by the Japanese poets might remain relatively unaffected but—to give one example—the dramatic diminution in the amount of imagery in the love poetry of the fourteenth century echoes the change in Chinese poetic ideals of the Sung dynasty. When we come to recent poetry, influenced by European rather than Chinese examples, it is possible to trace the rapid shifts from romanticism to symbolism and on to surrealism. Though the bulk of Japanese prose and poetry composed in any age was conservative, one part was sensitive to change from both foreign influences or native popular literature. The constant search by the court poets for new modes of expression served as a counterforce to the seemingly endless repetitions of the themes and language of the early collections. Haiku poetry, though eventually it became imprisoned in conventions no less stultifying than those of the tanka, achieved its eminence because seventeenth-century poets wished to express themselves in contemporary language on contemporary subjects. This involved the introduction of words of Chinese origin and also of Chinese allusions and imagery, contemporary only in the sense that they meant more to these poets than the worn-out themes of the tanka.

Yet with all the exceptions we may enumerate, some very important, we must conclude that the tone and direction of Japanese literature was established in the tenth century, in the poetry and criticism of *Kokinshū* and in the prose of *Genji Monogatari*. However strong the reactions to these standards at various times, most poets and prose writers, ultimately reverted to them. This meant that, just as the Japanese language was enriched but not basically altered by foreign importations, the literature which grew from the language shows a striking consistency through the centuries despite surface changes. This consistency was deliberate: allusive variation (*honkadori*), which sometimes involved a poet's borrowing as many as three of the five lines of a tanka when creating a "new" poem, was not only recognized as legitimate but was an especially important poetic device. A glance at the index to poetry in the imperial anthologies reveals an astonishing number of identical first lines. Even within the single collection *Kokinshū* nine poems have as a first line the single word in five syllables *harugasumi* (spring mist); two of them have identical second lines as well. Certainly the intent was not plagiarism. Instead, we recognize a verbal equivalent to the innumerable paintings of bamboos or pines, where the subject matter, materials, and composition are more or less determined, but individual genius manages, nevertheless, to infuse the work. Japanese poets and painters normally avoided surpising or novel themes, finding it a greater proof of artistic excellence to depict well the familiar subjects than to startle with superficial ingenuity. Just as the blandest sonata by Haydn may serve as a better indication of a pianist's talent than a difficult modern composition which demands dexterity rather than skillful interpretation, in Japanese poetry the use of a restricted number of themes, presented in a prescribed form with a rigidly limited vocabulary, served as a better guide than "spontaneous" works which showed no knowledge of tradition.

In Chinese literature, too, extensive allusions were often made to poetry of the past, but the Japanese practice need not be attributed to Chinese influence. Not all Chinese influences were absorbed. Indeed, Japanese literary individuality shows itself most conspicuously in the choice of material or poetic concepts borrowed from the Chinese. The first anthology of poetry in Japanese, *Manyōshū* (*c.* A.D. 777), gave Japanese expression to many themes of Chinese poetry—the delights of a royal excursion, the sorrows of poverty, the pleasures of drink—but the canons of Japanese taste enunciated in the preface to *Kokinshū* allowed no place for these themes, and they disappeared from later tanka, having been adjudged unsuitable to the Japanese tongue. The hackneyed "elegant" themes of poetry or painting, sanctified by long usage in China, included some the Japanese found uncongenial. "Monkeys crying in a gorge," for example, though often prescribed as a set theme at the palace poetry competitions, rarely evoked a meritorious response.

Perhaps the central factor of Japanese literature—if not of the entire traditional culture—was the love for and rejection of Chinese influence. The great, central Chinese culture asserted itself with overwhelming authority on surrounding cultures, making native traditions seem primitive or even barbaric. Some neighboring cultures vanished, unable to withstand the evident superiority of Chinese civilization. Others, like those of Korea and Vietnam, were so profoundly colored by Chinese usage that their peoples adopted Chinese names, observed the Chinese calendar, wrote their poetry in Chinese and, even as late as the eighteenth century, devoted their fiction to the lives of Chinese people in China, as if the lives of Koreans or Vietnamese were inadequate subjects for novels. Japan, thanks to its island situation, was better placed to resist Chinese influence. For a time, in the ninth century, it seemed possible that adulation of Chinese culture might lead to the same results in Japan as in Korea or Vietnam, but the claims of the Japanese language asserted themselves in time to forestall this danger. A love of Chinese literature, whether the poetry of Po Chü-i or the prose of Ssu-ma Ch'ien, deeply affected Japanese writers of the tenth and eleventh centuries, but the best writing, nevertheless, was in a language virtually untouched by Chinese influence, and described the actions and emotions of Japanese people living amidst contemporary surroundings. Some Japanese, it is true, were so devoted to Chinese culture as to affect Chinese habits and write classical Chinese exclusively, but in each age there were also men who rejected China utterly, insisting that China had nothing to teach the Japanese. The latter group included Sugawara no Michizane (898–981), the stateman and poet worshiped today as the god of learning, and Sesshū (1420–1506), the most celebrated Japanese painter.

The love and rejection of China is a strand running through Japan's entire cultural history. Rejection of Chinese civilization in some cases was occasioned by the dissimilar climate and geographical situation. The outlook of people living on narrow patches of flat land bordered by mountains on one side and the sea on the other not surprisingly differed from that of people living on the broad plains of China, as the perpetually humid Japanese climate also inevitably inspired a different range of expression from the dusty winds of north China. To put the matter in the most extreme terms: an English poet might well compare his sweetheart to a sunny summer's day, but an Indian poet, dreading the blazing sun of his country, likened his sweetheart to a cloudy, rainy day. Similarly, the Japanese poets, living by clear rivers and the lovely Inland Sea, were apt to compare lovers to seaweed bending together or the certainty of their love to a great ship riding the waves, but such imagery would not readily occur to a Chinese poet who knew only turbid rivers or the menacing ocean. The importance of the seasons in Japanese literature has been attributed to their sharp demarcations in the Japanese year, sharper than in China. Anthologies of poetry, beginning with *Kokinshū,* were divided into books of spring, summer, autumn, and winter poetry, and the poets assigned a season to each sight of nature, even if (like the moon) it could be observed throughout the year. Mention of the season became an absolute necessity in haiku poetry; haiku which lacked a word denoting the season were dismissed as "miscellaneous" verse. Even plays were assigned a season. A Nō play was normally performed only in the month it described, and Kabuki plays, which depict events extending over months or years, were by tradition staged in the appropriate season. Folklorists have suggested that the insistence on the season was due less to a poetic awareness of clearly defined seasonal variation than to a primitive identification of prescribed rites with a particular time of year. Ghost plays even today are generally performed in summer, not because the audience welcomes chills of fear during the oppressive heat, but because in ancient times ghosts were believed to walk in summer. Despite such qualifications, the exceptional importance of the seasons in Japanese literature distinguishes it from Chinese or European writing.

For all their awareness of the seasons, the Japanese were little interested in "nature" as the term is used in Western literature. Most Japanese poets appreciated "nature" in a garden rather than in a forest or lonely moor. The flowers they mentioned in their works were prescribed. A poet could not write about a flower merely because it had struck his fancy during a walk in the country; unless a precedent could be found in *Kokinshū* or another early collection, he hesitated to risk dangerous innovation. Unlike his Western counterpart, moreover, the Japanese poet-traveler evinced scant curiosity about unspoiled, unvisited spots; instead, he traveled specifically to observe with his own eyes the beauties of nature which had inspired earlier poets, hoping that he might also be inspired. Nature was admired through the poetry of the past, and the pleasure of discovery was less savored than that of rediscovery. Japanese poets lived more in poetry than in nature, and because poetry belonged mainly to an aristocratic tradition, the beauties of nature meant what the nobles admired and considered to be in good taste.

Emphasis on good taste meant that the earthy imagery found in some Chinese poetry was rejected even by Japanese imitators, not because inapplicable to the Japanese climate or landscape but because it was considered coarse. The virtual absence in Japanese literature—at least until the seventeenth century—of the kind of earthiness found in such Chinese similes as "hair black as a mud-snail's bowels" or "a neck white as lard" indicates how strongly aristocratic tastes dominated expression. Folk songs and folk tales existed in Japan, no less than elsewhere, but it often fell to a noble —in one case an emperor—to select and compile this material, inevitably "purifying" it in the process. The literature and theatrical entertainments of the common people again and again provided a stimulus to the stagnant court writings, but these fresh influences were soon subjected to purification and refinement. *Renga* and the Nō plays are two examples of popular creations which developed into highly aristocratic arts. Moreover, the common people in the end often adopted the tastes and even the poetic fancies of the nobility. The exaltation in court poetry of cherry blossoms above all other flowers eventually resulted in ornamental cherry trees being planted in every corner of Japan, and the symbolism of the blossoms falling after a brief moment of glory was appreciated by literate farmers, though farmers in other countries probably would have preferred a tree which bore not only blossoms but fruit. When compared to popular —let alone aristocratic—Japanese equivalents, the most refined Chinese novels and plays often seem coarse. This is not necessarily an adverse judgment on Chinese literature: works of literature without a touch of the common or even the vulgar may seem precious or insubstantial. Certainly, anyone obliged to read through a second-rate anthology of Japanese court poetry might well develop a hatred of the elegant cherry blossoms and reddening maple leaves and yearn instead for the sights and odors of daily life. The aristocratic tastes of the Japanese are best displayed in the Nō plays of the fifteenth century, but when the poetic intensity falls below the highest level a play may disappoint audiences with its lofty, unperturbed good taste; in the triumphs and failures of aristocratic taste one is reminded of seventeenth-century French drama. But Japanese literature, unlike European, was aristocratic not only in tone but in authorship; typically, the first anthologies of Japanese poetry in Chinese were arranged not by subject or date of composition but in descending order of the authors' ranks.

Love of Chinese and (in more recent times) European literature has been tempered by Japanese awareness that they do not accord entirely with Japanese taste. At times the Japanese have exaggerated the differences; not content with noting that Chinese or European literature is more intellectual than their own, they have asserted that it is excessively intellectual and that it lacks the simplicity and sincerity of Japanese writing. Again, Japanese have frequently opined that no foreigner can truly understand their literature. The island situation, which saved Japan from military and cultural invasions, also fostered insularism. The relative homogeneity of the Japanese people, despite their mixed origins, accounts for a national solidarity rare among large nations. The fact that until 1945 hardly any foreigners read the Japanese language reinforced this sense of solidarity; Japanese authors could relate secrets to an audience numbering in tens of millions without danger of outsiders eavesdropping. During the long isolation of the Tokugawa period, when for almost 250 years prior to Commodore Perry's "opening" the country in 1853 Japan was virtually sealed off from foreign intercourse, Japanese literature became so private, so concerned with details known only to persons inside a closed society, that scholars today find it almost impossible to unravel all the allusions. The Japanese have frequently been taxed with the crime of imitation, and glaring instances have been held up for condemnation, but it would be truer to say that insularism or an excessive particularism, rather than a proclivity towards imitation, has been the weakness of much Japanese writing. It surely makes little difference to a reader's appreciation of Wordsworth and Keats whether or not he is familiar with the lesser celandine or the cries of the nightingale, but Japanese critics often assume that a reader unacquainted with the blossoms of the *hagi* (the so-called bush clover) or the cries of the *uguisu* (a type of warbler) will miss the significance of a poem mentioning them. If these critics are correct, Japanese poems are remarkably precise in their overtones, though they may lack the universality at the heart of the best poetry. But they are probably wrong; despite difficulties in translation, the merits of great Japanese poetry are discernible even to foreigners because they derive ultimately from common roots of human feelings.

The dissimilarity of Japanese and Western traditions, however, makes comparisons only fitfully meaningful, and value judgments based on one set of standards obviously cannot be indiscriminately employed with works based on another. It would be as foolish to reproach the Japanese poets for their failure to treat more down-to-earth themes as it would be to reproach a Western poet for failing to maintain a perfect consistency of tone throughout every syllable of his poems. Similarly, the importance of a particular genre in one literature does not establish it as being universally important. The illiterate question frequently asked of scholars from remote parts of the world, "Who is the Shakespeare of your country?" is indicative of the assumption that the greatest writer of a country will prove to be a dramatist, though obviously this is a foolish assumption. Yet once we have freed ourselves of any lingering belief that Western literature provides a norm against which other literatures must be measured, we cannot fail to be struck by the immediate intelligibility of the best Japanese literature and by the surprising (though coincidental) resemblances with European literary developments. By historical accident, moreover, we in the West are now able to appreciate the excellences of Japanese literature, drama, and art in a manner impossible for Europeans in the past. Simplicity, understatement, ambiguity—qualities marking so much of Japanese artistic expression—are more prized by us than the picturesqueness, richly decorative effects, and lifelike depiction of objects which European visitors to Japan in the nineteenth century sought. Japanese influence, both in poetry and painting, accounts in part for our greater understanding but, more importantly, our coincidental discovery that art may be an interpretation of life rather than a mirror has led us to find in Japanese literature, whether the classical poetry, *The Tale of Genji,* or the Nō plays, a striking "modernity" of effect. A study of the background may disillusion us as we come to realize that unfamiliar religious or aesthetic beliefs underlie what we took for "modern" feelings, but Japanese literature, examined in terms of its historical development, reveals as much about Western literature as about itself, for in its choices—its conspicuous preference for the suggestive and indirect rather than the explicit and forceful—it demonstrates that the choices made by Western literature were by no means inevitable.

Literature of the Ancient Period

The oldest surviving Japanese book, *Kojiki,* was presented to the court in 712. The preface states that the text was transcribed from the oral narration of one Hieda no Are, a man who could repeat anything he had once heard; it also mentions earlier records, including a chronology of the Imperial House and legends of the gods, which were no longer extant. The intent of *Kojiki* was probably the same as that of the lost books: to justify the claims of the Imperial House to rule Japan by tracing its pedigree to the origins of the country. *Kojiki* is divided into two main parts, one dealing with the age of the gods, the other with the successive reigns of the emperors beginning with the legendary Jimmu, whose "coronation" was arbitrarily dated 660 B.C. Clearly, the compilers of *Kojiki* conceived of the book as a historical and religious document rather than a work of literature; nevertheless, Japanese scholars have devoted immense care to the text, and there have been controversies as to the reading and meaning of even the least impressive song. Although *Kojiki* is mainly in prose, it also contains poems supposed to have been composed by the gods, the emperors, and other personages on stated occasions. The prose on first examination looks like an exceedingly barbarous Chinese, but the great scholar Motoori Norinaga (1730–1801) spent thirty years of his life establishing a text read throughout in pure Japanese. Probably, as recent scholars have suggested, the text was intended to be read without consideration of the pronunciation. The Chinese characters, the only means of writing known to Japanese at the time, were totally unsuited to recording the Japanese language, but they possessed the advantage (not shared by phonetic scripts) of being able to communicate ideas without the intermediary of sound, rather as the number 25 communicates a specific quantity to people all over the world regardless of how they pronounce it. Scribes may have used Chinese characters as signals to the meaning of the text of *Kojiki* without worrying about how they would be pronounced. When it came to the poetry, however, the sounds themselves were important, and the Chinese characters were therefore employed for their phonetic value in transcribing Japanese.

An understanding of *Kojiki* has always been impeded by the religious or nationalistic sentiments it has inspired. Though it contains no ethical teachings or dogma, it is the sacred book of the Shintō religion. It begins with the creation of the world. The islands of Japan were begotten by the copulation of Izanagi and Izanami, the first man and woman, but other countries were formed of mud coagulated in the sea. This distinction established Japan as superior to all other countries; it also made the emperor, whose ancestors were also Izanagi and Izanami, a blood relation of the land he ruled, the strongest possible claim to sovereignty. At times when veneration of the Imperial House was particularly strong (e.g., during the war years 1941–45), *Kojiki* studies flourished and exaggerated claims were made, especially for the literary value of the songs. More recently, *Kojiki* has been discussed as folklore sharing themes with similar works elsewhere. The fables and legends have been analyzed for what they reveal of the early religious life of Japan rather than as examples of literature, much less as scriptural truths.

Eight years after the completion of *Kojiki, Nihon Shoki* (Chronicles of Japan; 720) was presented to the court. It is curious that a new national history should have been needed so soon after the first one. Probably the court felt Japan must be provided with a history in proper Chinese which could be displayed to Chinese or Korean visitors as proof that Japan had a long and glorious past. The compilers embellished their accounts of the successive reigns by putting into the mouths of Japanese emperors speeches taken word-for-word from Chinese or Korean histories, and even by making of one emperor (about whom *Kojiki* says almost nothing) a monster who delights in evil-doing, entirely in the continental traditions.

Kojiki and *Nihon Shoki,* for all their tendentious qualities, are the chief source of information about ancient Japanese history. Their intrinsic literary merits are slight, but the legends recorded in their pages recur countless times in later literature. Moreover, the poetry, for all its crudity, already possesses characteristics of the mature writings. The first poem in *Kojiki* is attributed to the god Susanoo:

1. *Yakumo tatsu*	4. We shall build a manyfold fence
2. *Izumo yaegaki*	2. A manyfold fence of Izumo
3. *Tsumagome ni*	1. Where many clouds rise
4. *Yaegaki tsukuru*	3. To shut in the bride—
5. *Sono yaegaki wo*	5. Oh, that manyfold fence!

This song has been interpreted in many ways, but probably it is a work chant, sung by members of a community when building a house for a bridal couple, or else a ritual song, imploring the protection of the gods of Izumo (still associated with marriage in popular belief) for the couple who will live in the new house. The poem is noteworthy in that it may be the earliest example of the classic Japanese verse form, the tanka, written in five lines of 5, 7, 5, 7, and 7 syllables. The regularity of the form—surprising in so early a text —may be product of some editor's reworking of a primitive song; nevertheless, it demonstrates that by 712, the date of the compilation of *Kojiki,* the tanka was a recognized form.

The poem is distinguished also by the use of the fixed epithet *yakumo tatsu* (where many clouds rise) in the first line, an attribute of the province of Izumo. Many other place names acquired such epithets, some based on topographical features, others on verbal associations. These epithets were known as *makura-kotoba* (pillow words), presumably because placed at the head of the poem. The poems of *Kojiki* and *Nihon Shoki* include about 130 varieties, usually in five syllables (to compose a line); *Manyōshū* has about 500 more, and some were still being invented in the seventeenth century. In time *makura-kotoba* lost their original meanings and became merely decorative; to omit the appropriate epithet before a place name was tantamount to disrespect. Similar but much longer epithets known as *jo* (preface) also made their appearance in *Kojiki.*

The Izumo poem also indicates the fascination which place names exerted on Japanese writers. Some poems in *Kojiki* and *Nihon Shoki* are hardly more than lists of names of places passed on a journey. They are forerunners of another important element in future Japanese literature, the *michiyuki* (travel description), found in almost every play and many novels. In a typical *michiyuki* the meanings of place names and their associations are woven into a description of the emotions of the travelers. The origins of place names always intrigued the Japanese; folk etymologies are prominent in the various *fudoki,* gazetteers compiled in the early eighth century. Again and again we find such examples as: "The place where he killed them brutally (*itaku*) is now called the district of Itaku; the place where he slew them swiftly (*futsu ni*) is now the village of Futsuna; the place where he killed them easily (*yasuku*) is now the town of Yasukiri. . . ."

Some poems in *Kojiki* and *Nihon Shoki* reveal an incipient literary sensibility, but nothing in either work prepares us for the magnificence of *Manyōshū*, the greatest collection of Japanese poetry. This is not entirely a matter of gradual improvement as time went on; the compilers, even when selecting primitive songs as old as some in *Kojiki*, were moved by literary tastes rather than by a pious intent of preserving the words of the sovereigns. The establishment of the first permanent Japanese capital at Nara in 710 ushered in spectacular advances in the arts of civilization, chiefly under Chinese influence. This influence is present in *Manyōshū*, not so much in the relatively few poems which are derived from Chinese models as in the superior literary awareness. *Manyōshū* may have been compiled originally to demonstrate that Japan could boast not only a long history but also a rich store of poetry, the mark of a civilized nation; a seventeenth-century scholar once described it as "the *Shih ching* of the East."

The title *Manyōshū* means literally "Collection of Ten Thousand Leaves," presumably meaning poems by "leaves." The number 10,000 was, of course, not intended literally; the collection in fact numbers some 4,500 poems by about 450 poets. Compilation was completed about 777. It is generally assumed that the poet Ōtomo no Yakamochi (718?–785) was the editor because the honorifics we should expect are not applied to his name. The collection includes poems written between the mid-seventh century and 759, and is arranged in twenty books.

Manyōshū, despite its eminence, was not an imperially sponsored anthology, and it differs markedly from subsequent anthologies in the variety of poetic forms, the subject matter, and the authorship. The tanka is overwhelmingly the predominant form, accounting for about 4,200 of the poems, but the *chōka* (long poems), although only 260 in all, impart a special grandeur to *Manyōshū*. In addition, there are some 50 poems in unusual, short-lived forms. The subject matter, presumably because no recognized code of poetic diction had been evolved, ranges from elegies on the deaths of emperors to songs of rustic sweethearts, and includes many themes which later poets would never have treated. Most *Manyōshū* poets, like those of later anthologies, served at the court, but the authors included soldiers on the frontier, farmers, and fishermen. These departures from what would become the standard form of the imperially sponsored anthologies—a collection of tanka written by court poets exclusively on themes approved of by the arbiters of good poetic taste—all contribute to *Manyōshū*'s unique importance.

The supreme poet of *Manyōshū* (and probably of all Japanese literature, though Bashō's admirers might question this) was Kakino-moto no Hitomaro. Little biographical data survives, but there is reason to believe that he died about 707, in his fifties. He had special attachments to Iwami on the Japan Sea coast, but his career was mainly at the court, then situated in the province of Yamato. Hito-maro, a kind of poet laureate, accompanied the emperor or empress on state visits, often commemorating these journeys in poetry. Even during his lifetime his greatness was recognized; the courtiers knew his poems by heart, and the farmers made them into folk songs. After his death his reputation continued to grow, as we know from the many imitations of his work.

Hitomaro's poetry is filled with an intense sincerity of expression which is his greatest glory. This sincerity of course does not imply a mere artless narration of his emotions; Hitomaro was a master of poetic techniques, whether in the use of imagery or in the choice of syntax. Nevertheless, his unmistakable conviction even when, in his capacity as poet laureate, he described the grief occasioned by the death of a prince he might never have known, gives his poetry a quality rarely attained by later poets when penning their exquisitely turned tanka on the scattering of the cherry blossoms or the blow-ing of the autumn wind. The later poets were not necessarily insin-cere, but their themes lent themselves to conventional melancholy or even gallantry; Hitomaro's poetry bespeaks a belief in the religious significance of addressing the dead and telling them that their glory will not be forgotten. It may be, as recent Japanese scholars have suggested, that the *chōka* originated in this reassuring of the souls of the dead, in the hope that they would not return as ghosts to plague the living; when once this belief waned, the *chōka* lost its reason for existence.

The *chōka* survived only as long as poets could approach Hito-maro's firmness of language and exactness of description. Perhaps alone among Japanese poets he combined a genius for amplitude with the more typical Japanese power of suggestion. The insistence on perfection of diction which colored poetics in later times made it almost impossible to compose extended works. If Milton, say, had fretted morbidly lest a single line of *Paradise Lost* fall below the excellence of the best parts, surely he could never have written his poem. In most extended Western poems the second or third stanza is less beautiful than the first, but the poets, sure that their themes demand amplitude, have not stopped at a single perfect quatrain.

In Japan, with the exception of Hitomaro and one or two other *Manyōshū* poets, notably Ōtomo no Yakamochi and Yamanoe Okura, the desire for perfection made men despair of extending themselves beyond the tanka. This meant that many subjects could not be treated at all, and others could only be hinted at, but the tanka poets, like sonneteers in the West, gladly accepted the narrow limits they had imposed on themselves. They arrived eventually at a perfect congruence between what they wished to express and what the tanka easily allowed. When longer and freer verse forms were introduced from the West in the nineteenth century, poets had to acquire the emotions proper to such expression before they could take advantage of their new freedom. Amplitude in poetry was especially hampered by a weakness of construction apparent in most extended Japanese works. Lacking the Greek traditions of the West, the Japanese did not conceive of a work in terms of a human body, perfectly proportioned; the emphasis in art was on smoothness of transition from one passage to another, sometimes without consideration of the whole. The linked verse of the sixteenth century affords the finest example of an onward-flowing, perfectly smooth composition which utterly lacks over-all unity. It closely resembles a horizontal scroll, meant to be seen in successive sections, each forming a perfect composition, rather than from one fixed point like a European painting.

Already in the *Manyōshū* we can see how the *chōka* gave way to the tanka. Yamabe Akahito wrote competent *chōka* but his fame rests chiefly on the "envoys," tanka appended to the long poems. These tanka suggest the burden of the *chōka* so effectively that the latter seem unnecessary.

A "feminine" tendency toward suggestion and intuitive perception, contrasting with a more "masculine" directness of utterance and concern over social or religious beliefs, may be traced in *Manyōshū*. Sometimes a poet wrote in both idioms, but a polarization gradually became apparent: the masculine style was channeled into the composition of Chinese poetry and prose, but women (or men when writing to women) expressed themselves in the tanka. The abandonment of the Japanese language by men when writing serious compositions was to mean that the literature of the Heian period, including the finest works of Japanese literature, was written largely by women. This was perhaps the only time that women have assumed so dominant a role in literary history.

Literature of the Heian Period (794–1185)

The first half of the ninth century is notable for several extensive anthologies of poetry in Chinese, continuing with greater skill the tradition begun with *Kaifūsō* (751). Prose in Chinese, especially the works of Kūkai (774–835), the founder in Japan of Shingon Buddhism, also attained high competence. The writings most remembered today, however, are the tanka composed by Ariwara no Narihira (825–80) and other members of the court. Narihira, the paragon of the Heian lover, wrote poetry which was melancholy rather than passionate, curiously lacking in masculine assurance; evidently this was the tone most successful when wooing a Heian lady. By contrast, the poetry of such women as Ono no Komachi (ninth century) and Ise (877?–939) is filled with emotions powerful enough to burst the confines of the tanka.

One cultural development made literature by women possible—the invention of *kana,* the Japanese syllabary. *Kana* replaced the cumbersome and confusing methods of writing Japanese found in *Kojiki* and *Manyōshū* with a simple and accurate system. Presumably *kana* was invented by someone familiar with Sanskrit—tradition ascribes it to Kūkai—but the time and circumstances are unknown. Women normally did not learn Chinese, so without *kana* they could hardly have written their lengthy prose masterpieces.

The first product of the new writing was *Kokinshū* (Collection of ancient and modern poetry; 905), consisting of 1,111 poems arranged in twenty books. The preface by Ki no Tsurayuki (859?–945) announced the ideals of Japanese poetry in terms that became definitive not only for Heian writers but for tanka poets as late as the nineteenth century. "Japanese poetry," he wrote, "has for its seed the human heart," an enunciation of his belief that the tanka must be emotional rather than intellectual. The specific occasions he considered likely to inspire poets included "when they look at the scattered blossoms of a spring morning; when they listen of an autumn evening to the falling of the leaves; . . . when they are startled into thoughts on the brevity of life by seeing the dew on the grass or foam on the water." Such subjects could indeed inspire beautiful poetry, but their gentle melancholy limited the range of expression, certainly in comparison with *Manyōshū.*

The *Kokinshū* poets are blamed sometimes for having injected into Japanese poetry an artificiality which vitiated the simple grandeur of

Manyōshū. Wordplays are easily managed in Japanese because of the many homonyms, and the *Kokinshū* poets often took advantage of them, not only to display their virtuosity but because wordplays were a legitimate means of enriching the content of the thirty-one syllables of a tanka. *Kokinshū* poets added depth to their poems in this manner, as a poem by Ono no Komachi shows:

Hana no iro wa	The flowers withered,
Utsurinikeri na	Their color faded away,
Itazura ni	While meaninglessly
Wa ga mi yo ni furu	I spent my days in the world
Nagame seshi ma ni	And the long rains were falling.

Nagame in the last line means "to brood" or "to stare," but is virtually identical in sound with *naga-ame,* or "long rains." *Furu* in the preceding line means either "to spend time" or "to fall" (as of rain). Thus two ideas coalesce: the poet spends her time staring outside broodingly; the long rains are falling. The faded flowers become one with herself: the blossoms have faded in the falling rain as her beauty has faded with time and as her days have passed in meaningless brooding. The effect of the wordplays clearly was not comic nor merely clever, but such virtuosity easily degenerated into artificiality or preciosity.

Kokinshū established not only the prevailing moods of Japanese poetry (which of course varied perceptibly according to the temperaments of different poets and the atmosphere of the times) but the thematic content. Like *Manyōshū,* it was divided into twenty books, but the contents were classified: six books of seasonal verse were followed by books of congratulatory, parting, travel, love (five books), mourning, and miscellaneous verse. The importance of seasonal and love poetry, accounting for more than half the total number of books, indicates what the Heian courtiers thought were the main functions of poetry. Courtship involved sending poems of both a seasonal and an amorous nature, and the contests at the palace in which participants were required to submit tanka on prescribed themes repeated this emphasis. Love became the chief subject of the tanka, but the joys of love were seldom described. The melancholy nature of the themes listed in the preface to *Kokinshū* dictated the moods in which lovers turned to poetry: the uncertainty before meeting the beloved, the anguish of parting, the hopeless realization that an affair has ended. Beginnings and ends, whether of love affairs or the blossoming of flowers, were deemed more poetic than the climactic moments, for the latter allowed no room for suggestion. Rarely does one encounter such familiar themes of Western love poetry as praise of the beloved one's beauty or delight in her charms; beauty in women as in flowers was made precious by its brevity of glory, and anticipated or regretted rather than enjoyed. The sacrifice of the central area of experience in favor of beginnings and ends deprived Japanese poetry of the power of Western examples, but given the shortness of the tanka and its prevailingly "feminine" moods, the *Kokinshū* and later poets chose wisely.

Ki no Tsurayuki, the compiler of *Kokinshū,* is famous also for *Tosa Nikki* (Tosa diary; 935), an account of his homeward journey to Kyoto from the province of Tosa, where he had served as governor. Tsurayuki wrote this diary in Japanese, though men normally kept diaries in Chinese; in order to escape reproach for adopting this unmanly style, he pretended that a woman in the governor's entourage had written the diary. Events of the journey, some quite exciting, and poems composed on various occasions make up the bulk of the work, which is given a peculiarly moving quality by repeated, half-spoken references to Tsurayuki's daughter who had died in Tosa and whose absence deprives the return to the capital of its joy.

Tosa Nikki is the earliest surviving example of an important genre of Japanese literature, the diary. Diaries were kept in every country, it is true, but normally they do not rank high among literary works. The Japanese found the diary particularly congenial, and developed it into a sophisticated literary form. The difficulties experienced in Japanese in constructing an extended work were alleviated by the day-to-day continuity of the diary, or by the successive events of a journey. Poetry could be included as part of the record of happenings, and the diarist's reflections gave the desired subjective, "feminine" quality. The literary diary easily passed from fact to fiction, particularly when the events described were recorded long after they occurred. The diary in fact influenced the development of the *monogatari,* the characteristic Heian form of narrative fiction.

Ki no Tsurayuki pretended he was a woman writing a diary; subsequent Heian diarists in the Japanese language were almost all women. *Kagerō Nikki* (Gossamer years; c. 974) describes the life between 954 and 974 of the author, a prime minister's wife. The first volume covers the period 954 to 970 in the manner of an auto-biographical novel; even the author confesses that her remembrances probably are tinged with fiction. The remaining two volumes cover only five years, and many entries were apparently made on the days indicated. The writer (known as "the mother of Michitsuna" because her own name is unknown) relates, with many touches of self-pity, her unhappy life with her husband. At first he had shown every sign of affection, but his attentions wandered to other women. When-ever he attempted a reconciliation, he was rebuffed by the author in wounded pride. She evidently assumed that readers would sympa-thize, and often we do, but her self-centered grievances are not en-dearing. She shows no interest in the thoughts or wishes of others, no ability to understand even her son, her only pleasure in life; her book is, in the most pejorative sense of the word, extremely femi-nine. So absorbed is she by her own griefs that, for instance, the sight of a dead body lying by the road neither frightened nor startled her. In one passage where she gloats over the death of a rival's child her obsession with her own griefs is displayed to the worst advantage. Yet her journal is extraordinarily moving, precisely because, by dwelling exclusively on universally recognizable sentiments, she makes us forget the vast differences separating Heian Japan from our world. Though fictional elements may be present, they are far from implausible or fantastic. *Kagerō Nikki* is an almost painfully honest work, unsparing of the author.

Two varieties of fiction survive from roughly the same period as *Kagerō Nikki*. The first, the "poem tale," originated in prefaces ex-plaining the circumstances under which a poem was composed, as found in *Manyōshū*. The tanka is so brief and elusive that often the full meaning escapes the reader unless he knows the background. *Ise Monogatari* (The tales of Ise), a ninth-century collection of 125 episodes ranging in length from a few sentences to several pages each, consists mainly of narrations of the events leading to poems by Ariwara no Narihira. The romantic nature of these episodes has given *Ise Monogatari* exceptional popularity through the centuries, though the work is neither profound nor sustained. The integration of prose and poetry was especially to affect later literature.

The second variety of early fiction was the fairy tale or fantasy. At the beginning of the ninth century a collection of Buddhist miracle stories *Nihon Reiiki* (Account of miracles in Japan) was compiled in Chinese by the priest Keikai. The fantastic elements remained prominent in later collections of religious and folk tales; in *Taketori Mono-gatari* (The bamboo cutter's tale), probably written in the late tenth century, a fairy tale with elements common to many countries was given more literary expression than any of the Buddhist tales. It tells of a childless old man who finds a tiny girl in a bamboo stalk. She quickly grows into a beautiful young woman, and is given the name of Kaguya-hime, "the shining princess." Many suitors are attracted, but she refuses to marry any man unless he proves himself by accomplishing an impossibly difficult task of her choosing. Each of five suitors, determined to win her, throws his energies and fortune into his assigned task, but all fail, to the evident relief and pleasure of Kaguya-hime. She next unwittingly attracts the emperor's attention. Unable to treat him in the same highhanded manner, she dissolves into a ball of light, to reveal that she is no ordinary mortal. In the end she departs the earth to return to her old home on the moon.

In *Taketori Monogatari* the detachment with which the fanciful incidents are related removes the story from the realm of the fairy tale. Kaguya-hime, unlike the serene and radiant princesses of most such tales, delights in the misfortunes of her suitors. The reader may well conclude that the author was slyly poking fun at the old-fashioned romance; certainly, there is none of the conventional wonder in the miraculous. The fantastic elements keep us from taking *Taketori Monogatari* seriously, but the comparatively well-organized story contrasts with the disjointed episodes of *Ise Monogatari* and other poem tales.

Ise Monogatari and *Taketori Monogatari* represent the two main streams of fiction before the emergence of the mature *monogatari* which combined them. An early product of the combination was *Utsubo Monogatari* (The hollow tree), apparently written late in the tenth century. It is a peculiarly awkward and confusing work, ranging in expression from unbridled fantasy to realistic description. It contains a high proportion of poems, and some chapters are so little related to the rest as to remind us of the poem tales, but an effort was made to preserve a single thread of story. Of late attention has been focused especially on the second section, describing the rivalry of the suitors of Princess Ate, a theme closely related to that of *Taketori Monogatari*. The suitors include not only nobles but men of humble station, to the delight of those scholars who resent the exclusion of the common people from works in the aristocratic tradition. However, the inartistry of *Utsubo Monogatari* is likely to interfere with enjoyment of its unusual but clumsy narrative.

Before the combined traditions of fiction could achieve literary distinction another element was needed—the introspection of *Kagerō Nikki* and other "feminine" writings. Murasaki Shikibu (978–1016?), whose own diary is a fine example of the genre, achieved the miraculous fusion of the different strands of existing Japanese prose in *Genji Monogatari* (*The Tale of Genji;* c. 1010), the supreme masterpiece of Japanese literature. A knowledge of the antecedents of *Genji Monogatari* does little to account for its brilliance, nor have the attempts of certain scholars to explain the work in terms of Chinese influence proved successful. *Genji Monogatari,* like the dozen other works of world literature which are its peers, eludes dissection of influences. It has been studied with immense devotion almost since its creation, and innumerable theories have been advanced concerning the reasons, circumstances, and techniques of composition, but Murasaki Shikibu's understanding of the human heart will forever compel our silent wonder. The judgment on *Genji Monogatari* most valid today is still that of Motoori Norinaga, who said that its theme was *mono no aware*—an almost indefinable term meaning something like "a sensitivity to things" or "an awareness of things." Unlike earlier Japanese fiction, it is concerned not so much with plot as with the portrayal of sensitive and believable people and their emotions. In this respect it may suggest a modern novel, though the careful reader will be aware of the nonmodern religious and social beliefs that shape the characters.

Genji Monogatari consists of fifty-four chapters, the first two thirds describing the peerless Prince Genji, the remainder devoted to the world after his death. Genji is the ideal Heian courtier: an accomplished poet, painter, dancer, musician, and even football player, his supreme gift is in the art most prized by Heian society, lovemaking. For the Heian courtiers love was not a onetime experience, but an art to be cultivated and afforded maximum artistic expression. *Genji Monogatari* relates the progress of many affairs, from the first tentative poems sent by Genji who has been intrigued by a woman's name or by a glimpse of her sleeve, to the bittersweet moments of parting after a single night or many years together. Genji's amorous involvements are numerous, but they are not calculable in the manner of Leporello's catalogue. He is an infinitely varied lover, from playful youth to demon lover, or from boy attracted by an older woman to father attracted by his supposed daughter. His mistresses range from the grandest noblewomen to insignificant creatures terrified by so magnificent a suitor. The reader can only feel that it would have been a criminal waste if, having fallen in love with one woman, Genji never looked further afield. Genji is unsuccessful only with his first wife; the author, instead of explaining the curious mutual hostility of a seemingly ideal couple, merely recounts their desperate attempts to understand why they cannot get along—a more subtle and convincing treatment of unspoken antipathy.

Genji is wholly believable, yet we realize that no person so flawlessly accomplished ever existed, and no society ever attained the aesthetic and emotional sophistication of his world. Our doubts are confirmed if we read Murasaki's diary or the third of the novel which takes place after Genji's death; the most accomplished princes, we discover, have failings. The world of Niou and Kaoru, Genji's successors, is still beautiful, but the Buddhist expressions of disillusion, so often on Genji's lips, now carry conviction. The world has become darker: Niou's affairs are cheapened by a shallowness which brings him conquests rather than love, Kaoru's by an incapacity to savor happiness. Niou and Kaoru, opposites though they are, are both incomplete reproductions of Genji, representing his romantic ardor and his sensitivity respectively. Not surprisingly, later generations found it easier to identify themselves with Niou and Kaoru than with the incomparable Genji; though Genji and his world were admired and envied, later court writings are dominated by Niou and Kaoru.

One other masterpiece of the same period may be mentioned with *Genji Monogatari;* this is *Makura no Sōshi* (*The Pillow Book;* c. 1002), a collection of essays and impressions by Sei Shōnagon. Japanese critics traditionally distingushed the *aware* of *Genji Monogatari* and the *okashi* of *Makura no Sōshi. Aware* meant the perception of the tragic implications of a moment or gesture hardly noticeable of itself; *okashi* the comic overtones of perhaps the same moment or gesture. The lover's departure at dawn evoked not only the wistful passages of *Genji Monogatari* but also the wit of Sei Shōnagon, who noted with uncanny precision the fumbling, ineffectual movements of the lover and the unpoetic irritation his unseemly haste or excessive concern over a mislaid article was likely to arouse in the lady. Murasaki Shikibu's *aware* is present throughout Japanese literature, for it fits the pattern of sensitivity expected of all under the spell of the aristocratic culture, but Sei Shōnagon's wit belonged to the Heian court at a particular moment of history. If George Meredith was correct, and wit exists only in a society where men and women meet on equal terms, the Heian period alone provided the necessary conditions for wit; in later times the role of Japanese women was so subservient that the give-and-take of wit was out of the question.

Literature of the Kamakura Period (1185–1333) and Muromachi Period (1333–1600)

The Heian court society did not collapse in a year or even a century. Long after its political power had been seized by military leaders and its economic basis was seriously weakened the court retained an unshakable prestige. Military men quite normally turned from warfare to composing poetry—certainly by the third generation —and the court poets became their mentors. But the removal of the effective capital from Kyoto to Kamakura at the end of the twelfth century deprived the court writers of the confidence to attempt another *Genji Monogatari*. The institution of a feudalistic system worked especial hardship on the position of the court ladies; after their brilliant literary productions during the Heian period it is sad to note that scarcely a woman writer is remembered between the thirteenth and nineteenth centuries. The poets, like the great Fujiwara Teika (1162–1241), reveal their alienation from society by an emphasis on other-worldly themes. A meaning had to be sought outside a world whose ideals were no longer those of the court poets. The symbolic poetry of *Shin Kokinshū* (New collection of ancient and modern poetry; 1205) represents perhaps the supreme achievement within the tanka form. The poets, unlike those of *Kokinshū* three centuries earlier, were worried and frightened; the fall of the cherry blossoms was sometimes the symbol of death. Teika (1162–1241), his father Shunzei (1114–1204), and the priest Saigyō (1118–90) were especially effective in evoking the lonely beauty of the monochrome, whose very lack of color could suggest more than the brilliantly tinted paintings of another age. Teika expressed this conviction perfectly:

Miwataseba	In this wide landscape
Hana mo momiji mo	I see no cherry blossoms
Nakarikeri	And no crimson leaves—
Ura no tomaya no	Evening in autumn over
Aki no yūgure	A straw-thatched hut by the bay.

In the bleak loneliness of the scene Teika sensed a beauty not found in the conventionally admired sights of nature.

The characteristic prose form of the Kamakura period was the war tale (*gunki monogatari*). The warfare described in these stories occurred in the twelfth century in a series of struggles which culminated in the Minamoto's triumph over the Taira. These war tales, for all the Japanese reputation as a martial people, reveal little pleasure in the deeds of war; instead, a sense of loneliness and a conviction of the meaningless of this world permeates the narrations. The Buddhism favored at this time had developed by way of reaction to the aristocratic religion of the Heian court. It emphasized that man could be saved only by recognizing his own nullity and throwing himself on the saving grace of Amida Buddha, who vowed to save all mankind. It also taught that the world is a place of suffering in the throes of the last phase of the Buddhist law, and that the only real world is that after death. Such beliefs provided the background not only for the war tales but for most other literature of the Kamakura period and succeeding ages.

The masterpiece among the war tales is *Heike Monogatari* (The tale of the Heike). Originally, it would seem, this was a chronicle of the rise and fall of the Taira (Heike) family, written by a court noble about 1225. Before long, however, the tale was being recited by entertainers who accompanied themselves on the *biwa,* an instrument resembling the mandolin. The dissemination of the original tale by many performers, each undoubtedly embroidering on the sections most congenial to his manner of narration, created an enormous variety of texts, but the main themes at least are common to all, and reflect the somber tone of the medieval era. *Heike Monogatari* opens with the celebrated words:

The sound of the bell of the Gion Temple echoes the impermanence of all things. The white flowers of the twin-trunked sal trees reveal the truth that they who prosper must die. The proud man is not for long, but vanishes like a spring night's dream, and the mighty man too perishes in the end, like dust before the wind.

The proud Taira Kiyomori indeed dies in agony, no one to comfort him, and the once-mighty leader of the Taira, Tomomori, commits suicide by leaping into the sea. At the end of the work we hear the bell toll at the Jakkōin, a tiny convent where the former empress, the daughter of Kiyomori and the mother of the drowned boy-emperor, lives out her remaining years in the tattered habit of a nun. Other memorable scenes (like the death of the young general Atsumori) have an intensely dramatic yet pathetic quality. It is small wonder that narrations of *Heike Monogatari* continued to move audiences for centuries, and that plays based on the deeds it records still dominate the traditional theater. *Heike Monogatari* is episodic, and sometimes the narration is interrupted by fussy details, but at its best it suggests with almost painful clarity the tragedy of life in a world of grief.

Hōjōki (An account of my hut; 1212) by Kamo no Chōmei (1153–1216), a poet and priest, is like a cry from the heart of medieval darkness. The author, after enumerating the natural disasters he had witnessed, which have made him realize the folly of possessions or pride in worldly achievement, describes the quiet beauty of life in a hermit's retreat. Yet even as he writes his words of comfort for those like himself aware of the terror of life in this world, he realizes that attachment to his hermitage, though it is only a hut with hardly an object inside, is a sin: attachment to *anything* of this world is a hindrance in the path of deliverance.

The Nō plays of the fourteenth and fifteenth centuries are largely concerned with this sin of attachment. An inability to forget life in this world prevents the dead from gaining release and forces them to return again and again as ghosts to relive the violence or passion of a former existence. Only prayer and renunciation can bring about deliverance; as long as the attachment persists there can be only the repeated bitterness of this world. The Nō plays, especially those of Zeami (1363–1443), are magnificently poetic, but possess almost no interest of a conventionally dramatic nature. Most plays present little conflict of character, plot development, or individuality in the personages, and hardly any movement except for the stylized dances which are their climaxes. The Nō plays are certainly not sermons, nor is it possible to compare them to the crude miracle and morality plays of medieval Europe. Zeami's treatises on the art of Nō display extraordinary perceptivity, and are still valid for the theater today. His aims are dramatic conviction and reality, but these ideals meant ultimates for Zeami and not the superficial realism of the Western theater. Some Nō plays, it is true, have little symbolic or supernatural content and are relatively close to works performed in other theaters; these represented one element in a total dramatic performance and

Zeami did not neglect to discuss the appropriate manner of acting and dancing their roles. The central element of a typical program of five Nō plays was to be found, however, in the highly poetic elusive masterpieces like *Matsukaze,* the most esteemed work of the repertory; they suggest a world invisible to the eye but evokable by the actors through the beauty of movements and speech (their *yūgen,* to use Zeami's word).

The Muromachi period, though sometimes dismissed as a "dark age" of Japanese literature, can boast, besides the Nō plays, tanka which are disturbingly "modern" in their complexity, new genres of both poetry and fiction, and highly evolved literary criticism. Underlying this literature were aesthetic principles owing much to Zen Buddhism and to the writings of Yoshida Kenkō (1283–1350), whose *Tsurezuregusa (Essays in Idleness;* c. 1330) at once crystallized century-old tastes and formed the tastes of many generations to come. The necessity that beauty be perishable, the importance of beginnings and ends (as opposed to the moment of full glory), the pleasure of the broken or imperfect were typical themes treated by Kenkō. Although a conservative constantly looking back nostalgically to a happier past, Kenkō actually voiced ideals entirely in consonance with the symbolism of the Muromachi writers.

Works in traditional forms, including *monogatari* in the Heian style, continued to be written by the court nobility, now an impoverished and powerless class, but as a result of almost incessant warfare from the middle of the fifteenth to the end of the sixteenth century, the city of Kyoto was destroyed, and with it much of the old aristocratic culture. The nobles were forced to flee from the capital, dispersing the court learning throughout the country, even as men of humble birth, taking advantage of the breakdown of the old order, were rising to literary eminence. Sōgi (1421–1508), the outstanding *renga* poet, became an arbiter of poetic taste no less respected and feted than the great Teika, though in earlier times his base birth would have made association with the nobility inconceivable.

Renga, the chief development in Muromachi poetry, was traditionally believed to have originated in ancient times. In *Kojiki* a traveler asks an old man the way to Tsukuba. His question is phrased in 5, 7, and 5 syllables, and the old man's answer in two lines of 7 and 7 syllables, completing a tanka. A single tanka was frequently composed by two people in this manner, but not until a third "link" was added, breaking the original tanka limitations, did *renga* emerge as a distinctive form. By the fourteenth century composing linked verse had become a popular pastime even in the countryside, where lonely men joined their fellows in poetry meetings. Gradually *renga* spread to the court poets, who saw the artistic possibilities of this diversion and drew up "codes" intended to establish *renga* as a full-fledged art. These codes made possible the masterpieces of the fifteenth century, but their insistence on formalities—how often a "link" on the moon might appear in a hundred links, which links must end with a participle and which with a noun, etc.—inevitably reduced the vigor and freshness of the early *renga,* itself a reaction against the excessively formal tanka. Nevertheless, the *renga* of Sōgi and his associates, notably the sequence *Minase Sangin* (Three poets at Minase; 1488), are unique in their shifting lyrical impulses, moving from link to link like successive moments of a landscape seen from a moving boat, avoiding any illusion that the whole was conceived in one man's mind. The associations evoked in one poet on hearing the link composed by another might be quite unlike what the first man had intended, but such unexpected shifts of direction were welcomed; they were abetted by the vagueness of the Japanese language, which allowed great leeway in interpreting the subject of a link.

The first verse of a *renga* sequence, the *hokku,* had to set the mood of the entire sequence by telling the season, the time of day, the place, the prevailing natural features. Eventually, the *hokku,* thanks to these characteristics, became an independent verse form, today generally known as haiku.

The short stories of the Muromachi period cannot be said to possess high literary value. Their plots are often marred by fantastic elements and their style is undistinguished. They are interesting because they fuse folklore with the language and sometimes the literary techniques of the older fiction, and because they describe not only the princes and princesses of the *monogatari* but Buddhist priests, merchants, bandits, and other members of a society frequently turned topsy-turvy by disorders. Even if many promising stories are ruined by absurdities before their course is run, for a few moments at least we have seen what life was like in an age of chaos and creation.

Literature of the Tokugawa Period
(1600–1867)

The restoration of peace and the unification of the country was achieved by 1600, the date of the Battle of Sekigahara, which established the Tokugawa family in power. For the next 250 years and more the country was to know uninterrupted peace preserved by the rigorous measures of a government organized on military lines. The successive shoguns had their capital at Edo, the modern Tokyo, but during the first half of the period the center of culture remained in Kyoto and the nearby commercial city Osaka. The three great cities each symbolized one aspect of the culture: Kyoto retained its aristocratic distinction and elegance, though the court nobles themselves had little importance; Osaka typified the contributions of the merchants to the new society; and Edo, at first a city populated by rough warriors, came to synthesize the tastes of the first popular, non-aristocratic culture.

The Tokugawa regime had for its state philosophy the Chu Hsi school of Confucianism. Much of what we now consider typical Japanese patterns of behavior—the rigid concepts of obligation, filial piety, loyalty, and the like—originated in the strict tenets of this variety of Confucianism, but it paradoxically also fostered the growth of the gay quarters and other amusements, considering them to be necessary evils in a well-run society. The Confucianist philosophers allowed romance no place in a man's life; marriage was a union of families whose purpose was the preservation of the family line, and a husband was not expected to show affection (let alone love) to the mother of his children. Marriage to the uncomplaining, inarticulate drudge who embodied the Confucian ideals of womanly behavior entailed few disagreeable complications for the man, but it was extremely dull. Quite naturally, he turned to prostitutes for more amusing female companionship. An elaborate hierarchy of prostitutes developed, and the gay quarters themselves became the subject of much literature and drama during the Tokugawa period. The rake who systematically exhausts the pleasures of all the gay quarters of Japan, or the hard-pressed merchant who finds himself torn between love for a prostitute and duty towards his wife and family became the heroes of comedy and tragedy. The arts, especially the ukiyo-e prints, brought publicity to courtesans and actors, the denizens of the "floating world."

Genroku, the name of the era 1688–1703, was the most brilliant period of Tokugawa culture, though the half century between 1680 and 1730 as a whole marked an expansive flowering of literature and the arts. The favored genres of writing were all Japanese in origin and hardly touched by outside influence because of the government's policy of isolation, which effectively cut Japan off from the rest of the world. Japan, turned in on her own resources as never before in history, produced a literature of a highly distinctive flavor, but it tended to become increasingly particular and private as the sources of universal themes dried up. In the latter part of the Tokugawa period especially the greatest ingenuity was devoted to devising surprising twists in otherwise familiar plots or to giving a surface freshness to an otherwise hackneyed poem by mention of a new fashion in costume, hairdress, or food. The results were usually ephemeral and are exceedingly hard to unravel today, but at least in the beginning the new culture was exciting.

A major forerunner of Genroku literature was the *haikai no renga,* a comic variety of *renga* composed in protest against the increasing formalization of what had begun as a popular form. The *hokku* of this humorous *renga* developed directly into the haiku of Bashō and his school, and the *renga* techniques helped to form the style of Ihara Saikaku (1642–93), the first important Japanese novelist for almost 500 years. Saikaku first won fame with his solo *renga* sequences, composing 1,600 verses on a single occasion in 1677, 4,000 verses in 1680, and the amazing total of 23,400 verses in one day in 1684. Obviously, the quality of these verses, composed at the rate of several a minute, cannot have been of uniformly high standard, but Saikaku's fertility of invention was unexcelled.

Saikaku's first novel, *Kōshoku Ichidai Otoko* (The man who spent his life at lovemaking; 1682), is the tale of Yonosuke, whose amorous exploits begin precociously in his seventh year, and who is last seen fifty years later as he sails off on a ship loaded with aphrodisiacs for an island populated exclusively by women. The manner and incidents hardly suggest that this novel was based on *Genji Monogatari,* but parallels in the text and even the number of chapters indicate that Saikaku was consciously attempting to write a Genroku equivalent of the Heian masterpiece. Yonosuke demonstrates none of the sensitivity or intelligence of Genji, but in a mechanical, uninvolved manner amasses a staggering total of amorous conquests.

The name Yonosuke was probably short for Ukiyonosuke, *ukiyo* being a key term in understanding Genroku culture. Originally it meant "the sad world," a typically Buddhist phrase, but by a pun came to mean "the floating world," or the world of uncertainties. For most peoples uncertainty has always seemed the source of grief (we need only recall the Greek chorus dolefully reminding us that we should call no man's life happy until he is dead), but in Genroku Japan it stood for the fascination of an endlessly changing, unpredictable world. To be abreast of the floating world was to be up-to-date, sharing in the latest fashions and slang, delighting in the momentary rather than in the eternal truths sought in the Nō plays or medieval poetry. Saikaku's novels are superficial alongside the great works of earlier Japanese fiction; their characters are hardly more than marionettes, but like marionettes they perform with deft exaggerations human actions. Saikaku's best work, *Kōshoku Gonin Onna* (Five women who loved love; 1686), is filled with revelations of the author's intimate knowledge of the foibles of his society. If we do not take his characters seriously, neither did Saikaku; he seems to be observing them through the reverse end of a telescope, maintaining his objectivity and detached humor even when describing the execution of an innocent person. Saikaku certainly did not hate his characters, but their tragedies, seen from his point of vantage, became the stuff of human comedy.

Saikaku's novels consisted of three main varieties: amorous tales, stories about merchants, and samurai tales. His amorous works display his flashing style at its most volatile and effective, recalling the comic *renga* traditions. His merchant stories are chiefly concerned with ways to earn or lose a fortune, but their apparently didactic intent is easily overlooked in the artful narration. Saikaku, ever the master of the telling detail, created figures of the floating world whose vitality makes up for their lack of depth. The samurai stories, Saikaku's least successful, reveal his admiration for the class but lack the incisiveness of his treatment of merchant society.

Saikaku is often contrasted with the playwright Chikamatsu Monzaemon (1653–1725), Saikaku being styled a realist and Chikamatsu a romanticist. Certainly Saikaku's portraits of prostitutes are completely unsentimental: the heroine of *Kōshoku Ichidai Onna* (The life of an amorous woman; 1686) enjoys her métier and at the end spends her decrepit old age in a hut named "The Hermitage of Voluptuousness." Chikamatsu, on the other hand, usually portrays his creatures of the demimonde sympathetically, insisting that even a common prostitute is capable of genuine affection. His heroines gladly choose suicide with the men they love in preference to being "ransomed" from their brothels by a despised suitor. It is cynically assumed therefore that Saikaku must have written the truth, but that Chikamatsu glossed over unpleasant realities in the interests of pathos; more probably, each man modified reality to suit his talents. Saikaku's hard-boiled prostitutes were no more typical than Chikamatsu's self-sacrificing victims of poverty and misfortune, but the former's comic purpose required him to de-emphasize the pathetic aspects of his characters. In one instance where both men treated the same story (the unpremeditated love affair between Osan, the almanac-maker's wife, and the clerk Mōemon) Saikaku's version remains comic even though the lovers are executed at the end, but Chikamatsu's tragic tone is scarcely relieved by a happy ending. The characters, once created by their authors, seemed to determine the comic or tragic effect irrespective of incidents.

Chikamatsu wrote mainly for the puppet theater (later called *Bunraku*), an art which had sprung up almost simultaneously with the beginning of the Tokugawa regime. He apparently preferred to write for puppets rather than actors because the latter, in the Kabuki tradition, considered the plays to be no more than vehicles, to be altered at their fancy. The puppets were less temperamental, but this theater imposed a special requirement of exaggeration, necessary in order to impart "human" qualities to wooden figures. Chikamatsu's texts represented a compromise between what he would ideally have liked to express and what his audiences were willing to accept. His plays contain flights of poetry that soared above the heads of the spectators but are also marred by absurdities introduced to appeal to audiences craving novelty and excitement.

Chikamatsu's plays included histories (*jidaimono*) based at least vaguely on the lives of historical personages, and domestic tragedies (*sewamono*) which treated the misfortunes afflicting merchants or samurai of low rank. Modern critics unaminously prefer the second category; the plays are better knit, more realistic, and more successful in terms of universally accepted standards. Chikamatsu's audiences, however, enjoyed the bombast and excitement of the texts of the historical plays, and the greater range of movement they afforded the puppets. Chikamatsu's most popular play, *Kokusenya Kassen* (The battles of Coxinga; 1715), is filled with extravagant and improbable doings, but it exploits the potentialities of the puppet theater better, than, say, a masterpiece like *Shinjū Ten no Amijima* (The love suicides at Amijima; 1720) which can be performed by actors as successfully as by puppets.

Chikamatsu's works are often discussed in terms of the conflict between *giri* (obligation) and *ninjō* (human feelings). The characters are constantly worrying about their obligations to their family or to society as a whole, sometimes evincing an almost ludicrous concern over appearances. When pressed to the wall, however, they are likely to give way totally to their emotions, abandoning any attempt at a rational solution. Jihei in *Shinjū Ten no Amijima* decides to commit suicide with the prostitute Koharu because he fears that otherwise his rival Tahei will ransom her, and he will be humiliated. Suicide, however, means leaving behind his wife and two small children; this fact does not deter Jihei, but before he and Koharu commit suicide they are at pains to die some distance apart so as to avoid giving offense to Jihei's wife, to whom both are obliged. The precipitate actions of Chikamatsu's heroes accord poorly with Confucian ideals, but Chikamatsu undoubtedly expected that audiences would sympathize with their emotionally pure, if rationally deficient, actions. The intensity of the emotions of Jihei, the owner of a paper shop, gave him the stature of a tragic hero. Aristotle might have denied that a man of so humble a calling could figure as the hero of a tragedy, but Chikamatsu was aware that tragedy struck irrespective of status. In this respect Chikamatsu's heroes are closer than Shakespeare's to those of modern theater.

Japanese drama after Chikamatsu did not develop along the lines of his best domestic tragedies. Instead, plays tended to be mixtures of historical and domestic elements, often also interlarded with comic relief. The most popular play of the traditional theater, *Chūshingura* (The treasury of loyal retainers, or forty-seven rōnin; 1748) by Takeda Izumo and others, is a superb example of how the faults of the puppet theater—the exaggeration, dependence on unexpected twists in the plot, thinness of characterization, conventionality of language, ineffectual structure—could be surmounted by a foolproof story, the vengeance wreaked by the forty-seven loyal retainers of the Lord of Akō. Later dramas, whether for the puppet theater or Kabuki, attained the heights of *Chūshingura* only intermittently, partly owing to the multiple authorship of most plays. This unevenness favored the practice, still observed today, of presenting only an act or two of a play, as part of a longer program.

Saikaku and Chikamatsu, though antithetically different in style and outlook, both belonged to the Genroku world. The third great figure of the period, the haiku poet Matsuo Bashō (1644–94), seems utterly aloof from the age, a throwback to the hermit-priests who had taken no interest in the vagaries of *ukiyo*. Bashō's detachment is often exaggerated: his early poetry had much in common with Saikaku's, and for all his devotion to Saigyō, Sōgi, and other poets of the past, he always insisted on freshness. He advised a pupil, "Do not follow in the footsteps of the men of old—seek what they sought." Nevertheless, we have only to compare Bashō's literary remains, easily contained in a single volume, with the multivolumed sets of Saikaku or Chikamatsu to detect a marked difference between their Genroku exuberance and Bashō's sobriety. He wrote little more than a thousand haiku in his whole life, less than many haiku poets have produced in a single year. This meant, of course, that Bashō's haiku were frequently revised. Although on occasion he would turn out impromptu verses, his memorable haiku were the result of three or more recastings. This spirit of perfectionism accounts for the length of time—five years—it took Bashō to write his most celebrated work, the travel diary *Oku no Hosomichi* (The narrow road of Oku; 1694), a mere thirty pages in most editions.

The haiku developed in Bashō's hands from the flashing moment of esprit typical of Saikaku into a distillation of the world in seventeen syllables. He described in his conversations the haiku ideals; his most important dictum was that the haiku must be both eternal and momentary. If it does not partake of the eternal qualities of literature, it will be ephemeral, but if it is eternal in the manner of the stale phraseology of the tanka, it will not be worthy of its traditions. The haiku must describe this particular moment, but the moment is of interest only against the background of timelessness. A haiku usually consists of two components: an unchanging factor, whether the expanse of the sea, an old pond, or the silence of the mountains, and a momentary occurrence which interrupts the eternal, making us realize its nature for the first time. A haiku composed on the *Oku no Hosomichi* journey reveals Bashō's artistry:

Shizukasa ya	How still it is!
Iwa ni shimiiru	Stabbing into the rocks,
Semi no koe	The cicadas' voices.

The stillness is the eternal component, interrupted by the momentary voices of the cicadas, so sharp they seem to stab into the rocks of the mountain. Only after the interruption are we aware of the otherwise imperceptible silence. The season, an essential element in the haiku, is disclosed by mention of the cicada (*semi*), an insect associated with late summer. The time of day is evening, when cicadas sing. The landscape is dominated by rocky crags. Even the sound of the words contributes to the effect: five of the seven vowels in the second line are *i,* suggesting the sound of the cicadas' trilling. The haiku is a perfect evocation of the place, a lonely temple built on the side of a mountain.

The two elements of haiku must be fused by the reader in an act of creation. A haiku is a failure if it simply describes a scene or makes a statement. The greater the tension between the two elements—the eternal and the momentary—the more successful the haiku. The haiku poets, sensing this, sometimes tried too hard and included elements whose relationship was excessively obscure; but just as a haiku's effect is slight if no distance separates the two elements—denying the reader the pleasure of a moment of creative intuition—it will be lost if the elements are so far apart that the reader cannot bridge them. Bashō, rejecting obscurity, insisted in his last period on "lightness" (*karumi*) as a touchstone of true haiku quality.

Bashō had many disciples, some still admired today, but the next haiku poet of first magnitude was Yosa Buson (1716–83). Bashō's manner was seldom successfully imitated even by his followers, if only because they lacked the intensity of Bashō's devotion to his art. Scholars of Bashō have pointed out the marked influence of Zen Buddhism in his haiku; they mean what they say on the surface but also present deeper insights into truth. Buson's haiku, like his paintings, are graceful and evocative, but lack Bashō's depth. He favored the use of the haiku to tell a story with a few artfully selected details, just as in the school of painting to which he belonged a few perfectly placed lines could suggest a larger scene and sometimes even a story.

> *Samidare ya*   The rainy season—
> *Taiga wo mae ni*   The swollen river before them,
> *Ie ni ken*   Two little houses.

Buson was preferred to Bashō by the poet and critic Masaoka Shiki (1867–1902), who especially admired Buson's ability to paint life. Shiki's judgment in turn affected many later haiku poets, and Buson's influence today is probably stronger than Bashō's.

By the early nineteenth century the Tokugawa culture seemed

to have exhausted itself, despite the persistence of novels, plays, and poetry in the traditions of Saikaku, Chikamatsu and Bashō. The novels had largely degenerated into frivolous tales purchased as much for their illustrations as their content; the theater had turned increasingly to the morbid and grotesque; the haiku, lacking the depth Bashō had given it, had become a kind of painting in words. Literature, deprived of any stimulus from abroad, had reached an impasse of repetition and threatened to turn into verbal equivalents of the ukiyo-e prints—elegantly composed, but two-dimensional and often superficial. Some writers reacted to these frivolous tendencies by choosing the opposite extremes. Takizawa Bakin (1767–1847), for example, relied on the war tales of medieval Japan and Confucian philosophy in writing his immensely long and desperately didactic novels, notably *Hakkenden* (Biography of eight dogs), over which he toiled from 1814 to 1841. Bakin's avowed purpose, as a samurai and a believer in Confucian morality, was to use literature as an instrument in "encouraging virtue and chastising vice" (*kanzen chōaku*). This unquestionably was his intent, but *Hakkenden* and his other novels were read mainly for the fantastic plots, involving prodigies, transformations, and a host of markedly non-Confucian themes. Bakin's novels enjoyed such esteem in their own time and later that W. G. Aston, writing in 1899 the first history of Japanese literature, reported that "nine out of ten Japanese if asked to name their greatest novelist would reply immediately 'Bakin.' " Certainly, the seriousness of tone and high moral purpose of Bakin's writings, for all their leavening of fantasy, contrasted favorably with the frivolity of most novelists of his time.

The late Tokugawa poets, including Tachibana Akemi (1812–68) in the tanka and Kobayashi Issa (1763–1828) in the haiku, showed their impatience with worn-out conventions by treating the humble, ordinary events of life rather than the obviously poetic themes, and Rai Sanyō (1780–1832), probably the greatest Japanese writer of Chinese poetry, expressed an intensity of concern with social and political problems quite foreign to usual poetic expression. But neither poets nor prose writers could come to grips with the serious questions of the age. State censorship inhibited writers, and the lack of external stimulus forced Japanese to plumb the nearly exhausted resources of their own literary heritage.

The arrival of Commodore Perry's fleet in 1853 ushered in developments which eventually destroyed the closed society of Tokugawa Japan and brought about the Meiji Restoration of 1868. In the sixteenth century Portuguese and Spanish missionaries had resided in Japan and won many converts to Catholicism, but the Japanese gained little knowledge of European literature from this contact. *Aesop's Fables* and possibly part of the *Odyssey* were known, and even exerted some influence on Japanese writing, but the lasting effect was slight. The European penetration of Japanese life after 1868, on the other hand, profoundly affected all forms of writing.

Modern Literature

The earliest literary reactions to the West took the form of satire directed against Japanese affecting Western ways, but bit by bit Western inventions were adopted into Japanese literature. The playwright Kawatake Mokuami, (1816–93), the only major author to have straddled the Restoration, mentioned trains, the telegraph, and the new penal code in his plays about gamblers and thieves. Japanese students returned from abroad with a knowledge of foreign literatures and began also to make translations and imitations. The Japanese have sometimes been taxed for their excessive proclivity for imitation, but a period of imitation was essential before Japanese writers could find their new voices. Imitation of Western examples, in fact, liberated Japanese from the stultification of a long period when literature had become excessively Japanese. Western influence, by providing new forms of expression, enabled the Japanese, at last members of the modern world, to be themselves, though it was not always easy for them to reject the themes and traditions of the past.

The literary revolution was first clearly enunciated by Tsubouchi Shōyō (1859–1935) in *Shōsetsu Shinzui* (Essence of the novel; 1885). Though an admirer of Bakin, Tsubouchi despised the productions of Bakin's imitators, who pandered to the public taste for lurid and erotic writings while professing their desire to "encourage virtue and chastise vice." His readings in European literature convinced him that literature must be an art and not mere diversion, and that it must depict life faithfully, rather than in ostensibly didactic terms. He believed also that the conventional literary language, used even in popular novels, was inadequate for modern fiction, and that Japanese must follow the Europeans in employing the colloquial. Tsubouchi's judgments were astute and laid the foundation for future literary developments, but his own novels and plays were more conventional than he intended, revealing the powerful attraction of the old literature even on the new iconoclasts.

Ukigumo (The drifting cloud; 1887–89) by Futabatei Shimei (1864–1909) was the first modern Japanese novel. The author, who had been educated at a school for training future Japanese officials in the Russian language, possessed an unusual familiarity with Russian literature, and his choice of the colloquial as a medium of fiction undoubtedly stemmed from this knowledge. The vivid style, no less than the novelty of the material, makes *Ukigumo* a monument of Meiji literature. The plot describes Bunzō, a young man of ability and honesty, who is unable to keep abreast of the new society because his gentlemanly scruples, a product of his samurai training, prevent him from toadying to superiors and otherwise acting in the "aggressive" manner expected of the new Meiji men. His failure to impose himself on society is matched by a failure to cope with individual members of the society; his samurai code of behavior makes him timid before the woman he loves and a figure of fun in the eyes of more aggressive associates. In the end he is reduced to a helpless irresolution which may remind us of Oblomov, the supreme example of the lethargic hero. But whereas Goncharov's "hero" embodies the foolishness and incompetence of the old aristocracy, Bunzō embodies its virtues, virtues without value in a changed world. It is easy to feel that Bunzō, for all his incompetence, is more worthy of our respect than the pushing new men dedicated to "self-help" in the Western manner.

The frivolity and ornamented style of the old fiction persisted in most Japanese writing even after *Ukigumo* showed the way to more advanced and psychologically absorbing fiction. Prose writers gradually adopted the colloquial, but poetry continued to be written for the most part in classical Japanese. The drama was most conservative of all. Some Japanese enthusiastically greeted both translated versions of European plays and modern Japanese works, but the public as a whole, accustomed to the spectacular Kabuki performances with their combinations of flamboyant acting, dance, and music, did not respond to plays in which a few drably attired characters sat and discussed their woes. When at last a Japanese public had evolved which was capable of appreciating modern drama, the motion pictures stole away this potential audience from the theater. The result has been that few distinguished works were written for the modern stage before 1949 when Kinoshita Junji (b. 1914) published *Yuzuru* (Twilight crane), a play that enjoyed extraordinary success.

Poetry in modern times has been guided by Western influence but shaped ultimately by the Japanese language. In the ancient past, when Japanese poets were directly inspired by Chinese works, they often described landscapes they had never seen because they had to adapt themselves to the natural expression of the Chinese language; but the Japanese poets who moved from romanticism to symbolism and from surrealism to dadaism, allying themselves with successive European fashions, were in no danger of losing their identity, if only because they wrote Japanese. A dadaist poem is as much Japanese as French, for it represents an attitude rather than a culture imposing national preferences. Japanese literature became part of the world literature for the first time, though this fact was not recognized elsewhere.

The creator of the modern poem was Shimazaki Tōson (1872–1943). Though influenced by Shelley and even by Christian hymns, his lyric poems remained distinctively Japanese in their expression, and they captured the imaginations of innumerable young readers, who identified the poet's romantic yearnings with their own. The outstanding Japanese poet of the twentieth century was Hagiwara Sakutarō (1886–1942). His point of departure was French Symbolism, but he soon displayed a totally individual style, expressing (most often in colloquial Japanese) the malaise of a sensitive man in an age of anxiety. His disciple Miyoshi Tatsuji (1900–63) captured with surpassing skill the music of Japanese, both the old literary language and the colloquial.

Despite the excellence of much modern poetry, whether in new forms of Western origin or in the tanka and haiku, forms given new life by Masaoka Shiki (1867–1902) and Ishikawa Takuboku (1885–1912), most Japanese used the words "modern literature" to designate fiction—the novel, novella, or short story. European influences were no less pronounced in fiction than in poetry, but Japanese taste more conspicuously affected these influences. The autobiographical novel, for example, stemmed from nineteenth-century European fiction, and was known as the "Ich Roman" to its Japanese creator, Mori Ōgai (1862–1922). By the late 1920s, however, this variety of fiction had assumed dominant importance, far exceeding its status in the West; some writers and critics considered it to be the only "serious" form. Again, Shimazaki and others adopted naturalism from the French in the early 1900s, but the humanitarian fervor of Zola's naturalism soon gave way in their writings to unadorned autobiographical descriptions closely related to the "Ich Roman." Other writers who began their careers by writing in a fashionably modern idiom turned back in later years to Japanese tradition.

A pattern may be traced in the careers of many figures of modern Japanese fiction. First, a novelist experiences a period of strong influence from a European literature (Russian for Futabatei Shimei, German for Mori Ōgai, English for Natsume Sōseki, French for Nagai Kafū, etc.); next comes a period when he incorporates European techniques in his writing; and finally, he rejects obvious Western influence in favor of traditional Japanese material. The pattern was naturally not followed exactly in all instances, but a glance at the career of Mori Ōgai or Natsume Sōseki, the two pillars of Meiji literature, shows striking similarities, though their novels are entirely different. Mori studied medicine in Germany from 1884 to 1888, and his first work, *Maihime* (The dancing girl; 1890), describes in unmistakably autobiographical terms the ill-fated romance between a Japanese student and a German dancer. This "Ich Roman" was followed by stories in a wildly romantic German vein. Mori's version of a German translation of Hans Christian Andersen's *Improvisatoren,* published between 1892 and 1901, was acclaimed as a masterpiece of Japanese style. His next important novel, *Gan* (The wild goose; 1911–13), is a romantic work with a symbolic title (the heroine, like a wild goose on a pond near her house, is destroyed by an act of cruelty) but it closely reflects life in Meiji Japan. Shortly after completing *Gan,* Mori turned to writing tales of samurai, apparently moved by the suicides of General Nogi and his wife after the Emperor Meiji's death in 1912. He rejected the techniques of fiction and avowed in a preface to one novel that he could vouch for the historical authenticity of every incident. No personal note survived in these objectively narrated stories, but clearly Mori looked at his samurai heroes with nostalgia and the eyes of an outsider; no samurai observer of the events related in, say, *Abe Ichizoku* (The Abe family; 1913) would have been so aware of the majestic beauty of the names of dead warriors listed in the story. Mori had returned to traditional Japan after a long immersion in Western culture, and he was tremendously moved by what he saw.

Natsume Sōseki (1867–1916) resided in England from 1900 to 1903 studying English literature, particularly the novels of George Meredith, whose influence is apparent in Natsume's early works. *Wagahai wa Neko de Aru* (I am a cat; 1905) and *Botchan* (1906) are imbued with a humor not often encountered in modern Japanese fiction.

Gradually, however, Natsume moved to more philosophical attitudes, attempting to depict the disastrous effects of self-centeredness. His masterpiece, *Kokoro* (The heart; 1914), tells of a man tormented by guilt over his betrayal of a friend. Natsume used the English word "egoism" to denote what he considered to be the root of unhappiness, and offered the formula *sokuten kyoshi* (to follow Heaven and shed the self) as a way of combating egoism. His shift from Western individualism to Oriental detachment was accompanied by increased interest in composing poetry in Chinese and a deepening tone of resignation in his fiction.

A similar pattern may be traced in the writings of Tanizaki Junichirō (1886–1965), who moved from an unabashed fascination with the West to a position of doubt and rejection—exemplified by his novel *Tade kuu Mushi* (Some prefer nettles; 1928)—to an absorption in the Japanese classics expressed not only in his original writings but in three complete translations of *Genji Monogatari* into modern Japanese. In his old age he reached a rather cynical acceptance of a world which he was powerless to change and which, he recognized, has its own wayward charms.

Modern Japanese fiction, though dominated by a dozen or so authors, is frequently discussed in terms of schools and subschools, suggesting that the literary principles of a group were more significant than the views of any individual. In one case this was true: the writings of the "proletarian" movement, though unequally endowed with literary value, were more important as an expression of the belief that writers must be concerned with social problems than as single works. Most products of this school today seem badly dated or even inept, but their concern over social injustice sometimes makes them moving documents.

The new important writers of the 1920s, like Akutagawa Ryūnosuke (1892–1927) or Kawabata Yasunari (1899–1972), though assigned to schools, shared with other members only a distaste for the ideologically motivated proletarian movement or for the Shirakaba group of aristocrats who used their writings to express Tolstoian ideals. Shiga Naoya (1883–1971), originally a member of the Shirakaba group, became perhaps the most influential writer of his time. His autobiographical works, known as *shishōsetsu* (I novels), usually described in a poetic but deliberately restrained manner the unexciting experiences of his daily life. His many disciples considered such writing to be artistically far superior to the creation of fiction, the work of mere storytellers.

The established novelists of the previous decade continued to publish important works in the 1930s, but the series of wars in China, culminating with the outbreak of the "Greater East Asia War" in 1941, led to increasingly severe restrictions on the literary productions even of well-known authors. Tanizaki's long novel *Sasameyuki* (Light snow; 1943–48, translated into English as *The Makioka Sisters*) could not be published during the war. With few exceptions, however, Japanese writers either cooperated with the government or attempted to avoid notice; there was no "resistance writing" directed at the militarists.

When the war at last ended in 1945 an exhausted Japanese nation turned to literature with great enthusiasm as an escape from harsh realities. Of the fiction from the war years only the writings of Dazai Osamu (1908–48) can still be read with admiration. Dazai's reputation was further enhanced in the immediate postwar period. His novel *Shayō* (The setting sun; 1947) was acclaimed for its bittersweet portrayal of the Japanese aristocracy in decline after the war; and his autobiographical *Ningen Shikkaku* (No longer human; 1948) profoundly moved many thousands of young intellectuals who identified themselves with the unhappy hero.

The postwar period saw a large outpouring of literature by established writers who had accumulated manuscripts they could not publish during the war. Kawabata in 1947 finally completed his masterpiece *Yukiguni* (Snow country; 1947), begun twelve years earlier, and was awarded the highest honors by the government after the publication of *Sembazuru* (Thousand cranes; 1948) and *Yama no Oto* (The sound of the mountains; 1951). At a time when most Japanese, stunned by their defeat in the war and reacting against the nationalist ideals that had involved them in great suffering, tended to reject their past, Kawabata still found inspiration in the wellsprings of Japanese taste and sensitivity even when he described entirely modern situations.

New writers also rose to prominence at this time, notably Ōoka Shōhei (b. 1909), whose novel *Nobi* (Fires on the plain; 1952), a description of the horrors of war as seen through the eyes of a Japanese private in the Philippines, was unquestionably the finest work to come out of the war. The devastation of the atomic bomb inspired much poetry and prose, but not until 1966 with the publication of *Kuroi Ame* (Black rain; 1966) by Ibuse Masuji (b. 1898) was an author successful in imparting literary distinction to his recounting of the terrible events in Hiroshima.

Perhaps the finest of the new writers to emerge after the war was Mishima Yukio (1925–1970). Mishima's first novel, the autobiographical *Kamen no Kokuhaku* (Confessions of a mask; 1948), immediately established him as a major writer. Mishima, however, turned his back on the world of the *shishōsetsu* and deliberately applied himself to the task of creating a world of fiction. Each work he published represented a new exploration of the novelist's art, including the sunny *Shiosai* (Sound of the waves; 1954), a Japanese equivalent of the celebrated Greek romance *Daphnis and Chloë;* the Dostoievskian complexities of *Kinkakuji* (The Golden Pavilion; 1956); and the realistic descriptions of contemporary Tokyo politics in *Utage no Ato* (After the banquet; 1960). Mishima also established a reputation as the leading dramatist of his day, writing plays that stemmed from the Nō and Kabuki traditions, as well as entirely modern dramas, such as *Sado Kōshaku Fujin* (Madame de Sade; 1965). His last work, completed shortly before his sensational suicide, was the tetralogy *Hōjō no Umi* (The sea of fertility; 1969–71), acclaimed by many as his masterpiece.

Abe Kōbō (b. 1924), though almost exactly a contemporary of Mishima's, did not gain general recognition until the publication of *Suna no Onna* (Woman in the dunes; 1963). Unlike Mishima, who constantly turned to Japanese classical literature for inspiration and who sought in many works to capture the particularities of life in Japan, Abe's novels and plays were intended to transcend the particular in an attempt to deal at the deepest level with the human condition.

A still younger generation of writers was represented by Ōe Kenzaburō (b. 1935), a powerful novelist whose concern with politics was expressed openly in numerous essays and indirectly in his fiction.

A large and generous public supported many writers and an astonishing number of literary magazines. Successful novels often sold 100,000 or more copies, and the works of the pioneers of modern Japanese literature, especially Natsume Sōseki and Akutagawa Ryūnosuke, were constantly reprinted, even though it no longer seemed possible that a single family in Japan could be without a set.

One important new development since 1945 was the appearance of many translations into English and other languages. Although this fame spread abroad did not directly affect the novelists in their work, they were aware that for the first time it was now possible for them to win an international audience. The award of the Nobel Prize in Literature to Kawabata Yasunari in 1968 was a source of profound satisfaction not only to writers but to the Japanese public as a whole, for it seemed clear recognition that Japanese modern literature had attained the highest level of excellence.

XIII

Economic

and Cultural

Geography

BY
NORTON GINSBURG

It is customary to say that the physical geography of Japan has continued its history and culture. It is less commonly said that the geography of contemporary Japan is a consequence in large part of its history and culture. Yet this is so. Given a set of natural conditions, an array of largely volcanic islands set in a shimmering sea, the far Western Pacific, the Japanese proceeded to create a landscape that is uniquely theirs. They distributed themselves and their works over the islands where they wished them to be, not merely where nature necessarily presented the best opportunities for occupancy. In short, the contemporary geography of Japan is a product of particular men with a unique culture, working out their history within a given environment which they have changed where they wished and where their technology permitted.

If these assertions seem paradoxes, there are yet others which form themes about which a description of Japan can be organized. One of these is the paradox of size. Japan is usually described as a small country, but this is according to Chinese, Indian, and North American standards. By European standards, Japan is relatively large. With its 143,750 square miles, it is more than half again as large as West Germany or the United Kingdom and larger than Poland or Italy, although it is only about the size of the state of Montana in the United States. Furthermore, in terms of population it ranks sixth in the world, following China, India, the USSR, the United States, and Indonesia.

Another contradiction is found in the assertion that Japan is an exceedingly crowded country. With a population density of 725 per square mile, it indeed ranks among the more densely populated countries. Yet that density is lower than that of the Netherlands or Belgium and only somewhat higher than that of West Germany, the United Kingdom, and Italy. Moreover, one of the most striking characteristics of the geography of Japan is the fact that so much of it lies empty. Clearly, this circumstance also requires explanation.

Finally, there is the paradox of the perception of Japan as a poor country, held not only by foreigners but by the Japanese themselves, along with the fact that Japan exceeds the United Kingdom in gross national product and surpasses many of the leading industrial powers of Europe in the production of steel and the consumption of energy, two of the better measures of economic development and power. Even on a per capita basis, where Japan ranks much lower, it now has attained Western European levels and lies around Italy on the scale of per capita income. Indeed, of all the countries of Asia, Japan is the only one entitled to the accolade "developed." Yet its economy is characterized by a pervading dualism that intrudes even into the industrial sector.

Location and Topography

The Japanese archipelago lies off the coast of eastern Asia, separated from the mainland by the narrow Straits of Tsushima and Korea, which together span 116 miles, and the Sea of Japan, at its widest some 550 miles. As in the case of the United Kingdom off the western coast of Europe, this insular character and separation has presented advantages and disadvantages at various periods in Japanese history. It has not necessarily made the Japanese better seamen, nor great world traders, nor a great naval power. On the contrary, it has contributed on one hand to long periods of isolation and on the other to the control of international and intercultural relations by various regimes. The Tokugawa shogunate was able to maintain a policy of seclusion for over 200 years as effectively as it did because Japan was an island country, and it was this characteristic that saved Japan from Mongol conquest in the thirteenth century. On the other hand, the seas are not only barriers but also avenues of communication, and it was across the straits between Japan and Korea that Chinese cultural influences moved with such authority and attraction that Japanese society became extensively Sinicized during the seventh century and thereafter. It was also over the seas that the first Europeans came to Japan, and eventually the "black ships" of Commodore Perry in 1853.

The archipelago itself consists of four main islands—Hokkaido, Honshu, Kyushu, and Shikoku—plus a host of lesser islands of which the largest is Sado off the west coast of Honshu. Of the four main islands, Honshu with 89,000 square miles is by far the largest; Hokkaido with 30,000 square miles is second; Kyushu and Shikoku following with 16,000 and 7,200 square miles respectively. In addition to these the Japanese Empire included as of 1940 the Kurile Islands (Chishima Retto), the Ryukyus, Taiwan, Korea, and Karafuto (southern Sakhalin), and it maintained puppet governments in Manchuria and northern China as well. As a result of the Pacific

War, Japan lost control of all of these territories, with the exception of the northern Ryukyus and residual rights to the southern Ryukyus (Okinawa), the later area being returned to her in 1972.

Structurally, the Japanese archipelago consists of the tops of mountains, mostly volcanic, which rise above the deep waters of the Pacific and form part of the circum-Pacific zone of active vulcanism. To the east is the Japan Trench, one of the deeper troughs of the Pacific Ocean, with depths over 30,000 feet; to the west is the Sea of Japan, also a deep-water arm of the great ocean, unlike the other seas of eastern Asia, which for the most part lie over the continental shelf. That these adjoining waters are deep is important in understanding some of the characteristics of Japan's climate.

In addition, Japan has a coastline of some 17,000 miles, representing a high ratio of coastline to land area. Much of this coastline presents inviting indentations and partially enclosed bodies of water like the Inland Sea, which provide natural harbors for fishing and for trade. In a sense, the Inland Sea might be regarded as one great harbor, with innumerable lesser harbors and shelters rimming its shores. Several great embayments, of which Tokyo and Ise Bays are the most noteworthy, appear on the Pacific coast of Honshu, and these also are the sites of great ports, handicapped somewhat, however, because of the shallow waters at the heads of these bays. With some exceptions, natural harbors are scarce on the coast of the Japan Sea.

Most of Japan is hilly or mountainous; only one quarter of its land area is in slopes of less than fifteen degrees. On a national and even regional scale, the natural landscape of Japan is typified by mountains and ocean, and there are few densely inhabited parts of the country that are not within easy access of both. Several mountain arcs, some partly submerged, converge upon Japan and form the spines about which the rest of the country is arranged. In central Honshu is the so-called Chubu (Central)Node, at which three such arcs intersect—the Northeastern, the Southwestern, and the Bonin, which enters Honshu through a chain of islands extending southward from Honshu. In west-central Hokkaido is a second node, created by the convergence of the Karafuto and Kurile arcs from the north and northeast, and the Northeastern arc from the southwest. Finally, in north-central Kyushu is the Kyushu Node, resulting from the intersection of the Southwestern arc and the Ryukyu arc which enters Kyushu from the southwest. These nodes and arcs for the most part are associated with some 180 volcanoes, many of them still active. These are least common in Shikoku and in the southwestern portion of Honshu known as Chugoku. In all, these ranges and mountains, with associated hill country, make cross-island communication difficult for Honshu. There is only one major break across the barrier, that associated with the Biwa Depression, of which Lake Biwa is the best known natural feature.

Along the margins of the islands, but not continuously, and within the uplands themselves, are a large number of relatively small aggradational plains and basins. All of these are covered or floored with alluvium, and their total area is no more than 15 percent of all Japan. The largest of these is the Kanto Plain at the head of Tokyo Bay, with an area of about 12,500 square miles. Others of importance include the Osaka Plain, the Ishikari-Yufutsu Lowland of Hokkaido, the Echigo or Niigata Plain of northwestern Honshu, the Nobi or Nagoya Plain of central Honshu, and the Tsukushi Lowland of northern Kyushu. Few of these lowlands are flat-floored. The Kanto Plain in particular is associated with two levels of alluvial deposits, one older than the other, and with foothills of the bordering mountains. These levels are marked by different types of land uses in keeping with variations in slope, soils, drainage, and natural vegetation. Most important, there is a dramatic coincidence between these lowlands and the distribution of both agricultural land and population.

Japan's soils closely reflect its surface configuration. Fully two thirds of Japan's soils are classified as lithosols, that is, immature soils without well-developed profiles, generally thin and infertile. These are largely mountain soils, with some beach sands and volcanic ash. Of the remainder, about 18 percent consists of so-called zonal and intrazonal soils, of varying degrees of fertility. The zonal soils are marked by altitudinal as well as latitudinal zonation, and range from podzols in the far north and at higher altitudes to gray-brown podzolics in intermediate locations and red-and-yellow podzolics in the lower latitudes. About 14 percent of the soils are classified as alluvials, relatively recently laid down by fluvial action, and are associated with lowlands. Since none of these lowland areas are structural or erosional plains, like those of the North American Middle West, for example, they contain no rich basic grassland soils.

Drainage patterns reflect both the terrain characteristics of the country and the abundant rainfall that occurs in most of upland Japan. Rivers are short and swift; the longest is not more than 200 miles in length. Most rise high on the slopes of the major ranges or peaks, hurtle downhill through deep V-shaped canyons which broaden toward the sea, and then debouch upon broadly deltaic lowlands across which they flow on elevated beds and with braided channels, dropping sediment wherever they can. During much of the year streams appear far too small to have created the valleys and alluvial lowlands of their middle and lower courses, and their beds appear gravel-strewn and dry; but during the early spring or at times of heavy typhoon rains they not only fill their channels to the brim but flow through or over them to inundate large areas of occupied lowland, spreading destruction with their floods. Few are navigable, except for very short distances and even then chiefly for small native boats and rafts; but they offer numerous possibilities for the development of hydroelectric energy. Until recently, therefore, most of the electrical energy developed in Japan was of steam origin. Despite the seeming abundance of surface water, however, the Japanese have long supplemented their water supplies with ground water drawn from wells. This source of water is used for irrigation or municipal and industrial water supplies, so much so that over 40 percent of all municipal water is supplied from ground water. Even more striking, the vast demand for water associated with urbanization and industrialization, together with ever higher demands for irrigation water, has resulted in acute water shortages in certain parts of the country.

If mountain, sea, and river are three essential natural ingredients of the Japanese rural landscape, forests are yet a fourth. More than 66 percent of the country is in forest; in addition, nearly 10 percent is in wasteland or scrub. In all, these areas are associated almost precisely with the uplands of the country. In their near-natural state about 1,500 years ago, and to some extent in the present, the forests of Japan displayed a marked latitudinal and altitudinal zonation. In the southwestern part of the archipelago, particularly at lower and middle altitudes, broad-leaved evergreen species predominated, mixed with some deciduous species, among which oaks were most conspicuous; at higher altitudes, various conifers appeared. In central Japan deciduous species predominated in ecological associations somewhat similar to those in the central part of the eastern seaboard of the United States, and included maple, oak, beech, poplar, and birch. Farther north, arboreal forest, dominated by needle-leaved evergreens, was prevalent.

In contemporary Japan, these basic patterns have been substantially modified. In the southwest, deciduous species introduced by men have come to be dominant, and at higher altitudes, as in all parts of Japan, planted stands, chiefly of conifers, dominate the landscape. Changes in the central and northern regions have been less dramatic, but planted forest accounts for over 25 percent of all Japanese forests, and most of it is coniferous—Japanese cedar, Japanese cypress, red pine, and black pine. Equally significant is the fact that over 36 percent of all forests are designated as suitable for fuel wood and only 27 percent for saw timber. Most of the remainder is either inaccessible or in neeed of reforestation. Over half of the forested areas are in the hands of private owners, chiefly in small plots which are harvested regularly for fuel wood. Apart from fuel wood plots, only a small proportion of all Japan's forests provide domestically produced timber, and the pressure on these areas is intense, with overcutting a continuous problem.

Climate

Except for land forms, and even there in part, the character of the nonmineral natural endowment of Japan is a function of climate. Five major elements help to explain the Japanese climate. The simplest is latitude. In a country that extends through 14 degrees of latitude, from 31 degrees north to 45 degrees north, differences in seasonal distributions of temperature are to be expected. Southwestern Japan has long hot summers and relatively short mild winters. Central Japan has hot summers and short cool-to-cold winters. Northern Japan has warm summers and long hard winters. Equally important, Japan is in a zone of convergence for several major high-altitude flows: from the west and southwest, the zonal westerlies and the tropical southwesterlies; and from the east, the tropical easterlies. The nature of their meeting over Japan varies with the time of year, but at all times it results in a play of frontal movements over the country and frequent variations in weather. The proximity of Japan to the largest of the world's continents also is significant, since surface flows over that continent, or toward it, reflect the differential heating and cooling of the great land mass as compared with the adjoining seas. Thus, during the winter months, Japan is inundated by outthrusts of cold, dry, polar continental air from the vicinity of Lake Baikal, and in summer by less forceful indrifts of moist warm tropical maritime air drawn toward the heated continent. Although this alternation of air movements is often termed "monsoonal," in fact this is not a correct term for the complex climatic mechanisms in the area of Japan. The fourth element is orographic, that is, it derives ultimately from the mountainous structure of the country. Given the extremes of relief and slope within short distances in Japan, climatic conditions vary substantially in places only slightly removed from each other. On a national scale, orographic conditions are important in contributing to the winter precipitation maxima along most of the Japan Sea coast of Honshu, exposed as it is to the forceful movements of polar continental air moving eastward across the Japan Sea from Siberia; whereas in most of Japan, the winter half year is characterized by little rainfall, the summer half year by 70 to 80 percent of the annual precipitation. Orographic conditions are also responsible for a "dry zone" in the Inland Sea region which lies in the lee of both the summer and winter flows of surface air.

Finally, the maritime variable is of importance in three ways. First, the southern coasts of Japan are washed by the famed Kuro Shio, the Black or Japan Current, the western Pacific's equivalent of the Atlantic's Gulf Stream. Constantly warm, the waters of the Kuro Shio substantially ameliorate the climate of much of Japan's Pacific coastal areas. Conversely, cold currents move down from the Sea of Okhotsk and wash the eastern coasts of Hokkaido as well as the western and eastern coasts of northern Honshu. Where these colder waters sink below the warmer waters of the Kuro Shio at about latitude 38 degrees north, marine life is particularly rich. Second, the fact that the Sea of Japan is a deep-water rather than continental shelf sea means that its waters are considerably warmer in winter than the adjacent continental land areas. Therefore, the lower layers of the dry polar continental air which moves out toward Japan from Siberia in the winter are warmed and made unstable, thereby contributing to the large amount of winter precipitation, often in the form of snow, that falls orographically in western Honshu. Third, southern and eastern Japan are subject to the onslaught of typhoons, especially in the autumn but also in the early spring, and these contribute to spring or autumn rainfall over large areas, sometimes hundreds of miles from the eye of the storms. Less often, the eastern areas are hit by giant waves called tsunami. These are caused by earthquakes in the circum-Pacific zone of orogeny and may travel thousands of miles across the Pacific before hitting Japan.

In simplest terms, the climate of Japan may be likened to that of the eastern seaboard of the United States, but with greater contrasts between summer and winter precipitation and with a prolonged rainy season in the late spring–early summer, called the "plum rains" or *baiu,* associated with the convergence of continental and maritime air masses over the archipelago during that season. Of considerable significance is the fact that, although rainfall is relatively abundant in Japan and is concentrated chiefly during the summer months, only in a few places does it reach the seventy inches over a four-month period that are necessary for the fruitful maturation of the rice plant, and this means that supplementary irrigation is essential for paddy cultivation almost everywhere in Japan.

Equally important for agriculture are regional differences in the length of growing seasons. In eastern Hokkaido the growing season averages about 120 days; in western Hokkaido, about 140 days. As one moves south through Honshu, except in the high lands, the growing season lengthens. In the Kanto area it is about 215 days; in southern Shikoku and Kyushu about 260 days. Since the southern part of Japan includes about half of Honshu as well as Kyushu and Shikoku, differences in growing seasons between, say, Kanto and westernmost Honshu are very slight. Growing seasons are longest not merely in the south but in those parts of southern Japan where the direct influence of the Kuro Shio is strongest. For raising a crop of early-maturing rice 140 days is ample, and rice is the chief crop even in Hokkaido, as well as in most of the rest of Japan. However, in Hokkaido a shorter growing season places stringent limits on agricultural technique and on the practice of double-cropping, virtually unknown there.

Mineral and Energy Resources

At the time of Japan's emergence as a member of the family of nations in the last quarter of the nineteenth century, she seemed to be relatively well-endowed with resources in addition to land, forest, and water. The archipelago is highly mineralized, and Japanese sword-steel and copper and bronze objects were long recognized to be of the highest quality. In fact, however, Japan's metallic mineral resources are modest, and few are of contemporary economic importance. Of these the most important is copper, mined chiefly in Akita Prefecture and in the Kanto area (120,000 tons ore content in 1970), but even copper production is no longer sufficient to meet domestic needs. Chromite, zinc, and lead also are relatively abundant, as are a vast array of nonmetallic minerals such as limestone, sands, clays, pyrites, and sulphur, found widely distributed throughout the country. Ferro-alloy minerals are almost entirely lacking, and iron-ore deposits, chiefly in Iwate Prefecture and other parts of northern Honshu, are sufficient to meet less than 5 percent of domestic demand. Oddly enough, salt, essential to the chemical industry, is not abundant, despite the surrounding sea. Most salt production is in the comparatively dry Inland Sea area, where sun-drying precedes artificial drying, and the annual production approaches 950,000 tons, less than a sixth of national needs.

In terms of energy resources Japan has, until relatively recently, been much better off. At the turn of the century, it appeared that Japan, with over 3 billion tons of confirmed coal reserves, had sufficient mineral fuels to supply her needs for decades to come at a production rate of 50 million tons a year, but the coal is of relatively poor quality, especially for coking purposes, and the measures are on the whole relatively thin and fragmented, which makes mining costs high. Furthermore, world energy production has been shifting rapidly toward petroleum and natural gas, and in these Japan is poorly endowed, although coal still accounts for 21 percent of all energy consumed, as compared with 70 percent for petroleum and 7 percent for hydroelectricity. Most of Japan's coal lies at the northern and southwestern extremes of the country, in northern Kyushu and west-central Hokkaido, the former being the older producing area and the site of Japan's early heavy industry. The Hokkaido fields are beginning to challenge the northern Kyushu fields as the country's prime producers, about 49 percent of the national production coming from them as compared with 37 percent from northern Kyushu. The trend away from Kyushu toward Hokkaido's more readily accessible fields is likely to continue. Petroleum deposits occur chiefly in northwestern Honshu, but these account for less than 1 percent of the national consumption, and natural gas is of slight importance.

However, the rivers of the country represent a generous domestic source of energy, and these have a potential of 22.5 million kilowatts of which nearly 75 percent already have been developed, chiefly through a host of relatively small run-of-stream plants. There are relatively few large storage dam and reservoir facilities of the sort found in the western United States, although a number of these have been completed since World War II. In fact, the installed capacity of nearly 20 million kilowatts represents a maximum seldom reached; firm capacity of the same installations lies closer to 12 million kilowatts. Expansion of capacity in any case appears unlikely, since the most favorable sites already have been developed, and competition from increasingly efficient thermal plants is too great. Hydroelectric sources in 1970 supplied about 30 percent of the electricity consumed in Japan, a striking decline from the 70 percent in 1957, and the situation in terms of gross installed capacity is almost identical, about 70 percent being in thermal plants. Many of the latter are auxiliary to the hydro plants, which suffer from lack of water during the drier parts of the year, and an increasing number are being constructed at tidewater locations as primary electricity suppliers. In short, the relative importance of hydro power in Japan is declining rapidly in favor of thermal, although in absolute terms electricity generation from fluvial sources continues to rise.

Land Use and Agriculture

One of the paradoxes in modern Japan is the relatively small amount of land that is intensively used. As noted previously, most of the archipelago is in forest cover and some is in waste land, the total coming to some 70 percent. Of the remainder, the largest single percentage is in agricultural uses, but this represents only about 18 percent of the total, the balance being in a variety of land uses, including small percentages in urban uses (about 4 percent), transportational uses, and the like.

The general pattern of agricultural land use conforms to that of the distribution of alluvial lowlands and basins, and these in turn are intimately associated with the distribution of population. Very little upland is in agricultural use, despite the use of lower slopes for various kinds of dry crops and for woodlots. In short, agricultural land in Japan is highly concentrated in a few limited areas, and most of Japan's population is associated with that distribution. Although, as noted, the over-all population density of Japan ranks below that of Belgium and the Netherlands, the physiological density of 4,700 per square mile, that is, the ratio between population and unit of cultivated land, is perhaps the highest in the world. In the agricultural areas it is true, as Archibald MacLeish has written, that "there is no getting away from men anywhere."

The cultivated area of Japan includes about 15 million acres, or about 16 percent of the total land area of the country. An additional 2 plus percent is in farmsteads, paths connecting houses and fields, waterways, and small grazing plots. The intensity of cultivation is remarkable. Scarcely a square foot of land remains unused, and in general that means cultivated. The Japanese farmer has lavished extraordinary care on his limited amounts of land, and in this respect Japanese agriculture has become a prototype of all that Asian agriculture is not but ought to be. Although the inputs of labor, fertilizer, and knowledge that go into Japanese agriculture have been rapidly increasing in the past two decades, even in the premodern period Japanese agriculture, a kind of intensive horticulture, was famous for its productivity per unit area cultivated.

Not all the land in Japan is of equal value, however. One Japanese geographer, Ogasawara Yoshikatsu, has divided Japan into a central zone of more intensive and a frontier zone of less intensive agriculture in terms of quantity of inputs, size of farms, and yield. The central zone in turn is divided into a core and a periphery, the core including the Inland Sea area and the extension of long-developed countryside along the famous Tokaido (Eastern Sea Road) from Kyoto to Tokyo. The fact that the term frontier zone can be used (for southern Kyushu, much of Shikoku, northeastern Honshu, and Hokkaido) is indicative of the relative inertia that characterizes an agriculture based largely on paddy cultivation. It clearly reveals the tendency to concentrate development in those areas best favored for paddy cultivation and earliest developed. It also suggests that Japanese agriculture is associated with favorable market locations, that is, the nearness to the larger metropolitan areas, and is becoming ever more so.

The pressures of increasing population on better agricultural land, especially in earlier times, led to the use of several agricultural practices, not confined to Japan by any means, but particularly characteristic of its agriculture.

The first of these is irrigation. Slightly over half of the cultivated land in Japan is under irrigation, and by irrigation is meant "controlled irrigation," not the natural inundation that is characteristic of the lower Nile basin. Even where the steeper paddy terraces rise up the lower slopes in the core zone of the country, water is led to the fields and down from one to another by a complex arrangement of diversionary ditches and viaducts. In cases where rivers flow above the level of the surrounding cultivated flood plain, their waters can be tapped easily without recourse to weirs; in other cases dams and weirs are used to divert water into a distribution system of ditches of varying sizes. Only in a few instances is ground water used for irrigation, and only within the past two decades has modern sprinkler irrigation begun to be employed, particularly on vegetable crops, but its use is spreading. Formerly water was raised from ditch to field by hand- or foot-driven pumps, but now most pumps are gasoline or electrically driven, and Japan exports large numbers of simple pumping devices to the Asian agricultural world. The use of controlled irrigation in paddy cultivation means an enormous investment in land improvements and a high order of inertia with regard to the size and location of fields. Each paddy field, even one elevated or depressed in relation to its neighbor only by inches, is a kind of terrace, which provides a substantial measure of water and erosion control. Soil erosion is a severe problem in Japan, as it would be in any country where slopes predominate, but it would be vastly more significant if wet-paddy cultivation were not so widespread.

A second practice is terracing, a term even more difficult to define than irrigation. Every paddy field is a terrace of sorts. Generally, however, the word is applied to the fields at levels more than a foot from one another, and these are commonly called "bench terraces." Throughout the core zone of Old Japan and even in the periphery terraced paddy fields rise along the margins of the alluvial areas on to the lower slopes of natural terraces or hill slopes. Elsewhere they are less common. Widespread though they are in parts of Japan, the bench-terraced, wet-rice fields are an anachronism in modern agriculture, and indeed in modern Japan. They are relics of an age when agricultural technology permitted increases in production only by expanding cultivated areas into immediately adjacent areas, no matter how unappealing. Such terraces represent enormously high investments of human energy, too high for a modern economy to countenance. Thus, virtually no bench-terracing has gone on for some years, although terraces less carefully leveled and buttressed are still being constructed in favored locations for dry crops such as vegetables, when the market prices are high enough.

The paddy field is a feature of Japanese agriculture, just as it is in middle and southern China and in parts of Southeast and South Asia, and is should properly be regarded as an artifact rather than a gift of nature. Each small field is surrounded by a low bund about a foot in height (on only one side in the case of bench-terraced fields), which helps hold water in the field. Eighteen inches to three feet below the surface is usually found a clay hardpan, created from the seepage downwards of fine particles and from conditions of generally poor drainage, albeit artificially induced. The field may be likened to a saucer with a raised lip—a receptacle. Held in the saucer is a quantity of structureless soil matter, so worked, beaten, and modified by men over centuries that it can scarcely be regarded as "natural," except in origin. This largely neutral stuff provides support for growing plants and acts as a medium through which these plants can be fed and watered. Into the receptacle and the soil medium goes seed or seedling, fertilizers, soil conditioners such as lime, and with them controlled quantities of water, which must be drawn off from time to time to facilitate weeding and ultimately harvesting. Thus, drainage is an important opposite side of the irrigation coin. The longer an area has been under wet-paddy cultivation, the more likely this ideal-typical model will be developed; and most of agricultural Japan has been under continuous cultivation, with the exception of Hokkaido, for several hundred years.

Another important practice is multiple-cropping. On the average one third of all fields in Japan is double-cropped. In part, this means the growing of a second, dry crop on wet-paddy fields after they are drained, commonly a winter grain such as wheat but sometimes vegetables or other grains. Double-cropping on paddy fields is restricted to that part of Japan south of the 37th parallel on the Pacific coast and the 35th parallel on the Japan Sea coast, primarily because the growing season is too short in the north for two crops, but also because of prolonged cloudiness on the Japan Sea littoral, which is, parenthetically, known as the "shady side" of Honshu. However, even in the climatically suitable areas about 40 percent of the paddy fields lies fallow during the winter season, primarily because of poor drainage. As for upland or dry fields, double-cropping is common everywhere except in far northern Honshu and in Hokkaido. A summer grain may be followed by a winter grain, or a winter grain by a crop of summer vegetables. In southwestern Japan, especially in the vicinity of the larger cities, three or more crops of vegetables may be raised, but under forced growing conditions. In any event, the cropped area in Japan is about 30 percent larger than the cultivated area.

Intercropping is a variant of multiple-cropping. A second crop will be planted between the rows of a standing crop well before harvesting. This practice may make harvesting of the first difficult, but it does permit higher yields per unit area cultivated.

Transplantation is yet another device directed toward raising yields from given plots of land, although there is some question as to whether it actually leads to higher yields of paddy itself. Transplantation is not practiced in Hokkaido where rice is sown broadcast, and the differences in yields appear small. However, transplantation does greatly extend the possibilities for double-cropping, since the seedlings need not be transplanted from the seedbed for several weeks, and this allows the winter crop already in the field greater time to mature and shortens the total time necessary for the maturation of the two crops. In the case of the rice plants, this permits earlier maturation and spares them from early frosts at harvest time in the fall. In addition, transplantation is a labor-saving device, since it concentrates the heavy investment of labor for weeding and cultivating during the early growth of the plant in very small areas; and it economizes on water, fertilizers, and insecticides during that period. It also helps align the rice plants in the field, and this in turn makes cultivation more convenient.

Finally, intensive fertilization is practiced throughout Japan. In the premodern period fertilizers were primarily natural, organic, and farm-originated; and they included nightsoil, manure, and waste materials, as well as cuttings from roadsides and hillsides. These materials are still important in the Japanese fertilizer mix, but they probably account for less than a third of all fertilizer inputs. Nightsoil and other wastes, as in China, came from the cities to the countryside and were one of the more important exports from urban to rural areas. The use of organic materials has declined for two reasons. First, the use of chemical and generally inorganic fertilizers has enormously increased even in the past two decades. Consumption of them has nearly tripled since 1950, and the Japanese fertilizer industry is one of the largest in the world, with surpluses for export. Second, the use of nightsoil has virtually ceased with the introduction of modern sanitation. It was nightsoil that carried most of the intestinal and other alimentary tract diseases that plagued the premodern world, and its use has been discouraged for several decades. Intensive fertilization, whether based on organic or inorganic fertilizers, is a prime characteristic of most of the Sinitic world. It has not been characteristic of the argiculture of most of the rest of Asia. The differences in yield between Japan and China on one hand and the rest of Asia on the other is substantially a reflection of the fertilizer factor. The crop-livestock associations in Japan by no means indicate a monocultural agriculture, but about 70 percent of the 19 million acres sown or harvested in Japan (counting multiple-cropping) are in calorie-producing crops—grains and starchy tubers. Most of the balance is in oil-seed crops, soybeans, or vegetables. Only 5 percent is in industrial crops. Paddy accounts for about 40 percent of the total, and it is the traditional basic crop throughout Japan. There are good reasons for this in that paddy yields a higher quantity of calories per unit area than any crop other than the sweet potato, which is held in low esteem. It also can provide, if not milled excessively white, protective nutrients of no small importance in a diet still heavily based upon rice as the food staple. Rice yields in Japan are not the highest in the world, but at 56 kilograms per hectare, they are exceeded only by Spain with 62. Yields in Italy and the United States are only somewhat lower than those in Japan, but in all three Western countries only good land is used for paddy production; in Japan, land of varying quality has long been used for rice production.

Wheat and barleys are the next most important grains, accounting together for less than one fourth of the total cropped acreage. Both tend to be concentrated in central and southern Japan, wheat often as a second and winter crop on paddy fields, the barleys more often grown on upland fields. Other cereals, such as millets, rye, maize, and buckwheat, also are grown, chiefly in upland areas. The total production of cereals other than rice amounts to less than 13 million metric tons, as compared with nearly 17 million for paddy.

Other crops include sweet potatoes, grown chiefly in southwestern Japan on crude upland terraces, and white potatoes chiefly from Hokkaido and northern Honshu. Together these two varieties of potato account for about 5 percent of the cropped area. Soy beans, other beans, and peas cover about 5 percent of the cropped area and vegetables also about 10 percent, although the economic returns from the vegetable areas near the larger cities tend to be higher than those for other crops. Specialized crops, in addition to vegetables, include fruits such as apples in northern Honshu; citrus south of 36 degrees; and pears, plums, and peaches in the Inland Sea area. Tea production tends to concentrate in Shizuoka Prefecture on slope lands not devoted to paddy cultivation. Oilseed crops, such as rape and sesame, are widely grown on small plots in central and southern Japan, and provide cooking fats and oils for what has been until recently a notoriously fat-short diet.

Nonfood crops occupy more than 10 percent of the cropped area. Of these, mulberry was long the most significant, but the acreage is less than a fourth of what it was in the prewar period, when silk-worm-raising provided a major source of income for farmers in the intermontane basins of central Honshu, although it still is a major feature of the crop-livestock association in the south. Now, fodder crops are more important.

The traditional role of livestock in Japan has been as draft animals, and cattle feed has consisted primarily of farm waste, including field stubble, and roadside and hillside cuttings. Meat was not an important element in the diet, nor was milk. This situation has been undergoing drastic change. Instead of one head of cattle for every five farms, there is now one for every two. Furthermore, a high proportion of these is raised for dairy products or for meat, rather than for draft purposes. In addition, swine have become important, and the swine population of nearly 7 million head represents an enormous increase over 1950. Only in Hokkaido, however, are sizable diary farms found. Elsewhere, livestock are raised in ones and twos as adjuncts, increasingly valuable, to cropping. Although 2.5 million acres of land are classified as "meadows and pastures" in Japan, in use-terms this figure probably is too high, since less than one-half of this has been improved, and much of it is relatively inaccessible and little used, even in Hokkaido.

Farms in Japan are very small. The average size for the nearly six million farms is about 2.5 acres, but this size varies with location. In southwestern Japan and particularly in the core zone, acreages are closer to 1.5 acres; in northern Honshu, they average over 3 acres; and in Hokkaido 12 acres is about the mean. Two thirds of all farms are under 2.5 acres, and about a third are less than 1.2 acres. These smaller units, except when used for vegetable production and some-times even then, are too small to provide a livelihood for their operators. Even in premodern times their operators sought auxiliary income from silkworm-raising, woodcutting, charcoal-burning, and casual labor for the gentry. In the early 1960s, about 78 percent of all farm households still depended upon outside sources, especially work in nearby towns and cities, for much of their income.

Prior to 1947 about two-thirds of Japan's farmers were wholly or partially tenants, but the Land Reform Law of that year radically altered the situation, so that by 1955 nearly that percentage of farmers owned all of their land and only about 5 percent rented all of it. Similarly, about 90 percent of the cultivated area in Japan is worked by owner-farmers. Thus, the burden of tenancy has been much diminished, but there is little evidence to suggest that this factor alone has resulted in higher yields, and the average size of farms has remained much as before.

Agriculture in Japan is largely village-organized. Most farmsteads are grouped with others into a village, usually agglomerated, in many cases elongated along roads, levee tops, or contours at the break between upland and lowland. Dispersed settlement is uncommon, except in Hokkaido and in areas of relatively recent reclamation. Agriculture is practiced to a large degree on a cooperative basis within villages or *buraku* and/or among them, the need for this cooperation being most evident in the administration of irrigation systems which often are shared among several settlements. Farmers' organizations and cooperatives also are important in marketing and in the purchase of fertilizers and other farm supplies.

Japanese agriculture has been experiencing remarkable changes in the postwar period and most markedly in the decade and a half since 1952. Although the number of farms has declined only slowly from over six million to about 5.3 million, increasing numbers of farm-households have become dependent upon income sources other than agriculture, and 42 percent are more dependent on other occupations than on agricultural ones. The farming population itself has been decreasing quite rapidly, especially in the period 1955–71. In 1955, it had been 15.4 million persons, or 37 percent of the working population; in 1971 it had fallen to 9.6 million or about one fifth of the national working population—all this after several decades of virtually no change. Since rural birth rates have remained relatively high, these data mark an acceleration in migration from rural to urban areas at a rate of about half a million each year. At the same time, the significance of agriculture in the total economy has declined. Whereas in 1955 agricultural income accounted for 17 percent of the national total, in 1968 it had dropped to just under 10 percent.

It would not be correct, however, to assume that agriculture in Japan is necessarily unhealthy. In fact, the incomes of farm families have risen markedly, and agricultural production has increased throughout the country; but incomes have not risen as fast as those in urban areas, and the drift to the cities is bound to continue. What appears to be occurring is a restructuring of agriculture as economic development is taking place.

As part of this restructuring, the relative importance of elements in the crop-livestock associations is beginning to change. Although dairy farming, for example, had been of modest importance in agriculture prior to World War II, by 1955 it accounted for about 9 percent of production, by 1960 about 15 percent, and by 1965 about 20 percent. The value of meat production rose at similar though less spectacular rates. On the other hand, the significance of grain and starchy tubers declined, though this was less true in the case of rice, which accounted for 38 percent of argicultural production in 1970, than for grains such as barley, buckwheat, and the millets. Substantial declines in relative importance also occurred for sweet and white potatoes as well as soy beans. However, these declines for the most part are relative and not absolute, except in the case of barley, traditionally a poor man's grain. In most instances, production increases have been on the order of a third since the early 1950s and have considerably exceeded population increases. In the case of rice, higher production has been aided by the mystique which the Japanese attach to rice production, by government price supports, and by Japanese preferences for their own rice varieties, which look, cook, and taste different from most of those grown elsewhere.

Ever since the beginning of the Meiji period Japanese agriculture has expanded its gross productivity and has kept pace with population growth. As of about 1900 Japan was importing close to 20 percent of the food requirements for a population of 44 million. In the 1940s the same proportion was being imported, but for a population of over 71 million. In 1965, the same situation held, but for a population close to a 100 million. Until about 1950 the Japanese diet remained very much the same as it had been half a century before, but with slightly larger increases in meat and dairy products. More recently, marked shifts in diet have been taking place, especially in urban areas, with greater emphasis on meat, dairy products, and wheaten baked goods. Agriculture has responded to these shifts, all associated with rapidly rising levels of living. Nevertheless, the contemporary Japanese diet still resembles its historical antecedents in that rice remains the staple, fish the primary source of animal protein, and bean preparations the primary source of vegetable protein, with vegetables added.

Japanese agriculture was able to maintain its high rates of productivity until after World War II largely through the application of science and engineering to traditional practices—improved water control, more efficient and enlarged consumption of fertilizers. These factors have continued to operate in recent decades as well, but mechanization also has played a role, perhaps less in increasing production as such than in making agriculture somewhat less labor-intensive and helping relieve peak labor shortages during certain times of the crop year. The almost complete electrification of the Japanese countryside, begun in the late 1920s, was an essential prerequisite. The development of gasoline engine-powered machines at scales adapted to local needs was another. Almost every Japanese farm is highly mechanized to the extent that most pumping of water and threshing of grain is done by small electrical or internal-combustion engines. More than half of Japan's farms have replaced draft animals with so-called garden tractors, usable in paddy fields of less than a tenth of an acre and capable of doubling as motive power to bring the farmers' crops to market or supplies to the farm. In addition, in many areas a gradual rationalization of fields has increased the amount of cultivable land and made cultivation easier. Transparent plastic coverings are employed to "force" rice seedlings in the seedbed and make earlier transplanting possible. Vegetable production has been similarly assisted, and multiple-cropping of vegetables, generally underreported, is said to have increased markedly.

The areal patterns of agriculture also have been changing. The primary rice-surplus areas in Japan have been shifting northward into northern Honshu and Hokkaido, especially the Japan Sea side of Honshu. Protected seedbeds and earlier maturing varieties have been important in making this possible. Greater emphasis is being placed on high-income crops such as fruits and vegetables, and more of these are being produced as major rather than auxiliary products. On the margins of the great cities former paddy land is being converted to vegetable plots which bring higher prices under a system of multiple-cropping. Lower value grains are declining in importance, and bench-terracing for new paddy fields has virtually ceased.

Equally significant, land reclamation for agriculture has slowed to a point where reclamation is barely keeping pace with losses due to expanding urban centers and competition with industrial land uses.

Each year there is a net loss in paddy land of perhaps 50,000 acres. There continues to be a net gain in dry fields, but most of these are in marginal areas in northern Honshu and Hokkaido, the productivity of which is naturally low. Clearly, Japan has reached the economic limits of the expansion of its cultivated area.

Fisheries

If Japan is not one of the major agricultural countries of the world, she easily qualifies as a major producer in terms of fisheries. In 1970 Japan's total fish catch was exceeded only by that of Peru. Her take was over nine million metric tons, roughly the equivalent of all the fisheries of northwestern Europe combined. Fishing is one of Japan's major industries, accounting for about 1.5 percent of the national product. Marine products have long been the major source of animal protein and certain protective nutrients in the Japanese diet. The typical Japanese meal even today consists of small amounts of fish, eel, crustaceans, and seaweed, in broth or dry, together with pickled vegetables and cool rice.

The seas about Japan are particularly rich in marine life, since they are the meeting place for cold and warm currents which bring large numbers of species into a relatively small area. In the north, herring, cod, halibut, crab, salmon, and other cold-water fish are most important; in more southern waters, sea bream, tuna, mackerel, and sardines are abundant. Herring and sardines are by far the most important species in terms of volume, though not value. Most of the catch is consumed within the country as food, but some is converted into animal feed or pressed for oil. Exports of fisheries products also are important. Although nearly 70 percent of the catch comes from coastal waters, an increasing proportion of this catch, as well as most of the catch from international waters, is of pelagic varieties, which since 1950 have grown in importance from less than a third to more than half of the total catch. This suggests that the near-shore waters have been overfished, but it also marks the expansion of Japanese fishing activities to all of the northern Pacific and their concentration in the hands of large, highly capitalized fishing companies based in the larger cities, at the expense of the small fisherman. Nevertheless, the coasts of Japan are dotted with perhaps three thousand fishing or fishing-agricultural villages which provide a modest livelihood for upwards of a million persons.

Seaweed and other exotic marine products are important elements in the Japanese mix of fisheries products. Fresh and brackish water fishponds also make their contribution, though the practice of raising carp and other freshwater fish in paddy fields has declined rapidly in recent years.

Fisheries production has increased rapidly since 1950, but from 1960 the rate of increase has been less rapid. International agreements are in part the cause, since in the Pacific many of these are directed toward restraining Japanese fishermen. However, the primary problem appears to be a limit on the size of marine harvest in the oceans near Japan.

Population

At the time of the Meiji Restoration the population of Japan was estimated at about 33 million. By 1900 it had increased to 44 million; by 1920 to over 55 million; by 1940 to over 71 million; by 1950, despite the war, to 83 million; and by 1960 to over 93 million. In 1967 the population reached 100 million. Thus, in almost precisely a century, Japan's population has trebled.

In spite of these dramatic figures, annual rates of increase were not exceptionally high, averaging about 1.5 percent for many decades. In the 1960s the rate of increase had fallen to about one percent, below that of France and considerably lower than that of the United States. Mortality rates have declined to levels comparable to or below those of Western Europe and North America, but birth rates have experienced sharp declines, especially since 1950. In 1949 the birth rate was 33 per 1,000; by 1961 it had declined to 16.8 per 1,000, one of the sharpest declines in history. The precise reasons for this drop are not understood. Perhaps the Japanese believed their own propaganda and that of foreign outsiders, which told them that their country was too small and too overcrowded to survive. Paradoxically, perhaps enough of them chose to take advantage of rising levels of living in the postwar period to act; more probably, the scars of war led many to look to the future with skepticism. Initially, abortion was the leading device for population control; but quickly birth-control devices came into prominent use. The present population of Japan is young, since the high birth rates of the pre-1950 period and declining death rates prior to that time are having their effect; but the population is aging as life expectancy has risen to Western levels, and it is expected that by the end of this century there will be severe short-ages of labor, since it will no longer be reproducing itself. Most of the population in Japan is where the arable land is, that is, in the lowlands and basins that have been cultivated for long periods of time. The reasons are simple, in that population and agri-culture in premodern and early modernizing Japan were highly associated in area. Agriculture demanded high labor inputs; trans-portation on the whole was poor; people lived where they could earn a living; and most of them earned their livings through agricul-ture. The present distribution of population is derived largely from the past, but there has been one major change: much, probably most, of the population of contemporary Japan lives in cities. It is important to realize, however, that most of Japan's cities are located where most of the people were in the first place. Therefore, both urbanization and population increase in Japan has reinforced the early pattern of population distribution. It remains more highly localized than ever before.

Rural Settlement

During the last century the rural population of Japan changed very little. At the beginning of that century it was over 30 million; in 1965 it was about 33 million, although by 1970 it was under 30 million. Clearly, the bulk of the population increase in Japan can be ac-counted for by cities, but urban population increases have had two sources, one of them natural increase, the other internal migration. The primary source of population increase in most of Japan's cities has been surplus population from rural areas, attracted by the op-portunities for employment and the general favorable living conditions that urban areas present. The story of contemporary Japan is, then, being written upon urban, not traditional rural, landscapes, which despite changes in organization and technology remain much as they were a century ago.

The rural population of Japan lives primarily in villages, ranging in size from several families to several thousands. Most of these are physically agglomerated or form a string pattern along roads, water courses, and seashores. A relatively small number are functional but not physical settlements, in that their houses are dispersed. Unfor-tunately, relatively few data are readily available concerning the size of these settlements and their precise distribution. Most data about them are submerged in a sea of information concerning the two basic rural administrative units recognized by the Japanese—the *mura* and the *machi*. In 1960 there were 1,031 *mura* and 1,924 *machi*, a marked decline from previous years because of progressive amalgamation of administrative units, especially since 1953. The word *mura* usually is translated as "village" and *machi* as "town," but these terms are misleading. The *mura* is in fact a rural township, composed of a number of physical villages and their lands, but not containing a real town of any size. A *machi* is a similar type of unit, but it also includes a sizable incorporated market town or towns.

In the administrative structure the *mura* and *machi* are equated with the *shi* or cities, the minimum population of which is set at 30,000. The next largest administrative unit is the *ken,* or prefecture, the equivalent of a province, of which there are forty-seven in Japan. Between the prefecture and *machi-mura* level is an intermediate rural territorial entity, the *gun,* which until 1927 was part of the official administrative hierarchy but since then is used primarily for postal and census purposes.

The number of *shi* in 1970 was 560, a vast increase over the 285 in 1953 when amalgamation into larger administrative units was accelerated. The rise in proportion of urban population from about 38 percent to 72 percent in 1970 was partly fictitious, since many of the newly created *shi* contain large rural areas within their official boundaries. In fact, some of the new *shi* have been termed "agricultural cities" since so high a proportion of their populations is not engaged in urban occupations. At the same time, many urban places are not recognized officially as such because they are under the official threshold of 30,000 population. It is probable that the true urban population of Japan is somewhere near 65 percent, and that it is rapidly rising.

In 1960, partly in response to these difficulties of measurement, the Japanese census established a category of so-called Densely Inhabited Districts (DID), areas with a population of 5,000 or more and densities of no less than 4,000 per square kilometer. In 1970 these areas included some 54 percent of the total population, although they accounted for slightly more than two percent of the national territory. These contained about 74 percent of all the official *shi* population, which occupied about 24 percent of that territory.

Urban Settlement

The cities of Japan fall into two major categories. The first of these composes a stratum of urban settlement widely distributed over the country which, for the most part, has its origins in cities established in premodern times. Many of these cities began as so-called castle towns, the seats of administrative authority and the sites of castles with masonry walls and moats in which lived the local lords and some of their warrior-vassals. It is estimated that there were 453 castle towns in Tokugawa Japan, of which 114 have continued as official cities, and many of the remainder as smaller places with some urban functions. The historic castle town was the center of a tributary region which it dominated. Its primary function was administrative and military, but it also was the chief market center for its region and it contained a number of artisans manufacturing consumers' goods for the daimyō, his samurai, and the wealthy merchants of the place. Inns, temples, and residential areas that were class-segregated completed the array of facilities within the city. Other places that developed into cities began as religious centers or as traffic stations on the major highways established during Tokugawa times. These various types of premodern cities form a dense network of cities chiefly in the 100,000 to 400,000 size category, about which the regional spatial economies within the country are organized. They are regional market and transportation centers, and many of them continue to have administrative functions as well. In fact, thirty-four of them also act as prefectural capitals.

Superimposed on this basic urban stratum is a layer of very large cities or metropolitan areas, the importance of which is national rather than regional in scope. Most of these multifunctional metropolises are found along the Pacific side south of the 37th parallel and are concentrated between Tokyo Bay and the eastern end of the Inland Sea. The largest of these is the Kanto metropolitan area, with a DID population of 18,200,000 in 1970, the largest cities of which are Tokyo (8,841,000), Yokohama (2,238,000), and Kawasaki (973,000). Next largest is the Kinki metropolitan area with a total population of some 11,468,000 in 1970. Osaka (2,981,000), Kobe (1,289,000), and Kyoto (1,419,000) are the largest cities within it. Third is the Chukyo metropolitan area, centered on the city of Nagoya (2,036,000) and lying between Kanto and Kinki. Finally, there is the much smaller Kitakyushu metropolitan area in northern Kyushu, which has a population of only 1,042,000. However, if the city of

Fukuoka thirty miles to the west is added, the total metropolitan population rises to a more impressive 1,896,000. In fact, Kitakyushu city came into being only in 1963, as the result of the amalgamation of the formerly independent but contiguous industrial cities of Moji, Kokura, Yawata, Wakamatsu, and Tobata.

Although it is possible to speak of the basic stratum of small- and medium-sized cities as indigenous and the larger overlayer as not, several of the metropolises had their origin in castle towns—Osaka, Tokyo, and Nagoya; and Kyoto was the traditional imperial capital, although in Tokugawa times the country was ruled from Tokyo, then called Edo. It was in the first three of these that much of the impetus for the modernization of Japan came to be centered, and they, and their satellite cities, are the most Westernized of the cities of Japan. All lie at the heads of large embayments in the southern coast of Honshu, and all share some of the same problems of that type of location—shallow, silting harbors and poor drainage in tidewater areas. For this reason Kobe and Yokohama were developed a few miles from the central cities to act as ports for them at points along the bays where deeper water was available. Only later did Tokyo and Osaka develop their own deepwater facilities, but these are still incapable of handling the largest deep-draft vessels, which use the wharves of Kobe and Yokohama. In the case of Nagoya, which began its modern development somewhat later than the others, a fine deepwater harbor has been created at the city itself, but Yokkaichi, on deeper water to the southwest on Ise Bay, has somewhat the same relation to Nagoya that Kobe and Yokohama have to Osaka and Tokyo respectively.

As of 1940, the existing hierarchy of metropolitan areas had already been established, and the largest cities accounted for about 20 percent of the total population of the country. Postwar recovery was slow. Even in 1960, 15 years after the close of the war, they accounted for only about the same percentage. In 1940, too, although Tokyo was twice the size of Osaka, the two were major rivals in commerce and industry. More than half of the central offices of large corporations were located in Osaka, an old commercial city which had a long tradition of manufacturing and commerce as well as excellent trade connections with the Asian mainland. Both Tokyo and Osaka, along with Nagoya, Yokohama, and Kobe, were severely damaged by fire-bombing during the war. More than three fourths of all the structures in central Osaka, for example, were thus destroyed. Kyoto, however, was spared. With the end of hostilities, reconstruction began, slowly at first, but with increasing speed as the economy began to reestablish itself. Tokyo began to rebuild much more quickly than either Osaka or Nagoya. The increased centralization of political functions associated with the Occupation was a major stimulus, and people moved toward the seat of power with unerring instinct. As a result, by 1955 Tokyo had regained its prewar population and more, but Osaka did not reach its prewar population size until 1961. Meanwhile, increased government regulation, and the convenience of being where the political action was, attracted the central offices of many major companies away from Osaka and to Tokyo. Although the weight of metropolitan dominance clearly has passed to the Kanto area, the Kinki area has been strengthened on the national scale by the partial integration of Kyoto within its functional metropolitan area. Furthermore, Nagoya's rate of growth has accelerated with the development of the national automotive industry, of which it is the major center, and it has proclaimed itself the regional "capital of central Japan" (the meaning of the term Chukyo).

Whatever their differences, the great cities are being brought into a single megalopolitan system in much the same way as the cities of the northeastern seaboard of the United States. Superior transportation facilities and the expansion of urbanized areas in central and satellite cities are leading toward the creation of a gigantic unified, though discontinuous, urban agglomeration with a population approaching forty million.

The smaller Japanese city has not been growing as fast as the larger, except for those in the vicinity of the metropoles, as in the case of Chiba city near Tokyo; and between 1960 and 1965 at least two hundred of them lost population. Thus, migrants from the smaller regional cities have joined those from the rural areas in moving toward the larger places.

The regional city has a distinct urban landscape. Most of it is covered with one- and two-storied wooden houses, largely unpainted and usually with earth-colored tile roofs. There are virtually no apartment buildings or others over three stories in height except in the central business districts (CBD) of some of the larger towns. There wartime destruction, followed by postwar reconstruction, growth, and rising levels of living, led to rows of ferroconcrete buildings, seldom over three stories and often covered with stucco of various shades. The CBD seldom consists of more than one or two main streets, and it usually contains a "ginza," or shopping district named after the one in Tokyo, one or more arcaded shopping areas, both parallel to and at right angles to the main streets. The CBD is near the railway station, the main means of interurban transportation in Japan, and across from the station is a bus depot, services from which fan out into the city's rural hinterland. The main commercial street in many cases extends well toward the other side of the city, where a cluster of public-administrative-governmental facilities, such as the City Hall and the fire and police stations, are located. If the city originally was a castle town, the castle or its remnants will be nearby. Thus, most Japanese cities display evidence of their dualistic history as both pre-modern and modern settlements—the modern business areas near the railway which first came to the city at its outskirts and attracted commercial activities to itself, and the traditional center of political power. Usually, a river, most often canalized, flows through the city, and some of its waters may have been diverted in earlier times to feed the moats surrounding the castle. Manufacturing activities are carried on throughout the city, the intermixture of land uses being commonplace in light of tradition, the dualism in the manufactural sector of the economy, and the general absence of rigorous zoning codes. Streets are narrow and unpaved in peripheral parts of the city.

In general, the smaller Japanese city is a compact "walking city," its streets being ill-suited to vehicular traffic except in the central business areas—and even there rather narrow. Little more than 15 percent of the gross urbanized area is in streets, as compared with 15 to 20 percent in most European cities and over 30 percent in Middle Western American cities. The break between urban and rural land uses generally is quite sharp. Within a hundred yards or so, one makes the transition between urban and rural; there are few attenuated ribbons of highway-oriented land uses on their fringes. Legally, however, the official city or *shi* contains a considerable amount of farm land and farming population within its boundaries.

The great city in Japan, on the other hand, is expanding in area and population at astonishing rates. Most of the population growth in Japan in the last decade is accounted for by the larger metropolitan areas. These metropolitan areas are fragmented among a number of administrative bodies in much the way that many American cities are, and the need for metropolitan organization and government is as acute in the Kinki (Osaka-Kobe-Kyoto) metropolitan area as it is in its Chicago metropolitan equivalent, which is about the same population size. Be that as it may, the great metropolises are the major magnets for migrants in Japan. Tokyo receives upwards of 150,000 net per year, and in certain postwar years has been known to receive and retain nearly 500,000, even apart from its university student population of over 300,000. Osaka and its associated cities have a large net influx of migrants, but the total is less than that of Tokyo. Nagoya has a large influx, but smaller than those of Tokyo and Osaka. Clearly, there is a relationship between size and therefore economic and other opportunity, and migration patterns, although Tokyo has the additional advantage of being known best to most Japanese through a national press centered there and television and radio programs which blanket the country. In general, growth also is related to population size, as are income levels. All the great metropolitan areas rank high on the scale of per capita income in Japan, with the Kanto, Kinki, Chukyo, and Kitakyushu areas ranked in that order, and immigration appears to be a partial function of this ranking.

The townscape of the great Japanese city resembles that of its smaller counterpart, but there are major differences as well. The low, even roof line, broken by a castle, as in Nagoya or Osaka, or by religious structures, as in Kyoto; the predominance of single-family dwellings mostly of wooden construction or of shophouses lining certain commercial streets; the paucity of streets, almost everywhere under 10 percent of the total urbanized area; the areal rather than lineal spatial principle of organization, as reflected in postal addresses; the contrasts between traditional and modern. However, the central business districts of the great cities consist of moderately high-rise, massive, modern buildings, most of which have been constructed since World War II, and the transportation system is mass-oriented and modern, with subways in the largest cities. Heights of buildings have been limited until 1965 due to national zoning regulations consequent upon the great Tokyo earthquake and fire of 1923, but with changes in design and construction methods, these limitations are being waived, and the skyscraper is beginning to appear.

There are also differences in functional organization, as well as similarities, between it and its Western counterpart. When compared to the American great city, the Japanese metropolis differs in two major respects. First, the separation of land uses which has become typical of most American cities is not nearly so common in Japan; and the separation of work place and residence has been less clear. Partly as a result and partly because of restrictions on building heights in the central areas, the central business districts in Japan tend to be much larger than those in their American counterparts. The central business district in Osaka, for example, is four or five times the area of that in Chicago, the central city of a metropolitan area of about the same size; and many land uses, such as wholesaling, which has been squeezed out of the centers of most American cities, lie well within the central areas in Japan. In fact, in Tokyo, partly because of the history of transportation development there and the situation of key railway stations and of the palace grounds, several huge outlying commercial areas have developed, one of which, Shinjuku, contains the largest department store in the metropolitan area.

More important, centrality continues at a high premium in Japan even for residential functions, and, with exceptions, the Japanese metropolis has had until recently few high-income or even middle-income suburbs similar to those found on the outskirts of most American great cities. On the contrary, such suburban development as took place found lower-income groups living along the urban-rural fringe, and the penalty for being poor meant traveling long distances to work. This situation has begun to change, however, not simply because of improved means of transportation and the rapid increase in the number of passenger automobiles, but more importantly because of government policy toward housing. That policy has encouraged the development of large, high-rise residential developments toward the outskirts of the metropolitan areas for middle-income white-collar workers. Furthermore, there was a massive migration to marginal areas during and after the war, because the more central areas had been so grievously damaged by wartime bombing and fires. As a result, middle-income "suburbs," or at least outlying residential areas, have begun to develop on a large scale as the spatial structure of residential land uses is being transformed.

Although manufacturing land uses continue to be found well within the central portions of the cities, the expansion of manufacturing activities is taking place primarily in two types of locations: first, outlying areas, chiefly upland, where land is relatively cheap and available, and second, on reclaimed land along the shores of the bays on which most larger cities are located. Thus, almost the entire shoreline of Tokyo Bay is being put to industrial land uses, to the neglect of recreational land uses and fishing activities. Of necessity, this land is low-lying, and much of it is vulnerable to tidal waves or storms associated with typhoons. Therefore, it has to be protected by costly sea walls which are constructed and maintained largely by capital-short municipal governments. The problem is exacerbated by the fact that most of the plants located on this land draw their water supply from ground water sources, through deep wells. This water is low-cost and generally pure; but one result has been a rapid decline of the water table and a slow subsidence of the reclaimed land (as well as much land reclaimed a century or more ago). Land subsidence and the associated problem of industrial-urban water supplies have been described by responsible officials as one of the more important economic problems facing the country.

Industrialization

Industrialization in Japan has been a concomitant of urbanization, and is said by some even to be its cause, although the distinction between cause and consequence is difficult to make. A century ago perhaps 5 percent of the labor force was engaged in secondary industries (including mining, manufacturing, and construction); in 1965 32.3 percent was thus engaged. Similarly, perhaps 10 percent was involved in tertiary industries, but in 1965 this figure had risen to about 43 percent. Although the labor force in agriculture had remained more or less the same, the relative importance of agriculture in employment had declined to about 23 percent. In addition, secondary industry has come to account for 39 percent and tertiary activities for 47 percent of the total national income.

These figures suggest that Japan has already made the transition from a largely subsistence-oriented, agriculturally occupied society to an industrial-urban one, in which service activities loom large, in less than a century. Moreover, in recent years the value of gross national product has risen at a rate exceeding 10 percent, doubling between 1958 and 1965, and the product per capita has grown at a rate of 9.4 percent. Exceeding these astonishing rates of growth has been that of manufacturing, the production indexes of which have nearly tripled in the same period. If other indicators are desired, one can observe that electricity consumption more than doubled during that time and by 1966 exceeded Italy's on a per capita basis.

Despite these remarkable changes, the over-all areal pattern of Japanese manufacturing has changed little since the prewar period. In fact, that areal pattern was well-established by World War I. There are four major industrial nodes in Japan. All of these are associated with the larger metropolitan areas and help support the proposition that industry, everywhere, is becoming increasingly market-oriented. The largest cities continue to attract more industry; the smaller proportionally less, despite the congestion and high land costs in the major metropolitan areas. Thus, the Kanto and Kinki areas together account for 56 percent of the value added by manufacturing. The Chukyo region (Nagoya) accounts for another 12 percent, and the northern Kyushu area about 5 percent. In short, the industrial belt of Japan forms a long, 600 mile, more or less continuous strip along the southern and Inland Sea coasts of Honshu to northern Kyushu. Each of the four nodes in that belt contains a substantial mix of industries, although there are important differences among them. Textiles and ceramics are most important and metal-refining least important in the Chukyo region; printing and publishing is most important in Kanto. Machinery is important in all three of these, but the automobile industry has tended to invest most heavily in the Chukyo region. The northern Kyushu area, much smaller than the others, has a heavy-industry, less diversified base and a smaller regional market, and it accounts for about one third of the pig iron produced and about one fourth of the crude steel produced in the country.

Industry also displays the dualism that pervades so much of Japanese society. About 90 percent of all the manufactural establishments in Japan employ less than 30 workers, and 98 percent less than 100. While these enterprises account for only 55 percent of all workers, this is still a high percentage for an advanced industrialized country. Although the trend is toward larger plants, the smaller establishments continue to perform valuable functions, in part as suppliers to the larger companies which depend on them for specialized processing, in part as training grounds for newly immigrated workers with lower skills than some of the larger modern plants require. It is these smaller establishments that are widely dispersed both within the metropolitan areas and throughout the country as a whole.

At the same time the traditional emphasis of Japanese industry upon textiles and similar so-called light industry has ceased. More than two thirds of the value added by manufacturing is associated with the heavier metal and chemical industries, and textiles and related industries account for no more than 10 percent of the total. Increasingly, too, Japan has become a maker and exporter of producers goods as well as consumers goods. There is virtually no product of the industrialized world that Japan does not produce, with the temporary exception of very large commercial computers, and in shipbuilding Japan leads the world. In 1970 Japanese yards launched 10.4 million gross registered tons of shipping, including 5.1 million tons of tankers, or about 48 percent of the world's total and several times the tonnage of the nearest competitor. With regard to motor vehicles, Japan is the second largest producer in the world, outranked only by the United States. With regard to steel, Japan ranks third, with 93,322,000 metric tons produced in 1970, more than trebling the output for the 60s.

Japanese industry depends to an extraordinary degree on imported raw materials. This fact explains in part both the location of industry at tidewater sites on one hand and the composition of Japan's import trade on the other. Japan is one of the world's great trading countries, and in 1971 had a gross commodity trade valued at 42 billion dollars. In all, foreign trade accounts for about 20 percent of the country's national product. Japan, like the United Kingdom, trades to live as well as to prosper. For decades Japan's commodity trade had displayed a marked imbalance in favor of imports. Commodity trade deficits were made up for by services such as shipping and banking, but the equilibrium was precarious. In 1965 the first substantial commodity trade surplus since the war was recorded, relatively small, to be sure, but indicative of the strength of Japan's marketing position on the world scene.

Imports include petroleum, iron ore, coking coal, cotton, lumber, wool, and foodstuffs, chiefly wheat and meat products, not rice. Exports consist almost entirely of manufactured goods, led by steels, ships, metal products, textiles, motor cars, and other manufactured goods, in contrast to prewar patterns when textiles led the field.

Trade orientations have been modified substantially since the war, but the United States continues to be Japan's major trading partner, sending 30 percent of imports and taking about 35 percent of exports. In the prewar period the United States also was the chief single foreign trading partner, but Japan's dependence on this partner was considerably less. At that time, if Japan's trade with her imperial territories were counted as foreign trade, about two thirds of all trade was with Asia. Now that percentage has declined to about one third and is likely to stay at that level, although trade with mainland China has begun to revive under stringently controlled conditions, and the export trade with it now ranks fifth, below that with the United States, Liberia (ships), Australia, and Hong Kong.

Japan's merchant marine developed as a concomitant of world industrialization, and in the prewar period Japan ranked third in world merchant shipping tonnages. Despite the ravages of the war, the Japanese merchant marine by 1970 had soared to 26.6 million registered tons, of which over 9 million was composed of tankers, a near-quadrupling of that tonnage in a ten-year period, and it now ranks behind only Liberia in total tonnage. More important, a substantial portion of Japan's overseas trade still is carried in foreign bottoms, and there is a net outflow of payments for shipping services which could only be balanced by a still larger merchant fleet.

Domestic Transportation

The domestic transportation network, which provides the sinews of the Japanese spatial system, also is heavily dependent upon marine transportation. About 42 percent of all domestic freight, as measured in ton-kilometers, is carried in coastal vessels, and this trade is a major employer of transportation personnel. Although almost all of the coasters are steam or motor vessels, many of them are very small and individually rather than corporatively owned. These serve the thousands of minor ports in Japan to which goods from the larger ports are transported in small quantities, and from which certain products may be carried to the larger centers, which thus act as entrepôts. Most cargoes carried are bulky and of relatively low value —petroleum and petroleum products, coal, gravels and sands, limestone, and construction materials—but even new automobiles are carried in specially adapted coasters. The coastal fleet also contains a number of modern passenger ships which ply the Inland Sea.

In terms of the value of commodities carried, the railways have been far more important than coastwise shipping. They have carried the prime responsibility for welding a cellular spatial economy into a well-integrated national system. Nevertheless, whereas both the volume of freight carried in coasters and its relative importance are likely to rise, it is probable that the relative importance of the railways will slowly decline, especially in competition with short-haul highway transportation. In freight terms, railway tonnages and ton-kilometers have been leveling off for several years. The percentage of freight attributable to railways decreased from 52 percent in 1955 to 19 percent in 1970, whereas that attributable to trucks increased from less than 12 percent to 39 percent. On the other hand, the railways appear to be doing better with regard to passenger traffic, and in 1970 they accounted for about half of all passenger-kilometers as compared with 82 percent in 1955, but this in the face of very large increases in the total numbers of passengers carried by all types of carriers.

Total railway mileage amounts to 16,835 miles, of which 12,981 miles are owned and operated by the Japanese National Railways, a government corporation. The national railways have been used by the central government as a device for economic development and national integration, but the privately owned railways also have had an effect on the areal organization and development of the country. Most of these are commuter lines which serve the larger metropolitan areas, and some have also acted as suburban real estate developers, as an important adjunct to their transportation activities. The private railways are primarily passenger carriers, unlike the national network which carries both passengers and freight.

The national railways are Cape-gauge (3′6″), a narrow gauge which has placed constraints on their ability to carry high-speed trains safely, though it is a matter of intense national pride that trains run on time. Seventeen percent of the national route mileage is double-tracked, and 42 percent is electrified, but the double-tracked and electrified portions of the system are those which carry the greatest amount of traffic, including the Tokaido Line and the Sanyo Line along the northern shores of the Inland Sea. On October 1, 1964, a new line was placed in operation—the New Tokaido Line, connecting Tokyo and Osaka with 515 kilometers of standard-gauge (4′8½″) track used by high-speed electric trains that make the journey, with stops at Nagoya and Kyoto, in three hours and ten minutes. The new line is an unqualified success, and construction already has been completed on an extension of it westward, as the New Sanyo Line, to Okayama, one of the several medium-sized cities identified by the central government as a focus for planned industrial expansion. The New Tokaido Line experiment has become a model for high-speed, medium-distance railways in other countries.

It is interesting to note that many of the railway lines are not profitable. About 90 percent of the route mileage of the national railway system is associated with unprofitable lines, and 41 percent of the operating revenues of the system comes from only the 10 percent that are profitable. This means that some curtailment of railway services is likely in the future, if alternative and cheaper means of transportation can be utilized. At the same time, the construction of tunnels between Honshu and Hokkaido (well underway) and tunnels or bridges between Honshu and Shikoku (in the planning stages), in addition to the existing tunnel between Honshu and Kyushu, should greatly improve the efficiency of the present system and those parts of it that are in greatest use. On the other hand, the electrified private commuter lines appear to be profitable.

The answer to more efficient short-haul freight transportation is the improvement of a truly backward highway network. Truck traffic now accounts for 39 percent of all ton-kilometers of freight carried, but these are almost all on hauls under 100 miles. The economic development of Japan, both prewar and postwar, was accomplished essentially without the automobile; but the motor vehicle population is increasing rapidly, and in 1969 was about fifteen million, as compared with less than two million in 1960. Well over half of these are commercial vehicles, many small, in contrast to the predominance of passenger vehicles in the United States. The total national highway network is only 21,000 miles, but there are an additional 100,000 miles of prefectural and local roads, some of which are paved. Although few of the national highways are suitable for long-haul truck transport, the volume of this type of traffic has been growing rapidly. As a major experiment, the controlled-access Nagoya-Kobe Expressway was completed in 1964, and it is being extended eastward to Tokyo, thus roughly paralleling the Tokaido Line. Other highways are being improved, and it is planned to integrate Shikoku into the Honshu highway network by at least two bridges across the Inland Sea.

Modern Japan has become a moderately well-integrated areal entity despite the handicap of multiple insularity. The core of the system consists of three major metropolitan population nodes—Kanto, Chukyo, and Kinki—served by highly efficient rail transportation, with improving highway and adequate air linkages supplementary, and evolving into a partially discontinuous megalopolitan structure not dissimilar to the northeastern seaboard of the United States. Beyond this core are a number of important regional subcenters, especially Kitakyushu, but also Hiroshima, Okayama, Sendai, Niigata, and Sapporo, in which investment is expanding and further industrialization proceeding with government support. These subcenters are linked with the core by well-developed transportation facilities, though not as efficient and modern as those at the core. In other areas, as in Shikoku, relative isolation has continued to hamper regional economic development, and the current stage of development in Japan involves the more intimate linking of these areas to the space-economy as a whole. All of these developments, however, account for only a very small proportion of Japan's national territory. Most of its landscape remains, superficially if not functionally, much as it has been for centuries, still bearing an uncanny resemblance to the Japan made famous by Hiroshige and Hokusai, a century and a half ago.

XIV

The Premodern

Economy

BY

E. S. CRAWCOUR

The economic aspects of Japan's development are of special interest because Japan was the first and is perhaps still the only Asian country which has achieved a substantial degree of modern economic growth. It comes as something of a surprise to us as Westerners that the Japanese have been so successful where other Asians have failed or not even made the attempt, and we are tempted to look for aspects of their history, society, or character that set them apart from other non-European peoples and which might therefore provide some sort of key to Japan's success. There is, in fact, probably greater diversity among Asian peoples than now exists between the peoples of European countries, and the Japanese are indeed different from other Asian peoples in all kinds of ways. To a large extent both the distinctiveness of the Japanese in Asia and the relative similarity of European peoples are a result rather than a cause of modern economic development. Nevertheless, we will find many aspects of Japanese economic development that are more reminiscent of the earlier development of European countries than of what we know of Asia today. We shall see how the Japanese economic system changed from a relatively unproductive premarket one, like that of the American Indians, to something having much in common with modern America. This process of improvement in material welfare is known as economic development. We shall see how a market economy evolved and how after much official hesitation it was finally adopted under the impact of internal circumstances and external pressures.

The Premarket Economy

The system by which goods and services are purchased and are distributed to consumers by being bought and sold in markets is so familiar to us that it is hard to imagine any other system. Yet on the time scale of human history this is a comparatively recent invention, and a thousand years ago there was hardly a country in which it had been adopted on a wide scale. In a premarket economy, such as that of the American Indians, for example, exchange of goods and services between one person and another is effected not by commercial transactions but by transfers governed by ritual or social custom or by forcible expropriation. Social custom may dictate that the menfolk supply the whole family with meat, while the womenfolk cook it. Within a wider family group or tribe some division of labor may be achieved by similar social conventions often supported by quasi-religious sanctions. The erection of quite elaborate buildings or the performance of impressive ceremonies may be possible on the basis of ritual contributions of goods and services, and the giving and receiving of ritual gifts may make possible exchanges of goods with distant communities. On the other hand, contributions may be exacted by force or the threat of it. A conqueror may acquire goods by plunder and services by taking slaves, or he may obtain the goods and services by regular tribute (now known as taxation). The degree of division of labor that can be achieved by these methods is, however, limited and the productive efficiency of the economy must remain correspondingly low. The bulk of the population must live basically on what they can produce and at best this can scarcely be much more than the necessities of life. Life at any level of material culture higher than bare subsistence can therefore be enjoyed by only a very small proportion of the population. This small group, usually selected on the basis of birth, constitutes a ruling aristocracy, which performs political or ritual functions for the community as a whole.

Such was the situation in ancient Japan. The objectives of the ancient Japanese economy were to supply this aristocracy with the resources to enable it to perform its often very expensive ritual functions—then thought to be important for the welfare of the community—, to maintain order and its own authority, and to achieve a level of material culture which would not suffer too much by comparison with that of other ruling groups in the more advanced areas of the neighboring Asian mainland. For the mass of the population, the economic objective was merely subsistence and even this was not always attained. In ancient Japan this system operated within a familial framework of control. A ruling family group (*uji*) exacted contributions of goods or labor services from the communities (*be*) under its control as well as enjoying directly the services of small groups of slaves (*yatsuko*). At such a low level of productivity, the work of the community was of necessity concerned mainly with producing food, but some groups were given land and protection because they possessed industrial skills required by the ruling family. Many of these groups of craftsmen were originally immigrants, not always voluntary, from the more advanced mainland.

About the end of the sixth century A.D. the rulers of Japan became interested in the superior culture of neighboring China. The adoption of this culture required the use of greater resources and, therefore, failing some general improvements in the productiveness of the

Japanese economic system, it could be enjoyed only by an even smaller group. This may have been one reason why the heads of the leading provincial families now became centralized around the imperial family at the national capital. As a result of this move, the flow of goods and services due to these provincial familial heads all went to a single center, and without these flows a city such as Nara, designed after the Chinese model, could not have been built at all. The imperial court now patterned itself on the Chinese and set about establishing a Chinese system of government based on a central administration. To finance this, the land of the home provinces and the other more accessible areas was declared public land and was allotted to the local people according to a checkerboard system of rectangular fields, traces of which survive in the Japanese countryside to this day. In return for the right to cultivate these lands, the cultivators were required to pay tribute to the central government.

These premarket flows of tribute certainly made possible in the narrow sphere of the capital a level of material culture far higher than Japan had previousy known, and perhaps as high as anything reached in the next four or five hundred years. The life of the aristocrats of the capital of those days may have lacked many amenities that we now consider indispensable, but to the average provincial Japanese it represented almost unimaginable heights of luxury. Visitors to the capital were spellbound by the magnificence of the public buildings, palaces, and temples and by the splendor of the nobility. In terms of the scale of the Japanese economy of those days the cost was enormous and, since the transport of tribute goods and services to the capital was also very expensive, the burden which these splendid works placed on the mass of the population must have been extremely heavy. Nevertheless, the force of traditional religious and familial sanctions by which tribute was required appears to have long continued undiminished, and at least some of the contributors seem to have taken a kind of vicarious pride in the gorgeous rituals of the capital. If there were voices of protest, their echoes have long since died away. Tribute took the form of rice and other foods, linen cloth, and a few other special products as well as labor services in the form of tribute men and women who served a term in the capital as servants, guards, and workmen of various kinds. Between the nobles and the temples exchanges took the form of gifts in kind. The aristocratic chieftains (including branches of the Imperial House) were awarded the income from lands in proportion to their rank and as salaries for their official posts or as rewards for meritorious services. There were thus two flows of tribute following the same route—one to the central government and one to the nobles. Since the nobles in fact occupied all the senior positions in the government it was not easy to keep these flows distinct and the tendency was for more and more to flow into the treasuries of the noble families at the expense of the government treasury. This tendency was formalized in the practice of granting to the estates of these nobles immunity from central government dues, and indeed a large degree of administrative independence. These immune estates, or *shōen,* grew not only by direct government grants, but also by reclaiming adjoining wastelands and by accepting lands in commendation from local landholders. Many *shōen* were also held by Buddhist temples and Shintō shrines.

This was the economic background of the political struggles which surrounded the rise of the Fujiwara family, and the system of government from the cloister of the retired emperor, though it would be unwise to look for a simple economic explanation of the complications of later Heian period politics. Meanwhile, in what were then the frontier provinces of the east of Japan, the imperial system penetrated only slowly. In these frontier areas, as in the old west of the United States, the man on the spot was the man in charge and local military strength carried more weight than legalistic determinations from the remote capital. Largely outside the imperial system, these eastern magnates reproduced a state of affairs such as might have existed in central Japan before the rise of the imperial system. As rights to income became more and more a subject of dispute between various factions in Kyoto, it was to these frontier warriors that interested parties turned in attempts to back up their claims with force. As a result the heads of these military groups acquired great power, and finally the military government known as the Kamakura shogunate was founded. The old system of flows of tribute to Kyoto, however, remained intact, and it was the duty of the shogun (or head of the military arm of government), as at least in theory an agent of the central government, to keep these channels open and to ensure that the tribute was in fact paid and that it reached its destination. To ensure this and to maintain public security, the shogunate appointed military officers alongside the civil governors and other officials appointed by the civil government. In practice disputes over rights to tribute were settled by the shogunal headquarters in Kamakura. Although these military officers naturally preempted a substantial share of revenue for their own purposes, the gap that this made in the flow of resources going to Kyoto was offset to some extent by the growth of the practice of commending private lands to Kyoto court nobles or influential Buddhist temples. While commendation involved payment of fees to Kyoto, the owners of the lands gained exemption from government supervision and taxation. By the fourteenth century only vestiges of the central government's official lands remained, and the bulk of cultivated land was held as estates, or *shōen,* by the Kyoto nobility who had acquired these lands either by official grant from the government or as a result of commendations. The flows of resources to Kyoto, therefore, continued with little change in form and direction even though their nature had changed somewhat. Thus the so-called feudal system of the Kamakura shogunate never entirely supplanted the central imperial system of civil government.

While these changes were taking place the productivity of the Japanese economy was gradually rising under the influence of a new wave of technical innovations from the mainland. Buddhist monks who came to Japan to propagate new doctrines propagated at the same time new crops and new ways of cultivating and processing them. Although the Japanese farmer still lived almost entirely on what he and his family could produce for themselves, some were able to produce a small surplus for exchange, even after contributing their share of taxes. Local fairs, often under the auspices of temples or shrines, enabled barter exchanges to take place and the existence of two centers of government, one at Kyoto and the other at Kamakura, as well as the development of some provincial centers and ports, brought possibilities of exchanges between one region and another. Limited as these possibilities still were, they represented some advance over the earlier system of one-way flows of goods and services to a single center.

It is tempting to speculate that, just as the immediate effect of introducing more expensive Chinese forms of material civilization may have been a centralizing influence in the Taika period, so the gradual improvement of productive techniques and growth of output may in time have made possible the development of a number of centers and the spread of a higher standard of living to a larger number of people, and perhaps of the vision of it to a great many more. Despite some technical progress, however, the possibilities of improvement remained limited by the lack of markets that alone could make further specialization and division of labor possible.

The Beginnings of a Market Economy

It was perhaps to be expected that, with the increasing productiveness of local regional economies and the growth of direct means of communication between different areas, possibilities of acquiring local wealth and power without dependence on or reference to a single center would increase. During the Heian period the capital at Kyoto was the only center where resources could be mobilized on a scale large enough to support pretensions to national power. But by the end of the Kamakura shogunate many regions provided an economic base capable of supporting local power independent of either Kyoto or Kamakura. Once this break-even point had been reached and passed, one local military official after another began to cut his ties with the shogunate. For some time contributions to the military budget of the shogunate had been largely retained by local agents, ostensibly in return for promises of loyalty and military services when called upon. The Mongol invasions and the inability of the shogunate to reimburse the heavy costs which these involved for its military agents in Kyushu, let alone reward them for their meritorious services, had shown clearly that the balance of power had swung away from the center in favor of the local authorities. Once ties with the shogunate were broken, local leaders no longer felt any obligation to protect the rights of the Kyoto court nobles, since this was the function of the shogunate. Local military agents had in any case been absorbing the functions of managers of noble estates for some time and by the fifteenth century were treating the estates as their own land. In the long period of wars that followed the collapse of the power of the shogunate, the ancient rights of the civil aristocracy finally went by the board, and there was no one to whom the legal owners of these rights could turn. Increasingly the estates lost their identity and were absorbed into the territories of local military magnates. Flows of tribute to the capital practically ceased, and members of the court nobility were reduced to earning their own living by acting as teachers of courtly arts or as advisers on etiquette to the leaders of the armies that one after another occupied the capital.

Though generally considered a "Dark Age," this period of endemic warfare was responsible for the beginning of a community of merchants and of a market economy. In general, the term "Dark Age" tends to be applied to a period in which one magnificent center is replaced by a number of lesser centers, since, even though the total resources of the economy may be increasing, they are being spread more widely, and no single center can rival the magnificence of the old capital. Although this must have been a "Dark Age" indeed for people who suffered the direct effects of war, in other ways it was a time of progress. Foreign trade developed greatly and Japanese not only visited the coasts of China—usually as pirates—but ventured as far afield as Indonesia, Cambodia, Thailand, Malaya, and the Philippines. These voyages were often backed by temples or important personages, and in the absence of markets the exotic imports were either stored up as wealth or given away, usually in return for favors or as the price of alliances. The wars of this period must certainly have required the mobilization and deployment of a far greater total of resources than was ever concentrated in Kyoto, and to mobilize them required new techniques of organization. The regular tribute of one's own territory could not provide the weapons and other military stores required for a campaign, so persons performing the functions of quartermasters general were retained to procure stores from wherever they were available.

These military commercial agents not only performed commissariat functions but also acted as ambassadors, messengers, transport agents, and intelligence officers. As the power and territory of their commanders increased, so the scale of their operations expanded and the agents of the greatest territorial magnates, or daimyō as they were called, handled what were for those days very large-scale transactions. As each daimyō employed several of these agents (some served more than one master) we have the beginnings of a community of traders trading with one another. Their operations were apparently not confined to working as agents, since many of them amassed huge fortunes of their own by trading on their own account. A famous story of two daimyō who were great military rivals at this time, Takeda Shingen of Kai and Uesugi Kenshin of Echigo, illustrates the need for interregional trade. Kai, having no coastline, was dependent on imports of salt, and when these were cut off by the enemy, Takeda's territory was in distress. When his rival heard of this he is said to have considered it an act unworthy of a warrior, since war was supposed to be purely a test of military prowess. He therefore invited his rival to send his purchasing agents to his own territory of Echigo, where he would instruct his own agents to supply them with salt at the normal price. Between regions that were not actually at war with one another, this type of trade must have already been quite common. The most convenient method of payment was gold, and a number of gold mines were opened or reopened at this time.

With the daimyō cutting off flows of tribute to the capital and gathering into their own hands all rights within their territories, the *shōen* became meaningless as administrative units. In their place the village became the basic unit of administration. The village was a community of farmers which was basically self-supporting. Taxes of various kinds were assessed on and paid by the village as a whole, and the headman of the village, who at this time was probably a military retainer of the daimyō, was responsible for apportioning the burden among the members of the village community. The farmers themselves lost their identity as members of an estate, and any rights they had enjoyed or obligations they had incurred vis-à-vis the noble proprietor of the estate were extinguished. Instead, they were confirmed as occupiers and cultivators of land in their village by the daimyō or his agent. They thus became registered cultivators (*hombyakushō*). To effect this change required some sort of land survey, and those daimyō who remained in control of an area long enough to do so (and in those confused times, not too many did) carried out a survey village by village. Grants of the income from lands were now made not by the central government but by the daimyō, and the unit of these grants for meritorious service and so on was the village. Each village had largely to fend for itself, and in the process became a tightly knit community owing taxes or services to a single overlord.

While daimyō organized interregional trade for their own purposes, villages began to trade more and more with each other. Local markets, which usually operated every fifth or tenth day, sprang up all over the countryside as the old organization of the *shōen* broke down. Small traders and guilds of artisans who had been granted privileged monopoly positions by the *shōen* proprietors in return for services rendered to the capital now found their position undermined; their appeals to the daimyō met with an unsympathetic response. The interest of the daimyō was not in bolstering the remnants of the old *shōen* but in facilitating the activities of their own agents and adherents. The *shōen* markets and guilds were therefore swept away along with the connections between the cultivators of the estates and the old estate proprietors. Their place was taken by a new system based on the daimyō and the village. Daimyō had a keen interest in the economic development of their domains as a source of war finance and actively encouraged their own groups of artisans and traders. To this end they standardized weights and measures, issued currency, and abolished barriers to commerce within their own domains. They issued licenses to their own commercial agents to trade anywhere within their domains free of tax or any other form of interference, and as their domains expanded these licenses became more and more valuable privileges. Such an official merchant serving two or three leading daimyō was free to trade without hindrance over a wide area.

When, toward the end of the sixteenth century, Toyotomi Hideyoshi gained control of virtually the whole of Japan, all these processes were expanded to national dimensions. Under Hideyoshi all the cultivated land of Japan was surveyed and its taxable income assessed. Around his great castles of Fushimi and Osaka flourishing communities of artisans and traders came into being. His own commercial agents held licenses which enabled them to trade freely all over the country as well as overseas, and some amassed huge fortunes.

In the course of surveying the land and registering its cultivators Hideyoshi carried out what is popularly known as the "Sword Hunt," in which farmers were disarmed and forbidden to carry weapons or defend themselves. This move, based on military and political necessity, had far-reaching results, since it made the military into a distinct political, social, and economic class. Over most of Japan it was now no longer possible to combine soldiering with other occupations. Many of the quartermasters general, who as fighting became less common were in any case more and more concerned with civilian trade, left the ranks of the samurai and became city merchants, though many retained at least social and some economic links with their former commanders. Established in Kyoto, Osaka, or Fushimi, it was they who became arbiters of taste and culture under Hideyoshi (the Momoyama period) and for the first two or three decades of the Tokugawa period.

Foreign contacts were greatly expanded by Japanese military operations in Korea and by the arrival of growing numbers of European missionaries and traders following in the footsteps of Francis Xavier. Like the Buddhist monks before them, the Christian missionaries brought new skills as well as a new faith. It was largely improvements in design and manufacture of armor and weapons, including firearms, and in castle architecture and ship construction learned from the foreigners that enabled first Oda Nobunaga and then Toyotomi Hideyoshi to gain control of Japan. By the end of the sixteenth century Japan was technically not markedly inferior to Europe. When Japanese and European fleets clashed in Southeast Asia, the Japanese were by no means always the losers, and the fact that no European country even attempted to conquer Japan as the Spaniards had conquered Mexico and Peru says something for the state of Japanese military technology at the time.

After the death of Hideyoshi, it looked for a time as though Japan might again dissolve into a long series of civil wars, but thanks to the military, diplomatic, and political skills of Tokugawa Ieyasu this was averted. Ieyasu came into possession of a country in which the market economy was developing rapidly, spurred on by the demands of military rivalry. For the first ten or fifteen years of the Tokugawa shogunate this development continued, but as the Tokugawa system took shape after the last remnants of opposition were crushed in the Osaka campaigns, this development was arrested and regulated, and the official political and economic philosophy of the Tokugawa period was firmly based on the ideas of a premarket economy. The Confucian political philosophy officially adopted by the Tokugawa government was based on the premarket economic conditions of China in the fifth century B.C.! Merchants, who had enjoyed such prestige in the Momoyama period, were placed at the bottom of the social scale, since in premarket economic theory they had no useful function. Farmers were forbidden to engage in any form of trade and were exhorted to live as frugally as possible on what they could produce for themselves. Exhortations to frugality were not designed to encourage saving for productive investment, but to limit the wants of the farmers to what they could produce themselves, since anything beyond that could be achieved only through the operation of a market economy. Regulations issued to villages in Japan contained such provisions as the following: peasants were not to leave their land; land was not to be allowed to go to waste, nor to be mortgaged for more than ten years, nor to be sold. No rice was to be sold until all taxes were paid; tobacco was not to be grown on existing cultivated land; the village was to provide labor and transport for official purposes as required; trees were not to be cut down without permission; gambling was forbidden; renting of land or buildings in the village without a license was forbidden; peasants were to work hard all the year round; commoners were permitted to wear cotton or hemp according to their station, and servants cotton only, but village headmen might wear coarse silk. In other regulations peasants were forbidden to use saddle cloths for pack animals or to hold elaborate festivals. In years of bad harvest they were forbidden to make rice wine (sake), or bean curd (*tōfu*) or to sell processed foods. They were urged to eat coarse grain rather than rice.

One reason for closing the country to foreigners and severely restricting foreign trade was that foreign trade activity encouraged the formation of markets in Japan. Trade was thus subversive from the economic point of view as well as in other ways. According to the Tokugawa economic theory even samurai were supposed to live on their military rations, which were distributed in the form of rice. Anything else they needed was supposed to be produced by their household or obtained by exchanging rice for it. As the custodians of the official order, samurai were not even supposed to know what money looked like, since in theory they had no use for it. The elaborate processions required to transport a daimyō to the shogun's capital at Edo and back to his own domain were needed partly to keep the daimyō poor, but the theory behind it was that the daimyō was supposed to bring everything he needed for his year in Edo with him from his territory. Ceremonial gifts of clothing or special foods, such as were typical of a premarket economy, were continued between shogun and daimyō right down to the mid-nineteenth century.

Why did the Tokugawa settlement set its face against commercial development? Perhaps part of the answer was sheer conservatism or the idea that such changes were likely to be socially and politically disruptive. One reason, however, stems from the fact that commercial development and the increase in productive efficiency that it made possible had been closely associated with the building up of military strength. Indeed, what other reason could there be in an age when improvement of the material life of the people was not an objective of the economy? In times of peace, such as the Tokugawa settlement was designed to preserve, economic development was therefore not only unnecessary but potentially dangerous.

All this was, of course, an ideal. In practice, the elaborate paraphernalia the daimyō so ostentatiously carted up from their domains was probably made in Edo anyway and bought there during an earlier term of duty at the shogun's court. Some market operations were clearly essential to the working of the Tokugawa system of government by the shogun and the territorial lords. Even supposing that farmers could be expected to live by subsistence agriculture, the daimyō and their retinues certainly could not. Taxes collected in rice had to be converted into cash at some stage to buy clothing, utensils, furniture (both military and household), stationery, and a host of other things. To sell their rice and to provide all these other things the shogun and the daimyō originally relied on the same kind of official commercial agents that had been employed during the wars—often on the same people or their descendants. These people were retained in an honorary capacity long after the development of markets had made their services superfluous and their functions completely formal. As early as the middle of the seventeenth century a highly organized rice market, banking system, and wholesale trading network had evolved in Osaka to cater to these needs and, since the service they offered was far more efficient, the daimyō soon turned to them. Nevertheless, the proprieties of premarket theory were observed by appointing these merchants to nominal posts in the daimyō households. The new merchant communities were tightly organized, with their own rules to ensure performance of contracts and to enable credit to develop, and the individual credit standing of each merchant firm was regarded as very important. All this was necessary because the government gave little protection to commercial transactions. Similar merchant communities, having similar relations with the daimyō, grew up on a much smaller scale in the castle towns of each domain. The relationship of government with the developing market economy was therefore complementary rather than competitive. It was a compromise in which government tried to reap the advantages of the more efficient market system wherever these could not be ignored, while at the same time trying to maintain the principle of a premarket economy for the country at large. As we shall see, it was an unstable and shifting compromise.

The Prelude to Modernization

The objectives of the Tokugawa system were to keep the peace, maintain the established order, and to ensure that the Tokugawa family retained control of Japan. After centuries of fighting, disorder, and lawlessness, the maintenance of peace and order was a great achievement; even if it involved a degree of supervision and control which gives the impression of a police state, it was a boon for which the Japanese people seem to have felt a great sense of relief when they realized that peace had at last come to stay. By the mid-seventeenth century the recollections of old people who had lived through the wars seemed like fairy stories to those who had grown up in the Tokugawa peace. At every opportunity the Japanese expressed their gratitude to the Tokugawa simply for the favor of being able to live, work, and (usually) eat, though it must be confessed that the fervor of these protestations tended to decrease as time went on. Beyond this the objectives of the Tokugawa system did not go. The maintenance of Japanese strength and prestige vis-à-vis foreign countries was an irrelevance during this period of seclusion and strict isolationism. As for raising national income or trying to provide a better standard of living for the people at large, nothing could have been further from the government's thoughts. One leading member of the early Tokugawa regime expressed the view that peasants should be handled so that they existed on the borderline between life and starvation. The official attitude was that any surplus above mere subsistence should be drained off in taxes, so that the ruling samurai class would remain strong and further development of a market economy in the countryside would be impossible.

The Japanese at large, however, understandably had other ideas. We may take it as axiomatic that everyone, given the choice, would prefer to be better off rather than worse off materially. Even Confucius acknowledged that everyone desires wealth and abhors poverty. For the Japanese of the Tokugawa period it was only the development of a market economy that could make this choice possible. On this point the aspirations of common people and samurai coincided. Comprising some 7 percent of the population, the samurai formed a far larger privileged group than the aristocracy of earlier centuries and only a market economy could supply the resources to support the ever-rising standards of living to which they also aspired. For the ruling class the problem was how to channel economic development in such a way that they could monopolize the benefits which flowed from it. This problem proved insoluble, with the result that the authorities were continually faced with the dilemma of either maintaining the premarket-oriented official ideology at the expense of their material welfare or enjoying the fruits of economic development at the expense of abandoning the official ideology to which they were bound by strong bonds of loyalty and solidarity. For us the choice would not be too difficult, but for the samurai class it represented the kind of deep conflict of interests that forms the theme of so much of the drama and literature of the period.

Two factors tilted the balance in favor of the development of a market economy, irrespective of official thinking. One was the official encouragement of more efficient farming in the interest of maintaining or increasing the amount of taxes farmers could pay. The lessons were well learned and applied, and by no means all of the results went in higher taxes. The other was the growth of large cities, whose inhabitants obviously could not grow their own food and had to buy what they needed from the surrounding countryside.

First let us look at the development of agriculture. Since farmers were supposed to be the backbone of the country, they were exhorted to be good farmers. In practice this meant opening up new land and making two stalks of rice grow where only one had grown before. The area of cultivated land roughly doubled during the Tokugawa period and there were slow but steady improvements in techniques of cultivation. By the mid-eighteenth century farmers in at least some areas of Japan could produce not only their own food needs and tax rice, but a substantial surplus of either food or industrial crops, such as cotton, for sale. They found that if they sold some of the crops, and used part of the proceeds to buy commercial fertilizers like fishmeal or seaweed from other parts of the country, even bigger yields and profits could be obtained. By taking advantage of the specialization and exchange that markets made possible, a better time could be had by all.

At the same time the growth of cities, and especially of the shogun's capital of Edo, provided a rising cash demand for food and other agricultural products. Swollen by large numbers of shogunal officials and the retinues of the daimyō required to reside there for terms of duty, as well as by the large numbers of civilians needed to attend to their manifold wants, Edo had grown to a city of almost a million inhabitants by the middle of the eighteenth century. Osaka, the center of official commerce, and Kyoto, the old capital and center of the silk textile and other luxury trades, had perhaps as many again between them. In the domains the larger castle towns were miniature Edos. This demand was met by more efficient farming. In a sense this urban demand created its own supply, since the commercial development that it implied itself made possible increased efficiency of production. The taxes that farmers were called upon to pay scarcely rose at all after the early eighteenth century, and so the proceeds of sales to the city formed a net addition to farmers' incomes. Having higher incomes, farmers wished to spend them, and this added to the demand for industrial products as well as for agricultural. Now that there were large numbers of people who no longer spun and wove their own cloth, cash demand for textiles grew very rapidly. The old guilds of weavers in Kyoto that had developed from the artisans who catered for an aristocratic market were totally unable to meet this new demand for more popular types of products and so textile wholesalers went out into the countryside for further supplies. In one rural area after another they encouraged cottage textile workers by advancing money or raw materials and contracting for the output of whole districts. The textile industry and other handicrafts became an important part-time activity of Japanese farmers, and the proceeds raised their cash incomes still further. In some districts, such as the Osaka Bay area, as much as half the rural population was engaged full-time in cottage industry and took no part in farming at all. With these new and comparatively profitable opportunities for additional employment, many farming households ceased to produce a number of the things that they had once made for their own consumption. As in the United States, homespun cloth, homemade pickles and sauces began to go out of fashion and store-bought goods began to take their place.

The village had come a long way from the subsistence farming unit envisaged in the seventeenth century. In the early seventeenth century the average farmer hardly needed cash and a gold coin was a very rare sight in the countryside. A hundred years later no one could get along without some cash income. In almost every village there were farmers and businessmen whose incomes and style of life put the local samurai officials to shame, and these businessmen-farmers tended to take over the positions of village leaders. Almost every village had its shops dealing in grain, oil, textiles, processed foods, wine, stationery, furniture, and tools, as well as hairdressers and members of other service trades. All this was, of course, unofficial and outside the system of trade recognized by the authorities for their own purposes. Still, as long as villages paid their taxes and did not make a nuisance of themselves, the authorities were usually content to let them run their own affairs.

By the nineteenth century, however, these unofficial industrial and commercial developments had gone so far that they were competing with the official system at an increasing number of points. When the official markets of Osaka and elsewhere asked for protection from the new competition, the authorities usually gave it, but in an increasingly halfhearted manner. Both shogunate and daimyō, becoming financially more and more embarrassed, were looking for any means of increasing their incomes. As early as the eighteenth century they considered shifting ground in their compromise with the market economy. Daimyō began to move into the business of industrial production and the marketing of industrial crops and handicraft products, in collaboration with new groups of merchants both in their own territories and in the commercial city of Osaka. Often the daimyō used their official privileges and immunities to by-pass the "official" trading system and retain a greater share of commercial profits for their own depleted treasuries. Even the shogunate under its minister Tanuma Okitsugu made some tentative moves in this direction in the late eighteenth century, but conservative opposition led by Matsudaira Sadanobu forced a reaction which sought to return to the original pre-market principles of Tokugawa government. By this time, however, trading was not confined to isolated acts of exchange but was an integral part of daily life even in the smallest villages. Once the material advantages of development along the lines of a market economy were clear, the official orthodoxy became a more and more expensive anachronism which the authorities could ill afford to maintain, particularly when some of the leading daimyō had already all but abandoned it.

A further attempt at revising the compromise with economic development was therefore made in the 1830s. Its guiding spirit, the shogunate's minister Mizuno Tadakuni, seems to have considered at one stage going all the way and organizing the market economy as a central government monopoly. This scheme was abandoned for financial and political reasons, but the compromise that was reached gave official recognition to the position of the "civilian" or unofficial market network. Retreat was now scarcely possible, and the arrival of the United States flotilla under Commodore Perry clinched the matter because in the interests of national survival adoption of the most efficient economic system available became essential.

The extent to which "modernization" of the Japanese economy had taken place in the last forty or fifty years of the Tokugawa shogunate is the subject of some controversy. Many Japanese scholars believe that the premarket "feudalism" of Tokugawa theory actually prevailed in practice right down to the Restoration and even beyond it well into the Meiji period. Others, as well as most Western scholars, on the other hand, recognize the developments of this period and regard them as a possible source of clues to explain the remarkable aptitude with which Japan responded to the challenge of Western industrial civilization. Nevertheless, it is generally agreed that commercialization had proceeded quite far, at least in the more advanced areas, and agriculture had made considerable strides, although industry was still by-and-large in the cottage handicraft stage. It would be a mistake to assign to these agricultural and commercial developments a role similar to that played by the agrarian, commercial or industrial revolutions in the economic history of England. Modern economic growth in Japan clearly starts as a response to outside pressures, and modern industrial techniques were clearly imported from the West. At the same time Japan's modern economic growth started from the existing traditional economic base and for nearly half a century most of the growth came not from modern Western-style industry but from increases in the output of Japan's own traditional industries. Initially the impact of the West on the Japanese economy was not technological but political. Overtures from the United States and the European powers appeared to the Japanese as a threat to their national identity and convinced her leaders that she could maintain her independence and self-respect only by matching the West in productiveness and military strength. That these new national objectives could not be attained as long as even a pretense of the old premarket Tokugawa economic ideology was maintained was abundantly clear. Therefore the arrival of Commodore Perry's flotilla started a chain of events which was to force the rejection of the shogunate and its restrictive attitudes to economic development and the unequivocal adoption of economic development as a national objective.

That Japan was able to react in this way was due to the developments that had already taken place, as it were unofficially, or at best with the uneasy acquiescence of the authorities. After all, other Asian countries such as China or Thailand were faced with the same pressures but their reaction was quite different from Japan's. Townsend Harris, the first resident representative of the United States government in Japan, had visited both of these countries before he came to Japan but his visit and those of other Europeans did not have the same consequences there. Some people have claimed to find something in the Japanese character that makes them particularly suited to modern economic development—something akin, perhaps, to the frugal, hard-working so-called Protestant ethic. Certainly, as we have seen, there was no lack of people ready and anxious to get on with the job of economic growth. Yet we do not really need to be psychologists to explain the Japanese reaction. Japan was already showing some signs of a quickening of economic growth. The market economy had already developed a long way and its economic advantages were becoming more and more widely recognized, even at an official level. The people of Japan were comparatively well-educated —perhaps not as well as the Americans of those days but at least as well as most Europeans—and the apparatus of government administration worked effectively and reached down to every member of the population. Even in the unfavorable Tokugawa environment the traditional economy was capable of supplying the restricted wants of the Japanese people. Given a little encouragement, it was capable of supplying a much greater demand. Equally important, the traditional economy was geared to contribute perhaps as much as a quarter of its total output in taxation, most of which was used to support a largely unproductive samurai class. Once the Japanese government adopted new economic objectives, access to this surplus was to be a key factor in government investment in modern productive facilities.

Economic Development Becomes a National Objective

If Japan began her history with an economic system similar to that of the American Indian, it was clearly very different by the time Perry arrived, and her reaction to the coming of the white man was equally different. As we have seen, Japan's response was to determine to catch up with the West economically and militarily in as short a time as possible. At that time this was by no means so fearsome a task as it would be today. Only thirty or forty years before Perry's expedition the United States economy had contained very large areas of subsistence agricuture. Water power had been the main alternative to muscle power and industry had been only just emerging from the cottage. It was in attitudes to economic progress that the great gap between Japan and the West lay, and it was in closing this gap that the work of the Restoration was crucial. The slogan of the new Meiji government was "Enrich the country and strengthen the armed forces," a slogan that had been out of fashion since the days of the daimyō wars almost 300 years earlier. Now it was applied not to a warring daimyō's territory but to a Japan more or less united against the outside world. To achieve these new objectives the new government appreciated the overriding necessity of pursuing the material advantages of the market economy. In deciding upon the context in which markets should operate, they adopted the form that had apparently been so successful in Great Britain and the United States, namely, free enterprise utilitarian capitalism. Indeed, at that time no proved alternative presented itself, and the decision was based more on expediency than on ideological conviction. There were a few intellectuals who, insofar as they understood free enterprise utilitarianism, wholeheartedly adopted its philosophy, but the government adopted the system in form, rather than unreservedly in spirit. Once the political decision had been made, however, it met a sympathetic response in many sections of economic life. Farmers who had been trying to run their farms on businesslike capitalist lines for a generation looked forward to official approval to get on with the job. "Unofficial" businessmen whose enterprise had been restricted rather than encouraged under the old system welcomed the change, and lower-ranking samurai, irked by the old system of status according to birth, were hoping for promotion according to ability. Hopes had already been raised by the opening of foreign trade (which the foreign powers insisted from the start should be based on private enterprise) and by the stimuli this gave to export industries such as silk production. Hesitant official moves toward a new accommodation with the market economy in the last years of the shogunate served to whet appetites for more thoroughgoing measures.

The institutional changes that followed the Meiji Restoration swept away the survivals of the premarket ideology. The old caste-like social classes of samurai, farmer, artisan, and merchant were abolished along with all restrictions on occupation, although ex-samurai would continue to refer to themselves as such for a long time. The hereditary salaries formerly allocated out of tax revenue were commuted to lump sums payable in government bonds. For most samurai this compensation turned out to be meager and they were forced to seek productive employment. For the former daimyō, however, the compensation was substantial and legislation enabling them to use their pension bonds as subscriptions to bank capital ensured that much of this newly created capital would be available for productive investment. With the abandonment of even the pretense of confining large-scale commerce to the agents of the shogunate and the daimyō, the privileges of the official merchants of Osaka, Edo, and the provincial castle towns ceased to have any meaning or value. Restrictions on land use and on the sale and mortgaging of land were removed, thus officially recognizing land as a form of investment, which unofficially it had been becoming for some time. In place of the customary taxes, generally payable in kind, a new national land tax was introduced, payable by the landowner in cash and based on the estimated productivity of the land. This move forced farmers into the market since they now had to sell their produce themselves to get cash to pay their taxes. Previously the concept of land ownership had been vague, and split between rights of cultivation—since Hideyoshi's time vested in the farming members of the village—and rights to tax revenue—which we have seen passing from *uji* chiefs to the central government and its courtiers and then to the daimyō. With the reform of the land tax, cultivators, who had once been people of a *shōen* and then members of a village community, became landowners (and taxpayers) in their own right, although even now the village retains some influence as a social entity. Not all inhabitants of villages were full members. Some were tenants or laborers and their status was virtually unchanged.

Soon after the opening of foreign trade in 1859 a beginning had been made in reform of the currency in order to bring it into line with overseas practice. This reform was followed up after the Restoration with some success, although it was nearly fifteen years before a really satisfactory system of currency was achieved. Moves were made to establish modern banks, a system of commercial law, stock exchanges, a communications network, and a national system of education. At first the impact of these changes on the life of the Japanese people was small, but they were of the utmost importance in creating an environment favorable to economic growth. A favorable environment, however, is not enough. Economic growth requires investment in equipment and materials, as well as businessmen to organize production and introduce technological improvements. In real terms, investment involves the use of resources over and above the requirements of current consumption, and the embodiment of these resources in relatively fixed productive form. Where did the resources for increasing Japan's productive capacity come from?

One source was provided by a redirection of existing flows of resources from consumption by more or less unproductive samurai and their dependents to government investment. In practice, tax revenue that had once been used to pay samurai was now available for government capital construction. After the Restoration samurai stipends ceased, and although some compensation was paid, it was on the whole meager, and in any case was paid not out of current revenue but in the form of long-term bonds. Even though taxes were reduced somewhat, the government retained control of very substantial resources. To the extent that tax reduction left funds in the hands of taxpayers, they also tended to use them more productively than had the samurai. This redirection made possible important government contributions to investment at a number of key points which were unattractive to private enterprise.

A second source of funds was the growth of the output of the traditional economy, mainly agriculture and cottage industry. This output more than doubled in the fifty years following the Restoration, thus making a bigger total of resources available. A part of the increase was needed to support a growing population and a further part went to provide a modest rise in standards of living, but the remainder could be channeled into investment. This great rise in output, unparalleled in Japanese history up to that time, was a result of a number of factors. Possibly the most important was the new official attitude which encouraged business enterprise instead of repressing it. A process of technological catching up was also important, and this included not only adoption of new techniques from abroad but also—and more importantly in the early period—the spread of the best traditional techniques from more advanced to less advanced areas within Japan. This diffusion of technical skills had been proceeding more or less continuously since the early days when the capital at Nara or Kyoto had been the only center of industrial arts, but the removal of restrictions after the Restoration greatly accelerated the process. The removal of restrictions, population growth, and an increased supply of money created an expanding market for the products of the traditional economy. It was most fortunate for Japan's economic development that the kinds of things people wanted to buy continued to be the kinds of things traditional industries could produce. Increasing production in that area did not involve much new investment, and what was required was provided very largely from within the traditional sector itself. Thus, existing forms of production were able to supply not only the needs of a growing population but also surplus for export and for investment in expanding and modernizing production. This was another key factor in Japan's modern economic growth.

Finally, resources for growth were obtained by some transfer of resources from agriculture and handicraft industries to more productive kinds of industry. A change from overwhelmingly agricultural to primarily industrial production is one of the outstanding features of economic growth everywhere, and so it eventually was in Japan. The extent of this structural change in the early phases of Japanese development tends, however, to be exaggerated, since what appears at first sight to be a very rapid movement of workers from agriculture to industry was in reality often only a move from one type of industry to another; namely, from rural cottage industry to small-scale factory industry.

Who were the businessmen, or entrepreneurs as they are sometimes called, who organized new industries and expanded old ones? It was once thought that most of the capital and initiative for modern industrial growth came from the government and the former samurai class, but if our assessment of the business situation at the time of the Restoration is correct, we would expect the "unofficial" businessmen to have been ready and waiting to grasp the new business opportunities opened up by the policies of the Restoration government. And so indeed they were. It was they who, even before the Restoration, took the lead in the export trade, and organized and financed the rapid expansion of export silk production. It was they who financed the expansion of traditional industry, both directly through their own industrial interests and indirectly through organizing and financing local banks. It was they who took the lead in local chambers of commerce and industry and who pressed for and largely financed local developments like port facilities. In the commercial field they created the new network of sales routes which by and large supplanted the old official system based on Osaka.

The old official merchants and merchant-bankers of Osaka with one or two exceptions failed to adapt to the new conditions. The Meiji government's recognition and encouragement of free enterprise market operations made their position something of an anachronism, bound up as they were with the requirements of the shogunate and the daimyō. Currency reform, especially the depreciation of silver in which their assets were expressed, dealt them a heavy blow and, coupled with changes in the flow of funds and goods, reduced the need for the exchange transactions between Osaka and Edo that had once been a key part of their business operations. Those who could went back to wholesale trading, but as local wholesalers rather than the controllers of national official commerce that they had once been. It was twenty or thirty years before Osaka recovered from these blows and at last began to develop new institutions and new industries adapted to the new situation. One firm stands out as an exception to the general experience. The famous firm of Mitsui, who had worked closely with the shogunate, managed to maintain their role as bankers to the new government, and they used both their government connections and their own business skill to achieve unprecedented prosperity.

The role of former samurai in the business enterprise of the Meiji period tends to be overrated. The investment by daimyō of their bond holdings to found a national bank has already been mentioned. The initiative was hardly theirs but seems to have been a government policy to insure them against depreciation of their pension bonds and to provide them with an income consistent with their elevated status. It is the lower ranking samurai, however, who are usually credited with spearheading economic modernization. Their role in staffing government economic administration was an important one, and in some fields in which the government had a special concern, such as shipping, strategic industries, and some branches of engineering, former samurai were prominent. In view of their higher level of education, experience of working within a large organization, and access to Western ideas and government contacts, however, they might have been expected to take a more active part. Possibly they were inhibited by their anticommercial Confucian upbringing. Although some succeeded, the performance of those who were given official help to set them up in business on the whole disappointed their sponsors. It is hard to say whether those who succeeded in business did so because of their samurai origins or in spite of them. Iwasaki, the founder of the Mitsubishi concern, had pretensions to samurai status but was noticeably lacking in samurai-type scruples, or for that matter in any other kind. In fact, he seems to have acquired samurai status to further his business ambitions. As we might expect, the contribution of the ex-samurai was more important in public life than in business. As officials, as policemen, and especially as teachers they played an important part in bringing Japan into the modern world.

The role of the government in setting Japan on the road to modern economic growth was a leading one and can be cited as one of the more successful examples of state participation in economic life. Its most significant contribution was, as we have seen, in providing a climate favorable to economic development and in creating the institutional basis for modern capitalism. In providing this climate, however, it tended to stress the needs of the state rather than the legitimate aspirations of the individual. Had some form of state socialism been available as a viable alternative, the Meiji government might well have found it more in tune with their sympathies. Except for military plants, early government attempts to engage directly in the building of modern industry were soon abandoned, but not before they had performed important pioneer service in giving many Japanese a glimpse of the new methods. In general, government investment was concentrated in those fields, such as public utilities and other social overheads, that were unattractive to private investment but made all the difference to the profitability of private business. Thus government enterprise complemented rather than competed with private enterprise, and this was one of the main reasons for the success of its role.

This transitional phase of Japan's modern economic growth was accomplished relatively smoothly because it released and utilized trends and energies already in existence. The dynamic for change from the traditional to a more modern order stemmed from the recognition that the Japanese were producers as well as subjects. For the authorities there was a conflict between keeping them in their traditional place as subjects and realizing their potential as producers, since the latter involved granting freedoms and incentives that made it difficult to achieve the former. In normal times in traditional Japan, the resources available to the government were adequate for its needs and it was therefore free to concentrate on maintaining the *status quo*. Even though traditional Japanese are presumed to have been similar to us in wishing to be better off rather than worse off materially if given the choice, their rulers were then under no compulsion to grant them that choice. When, however, the government was faced with a need for increased resources that could not be met by territorial expansion, it was prepared to permit and indeed actively promote changes designed to raise the effectiveness of the population as producers. An awareness of a need for increased resources had arisen in a mild form as a result of financial difficulties as early as the seventeenth century, but attempts to meet the need by permitting economic change within carefully circumscribed limits proved inadequate and difficult to administer. The demands imposed by the opening of Japan in the mid-nineteenth century required far more thoroughgoing changes emphasizing the role of Japanese as producers. That concern with their status as subjects, though modified somewhat, nevertheless remained strong is attested by the strenuous efforts of the Meiji and later governments to inculcate in every Japanese a sense of the national polity and what it meant to be a Japanese. Attempts to raise national strength by overseas territorial expansion rather than make further adjustments at home could possibly be regarded as evidence that this mechanism was still operating in the 1930s. It was not until after Japan's defeat in the Pacific War that an entirely different and more democratic dynamic of growth began to operate.

XV

The Modern

Economy

BY

E. S. CRAWCOUR

The Growth of the Modern Sector

The twenty or thirty years that followed the Restoration saw the creation of a climate favorable to economic development, and large numbers of Japanese were quick to take advantage of it. Thanks to their activities a whole new network of commerce developed from the unofficial beginnings in the first half of the nineteenth century. Instead of existing outside or alongside the old commercial system based on privilege and designed to serve the needs of government and the governing class, it now replaced that system. That such a major adjustment could be made within the short space of ten to fifteen years clearly demonstrates the enormous energy released by the post-Restoration changes. At the same time similar energies were producing very rapid growth in traditional industries, not only in those, such as raw silk, stimulated by new overseas demand, but in industries catering to the daily wants of the Japanese. It was this kind of development rather than the establishment of modern Western-style industries that was responsible for the rapid growth of industrial output in the nineteenth century. Here may well be one of the secrets of Japan's rapid economic growth. Japanese businessmen and manufacturers did not sit around waiting for someone to build big Western-style plants, but got on with the job of increasing production in areas that were already familiar to them. This was possible because there was an existing structure capable of supplying Japanese wants and because in many fields foreign suppliers were not in a position to compete in supplying the kinds of things that Japanese consumers wanted.

Although Western-style factories had been built by some daimyō domains for special purposes as early as the 1850s, a process that was continued by the Meiji government, those were small plants, few in number, and mainly concerned with defense or with the supply of some new product (such as glass or cement) that could not be procured otherwise, at least not without a disproportionate expenditure of scarce foreign exchange. Others, like repair facilities for ships and machinery, had of necessity to be built in Japan, since by their nature they could not be obtained in the form of imports. These activities cannot realistically be regarded as the beginning of a process of modern industrial development, and their main importance was the educational one of familiarizing a number of Japanese with some aspects of modern industry. It was only around 1890, after a preparatory period of some twenty years, in which the annual output of the existing Japanese economy had already roughly doubled, that a continuing process of industrialization based on Western technology really got under way.

Some scholars have regarded Japan as an example of a country that successfully industrialized from the low initial level of incomes typical of an Asian country. Even in 1868 Japan may have been at a somewhat higher economic level than most Asian countries at that time, but if we date the beginning of the process from around 1890 there is no doubt that she was by then already well ahead. This is not to underestimate the value of the government contribution in laying the institutional and physical foundations in the interval. As we have seen, this was a crucial factor in the expansion of the traditional economic base and ultimately of modern economic growth. And it was in the twenty years following the Restoration that Japanese businessmen accumulated the capital and knowledge that would later enable some of them to adopt Western technology. But the growth of modern industry really began in the decade preceding the Sino-Japanese war.

The first industry to modernize was the cotton spinning industry. Small spinning mills had been built more or less experimentally as early as 1868, and a number were started on government initiative in the 1880s. In 1883 the first large-scale modern cotton spinning mill was founded. Significantly enough, businessmen who had accumulated funds in commerce and traditional industry played a leading part in it. It was a success and the industry expanded rapidly through the 1890s. Although imports of cotton yarn continued to rise up to 1888, by the end of the century Japan, from being a substantial importer of cotton yarn, had become a net exporter. The cotton weaving industry remained largely a cottage handweaving industry until at least 1890. In fact, because the Japanese value individuality and craftsmanship in their everyday clothing, as in other articles of daily use, the handweaving of cotton remained of some importance as long as the kimono was the everyday dress of Japanese women. In the last two decades of the nineteenth century a number of other modern industries were established or reestablished on modern lines. In the former category were the manufacture of cement, beer, and glass and in the latter, papermaking, sugar refining, and some other food processing industries where the advantages of large-scale operation were particularly great.

Some progress was made in coal and copper mining before 1900, but by no means all of the increased output was produced by modern methods. In engineering, iron and steel, shipbuilding, and other heavy industries, only small beginnings were made before World War I. To the outside world Japanese military victories over China in 1895 and over Russia in 1905 seemed dramatic evidence that here was a vigorous young industrial nation. And so they were but, despite the progress already made, these victories could not have been achieved without imported steel and imported warships.

Why did about thirty years elapse between the decision for economic development and the beginning of a modern industrial sector? So many people have commented on the speed of Japanese development that this may seem almost an impertinent question. Nevertheless, a thirty-year gestation period would probably seem a long time to an underdeveloped country of today and the answers may be instructive. First there is the simple answer that change takes time—time for a sizable number of people to acquire knowledge and overcome hesitation about investing in a completely unfamiliar operation. Second, what more than anything else distinguishes modern industry from earlier methods of production is that it requires large amounts of capital. In the early years of the Meiji period few people outside of the government had access to funds on a sufficiently large scale, and they were not necessarily interested in investing them in modern industrial plants. By the late 1880s five important things had happened. A number of enterprising businessmen had accumulated substantial funds in traditional industry and commerce; financial institutions had been established to help channel funds into the hands of those who were prepared to use them productively; financial stability had been achieved after the hectic financial strains of financing the Restoration and its aftermath; the government had provided some of the basic services without which modern industry cannot function profitably; and, perhaps most important of all, the economy had become productive enough to be able to set aside a part of its productive efforts for factory building without undue strain and to provide a mass market for the resulting products of modern industry.

Impatient Japanese modernizers of the 1870s and 1880s were sometimes critical of what appeared to be the caution and conservatism of Japanese business, although a few recognized that lack of capital, experience, and clear profit opportunities were usually the reason for it. In this case caution may well have paid. By at first making haste slowly the Japanese avoided costly mistakes (though by no means all of them). During these thirty years, moreover, industrial technology in Europe and America was advancing far more rapidly than ever before. In most fields the machinery and methods of the 1870s were ludicrously outdated by those of the 1890s. By concentrating on social overhead and public utilities, in which as it happened technological progress was rather slower, the Japanese were able to avoid the alternative of either being stuck with outdated plants or having to carry out a costly program of reequipment. This is, of course, not an argument for indefinite postponement of industrialization. It worked in Japan at that time because in the meantime there were other profitable avenues of investment. When modern industries were established, the choice of industries for modernization was made—apart from strategic industries—on sound business lines rather than from considerations of national prestige. Thus those industries, like cotton spinning, in which even the most advanced techniques of those days involved large amounts of labor, were adopted first, since it was these that promised the greatest advantages to Japan, with her relatively abundant labor and little capital.

Stimulated by the demands of the Russo-Japanese war, modern industry had by the eve of World War I reached a stage where it was in a position to take advantage of the opportunities for expansion that came with the outbreak of war. Allied demands for supplies and shipping were insatiable. More importantly, with the European powers fully occupied in trying to destroy one another, their markets in Asia and other parts of the world were left wide open for Japanese industry. Instead of the deficits in international trade that had been typical of the prewar years, Japan now had a large export surplus. Although technically engaged in the war on the side of the Allies, Japan's military contribution was negligible. Instead she concentrated all her energies on expanding her industries and overseas markets as rapidly as possible. By the end of the war Japan found herself with huge amounts of overseas currency, and a modern industrial sector large enough to play a leading role in her economic life. No longer did the modern sector have to rely for its expansion on capital accumulated in agriculture or traditional industry. Expansion could now be financed out of the profits of modern industry itself. A large part of the expansion was in fact financed and undertaken by large and successful business combines (zaibatsu) that had been in on the ground floor of modern industrial growth and were able to channel the profits of existing operations into more and more new fields through their own banking facilities.

The Double Standard

With the emergence of a modern sector, the Japanese economy operated, as it were, at two levels. On one hand was the traditional economy, consisting of agriculture and traditional industries using traditional methods of production and organization—though often improved, by the use, for example, of electric power—and including industries that produced new products (electric light bulbs, bicycle parts, toys) by traditional small-scale labor-intensive methods. On the other was the modern sector, using Western techniques of production and organization and requiring large amounts of capital equipment with correspondingly higher output per worker. An economy in which these two kinds of activity exist side by side is sometimes called a "dual" economy. This situation contributes to the popular impression of Japan as a land of contrasts between the traditional and modern. It arose in Japan, as in other densely populated countries where industrialization began rather late and proceeded rapidly, because capital was not spread evenly throughout the economy, but was invested selectively in certain areas. Thus economic growth did not raise output per worker and incomes in all sections of the economy at the same rate. In agriculture change was relatively slow and involved no departure from traditional small-scale farming practice. Agricultural output did rise by an average of about 2 percent a year until the 1920s, and this growth was an important factor in enabling growth to take place in other sectors. From the 1920s, however, agricultural output and farm incomes rose very little, and with cheap food coming in from Japan's overseas territories and the collapse of the silk market in the world-wide crash of 1929 the economic position of Japanese farmers actually deteriorated. In traditional industry, output per worker (productivity) was from the start higher than in agriculture and also rose faster, although because of the existence of a pool of farmers or cottage workers prepared to enter industrial employment for a rather small increase in earnings, wages in traditional industry did not rise as fast as they might otherwise have done. Eventually it was in modern Western-style industry that productivity increases were most spectacular and most sustained.

Even though workers were far more productive using advanced equipment in the modern sector, why should their employers have paid them more than their less productive brethren in traditional industry, since there was no shortage of workers anxious to move up from traditional to modern employment? The answer is not simple, but seems to be connected with early shortages of trained labor and with the business fluctuations that followed the World War I boom. Wages in the modern sector tended to rise more during booms and fall less during slumps, creating a widening gap between wages in the two sectors. The 1920s were remarkable for the frequency of business fluctuations. The wartime boom was followed by a short recession from which Japan was recovering, with the help of reserves accumulated during the war, when she was hit by the great earthquake of 1923. This was followed by a reconstruction boom followed by another recession brought on by an untimely return of the yen to the prewar gold parity. On top of this came the world-wide depression of 1929–30. Through all these fluctuations the modern sector continued to grow rapidly. Although succeeding slumps weeded out weaker firms, their place was taken by others, especially by the zaibatsu whose economic and political power reached a peak as a result. The effect on agriculture and traditional industry, however, was quite different. Hit hard by falling demand and prices during the slumps, relief during periods of business recovery seemed always too little and too late. For farmers in particular, the collapse of the American silk market in 1929 meant the loss of a vital source of income.

Thus, in a sense, the traditional sector continued to subsidize the growth of the modern sector, though in a new way. Whereas in the nineteenth century the traditional sector contributed taxation, savings, and manpower, now it contributed through absorbing economic fluctuations in the form of cuts in income and living standards. By supplying food and consumer goods at low prices to workers in the modern industrial sector it enabled modern industry to keep costs down, strengthen its competitiveness in world markets, and maintain profits which could be plowed back into further growth. From the standpoint of the economy as a whole, therefore, the two sectors were complementary rather than competitive, although it must be admitted that the traditional sector got the short end of the stick. Traditional industry contributed to the modern sector in other ways as well. Parts that could be produced or processes that could be performed cheaply by the traditional labor-intensive methods were often subcontracted out to small workshops by large-scale manufacturers. Sometimes even complete products were subcontracted and resubcontracted at very low rates, the large firm playing no physical part in the process at all, but nevertheless reaping a substantial profit.

By the early 1930s output per worker was four to five times higher in the modern sector than in the traditional, and wages were two to three times higher. While profits in the modern sector were high, in the traditional sector they were close to zero or even negative, in the sense that the owner of a traditional business barely made the equivalent of his own and his family workers' wages. In addition, working conditions and fringe benefits were incomparably better in the modern sector.

There is no doubt that the dual structure worked to promote rapid growth of the modern sector. The high proportion of income going into profits served to raise the rate of saving and investment, and lower costs made it possible for modern industry, despite some continuing technical backwardness, to break into world markets and reap the economic advantages of consequent increases in the scale of production. On the other hand, the possibility of pushing burdens of adjustment onto the traditional sector sometimes delayed badly needed rationalization within the modern sector. Nevertheless, on balance, it seems highly unlikely that Japan could have made such rapid economic progress if she had attempted to advance equally on all fronts. To measure progress simply by the growth of industrial output, however, is to neglect the serious social and political problems raised by the existence of the dual structure. Although all Japanese may initially have taken pride in their country's progress, the question of "progress for whom?" was bound to arise sooner or later. To farmers suffering real hardships in the 1920s and early 1930s economic development must have seemed a frustrating process. In particular, for a nation proud of its identity as one homogenous family under the emperor, the existence of two groups divided by different standards of living and different ways of life was bound to produce strains and tensions. Eventually, perhaps, the farsighted could envisage the modern sector growing to the point where it would absorb the whole population, but in 1930 this was still a long way off. The modern sector was barely growing fast enough to provide employment opportunities for the increase in population of working age, let alone for those working at low standards in the traditional sector. In the late 1920s the plight of those whom progress had passed by prompted many to ask whether the price of progress was not too high and to think about radical solutions. For the first time the idea of popular welfare as an economic objective came to the fore. The reaction of the government, controlled by a combination of the heirs of the Meiji nation-builders and the representatives of zaibatsu interests, was strongly negative. The proponents of popular welfare were branded as socialists or communists, as indeed many of them were, and their ideas as "dangerous thoughts." It was in the army that various streams of dissatisfaction became focused into a restatement of objectives. The army provided a meeting ground for soldiers who were mostly farm boys and young officers who were often landowners' sons. Both groups found the idea of a Japan controlled by business considerations disgusting. In the process, the idea of popular welfare as an economic aim became submerged in a vague and sometimes semimystical doctrine that popular welfare and national destiny were not conflicting objectives, but that given the right leadership popular welfare could be achieved *through* the pursuit of national destiny. How mistaken this doctrine was is now obvious. It is not the task of this chapter to tell how, with the help of terrorism and political blackmail, the military took control, but it should be noted that the situation arose directly out of the dual economic structure and that the idea that the modern sector should work for the nation and not the nation for the modern sector enjoyed a wide measure of support.

Once in power, the military moved to speed up the growth of heavy industry and the engineering industries. In doing so they could scarcely avoid relying heavily on the resources of the zaibatsu, but at the same time they were able to reestablish a measure of supervision over their activities. Efforts were concentrated on building up military potential and on promoting export industries that would earn the means of paying for heavy imports of equipment and strategic materials. In the traditional sector steps were taken to help farmers and small manufacturers improve production methods, effect economies through cooperative action, and market their products more effectively, especially for export. To these ends cartels and cooperatives were formed extensively with official encouragement; systems of inspection were instituted to maintain quality and facilitate marketing; and credits were made available to exporters to enable them to sell abroad on favorable terms. Overseas, the army moved into Manchuria and the government promoted huge investments there designed to build the newly created puppet state into both a major source of raw materials and an industrial base. Significantly enough, most of the expansion in Manchuria was entrusted not to the old zaibatsu but to new concerns more amenable to military interests and more dependent on official protection.

All this activity involved huge expenditures, and heavy government spending brought rising prices and business prosperity. For the mass of the Japanese people times had never seemed so good as in the middle and late 1930s. Controls were not yet burdensome and even the outbreak of full-scale war in China hardly cast a shadow on the general atmosphere of well-being. After all, thought most Japanese, it was a small price to pay for continued prosperity in a period when more peaceful countries were still floundering in the aftermath of world depression. But the situation was not viewed so complacently abroad. Competition from Japanese exports, which other countries considered unfair competition, aroused rising hostility and retaliation in the form of high tariff barriers and other obstacles to the export of Japanese goods. Japanese activities in Asia and the Pacific were viewed as a threat to United States interests, and the Japanese plea that expansion on the mainland was essential to secure raw materials and export markets for legitimate economic development met with a cold reception. With the imposition by the United States and other countries of embargoes on trade with Japan it became clear that war in the Pacific was practically inevitable. Even then, despite some shortages and rationing of industrial materials, prosperity continued, and the Japanese were not called upon to make painful sacrifices. Setbacks in other markets were largely offset by increased exports to the Asian mainland. It would be a mistake to attribute the outbreak of the clash in the Pacific solely to economic factors; strategic, ideological, and foreign policy factors were also involved. Nevertheless, there is no doubt that Japan's economic expansion, which had been acclaimed abroad forty years before, was now exciting suspicion and anxiety.

The early victories of the Pacific War seemed almost ridiculously easy, and only the more knowledgeable and farsighted could foresee the disaster that would inevitably result. In 1941 the policies followed since the early 1930s seemed a resounding success. Japanese industry had indeed made great strides. Between 1930 and 1940 the output of her manufacturing industry doubled and even the output of agriculture and other primary industries rose by some 25 percent. Since a part of this increase took the form of military goods and capital equipment, the standard of living of the ordinary Japanese did not rise in the same proportion, but nevertheless improved noticeably. Not only in volume but also in quality and technical sophistication the modern industrial sector made notable progress, as the performance of Japanese planes in the Pacific War amply demonstrated. These advances were by no means limited to the iron and steel and munitions industries but were shared by general engineering, shipbuilding, chemicals, and even textiles, particularly in the new field of synthetics.

The behavior of the Japanese economy during the war is something of a digression from our main theme of economic development and need not concern us here. Economic controls became more rigorous, but even so shortages of essential materials and the destruction of shipping and industrial plants by United States bombing had crippled Japan's war potential and seriously disrupted her whole economic life well before the first atomic bomb was dropped. By the time the Japanese government finally brought itself to accept defeat, almost half of Japan's modern industrial capacity had been destroyed and her population had been reduced to a level of economic life at which the sole and overriding aim was sheer survival from day to day. In August, 1945, many Japanese believed that they would never live a good life again.

A Fresh Start

Just as the Meiji Restoration heralded the adoption of modern economic development as a national objective, so defeat was significant for the new economic objectives that arose from it. The idea of achieving popular welfare through the pursuit of national destiny was thoroughly discredited and the nation's right to wage war was renounced absolutely. The improvement of the economic life of the Japanese people and the attainment of Western standards of living were adopted as the major if not ultimately the sole aim of economic growth. It is sometimes suggested that adoption of these new objectives was more or less forced on the Japanese by the Occupation, and that they represented a departure from established Japanese attitudes. In general, however, Occupation policies were effective only in so far as they were in accord with Japanese aspirations. Athough there may have been a few diehards who could not reconcile themselves to the change, for the mass of the Japanese people these goals represented the fulfillment of hopes that had been held, if not fully expressed, since at least the 1920s.

That these hopes were finally realized, however, was due in no small measure to the presence of the Occupation and its policies. Had it not been for the prompt and massive economic assistance provided by the United States, the Japanese economy would probably have relapsed into a state of anarchy. Once some semblance of normal life had been restored, the policies of the Occupation concentrated on ensuring that Japan would never again have the economic potential to wage war. All those who were thought to have made a significant contribution to Japan's war effort or who were closely connected with the military were removed from their positions in government or business and forbidden to take any part in the economic life of the country. The zaibatsu combines, which were rightly thought to have played a major part in the organization of the wartime economy, were dissolved, and the large number of enterprises that they had formerly controlled were required to operate as independent units. These policies may have contributed to the demilitarization of the Japanese economy, but they also reduced the chances of economic recovery. The purge removed from economic life most of the businessmen and managers best fitted to get production going again, and although many of them continued to give advice from behind the scenes they were often sorely missed. Many former zaibatsu enterprises also found difficulty in operating in the peculiarly difficult postsurrender years without the managerial and financial links that had long been their strength. But this was of no great concern to the Occupation at that time. Their directives were to demilitarize and democratize Japan and they had no specific instructions to rebuild her economy beyond providing assistance in the relief of suffering.

In the economic field democratization took the form of encouraging the labor movement and carrying out a land reform. Previously, such organized labor as there was consisted of officially sponsored associations of employees to act as a channel for government and company directives, encourage patriotic effort, and increase production in a way reminiscent of labor unions in other totalitarian countries. The idea that workers should organize to raise wages and improve working conditions through collective bargaining had been regarded as subversive and un-Japanese. An American-style labor movement was unfamiliar to the Japanese and was largely either uncomprehended or interpreted as a first step in the direction of communist socialism. Despite extensive educational campaigns, therefore, few unions operated in the way expected of them. In smaller plants, which collectively still employed the majority of the industrial labor force, the organization of labor made practically no headway at all, and laws governing employment and working conditions, enlightened though they were, could not be enforced in this sector which, as we have seen, depended for its operation on substandard wages and conditions of employment.

The land reform was very much more successful. Its aim was to redistribute land from large landlords to cultivating farmers and so to remove both a source of agrarian unrest and a reactionary landlord class. Both these objects were achieved. Landowners were removed from political influence with little resistance on their part. Farmers were relieved of the heavy burden of rent that had been a major source of their discontent and as a group have remained a strongly stabilizing influence in Japanese political life. Economically, transfer of ownership to the cultivators has encouraged investment in farming and has made it politically easier for the government to give support and protection to agriculture.

Economic recovery, however, began slowly in the years immediately following the war. Agriculture benefited from food scarcity and high prices for its products for, although food was rationed and prices pegged, a good deal of food was sold unofficially at much higher prices. Small-scale industry, the heir of the traditional industrial sector, also prospered in this period of general scarcity and steeply rising prices. Small workshops that could turn out household goods with makeshift equipment and using scrap materials made good profits. The modern industrial sector could not adjust so rapidly, and its recovery was not helped by the suspicion with which it was initially viewed by the Occupation authorities. In 1948, however, Occupation policy underwent a change. With the emergence of the cold war situation and developments in China, the United States began to see Japan as a counterpoise to rising Communist influence in Asia and as the industrial bastion of the Free World in East Asia. The revival of modern industry in Japan was now seen by the United States (though not at that time by all of her allies) not as a threat but as a necessity.

The aims of the Occupation shifted to economic stabilization and reconstruction. One of the most serious obstacles to this was monetary instability. Following the breakdown of economic controls at the end of the war, prices rose at a very rapid rate and by 1948 were over a hundred times higher than they had been three or four years before. Moreover, despite the reestablishment of rationing and price controls, they were still rising and the instability and uncertainty that this caused seriously hindered the recovery of industry and especially of overseas trade. On the recommendation of the Occupation authorities, government spending was curbed, bank credit restricted, taxation increased, and in general measures were taken to reduce the amount of money in circulation. With the government and banks treating money with a little more respect, its value ceased to fall so quickly, although it still required forty bills of the highest denomination issued to make a payment equivalent to ten dollars. The actual level of prices, however, did not matter greatly as long as they could be kept relatively stable, and this was achieved. Now that the aim was to get Japanese industry back on its feet, the Occupation attitude to the zaibatsu changed and no further action was taken to complete their dissolution after late 1949. Shortly after this, victims of the economic purge were reconsidered and many key men were permitted to resume their jobs. Moreover, the policy was now to concentrate reconstruction in key industries and in the most efficient firms, which in practice often meant former zaibatsu enterprises. These firms were given first claim on scarce raw materials and credit and were awarded the lion's share of government contracts. The official attitude to the trade union movement also changed, since it was feared that Japanese misconceptions about the role of democratically organized labor or the misuse of the labor movement for political purposes might hamper economic recovery.

Although some of the more radical Japanese feared that the new look in Occupation policy represented a retreat from democratic ideals, it was clearly necessary if the objective of raising Japanese living standards was ever to be attained. At any rate it was effective, and by the outbreak of the Korean War the Japanese economy was stabilized and functioning reasonably normally, if still at a low level. It was fortunate indeed for Japan that these steps had been taken when they were, and that her industry was in a position to profit from the large flow of United States procurement orders that came with the outbreak of fighting in Korea. Thanks to this timely event, recovery proceeded rapidly and most rapidly in the sector where it would ultimately do most good, namely, in the increasingly productive modern industrial sector, which expanded at a rate approached only in the boom of World War I. By 1953 the economic scars of the Pacific War had been all but obliterated and output per capita was close to the level of the mid-1930s. Recovery was fastest in basic industries and engineering but, because destruction had also been most extensive in these industries, they had only just regained their prewar importance in the economy by 1953. The high rate of growth that enabled Japanese output roughly to double in the first eight or nine years after the surrender was due to a number of factors, including economic assistance from the United States, the Korean War boom, and a rather high rate of investment, but most importantly to the fact that reconstruction from an abnormally low level is always easier and cheaper than new construction. By repairing damage and replacing installations at various key points, the whole productive apparatus could be restored to working order at relatively little cost. It might have been expected that once this phase of reconstruction was over the rate of further growth would be slower. What happened in fact was just the opposite.

A Methodical Miracle

From 1954 to 1961 the output of the Japanese economy grew by an average of about 9 percent a year. This is an extremely fast rate—around 3 percent a year is considered a good performance for an advanced industrial country like the United States. Since 1961 growth has been even greater and has averaged the high figure of over 11 percent a year. This was no longer a question of relatively simple reconstruction from an abnormally low level. It involved establishing and developing whole new industries like petrochemicals and electronics that were either nonexistent or insignificant before the war. To many observers this growth has seemed something of a miracle, but if it was a miracle it was man-made and largely planned. This does not mean, of course, that any other country, the United States, for example, could achieve similar rates of progress if only it tried hard enough. Japan's performance in recent years depended on a number of factors which were peculiar to Japan.

First, Japanese development has proceeded more or less in accordance with a conscious plan or strategy. Japan is not and never has been a highly planned or controlled economy, but at least since 1949 government agencies, and in particular the Economic Stabilization Board (later renamed the Economic Planning Agency), have made projections and laid down guidelines for economic growth. The core of the strategy was to concentrate efforts in those sectors in which output per worker was highest and was also rising fastest. Although this policy would intensify the dual structure and widen the gap in productivity and living standards between the modern and traditional sectors, it was thought that there was a good chance that the modern sector could be made to expand fast enough to draw up more and more people into high-productivity, high-wage employment, and thus eventually solve the dual structure problem by absorbing the whole population. This, it was felt, was the only feasible way of achieving the objective of raising Japanese living standards to a level comparable with those of advanced industrial countries. Meanwhile, as one minister of finance rather tactlessly put it, if some people in agriculture and small business suffered this was simply a price that had to be paid for achieving the over-all goal. Some may have suspected that the choice of this strategy was influenced by links between the government and big business, but the choice was generally approved, and it was believed that ill effects on the small business sector could be mitigated by subsidies and other forms of assistance. At the end of 1960 the government embodied its ideas in a plan for doubling the national income by 1970. This was not a plan in the sense of the economic plans of the socialist countries. It was more of an architect's drawing of what the economy might look like if its output doubled over this period. Nevertheless the consequences were worked out in some detail, showing what kinds of increases would be required in various industries; how much investment in new and better equipped factories would be needed to produce the increased output; how many new jobs would be created in each industry and where the extra workers might come from; what level of imports would be required and how exports might expand to pay for them. All these things were calculated with some precision, based on what was known or assumed about the relationships between various aspects of the economy.

Taking the years 1957–58 as a basis for comparison, the plan envisaged that national income would be 2.7 times as high in 1970, giving an average income per capita of $578.00—a little higher than in Italy but less than half the level in West Germany at the time the plan was made. The major increases were to be in manufacturing output, which would need to increase to 4.3 times the 1957–58 level. The greatest relative increases were scheduled for industries like chemicals, electronics, and automobiles, which required expensive equipment per worker but in which workers were most productive. No compulsion was involved, but it was clearly implied that the government would frame its policies and use whatever powers it possessed in the economic field to guide development along the planned lines. The existence of the plan had favorable effects on the rate of growth in several ways. Assured that the government was behind them and would take all possible measures to maintain favorable conditions for the growth it had planned for them, large firms invested confidently in expanding their capacity. If all industries were to base their production plans on the guidelines, each one of them could feel better able to anticipate the market conditions for its materials and products.

This assured the maintenance of the second condition for rapid growth, namely a high rate of investment. For people to produce more with the same amount of effort, they must be supplied with more efficient machinery with which to work. Producing this machinery and adding to the stock of buildings, power plants, transport facilities, and so on to go with it instead of producing goods for current consumption is investment. Investment means forgoing, at least temporarily, a part of production that could otherwise have added to the current standard of living in return for more production, and presumably higher living standards, in the future. Since the beginning of modern economic growth the Japanese have plowed back in this way a high and rising proportion of their output. Even before the Income Doubling Plan was published, about a third of all output was being invested, and in the years following 1960 the proportion rose to almost half. This was far higher than the 20 percent invested before the war and well above the rate of investment in any other country in recent years. About half of this investment went into manufacturing plant and equipment and, as planned, increased the importance of this highly productive modern sector in the economy.

When new plants were built, they naturally embodied the latest technological improvement, and this technological advance was a third major source of rapid growth. Its effects were particularly striking for two reasons. First, there was a very large backlog of technology. There were many fields in which Japan had never caught up with the best technical standards even before the war and, cut off from access to new patents and processes during the war, she fell even farther behind. The speed of world technological progress during and after the war was very fast indeed with the development of new materials like plastics, new products like television sets, and new methods of production like automation. This very wide gap between Japanese practice and world standards made correspondingly great improvements possible. Technical agreements between Japanese and foreign—mainly United States—companies were coordinated and facilitated by the Japanese Ministry of International Trade and Industry. Japanese companies were able to take advantage of these arrangements because of the postwar expansion of education facilities, especially in the fields of engineering, science, and technology. As we noted in the previous chapter, Japan started her modern economic development with a comparatively high standard of education, and investment in education has paid off ever since. Even now, almost all the patents in the textile, chemical, electronic, and automotive industries are foreign owned but, if few technical breakthroughs have actually been made in Japan, her well-trained scientists and technicians have been able to adapt techniques to Japanese conditions. The second factor that intensified the effect of technology on growth was the large amount of investment in new plants. Because such a large proportion of Japan's industrial capacity was either destroyed or scrapped during or just after the war, nearly all the equipment she is now using is less than ten years old and embodies the new technology. The speed of this technological progress has revolutionized many sectors of Japanese industry. Whereas other countries once complained that the competitive strength of Japanese industry was based on her exploitation of cheap labor, now the image of her industry is one of advanced technology and high-grade precision products.

The speed with which Japan built new factories not only enabled her to take advantage of technical progress; it also made it possible for increasing numbers of Japanese to work more productively than they had before. As had been planned, the expansion of the modern industrial sector provided highly productive jobs for people whose labor, on farms or in small ill-equipped workshops, had previously been far less productive. The very size of the gap between the two parts of the dual economy made the gains from moving workers from one side to the other all the greater.

As a result of the very rapid expansion of modern industry the goal of doubling the national income was reached ahead of schedule and Japan took a long stride toward becoming a thoroughly modern industrial nation. In the process, modern industry not only absorbed all the increase in the labor force over the period but also drew very substantial numbers of workers out of agriculture and small-scale industry. From 1955 to 1965 the proportion of the labor force engaged in agriculture, forestry, and fisheries fell from 40 percent to 26 percent, while the proportion engaged in manufacturing industry rose from 18 percent to 24 percent. Each subsequent year has seen a further accentuation of these trends.

Measured by output, the change in the relative importance of the two sectors was even more striking. The share of gross national product produced by agriculture, forestry, and fisheries fell from 23 percent in 1955 to less than 9 percent in 1965, while that of manufacturing industry rose from 23 percent to over 33 percent. Within manufacturing, employment rose fastest in large-scale modern industries like heavy engineering, automobiles, chemicals, and electronics. The composition of Japan's exports changed in the same fashion, with the share of such typical prewar exports as textiles, chinaware, toys, and other products of light industry falling and that of ships, steel products, automobiles, large generators, and industrial machinery rising.

The growth of exports played a crucial part in allowing rapid growth to continue. Increased industrial activity not only brought bigger demands for industrial raw materials like coal, petroleum, and iron ore, but with more people holding better jobs and enjoying higher incomes, the Japanese also wanted more imported goods for their own consumption. Unless these supplies could be imported from abroad there would be shortages leading to bottlenecks and price rises, which would in turn make it harder to sell Japanese goods overseas at competitive prices. Fortunately, the industries that were growing most rapidly in Japan were those for whose products world demand was also rising fastest. Despite this and very active trade promotion, Japan's exports would not have been sufficient to pay for all the imports she needed had not foreigners been prepared to supply funds both through direct and indirect investment in Japanese industries and through the granting of credit to Japanese customers. Even so, the tempo of growth had to be slowed from time to time to prevent rising prices jeopardizing Japan's overseas earning capacity. Consequently, spurts of growth were followed by periods of consolidation in which growth continued but at a slower rate.

Rising prices were only symptoms of shortages and imbalances brought on largely by the speed of growth itself. The most fundamental shortage was a shortage of labor. Until the 1960s, whenever the growth of the modern sector required more workers, they were always freely forthcoming from the large reservoir of lower paid workers in agriculture and small-scale industry. Over the last few years, however, this reservoir, which in the past had seemed almost inexhaustible, has begun to dry up, or at least to flow less freely. Because of its increasing productivity modern industry was able to cope reasonably well with the demands for higher wages that a tighter labor market brought. Small business, however, was able to pay higher wages only by passing their cost on to the consumer in the form of higher prices. As it happens, most of the things, such as food and clothing, that Japanese buy and consume as individuals are produced by farmers and small-scale manufacturers who have not been able to raise productivity fast enough to avoid raising the prices of their products. Rising living costs have therefore deprived the Japanese of the gains from economic growth to such an extent that the Income Doubling Plan was widely criticized as being in reality more of a Price Doubling Plan. To some extent it was inevitable that some part of consumption would have to be forgone in the interests of a high rate of investment in plant for further growth, but it was widely felt that the government might well do a little more to spread the burden more equitably. The planners, however, felt that any move in this direction would reduce the rate of saving and investment because wage earners do not save and invest as high a proportion of their earnings as large corporations and their owners do. The expansion of modern industry and the success of the plan to raise living standards by providing modern high-wage employment for all might therefore be endangered by distributing the fruits of growth prematurely.

The government therefore decided to approach the problem of easing the transition from a different angle. In 1965 a Medium Term Economic Plan was published which aimed to correct some of the imbalances but with a minimum reduction in the rate of growth of the modern sector. This was to be achieved by devoting more attention to improving the efficiency of agriculture and particularly of small business. This would help to keep consumer prices down and at the same time raise the incomes of people who for one reason or another could not be transferred to the modern large-scale sector. At the same time the plan provided for an attempt to overcome the serious lag in housing, transport, and other public services. These social overheads, as they are sometimes called, make an important contribution to living standards but do not contribute directly to the growth of industrial capacity. They had, therefore, tended to be overlooked in the single-minded effort to expand the modern industrial sector. Crowded trains, substandard housing, and almost permanent water restrictions in the big cities were becoming something of a national disgrace.

In the event, efforts to ameliorate the less desirable effects of rapid economic growth were outpaced by even faster industrial development aimed particularly at increasing the competitiveness of Japanese products in world markets. More substandard housing was built to form sprawling satellite towns around the major cities, and transport and communication facilities were improved and expanded. But crowding and environmental pollution continued unchecked and cynical Japanese observed that Tokyo's efficient and non-pollutant streetcars had been sacrificed to the cars and buses of the export-oriented automobile industry. Consumer prices, far from stabilizing, rose even faster, land prices soared and, as reserves of manpower and space approached exhaustion, wholesale prices also began to climb steadily.

Between 1962 and 1971 the output of the Japanese economy rose by about two and a half times in real terms to become the world's third most productive nation after the United States and the Soviet Union. Over the same period exports rose more than fourfold in current prices. The proportion of the labor force engaged in agriculture further fell to 20 percent (16 percent in 1972) while that in manufacturing rose to 27 percent. Despite rising prices, Japan's exports soared and reserves of foreign exchange accumulated at such a rate as to contribute significantly to a world currency crisis. Even revaluation of the yen by about 30 percent relative to the United States dollar has so far failed to dampen Japan's economic expansion more than momentarily.

As a result of this continued expansion, the end of the dual economy is at last within sight. The two processes of raising output per capita in the modern sector and transferring workers from less productive to more productive types of employment have transformed the life of the average Japanese. In the 1950s the security of employment in a large modern company at good wages and with good working conditions was the privilege of a small minority. Now it is something that the majority of Japanese can at least aim for with some hope of success. Food costs may be high but very few indeed go hungry. Housing may be cramped but most Japanese manage to squeeze into their homes refrigerators, television sets, washing machines, and other appliances which twenty years ago few Japanese had even seen. Working hours are shorter than they were, and many have the means to enjoy their extra leisure in ways that once only the richest could afford.

Prospects and Problems

For at least fifteen years both Japanese and foreigners have been asking how long Japan's rapid growth can be maintained. It has generally been assumed that at least some of the factors that have made this growth possible up to now cannot be expected to operate indefinitely. As the dual structure approaches its end and the low-productivity sector becomes smaller and smaller, while the gap between it and the modern sector also begins to narrow, the possibility of large percentage gains in total output by transferring workers from one to the other will be sharply reduced. Deprived of this flow of workers, the modern sector will face labor shortages and pressure for higher wages that will make it harder to keep costs and prices down. In effect, what this means is that in a tighter labor market demands for higher immediate returns from growth in the form of a better life will carry more weight. In fact, they could scarcely be ignored, since an attempt to maintain the same rate of investment and growth regardless of higher wages would lead to rising prices, greater demands for imports, fewer sales overseas to pay for these imports, and a consequent serious drain on Japan's reserves of foreign currency. Maintaining expansion of export markets at the rate required for rapid and reasonably stable growth would not be easy in any case. Japan has been fortunate that world demand has been growing since the war, particularly for those products which she is producing in increasing quantities.

Another difficulty facing Japan is that the backlog of technology that has played such an important part in recent growth is not inexhaustible. Once Japanese technical standards catch up with those of more advanced industrial countries, as in many fields they soon will do at the present rate, further improvements will have to be at a rate no faster than in other countries. Even if the Japanese were to become world leaders in technological progress it would necessarily be at a slower rate and at a higher cost in research and experiment than it has been in the past. Given the prospect of these profit-reducing trends it is doubtful that investment, the mainspring of growth, will continue indefinitely at recent levels.

In view of all these possibilities it has long seemed likely that Japan's rate of economic growth would eventually fall. The important question is when will this actually occur. In fact the performance of the Japanese economy so far indicates that these restrictions on its rate of growth will come into operation much later than once fore-cast. Some Japanese projections now see Japan overtaking the United States economically by 1985. One American analyst has even pre-dicted, in what at times reads like a scenario for economic science-fiction, that the process of growth will continue unchecked by any of these factors until Japan dominates the world economy by 1990. Even though earlier predictions of a cooling-off of growth were off in their timing, the basic considerations behind them still hold good, and fur-ther external and domestic checks can be anticipated as growth con-tinues. Japan's economy is already so large that she can no longer afford to ignore the effects of its growth on other countries and on the whole system of international trade and payments. Foreign reaction is already building up and Japan may have to exercise some restraint if she is to avoid producing international tensions disruptive to the world economy and potentially ruinous to herself. These effects will become more important the bigger the Japanese economy becomes.

Within Japan, too, there is a rising groundswell of disillusionment with the idea of growth for its own sake and some scepticism about whether the rising national income has increased actual welfare and provided a better life. Just as Japanese around 1930 began to ask the question "Progress for whom?" so now many are asking "Growth for what?" While in terms of national income per head Japan moves ahead of one European country after another and is forecast to overtake the United States in the 1980s, many feel that this is not a fair compari-son of actual living standards or quality of life. If the yen is so strong abroad, they ask, why does it buy so little at home?

There is, in fact, no way of making any accurate comparison be-tween the living standards of Japanese and, for example, Americans. Such a comparison involves making judgments about such things as whether Japanese enjoy raw fish as much as Americans enjoy steaks or whether Japanese sleep better on mattresses on the floor than Americans do in beds. The usual way of making a rough comparison is to value all the things Japanese (including Japanese corporations and government) buy at the prices they are prepared to pay for them and all the things Americans buy at the prices Americans are pre-pared to pay for them, expressing both sets of prices in dollars at the current rate of exchange. These figures are given in a form which rep-resents the value of goods and services available per capita if the total national output were divided equally among all members of the popu-lation which, of course, it is not. Moreover, this figure is not a very good indicator of standards of living since it is calculated on the basis of total production and ignores the composition of that production. It includes, for example, some products, such as munitions, which do not contribute directly to living standards.

As regards the way in which income is distributed among persons, there are many Japanese who feel that more could be done to make incomes less unequal. Some Japanese feel that the economic growth of the past twenty years has benefited large corporations and their owners, who have been able to build up large assets to a disproportionate extent, and that as a result the standard of living of the average wage earner has been lower than it might otherwise have been. In other words, they feel that economic growth should pay a higher dividend now rather than continue to plow back profits.

More recently dissatisfaction has focused on the composition of Japan's output. Too many resources, it is argued, are being devoted to producing goods for export at competitive prices and too little to increasing the availability of goods and amenities for home consumption. There is a feeling that by being forced to accept increasing living costs, smog, urban congestion, water pollution, noise, and general ugliness, the average Japanese is subsidizing export growth at the expense of the quality of life in Japan. Inadequacies in housing, public transport, water supply, sewage, telephone service, road and other public utilities certainly make life unpleasant for the Japanese and given the choice, most would probably prefer to see more spent on supplying deficiencies in these fields than on maintaining the present high rate of growth of total output. Faced with mounting pressure from abroad to reduce her surpluses of foreign exchange earnings, the government itself is now talking about policy changes along these lines. The readjustments required are too far-reaching to be made in a short time, but if and when they do occur they will have the effect of reducing the rate of growth of total national output, though not necessarily of living standards.

In summary the economic problems now facing Japan are largely consequences of her development. They call for structural changes to cater to the changing demands of a now relatively affluent society and to adjust to her integration into the world economy. There is no obvious reason why, given time, she should not make these adjustments successfully, and if in the process her rate of growth should fall somewhat from its current very high level this would scarcely be disastrous or inconsistent with the overall objective of raising Japanese living standards.

The Relevance of the Japanese Experience

In these chapters we have seen Japan develop from a primitive state to one standing by the measure of per capita income in at least the lower ranks of the modern industrial nations. Although she has faced problems and made mistakes over the last hundred years, her performance has been so much better than that of any other non-European country that we tend to think, rather condescendingly perhaps, that it was a really exceptional phenomenon. Actually, investigations by psychologists and sociologists have not come up with any very obvious reasons why Asian or other non-European countries could not achieve results similar to Japan's if they were given similar opportunities. It has therefore been suggested that Japan's experience might well serve as a model for other countries starting from a low level of economic life based on small-scale peasant rice farming at least superficially similar to Japan's situation a century ago.

If Japan's experience could be applied in this way, it would be a pity not to make use of it, but it is worth examining whether this is really the case. Let us first summarize the important factors in Japan's economic development. She began with an economy that was not much more productive than those of other Asian countries of the time but was in the main capable of attaining its objectives of maintaining the population at a low level and providing the resources to keep the samurai and especially the Tokugawa shogunate in power. Because she was practically cut off from international trade, she of necessity possessed a full range of industries to supply her own needs, and industrial and commercial development was beginning to accelerate gradually over a large part of the country in defiance of official theory though sometimes with official encouragement. Once Japan, under pressure from outside, got a government committed to encouraging economic development in the national interest, the traditional economy responded quickly and grew rapidly. Meanwhile the government, well placed by its tradition of high taxation and economic control, was able to prepare the ground for the development of a modern sector. Japan had very good supplies of business skill and labor, and poverty of natural resources was not yet a problem. Within twenty or thirty years a modern industrial sector was growing nicely in selected fields, supported at first by tax funds and fiscal policies and later, as the dual structure developed, by lower incomes and living standards in the traditional sector. Thus, even though the emergence of the dual structure created problems, it was a growth-promoting factor. Concentration of modern industry in a few large firms made possible economies of scale at an early stage. Military demands were a stimulus to industrial development and the booms of World War I and the Korean War were also growth-promoting factors. Whether the Pacific War was an integral part of Japan's growth process or a departure from it is a question we cannot answer here. Since the Pacific War rapid investment and a backlog of technology have enabled the modern sector to expand very quickly and effect a dramatic rise in the output of people it has drawn into modern industry from much less productive employment.

Conditions in most of the underdeveloped areas of today are very different from those in nineteenth-century Japan. Few of these areas have the sense of national cohesion that has been characteristic of Japan from the beginning. Nor do they have the human resources in the form of experienced businessmen and good quality labor. Many are still predominantly at the stage of subsistence agriculture that Japan left behind well over a century ago. If they have any kind of stable government at all, it seldom has any very consistent economic objectives or much influence on economic life. The economic theories of the Tokugawa shogunate may not have been favorable to economic development, but the fact that Japan had reached a stage where the government could have a theory at all and actually put it into practice with some degree of effect gave her an incalculable advantage.

It seems highly unlikely that traditional industry elsewhere could play the vital role that it played in Japan. In many of the underdeveloped countries of today the traditional industrial system ceased to function as a comprehensive going concern long ago and was replaced by European manufactures imported in exchange for the products of tropical agriculture, minerals, or other raw materials. From the point of view of economic objectives, also, they are in a less favorable position than Japan was in 1868. The idea of economic development as a means of meeting a military threat is unrealistic today. In fact, it would almost seem that it is now the least developed areas that are least vulnerable to military pressure and best able to resist it. Strongly nationalistic grounds for economic development now meet with an unfavorable reaction from the outside world, and the sort of objectives, such as raising living standards, that do find favor outside, do not always have a natural appeal to those in power within the country at its present stage of political development. World economic conditions, too, are less favorable for a country wishing to embark on a process of economic growth than they were a century ago. World trade in the kinds of things backward agricultural countries produce is now declining rather than growing.

Because conditions both within the underdeveloped countries themselves and in the world at large are so different from those in which Japan found herself in the nineteenth century, it is doubtful whether Japan's course could now be imitated with any hope of success. One may doubt also whether many countries would really want to follow it. In the first place, although Japan's progress may seem to us to have been rapid, underdeveloped countries of today may not be prepared to wait a hundred years to reach the level of present-day Japan. In the second place, some of the features of Japan's growth, such as unequal income distribution, private monopolies, or a high rate of more or less forced saving for the sake of higher future output, might well be less acceptable now than they once were in Japan. It may even be that countries that did not begin their modern economic growth in the nineteenth century have now missed their chance and will have to wait a long time for another opportunity. On the more optimistic side, however, there are new ways of doing things in economic development, as in other fields, and out of these alternatives may come a new path of growth that could be followed with better results than that which, all things considered, served Japan so well in the past.

XVI

Japanese Society:

A Sociological

View

BY
KOYA AZUMI

This chapter has the dual purpose of informing the reader of some important features of Japanese society and of arguing in the process for a universalistic approach to the study of Japan. It is often claimed that Japan is unique in being the only non-Western society to have achieved a high degree of industrialization. The claim is probably correct, but academically the observation entails a number of problems. For instance, one problem is the meaning, or lack of meaning, of the term West itself. This is an elusive, nonanalytical term connoting a whole host of dimensions that are left unarticulated. The geographical division of the world into East and West is perhaps convenient, but hidden assumptions about the differences between East and West cloud our analysis. To attribute the differences we perceive in world view to this geographic distinction is to offer no explanation at all.[1] A second problem relates to methodology and it concerns what we make of Japan's uniqueness. The idea that Japan is unique is perhaps responsible for the large number of studies of that country which have taken a particularistic in contrast to a universalistic approach.

Since sociology was born with the rise of modern society in Europe, one of its major concerns has been the processes and consequences of industrialization. What were the qualities of the societies which have successfully industrialized that set them apart from those which have not? If these qualities are universally the same, then did Japan possess the same ones that were present in other industrialized societies? Inasmuch as sociological theories of industrialization and its consequences have been based primarily on the experiences of the West, does the data of the Japanese case require modifications in those theories? Does the Japanese case exemplify a new pattern likely to be followed by other latecomers to industrialization? These are some of the questions that have been posed by sociologists. No definitive answers to them have been possible, but the queries have helped to clarify certain points important to an understanding of Japanese society.

Japanese Modernization

Studies investigating why Japan was able to modernize have, of necessity, focused their attention on pre-industrial Japan. A study

1. When I use the word West in this essay, I mean no more than the geographic region.

published by Marion Levy in the early 1950s is a good example to consider. He compared Japan with China, a society in the same civilization zone and one from which Japan had borrowed many ideas and institutions. If exposure to the West, the availability of natural resources, and past contributions to science and technology facilitate modernization, then it is China and not Japan which should have modernized. Why then, he asked, of these two countries had it been Japan which was able to modernize despite the seeming advantages over her possessed by China?

A discussion of change must always consider the relative importance in a given case of external as compared with internal factors. For both China and Japan external influences (mainly Western) were dominant and the answer to Levy's question might have lain in the differing nature of the external influences to which each society was exposed. However, Levy claims that these influences were identical, and therefore a comparative study of modernization in these two societies can ignore external influences. The explanation of the large difference in the modern development of these two countries must be found, he argues, in differences between the two societies in their premodern stages. He consequently undertakes a lengthy comparison of China and Japan with respect to their traditional social structures.

His study makes evident that in the traditional stage, despite a large number of similarities, some crucial differences between the two societies existed. China was a family-oriented society to a much greater extent than Japan. As in any society, the family was, of course, an important institution in Japan, too, but political institutions took precedence over the family. In an extension of Levy's argument, another scholar has suggested that "one major nonfamily type of relationship, that of lord and retainer, *samurai* and vassal, patron and protégé, was applied to almost every possible social situation *and was even the model for family relations.*" Politically, the source of legitimacy was the emperor and that source has been particularly stable because the position was hereditary in a line of sovereigns unbroken since the mythological origins of the nation. Other families may have assumed the shogunate and been the actual rulers of the land, but they had always ruled in the name of the emperor. In contrast the Chinese polity had from ancient days the notion of the mandate of heaven—the sovereign who in fact ruled well had the mandate of heaven to rule. A crucial element in this notion was that the people had the right to judge the ruler and anyone who believed the current sovereign not to have the mandate of heaven had the right to over-throw him. The idea that the people at large were the source of po-litical legitimacy introduced an element of instability into the Chi-nese polity. As a result the history of China is filled with the comings and goings of dynasties. According to Levy, the ever present possi-bility of political unrest had consequences for people's long-range planning, perhaps most importantly in the way capital might have been invested.

Reflecting the Confucian emphasis on the production of goods, especially food, the ideal class structure of both societies recognized, in descending order of prestige, the following four classes: (1) the gentry in China and the samurai in Japan; (2) farmers; (3) artisans; and (4) merchants. That the merchant occupied the lowest position in both societies is interesting and perhaps has had its effects upon modernization. Merchants, after all, normally play a vital role in industrialization and perhaps more importantly industrialization al-ways involves an enlargement of merchant activities. There was, however, one significant difference between the position of the Chinese merchant and the Japanese merchant. China was an open society and people could change occupations, rising or falling across class lines. Given the universal proposition that people desire to maintain or improve their self image, it is not surprising to find that many Chinese merchants were motivated not to be merchants. A prosperous mer-chant frequently bought land and invested in the education of his son, who could then compete in the civil service examinations. If success-ful, the son would become a member of the gentry class and in the process raise the social status of his whole clan. In Japan there was a closed society: social mobility was impossible in theory and virtually impossible in reality. The Japanese merchant was motivated to do a good job in his own occupation, to be a good merchant and to seek to make his son a good merchant after him. Adoption was the one in-stitutional mechanism which allowed some social mobility and in-troduced some flexibility into the rigid hereditary occupational system. When the biological heir was lacking in the appropriate talents, it was possible to fill a position with an adopted heir equipped with the abilities necessary to discharge it efficiently.

Tokugawa Japan was a rigid society partly because the shogunate had to live with some 250 daimyō, each somewhat independent in his own domain. In order to avoid a disintegration of control various devices were used by the shogunate to keep deviations from developing not only on the level of the domain governments but also on the grass roots level. Thus in Japan there were two effective channels of social control operating: the family and the political system. This, Levy contends, helped to keep deviance low when Japan began to industrialize. In China, on the other hand, only the family performed this function and the network of control began to be ineffective when the modernizing process geographically separated individuals from those family members who would by tradition have made decisions for them. In sum, Levy's findings are that the single major difference between traditional China and Japan was that Japan was feudal and China was not, a point to which we shall return.

Levy's study was by design confined to China and Japan. It is highly debatable whether the two factors he uncovered—the primacy of political values and the closed society—can be thought of as prerequisites for modernization applicable to all societies. Another debatable point in Levy's work is the assumption that the external influences on China and Japan were identical. Sociologists have a tendency to look for internal sources of change, but a case could be made for explaining the contrasting development of modern China and Japan in terms of the context of world power politics and differing external influences.

We should move on now from Levy's limited approach to a more general framework in terms of which all societies can be studied and universal propositions established. One of the great sociologists who developed such a general framework is Max Weber. His orientation, insights, and arguments have been points of departure for many scholarly works published in the past few decades. Weber was particularly intrigued by the things which appeared to have made the West unique among civilizations. Most prominent among these was the institutionalization, i.e., the making pervasive and legitimate, of the scientific outlook and capitalism, meaning by the latter the disciplined and rational pursuit of profit combined with a sense of moral responsibility. Though some writers of his period were led by a biological determinism to attribute the "apparently more advanced" state of the West to the "superior race" of its people, Weber looked rather for the cultural factors that set the West apart from other civilizations.

Partly in response to the Marxian thesis that the ideas men hold are a product of their station in the class structure of their society, Weber argued the opposite: men's values and view of the world are a more important influence on their actions than is their social status or the mode of production of their society. Weber engaged in a comparative study of the major world cultures and emerged with the fascinating theme that what made cultures different was the varying extent to which religion, especially the object of religious loyalty, was entangled with other social institutions. What made the West unique was the notion developed by the prophets that God was apart from and not to be identified with the earthly office of political rule. This idea, Weber believed, was a breakthrough that had profound effects on the course of the West. With it there arose the possibility of conflicting political and religious loyalties. It also provided the basis for the development of individualism since a man judged himself not by the standards of his political superiors but by those of his religious beliefs, the latter taking supremacy over his other commitments. The separation of the sacred from the secular social nexus and the avoidance of contamination by secular commitments is shown in an extreme form, for example, by the institutionalization of celibacy for the clergy in the medieval period. Celibacy coupled with monasticism eliminates kinship entanglements. The separation of the sacred from the secular and man's subjection to both was then for Weber a crucial factor which distinguished Western civilization from the other major cultures.

Subsequent to the prophets' idea of God the second important breakthrough was the Protestant Reformation, a movement from which sprang concepts leading the West into industrialization. In his classic, *The Protestant Ethic and the Spirit of Capitalism,* Weber attempts to establish a link between man's beliefs and his actions in nonreligious spheres. An affinity is suggested between the capitalist spirit and the Protestant ethic, especially the latter's definition of work as virtue and hence a moral responsibility. For Weber capitalism and industrialization were not consciously intended results but rather the unanticipated consequences of behavior motivated largely by religious beliefs. Granted that change is taking place and the following statement is probably an over-generalization, nevertheless during this century in America and in the West in general hard work has been considered a good thing: one is supposed to work hard and one even feels guilty if one does not. This, of course, is not the only definition of work possible. Work can be defined as a necessary evil, as it was during the medieval period when virtue lay in meditation and prayer. The change in the definition of work from being a necessary evil to being a virtue was facilitated by the Protestant Reformation, especially by the Calvinist notion of predestination. One's fate in the eternal life to come was determined already by God, this doctrine proclaimed, and there was nothing that could be done to alter it. It was a sign of insufficient faith, Calvin declared, to have any doubt that one was included amongst those elected to be saved by God. To eliminate all doubt unceasing work in one's occupation was suggested. Hard work was defined then as a religious act and a sign of the quality of one's faith. And yet one was not to enjoy the material fruits of one's labor, for thrift and frugality were called for as part of a life lived to God's glory. Wealth had to be accumulated without being expended on earthly enjoyment. Thus the accumulation of wealth came to be as much an indication of one's religious state as was hard work. From this developed accumulation and capitalism, but once it had been institutionalized capitalism no longer needed the religious motivation that had provided the impetus for its growth.

If Weber's hypothesis is universally applicable and therefore a Protestant ethic is a necessary condition for industrialization, we should find that all cases of industrialization have had a Protestant ethic. Japan, a non-Christian nation far removed from the West, would appear to be a strategic research site for testing Weber's thesis. Does the Japanese case refute him, uphold him, or demand some modification of his thesis?

Robert N. Bellah squarely met these questions in his *Tokugawa Religion,* a most penetrating and intellectually stimulating work on pre-industrial Japan. He asked if in Japan there was an ethic which was the functional equivalent of the Protestant ethic. In contrast to the West but in common with other civilizations, Japan displayed an identity or mutual legitimation between political and religious institutions. Both religious and political authority resided in the emperor and there was no institutional separation of the sacred from the secular. There was no basis for the social development of conflicting political and religious loyalties. Social institutions constituted a more or less coherent and harmonious whole.

In his analysis of Japan Bellah owes much to the power of a general framework for the comparative study of societies developed by Talcott Parsons. One of Parsons' concepts was that of "functional imperatives," namely, the basic needs that must be met by any society if it is to exist. Parsons specified four such needs and suggested that a certain value had to dominate in the task of meeting each of these needs. He also held that societies varied in the degree to which the pursuit of each of these four needs was thought important. For example, in America today the economy is the primary social institution organized to meet the society's "adaption" need. The values which are dominant are universalism and performance, the combination most suitable for a society with that kind of emphasis. Parsons believes that in an industrial society universalism and performance will be the main values. It was the role of the Protestant Reformation to increase the West's stress on those values.

In determining what Tokugawa Japan's values were, Bellah looked at the way in which the functional requirements of the society were met and concluded that the dominant values were particularism and performance, that is, the values which further the "goal attainment" need of society. In short, he found that political values took precedence over other values. Values which helped to attain the society's collective goals were highly esteemed. The other values—economic, integrative, and cultural values—were subordinate to the political values. In economic matters, for instance, universalism and performance were valued to the extent that they furthered the goal attainment of collective values. Or, to take another instance, scholarship was not esteemed in and of itself but only as a means to an attainment of other goals. To sum up, in pre-industrial Japan Bellah sees a great deal of utilitarianism and collectivism. The function of nonpolitical social institutions was to support political values.

By the Tokugawa period religious thought had evolved beyond the magical stage and had reached the ethical-philosophical stage. The central concept of religious action was *hōon,* or repayment for blessing received. One is given the blessing of life, of nurture, etc., by one's superiors and the grateful repayment of these favors was thought of as a religious act. *Hōon* was not to take the passive form of reflection and meditation but was to be voluntary acts in the service of one's superiors. There was no conflict over which superiors—for instance, one's domainal ruler or one's parents—had priority since the value system had predetermined that filial piety was subordinate to and found its fulfillment in political loyalty. Moreover, the object toward which one's loyalty was directed was not so much the occupant of a position as the position itself. This eliminated any possibility of a crisis of loyalty arising when there was a turnover in the occupants of a position or a position was assumed by an incompetent. In this way Tokugawa religion supported the societal value of the primacy of the political.

As a case study of religion supporting the political values, Bellah considered at length a religious movement called Shingaku, which had a large following and attracted adherents particularly among the merchant class. The merchant class was receptive to Shingaku because its teachings gave legitimation to the occupation of merchant and to the pursuit of commercial profit whereas Confucianism regarded mercantile activity with suspicion since it did not involve the production of goods. The lesson Bellah draws from his study of Shingaku is that political values took primacy over those other social institutional realms and that other institutional values supported the political values, thus making the social structure "rational," consistent, and coherent. In this way different social institutions were interlinked in support of the values of performance and particularism. Hard work was highly esteemed and had a religious connotation so long as the work being done was for one's political overlord. In a way the Protestant ethic equivalent was there, but the object of worship was entangled with earthly offices. Economic values were highly valued to the extent to which economic activities aided in the pursuit of political goals. Thus the rationalization of economic activities was not opposed so long as it did not get out of bounds and jeopardize political values.

In addition to the parallel between the Protestant ethic and certain Japanese religious values, another similarity between Japan and the West which historians have noted is the existence of a feudal system and some scholars have suggested that this feudalism served to facilitate rather than hinder modernization. However, objections can be raised to using "feudalism" as a universally applicable concept. The notion of feudalism is really European in origin. This form of social organization was undoubtedly real in a particular region at a particular time in human history, but to take a general description of it and apply it to other societies risks the danger of oversimplifying the concept and of ignoring the particular context in which it was observed in Europe. It has even been difficult to get a definition of feudalism acceptable to both sociologists and historians.

Dealing with this problem in Japan, John W. Hall reviewed the definitions of feudalism offered by various scholars and concluded that they more or less agreed on the following three points: (1) feudalism is a lord-vassal complex of military origin in which the relations are personal rather than contractual; (2) it is a closed class system in which arms bearers constitute one class; and (3) it rests on a landed or locally self-sufficient economic base, with a relatively immobile population in direct personal subordination to the land manager. Hall then considered whether Japan at any time exemplified the model. He suggested that some of these features were to be seen as early as the eleventh century and some as late as the nineteenth century, but that it was during the early sixteenth century that "Japanese society gave every indication of conforming in general outline to the ideal type itself." However, even though some variety of "feudalism" be accepted as existing at some point of time in traditional Japan, feudalism has not been demonstrated to be a prerequisite of modernization.

In the search for factors which may have facilitated Japan's modernization some writers have emphasized its remoteness and relative isolation. This, they argue, fostered homogeneity and a sense of oneness among its population. The decision to open the doors to the West and then to industrialize was no doubt aided by this national consciousness and by the desire to push the nation forward to an equal footing with the encroaching nations of the West as quickly as possible. In order to accomplish this national objective Japanese society was rather well prepared. It had a population dedicated to hard work for the attainment of collective goals. The 250 years of relative peace had developed within the warrior class men experienced in running bureaucracies and a sizable group of scholars. By the end of the Tokugawa period probably as much as half of the adult male population was literate. And perhaps most important of all, the population was imbued with the ethic of service and loyalty. With the Meiji Restoration all the domains were abolished and political rule was centralized, but the disruptions in the web of social networks were not as great as might have been expected. Japanese loyalty was an institutional loyalty aimed less toward a particular person than toward his office and this in turn demanded that the occupant of an office aim his loyalty toward a higher office, culminating in the nation itself and its symbol, the emperor.

Japanese Culture

In retrospect it is now clear that World War II provided for Americans a great impetus to the study of Japan. Though the Japanese authorities curtailed the study of English and banned the music of enemy composers, the Americans rushed to study the Japanese on the theory that to win a war one must understand the enemy.

One of the scholars mobilized to further this purpose was the noted anthropologist Ruth Benedict, and as a consequence of her investigations she wrote *The Chrysanthemum and the Sword*. Benedict studied Japanese culture at a distance and without ever setting foot in Japan. Her sources were Japanese immigrants and their descendants in the United States, Japanese films, prisoners of war, and whatever written materials on Japan she could locate. The outcome of her work was a fascinating book filled with innumerable insights and bewitching effects. It has perhaps had more influence on Japanese studies than any other single work.

As a cultural anthropologist Benedict was especially interested in deciphering patterns of culture. Out of a mass of varied data she isolated several important themes in Japanese culture. Among them the importance of hierarchy, the notion of "taking one's proper station," and the concept of obligation. The Japanese "reliance upon order and hierarchy," she observed, "and [American] faith in freedom and equality are poles apart. . . ." Hierarchy is taken for granted in the Japanese world view and is assumed to be necessary for ordering any social group, be it family, community, or nation. The maintenance of hierarchy and thus order is built into the prescriptions of behavior considered appropriate for a person on the basis of his sex, age, birth order, and lineage. Social distance among men is manifested in the use of the language itself, which contains a number of honorific and humble forms designed to reflect clearly the relative rank differences among the parties in interaction. "Behavior that recognizes hierarchy," Benedict wrote, "is as natural to [the Japanese] as breathing." Since hierarchy is the basic manner of social organization, it then follows that each party must take his proper station within the system. There is, therefore, a great sensitivity to behaving in ways appropriate to one's status.

Benedict also called attention to the fact that a person's conduct in social life is governed by the obligations of *on* and *giri*. In contrast to America where people consider themselves "heirs of the ages," the Japanese consider themselves debtors to the ages. Men are indebted not only to the past but also to the emperor, the nation, parents, and teachers. It is the need to repay these debts which furnishes the motivations for a person's action. *On* refers specifically to the obligations passively incurred toward important benefactors such as the emperor, the nation, the law, parents. It is one's *gimu* (duty) to work hard to repay these benefactors, but the debt is life long and is never considered to be fully paid. One is obliged, however, to repay the mathematical equivalent of *on* (whether the original benefaction be money, a favor, or a gift) within certain time limits if the benefactor is less closely related. Toward friends, workmates, distant relatives, and other persons of a status equal to or inferior to oneself one is said to have incurred *giri*. Though one may not be genuinely willing to do so, the *giri* relationship will nevertheless oblige one to come to the aid of these persons if ever the need should arise. *Giri,* according to Benedict, is a specifically Japanese notion and has no possible English equivalent. She quotes in translation a Japanese dictionary definition of *giri:* "righteous way; the road human beings should follow; something one does unwillingly to forestall apology to the world." The Japanese are bound by a "circle of *giri"* and lest they incur further *giri* they "walk warily in a complicated world."

The Chrysanthemum and the Sword is full of interesting stories well designed to illustrate the contrast between Japan and the United States. Fascinating as the book is, however, it must be regretfully stated that it has probably done more harm than good. In postwar Japan it created a sensation, coming as it did at a time when many people were in search of a new meaning for their lives and were prone to self-analysis. In the United States it set the tone of Japanese studies for many years and is still widely read. Her study of Japan is an example of a particularistic approach, and is in sharp contrast to the universalistic approach exemplified by Bellah. Her approach is devoid of an articulated general framework which may readily be applied to all societies and chooses to describe what it does deal with in an *ad hoc* manner and without any apparent reason. Benedict had a professional interest in differences and though there is nothing wrong *per se* with such an interest her emphasis on differences had the effect of portraying the Japanese as a wholly strange and alien people.

Differences are valuable. Imagine how dull a place the world would be if there were no differences. If there were no differences among men, I am sure we would create them. Anthropology has made a great contribution in making us aware that there are different ways of meeting the same needs. Along with that perspective came the notion of the relativity of cultural values, anthropology's greatest contribution. However, an awareness of differences must not be permitted to lead to an overemphasis of them. Though societies may differ in the ways they meet the needs they share in common, they are basically more alike than different. Benedict's thesis that hierarchy is important to the Japanese is true, but hierarchy is a phenomenon found everywhere. Her discussion of *on* and *giri,* made more mysterious by her use of the original language, is a good example of a focused blindness. The idea of obligation and debt exists in all societies, including that of the United States. She spends many pages discussing the repayment of *on* as if it were a peculiarly Japanese trait, but reciprocity and exchange are basic to the fabric of social life in any society. Indeed, many sociologists—such as George Homans, Alvin Gouldner, and Peter Blau—have built sociological theories based on the concept of exchange. The extent to which authority relations are diffuse [2] and social relations are hierarchical is probably greater in Japan than in other industrial societies, and in this respect Benedict's point is well taken. But the days of the double standards are gone. Kipling to the contrary, notwithstanding, East and West, men and women, white and colored, the twain shall meet and never part.

The ideal of social science is to formulate concepts and propositions which are universal and can be applied cross-culturally. It is to be admitted, however, that the idea has arisen that social science is the cultural product of the West and contains its own built-in ethnocentrism. Sometime ago I heard a scholar in Korea argue very forcefully that American social science was inadequate for the analysis of Korean culture. He felt it was incapable of articulating the essence of Korean society and the spirit of the Korean people. I have no doubt that we should remain sensitive to the possible limits of our concepts and propositions, but if the perspective of social science as developed in the West is inadequate, that must be demonstrated by the creation of a new and better social science.

One recent attempt to develop a somewhat new approach to the analysis of Japanese society is Nakane Chie's book, *Japanese Society.* Her analysis is based on two concepts: "attribute" and "frame." By "attribute" she means ascribed or achieved social status. An "attribute" refers to membership in a caste, an occupation, a kinship group, etc. The concept of status is, of course, one of the most basic in sociology, and the sociologist would be lost without it. The new part of her approach is the concept "frame," which Nakane considers to be

2. This term is used by sociologists to describe a situation where a person's superior in one organizational context tends to exercise authority over that person in areas of life beyond the specific sphere of organization involved.

much more important in Japan than "attribute." By "frame" she means "a particular relationship which binds a set of individuals into one group." A "frame" circumscribes men of different "attributes" and gives them a stronger sense of identification with each other than with persons of the same "attribute" who are in other "frames." For instance, the members of a village, or a university, or a business firm constitute a "frame." Because in Japan the "frame" is of relatively greater importance than in other societies, a person relates himself to the outside not by identifying himself with a particular occupation (an "attribute") but by identifying himself with his "frame." The employee of a business firm is likely to say, "I am from Company A" rather than "I am an engineer." In each "frame" hierarchical ranking is of paramount importance and the basis of ranking is not merit but seniority. The members of a "frame" tend to limit most of their social relations to other members and it is a cardinal rule that conflict within the "frame" be avoided at all costs. The basic unit of Japanese society, Nakane argues, is the "frame" and just as each member is ranked within the "frame" so each "frame" is ranked in Japanese society. One might visualize Japanese society, therefore, as a pyramidal structure of "frames" with each "frame" itself being a pyramid. A vertical principle of organization pervades Japanese social life, Nakane believes, and is the key to understanding Japan. This principle has been the one persistently stable element in Japanese social organization and has remained unchanged by industrialization.

In my own mind it is open to question whether this vertical principle central to Nakane's analysis will persist in Japan in the future or has in fact remained unchanged during the last hundred years. As the following discussion of the consequences of modernization makes clear, neither Japan nor any other society can remain unaffected in its social structure when it industrializes. Certainly it can not maintain a univalent structure. In the new circumstances few persons can remain, to use Nakane's terminology, in one "frame"; most people develop affiliations with a number of "frames" and the demands of these different "frames" may very likely not be compatible with each other.

Consequences of Modernization

Industrialization necessarily transforms social structure. Concentration of population in urban centers, growth of specialists, mass and prolonged education, decline in the birth rate, decentralization, a rise in individualism are all phenomena that accompany industrialization. Whether Japan with its supposedly different cultural base will follow the expected pattern and further what form postindustrial society will assume have been questions of both general and scholarly interest. Are all industrializing societies becoming alike? Will they eventually converge, or will they continue to exhibit certain differences?

One work on post–World War II Japan which has a bearing on the answer to these questions is James C. Abegglen's *The Japanese Factory*. It has caught the attention of those interested in the convergence theory and stands among the most frequently cited books in the sociology of organizations. Abegglen investigated Japanese factories in the mid-1950s and pointed out two features that appeared to depart radically from the familiar American pattern. One is the practice of what he called lifetime commitment. Once a person has joined a firm, both the employer and the employee are bound together so that the employee never is laid off nor will he quit for employment elsewhere. Thus, Abegglen said, mobility is virtually nonexistent in the Japanese labor market. The second distinguishing feature of the Japanese system is a method of compensation based not so much on job performance as on seniority and education. One can find, therefore, two men doing exactly the same work but receiving radically different wages. Furthermore, even if there is no business expansion or rise in productivity, the labor costs of a firm go up automatically every year.

From the American perspective these practices make no sense and are certainly no way to run an organization, especially an economic organization functioning in a competitive market place. And yet the Japanese economy has been surging ahead at a phenomenal rate, a contradiction which obviously requires an explanation. Abegglen's solution was to link these features to Japan's feudal tradition. "At repeated points in the study of the factory," he wrote, "parallels to an essentially feudal system of organization may be seen—not, to be sure, a replication of feudal loyalties, commitments, rewards, and methods of leadership but a rephrasing of them in the setting of modern industry." The Japanese case, he concluded, suggested that the experiences and organizational system of the West were not necessary to the introduction of industry into another social system.

Abegglen's observations and interpretations intrigued the imagination of social scientists. The Japanese were particularly interested:

the book was translated into Japanese and sold many copies. Its reception was especially good among professional business managers, who were then under attack for being traditional, feudalistic, and backward. They were delighted that an American observer saw functionality in practices that many Japanese thought were feudalistic and outmoded. However, to suggest the cultural relativity of management principles is almost to deny the foundations of sociology, which assumes that there are constant laws that govern the social as much as the physical. Critical comments on the book touched on two aspects: facts and interpretation. Abegglen's conclusion about labor mobility has to be qualified by noting that lower labor mobility is associated with male rather than female labor, with white-collar rather than blue-collar labor, and with large rather than small firms. These are rather large qualifications. For example, only a small proportion (about 16 percent in the 1960s) of the manufacturing labor force work in firms with more than 1,000 employees. Labor mobility in Japan, far from being virtually non-existent, was, according to government surveys, roughly 25 percent a year at the very time Abegglen was doing his field work. This rate is about half the United States rate, but it is on a level with the rates of the industrial societies of Europe. Perhaps it is the United States rate which is the exception and requires an explanation.

An empirical study directly aimed at analyzing the system of lifetime commitment did not appear until 1971. The investigators, Marsh and Mannari, studied in detail a 1,200 worker plant belonging to a large (13,000 employee) electric appliance firm. In the year previous to the investigation the plant had experienced a separation rate of 7 percent, a rate much lower than the national average. Marsh and Mannari make a distinction between two types of lifetime employment. One is the moral type, in which the worker stays with the same firm for the entire duration of his career for moral reasons. This is the type which Abegglen suggested was predominant in Japanese employment. Their second classification is the status enhancement type or utilitarian type, in which the worker stays on with the same firm because he considers it in his best interest to do so since his rank and wages will improve with his seniority. Marsh and Mannari found that only 12 percent of the employees accepted lifetime commitment as a moral value and were therefore to be classified as belonging to their first type. National statistics also indicate that over two thirds of all worker separations have been voluntary and for personal reasons. This demands a modification of the Abegglen statement that "the worker . . . is bound, despite potential economic advantages, to remain in the company's employ." The over-all picture that emerges out of this and other studies of Japanese workers is that they are in no way fundamentally different from their counterparts in other societies. It must be concluded, then, that Abegglen's study is still another example of a particularistic approach. His reader is left with the impression that Japanese organizations are radically different from those in the West, but a closer look at his facts leaves us wondering exactly in what respects and to what degree they really do differ.

The issues that are raised implicitly in Benedict and explicitly in Abegglen have to do with the nature of industrial society and man's place in it. Sociology from the days of the founders to the present has assumed that industrialization entails differentiation and that in the process of this differentiation men are gradually freed from the bonds which restrict their minds and bodies within the tightly knit social nexus of the traditional community group (*gemeinschaft*). Abegglen concluded that the Japanese case departed from the expected, but Marsh and Mannari have shown that Abegglen exaggerated the situation and that the expected patterns hold in Japan as well. Can we say then that Japanese society is now exactly like other industrial societies and there are no observable differences? The answer is that the direction of change in Japanese society supports the convergence theory, but that there still remain numerous social and cultural differences attributable to differences in origin and to variations in the wider world context to which each nation has been exposed.

Some years ago a number of social scientists who had worked on Japan held a conference on the question of convergence. Ronald P. Dore prepared a series of six hypotheses for the conference and they are worth repeating:

1. The criteria determining status in social organizations tend to change, showing less emphasis on birth and seniority and more on merit.

2. Relations of authority become more circumscribed, more specific to the particular narrow functions of the organization and less "relations of the whole man."

3. In consequence, the "volume" of authority exercised by superiors vis-a-vis inferiors tends to diminish; there is less social distance between statuses; there are fewer formal marks of deference required in speech, gesture, etc.

4. A greater range of the individual's behavior is the result of choice between conscious alternatives rather than the following of tradition.

5. A greater range of an individual's choices is determined by reference to his own well-being or that of certain other specific individuals and less by reference to the well-being of some group to which he belongs.

6. A greater range of an individual's behavior is based on rational secular premises and with reference to situations and events beyond his personal experience.[3]

These hypotheses are based on the patterns for variations of social relations established by Parsons, which in turn are drawn from a number of classical dichotomous formulations for contrasting modern with premodern society. Using these hypotheses, Japan becomes a case with which to test the issues of general sociological theory and thus the approach is a universalistic one. On the most general level and in terms of direction of change, all these hypotheses are upheld by the Japanese case. Although we cannot determine the degree of change with quantitative precision, in terms of these hypotheses Japan today is decisively more modern than it was a hundred years ago. Dore concludes, however, that there is more evidence of change in the direction of equality than in the direction of individuation. There are also further modifications which are in order. As implied previously, Tokugawa Japan had an ideology which valued merit and, although the allocation of occupations on the basis of ascription was dominant, there was no ideological justification of the hereditary principle. The over-all shift in emphasis from ascription to achievement, moreover, has not been unilinear. Rather, there is evidence that during the last three centuries there has been a cyclical change in this respect. Hereditary rule did not become institutionalized until the middle of the Tokugawa period. Of course, now the long-term cyclical change has probably become unilinear in the direction of greater emphasis on achievement and it is doubtful that there will be any reappearance of a hereditary principle.

Is Japan, then, now an open society? A few solid empirical studies show that the rate of social mobility in Japan is comparable to those in other industrial societies. Some outstanding individual instances are often cited: the marriage of Crown Prince Akihito to a commoner; the Japanese representative of the Horatio Alger theme, Matsushita Kōnosuke, the founder of the Matsushita Electric Company whose

3. Ronald P. Dore, ed., *Aspects of Social Change in Modern Japan* (Princeton, 1967), pp. 4–5.

Panasonic products are to be seen everywhere. There are those, however, who insist that there are qualifications which must be made in the over-all picture of an open society. Most frequently cited is the importance of the particular school, especially the particular university, one attends as a major determinant of a person's life chances. Study after study shows how disproportionate is the representation of Tokyo University graduates among the occupants of elite positions. To this must be added the general importance of the university one has attended in obtaining employment with prestige firms. Of course, inasmuch as entrance into a university is competitively determined, merit does play a role. Nevertheless this educational situation combined with the persistence of factions in political parties and other areas of life has led some scholars to call Japan an open society with closed components. One also frequently hears of the continuation of discrimination against the descendants of the outcaste groups. Though legally emancipated a hundred years ago and physically indistinguishable from other Japanese, the Eta remain degraded and oppressed. Similarly, one should note the legal and other discrimination against the non-Japanese residents of Japan, most of whom are Koreans.

Concerning the second and third hypotheses, one can say with confidence that during the last hundred years authority relations have become less diffuse and deference behavior less pronounced. The extent of change appears, however, to be much less than has occurred in other industrial nations. Thus it is not at all unusual for a superior in one organizational context (e.g., school, place of employment) to assume and be expected to assume a wider role in the life of his subordinate (e.g., as marriage go-between). Fringe benefits for employees are also normally much broader in scope than in the United States. As for deferent behavior, it is still visible, but one form of bowing—*dogeza,* kneeling down on the street—is today unthinkable. Dore points to one difference between European and Japanese history to explain the unusual degree of diffuseness in authority relations. Since in Japan the end of feudalism came quite suddenly, its ideology of unconditional loyalty still persists and mitigates against the narrowing of authority relations to specific organizational contexts.

The fourth and fifth hypotheses relate to individuation. Sociological theory predicts that as society becomes industrialized a person becomes increasingly more able himself to select his course of action from among a number of alternatives and he makes his choice more for his own interests than for the interests of others. This prediction is borne out by Japanese developments. Nevertheless, compared to other industrial societies the range of choice is smaller and the extent to which one considers the interests of others is probably greater. The procedure for choosing a marriage partner is a good illustration of this. The love marriage, as opposed to the traditional arranged marriage, has become not only respectable but preferable. Studies indicate that the proportion of Japanese who prefer love marriages to arranged marriages has increased and so has the proportion of married couples who say their marriage was based on love. The love marriage, however, is an ideal whose implementation encounters a number of obstacles. The reality has not caught up with the ideal and has failed to provide the institutional mechanisms necessary to facilitate love marriages. Dating has not as yet become widely practiced in Japan. Consequently it is very difficult for young people to become casually acquainted and then develop a continuing relationship without the parents and other seniors involved becoming worked up over the situation. Coeducation has narrowed the distance between the sexes, but students do not yet usually have the economic base for a marriage without subsidies.

It should be pointed out that there has been a qualitative change in arranged marriages also, a change in a direction which tends to uphold our hypotheses. In arranged marriages nowadays, as before, written background statements and photographs are exchanged via a go-between. If both parties are willing, a personal meeting, called an *o-miai,* is arranged. If both parties are still willing, and here the decision is made by the two persons themselves although they are likely to consider the views of others, they will go out socially together more and more, but the more they go out together the greater the pressure on them to make a decision. A person can have a number of *o-miai.* However, one cannot enter into the *o-miai* lightly, since it is a formal process involving more than the two persons. As the number of *o-miai* increases, people will begin to say "What's the matter with him?" or perhaps more commonly "What's the matter with her?"

With regard to individuation it should also be pointed out that choice of occupation is limited unless a decision has been made relatively early in the process of formal schooling. Once a person has entered a university it is rare for him to change his major, let alone transfer from one university to another. Moreover, once a person's educational path has been determined he does not have a free choice in selecting the particular firm or government agency in which he will seek employment. Individualism can hardly be exercised where realistic alternatives are limited and the alternatives must be pursued within a tightly knit web of human networks. Group affiliations are still of paramount importance in Japan and individuation has not progressed as far as it has in Europe. One reason for this is, as Dore points out, that "the Tokugawa society of a century ago had a more tightly organized structure of corporate groups than was found in Europe, even perhaps at the height of European feudalism." It is plausible, following Bellah, that this is related to the absence in Japan of the religious notion of man's equality before God.

Dore's sixth hypothesis deals with an area in which there has been little research. It is true that during the last hundred years of industrialization mass education and mass communication have done much to widen horizons for the Japanese. Still, during the same period there have arisen some extreme forms of nationalism and religion. However, it is perhaps reasonable to expect that during such a period of rapid social change there would be much strain and this strain could be lessened by such revitalization movements. The "rationality" of the extreme nationalist movements can be questioned, but a look into the dogma of some of the more popular religious movements reveals an unexpected amount of secularism. The largest such movement, Sōka Gakkai, can be better understood not so much by the religion's belief in the supernatural as by the largely latent psychological and social functions it has provided for its members.

In conclusion, Japanese society has changed in the expected direction and is likely ultimately to converge with other industrial societies, but there remain a number of contrasting differences. These differences are largely attributable to variations in the premodern stages of these societies, but the course Japanese society has taken must also be considered in the larger context of her international relations. Sociologists have thus far paid more attention to the internal dynamics of society than to the external influences from which no nation can today remain isolated. Perhaps the time is ripe for us to consider the world as a single social system and each nation but one of its units.

XVII

Modern Political

Institutions

BY
ARDATH BURKS

Although extravagant Japanese claims should be treated with due caution, it is true that Japan's political institutions represent a unique system. Whether regarded as the first of Asian nations to modernize, or as the sole persistently Asian country among modern industrial. states, Japan offers a rather unusual case study in what is called political development. Once referred to along with Germany as a "late developer," Japan obviously lost its underdeveloped status long before most other countries of Asia, Africa, and even Latin America. It was, in other words, late only in comparison with countries of Western Europe and North America. The Japanese case in political modernization, therefore, now seems as remote from the experiences of other Asian nations as do the prior examples drawn from European and American historical development.

On the other hand, Japanese political experience has in itself great interest, for the political structure and behavior of every nation are rooted in that nation's basic culture and Japan's political institutions therefore offer a valuable clue to the understanding of Japanese culture. As Warren Tsuneishi put it:

Japan, in short, constitutes a unique polity, which should not be surprising given the particular forces that have molded and shaped her over the centuries. These forces have been both physical and cultural; they include her geographical background and location at the very edge of the Sinic node of civilization; her economic foundations and human resources; and certain pervasive features of her historical past which impinge upon her present constitutional structure and political processes.[1]

Nor is the Japanese case totally irrelevant to a general theory of political modernization. Indeed, it throws additional light on the complex process of modernization, considered carefully in other than an ethnocentric fashion. It also reflects in an unusual manner the axiom that "traditional" and "modern" characteristics not only can but must coexist.

Instability and Stability

Admittedly the terms "modern" and "modernization" remain as yet undefined; nevertheless, they are useful labels for social characteristics that we know exist. Vague and sweeping as they are, certainly the words are more meaningful than the Marxist "mode of production"

1. Warren Tsuneishi, *Japanese Political Style* (New York, 1966), p. 2.

(primitive, slave, feudal, capitalist, socialist), which makes political institutions the handmaidens of stages of economic growth. Even in non-Marxist theory "modernization" is frequently identified with "industrialization," yet, however significant a factor it may be, "industrialization" is obviously only a part of the whole process.

Japanese society, like that of any other country, has of course felt the effects of a very basic change, namely, the great multiplication of human power through mechanization and, later, through the use of nonanimate sources of energy such as coal, steam, oil, and, most recently, atomic power. Japan, like the rest of the world, has felt the impact of these successive waves of inanimate energy, beginning in the eighteenth, but becoming most significant in the nineteenth and twentieth centuries. Far more subtle and basic, as former Ambassador Edwin O. Reischauer has pointed out, are certain factors and their effects on social structure:

One such factor, I believe, is the development of the scientific method, that is the concept of purposeful experimentation leading to new discoveries and inventions. Back of the development of the scientific method is probably something even more basic, namely the concept of "progress." [2]

This is the significant factor in modernization which the philosopher Charles Frankel called "changes in the concept of social time."

One of the simplest everyday definitions of modernization involves this very sense of change. A traditional society with traditional political institutions (let us say, those of early Tokugawa Japan between 1600 and 1750) produces one generation after another which finds it impossible to think that any succeeding generation will be born and nurtured in a different environment. A modern society with modern political institutions (for example, those of the late Tokugawa and Meiji period) finds change desirable and even inevitable. Political institutions are resultants from changing forces, from instability, if you will; political institutions are also deliberately used for "purposeful experimentation" toward further change. Change, however, is always surveyed from the bench mark of tradition.

This is why the label "Westernization" has been largely abandoned in describing modern Japanese political development. The concept of progress and the restlessness of change is a worldwide phenomenon,

2. Edwin O. Reischauer, "Toward a Definition of 'Modernization,' " in *Nichibei Fōramu* (*Japan-America Forum*), XI (January 1965), 10.

affecting the West itself. Granted, change and the impact of the West on Japan did overlap during the nineteenth century; the eventual result, nevertheless, showed clearly that modernization and Westernization must be thought of as two distinct processes.

Paradoxically, the impact of the Allied—largely American—Occupation of Japan (1945–52) illustrates much the same point. There are still those who like to think that the true modernization of Japanese society and political institutions began only after defeat in the Pacific War and the Occupation. More objective observers, with a longer historical perspective, have rather adopted the description of that momentous period chosen by Kawai Kazuo, "Japan's American interlude." The term "interlude" quite properly suggests not only what went on in Japan long before the Occupation but also what must be taken into account afterwards.

When one considers the tremendous changes which have occurred in Japan over the past century; and when one considers the enormous impact of her twentieth-century imperialism, aggression, war, defeat, and the Occupation, he cannot help but be astounded at the relative stability of formal political institutions since the 1952 peace treaty. In the 1950s even expert observers were gloomy in estimating the staying power of a largely alien-inspired political structure. As Japan approached the time to recover the exercise of sovereignty, it was fashionable to predict that a reverse course would soon restore Japan to a traditional political style.

After all, the new Constitution was drafted in record time in English under largely American authorship. Only then was it conveniently translated into Japanese. Drawn up in 1946 by American officials in the Government Section of Headquarters, Supreme Commander for the Allied Powers (SCAP), the so-called MacArthur draft for all practical purposes became the Constitution of Japan. The product of persuasion, cajolery, and some threats, this organic law was in fact imposed on the Japanese and in parts its language sounded strange to Japanese ears. All the more surprising that this Constitution has yet to be formally amended; that today the most informed predictions allow little chance for wholesale revision.

For this seeming paradox there are several reasons. For one thing, the Occupation itself was carried off with a minimum of friction. A people who had never been defeated or occupied faced another people who had never defeated and then occupied such a large and populous country. Both played their difficult roles so well that an amazing reservoir of good will was created. Yoshida Shigeru, who was prime minister during most of this critical period, wrote: "Judged by results, it can be frankly admitted that Allied (of course, predominantly American) occupation policy was a success." There was, in other words, little or no backlash.

For another thing, the framework of government inherited from the Occupation period was never so inflexible as to rule out further change. Although it has not been formally amended, the Japanese Constitution—like its American counterpart—has permitted informal revision. A few examples include: covert and limited rearmament (despite the famous Article 9, which at first seemed to rule out armed forces); a departure in practice from imported American principles of federalism (more specifically, movement from the local autonomy called for in Chapter Eight to the more familiar procedures of a unitary state); and the reestablishment to some extent of the centralized control of fiscal policy, police, and education. These were safety valves which siphoned off pressure toward outright amendment of the Constitution.

Finally, and this brings us around full circle, beginning about 1948 socio-economic changes within Japan made what had originally appeared to be an overly idealistic constitution a rather more practical organic law. It was almost as though the Japanese, with American help, had put up an elaborate but temporary scaffolding, within which reconstruction, using largely Japanese materials, steadily moved toward a brand-new political structure. Like most ultramodern Japanese architecture, however, the building incorporated traditional elements of design.

In other words, the miraculous success of post-treaty Japan cannot be attributed solely to the wisdom of the Occupation forces nor to the admittedly constructive cooperation on the part of the occupied Japanese. As ex-Ambassador Reischauer has pointed out, modernization did not begin with the "American interlude," but has been proceeding in fits and starts for a century. Scholars have been increasingly fascinated by the idea that Japan's long experience with feudalism may have had something to do with the speed and success with which Japan was able to modernize. In this sense, Japan early displayed signs of incipient modernization not found in other Asian countries; it began to modernize earlier and more easily than other countries outside the West; and it shared certain historical characteristics with Western countries.

It is important to remember that a century ago the Meiji modernizers very carefully eliminated conventions that proved harmful and
were obstacles to achieving the goal of an enriched nation and a
strong country; equally carefully they kept traditions that proved useful for further change. In the post-treaty period, the Japanese had a
threefold task in restructuring political institutions: further to eliminate conventions inherited from the prewar period; to weed out purely
alien institutions inappropriate to Japan; and to continue traditions
which were practical.

It was not by accident that Allied officials referred to the removal
of obstacles to "the revival of democracy" in Japan. There had been
a relatively strong Japanese tradition—the oldest outside Western
Europe and North America—of political parties, elections, a cabinet,
and a parliament, which had tried to aggregate the multiple interests
of the public. To these institutions were added, during the postwar
and post-treaty period, a stake in the "peace constitution," in democratic procedure, and in civil liberties shared by peasants, professors,
women, students, labor union members, and the news media of Japan.

The Occupation is even more dramatically illuminated as an interlude when we turn to examine what has happened since its end. To
borrow a phrase from contemporary writing on economic history,
since the peace treaty Japan has entered upon a second-stage "take-
off" into modernization. This phase has been marked by further
urbanization at a geometric rate of speed, the growth of a new white-
collar middle class, and what seems to be almost an obsession with
durable consumer goods. So far at least, as we shall see, the Japanese
have been able to carry into this stage a large measure of traditional
behavior with which to protect themselves against the shock waves of
rapid change. But the real test, as between stability and instability, is
yet to come. Like all very advanced countries, including the United
States, Japan is even now experimenting with the tensile strength of
its post-treaty political institutions when they are subjected to the
strain of issues like war and peace, the gap between rural and urban
society, and the desire for individual liberty versus community order.

Political Culture: Society beneath the State

Contemporary political scientists, whether American or Japanese,
have been conducting a search for more meaningful measurements
with which to understand across cultural boundaries in a truly com-

parative fashion governments, political institutions, and political behavior. Such efforts by Americans have been inspired and aided to no small degree by the need to grasp institutions rooted in unfamiliar (so-called non-Western) cultures. Because of the very intimate relationship between the United States and Japan in recent years, Americans have perhaps progressed furthest in collecting data on Japanese government and politics.

With regard particularly to Japan, observers by and large have abandoned the older and simpler method which was limited to the description of formal institutions of government. Concern has rather been expended on concepts of culture in general, on which political culture in particular is based; on tradition, transition, and modernization in general, within which political development is worked out; on political behavior and ideology which, when understood, help to reveal the real functions of the political institutions.

To repeat, to say that modern, post-treaty Japanese political institutions—like social institutions any time, anywhere—are rooted in traditional Japanese culture is neither to state a truism on one hand, nor to engage in contradiction on the other. Culture, according to anthropologist Clyde Kluckhohn, refers to "those selective ways of feeling, thinking, and reacting that distinguish one group from another—ways that are socially transmitted and learned (with, of course, some change through time) by each new generation." One can, then, presumably speak with assurance about Japanese culture (as compared across space with American); within Japan, about traditional culture (as compared across time with modern); and more specifically, about Japanese political culture. Such terms are now in more common use than "national character," a phrase which was popular just after World War II.

More behaviorally inclined social scientists generally accept the proposition that culture so defined gives birth to, nurtures, and supports the political institutions of a nation, particularly those which survive and thrive. It is more controversial to contend that wide distribution of a certain personality type in a given country is revealed by the nature of its political regime or ideology (for example, democracy or totalitarianism). For our purposes it is less debatable to say that such a broad approach puts more formal political institutions in the proper perspective, in the light of political culture, behavior, and ideas. This permits a dynamic, rather than a static, interpretation, taking account of tradition, transition, and modernization.

It is often noted with some surprise that "modern" Japanese political culture is still indelibly marked by "traditional" Japanese social values. These are usually summarized as follows:

(1) values are achieved mainly in groups, that is in the community (*gemeinschaft, kyōdōtai*), and are
(2) endowed with a semisacred quality (that is, they are *Japanese* values) and are transmitted through
(3) symbolic heads of family-style groups, which have a peculiarly vital role (in a patriarchal, hierarchical society), to
(4) individual Japanese, who receive a continuous flow of blessings and, in return, are freighted with obligations to the group; finally
(5) there is no universal ethic: ideas, ethics, education, science, politics—these are vital only in so far as they are vital to the group, and not as ends in themselves.

With regard to such older values, several comments need to be made. Often the interpretation of political development (including analyses by some Japanese) implies the elimination of such traditional values, a regular evolution out of the old into the new. Otherwise, the society is not modern, represents "abortive modernization," or shows signs of "feudal residues." Once again, the Japanese case challenges such a simplistic thesis. Obviously, the value pattern sketched above has provided a firm foundation for Japanese modernization and even for the second-stage take-off. Emphasis on group loyalty, group coherence, a relatively greater emphasis on obligations (rather than rights) of individuals—a complex quite different from Western patterns—illustrate how "modern" coexists with "traditional," in fact, how traditional characteristics are of positive value to the modernization process. Finally, the values do not remain exactly the same: they are, to borrow a figure of speech used by Arnold Toynbee to epitomize this social fact, old wine in new bottles.

In short, a sure way to interpret the workings of post-treaty political institutions in Japan is first to examine subtle changes in Japanese political culture, in the society beneath the state. Such changes include in Japan, as elsewhere, the steady rise in functions of what we call "the administrative state." Modern government reaches out further, in both input and output functions, and touches more and more Japanese. Government can be used, indeed, it is expected that it will be used, for "purposeful experimentation" and change, if not progress. But Japanese political institutions are in turn affected by a wider political public. Certainly one mark of modernity in Japan is the exceptional rate of literacy, the highest in the world. Japan is saturated with newspapers, a wide variety of magazines, and alert radio-television broadcasting. It has a mature system of schools and universities. The public has wide general access to up-to-date information about its own and other governments. Both the government (the majority) and the opposition (the minority) can and do use these facilities to educate, to inculcate, or even to try to mislead the public. According to the constitutional framework already mentioned, however, they cannot suppress sources of information and dare not ignore them. In short, ideology—commonly shared beliefs and perception of change itself—powerfully affects and is affected by political institutions. This is ground which is hard to survey and which has been only crudely mapped.

From a few sound public opinion-political attitude surveys already conducted in Japan, we can surmise that the Japanese are probably not yet unalterably committed to any ideology which might determine the exact shape of future political institutions. What emerges are profiles of contemporary political culture which contain substantial elements of traditional attitudes: emphasis on the family, the group, and the nation over the individual; and on discipline and duty over freedom; persistent distinctions of status over social equality. Alongside these elements is evidence that a younger, better educated, more scientifically inclined generation is moving toward egalitarianism if not democracy. Surprising, if not viewed in light of the aforementioned coexistence of tradition and modernity, is the fact that while labels like "democracy" and "liberalism" evoke favorable responses from the Japanese, "socialism" is also viewed favorably and "capitalism" is almost universally held in low esteem.

It is entirely too early to jump to the conclusion that Japan, like modern Western societies, is witnessing "the end of ideology." It is intriguing, however, to speculate on developments whereby a relatively open society with democratic political institutions, supported by a high degree of economic affluence, and marked by a new, emergent, white-collar, urban middle class seems to grow intensely pragmatic and apolitical. An answer to the question "What sort of political institutions best suits such a people?" remains to be discovered both in the West and in Japan. For the present, even a cursory survey of contemporary political culture—of society and attitudes beneath the state—goes a long way toward describing not only the kind of political institutions Japan now has but also how they work.

The Establishment, a Pluralistic Hegemony

In the light of what has already been said, it should come as no surprise to learn that post-treaty Japanese political institutions have been dominated by conservatives. This is to say that amidst change those who wish to conserve some Japanese traditions have by and large grasped and held on to the levers of power.

A century ago the Meiji modernizers, once referred to as the first modern mercantilists, overcame Japan's crisis of security and brought the country out of isolation. They established a tradition which has been called "conservative modernization." In the interwar period, it is true, Japanese engaged in a disastrous flirtation with radical-reactionary tendencies. Partly because of unfavorable internal and external conditions, the pendulum swung to the extreme of romantic nationalism and traditionalist reaction. War, defeat, and the Occupation brought far-reaching changes in the society, which were reflected in new post-surrender political institutions.

Under the prodding of the Occupation not only was a new constitutional framework erected but large sectors of the older political leadership were dismissed or temporarily purged. Most striking in a modern state was the removal of the military elite from the center of governmental gravity. The zaibatsu, or business combines, were at first reduced in importance and then reshaped within the post-treaty economy; land reform basically modified class relations at the rice roots level; and more openly competitive associations (political parties, private business organizations, labor unions, and a network of mass media) made their appearance. Despite wide-ranging changes, however, the over-all impact of "directed change" under the Occupation—particularly after American policy shifted from reform to reconstruction—was conservative.

Above all, rapid growth since the peace treaty has guaranteed a new breed of conservatism. What one Japanese writer has referred to as a "pluralistic hegemony" shared by many groups has deliberately conserved Japanese values while engaging in further modernization. Japanese conservatives might be referred to, in American terms, as the Establishment. It consists of the majority Liberal-Democratic

Party government, business and industrial organizations, and the closely allied civil service bureaucracy.

Post-treaty Japanese political institutions have to no small degree owed their stability to two gambles early and consciously made by the Establishment. To paraphrase previous surrender terms, enduring the unendurable, conservative governments have purchased security by placing Japan under the American nuclear umbrella. The cost was signature of the Japan-American security treaty, first signed along with the peace treaty in 1952; renewed after a bitter struggle in 1960; and continued by mutual agreement in 1970. For one brief historical moment, in the riots of 1960, there was a real risk that the arrangement would uproot the transplanted political institutions themselves. On the other hand, the Security Treaty has had other effects on political structure: for a medium-range power, Japan spends as little of its public budget on arms as any nation in the world. There is no longer in the Establishment a military elite. The defense agency does not even enjoy cabinet status.

The other gamble by the conservatives was to pledge achievement of an unprecedented and unparalleled growth rate which would double national income in ten years. The results have been beyond the wildest dreams of the most sanguine politician, for Japan doubled its income in only seven years. Although much noise is made by the opposition, as well as by the Establishment, over issues of foreign affairs, every post-treaty cabinet has paid primary attention on a day-to-day basis to questions of full employment, gross national product, and balance of payments. What Lawrence Olson has called "economism" has therefore left its stamp on political institutions.

The Establishment has been faulted by Japanese critics, who say that it has been marked by "bureaucratic leadership," characterized by passivity, and weakened by failure to search out new approaches to problems. These have been the specific characteristics of recent cabinets led by Prime Ministers Ikeda Hayato, Satō Eisaku, and Tanaka Kakuei, say the critics.

In other words, rather than creating new values, bureaucratic leadership is satisfied merely to represent the old; rather than blazing new trails, it falls into step with the natural development of society and handles all problems through established social mechanisms. Because of this it is unfit to cope with social upheavals such as those wrought by economic panic. It is effective only when conditions are favorable enough to allow a normal development of society.[3]

As a matter of fact, this is as good a definition of modern Japanese conservativism as possible. Fortunately for the Establishment, conditions have remained favorable, the gambles have paid off. What the opposition is reluctantly coming to realize, as we shall see below, is that political institutions in modern so-called capitalist societies are effective instruments with which to make economic panics improbable if not impossible. However, the risk of national security is a matter uncomfortably beyond Japanese control. Escalation of conflict might well run beyond the control of any system of political institutions.

A less flattering view of the stability of Japan's political institutions and of their dominance by the Establishment might see the majority of the Japanese public armed with relative security (provided from the outside), enjoying increasing levels of prosperity (even though the fruits are unevenly distributed), and content to drift with the currents of progress. Whatever the reason, the conservative coalitions have rolled up impressive (if slightly decreasing) majorities. In the thirty-third general election for the House of Representatives (held in December, 1972) votes and seats (as compared with the previous elections) were distributed as shown in Table I.

Another unflattering interpretation of conservative strength can be quickly surmised from even a brief scanning of these election statistics. Obviously Japan has not yet faced the reapportionment struggle triggered by recent Supreme Court decisions in the United States. The total number of conservative seats (held by the ruling Liberal-Democrats) represents a considerably higher percentage than does the total vote for conservatives. Distribution is gerrymandered so that conservative bastions in the more traditional countryside are overrepresented as compared with opposition bases in the cities, where organized labor tends to support the Socialists.

Paradoxically, distribution of votes and seats to the combined opposition has also lent post-treaty Japanese political structure an element of stability. So-called progressive or left-wing parties have regularly managed to garner a little more than one third the popular vote and seats in the House of Representatives. And this strength has allowed them to block amendment to the Constitution, since revision

3. Shinohara Hajime, "The Leadership of the Conservative Party," *Journal of Social and Political Ideas in Japan,* II, No. 3 (December, 1964), 40.

TABLE I

Distribution of Votes and Seats in Lower House Elections 1963–1972

Party	Year	Popular Votes	Percentage	Diet Seats	Percentage
Liberal-	1963	22,423,915	54.7	283	60.7
Democrats	1967	22,447,834	48.8	277	57.0
	1969	22,381,566	47.6	288*	59.2
	1972	24,563,078	46.8	271*	55.2
Socialists	1963	11,906,766	29.0	144	30.8
	1967	12,826,099	27.9	140	28.8
	1969	10,074,099	21.4	90	18.5
	1972	11,478,600	21.9	118	24.0
Democratic	1963	3,023,302	7.4	23	4.9
Socialists	1967	3,404,462	7.4	30	6.2
	1969	3,636,590	7.8	31	6.4
	1972	3,659,922	7.0	19	3.9
Communists	1963	1,646,477	4.0	5	1.0
	1967	2,190,563	4.8	5	1.0
	1969	3,199,031	6.8	14	2.9
	1972	5,496,697	10.5	38	7.7
Kōmeitō	1963	—†	—†	—†	—†
	1967	2,472,371	5.4	25	5.1
	1969	5,124,666	10.9	47	9.7
	1972	4,436,631	8.5	29	5.9
Minor	1963	59,765	0.2	0	0
Parties	1967	101,244	0.2	0	0
	1969	81,373	0.2	0	0
	1972	143,019	0.3	2	.4
Independents	1963	1,956,313	4.7	12	2.6
	1967	2,553,988	5.5	9	1.9
	1969	2,492,559	5.3	16	3.3
	1972	2,645,530	5.0	14	2.9
Totals	1963	41,016,540	100.0	467	100.0
	1967	45,996,561	100.0	486	100.0
	1969	46,989,884	100.0	486	100.0
	1972	52,423,477	100.0	491	100.0

* After the elections of 1969 and 1972, admission of 12 and 9 of the conservative independents boosted the LDP totals to 300 and to 280 respectively.
† The Kōmeitō first ran for the lower House of Representatives in 1967.

requires the concurrent vote of two thirds of all members of each chamber in the Diet. It is an irony of history that the conservative majority, which has favored the American security alliance, has been strongest in advocating amendment of the American-inspired Constitution; while the "progressive" opposition, which has opposed the security system, has been strongest in defending the organic law as it is. As one Japanese observer put it, the Japanese public in its unconscious wisdom has regularly returned a conservative majority, but not with sufficient strength to alter the structure of government.

Lack of space in this survey of Japanese politics prohibits a detailed account of conservative strengths. The highlights of success can, however, be brought out. It is best to have begun with the Diet and elections, for constitutionally, politically, and morally the government is regularly subject to public audit; the Establishment is at least indirectly accountable to the Japanese people, and the majority is subject to minority pressure. Having been successful in every postwar election save one (which produced a coalition Socialist government), the Establishment may and (as the opposition charges) often does exercise a "dictatorship of the majority." Nevertheless, the almost unassailably popular economic policy and the less popular security alignment with the United States have enjoyed majority support, if we can believe public opinion polls. Finally, in what has been dubbed a "one and a half" (rather than a two) party system, the conservatives have enjoyed the universal political advantage of running for office while controlling the government with all the attendant advantages of patronage.

It has been charged that the conservative Liberal-Democrats are only the "party of business." With such a strong emphasis on reconstruction and economic growth in the post-treaty period, business has provided them a strong support base. And to the interlocking directorate which is the Establishment, business organizations have given seen and unseen leadership, legal and extralegal financial support. It is important to remember, however, that the Establishment itself is a "pluralistic hegemony," business organizations differ, and they lodge different demands with government. For example, the Federation of Economic Organizations (Keidanren) is a loose confederation of mostly big industries, which has the wherewithal to contribute millions to the conservative cause. There is some overlapping in membership with the Federation of Employers' Organizations (Nikkeiren), which specializes in labor-management problems. Many of the new breed of entrepreneur are also members of the very special Japan Committee for Economic Development (Keizai Dōyūkai). As one might suspect, the JCED watches trends in international trade carefully. Incidentally, this relatively progressive group has pressed the Liberal-Democrats for party reform. Finally, there is the older and staid Japan Chamber of Commerce and Industry, which represents medium and small, rather than large, enterprises.

It is also important to keep in mind that conservatives have won support from the farmers (through their Agricultural Cooperative Associations) and from white-collar groups in the cities. It may be, as has been pointed out, that the latter are actually apolitical and conservative out of inertia. The fact remains that conservatives enjoy nationwide support in every sector of the population.

Critics of the conservatives have also claimed that Liberal-Democrats have turned the entire government bureaucracy into a permanent apparatus for maintaining and expanding their own power. This charge may be true, but it is just as accurate to say that the party itself has become increasingly bureaucratized. True, the majority of Diet members are so-called pure politicians. That is, they have not had careers in government bureaus and have usually risen from elected offices at the local or prefectural levels. The best-mapped path to the highest political posts, however, is (as it has been in the past) through a career in the bureaucracy.

Indeed, although bureaucrats too are now indirectly accountable to the public, it is safe to say that the social base of Japanese bureaucracy has been as little changed by defeat, Occupation reform, and rapid change as any sector of Japanese government. Very recent studies of the higher civil service have shown that its ranks are filled from top-ranking university graduates; that these in turn come overwhelmingly from one institution, Tokyo University; and that the milestones of success in the bureaucracy are measured by seniority from the date of graduation.

Although constitutionally the Diet is supposed to be "the highest organ of State power" and "the sole law-making organ of the State," the rule-making and regulatory authority centered in the administrative process is enormous.

There are several reasons for the bureaucracy's strategic position. First, in Japan's long modernization process the bureaucracy was the first sector of government to emerge, producing the famous "ministers of modernization" of the nineteenth century. Second, mobilization for modern war further strengthened the strategic position of the bureaucracy. Third, even in defeat, and especially under the Occupation, directed change demanded clean lines of authority from SCAP to the Japanese government. Effects of the "American interlude" reinforced the universal tendency, shared by Japanese, to move into the era of the administrative state, which requires ability, specialized knowledge, and prestige. Fourth, as we have seen, the Establishment (including the bureaucrats) have effectively used the powers of government after the second-stage take-off to launch the state into an orbit of economic affluence.

These are also the reasons why the cabinet (constitutionally responsible to the Diet in a British-type cabinet-style parliamentary system) may be more significant in its role as head of the civil service than as leader of the Diet. Recently the cabinet has consisted of twelve ministries: Finance (inner citadel of the bureaucracy), Justice, Foreign Affairs, Education, Health and Welfare, International Trade and Industry, Agriculture and Forestry, Transportation, Postal Services, Labor, Construction, and Local Government. Equally or more important is the increasingly vast Office of the Prime Minister, which embraces all functions of the administrative state not assigned to one of the ministries. Japanese tradition is reflected in the fact that the office now has jurisdiction over Imperial Household affairs, defense matters, and police problems. The most modern functions are represented by those of its agencies concerned with administrative management, economic planning, science and technology, and atomic energy.

Again, in the interlocking directorate which is the Establishment there is a very close relationship among leading bureaucrats, private business interests, Diet politicians, and Liberal-Democratic Party leaders. To say that this pluralistic hegemony is conservative is perhaps still not to say quite enough. It is true that the Establishment prefers a new kind of aristocracy, order, property, patriotism, and pragmatism. These characteristics have led Americans in particular into a congenial relationship with Japanese, on the correct assumption that both peoples are anticommunist. And such common tendencies have also led to puzzled shock on the part of Americans when Japan has seemed to become a "reluctant ally," either in the 1960 demonstrations against the security treaty or in the Japanese unwillingness to contribute to the Allied effort in Vietnam.

The real point is that there are important differences between conservatism in post-treaty Japan and the conservative persuasion in the United States. It is very doubtful, for example, that the Establishment in Japan originally entered into alliance with America out of any deep ideological affinity. Rather, it was a policy bred of pragmatic calculation. Beneath the alliance of convenience and behind the superficially similar conservatisms are entirely different traditions. Enough has been said about political culture to demonstrate that the Japanese conservative still emphasizes the group over the individual; individual obligations over individual liberties; the place of an individual in a hierarchy over social equality and freedom. Thus does conservative, modern Japan continue to feed on tradition.

Nowhere is this more apparent than in the makeup and functioning of the majority Liberal-Democratic Party itself. From one point of view, the party seems to illustrate Japan's lag behind other advanced countries in producing broadly based national parties, for it is really a confederation of readily identifiable factions whose interminable maneuvers are frequently criticized by Japanese commentators. Although the prime minister is technically elected by a formal resolution of the Diet, it is apparent that his choice is determined by factional forces within the perennial majority party. Even more apparent is the balancing of factions in the prime minister's choice of his cabinet colleagues.

From another point of view, factions represent the marriage of the traditional with the modern. Because conservatives have enjoyed an almost permanent monopoly of power, the completely modern function of aggregation—a term political scientists use for the process of selecting policies and politicians—is carried out through factions. In other words, the subtly different conservative interests among different parts of the pluralistic hegemony are rather effectively mirrored in the factions. The very oldest Japanese tradition of parent-childlike relationships (*oyabun-kobun*) is translated into a modern complex of personal local support groups (*kōenkai*). Diet members tap sources of power in traditional constituencies (*jiban*) and carry political energy along the transmission belts of local support associations. At the top of the party, faction leaders enjoy the almost feudal loyalty of political samurai. On the floor of the Diet and in committees, leagues of factions form modern study groups to hammer out policies.

Two other features of the post-treaty Establishment require mention. To the outsider conditioned to images of an older, mysterious,

Oriental Japan, there will seem to be a major omission in this description of conservatism. Where does the emperor fit into this picture of political structure? First of all, Japanese tradition had long since dictated that the emperor was to be an important but ceremonial symbol of the state rather than an operating executive. The lingering doubt that the emperor was ever literally a god was cleared up in 1946, when he explicitly denied that his ties with the Japanese people rested on myth. In the Constitution, the emperor became the "symbol of the state and the unity of the people."

This means that the emperor legally exercises no power and is subject to the authority of the cabinet. As a representative of conservative tradition, however, he is an important symbol. Indeed, the opposition has charged that the Imperial House has been subtly used to bolster the conservative position in government, for example, through the "crown prince boom." Whether this is true or not, the status of the imperial symbol will change further only with long-range alterations of Japanese society, shifts in family relationships, and the erosion of the patriarchal principle.

To an American knowledgeable in the ways of his own politics the other interest group which seems to be missing in Japanese government—especially in a conservative Establishment—is the legal profession. In the American system, law is a major pathway to political power. A majority of the members of Congress are lawyers by training. We are proud to say that ours is a government of laws and not of men. Two of the most important governmental decisions which have recently revolutionized American life—against segregation and for reapportionment—have emanated from the court system.

As a matter of fact, Japanese laws and the judicial system are probably the political institutions most closely modeled after Western, specifically American, models. Under Occupation prodding, the court system was separated from the otherwise unified cabinet-parliamentary structure. Under American influence, the Japanese gave the Supreme Court the power of judicial review (Article 81 of the Constitution). The Supreme Court has, however, only warily exercised this unfamiliar power. Nonetheless, as Dan Henderson and James Anderson point out in the following chapter, Japan has moved from "rule-by-law" to "rule-of-law."

Japanese society, particularly at the rural level, has traditionally preferred informal means of settling disputes. The custom of consensus and the habit of harmony have until very recently inhibited the practice of adversary law. The relatively undramatic role of the judicial system in Japanese governmental practice rather faithfully reflects Japanese tradition.

Sources of Unrest and Channels for Dissent

This picture of post-treaty Japanese political institutions has dwelt thus far on the highlights of stability amidst growth, conservative modernization, and rule by the Establishment. But growth, as Americans are beginning to understand, also presents problems. And problems give rise to political unrest and offer opportunities for dissent from majority rule.

For example, all of Japan's political parties have in fact come up against the increased political apathy of the new middle class, a studied indifference which is compounded of extreme pragmatism, expanding technology, and increased bureaucratization. In other words, there is a fine line between the stability of political institutions and the inertia of their clientele.

Perhaps inertia is not the correct word. Probably no other modern government is as severely attacked by its people as is that of Japan, and this characteristic is faithfully mirrored in the large, vigorous, and independent press. Japanese observers have offered two reasons for this interesting tendency: increasing competition in the journalistic world and degradation of the politician in mass democracy. At best, Japanese newspapers are strictly neutral and take an impartial stand with regard to political parties and candidates even during elections. At worst, the mass media often appear hypercritical and even cynical. The most hopeful estimate is that the press is by and large independent and engaged in free competition in the market of ideas.

One difficulty is that middle-class skepticism is bounded by sharply polarized "conservative" and "progressive" forces. Too often the conservative majority stresses governmental authority at the expense of minority rights. Above all, conservatives are distrustful of Marxism and anyone whom they regard as a Marxist. And many leaders of the organized opposition in Japan are Marxists of some sort or those whose thinking and language have been colored by the dogma of Marxism.

Until very recently the only major and effective opposition to the Establishment was provided by various kinds of socialist parties. In June, 1947, Katayama Tetsu became prime minister and formed the first Socialist Party government in Japan's history. Unfortunately for the Socialists, they came to power when Japan was at low ebb economically and the coalition cabinet fell in 1948. Since then, never tempered by responsibility for governing nor even moderated by the probability of coming to power, "progressive" leaders have increasingly perceived politics as a struggle and regarded political issues in doctrinaire terms.

As for interest groups behind the "progressives," the predominant characteristic of Japanese socialists is that they have built largely one-pressure-group parties. Their political parties have remained small. In recent years the Socialist Party has had only about 60,000 members, but they can count on large blocs of voters to support them at election time. Labor unions have provided the mass support. In fact, at prefectural levels the interlocking directorate of party and union officials has been striking. Incidentally, as Japan's labor movement has split, so have the socialists divided.

Put the other way around, to the left and also outside Japan's rapidly increasing middle class, is an interest bloc consisting of the great labor federations. Enjoying too close ties with the socialist parties, organized labor has been out of touch with the middle class, although it has received some support from intellectuals, professors, and students. Labor organizations, too, have been characterized by rigid ideology, intense factionalism, and political platforms largely out of touch with the phenomenon of the consumer economy.

It has been charged that Japan's labor movement has not been characterized by practical codes of procedure formed out of experience with collective bargaining and strikes for better working conditions. Rather, labor leaders, too, have been obsessed with dogma inherited from Marxism-Leninism, which they learned when they were young. The posture of trade unions has been predominantly political and geared to "confrontation" and "struggle."

Alongside the socialists and labor have also stood many of Japan's so-called intellectuals (the *interi*, that is, almost anyone with a college education). In this sector, too, the older generation has been greatly influenced in its thought patterns by Marxism. Consequently, as one Japanese observer put it, an opinion gap exists between this type of intellectual, on one hand, and the Establishment and the middle class, on the other.

A source of internal friction among "progressives" has been the age brackets into which they fall. Top socialist and labor leaders have been mostly veterans of the suppressed prewar social democratic movement: they were nurtured in a hostile environment, trained in mass struggle, steeped in theoretical controversy, and practiced in factional infighting. Paradoxically, doctrinal positions of "progressive" politicians have encouraged tightly bound groups entirely compatible with the traditional parent-child relationships.

Support for the "progressive" parties also flows out of the tensions of growth itself. Although they have never fully capitalized on potential sources of strength, socialists have drawn support from some professional and technical personnel, some white-collar workers (including low-level bureaucrats), small merchants, youth, and women. These sectors have been attracted by opposition to the "black mist" of corruption in the Establishment, to rearmament, to the American presence in military bases, and to revision of the Constitution. The urban proletariat, referred to by one observer as "industrial peasants," have shown a marked penchant for bowing to authority on one occasion and embracing political radicalism on another. These characteristics are also found among some white-collar workers, for example, members of the powerful Japan Teachers Union.

Turning from informal groups and more highly organized interests behind the opposition to formally established channels for dissent, in the postwar period the earliest opposition to the Establishment was supplied by the Socialist Party of Japan. Established in November, 1945, this party represented diverse elements inherited from prewar social democracy, a conglomeration of a revived postwar Left and traditional factionalism. Right-wing and left-wing socialists parted company over the issue of the peace treaty. A complex compromise brought them back together in October, 1955, but this truce actually did little to close the gap between two different concepts of the Socialist Party's nature. These had been obvious since the first postwar (1945) party convention at which the left wing argued that the party should be based on the working—especially industrial labor—class while the right wing insisted that it should reflect the interests of all "revisionist" strata.

In 1959 a long simmering rebellion against domination of the Socialist Party by left-wing and labor factions, against preoccupation with politics as a "class struggle," and against Socialist contempt for parliamentary procedure led a leader who had been deputy prime minister, Nishio Suehiro, to bolt with about forty members of his faction in the Diet. In 1960 the rebels established the Democratic Socialist Party. Promptly denounced by the parent party as a "bourgeois" faction, it aims at a position somewhere near the middle in the confrontation between Socialists and Liberal-Democrats.

Steadily improving economic conditions in Japan may well give the new party a more important position, like that of moderate socialists in Western Europe or of the Labour Party in Great Britain, but the Democratic Socialist Party as yet has been unsuccessful in attracting a significant proportion of the "progressive" vote. In the 1972 elections it commanded only 7 percent of the popular vote (as against almost 22 percent for Socialists) and held 19 seats in the lower house (compared with 118 for the Socialists). As has been previously indicated, labor unions behind the socialist parties have been similarly split: the General Council of Trade Unions (Sōhyō) has ranged behind the Socialists; the All-Japan Congress of Trade Unions (Dōmei Kaigi), behind the Democratic Socialists.

In the post-treaty period (especially since 1957) perhaps the most important effects on the socialist opposition have arisen from the profound changes which have affected Japan's industrial relations, the environment of proletarian politics. These include the spectacular economic growth; technological innovations with shifts in industry and attendant alterations in the use of the labor force; increased productivity of labor; modernization of labor-management relations; an improvement in the income, consumption level, and welfare of most Japanese workers.

Further considering "progressive" opposition, a distinction must be drawn between the influence of Marxist ideology (as it has permeated labor organizations, the *interi,* and socialist parties) and the role of the Japanese Communist Party in political institutions. The latter has grown to be the third ranking opposition party (commanding 10.5 percent of the popular vote and capturing 38 lower house seats in the 1972 election). Moreover, the party boasts a membership larger than those of all other left-wing parties combined. Still hampered by splits among pro-Chinese, pro-Russian, and neutral wings, the JCP has nonetheless been increasingly successful, particularly at the local level. By deliberately adopting pragmatic policy stances, by identifying serious issues in the growth syndrome—inflation, pollution, and corruption—and by carefully backing attractive candidates, the Communists have often provided a core for coalitions which have upset LDP incumbents at the local level, specifically in urban centers.

Far more strident (possibly because emerging so recently and so rapidly) are the voices of unrest raised by the Sōka Gakkai (Value Creation Society), a religious association. Highly successful in coupling tradition—almost romantic reaction—with promised solutions to problems inherent in growth, the Sōka Gakkai has appealed to students, to the sick, to the poor, and to the displaced, who face difficult problems of adjustment in an otherwise affluent society. All its members nominally belong to the old Nichiren sect of Buddhism, which has been traditionally nationalistic and intolerant of other religions. On the other hand, it has used the most modern organizational methods, its smallest cells meeting frequently to air personal problems, to confess to weakness, and to testify to the force of their religion. Sōka Gakkai claims some fifteen million members.

The Kōmeitō (Clean Government Party) is the formal political organization of Sōka Gakkai. The party entered the political lists slowly and carefully, first in local government contests, then in elections for the upper house of the Diet, and finally, in 1967, in the election for the lower house. In the latter election it won more than 5 percent of the popular vote (higher than the Communists) and captured 25 seats. In the 1969 lower house election it obtained 10 percent of the popular vote and increased its seats to 47; but in the 1972 election, Kōmeitō votes fell sharply to 8.5 percent, generating only 29 seats.

Kōmeitō and its parent Sōka Gakkai, from which the party has nominally been separated, would seem at first glance to belong on the extreme Right. Vigorous proselytizing, emphasis on discipline, familial face-to-face organization, nationalism, and exclusivism in religious beliefs appeal to the deepest Japanese traditions. These characteristics are ominously remindful of prewar ultranationalistic movements. Yet much of the approach of the Gakkai is ultramodern and even sophisticated. Business has contributed great material wealth, certainly in the form of spectacular temple architecture. There is also a widespread network overseas. Though in its early phase the party tapped the roots of malaise amidst affluence, it has more recently come to grips with the pragmatic outlook and apolitical attitude of Japan's new white collar middle class. The Kōmeitō bears close watching, for it may well have solved the problem of how best to meld the traditional and the modern and to win large sectors of an otherwise indifferent middle class.

Testing Grounds for Japanese Political Institutions: Constitutional Revision and Law

Despite strident voices of dissent from "progressives" and what might be called calculated inertia on the part of conservatives, Japan's political structure has demonstrated a rather surprising stability in face of the maladjustments resulting from rapid growth. As Robert Ward so well expressed it: "Thus in eighteen years' time the most remarkable facts about the constitution have been its stability, the degree to which both people and government have accepted and adjusted to its spirit and its institutions, and the measure of democracy that it has helped bring to present-day Japan." [4] Of course, Japan has been able to afford stability because the country has achieved so much in the economic field. It would be unwise to attribute this success solely to political institutions; but it would be equally unwise to claim that the latter have had no effect at all.

When, a number of years after the end of the Occupation, the government established a Commission on the Constitution to study the circumstances of its adoption and the effects of its application, there were predictions—dire by the "progressives," hopeful by the conservatives—that sooner or later the organic law would be revised. The most avid revisionists relied on the fact that the Constitution had been written and enacted in the most humiliating circumstances for Japan. In spirit and in wording the document was alien.

Now it is apparent that revision will come later rather than sooner. There are several reasons for this prediction. For one, the crisis of 1960 involving the renewal of the American security treaty intervened between adoption of the Constitution and the final report of the commission. The street demonstrations of the early 1960s had a sobering effect on all concerned. Even conservatives, who favor revision, realize that this is precisely the type of issue on which the opposition can focus vigorous and even successful attacks. Caution overrules daring and the conservative majority is content to leave well enough alone. The socialist opposition—together with the Kōmeitō, incidentally—is dead set against any revision. And the opposition has, with the passage of time, a more strongly entrenched position as everyone becomes more and more adjusted to the legal

4. Robert E. Ward, "The Commission on the Constitution and Prospects for Constitutional Change in Japan," *The Journal of Asian Studies*, XXIV, No. 3 (May, 1965), 402.

framework. Conservatives, as was pointed out, have discovered semi-legal and extralegal means of reinterpreting the organic law.

Certainly it can safely be said that in the near future, with informal revision—as against formal amendment—of organic law, the Supreme Court of Japan will play a less spectacular role than does its counterpart in the United States. After all, the American court too was very cautious in its early history. There is also the cultural lag between the formal legal changes brought by legislative and administrative agencies and the Japanese tradition not to use legal means for the settlement of disputes. It will be interesting to watch the quiet social revolution beneath the state, as it brings actual conditions into line with the prematurely and formally defined civil liberties of Japanese individuals.

Then again, it will be equally fascinating to see how much sooner Japanese law will have to adjust in turn to community demands for authority and orderly procedure. In some judicial institutions—for example, the unique Family Court of Japan—the traditional and the ultramodern blend nicely to move principles of law in parallel with up-to-date social welfare functions. In any case, the fine balance between the need for order in society and the desire for individual rights has already attracted the attention of Japan's best legal minds.

The Diet in Action and Inaction

Constitutionally the Diet is supposed to be "the highest organ of State power." Formally it is the only institution empowered to make laws. From one point of view, this situation is in great contrast to that under the Meiji Constitution. Before the war, emergency decrees could be made in the name of the emperor, and the cabinet had power to implement them with the force of law. Furthermore, a considerable area was outside the jurisdiction of normal law-making procedure: questions of Imperial Household affairs, the budget (if it were not promptly passed), security strategy, military matters, and administrative structure.

Actually, changes under the new Constitution are more than formal. It is a fact of political life that the Japanese government has become Diet-centered; delegates of the people are infinitely more powerful. Nevertheless, in the mixture of tradition and modernity which is Japan's polity, the system works out in unusual ways.

Consider the fact, for example, that although Japan is not a federal state (like the United States) but rather a unitary cabinet-style parliamentary government, nevertheless there is a bicameral type of legislature with an upper house designed to give functional representation. Early drafts of the Occupation-born Constitution contained only one house. In one of the few cases where Japanese influenced the eventual structure of their government, the final draft provided an upper House of Councilors as well as a lower House of Representatives.

As a result, the upper house of the Japanese Diet represents a somewhat unsatisfactory compromise. Consisting of a total of 250 members, the House of Councilors has 150 members popularly elected from prefectural voting districts, that is, on the basis of geographic constituencies. The other 100 members are elected at large. The latter do, then, functionally represent nationwide associations and interest groups. Increasingly, however, the upper house has taken on a party composition closely resembling that of the lower and it has become politicized in the same proportions.

Perhaps more serious is that informally the Diet does not actually make laws. Most bills originate—as they generally do in parliamentary governments—in the ministries. They are subject to committee surveillance, which in effect means they are the products of interfactional adjustment within the Liberal-Democratic Party, representing the Establishment.

Doomed to a position of almost permanent minority, the opposition has often chosen not to abide by ordinary parliamentary rules. In a disturbing number of cases they have abstained entirely from participation in the Diet, have seized control of the floor by force, have physically interfered with the Speaker, and have even encouraged mass demonstrations in the streets surrounding the Diet. All of this, of course, is faithfully reported in the alert press and the cynicism of middle-class readers is heightened. The impasse raises serious questions about the future of democracy and the fate of parliamentary procedure.

Rural and Urban Bases

The majority Establishment too faces its problems. These are related, in part, to perhaps the most profound change in the basic Japanese society underneath contemporary political institutions.

Enough has been said to make the point clearly that modern Japanese political institutions have a strong strain of traditional political behavior. This is certainly one of the reasons for their stability. Such traditions, of course, matured when Japan was still largely an agricultural, rural society. Even today, the Establishment—more specifically, the Liberal-Democratic majority—enjoys disproportionate support from the gerrymandered election districts throughout Japan. This is a familiar story: in Japan, as in America until recently, it took fewer rural voters to elect a presumably conservative candidate than urban voters to elect a presumably "progressive" candidate. Even without reapportionment, it is precisely in the relation between rural and urban areas that the most dramatic shifts are taking place in Japan today.

Briefly, between 1955 and the 1960 census, Japan's population increased by 4.14 millions (4.6 percent) to a total of 94,410,000. In twenty-six (more than half the) prefectures, however, population actually declined; in the remaining twenty the increase was well above the national average (ranging from 4 to 10 percent). As is well known, the bulk of the Japanese were settling in a vast conurbation in the Pacific Coast belt. Even more startling was the concentration in the six largest cities: Tokyo, Osaka, Nagoya, Yokohama, Kyoto, and Kobe. By October, 1960, Tokyo and Osaka, the two biggest metropolises—Doxiades, the Greek city planner, would call them megalopolises—accounted for one third the total population of Japan. Most amazing, one in ten Japanese had come to live in Tokyo.

More recent statistical data on population, released December 2, 1965, showed a continuation of the flight from the farm and the trend to the city. Japan's population had increased since 1960 by 4.8 millions (5.2 percent) to a total of 98,281,955. Again twenty-five (more than half the) prefectures decreased and twenty-one increased in population. Kanagawa, which adjoins Tokyo on the south (and includes Yokohama), had jumped 28.7 percent. Tokyo had reached a population of 10,880,000. The Osaka metropolitan area had a population of 6,660,000.

The first and most obvious thing to say about these revealing statistics is that such a major shift in population is having and will continue to have a profound effect on the shape of Japan's political institutions. On the face of it, the traditional rural bases of the Liberal-Democratic Party are steadily being eroded away. The great opportunity for the conservatives—as for the opposition—lies in the new middle class. So far, at least, the Establishment has been able to command enough loyalty from this pivotal sector to guarantee continued success at the polls. Stability, rewards from economic growth, a policy of peace—all have worked in favor of the conservative majority.

The Liberal-Democratic Party, however, faces a dilemma. Having deliberately chosen a policy of further directed change, of conservative modernization, the party has seen its subsidies and patronage flowing back out into constituencies where the primary emphasis has been on further industrialization, further urbanization. To say that these trends will inevitably work toward a victory of the Socialist Party is to repeat a prediction which has proved to be wrong in the past. It is hard to foretell what effect the growth of an urban white-collar class will have on the distribution of votes. It may increase the power of the urban-based Socialists; with a further shift to the suburbs, it may supply a larger bloc of votes to the Liberal-Democrats; or with some measure of disillusionment and alienation amidst adjustment, it may swell the ranks of a party like the Kōmeitō.

In any case, Japan has certainly joined the ranks of the most modernized states of the world. It is now fully under the influence of the flight from the farm, what has fittingly been called by Ernest Weissmann of the United Nations "the twentieth century's great migration."

Conduct of Foreign Relations and Maintenance of Security

Certainly one of the clearest signals that a country has entered the later stages of modernization is the fact that it finds necessary the building of political institutions with which to conduct foreign relations. Diplomacy, which is the implementation of decisions in this field, defines rather precisely the country's political commitments. It is one of the greatest challenges to statesmanship to balance alongside these commitments a state's capabilities. These include a sophisticated nervous system of strategic intelligence, bone structure of domestic economic performance, and muscles of mobilization. In an ideal world effective diplomacy will rule out the probability of war; in the real world diplomacy must always be carried on in light of a grim alternative, the possibility that the state may have to use force. In this sense a country is in deep trouble when its commitments outrun its capabilities.

Japan of the 1940s has been denounced for being aggressive, imperialistic, and warlike. Technically, it would be just as accurate to say that in those days Japan suffered greatly because its outmoded political institutions were so constructed as to deny a viable balance between commitment and capability. Studies immediately after the war clearly pointed out that, dedicated to war though Japan was, surprisingly the nation never fully or rationally mobilized its economic resources for the campaign; that, totalitarian as the state tried to become, even its armed forces were never fully coordinated. These were two important reasons for defeat.

In the post-surrender period Japan was not, of course, in control of its foreign relations. One of the very first steps taken by the Supreme Commander for the Allied Powers was to channel all foreign contacts, in or out, through his headquarters. As the Occupation drew to a close, the Japanese assumed greater and greater responsibility for the exercise of their own sovereignty.

There are those Japanese who claim, however, that to this very day their nation has not fully recovered the power to conduct its own foreign relations, has not been able to move "from dependence to independence." Japan obtained a peace treaty, the argument continues, only by accepting unequal status under the American security treaty. Her armaments are closely geared to the defensive (and critics would add, offensive) position of the United States.

It is a moot point whether this continued dependence is a product more of American will or of Japanese choice. The Establishment in control of Japan did, as we have seen, deliberately choose to pay the cost of externally provided security in return for the profit to be made from rapid economic growth.

Certainly the climate of post-treaty Japan, the tendency toward pacifism after a disastrous war, has had an important effect on the country's political structure. No cabinet, despite an understandable desire for greater independence in foreign affairs, has dared suggest a sizable increase in military capability. Japan literally is unable in a neutral fashion to pledge support to even a United Nations peacekeeping force. Although covert rearmament has produced self-defense forces capable of handling a rearguard defense with conventional arms, there are constitutional, political, and moral objections to increasing capability to such an extent that Japan could make commitments appropriate to even a medium-range power.

Furthermore, it is precisely in the areas of conduct of foreign relations and security policy that the greatest gap between conservative and opposition viewpoints exist. The most rigid polarization between political forces is there and, as the 1960 demonstrations indicated, there, too, is the most severe test of the viability of otherwise stable institutions.

Japan has been able to make a comeback on other fronts. Soon after the peace treaty, the country proudly became a member of the United Nations and has, within limits, played an important role in that and in other international organizations. On the cultural front, in 1964 the world was surprised and pleased by the manner in which Japan played host to the Olympic Games. Symbolically, this event was an important milestone to many Japanese. Perhaps more significantly, the nation later welcomed the International Bank for Reconstruction and Development (World Bank) and the International Monetary Fund in an annual convention. In the minds of the delegates who attended these meetings, there was no doubt that post-treaty Japan had become, in former Ambassador Reischauer's phrase "a large, an important power." An image reinforced by Osaka's Expo '70, the first major world exhibition held in Asia.

Japan's Foreign Ministry, in a position to tap an advanced and highly selective system of higher education, sends out to the world a corps of diplomats second to none in intelligence, sensitivity, training, and performance. Nevertheless, limits on the country's capabilities—and particularly in force components—led one cynical statesman to dub Japan's representatives "transistor salesmen."

Why should Japan not be content with limited capabilities and therefore limited commitments? Will Japan soon reshape its political institutions to allow greater capacity, particularly in the field of rearmament, and therefore greater independence and wider responsibilities? This side of the coin is invisible. To describe it is to engage in speculation, which is dangerous. Only the most general alternatives can be summarized.

First, it should be recognized that no power—not even a major state—can be absolutely certain that its commitments in foreign affairs and its domestic capabilities will remain in perfect balance. Even the apparently free superpowers regularly demonstrate the capacity for misjudgment: for example, despite application of enormous power, the United States found the situation in Vietnam beyond its leverage. Indirect assignment of capabilities by the Russians to the Middle East may also turn out to be a massive miscalculation. The sheer enormity of problems involved in planning in a nuclear age, plus the

Japanese tendency toward fatalism, has tended to underwrite the *status quo* as far as political structure is concerned. Prosperous and strong in the economic field, Japan has shown little tendency to experiment in foreign and security matters.

In the short range, unless there be a severe depression or an enforced involvement in war, Japanese political institutions are apt to remain unchanged. It is difficult to see, however, how the Establishment can long withstand the pressure from a distinctive, capable, and proud people to seek an identity of their own making. Some have predicted that it might well be the Socialists, inspired by hopes for real independence, who will suggest a breakthrough. The purposes would be to return the conduct of foreign relations fully to Japanese control, to develop a military capability not to be contributed to an alignment but to guarantee security through nonalignment.

Of all the problems faced by the modern state, those linked with diplomacy, peace, and war offer the harshest testing grounds for the staying power of political institutions. This is because they involve both internal, or flexible, and external, or inflexible factors. If it were clear exactly what kind of political institutions are best suited to withstand severe world crises—institutions which nicely balance commitments and capabilities—there might be no crises! Japan can be expected to move somewhat closer to a practical compromise: to continue to use institutions which are both appropriate to Japanese tradition and, hopefully, also suited to constant rapid change.

XVIII

Japanese Law:

A Profile

BY
DAN F. HENDERSON
AND
JAMES L. ANDERSON

General Concepts

The purpose of this chapter is to describe the salient characteristics of the Japanese legal system. We will try to answer the question "What is Japanese law like?" rather than the question "What is Japanese law?" To resort to analogy, this is not an attempt to delineate, as on illustrated plates in a physiology text, every bone, nerve, muscle, and organ in the body of Japanese law. We seek to sketch in only the skeletal outline, to provide a profile of the Japanese legal order and to portray its most characteristic features.

Prior to any consideration of Japanese law proper, several fundamental concepts must be introduced and explained, for they are basic elements of several major themes which run through this chapter.

Law. Bear in mind that the law or laws of a country are both a reflection of its culture and an instrument of deliberate social control. In the United States, for example, our Puritan heritage has been mirrored in Sunday blue laws. Tax laws, on the other hand, are one of the most effective means of implementing public policy.

Public law and private law. Public law defines the rights and duties of the individual in relation to the state (e.g., constitutional law, administrative law) and the power relationships between superior and inferior officials. Private law defines the relationships between individuals (e.g., the law of contracts, property, torts). This distinction may be challenged on theoretical grounds, but it has a settled position in Japanese law.

Feudalism. For legal purposes, feudalism includes a contractual element, the personal homage of a man to his lord, symbolized by the oath of fealty and the reciprocal property right in an enfeoffment of land or other property. The term is often used, especially in Japanese writings, to refer pejoratively to the "old regime."

Justiciable rights. In the juristic sense a right is something which an individual is entitled to have or to do or to receive from others within the limits prescribed by law and with the assistance of law. A justiciable right is, then, simply a right which an individual can have vindicated in a court of law. The line which separates justiciable and nonjusticiable rights is often wavering and blurred. Consider, for example, the "right" of privacy. In the United States an individual who is a "public figure" may have some sort of moral right to privacy, but he does not have a justiciable right under which a court of law will prevent stories and articles about him and photographs of him from appearing in the press. However, those of us who are not public figures have some such right. Similarly, under our laws of libel and slander, we have no justiciable right which protects our good name in private. We have no legal recourse against a man who comes to us in private and falsely and maliciously accuses us of all manner of heinous crimes. But we do have a justiciable right to maintain our reputation before the public, and if the same man makes the mistake of falsely accusing us of a crime before other persons, the courts will vindicate that right.

Right consciousness. As used in here, right consciousness implies not only an awareness of one's individual justiciable rights but also a willingness to resort to the courts for their vindication. In tracing the growth of right consciousness among the Japanese, we must take care to avoid ethnocentric value judgments. Compared to litigation-minded Americans, Japanese may appear to possess a relatively low right consciousness. It it natural for us to consider that a low level of right consciousness is symptomatic of the law's ineffectiveness in a given area. Witness, for example, the efforts which are now being taken in this country to educate the poverty-stricken to a greater awareness of their justiciable rights. It does not necessarily follow, however, that the degree of right consciousness which is desirable in our society is also desirable in Japanese society, where, as we shall see, there are other means of settling disputes, which apply to rights broader than justiciable rights.

The language barrier. A word of caution is in order. The use of English equivalents to describe Japanese legal concepts has its hazards. Without a rather detailed explanation of the Japanese term being translated, one is never quite sure whether the English equivalent represents a legal concept which is identical to, merely approximates, or is miles apart from its Japanese counterpart. For example, even such a basic concept as *keiyaku* is fraught with potential misunderstanding for the Anglo-American lawyer, because the English equivalent of *keiyaku,* "contract," connotes a set of subconcepts concerning formation, performance, discharge, and remedies for breach of "contract" which frequently differ substantially from their Japanese counterparts. However, because this chapter is concerned with the major characteristics of Japanese law rather than with a detailed exposition of its specific provisions, we will proceed to move blithely over this language barrier.

Historical perspective. The foreigner who seeks to understand the legal order in Japan's changing society must study this legal order in its historical perspective, as a system with roots in the Tokugawa period which has been formally, though not completely, transformed through the adoption of a predominantly German-type civil law system in the late nineteenth century and further modified during the Occupation period following World War II by sweeping democratic reforms and the imposition of a constitution patterned after that of the United States. The foreigner who ignores this historical perspective, who concentrates exclusively upon the "book law" to be found in the codes, statutes, and judicial decisions, while overlooking the "living law" of fundamental attitudes and customs which has influenced the adaptation of book law, which affects the application of book law, and which sometimes operates in serene disregard of book law, is like a tourist who, with his eyes glued to his guidebook, attempts to cross a crowded Tokyo street oblivious to the kamikaze taxicabs. Accordingly, the characteristics of Japanese law considered in this chapter—more particularly, the "living law" of attitudes and customs —will be traced from their origins in the Tokugawa period through the adoption of the codes following the Meiji Restoration into the postwar period of Japan's democratization.

Civil Law and Common Law Systems

To understand what is specifically Japanese about Japanese law, it is first necessary to know something about the two major systems into which the world's modern legal orders are divided, civil law and common law. For, although the American Occupation and the imposition of an American-style constitution entailed a considerable common law influence in postwar Japanese law, nevertheless, the formal structure of the modern Japanese legal order remains that of continental European civil law. Many, if not most, of those features of Japanese law which puzzle the Anglo-American lawyer are not at all peculiar to Japanese law, but are rather typical features of European civil law.

The common law was born in England. Before there were courts there were customs. When parties brought a dispute before a judge, the judge attempted to settle the dispute according to applicable custom, and to this extent custom was a source of law. Precedents, i.e., prior judicial decisions, furnished guidelines for subsequent judicial decisions, and in this way precedent became a source of law. Haphazardly at first, and later more systematically, judges developed a body of rules and principles derived from their own prior decisions. "Common law," then, refers not only to the body of old English law but also to the fact that it was developed by judges on a case-by-case basis, i.e., judge-made law rather than legislated law.

Today the laws of the common law countries, principally England, the Commonwealth countries, and the United States, include not only judge-made laws but also many laws enacted by their respective legislatures. Nevertheless, the legal systems of these countries remain basically common law systems, and their judges continue to "make" law as cases arise by applying precedents to the settlement of disputes.

Japan, in the late nineteenth century, adopted a system of law which Anglo-American lawyers usually call "civil" law. This nomenclature causes some confusion, for in this system, which is represented principally by such continental European countries as Germany and France, "civil" law means private law, as opposed to public law, a dichotomy which is fundamental to this system. It might be more accurate to call this noncommon law system continental law or code law, but "civil" law will do, as long as we keep in mind that the term has an entirely different meaning within the system. The private ("civil," remember) laws in these countries are rooted, however remotely, in the ancient Roman law codified in the Emperor Justinian's *Corpus Juris Civilis*.

A code is a complete system of legislatively enacted law systematically arranged and designed to set forth the principles of an entire field of law. Codes may be found even in common law countries, as, for example, the Internal Revenue Code and the Uniform Commercial Code in the United States. However, in civil law countries the codes are the basic, if not the exclusive, source of private, commercial, criminal, and procedural law. The codes are actually not the exclusive source of law, for they are supplemented by innumerable statutes which treat problems not specifically dealt with in the codes. Since the codes regulate the basic legal questions in their respective fields, their provisions represent the primary basis for decision in individual cases. All special statutes are read and interpreted in the light of the codes, wherever the special law is incomplete. There is thus a great difference in the application of statutes in civil law and common law countries. If an Anglo-American lawyer cannot decide a particular problem on the basis of the wording of the applicable statute, he looks for a precedent whether the decision was rendered before or after the enactment of the statute. If a French or German lawyer, on the other hand, has the same difficulty in reading a statute, he consults the possibly applicable codes, for in theory the codes, together with their supplementary statutes, are supposed to constitute a complete or "closed" system of law, according to which any legal problem can be solved.

The above gives some idea of the theoretical differences between the two systems. It is more difficult to state accurately the practical functional differences. For as a matter of fact lawyers and judges in civil law countries do cite prior judicial decisions. Whether, however, these decisions have the same force as precedents in common law countries is another matter. In common law countries precedent is a source of law. In civil law countries, though supreme court decisions are in practice treated by lower courts as authoritative, even binding interpretations of statutes and code provisions, these decisions are not regarded as a source of law. When the statute is changed, the decisions lose their significance. The common law rule that statutes are interpreted in the light of cases which formed the law before the statute was enacted is literally alien to civil law thinking; for to this mentality precedents can only follow and interpret statutes, not precede or underlie them.

The style of legal analysis in civil law and common law systems reflects this fundamental difference. When the lawyer in common law countries prepares an argument, he searches for prior cases in which the fact pattern is identical, similar, or analogous. More specifically he is seeking for citation in support of his positions a judicial "holding." A "holding" may be roughly described as a rule embodied in a fact pattern. The "holding" may be stated broadly or narrowly, depending on how closely the rule element is tied to the fact element. The common law lawyer will often go farther than the "holding" and also seek out the reasoning which led the court to its decision. As we have seen, court decisions do not represent a source of law in civil law countries, and lawyers there tend to use precedents in an entirely different manner. The civil law lawyer will look for a supreme court decision in which a statute is interpreted. He will quote passages from the opinion which he regards as authentic interpretations of the statute; the factual pattern of the case is of little importance to him, for he is educated to think in highly abstract terms, of rules divorced from facts rather than of rules embodied in fact patterns.

In the past several decades the methodological distinctions between common law and civil law have become blurred. Legislatively enacted statutes have come to play an increasingly important role in Anglo-American law. Civil law courts, on the other hand, have felt less restricted by specific code provisions and have allowed themselves more liberty in reaching just decisions by employing broad equitable considerations. In short, while precedents remain the primary source of law in common law countries and codes and their supplementary statutes remain the primary source of law in civil law countries, statutory law is coming to occupy an increasingly important position in common law countries while civil law countries are placing more emphasis on precedent.

The distinction between public law and private law has been of prime importance in civil law countries, especially in the prewar period; it is a matter of little concern in common law countries. In civil law countries the regular courts have jurisdiction over only civil (private) and criminal law cases, not over public law cases, which are decided by special administrative courts. In this respect, as we shall see, postwar Japan has departed from the civil law system.

The fundamental differences between principles of trial procedure and evidence in the two systems stem from the tradition of trial by jury in common law countries and the almost total absence of jury trials in civil law countries. The rules of evidence in common law systems are designed to insulate the jurymen from proffered testimony or documents which are, as any Perry Mason fan knows, "irrelevant, immaterial and incompetent," that is, which would tend to mislead the jury. Such rules are absent in civil law countries. The admissibility and relevance of evidence is left to the discretion of the judge, who is presumably better able than a jury of laymen to separate the wheat from the chaff.

Common law trials reflect the adversary system, which characterizes common law dispute settlement. The theory is that out of the clash between counsel for the opposing parties, the jury and judge will be able to synthesize the truth. In civil law countries, however, the initiative of the trial is carried by the judge rather than by counsel for the disputant parties. Examination of witnesses is the responsibility of the presiding judge. Counsel may request that the judge ask certain questions or may with his permission ask questions themselves, but the primary responsibility for questioning witnesses remains with the judge. The foregoing discussion of the common law and civil law will be of help in understanding Japanese law, which has absorbed infusions from both systems in the past century.

Rule-of-Status:
The Tokugawa Period (1600–1867)

Two principal systems, corresponding roughly to the public law-private law division in modern civil law countries, determined the legal or quasi-legal relationships of Japanese under the Tokugawa shogunate: 1) public—the decentralized feudal law system in which administrative power was directed downward from shogun to daimyō and lesser lords connecting them with the nonfeudal officials, the village headman, the heads of five-man groups, and finally the heads of families; 2) private—the customary law governing the private relationships and transactions of Japanese on all levels of the status hierarchy.

Tokugawa society was characterized by 1) a highly decentralized feudal structure, and 2) an intricate status hierarchy. So complete was feudal decentralization under the Tokugawa that only approximately one fourth of Japan was governed directly by the shogunate. The rest of the country was divided into roughly 250 domains governed directly by their local daimyō, who remained, of course, subservient to the shogun, but who exercised a nearly autonomous feudal authority over their own domains. But the relationships of feudalism (that is, fealty and enfeoffment) were employed in the public law (power structure) only amongst the warrior class. Feudal relationships did not exist within the Japanese village. The feudal power structure connected with the rest of society at the point of the village headmen who were responsible to the domain lord but administrated the village in a bureaucratic fashion. The headmen had complete and direct authority over the villages, which thus had much autonomy as well as a collective responsibility for any default in fulfillment of duties to the daimyō. The villagers were divided for administrative purposes into five-man groups composed of family heads. Down this decentralized feudal structure to the bureaucratic village—from shogun through daimyō and eventually to the family heads—flowed Tokugawa public law and administrative power.

At the heart of the Confucian natural-law philosophy of the Tokugawa shogunate and, naturally, at the heart of its feudal administration was the principle that men are unequal. Consequently, it was regarded as natural, just, and "legal" that Tokugawa subjects be governed accordingly. This principle received particularly harsh application in the general refusal to entertain appeals by inferiors in the public law hierarchy against the discretionary actions or decisions of their superiors, who, although their discretion was self-limited by the behavior patterns expected because of their status—a kind of *noblesse oblige* —were simply not accountable to or on behalf of their inferiors. Thus villagers had no right of appeal against village headmen, who in turn had no right of appeal against their daimyō, etc. In sum, Tokugawa underlings had no "rights" assertable against their superiors; they had only duties. The administrative lawsuit found in modern public law simply did not exist. Even the word for "right," in the sense of a concept corresponding to "duty," was lacking in the Japanese language until the latter part of the nineteenth century when *kenri* was coined during the period of Western code adoption. This lack of redress against discretionary authority in the Tokugawa administration is the outstanding characteristic of the Tokugawa "public law," which has for this reason been described as a rule-of-status.

The intricate Tokugawa status hierarchy classified all Japanese into four major status groups—in descending order: the ruling samurai, farmers, artisans, and tradesmen (*shi-nō-kō-shō*)—and, within these major status groups, into smaller status groups. The Confucian patriarchal family system was, in microcosm, a model of the whole status structure of Japanese society: father over family, husband over wife, older son over other children, etc. The previously described Confucian natural law principle that men are unequal was mirrored in the status hierarchy of Tokugawa society.

Private law disputes were settled according to locally diverse customary law and the process usually involved some form of conciliation procedure, for conciliation was the favored device of Tokugawa dispute settlement.

Most private disputes on the village level were settled by didactic, or coerced, conciliation, as opposed to voluntary conciliation. An insistence upon a clear-cut, all-or-nothing decision in favor of one disputant rather than a compromise settlement in which each disputant conceded something was regarded as inimical to group harmony. To the litigation-minded American, this willingness to sacrifice one's rights in a compromise settlement for the sake of group harmony may indicate a lack of individual right consciousness. It certainly leads one to speculate whether, if Solomon had possessed the mentality of a group of Tokugawa villagers, he really would have cleft the baby in twain and given half to each woman. In any event, this insistence on conciliation and compromise settlement of disputes between equals in the status hierarchy bespeaks an emphasis on group harmony and social duties which has been alien to American legal thinking.

Actually, in spite of this strong preference for local conciliatory dispute settlement, there were quasi courts in Tokugawa Japan to which a determined disputant could bring suit. When speaking of "trials" and "judicial decisions" in the Tokugawa period, we are, it should be borne in mind, using these terms loosely; there was no independent court as such in Japan until 1875, eight years after the close of the Tokugawa period; "judges" were members of the Town, Finance, and Shrine-and-Temple Commissions (administrative officers); and although the parties might have enjoyed the benefit of legal advisers, they were not represented by these advisers before the commissions. We must also remember that under the decentralized structure of Tokugawa feudal society, each daimyō exercised a nearly autonomous authority over his own domain. Thus, except in diversity cases (*shihai chigai*) involving parties from different domains, the shogunate "courts" had no jurisdiction.

The diversity cases arose out of 1) the growing commercial activity of merchants, with their attendant disputes over money, and 2) the fact that when the disputants were registered in different domains, the daimyō of neither disputant had normal feudal jurisdiction. In such cases the shogunate was obliged to accept jurisdiction. Out of the techniques evolved in settling these diversity cases arose the only substantial body of truly national and justiciable private law in Tokugawa Japan.

Even in diversity cases a claimant could bring suit only after securing the approval of his village and his daimyō, for even private suits with those outside the local community were regarded as group matters.

Tokugawa "trials" were characterized by 1) a policy of "individualizing" in deciding cases, and 2) pressure on the parties to compromise their disputes by conciliation even after commencement of suit. The policy of individualizing, that is, of deciding each case on its own merits rather than according to general principles or precedents from prior decisions, was due to two factors. First, there were very few written rules in the area of civil law, which was governed largely by ancient local custom, called the Great Law (*taihō*). Second, there was the basic principle that Reason (*dōri*) should supersede the Great Law of custom. An example of the official attitude toward this policy of individualizing appears during the reign of the second shogun, Hidetada (1605–23). Shimada, an Edo commissioner, had requested permission to make available to his successors compilations of precedents which he had built up during his term in office. The shogun denied permission on the grounds that such reliance on precedents might dull a judge's sense of justice. Though in the later Tokugawa period precedents were indeed compiled and relied upon extensively, the basic theory remained unchanged.

Even in diversity cases, however, conciliation continued to be the favored device of Tokugawa dispute settlement. The "judges" endeavored to avoid rendering a clear-cut decision for either party, and subjected the parties to pressure to agree to a compromise settlement.

In conclusion, it should be observed that the reluctance of Japanese during this era to seek justice in formal judicial proceedings and their preference for out-of-court settlement through some form of conciliation were the most enduring attitudes toward dispute settlement.

Rule-by-Law in the Meiji and Post-Meiji Period (1868–1945)

After the startling arrival of Commodore Perry and his black ships in Edo bay, the world began to press in. Japan's isolation policy collapsed and the Great Powers forced upon Japan treaties which included humiliating provisions for extraterritoriality. By virtue of extraterritoriality, if a citizen of these foreign powers committed an offense in Japan, he was to be tried by a representative of his own country in Japan, according to the substantive laws and procedures of his own country. This insistence upon extraterritorial rights was indicative of the foreign powers' belief that Japanese law was too barbaric to be entrusted with trials of their citizens. Furthermore, these unequal treaties deprived Japan of its customs autonomy. The effect of this provision was the loss of protection for Japan's domestic industry against foreign imports. It further deprived the Japanese government of needed customs revenue. Finally, the rapid expansion of trade, without tariff curbs, resulted in a surplus of imports; the resulting flow of gold and silver from Japan disrupted the stability of currency and the establishment of government financial policies. Knowing that they could not persuade the powers to revise these unequal treaties until Japan had adopted a legal system acceptable abroad, and now fired with determination to prepare their country for the demands of the modern world into which it had been so abruptly thrust, the Japanese sent their brightest young men abroad to study Western legal systems (and politics, economics, science, industry, warfare, etc.).

Initially influenced by French law, and to a much lesser extent by Anglo-American common law, the Japanese eventually adopted a civil law system which retained some French features but was largely patterned after that of Bismarck's Germany, one of the most fundamental structural principles of which was a division between public law and private law.

This period in the history of Japanese public law is described as a rule-by-law, a system of administration under law; administrative discretion was no longer unbridled but there was as yet no legal limitation on the legislative formation of that law. Rule-by-law is to be distinguished from the rule-of-law, whereby not only administrative discretion but also legislation is limited by fundamental human rights and the electoral process. The rule-by-law was taken by the Japanese from the German *Rechtsstaat,* characterized by an absolute central authority and rules governing subjects and officials, but not lawmakers. When it is said that in Japan rule-by-law took the form of legal limits on the administrative exercise of power but no limits on legislative power, it should be added that one effect of the public law–private law division in Japan was to leave officials still above the law. This effect will be discussed later.

Rule-by-law was accomplished in Meiji Japan through four phases. First, through the creation of a centralized administrative system, with criminal law and courts backing it up. Second, through the leveling of the old status hierarchy to a single legal status, that of subject of the emperor. Third, through a constitution, promulgated as a gift from the emperor to his subjects. Fourth, through the adoption of German-type codes to govern the whole private law field, thus replacing the traditional customary law which had hitherto regulated relations between private citizens.

These four phases were accomplished in two stages. Between 1868 and 1882 administration building and status leveling had largely been accomplished, along with criminal laws which functioned partially as an auxiliary of administrative power. The second stage, codification, lasted, roughly, from 1882 to 1898.

The enormous accomplishment of the first stage can only be appreciated in light of what we have seen above of the all-encompassing complexity of Japanese feudalism and the status structure of its society. During this period the feudal order was demolished; in place of the multilayered status society in which the Japanese had formerly stood, either as warriors, farmers, artisans, or tradesmen, there was now one status shared by all, that of subject of the emperor.

As noted above, the daimyō exercised autonomous administrative jurisdiction within their own domains. This autonomous jurisdiction extended also to criminal law; the decree of judicial autonomy (*jibun shioki-rei*) promulgated by Tsunayoshi in 1697 confirmed the daimyō's exclusive jurisdiction within his domain to apprehend, convict, sentence, and execute the heaviest penalties upon persons registered in the domain. This vestige of decentralized feudalism was removed in 1868, when the Tokugawa Criminal Code (*osadamegaki*) was applied to the whole country. It was soon supplemented by criminal laws of Chinese origin, which were replaced in 1882 by the Old Criminal Code and the procedural Code of Criminal Instructions, patterned after French criminal law. As the first Western-style codes adopted in Japan, they marked the end of major Chinese influences on Japanese law.

Other criminal laws, in addition to the above-mentioned codes, were passed during this period to provide "muscle" for the newly erected administrative structure. The mere mention of the titles of these special police laws is enough to give a general idea of their character: Police Regulations on Public Meetings, the Press, Libel, Book Censorship, and Peace Preservation.

The second or codification stage of legal reform began with the adoption of the French-style penal codes in 1882. This was followed in 1889 by the adoption of the Meiji Constitution, which provided, for the further codification which immediately followed, a formula of rule-by-law: governmental power to be exercised in accordance with law rather than according to the discretion and status of administrative officials who were responsible only to their superiors. Note, however, that in one sense discretionary power still remained; it was now wielded by the legislature instead of by feudal officers. Law was to be merely a tool of legislative power, not yet a limitation upon it. And though legislative power resided formally in the emperor, it was actually in the hands of a small oligarchic group of Meiji leaders.

Under the Meiji Constitution sovereign power resided in the emperor (Article 4), who was to exercise his lawmaking power through the Diet (Article 37). Legislation, which was thus regarded as an instrument of the emperor and sometimes embodied in imperial decrees, was supreme; the role of the ordinary and administrative courts in enforcing legislation illustrates the judiciary's humble position and the meaning of rule-by-law.

The Meiji Constitution followed the German practice of separating law into public and private law. Accordingly, it provided for separate courts to handle (1) administrative, and (2) civil and criminal cases. Although not enjoying the supremacy of the legislature, the judicial branch under the Meiji Constitution became independent of the legislative and executive branches, not only in theory but in one important sense also in practice: neither judicial superiors nor the executive branch interfered in the disposition of specific cases. Judicial personnel administration was designed to provide professionally qualified and impartial judges, but until 1947 it remained subject to the justice minister.

In 1868 the old Tokugawa administrative commissions (*bugyō*) were designated "courts," and their judicial and administrative functions were initially confused. Gradually, however, the new courts were freed of their administrative character. In 1875 local governors were prohibited from acting as judges. Finally, in 1890, the Law on the Constitution of the Courts formally decreed the separation and relative independence of the judicial branch.

The infant judiciary soon had occasion to exercise its constitutionally guaranteed independence. In 1891 a Japanese policeman, Tsuda Sanzō, wounded the crown prince of Russia (later Nicholas II) at Otsu. The law provided only life imprisonment for attempted murder. Although the Japanese government, which for diplomatic reasons wanted the death penalty to be imposed, exerted considerable political pressure, the court which tried Tsuda chose to observe the law and confined its sentence to life imprisonment.

As noted, one shadow from the Tokugawa period still hung over the independence of the courts; the entire court system was under the justice minister. Nevertheless, although the minister selected, promoted, and assigned judges, there is little evidence of his interference in the handling of specific cases.

The division of the courts into regular courts, which handled civil and criminal cases, and a single and rather ineffectual administrative court was evidence of a significant failure of the new regime to break cleanly with the Tokugawa tradition of discretion-exercising administrative officials from whose decision there was no appeal. However, since this public law–private law judicial division was the pattern of the civil law system which Japan adopted, nothing else could have been expected. Indeed, the Japanese probably found the civil law pattern congenial to their traditions. The administrative court did provide an opportunity for appeal from a decision of an administrative official, but only as to those decisions which were not matters of administrative discretion—and much was left by law to the unchallengeable discretion of officials. Moreover, judicial appeal was possible only after all channels of administrative appeal to administrative officials had been exhausted. Finally, the aggrieved individual who had demonstrated that the contested decision was not a matter of official discretion, who had exhausted the channels of administrative appeal, and who had satisfied the administrative court that the matter was within its highly limited jurisdiction—this pertinacious claimant had only one chance to win judicial vindication, for administrative court decisions were not appealable. Small wonder, then, that relatively few Japanese sought to assert their rights, vis-à-vis administrative decisions, in the administrative court.

The procurator (an official analogous to our prosecuting attorney) was also in many ways reminiscent of the past. In criminal cases he enjoyed a semijudicial status; he wore judicial robes, sat on the level of the judge (above the defendant and defense attorney), and was thus in an excellent position to intimidate the accused and his attorney.

Lawyers were not specifically provided for in criminal actions until the Criminal Code of 1882. Even the law of 1893 left the Japanese lawyer with a restricted, passive role; he was not even given the right to question witnesses directly.

The Civil Code and the Commercial Code, which became effective in 1898 and 1899 respectively, were based principally upon German law. Curiously, the draft German Civil Code, upon which the Japanese Civil Code was modeled, did not become effective in Germany until several years later. The period of intensive scholarly analysis and comment upon the new law, roughly the first twenty years of this century, also witnessed a heavy borrowing of German scholarly methodology. How this came about is an interesting chapter in Japanese legal history.

As we have seen, the Criminal Code of 1882 was based on the French Criminal Code. On the verge of the enactment of three more French-style codes (the Commercial Code, Civil Code, and Code of Civil Procedure), a controversy erupted among Japanese legal scholars which caused the postponement of the Civil Code until 1898 and the Commercial Code until 1899; the Code of Civil Procedure was finally permitted to take effect in 1891, as originally planned.

This "postponement controversy" began as a dispute between the English-trained Japanese jurists (the "postponement school") and the French-trained Japanese jurists (the "immediate enforcement school"). The English-trained jurists, who were not simply arguing for the adoption of an English-style common law system rather than the French-style code system, contended that postponement would, first, permit a more deliberate and scientific selection of legal models instead of what they considered an overemphasis on French law, and, second, allow a better synthesis between Japanese customs and code law. The French-trained Japanese jurists possessed an understanding of "natural law" principles which led them to believe that the French-style codes embodied principles universally applicable and that they therefore need not be specifically accommodated to Japanese custom. The postponement school won out, temporarily, and the largely German-style codes which were finally enacted did contain some elements of Japanese customary law; especially important were certain traditional Japanese family institutions preserved in Books IV and V of the Civil Code.

The German-style codes won out in the end over the French-style codes because they were newer and were regarded as more perfect arrangements. But why was a common law system never seriously considered by the Japanese? Two principal reasons may be suggested, one academic and one eminently practical. First, a law based on abstract rules can more easily be transplanted to foreign soil; the principles of abstract logic are basically the same in all countries. But Anglo-American common law, a comparatively haphazard accretion of judicial decisions derived from concrete cases, may be too intimately intertwined with a particular culture to be readily adopted by another. Second, just as one of the most compelling reasons for the codification of French, Italian, Swiss, Spanish, and German law was the desire of these countries to "nationalize" their laws and thereby contribute to national unity, so was the adoption of a code system regarded by the Japanese as a means of unifying and consolidating their new national order.

The Postwar Rule-of-Law

The idea of the rule-of-law springs from a view of man as an individual with rights which are to be safeguarded from the unlimited action of either individual administrators or lawmaking bodies. All, even the lawmakers, are subject to the rule-of-law.

In England the idea of rule-of-law has been embodied in a parliamentary form of government in which parliamentary and administrative law techniques have been developed to insure individual liberties and official responsiveness to the will of the electorate. The rule-of-law in the United States has taken form in a written constitution and judicial supremacy.

The legal and political institutions which carry out the rule-of-law in postwar Japan clearly reflect their mixed Anglo-American heritage. The new Constitution provides for the "dual supremacy" of the Diet and the judiciary. Structurally, the Japanese state is patterned after England: a symbolic head of state and a union of executive and legislative power in parliamentary government. The Diet is the highest organ of state power, and the sole lawmaking organ of the state. But the Constitution also provides for judicial supremacy. The Supreme Court is explicitly granted power "to determine the constitutionality of any laws, orders, regulations, or official acts."

An important element of Japanese judicial supremacy was the liberation of the courts from the supervision of the justice minister. The whole judicial power is now vested in the Supreme Court and in such inferior courts as are established by law. Even procurators are subject to the rule-making power of the Supreme Court. Attorneys now have equal status with procurators in court.

An enormous practical contribution to the Japanese rule-of-law was the abolition of the old separate administrative court system. Now all cases, administrative as well as civil and criminal, fall under the jurisdiction of the regular court system. Now, at least in the eyes of the court, government officials and aggrieved individuals stand on equal footing; officials are, legally, "public servants," and as such accountable to individual members of the public for their conduct and decisions. But note the qualifications, "in the eyes of the court" and "legally." The Tokugawa Confucian notion of a superior officialdom whose only responsibility to the people was a self-imposed *noblesse oblige* was not completely expunged during the post-Tokugawa era of rule-by-law in which the system of a separate administrative court tended to discourage, rather than encourage, individuals from seeking judicial redress of their rights. The traditional attitude of "look up to officials" and "down on the people" (*kanson mimpi*) has continued into Japan's postwar age of democratization, though it does seem to be weakening year by year.

Nevertheless, the unified judicial system, by making access to the courts easier for aggrieved individuals, by placing both parties, the private citizen and the official, on equal footing in court, and by making lower court decisions appealable in public law cases, has encouraged the development of individual right consciousness vis-à-vis officialdom and has begun to lay down basic guidelines for official conduct and decision-making. Several recent cases involving the tax bureau have clearly established the principle that official agencies in notifying individuals of adverse rulings-on-review must include specific reasons for the ruling in order to insure against arbitrariness in official decision-making. Even more recently, in a case involving the rejection by the Tokyo Land Transportation Office of an individual's application for a license to operate a taxi, the Tokyo High Court, emphasizing the need for eliminating arbitrary decisions and insuring fair procedure, ruled that administrative agencies must establish concrete standards for reviewing contested decisions prior to the hearing at which these standards are to be applied and that the officials conducting the hearings must understand and apply these review standards. However, in ruling favorably for the license applicant the court nevertheless stated that it was not necessary for administrative agencies to make their review standards known either to individual applicants or to the public generally. Thus, the question of *naiki* (internal and ordinarily undisclosed administrative procedures) remains to be settled by some future court decision.

We have already noted three major constitutional changes adopted to implement the rule-of-law in Japan through judicial supremacy. First, the regular court system was freed from the administrative supervision of the justice minister and is now administered by the

Supreme Court, which also has rule-making power. Second, the separate administrative court system for suits against officials was abolished, and the regular courts were granted jurisdiction over cases involving complaints of official misconduct or abuse of authority. Finally, the Supreme Court now has the power of reviewing all legislative, executive, and administrative acts for constitutionality. This power of review is intended to enable the court to fulfill one of its chief functions, the enforcement of the bill of rights of the new constitution against administrative or legislative infringement.

The Supreme Court has made several decisions concerning the nature of its power of review. First, the court will settle only those questions of constitutionality which arise out of concrete cases or controversies; it will not consider abstract questions of constitutionality. Second, the power of constitutional review may be exercised by lower courts as well as by the Supreme Court. Third, even the judgments of lower courts can be "declared unconstitutional."

Right Consciousness and the Social Efficacy of Japanese Law

In the area of private law the manner in which disputes are settled is an important index of the existence, nature, extent, and consciousness of justiciable rights in any given society. To contrast the traditional American and Japanese attitudes toward disputes settlement, we might characterize the American attitude as "I'm right and he's wrong. I'll take him to court, and the court will tell him so." The Japanese attitude, on the other hand, seems to place more emphasis on group harmony than upon vindication of individual rights: "I'm right and he's wrong, but for the sake of group harmony it is better to compromise than to go to court." For the American, his rights and his free access to courts for vindication of his rights are only two sides of the same coin; a legally unenforceable right is hardly better than no right at all. Accordingly, the traditional Japanese propensity to settle private disputes by resorting to nonlegal or sublegal conciliation techniques appears to the litigation-minded American as evidence of lack of right consciousness and as undermining the foundations of the rule-of-law.

However, such a pessimistic appraisal of the level of right consciousness among the Japanese and the social efficacy of their laws ignores at least two important considerations, one sufficiently pragmatic to satisfy even the most litigious American and one of a more speculative nature. First, litigation is expensive. If Tanaka claims that Yamamoto owes him 100,000 yen and Yamamoto says he owes only 50,000 yen, and if the lawyer's fees and court expenses involved in taking Yamamoto to court and getting a judgment for 100,000 yen are going to consume a considerable portion of the judgment, Tanaka is obviously going to be ahead by compromising with Yamamoto and getting, say, 75,000 yen without the trouble, time, and expense of hiring a lawyer and waiting for the court to vindicate him. Moreover, perhaps Tanaka lacks the money to retain a lawyer. Second, it is conceivable that amicable, voluntary conciliation and compromise techniques of dispute settlement reflect a more civilizeᴅ way of coexisting with one's fellows in a crowded, complex society than does a hair-trigger readiness to sue.

In any event, from Tokugawa Japan down to the present most private disputes have been settled through various techniques of conciliation, including informal conciliation (*jidan*), court conciliation (*chōtei*), and court compromise (*wakai*), all of which seem to have contained an element of coercion until after World War II. It is this coercive conciliation, in contrast to voluntary conciliation, which is inimical to the spirit of the rule-of-law, not to mention the fact that it is a violation of the citizen's right of access to the courts guaranteed in Article 32 of the new Japanese Constitution.

In 1960 the ꜱupreme Court in deciding the case of *Nomura v. Yamaki* addressed itself to this very problem and held that a prewar compulsory conciliation statute could not be permitted to deprive a citizen of his right of access to the courts. Apart from the fact that in Japan judicial decisions do not "make" the law as they do in common law countries, *Nomura v. Yamaki* is not binding precedent because the statute authorizing the type of court conciliation (*chōtei*) involved in the case had been repealed prior to the decision. Nevertheless, the court's discussion of this case reveals a fundamental principle which extends far beyond the limits of this particular case: conciliation must be voluntary; otherwise it is a violation of the citizen's right of access to the courts as guaranteed by Article 32 of the Constitution.

The case developed out of a house evacuation dispute. The lower court referred the matter to conciliation, but after the landlord and tenant failed to reach a conciliation agreement, the court ordered the defendant (tenant) to vacate without further trial. The 1932 conciliation statute on which the court relied (and which was repealed before the appeal was decided by the Supreme Court) was *Kinsen saimu rinji chōteihō,* of which article 7 provided: "When the court deems it proper in cases where a conciliation is not reached in the conciliation committee, the court on its own authority may make a substitution of judgment for conciliation. . . ."

On appeal, the Supreme Court held nine-to-six that the lower court's judgment applying the compulsory conciliation provision had deprived the defendant of his constitutional right of access to the courts (Article 32) and a public trial (Article 82).

A postwar trend of growing popular preference for litigation over statutory conciliation has been observed. During the twelve-year period 1950–62 the ratio of cases filed for litigation and conciliation has shifted from roughly 40:60 in 1950 to 60:40 in 1962 in favor of lawsuits. It should be noted, however, that these figures do not reflect the amount of traditional, informal conciliation which goes on outside of statutory conciliation. There is considerable evidence that such informal conciliation is extensive. First, in 1958 the Tokyo police handled 21,596 conciliation cases, while only 6,815 were filed with the Tokyo district court. Second, over 90 percent of Japanese divorces are divorces by agreement. Third, according to a recent survey in Shimane Prefecture, 80 percent of those surveyed would prefer consulting informal conciliators to going to court.

Assuming that Japanese become involved in approximately as many disputes as Americans, further evidence of their continued preference for traditional informal conciliation over judicial determination of their rights may be found in a comparison of the relative number of lawsuits brought in each country. In California, for example, in 1959–60 there were fourteen times as many lawsuits per capita filed as in Japan, including Japanese court conciliations. Excluding cases of court conciliation (as opposed to actual litigation), the ratio rises to twenty-three to one.

In addition to the factors already considered, the paucity of lawyers in Japan may be another reason for the continued preference for informal conciliation over litigation. In 1968, there was one lawyer (total, 8,210) for every 12,500 people in Japan, whereas in the United States there was one lawyer (total practicing, 200,586) for every 950 people.

Several factors help account for the small numbers and relatively low prestige of Japanese lawyers. The national legal examination constitutes a very fine needle's eye for candidates. On the average, scarcely more than 4 percent of those taking it each year manage to squeeze through. Moreover, the income of lawyers is not very high. In addition, the Japanese lawyer's traditional role has been hampered by the old court procedures under which he played such a passive part in trial proceedings, by the Japanese preference for conciliation rather than litigation, and by the fact that nonlawyers are permitted to exercise functions which in the United States would be the exclusive domain of lawyers. For example, the patent specialist (*benrishi*) handles patent, utility model, design, and trademark questions; the tax specialist (*zeirishi*) drafts tax returns; the legal scrivener (*shihō shoshi*) drafts various legal documents; and the legal staffs of many companies and government agencies are comprised of graduates of university law departments who have failed to pass the national legal examination, or have chosen not to take it.

Family Law

Until 1948, when the new family law was made effective, the basic unit of Japanese society was the family, not the individual. As we have seen, as far back as the Tokugawa period, the hierarchical family system in which father stood over family, husband over wife, eldest brother over younger children, etc. was a microcosmic model of Japanese society. In 1898 Books IV and V of the Civil Code incorporated many features of the old family system.

Before World War II, marriage constituted an alliance between two families rather than a union of two persons. Divorce was an exclusively male prerogative until the Meiji period. Children were bound to obey their parents, but parents had no obligation toward their children. Children were in many instances regarded as "property"; daughters of impoverished families could be, and were, "sold" to houses of prostitution.

The new postwar Constitution established the equal rights of husband and wife, equality of the sexes, and the inviolability of the individual (Article 24), and provided for equality for all persons before the law (Article 14), thus abolishing the legal foundations of the old family system. Under the new family law, which took effect in 1948, marriage is recognized as a union between two individuals based on their free agreement rather than a transaction between two families. The former limitations on the legal capacity of married women have been abolished. Parental power is now exercised by both father *and* mother over children under the age of twenty. Children reaching majority become equal with their parents before the law.

Sources of Japanese Law: Codes, Equity, and Cases

The Japanese attitude on the sources of law might be summarized in this way: the source of modern Japanese law is its politically organized society speaking through its legislature. Therefore, the codes and statutes are the prime source of law (as standards for application in court). But the statutes themselves explicitly provide for the incorporation of other sources of law into the system. For example, custom and customary law, as well as certain broad principles of equity (*jōri*), supplement legislation. Although court decisions and scholarly treatises are not exactly law, they are highly useful in understanding the refinements of the law's application. In practice, if not in theory, higher court decisions are usually treated as authority and, hence, as law. This is particularly true of Supreme Court decisions. But even a lower court's own prior decisions will ordinarily be respected. This capsule description of the modern Japanese attitude toward sources of law serves to exemplify the mixed ancestry of law in Japan: custom and "equity" (*jōri*) from Tokugawa Japan; codes from continental Europe; and the case law approach from England and America. It may also indicate that, like so many other originally foreign things adopted by the Japanese, Japanese law will grow increasingly less foreign and more specifically Japanese.

Appendix: Maps

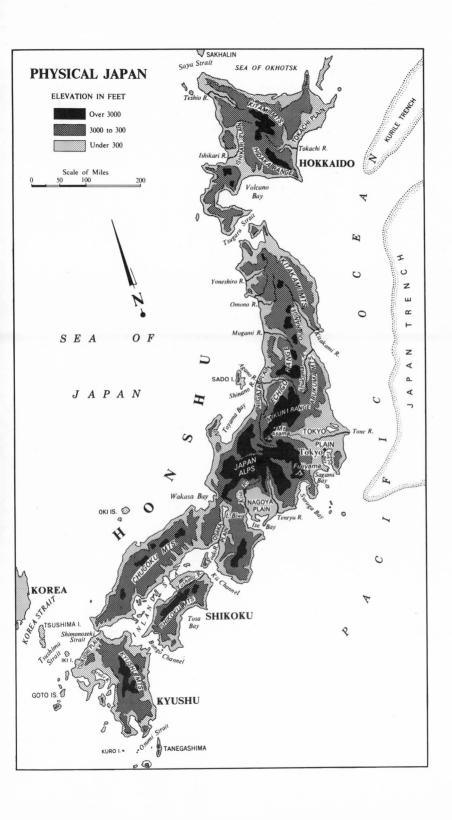

PHYSICAL JAPAN

ELEVATION IN FEET

- Over 3000
- 3000 to 300
- Under 300

Scale of Miles

0   50   100   200

N

SAKHALIN

Soya Strait

SEA OF OKHOTSK

Teshio R.

KITAMI MTS.

TOKACHI PLAIN

HIKARI PLAIN

Ishikari R.

HIDAKA RANGE

Tokachi R.

HOKKAIDO

Volcano Bay

KURILE TRENCH

Tsugaru Strait

KITAKAMI MTS.

Yoneshiro R.

OU RANGE

Omono R.

Kitakami R.

Mogami R.

ABUKUMA MTS.

SEA OF JAPAN

Agano R.

ECHIGO RANGE

SADO I.

NIIGATA PLAIN

Shinano R.

Toyama Bay

MIKUNI RANGE

MT. Asama

Tone R.

TOKYO PLAIN

Tokyo

JAPAN ALPS

Fujiyama

Sagami Bay

Wakasa Bay

NAGOYA PLAIN

Suruga Bay

OKI IS.

L. Biwa

Tenryu R.

OSAKA PLAIN

CHUGOKU MTS.

KISO R.

Ise Bay

JAPAN TRENCH

PACIFIC OCEAN

KOREA

Yodo R.

Kii Channel

INLAND SEA

SHIKOKU MTS.

SHIKOKU

Tosa Bay

TSUSHIMA I.

Shimonoseki Strait

CHIKUGO PLAIN

Bungo Channel

IKI I.

Tsushima Strait

KYUSHU MTS.

GOTO IS.

KYUSHU

Osumi Strait

KURO I.

TANEGASHIMA

PROVINCES OF
TRADITIONAL
JAPAN

░ Important Daimyō domains

━━━━ Provincial boundaries

Scale of Miles
0   50   100   200

J   A   P   A   N

HOKKAIDO

Matsumae

MUTSU

Morioka

DEWA

SADO I.

Niigata

ECHIGO

IWASHIRO

IWAKI

NOTO

ETCHU

KAGA

KOZUKE

SHIMOTSUKE

Nikko

HITACHI

ECHIZEN

HIDA

SHINANO

MUSASHI

SHIMOSA

WAKASA

MINO

×Sekigahara

KAI

Tokyo (Edo)

TAMBA

L. Biwa

OWARI

Nagoya

Kyoto

OMI

SAGAMI

Yokohama

KAZUSA

SETTSU

YAMASHIRO

MIKAWA

SURUGA

Kama-
kura

AWA

Osaka

IGA

TOTOMI

Odawara

Uraga

KAWACHI

Nara

ISE

IZU

YAMATO

Yoshino

SHIMA

II

SHICHITO

P   A   C   I   F   I   C   O   C   E   A   N

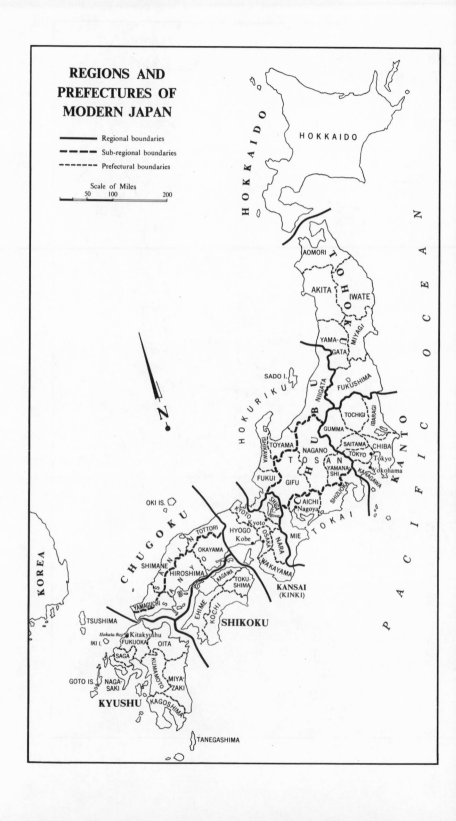

REGIONS AND PREFECTURES OF MODERN JAPAN

——— Regional boundaries
– – – Sub-regional boundaries
- - - - Prefectural boundaries

Scale of Miles
50   100   200

HOKKAIDO

HOKKAIDO

N

PACIFIC OCEAN

TOHOKU

AOMORI

AKITA   IWATE

MIYAGI

YAMA-GATA

FUKUSHIMA

SADO I.

HOKURIKU

NIIGATA

TOCHIGI

IBARAGI

KANTO

GUMMA

ISHIKAWA

TOYAMA   NAGANO

SAITAMA
TOKYO

CHIBA

HIBU

TOSAN

YAMANA-SHI

Tokyo
Yokohama

KANAGAWA

FUKUI   GIFU

SHIGA

AICHI
Nagoya

SHIZUOKA

OKI IS.

CHUGOKU

SHIGA
L.
Biwa

KYOTO

Kyoto

TOKAI

TOTTORI

HYOGO
Kobe

OSAKA

NARA

MIE

SANIN

OKAYAMA

SHIMANE   HIROSHIMA

SANYO

KAGAWA

TOKU-SHIMA

WAKAYAMA

KANSAI
(KINKI)

KOREA

YAMAGUCHI

EHIME   KOCHI

SHIKOKU

TSUSHIMA

Hakata Bay   Kitakyushu

IKI I.   FUKUOKA   OITA

SAGA

GOTO IS.   NAGA-SAKI   KUMAMOTO   MIYA-ZAKI

KYUSHU   KAGOSHIMA

TANEGASHIMA

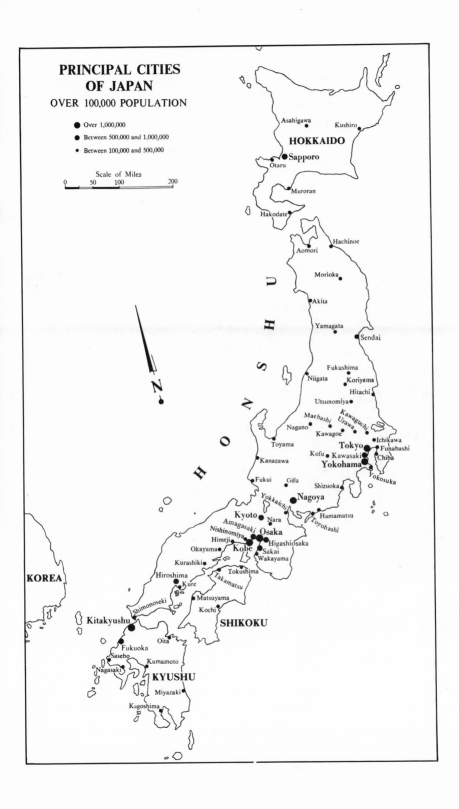

PRINCIPAL CITIES
OF JAPAN
OVER 100,000 POPULATION

● Over 1,000,000

● Between 500,000 and 1,000,000

• Between 100,000 and 500,000

Scale of Miles

0   50   100   200

HOKKAIDO

Asahigawa
Kushiro
Sapporo
Otaru
Muroran
Hakodate

Hachinoe
Aomori
Morioka
Akita
Yamagata
Sendai

H O N S H U

Fukushima
Niigata
Koriyama
Hitachi
Utsunomiya
Kawaguchi
Maebashi
Urawa
Nagano
Kawagoe
Toyama
Tokyo
Ichikawa
Kofu
Kawasaki
Funabashi
Kanazawa
Yokohama
Chiba
Fukui
Gifu
Yokosuka
Shizuoka

Nagoya

Yokkaichi
Kyoto
Nara
Hamamatsu
Amagasaki
Toyohashi
Nishinomiya
Osaka
Himeji
Higashiosaka
Okayama
Kobe
Sakai
Kurashiki
Wakayama
Tokushima
Hiroshima
Takamatsu
Kure
Matsuyama
Shimonoseki
Kochi

SHIKOKU

KOREA

Kitakyushu
Oita
Fukuoka
Sasebo
Kumamoto
Nagasaki
KYUSHU
Miyazaki
Kagoshima

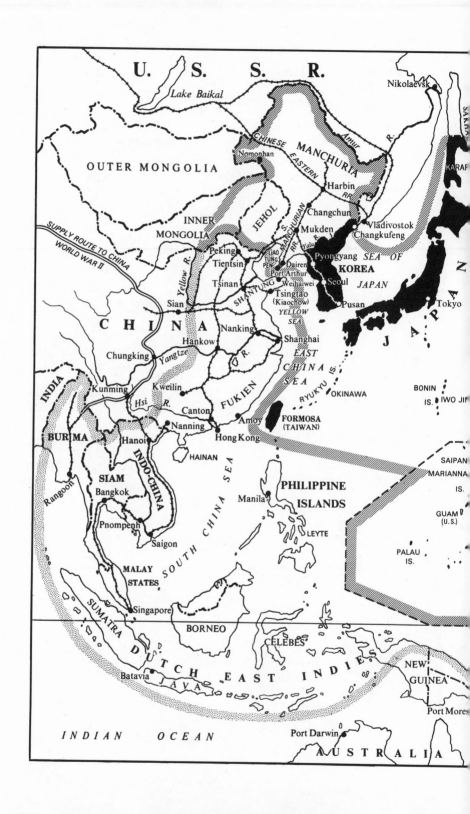

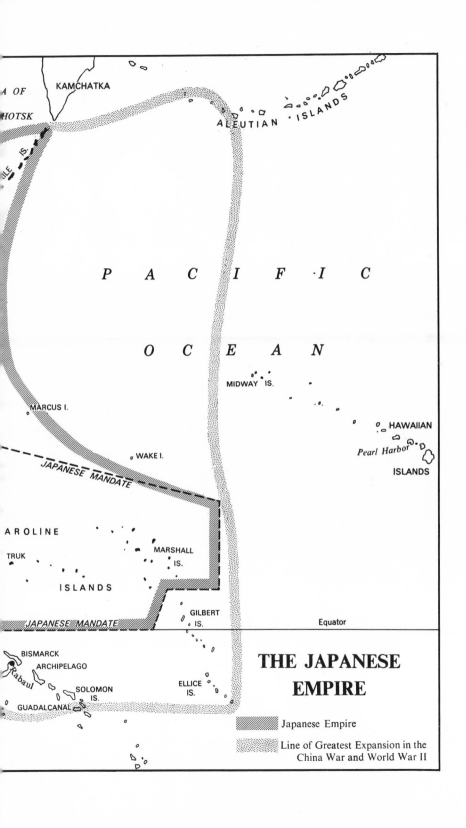

THE JAPANESE
EMPIRE

For Further Reading

A reader may wish to pursue further almost any subject taken up in this book. If so, he will find useful guides in H. Paul Varley, *A Syllabus of Japanese Civilization,* 2d ed. (New York, Columbia University Press, 1972) and Hyman Kublin, *What Shall I Read on Japan,* 11th ed. (New York, Japan Society, Inc., 1973). The latter book may be procured from the Japan Society, Inc., 333 East 47th Street, New York, N.Y. 10017 for the price of the postage. Varley's book is a chronologically arranged outline of the major developments in Japanese political and cultural history. It includes descriptions of other texts and suggestions for additional reading. Kublin's book is an annotated, topically arranged guide to a hundred or so judiciously chosen books on all the most important aspects of Japan and the Japanese. The great virtue of these two works is that they are periodically updated and that they recommend material of a level and quantity well within the capabilities of beginners.

Readers who wish to pursue a topic in extensive detail should consult Association for Asian Studies, *Cumulative Bibliography of Asian Studies 1941–1965* (Boston, 1969) and *Cumulative Bibliography of Asian Studies 1966–1970* (Boston, 1969). Material published after 1970 can be located in the annual *Bibliography of Asian Studies for 1971* and subsequent years. Such readers are also referred to Bernard S. Silberman, *Japan and Korea. A Critical Bibliography* (Tucson, 1962) and Hugh Borton and others, eds., *A Selected List of Books and Articles on Japan in English, French and German,* revised and enlarged (Cambridge, 1954). Teachers will find particularly useful John W. Hall, *Japanese History, New Dimensions of Approach and Understanding* (Service Center for Teachers of History Publication No. 34), revised ed. (Washington, D.C., 1961).

Index